Toward a Green Society

Hong Dayong · Fan Yechao
Editors

Toward a Green Society

The Practice and Impacts of Environmental Governance in Contemporary China

中国人民大学出版社
CHINA RENMIN UNIVERSITY PRESS

palgrave
macmillan

Editors
Hong Dayong
Renmin University of China
Beijing, China

Fan Yechao
Minzu University of China
Beijing, China

Translated by
Zhang Xiaohong
Department of Social Work
School of Philosophy and Social Development
South China Normal University (SCNU)
Guangzhou, China

ISBN 978-981-96-5110-8 ISBN 978-981-96-5111-5 (eBook)
https://doi.org/10.1007/978-981-96-5111-5

Jointly published with China Renmin University Press
The print edition is not for sale in China (Mainland). Customers from China (Mainland) please order the print book from: China Renmin University Press.
ISBN of the Co-Publisher's edition: 978-7-300-28328-9

Sponsored by Chinese Fund for the Humanities and Social Sciences (本书获中华社会科学基金资助)

Cover credit: @Maram_shutterstock.com

This Palgrave Macmillan imprint is published by the registered company Springer Nature Singapore Pte Ltd.
The registered company address is: 152 Beach Road, #21-01/04 Gateway East, Singapore 189721, Singapore

The original version of this book has been revised to update the translator's name and affiliation as requested. This update has been applied across all corresponding renditions of the book. No other changes have been made to the content.

Preface

Academic research is inherently a work in progress. In 2012, I completed the data cleaning for the 2010 China General Social Survey (CGSS) and published my work *Social Bases for Environment Friendly Society: Empirical Studies on Environmental Concern and Behavior of Urban Residents in China*. After this, I began considering the idea of spearheading related projects to expand the research on public environmental concern and behavior in China. In 2013, the Sociology Theory and Method Research Center at Renmin University of China, a key research base for humanities and social sciences supported by China's Ministry of Education, called for bids for major research projects. I organized and submitted a proposal for "Research on the Environmental Awareness of Chinese Urban and Rural Residents in the Perspective of International Comparison", and fortunately was approved to establish the project (Project No. 13JJD840006). This book represents the final research outcome of that project, which passed expert evaluation and was officially completed in August 2019.

The core theme of this book is exploring the new transformation trends in Chinese society based on the development of environmental issues, environmental governance practices, and the strengthening of environmental concern and the associated behaviors. Even in the days of the earliest humans, the relationship between humanity and the environment was marked by both opposition and unity. On the one hand, obtaining resources from the environment is essential for human survival and development. Human activities, whether in production or in daily life, inevitably impact the environment, leading to its consumption, degradation, or even destruction. On the other hand, excessive resource extraction and environmental destruction ultimately threaten human survival and development. Therefore, human societies have consistently incorporated environmental factors into social construction. This has transpired through different stages of productive development, and under various social systems. The relationship between the environment and society is inherently dynamic and evolving. Since the Industrial Revolution, the evolution of environmental issues has become a factor driving the transformation of modern society. As such, analyzing this transformation process, its manifestations, and its underlying mechanisms is an important topic in environmental sociology.

Over 20 years ago, when I was studying the relationship between China's social transformation and the evolution of environmental issues, I realized that the relationship between human society and the environment is dynamic and dialectical. I have contended that China's rapid industrialization and urbanization have been the direct causes of environmental degradation. Moreover, the growing consumerism in China has added pressure on the environment, and expanding regional disparities have made it even more difficult to curb environmental decline. Furthermore, the shift from a planned economy to a market economy has led to a loss of control, complicating environmental governance, which in turn has resulted in growing environmental pressure. At the same time, China's shift from a closed to an open society has facilitated the social construction of environmental issues. Meanwhile, policy adjustments to address environmental degradation have promoted the institutionalization of environmental protection, and the shift toward democratization has provided new possibilities for improving environmental governance. These factors have all been favorable to alleviating environmental pressure.

I have also maintained that China's environmental governance should pursue the path of regulating development goals and managing consumption demands. The key issue lies in promoting changes in the social system itself, which is part of the new transformation in the modernization process. I summarized these views in what I called the "social transformation paradigm" for environmental issues, which was reflected in my 2001 book *Social Changes and Environmental Problem in China*. This work explores the social causes of environmental problems.

Next, I shifted my focus to the social impact of environmental issues, specifically examining the impact of environmental pressure on the public's environmental concern and behavior. In 2003, I helped design the environmental concern and behavior module for the China General Social Survey initiated by Renmin University of China and the Hong Kong University of Science and Technology. With the assistance of Professor Li Lulu, then Director of the Department of Sociology at Renmin University of China, I obtained nationally representative survey data that, though not without its flaws, was invaluable. Based on this data, my team and I conducted a series of empirical studies, which were eventually compiled into the book *Social Bases for Environment Friendly Society*, published in 2012 by Renmin University Press. This book offered preliminary analyses of environmental concern measurement, its structure, influencing factors, and citizens' environmental behaviors. Key contributions included identifying that the environmental concern scale widely used in Western environmental sociology cannot be directly applied to China; the idea that environmental concern is a complex and constitutive concept; and an analysis of the relationships between environmental concern and factors such as gender, age, residence, socioeconomic development, and environmental conditions, testing existing theoretical hypotheses. Some findings were consistent with those of Western scholars, while others differed. The book was translated into English in 2018.

Because the environmental module of the 2003 China General Social Survey was limited to urban areas and there were some missing regional samples, the existing research could only be considered preliminary. During the course of the research, my team and I were constantly working to develop a new survey, and in 2010, this opportunity came to fruition. Once again with the support of Professor Li Lulv, the 2010 China General Social Survey included the environmental concern and behavior module I had designed, as well as the environmental module from the International Social Survey Programme (ISSP). This allowed for a random sampling of urban and rural areas across China, and the ISSP environmental module was conducted simultaneously in several major countries around the world. This provided the most authoritative environmental concern and behavior survey data available at the time, enabling both urban-rural comparisons and international comparisons. The original intention of this book was to use this authoritative dataset to remeasure and further investigate Chinese public environmental concern and behavior, while also conducting international comparisons.

However, as the research deepened, I increasingly realized that an analysis and discussion of environmental concern among urban and rural residents in China cannot be separated from the social responses to environmental issues, specifically contemporary environmental governance practices in China. As a subjectively constructed "social fact", residents' environmental concern is largely a special manifestation of China's increasingly serious environmental problems and the intensification of environmental protection efforts. Meanwhile, residents' growing environmental concerns have not only driven changes in contemporary Chinese environmental governance models, but have also served as an important force in leading broader societal transformation. For this reason, I expanded the scope of the project, not only conducting an in-depth comparative empirical analysis of Chinese residents' environmental concerns using survey data, but also situating the emergence and consequences of residents' environmental concern within the narrative of contemporary environmental change and social transformation in China. Ultimately, the book became *Toward a Green Society: The Practice and Impacts of Environmental Governance in Contemporary China*.

Based on the analytical framework of objective issues, subjective cognition, and social construction, this book focuses on the mutual construction and co-evolution of contemporary Chinese environmental governance practices and social transformation. It includes analysis of the environmental quality improvement process, the evolution of public environmental concern and behavior, and the resulting transformations in environmental governance models and social construction. The book is divided into three parts: the first part, "Environmental Issues and Governance Practices" (Chapters 1–6), examines major environmental issues in urban and rural China, such as air pollution, water pollution, and waste pollution, analyzing their history and current status, with a focus on the associated environmental protection policies and practices. This part explores the objective foundation for China's transition to a green society. The second part, "Environmental Concern and Behavioral Tendencies" (Chapters 7–12), analyzes changes in public environmental concern and behavior based on China's environmental issues and socioeconomic development. It discusses urban-rural differences in environmental concern, age differences, and the impact of economic growth on public environmental concern and behavior, particularly exploring the correlation between air pollution and residents' intention to migrate in a case study of one city. The third part, "Governance Transformation and the Green

Society" (Chapters 13–18), examines China's governance transformation in the context of addressing climate change and air pollution, focusing on the macro trends and challenges of green society development in China.

Some of the key findings of the book include: (1) the complex relationship of mutual construction and co-evolution between the environment and society, which not only affects the quality of the environment itself, but also changes the process of social development; (2) overall, residents' environmental concerns have gradually increased and played an important role in this complex interaction, yet there are social demographic differences, and international comparisons show that the development of environmental concern among Chinese residents is unique; (3) changing social structures have enhanced the openness and complexity of environmental governance, leading to a new environmental governance model with Chinese characteristics; (4) environmental governance practices have triggered overall social changes in China, and a green society is emerging, although challenges remain; (5) unwaveringly advancing ecological civilization construction, particularly cultivating, guiding, and strengthening the internal driving force for society to protect the environment, and further improving the institutional arrangements for complex governance, are crucial to the modernization of environmental governance and social transformation.

This book's innovative academic contributions include: (1) the introduction of two scales for measuring public environmental concern and environmental knowledge in China—the CNEP and the CEKS; (2) the empirical testing and discussion of theories such as "post-materialism", "differential exposure", "differential occupation", "differential experience", the "Bartel model", "social constructivism", "global environmentalism", "ecological modernization", the "environmental Kuznets curve", "push-pull theory", "stress-threshold theory", and "environmental justice", as well as new insights into these theories; (3) the creative introduction of analytic concepts and theoretical propositions with Chinese characteristics, such as the "environmental belief system"; "performance expectation theory"; "complex environmental governance"; and "green society construction"; and (4) a theoretical summary and analysis of China's unique environmental governance model and social transformation direction.

We realize that there are still some areas in the book that need improvement. First, although the book highlights a central theme, the system is not yet rigorous, especially in terms of constructing more precise theories, concepts, and analytical frameworks around the core issues of the research. Second, in terms of analyzing environmental issues and governance, although we have addressed several major areas of concern, our analysis is still not comprehensive, deep, or detailed enough, and it focuses on the national level, with insufficient analysis of local and global environmental issues. Third, the research process took a long time, and due to the lack of up-to-date authoritative data for comparison, some conclusions may not align with current realities, requiring further testing and revision. Finally, because multiple team members participated in the research, the approaches, variables used, presentation styles, and quality of the work varied, despite our best efforts to make the needed improvements. We sincerely welcome readers and fellow scholars to provide critique and encouragement, which will aid in advancing our research.

The team members who participated in the project at different stages of application and research were Dr. Lu Chuntian from the Department of Sociology at Xi'an Jiaotong University, Dr. Peng Yuanchun from the Department of Sociology at Central South University, Dr. Fan Yechao from the Department of Sociology at Minzu University of China, Dr. Zhang Feinan from the Social Research Institute of Heilongjiang Academy of Social Sciences, doctoral student Qu Tianci and master's student Deng Xiaqiu from Renmin University of China, Dr. Shi Chaoyi from the Department of Sociology at East China University of Science and Technology, Dr. Gong Wenjuan from the Institute of Population and Ecology at Xiamen University, Dr. Ma Guodong from the Social Research Institute at Ningxia Medical University, Dr. Tong Zhifeng from the Department of Sociology at Zhejiang University of Finance and Economics, Dr. Zhang Jinjuan from the Department of Sociology at Anhui Normal University, Dr. Xiao Chenyang from American University, Dr. Wang Yujun from the Department of Sociology at Renmin University of China, Dr. Wu Liufen from Guangxi University of Finance and Economics, and Professor Song Guojun from the School of Environmental Studies at Renmin University of China. Dr. Lu Chuntian made important contributions to the project design phase.

The final writing of the book involved the following contributions: Fan Yechao, Chapter 1; Shi Chaoyi, Chapter 2; Gong Wenjuan and Zhao Zhao, Chapter 3; Ma Guodong, Chapter 4; Tong Zhifeng, Chapter 5; Zhang Jinjuan, Chapter 6; Fan Yechao and Hong Dayong, Chapter 7; Hong Dayong, Fan Yechao, Deng Xiaqiu, and Qu Tianci, Chapter 8;

Xiao Chenyang (translated by Fan Yechao), Chapter 9; Peng Yuanchun, Chapter 10; Hong Dayong, Fan Yechao, and Li Peifan, Chapter 11; Hong Dayong and Fan Yechao, Chapters 12 and 17; Hong Dayong, Chapters 13, 15, and 18; Wu Liufen and Hong Dayong, Chapter 14; Lu Chuntian and Hong Dayong, Chapter 16. I sincerely thank all team members for their cooperation.

I would like to particularly highlight my former master's and doctoral student, and now associate professor Fan Yechao at the Department of Sociology at Minzu University of China, for his role in the writing of this book. He is a diligent and insightful young scholar, and a core member of this research team. He not only participated in much of the research and writing, but also assisted me in contacting team members and editing the manuscript. I believe he has a bright academic future ahead of him. In addition, my current doctoral students He Junli, Guo Hanxiao, Li Yang, and Minzu University of China master's student Liu Mengwei also made important contributions to the final compilation of the research results, for which I thank them sincerely.

Some of the contents of this book have been published as papers in journals such as *Sociological Review*, *Sociological Research*, *Social Studies*, *Journal of Renmin University of China*, *Youth Studies*, *Journal of the Central Party School*, *Social Science Research*, and *Society & Nature Resources*. On behalf of the research team, I would like to express my gratitude to these journals for their support and professional suggestions. Ultimately, the book was published, thanks to support from the Sociology Theory and Method Research Center at Renmin University of China and Renmin University Press, and especially the efforts of editors Pan Yu and Sheng Jie.

As the project comes to a close, I cannot help but remember my late mentor, Professor Zheng Hangsheng. During my doctoral studies, he supported my research in environmental sociology. When I spearheaded this project in 2013, he was the director of the Sociology Theory and Method Research Center at Renmin University of China, and he gave me invaluable project design advice. It was with great sadness that he passed away during the course of this project. This book is dedicated to his memory.

Beijing, China
Chinese New Year 2020

HongProf. Dayong

Contents

Notes on Contributors

Deng Xiaqiu holds a Master's degree in Sociology from Renmin University of China.

Fan Yechao, Ph.D. in Sociology, is an associate professor at the Department of Sociology, School of Ethnology and Sociology, Minzu University of China. Fan is mainly engaged in teaching and research in the fields of environmental sociology and social theory.

Gong Wenjuan, Ph.D. in Sociology, is a professor in the Department of Sociology at Xiamen University. Her research interests include social impact assessment of environmental issues, public responses to environmental risks, collaborative governance of rural ecological environments, environmental social governance, and environment-health interactions.

Hong Dayong, Ph.D. in Sociology, is an environmental sociologist in China. Hong was previously a professor at the Research Centre for Sociological Theory and Methodology of Renmin University of China, Vice-President of the Chinese Sociological Association. He has published books such as *China's Social Transformation in the Perspective of Ecological Modernization* (2014), *Social Base for Environmentally Friendly Society* (2012).

Li Peifan, Ph.D. in Sociology, is a researcher at China Energy Investment Corporation.

Lu Chuntian, Ph.D. in Sociology, is a professor in the Department of Sociology at Xi'an Jiaotong University. His research spans quantitative sociological methods, environmental sociology, and social stratification.

Ma Guodong, Ph.D. in Sociology, is a professor at the School of Humanities and Management, Ningxia Medical University. His research areas include environmental sociology, health management, and social security.

Peng Yuanchun, Ph.D. in Sociology of Renmin University from China and Postdoc in Philosophy from Central South University, is born in September 1981 in Longhui, Hunan. He is an Associate Professor, Intermediate Social Worker, and Master's Supervisor. Specializing in environmental sociology, social development, and social policy, he also serves as a Council Member of the Environmental Sociology Professional Committee, an Associate Researcher at Renmin University's Center for Sociological Theory and Methods, and a Researcher at the Institute of Environmental Sociology at Renmin University of China.

Qu Tianci holds a Ph.D. in Sociology from Renmin University of China.

Shi Chaoyi, Ph.D. in History, is an associate professor in the Department of Public Administration at East China University of Science and Technology. Her research focuses on environmental governance, administrative divisions, and toponymy management.

Tong Zhifeng, Ph.D. in Sociology, is a professor at Zhejiang University of Finance and Economics. His research focuses on social governance and its legalization, sociology of law, environmental governance, and social work.

Wu Liufen, Ph.D. in Sociology, is an associate professor at the School of Public Finance and Public Administration, Guangxi University of Finance and Economics. Her research interests include environmental sociology and social governance.

Xiao Chenyang, Ph.D. in Sociology, is a professor in the Department of Sociology at American University. His research specializes in environmental sociology.

Zhang Jinjun, Ph.D. in Sociology, is a professor at the Law School of Anhui Normal University. His research interests include environmental sociology, sociology of history, social policy and development, and social work theory and methods.

Zhao Zhao holds a Master's degree in Sociology from Xiamen University.

List of Figures

List of Tables

PART I

Environmental Issues and Governance Practice

This section explores several prominent environmental issues in both urban and rural China, such as air pollution, water pollution, and garbage pollution. It includes analysis of these issues from both a contemporary and a historical perspective. In doing so, it reveals the environmental policy practices related to these issues, and also offers analysis of the objective basis within Chinese society's progress toward a green society.

CHAPTER 1

Air Pollution and Its Governance in Urban Areas

Fan Yechao

With the rapid development of China's social economy and improvement in standards of living, the general public's demand for environmental quality has also been on the rise. In early 2020s, the problem of smog-based urban air pollution attracted widespread attention. Frequent, persistent, and severe urban air pollution has prompted the government to intensify air pollution management policies to better respond to the new demands of the people. In this chapter, we review the historical evolution of China's urban air pollution problem, discuss China's air pollution prevention and alleviation policies at different stages, and explore a series of extraordinary actions the Chinese government has undertaken in recent years to combat air pollution. We also examine their positive effects on urban air quality. We do so by exploring the main concepts underlying air pollution, as well as its geographic distribution, hazardous consequences, and evaluation criteria.

Y. Fan (✉)
Department of Sociology, School of Ethnology and Sociology, Minzu University of China, Beijing, China
e-mail: fanyechao@ruc.edu.cn

D. Hong and Y. Fan (eds.), *Toward a Green Society*,
https://doi.org/10.1007/978-981-96-5111-5_1

1.1 Overview of Air Pollution

1.1.1 Basic Concepts of Air Pollution

Air pollution, also known as atmospheric pollution, usually refers to "the phenomenon in which the concentration of pollutants in the atmosphere reaches such a harmful level that it destroys the ecosystem and the conditions for the normal survival and development of human beings, and causes harm to people and things" (Qian 2011: 92). The substances that cause air pollution are called air pollutants. Scientific research has revealed more than 100 types of air pollutants, and common air pollutants emitted into the atmosphere by human activity include sulfur dioxide (SO_2), nitrogen oxides (NOx), carbon monoxide (CO), volatile organic compounds (VOCs), ozone (O_3), inhalable particulate matter (PM_{10}), and fine particulate matter ($PM_{2.5}$)[1] to name but a few. The sources of air pollutants, i.e., air pollution sources, can be divided into fixed sources and mobile sources, according to their movement, or lack thereof. Fixed sources refer to pollutants discharged from fixed locations, such as pollution sources from various factories and enterprises, as well as household stoves. Mobile sources generally refer to sources from means of transportation, such as gas-powered motor vehicles and ships which emit pollutants into the atmosphere during operation. This is characterized by small-scale dispersal, large quantities, and frequent flow (Li et al. 1997: 41).

The production of air pollution is directly related to the accumulation of air pollutants in the atmosphere. When there was little human activity, air pollutants, which originate mainly from natural processes, generally did not accumulate to create air pollution, due to the atmospheric environment's capacity for self-purification. However, with the increase in human activity which has accompanied industrialization and urbanization, social processes (e.g., industrial emissions, automobile exhaust) have become the main sources of air pollution. Moreover, when the accumulation of pollutants reaches a level that seriously exceeds the atmosphere's self-purifying capacity, air pollution is easily induced. In this sense, it is the

[1] Both RSP and fine particulate matter are particulate matter, i.e., a wide variety of solids, liquids, and aerosols in the atmosphere other than gases, including dust, soot, smog, and total suspended particles (TSP). The difference between PM and fine particles lies in the size of the particles, which have aerodynamic equivalent diameters of less than 10 micrometers and 2.5 micrometers, respectively.

long-term negative impact of human activity on the atmospheric environment that breeds air pollution. Thus, what appears to be a sudden air pollution phenomenon is mostly an early ecological warning indicating that pollutants have far surpassed the atmospheric environment's self-purifying capacity.

Common types of air pollution include soot pollution, petroleum pollution, compound pollution, and special pollution (Liu and Zhang 2012: 110). Soot pollution refers mainly to pollution caused by the emission of sulfur dioxide, particulate matter, and other pollutants during the burning of coal, as well as the pollution caused by the secondary pollutants generated by chemical reactions between these pollutants. Petroleum-type pollution refers to pollution caused by pollutants such as those released from the atmosphere during the production and use of petroleum products (especially in the process of driving automobiles). Compound pollution is a combination of soot and petroleum pollution. This is a special type of air pollution which is related to coal, petroleum, and other energy sources. In addition to air pollution related to energy use, there are also several special gaseous pollutants which are discharged into the atmosphere due to the local or limited area of the special air pollution phenomenon. These include nuclear industry emissions (radioactive dust and exhaust), chlor-alkali plant emissions of chlorine-containing gases, phosphorus fertilizer plant emissions of fluorine-containing gases, and other special air pollutants caused by the pollution.

1.1.2 *The Hazards of Urban Air Pollution*

Although the atmosphere is continuous and dynamic, air pollution is usually distinctly urban in terms of its frequency of occurrence. In most cases, air pollution is more serious and more noticeable in urban areas than in rural areas, with their larger populations, more densely packed factories and enterprises, and heavier vehicular traffic. For example, according to the 2013 China General Social Survey (CGSS), 53% of urban respondents reported that air pollution was "severe" in their neighborhoods, compared to 25.7% of rural respondents. In addition, many of the most well-known air pollution events in history have occurred in large industrialized metropolitan areas, such as the Great Smog of London, and the photochemical smog in Los Angeles. It is for these reasons that air pollution has long been regarded as an "urban disease", and the severity of air pollution in a given area over a given period of time is usually assumed to be closely related to its level of urbanization.

Air pollution has multiple harmful effects. Firstly, many air pollution events result in reduced air visibility, which can lead to serious traffic accidents, causing casualties, and more commonly, the obstruction of sea, land, and air transportation, inhibiting both the daily routines and the work of individuals. Secondly, studies have confirmed that many air pollutants are toxic, or have strong associations with toxic substances (e.g., heavy metals, microorganisms) which can invade the human body through a variety of pathways and cause varying degrees of intoxication. Long-term exposure to air pollution can also increase the incidence of cancer and infant mortality in a region (Pope III et al. 2002; Kelly and Fussel 2015). Again, heavy air pollution can stimulate the visual center of the brain, which can lead to depression, pessimism, and other negative emotions, which in turn can harm mental health (Bullinger 1989). Finally, over the long run, air pollution may indirectly cause a series of harmful consequences such as material damage (e.g., the corrosion of metals and the destruction of building materials), lowered food production, water pollution, and global climate change.

1.1.3 Air Quality Assessment

Air quality standards are defined as the maximum permissible mass concentrations of various pollutants in the atmosphere within a period of time. These are the environmental quality objectives established to realize the requirements of a country's environmental policy, and are also the basis for evaluating air quality (Li and Shen 2003). As of this writing, most countries and regions throughout the world have established air quality standards, and the United Nations World Health Organization (WHO) has also established air quality guidelines on a global scale. As scientific research on the effects of air pollution on human health become increasingly more in-depth, the air quality standards of different countries and regions are regularly being adjusted. As such, the air quality standards of the United States, the European Union, and the World Health Organization (WHO) have been revised several times over the years.

The earliest air quality standard in China was the *Atmospheric Environmental Quality Standard* (GB3095-82), which was enacted in 1982 and revised twice, in 1996 and 2000. The current air quality standard in China is the *Ambient Air Quality Standard* (GB3095-2012), which was released in 2012, and stipulates the classification of ambient air functional zones, the grading of standards, pollutant items, averaging time, concentration limits, monitoring methods, validity of data statistics, implementation, and supervision. On this basis, the former Ministry of Environmental Protection (MEP) also synchronized the introduction of the *Ambient Air Quality Index (AQI) Technical Provisions (Trial)*, which stipulates the grading scheme for air quality assessment. Compared with the old version of the standard, China's current air quality evaluation standard has increased the monitoring of fine particulate matter and tightened the concentration limits of pollutants such as inhalable particulate matter and nitrogen dioxide. However, compared with international standards, China's current air quality standards are weak overall, and thus, it still relies on the World Health Organization's Phase I target values (Dong et al. 2015).

1.2 The Evolution of Urban Air Pollution in China

Using written records and official atmospheric monitoring data, this section reviews the evolution of urban air pollution in China since 1949. As discussed earlier, air pollution is not a sudden phenomenon, but rather cumulative and gradual. Therefore, it is rarely possible to identify specific points in time during which air quality changes have occurred. Nevertheless, we can generally identify 1972 as a pivotal year, dividing the evolution of urban air pollution in China into two phases. The early phase was the incubation period of air pollution in China. Formal pollution prevention and alleviation had yet to be implemented, and the deterioration of air quality was in a long-term state of laissez-faire. In the latter phase, air pollution management was formally incorporated into the national agenda, and the atmospheric environment began to be simultaneously subjected to the tension between pollution and alleviation measures, resulting in a complex change trend.

1.2.1 Urban Air Pollution Prior to the 1970s

Prior to the 1970s, when China's environmental protection endeavors officially began, there was limited awareness of environmental protection in Chinese society, in either the government or the private sector. Nonetheless, there is ample evidence that air quality in many of China's urban areas (especially in industrial cities) had begun to deteriorate, and that air pollution was already visibly occurring between the founding of the Peoples Republic of China and the end of the 1960s. By the early 1970s, the atmospheric environment in many areas was severely polluted, and this had already begun interfering with people's work and daily lives. A government document from 1973 shows that from 1967 to 1972, dye factories in the city of Lvda (present-day Dalian) emitted toxic gases, causing at least 20 poisoning incidents involving over 200 people. The Hada Bay Industrial Zone in Jilin City had been discharging 23 billion cubic meters of sulfur dioxide and other toxic gases annually. The resulting smoke and dust pollution in the area posed a danger to residents' health. People in cities such as Zhuzhou, Jilin, and Guangzhou also petitioned their local governments because of the emission of exhaust gases and smoke from local factories, which evolved into mass incidents (Qu and Peng 2010: 316–317). Most urban air pollution in this period was caused by the increase of industrial soot and exhaust emissions, mainly soot pollution, with some special pollution. However, the scope of influence was typically small and localized.

The deterioration of urban air quality prior to the 1970s was mainly related to China's large-scale industrialization at that time. In the early years of the founding of the People's Republic of China, Chinese society initiated comprehensive industrialization construction, and systematically developed industrial production (especially heavy industry). During this process, the proliferation of industrial output became a driving force for the national economy's recovery. Between 1949 and 1952, the value of China's industrial output increased from 14 billion yuan to 34.9 billion yuan, and the percentage of heavy industry in total industrial output increased from 56.4% to 64.2%. Meanwhile, the proportion of light vs. heavy industry decreased from 73.6% vs. 26.4% to 64.5% vs. 35.5%. During the First Five-year Plan period (1953–1957), the annual average growth rate of industrial output reached 18%, the percentage of modern industry among industrial output increased from 64.2% to 70.9%, and the percentage of heavy industry among industrial output rose from 35.5% to 45%. Between 1958 and 1976, despite the slowdown in industrialization due to the disruptions of the Great Leap Forward and the Cultural Revolution, gross industrial output still grew at an annual growth rate of 9.3%. The petroleum industry's percentage of the gross industrial output also rose from 1.1% to 6.2%, and the chemical industry's proportion of gross industrial output rose from 6.8% to 11% (Li 2009: 2–3). The remarkable industrialization achievements of this period came largely at the expense of the environment, with air pollutants from industrial emissions proliferating, and air quality in many industrial cities deteriorating.

The destructive effects on the atmospheric environment wrought by the social disorder brought about by the Great Leap Forward and the Cultural Revolution during this same period should not be underestimated. During the Great Leap Forward, a nationwide iron and steelmaking frenzy was launched under the erroneous guidance of the leftist leadership. In the second half of 1958 alone, tens of millions of people were mobilized from all parts of the country to produce iron and steel on a massive scale. They built at least 600,000 crude iron and steel furnaces, 59,000 small coal kilns, 1,000 small power stations, 9,000 small cement factories, and 80,000 factories for repairing farm implements. The number of industrial enterprises ballooned from just over 9,000 in 1957 to 310,000 in 1969. This aggressive industrialization strategy led directly to the creation of a large number of industrial enterprises. It also led to rapid deterioration of the ecological environment in many regions in a short period of time, with laissez-faire industrial emissions standards also leading to smoggy air pollution in many locales (Qu 1988). During the Cultural Revolution, the "Third-Front Construction" project implemented the misguided policy of "relying on the mountains, scattering and entering caves". This resulted in many factories emitting large quantities of hazardous substances that were located deep in the mountains and valleys with poor air dispersal conditions, which also caused serious air pollution in localized areas. For example, in Panzhihua City, the iron and steel industry boomed in the mid-1960s, but the excessive industrial emissions and poor air dispersal conditions caused serious air pollution, and there were elevated rates of lung cancer among workers (Shapiro 2001: 139–194).

In the nearly two decades since the founding of Peoples Republic of China, air quality in China's urban areas as a whole has gradually deteriorated due to rapid industrialization and social unrest, and air pollution has been particularly prominent in certain industrial urban areas. Although the government had exerted some effort to reduce industrial emissions and soot during this period, the limited understanding of air pollution and the lack of effective pollution alleviation measures were insufficient to address the root causes of the problem. As a result, air quality in many urban areas continued to decline.

1.2.2 The Evolution of Urban Air Pollution Problems Since the 1970s

In June 1972, the Chinese government sent representatives to Stockholm to attend the United Nations Conference on the Human Environment. This marked the beginning of China's modern environmental protection endeavors, and air pollution prevention and alleviation were formally launched. Since then, there have been several important changes in China's urban air pollution. Firstly, the types of air pollution have become more complex, evolving from the dominant soot-based pollution to compound pollution. Secondly, the scope of air pollution has continued to expand, with a trend from localized pollution to widespread pollution. Thirdly, air pollution is becoming an important social issue, and public awareness of the issue is escalating. The following is a detailed analysis of each of these changes.

1.2.2.1 The Complexity of Pollution: From Soot-Based Pollution to Compound Pollution

As discussed earlier, prior the 1970s, the most common type of urban air pollution in China was soot-based pollution caused by the emission of sulfur dioxide and particulate matter such as soot from factories, along with several specialized types of pollution. Although the state took many measures to reduce emissions of sulfur dioxide and industrial soot, beginning in the 1980s the intensifying trend of soot pollution was curbed, but it remained serious (Qu 1988). In 1981, the State Council approved the United Nations Environment Program (UNEP) and the World Health Organization (WHO) to implement air quality monitoring in the five Chinese cities of Beijing, Shanghai, Shenyang, Xi'an, and Guangzhou. This was the first time that China's air quality monitoring system had been approved. This was one of the earliest air quality monitoring programs in China. The results of that year's report showed that the concentration of dust in Beijing, Shanghai, Shenyang, and Xi'an had exceeded the standard, while the concentration of sulfur dioxide in Beijing, Xi'an, Guangzhou, and Shenyang had exceeded the standard to varying degrees. These air pollutants originated mainly from the coal burning process in industrial production and daily life (Environmental Health Monitoring Station of the Chinese Academy of Medical Sciences 1983). Coal smoke pollution was the main cause of sulfuric acid rain in China, and in March

1982, the State Council Leading Group Office of Environmental Protection conducted a nationwide mapping survey of acid rain. They found that acid rain was already widespread in Southwestern, South-central, and Eastern China at that time, with a tendency to worsen progressively from the North to the South (Jibin and Chen 1982).

It was not until the beginning of the twenty-first century that soot-based air pollution began to ease. As shown in Fig. 1.1, China's industrial sulfur dioxide emissions peaked in 2006 and then trended downward. By 2015, the total emissions had returned to the levels of the early twenty-first century. Similarly, industrial smoke (dust) emissions have also trended downward since 2005. Also, since the start of the twenty-first century, among cities monitoring precipitation, the percentage of cities experiencing acid rain decreased from 61.8% in 2000 to 36.1% in 2017. Based on the air pollution index (API) released by the national environmental protection department, there has indeed been an overall trend of improvement in China's urban air quality (Li et al. 2012). These results indicate that air pollution prevention and mitigation efforts in the early decades of the new millennium have produced initial results, and China's soot-based pollution is now under effective control.

Despite the significant progress made in the alleviation of soot-based pollution, actual air quality in Chinese cities has not improved significantly, and has even worsened in some areas. This is mainly due to the

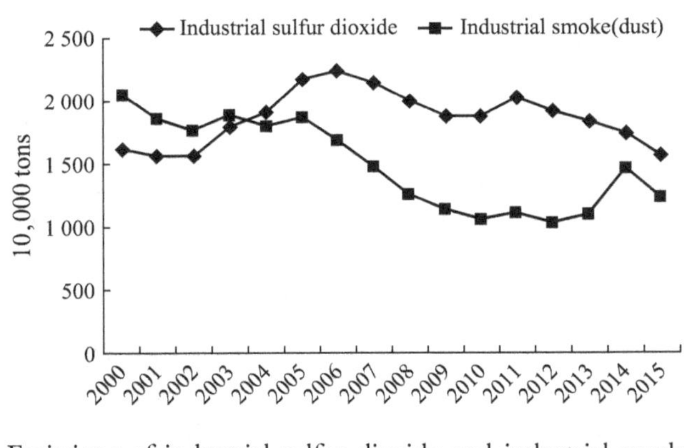

Fig. 1.1 Emissions of industrial sulfur dioxide and industrial smoke (dust) in China, 2000–2015 (*Source* Bulletin on the State of the Environment in China, 2000–2015)

fact that the type of air pollution in China has changed over time. As of this writing, China's air pollution has evolved from the original soot-based pollution to a composite type of pollution that is a combination of soot-based pollution and petroleum-type pollution (Chinese Academy of Engineering, Ministry of Environmental Protection 2011: 469). In order to cope with this new type of pollution, China revised the air quality evaluation standard in 2012, and formulated the *Ambient Air Quality Standard* (GB3095-2012) and began using the Air Quality Index (AQI) to evaluate air quality. Based on this new evaluation standard, the 2013 *Bulletin of China's Environmental Conditions* showed that of the initial 74 cities monitored nationwide, only three—Haikou, Zhoushan, and Lhasa—had achieved acceptable air quality levels, with 95.9% of cities failing to achieve acceptable air quality levels.

The manifestation of compound air pollution is centered on the frequent occurrence of hazy weather in years leading up to this writing. Strictly speaking, "haze" is not a scientific concept. As of this writing, the Chinese scientific community often uses the term "haze" or "gray haze", which refers to "a large number of very fine dry dust particles, etc. floating uniformly in the air, obscuring the view so that horizontal visibility is less than 10.0 kilometers" (China Meteorological Administration 2003: 23). Several scientific studies have analyzed the long-term trend of haze in China between 1951 and 2005 based on the data from ground meteorological stations across the country. These studies have shown that the number of hazy days in China has increased significantly since the 1980s. Moreover, hazy days have been quite common in most of the eastern parts of the country, and in large urban areas, throughout the twenty-first century (Wu et al. 2010). The causes of urban haze are complex. Scientific studies have shown that there are multiple sources of atmospheric $PM_{2.5}$, the main culprit of haze. These can be categorized into primary and secondary sources. The former includes sources such as coal burning, industrial production, motor vehicle emissions, and dust. The latter refers to gaseous pollutants that undergo "gas-particle transformation" (condensation, adsorption, reaction, etc.) in the atmosphere to produce $PM_{2.5}$ (He et al. 2013). In terms of external factors, factors such as subsurface characteristics, weather processes, atmospheric circulation, and climate change can also indirectly affect the formation of haze (Wang et al. 2013, 2014). In other words, the causes of haze may vary in different cities or regions, and even in the same city. Additionally, the main causes of haze may change from season to season. Despite the complex causes of haze, there is a consistent view that unlike traditional soot-based pollution, the sources of $PM_{2.5}$ that cause haze include not only traditional industrial emissions, but also motor vehicle emissions, which account for a significant portion of the haze problem. For example, the Beijing Municipal Environmental Protection Bureau released a new round of Beijing $PM_{2.5}$ source analysis results in 2018 which showed that local emissions had accounted for two-thirds of the main sources of $PM_{2.5}$ in Beijing throughout the year. Mobile sources contributed the most to local emissions at this stage (45%), and industrial sources and coal burning contributing only 12% and 3%, respectively.[2]

The production of composite urban air pollution is related to China's rapid industrialization, urbanization and other macro-social development processes that transpire during this stage (Koo et al. 2014); it is an important manifestation of the increasingly acute contradiction between development and the environment. During the first 40 years of the Reform and Opening-up, China has made remarkable achievements in social development. From 1978 to 2018, China's gross domestic product (GDP) grew from 367.9 billion yuan to 82,075.4 billion yuan, and it surpassed Japan to become the world's second-largest economy in 2010. During the same period, China's urban population as a percentage of the total population grew from 17.9% to 59.6% for a total of 831.37 million people. The rapid social development at the macro level has been built upon massive energy and resource consumption. From 1978 to 2017, China's total energy consumption increased from 571.44 million tons of standard coal to 449 billion tons. The resulting consequences were direct and indirect pressure on the atmospheric environment from human activities. This constituted the background for the production of compound air pollution in China at this stage.

Moreover, compound air pollution is also closely related to changes in the daily lives of Chinese urban residents, especially changes in modes of transportation. As mentioned earlier, compound air pollution is a type of air pollution that includes both soot-based pollution and petroleum-based pollution, and the main source of petroleum-based pollution is mobile sources, i.e., motor vehicle emissions. In 1978, there were only

[2] Beijing Municipal Bureau of Ecology and Environment. Latest scientific research results of the new round of Beijing $PM_{2.5}$ source analysis officially released. (2018-05-14) [2019-07-22]. http://sthjj.beijing.gov.cn/bjhrb/xxgk/jgzn/jgsz/jjgjgszjzz/xcjyc/xwfb/832588/index.html.

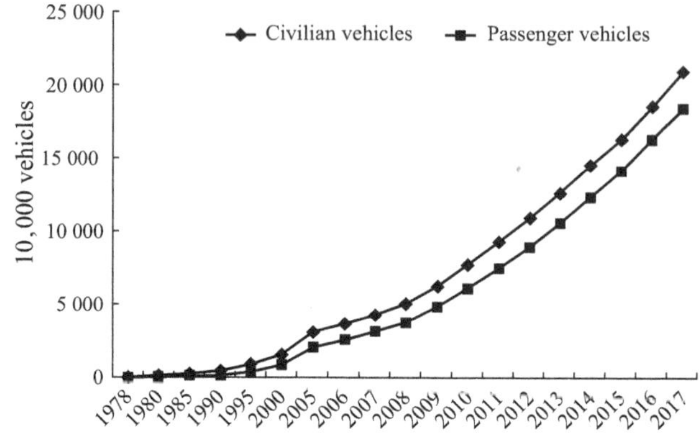

Fig. 1.2 Growth of civilian and passenger vehicles in China, 1978–2017 (*Source* 2018 China Statistical Yearbook)

1,358,400 automobiles in China, of which only 259,000 were passenger automobiles. However, since the 1990s, the number of automobiles in urban areas has grown exponentially with the improvement of urban living standards (see Fig. 1.2). According to data from the 2018 China Statistical Yearbook, by the end of 2017, the number of automobiles per 100 households among the country's residents had reached 29.7. This data indicates that China became an "automobile society" at this stage (Wang 2011). The advent of the automobile society reflects the increasingly important role of automobiles in the daily mobility practices of urban residents. If pollutant emissions from the use of automobiles are included, this also represents the expanding negative impact on the atmospheric environment caused by modern urban life.

1.2.2.2 The Delocalization of Pollution: From Localized Pollution to Widespread Pollution

Since the 1970s, the delocalization of urban air pollution in China has become increasingly prominent. According to the Environmental Flows Theory in environmental sociology, due to the connectivity of the ecosystem and the increasing social links between different regions, more and more environmental problems nowadays are characterized by delocalization, i.e., the variety of material flows across boundaries plays an increasingly important role in the emergence of environmental problems (Fan 2018). The emergence of urban air pollution in China is firstly manifested in the spread of air pollution from urban to suburban areas, and especially rural areas, resulting in a drop in air quality in some rural areas. Especially since the 1980s, with the emergence of township and village enterprises, the proliferation of small cement factories, brick kilns, and ceramic factories has caused serious damage to the air in rural areas, resulting in excessive rural air pollution in the 1990s (Jiang, and Li 1994; Li et al. 1999). However, in the twenty-first century, with the decline in township and village enterprises and the increase in national investment in environmental protection in the countryside, air pollution in rural areas of China has begun to subside, and air quality has improved.

The delocalization of urban air pollution in China has also been highlighted by the fact that the flow of air pollutants has broken through small, localized urban boundaries, and its dispersion is gradually becoming widespread. In the years leading up to this writing, air pollution has increasingly become a regional threat. For example, in 2013, China suffered its worst hazy conditions in 52 years, with haze incidents affecting more than 100 cities in 25 provinces (accounting for a quarter of the country's land area). Roughly 600 million people were affected, with the Beijing-Tianjin-Hebei metro area, the three Northeast provinces, and the Yangtze River Delta being the hardest-hit areas. Again, the 2017 China Climate Bulletin showed that from December 30, 2016 to January 7, 2017, widespread haze appeared in the central and southern parts of Northeast China, the eastern part of Northwest China, most of Northern China, Huanghuai, Jianghuai, Jianghan, Central and Northern Jiangnan, central Southern China, and the Sichuan Basin. Severe haze appeared in central and southern Northern China, Huanghuai, most of Jianghuai, central Liaoning, Guanzhong, and Shaanxi. Affected by this, haze warnings were issued in many places in Beijing, Tianjin, Hebei, Shandong, and Henan. Flights at many airports were delayed or canceled en masse, and many highways were forced to close. As of this writing, air pollution is most frequent in the Beijing-Tianjin-Hebei region, the Yangtze River and Pearl River Deltas, and the Fenhe Plain, and these regions have become the focus of China's air pollution mitigation efforts.

1.2.2.3 Public Concern Over Air Quality Continues to Grow

The constructivist paradigm in environmental sociology suggests that objective environmental conditions in a society do not become problems on their own, and that the emergence of any environmental problem depends on a joint construction process between scientists, governments, and media, among other actors. Only when it is widely recognized as a concern and action is needed in response, does a particular change in environmental conditions constitute a problem (Hannigan 2009; Gong 2011; Hong 2017). The presentation of urban air pollution as a category of environmental problems in China is also characterized by a typical social construction, as the Chinese public's perception of air pollution has transformed over the past decades. In the 1970s, when China's environmental protection program was in its nascence, both the government and the private sector had a minimal understanding of environmental protection. Even though urban air quality had deteriorated, only limited social concern could be aroused. However over time, public awareness of urban air pollution has grown. A sample social survey conducted by Lu Shuhua (1994) in Benxi City, Liaoning Province, in the early 1990s found that more than 80% of its residents had clearly perceived the deterioration of urban air quality caused by industrial emissions. Some respondents even expressed their concerns about air pollution in interviews. In the spring of 2014, the China Survey and Data Center at Renmin University of China was commissioned to conduct a telephone survey entitled "Beijing Residents' Haze Perceptions and Behavioral Responses". The results of the survey showed that 76.6% of the respondents believed that the haze phenomenon was serious in Beijing at that time, and the majority of the respondents reported that the haze had detracted from their daily work and livelihood, their physical health, and their mental health, making environmental protection the most important issue of concern to Beijing residents (Hong and Fan 2014). The public's general concern about urban air quality indicates that in contemporary China, air pollution has become an issue of common concern for the greater society.

Although growing public concern about air quality is in some sense a reflection of the fact that the atmospheric environment is indeed deteriorating, the issue of air pollution in China can also be viewed as socially constructed. The process of constructing the issue can be characterized in three ways. First, since 1972, with support from the Chinese government, specialized scientific research on air pollution gradually began, and the danger of air pollution in China started receiving systematic recognition. Furthermore, as a basic national policy, China's environmental education has long involved special presentations on the hazards, causes, and prevention of air pollution, and the importance of air pollution has gradually been popularized among different school-age groups. Finally, media publicity and reporting have also contributed to the focus on air pollution.

China's urban air pollution has a long history, and it is a phenomenon which appeared even before the 1970s, and even in some areas, it was very serious. Over the past 40 years, air pollution has undergone a transformation from localized soot-based pollution to wide-area composite pollution, and the overall understanding of air pollution among Chinese society has become clearer during this process.

1.3 The Evolution of Urban Air Pollution Mitigation Policies

Air pollution prevention and mitigation policy is a series of management measures adopted by the state to protect air quality. This includes not only environmental laws and regulations, but also all related policies and measures beyond environmental laws and regulations. China's air pollution prevention and mitigation policies have evolved along with the evolution of air pollution. In the process, with accelerating industrialization and urbanization, and the increasing pressure of social life on air quality, China's air pollution prevention and mitigation measures and methods have been continually adjusted. The evolution of China's urban air pollution prevention and mitigation policy has gone through four stages: initial establishment, rapid development, the prevention and alleviation of acid rain and sulfur dioxide pollution, and regional joint prevention and mitigation.

1.3.1 Initial Establishment (1973–1977)

In 1972, the Chinese government sent representatives to attend the United Nations Conference on the Human Environment held in Stockholm. The following year, the First National Conference on Environmental Protection was held in Beijing, thus opening the way for China's environmental protection endeavors (Qu 1999). The conference adopted *Several Provisions on the Protection and Improvement of the Environment*, the first regulatory document on environmental protection issued by the Chinese government since the founding of the People's Republic. The main points of the document were: Urban air pollution should be mitigated through the rational layout of industries, and effective measures must be undertaken to eliminate smoke and dust from the exhausts of all establishments. Fuel alternatives to coal should also be developed in a planned and systematic manner and district heating should be promoted. Air pollutants that must be emitted from industrial production should be utilized in a comprehensive manner, or purified as much as possible. On the basis of the *Several Provisions on the Protection and Improvement of the Environment*, the Chinese Government also issued the "Trial Standards for the Emission of Industrial (Three Wastes)" in the same year in order to better prevent environmental pollution caused by the emission of the industrial "three wastes". In terms of air pollutant emissions, the standards are based on the degree of harm they cause the human body and also account for existing conditions in China. The Chinese government set tentative emissions standards for the height of smokestacks, emissions volumes, and emission concentrations of 13 types of harmful substances in five industrial sectors. The harmful substances included sulfur dioxide, carbon dioxide, hydrogen sulfide, fluoride, nitrogen oxides, chlorine, hydrogen chloride, carbon monoxide, sulfuric acid (spray), lead, mercury, beryllium, soot, and production dust.

Under the guidance of the *Several Provisions on the Protection and Improvement of the Environment* and the *Trial Standards for the Emission of Industrial* (Three Wastes), China's air pollution prevention and mitigation efforts were formally launched. In the years that followed, several cities implemented air pollution mitigation measures focused on eliminating smoke and dust. However, due to the interference of the Cultural Revolution, although the national air pollution mitigation measures had been implemented in localized areas and achieved some results, the measures were unable to curtail the deterioration of China's air quality. Nevertheless, it is important to note that the air pollution prevention and mitigation policies of this period were established from a blank slate, marking the end of the long-term laissez-faire regulation of air pollution in China's cities, the significance of which is self-evident.

1.3.2 Rapid Development (1978–1994)

In March 1978, the Constitution of the People's Republic of China was adopted at the first session of the Fifth National People's Congress. The Constitution specifically addressed environmental protection: "The state shall protect the environment and natural resources and prevent pollution and other public hazards". For the first time since the founding of the People's Republic of China, the formulation and implementation of national environmental policy was constitutionally guaranteed, and China's air pollution prevention and mitigation policy entered a period of rapid development.

On the basis of the constitution, the prevention and mitigation of air pollution in China began to be codified into law. In September 1979, the Standing Committee of the National People's Congress adopted the *Environmental Protection Law of the People's Republic of China* (for Trial Implementation) at its 11th meeting. The declaration of the Environmental Protection Law marked the end of the period of unreliable environmental protection in China, clarified the objects and tasks of environmental protection, determined the basic policy and the "whoever pollutes, whoever treats" policy. It also stipulated the establishment of environmental protection management organizations and their duties. Articles 18 and 19 of the law contain specific provisions on emissions standards for air pollutants, the development of clean energy, and the promotion of district heating. In September 1987, the Standing Committee of the Sixth National People's Congress, at its twenty-second meeting, considered and adopted the *Law of the People's Republic of China on the Prevention and Control of Air Pollution*. This legislation regulated the sectors that produce soot and other air pollutants in fields such as industry, civil use, transportation, and construction, and assigned environmental protection agencies the responsibility for the prevention and mitigation of air pollutants. In May 1991, the State Environmental Protection Bureau issued *Detailed Rules for the Implementation of the Law of the People's Republic of China on the Prevention and Control of Air Pollution*, which provided specific explanations and supplements to the *Law of the People's Republic of China on the Prevention and Control of Air Pollution*.

Additionally, the mitigation of industrial pollution sources has become the key target of air pollution alleviation in the new period, and the state has enacted numerous policy arrangements both prior to and since this shift. In 1981, the State Council issued *Decision on Strengthening Environmental Protection in the Period of Adjustment of the National Economy*, which initiated focus on the problem of serious pollution from factories and enterprises in residential areas, water source protection areas and tourist areas, requiring that boilers in factories be either equipped with dust collectors or implement effective measures to eliminate smoke and dust, and levying sewage charges on enterprises that emit pollutants exceeding the national standards. In February 1983, the State Council issued *Regulations on Combining Technological Reforms to Prevent and Control Industrial Pollution*, stipulating that when industrial enterprises implement technological reforms, they should emphasize the prevention and mitigation of industrial pollution, and improve the utilization rate of resources and energy through the adoption of advanced technology and equipment, so as to eliminate pollutants in the production process. Against the background of the proliferation of air pollution from cities to rural areas, the State Council issued *Regulations on Strengthening the Environmental Management of Townships and Street Enterprises* in September 1984. This prohibited townships and street enterprises from engaging in seriously polluting production projects, and required townships and street enterprises that discharged the three wastes of industry to collect sewage and urged them to curb them by a deadline. In July 1987, the State Council's Environmental Protection Committee considered and passed *Measures for the Administration of Urban Smoke and Dust Control Areas*, proposing to quantitatively limit the concentration of smoke and dust emitted from various furnaces and industrial production facilities within the areas delineated by city streets and administrative districts such that they would meet the prescribed standards. In September 1992, the State Environmental Protection Administration, the State Council's State Price Administration, and the Ministry of Finance and Economic and Trade Office jointly issued the *Pilot Program for Levying Industrial Coal-Fired Sulfur Dioxide Emission Fees*. It identified Guizhou and Guangdong provinces and cities including Chongqing, Yibin, Nanning, Guilin, Liuzhou, Yichang, Qingdao, Hangzhou, Changsha, and nine others to implement a pilot program for collecting industrial coal-fired sulfur dioxide sewage.

Finally, other air pollution prevention policies of this period also targeted the transformation of domestic energy in urban areas and the mitigation of pollution from mobile sources. In 1981, the State Council issued *Decision on Strengthening Environmental Protection in the Period of Adjustment of the National Economy*, in which it was proposed that low-sulfur and low-volatile coal be supplied to the civilian population as a priority, and centralized heat supply and combined heat supply be promoted in urban planning and construction, with the planned development of gas and the rational use of liquefied petroleum gas (LPG). In October 1984, the State Council's Environmental Protection Committee issued *Provisions on Technical Policies of Preventing and Combating Soot Pollution*, which offered specific provisions on the technical policies of centralized urban heating and urban gasification. In July 1987, the State Council's Environmental Protection Committee and six other ministries considered and *passed Interim Measures on Developing Civilian Coal*, which proposed accelerating the promotion and development of civilian coal. In August 1990, the State Environmental Protection Bureau, in conjunction with several other departments, issued *Measures for the Supervision and Management of Vehicle Exhaust Pollution*. This directive required that the exhaust pollution from automobiles and their engine products be included in the supervision and mitigation of automobile exhaust pollution, and that automobile exhaust pollution must meet emissions standards set by the State.

Overall, the period from 1978 to 1994 was an important period for the development of air pollution prevention and mitigation policies in China, and many related policy arrangements were implemented in succession, reflecting the state's emphasis on the air pollution problem. These policies also denoted the specific direction for the curbing of urban air pollution, which had become increasingly serious at that time.

1.3.3 The Prevention and Mitigation of Acid Rain and Sulphur Dioxide Pollution (1995–2009)

Since the mid-1990s, China's air pollution problems, characterized by acid rain and sulfur dioxide pollution, have become increasingly prominent, and the mitigation of acid rain and sulfur dioxide pollution have become the focus of China's air pollution prevention and mitigation work. In August 1995, the Standing Committee of the National People's Congress passed the *Law of the People's Republic of China on the Prevention and Control of Air Pollution*. It stipulated that the country should designate an Acid Rain Control Zone and a Sulfur Dioxide Pollution Control Zone ("the two control zones") and strengthen the alleviation of acid rain and sulfur dioxide pollution within the control zone. In January

1998, the State Council approved the *Acid Rain Control Area and Sulfur Dioxide Pollution Control Area Delineation Program* formulated by the State Environmental Protection Bureau, which defined the "two control zones". This included the four municipalities directly under the central government, 21 provincial capitals, and 175 cities and districts at the prefectural level or above, with a total area of about 1.09 million square kilometers (11.4% of the national territory). The program also proposed pollution alleviation objectives for the two control areas by the years 2000 and 2010. In 2002, the State Council approved the *Tenth Five-Year Plan for Prevention and Control of Acid Rain and Sulfur Dioxide Pollution in Two Controlled Areas*. This directive set reduction targets for 2005 for sulfur dioxide emissions and acid rain pollution in the two controlled areas, and proposed specific emissions reduction measures. In 2007, the National Development and Reform Commission (NDRC) and the State Environmental Protection Administration (SEPA) issued the *11th Five-Year Plan for Sulfur Dioxide Control in Existing Coal-fired Power Plants*, proposing a goal of reducing the total sulfur dioxide emissions from existing coal-fired power plants by 61.4% during the 11th Five-Year Plan period. In January 2008, the State Council approved the *National 11th Five-Year Plan for Acid Rain and Sulfur Dioxide Pollution Prevention and Control*, proposing that China's total sulfur dioxide emissions be reduced by 10% from 2005 to 2010, effectively mitigating acid rain pollution and reducing sulfur dioxide concentrations in urban air. In addition, in order to implement the newly revised *Air Pollution Prevention and Control Law of the People's Republic of China* in 2000, the state also issued the *Regulations on the Classification of High-Pollution Fuels* and the *Technical Policy for the Prevention and Control of Sulfur Dioxide Emissions from Coal Combustion*, in 2001 and 2002 respectively. This required all cities to demark urban prohibition zones for high-pollution fuel to alleviate soot pollution.

Total volume reduction was also an important strategy in China's air pollution prevention and alleviation efforts during this period. Prior to 1996, China's pollution management strategy had been based on pollutant emission standards, that is, relying on reducing pollutant emission concentrations in order to implement environmental policies and environmental management (Song 2000). In August 1996, the State Council issued the *Decision on Several Issues Concerning Environmental Protection*, proposing the implementation of total pollutant emissions management. This policy proposed the establishment of a national indicator system for the total amount of major pollutant emissions, and a system of regular announcements. It also required provinces, autonomous regions, and municipalities directly under the central government to keep the total amount of major pollutant emissions under their jurisdiction within the national total emissions indicators. During this period, the relevant policy arrangements for the prevention and alleviation of sulfur dioxide pollution were the embodiment of the total volume reduction strategy.

Driven by these national policies, between 1995 and 2009 China made significant progress in alleviating acid rain and sulfur dioxide pollution. National environmental monitoring data show that the frequency of acid rain in China has been declining since 2007, and the amount of acid rain in the country as a whole has decreased (Xie et al. 2012). In addition, China's total sulfur dioxide emissions peaked in 2006, and has been declining ever since (see Fig. 1.1).

1.3.4 Regional Joint Prevention and Alleviation (2010–Present)

The territorial nature of air pollution largely determines the magnitude of the challenge of air pollution management. Although territorial management can play a role in improving air quality at the local level, it is usually unable to properly address air pollution on a larger spatial scale and across geographical boundaries. For this reason, air pollution management requires the cooperation of governments and environmental protection departments in different locales and at different levels, based on which enterprises and social forces should be introduced to participate in the mitigation process to improve its effectiveness. In recent years, the effectiveness of the traditional territorial governance model has faced great challenges as air pollution has become increasingly widespread. At the same time, the frequent occurrence of large-scale hazy weather has increased public concerns over air quality. Against this backdrop, China's air pollution management policy has undergone a transformation. Since 2010, the Chinese government has accelerated the pace of air pollution management policies (Zhang, and Wu 2010), and air pollution management has received unprecedented attention and support. The new air pollution prevention and management policy emphasizing joint regional prevention and alleviation indicates that China's air pollution management has begun to break through the limitations of traditional territorial management in order to better adapt to the changing dynamics of air pollution, which is becoming increasingly complex.

In May 2010, the State Council issued *Guiding Opinions on Promoting Joint Prevention and Control of Air Pollution and Improvement of Regional Air Quality*. This directive proposed the establishment of a joint prevention and alleviation mechanism for air pollution by 2015, and the enactment of a system of laws, regulations, standards, and policies for regional air pollution management. This was China's first comprehensive air pollution prevention and alleviation policy, and it clarified the guiding ideology, objectives, and key measures for air pollution prevention and alleviation at this stage. In November of the same year, the Ministry of Environmental Protection (MEP) issued the *Notice on the Preparation of the Joint Prevention and Control Plan for Air Pollution in Key Areas during the 12th Five-Year Plan Period*. This resulted in the establishment of regional air pollution management programs in three major regions—the Yangtze River Delta (YRD), the Pearl River Delta (PRD), and Beijing-Tianjin-Hebei (BTH), and in six urban clusters—Chengdu-Chongqing, central Liaoning, the Shandong Peninsula, Wuhan, Chang Zhu Tan, and the west bank of the Taiwan Strait (Three Regions and Six Groups). In September 2012, the State Council approved the *12th Five-Year Plan for Prevention and Control of Air Pollution in Key Regions*, proposing the joint establishment of regional air pollution prevention and alleviation mechanisms in 13 key regions such as Beijing-Tianjin-Hebei, the Yangtze River Delta, and the Pearl River Delta by 2015. In September 2013, the *Action Plan for Prevention and Control of Air Pollution* issued by the State Council proposed policy measures to establish a mechanism for regional collaboration and to coordinate regional environmental governance. In 2015, the newly revised *Law of the People's Republic of China on Prevention and Control of Air Pollution* formally incorporated the establishment of a joint prevention and alleviation mechanism in key regions into law. In February 2017, the MEP, along with the Air Pollution Prevention and Control Cooperation Group of Beijing-Tianjin-Hebei and Surrounding Areas and relevant danwei, formulated the *2017 Air Pollution Prevention and Control Work Plan for Beijing-Tianjin-Hebei and Surrounding Areas*, and increased the intensity of air pollution management in the "2 + 26" cities[3] along the Beijing-Tianjin-Hebei air pollution transmission channel.

[3] The "2 + 26" cities were Beijing; Tianjin; Shijiazhuang, Tangshan, Langfang, Baoding, Cangzhou, Hengshui, Xingtai, and Handan in Hebei Province; Taiyuan, Yangquan, Changzhi, and Jincheng in Shanxi Province; Jinan, Zibo, Jining, Dezhou,

By reviewing China's relevant policy arrangements for air pollution prevention and alleviation since the 1970s, we can draw two conclusions. First, the Chinese government's scientific understanding of air pollution is constantly deepening, and it has long emphasized air pollution management. Second, China's air pollution prevention and alleviation policies are in-step with the evolution of air pollution. In response to the dominant characteristics of air pollution at different stages, the country has enacted corresponding policy arrangements in a timely manner.

1.4 New Trends in Urban Air Pollution Against the Backdrop of "Iron Fist" Pollution Management

China's environmental protection work has been implemented in an orderly manner since the 1970s, and by the beginning of the twenty-first century it had begun to bear fruit. As such, the trend of continuous deterioration of the ecological environment has gradually eased. Nevertheless, in the decade leading up to this writing, China's economic and social development has caused immense environmental pressure, and several prominent environmental problems have intensified, arousing social concern. Furthermore, conventional environmental protection measures have been unable to respond to the public's growing demand for a cleaner environment. Beginning in 2012, China entered an era of "iron-fisted pollution management" and "declaring war on pollution". The Chinese government launched a series of extraordinary measures to strengthen the governance of several prominent environmental problems, including air pollution. Against the backdrop of the era of iron-fisted pollution management, China's urban air pollution management is facing unprecedented opportunities, with several impressive achievements having been made.

Liaocheng, Binzhou, and Heze in Shandong Province; and Zhengzhou, Kaifeng, Anyang, Hebi, Xinxiang, Jiaozuo, and Puyang in Henan Province.

1.4.1 *The Advent of the "Iron Fist Pollution Management" Era and the Extraordinary Treatment of Air Pollution*

Facing increasingly severe ecological and environmental conditions, the 18th National Congress of the Communist Party of China (CPC) held in 2012 proposed emphasizing the construction of "ecological civilization", and integrating it into all aspects of economic, political, cultural, and social construction. It also proposed endeavoring to "build a beautiful China" to achieve the sustainable development of the Chinese nation. In a September 2013 conversation with entrepreneurial representatives at the Summer Davos Forum in Dalian, Premier Li Keqiang said:

> The Chinese government will firmly follow the path of green development. At the same time, we must strike with an iron fist to rectify existing pollution. We will start with the air, water and soil, which directly affect human health, increase the intensity of remediation, and resolutely eliminate outdated production capacity.[4]

The 2014 *Government Work Report* further clarified that the Chinese government would strengthen pollution prevention and alleviation, and resolutely declare war on pollution. With promotion from the Party and the government, China's environmental protection had ushered in a new era of iron-fisted pollution management.[5]

In the era of iron-fisted pollution management, the Chinese government has formulated a special plan to improve air quality across the country in a step-by-step manner, in response to the complex regional problem of smog-based air pollution. In September 2013, the State Council issued the *Air Pollution Prevention and Control Action Plan* (APPCAP), which focused on the prevention and alleviation of $PM_{2.5}$ pollutants, and proposed 10 articles including 35 measures for the alleviation of air pollution. This marked the official launch of the first phase of the air pollution management work. APPCAP's goals and specific five-year targets are: overall improvement of air quality across the country;

[4] Li Keqiang: Chinese government firmly takes green development path. (2013-09-10) [2019-07-22]. http://cpc.people.com.cn/n/2013/0910/c64094-22875570.html.

[5] Multi-departmental joint action on China's iron-fisted pollution management gets real (2014-06-13) [2019-07-22]. http://paper.people.com.cn/rmrbhwb/html/2014-06/13/content_1440894.htm.

a substantial reduction in heavily polluted days; and significant improvement in the air quality in Beijing-Tianjin-Hebei, the Yangtze River Delta, the Pearl River Delta, and other areas. The next goal over the following five years was gradual elimination of heavily polluted days and significant improvement of nationwide air quality. By 2017, the PM_{10} concentration in prefecture-level and above cities had dropped by more than 10% compared with 2012, and the number of days with good air quality had increased every year. The $PM_{2.5}$ concentration in Beijing-Tianjin-Hebei, the Yangtze River Delta, the Pearl River Delta, and other regions had also dropped by about 25%, 20%, and 15% respectively, with the annual average concentration of $PM_{2.5}$ in Beijing stabilized at about 60 $\mu g/m^3$. APPCAP is a major strategic plan to promote air pollution management in the new era, and it is also China's first national clean air plan with air quality target objectives. It demonstrates the current Chinese government's confidence and determination in its air pollution management.

In order to implement APPCAP, the State Council and local governments signed target responsibility letters, implemented annual implementation assessments, and each province, autonomous region, and municipality also formulated its own implementation plan in light of its actual conditions. In 2013, the central government started establishing "special funds for the prevention and alleviation of air pollution" to support the implementation of key APPCAP tasks. By the end of 2017, the cumulative investment had reached 63.3 billion yuan. Provinces, cities, and counties have also implemented corresponding funds for air pollution management. In addition, the MEP has also conducted central environmental protection inspections in all provinces, autonomous regions, and municipalities across the country, and interviewed government officials who have failed to alleviate air pollution. Since April 2017, the MEP has dispatched 5,600 environmental law enforcement personnel across the country to implement a year-long intensive inspection of the 2 + 26 cities in the Beijing-Tianjin-Hebei air pollution transmission channel. In September of the same year, it also sent its direct subordinate units to implement daily inspections in various districts and counties (Wang et al. 2018). The 2017 Communiqué on the Status of China's Ecology and Environment issued by the Ministry of Ecology and Environment summarized the implementation of the APPCAP from 2013 to 2017 with the following accomplishments:

- It eliminated most coal-fired small boilers in built-up areas of cities at the prefecture level and above.
- It eliminated more than 200,000 coal-fired small boilers below 10 tons in developed urban areas.
- The transformation of 700 million kilowatts of ultra-low emissions coal-fired power plants was completed.
- Nation-wide "V motor" vehicle emissions standards and oil standards were implemented.
- All "yellow-label" vehicles[6] were eliminated, and a cumulative 1.8 million new energy vehicles were put on the road.
- The promotion of the ship emission management area plan.
- The launch of a research project on the causes and treatment of heavy air pollution
- The implementation of comprehensive air pollution management in autumn and winter in Beijing-Tianjin-Hebei and surrounding areas
- The Cleaning and rectification 62,000 gas-related 'scattered pollution' enterprises
- The completion of the annual task of replacing coal with gas or electricity, and reducing the consumption of loose coal by about 10 million tons
- The implementation of the peak shifting production of industrial enterprises in the heating season; Tianjin, Hebei and the Shandong Bohai Rim ports each switched their coal collection and distribution ports to railway transportation.

In sum, the APPCAP can be regarded as a "strong medicine" specially prescribed by the Chinese government to improve air quality in the new era. Its implementation has expedited the process of air pollution management in China.

A new phase of China's extraordinary air pollution management work is now underway. 2017 was the final year of the APPCAP. In order to consolidate the hard-won results of air pollution management, the State Council officially released *Winning the Three-Year Action Plan for*

[6] "Yellow-Label Vehicle" refers to vehicles with high-pollution emissions, specifically gasoline-powered vehicles that do not meet National Emission Standard I or diesel-powered vehicles that do not comply with National Emission Standard III. These vehicles are labeled with a yellow environmental protection emblem, hence the designation "Yellow-Label Vehicle".

Defending the Blue Sky (hereinafter referred to as the Action Plan), which deploys the new phase of air pollution management. The goals and targets set by the Action Plan are as follows:

- Within three years, significantly reduce the total emissions of major air pollutants, greenhouse gas emissions, concentrations of $PM_{2.5}$ and the number of heavily polluted days; significantly improve the ambient air quality, and enhance people's sense of blue-sky happiness.
- By 2020, reduce the total emissions of sulfur dioxide and nitrogen oxides by at least 15% compared with 2015.
- Reduce concentrations of $PM_{2.5}$ in cities at the prefecture level and above by at least 18% compared with 2015.
- Increase the ratio of good air quality days in cities at the prefecture level and above to 80% or better, and reduce the ratio of heavily polluted days to 25% or less of what there was in 2015.
- Provinces that have completed the goals and tasks of the 13th Five-Year Plan ahead of schedule should maintain and consolidate the improvement; those that have not yet completed them should ensure that the binding goals of the 13th Five-Year Plan are achieved.
- Beijing's ambient air quality improvement targets should be further improved on the basis of the 13th Five-Year Plan targets.

The Action Plan is the second national clean air plan since the APPCAP, and its implementation has demonstrated the determination and commitment of the Chinese government to continue to combat air pollution with an iron fist. It is reasonable to believe that this will lead China's air pollution management to new heights in the present and in the future.

1.4.2 Recent Improvements in Urban Air Quality

Since the implementation of the "Iron Fist Pollution Management", there has been significant improvement in China's air quality. In February 2012, the *Ambient Air Quality Standards* (GB3095-2012) was officially released, providing a new reference standard for the evaluation of air quality. Beginning January 1, 2013, a total of 74 cities directly administered by the central government, provincial capitals and cities with separate plans, as well as 496 monitoring points of the national ambient air monitoring network in key regions such as Beijing-Tianjin-Hebei, the Yangtze River Delta, and the Pearl River Delta, began monitoring air pollution using the new standards. Using the monitoring data released by the government between 2013 and 2017, we can analyze recent trends in air quality in major cities and key areas in China.

We can see the monitoring results of some major air pollutants in key cities across the country in these years. Between 2013 and 2017, 74 Chinese cities implemented concentration monitoring of six major pollutants: SO_2, NO_2, PM_{10}, $PM_{2.5}$, O_3, and CO. The percentage of cities that met the annual average concentration limits of each pollutant in all monitored cities were calculated according to air quality standards (see Table 1.1).

As shown in Table 1.1, since 2013, the compliance of major air pollutants in major cities nationwide has improved. The monitoring results of 74 cities nationwide show:

- The percentage of cities meeting the standard for NO_2 increased from 39.2% in 2013 to 52.7% in 2017.
- The percentage of cities meeting the standard for PM_{10} also increased from the initial 14.9% to 43.2%, an increase of nearly 30%.
- The percentage of cities meeting the standard for $PM_{2.5}$ in 2017 was six times more than that of 2013, even though the percentage of cities meeting the standard for PM was only 25.7%.

Table 1.1 Percentage of cities meeting the standards for major air pollutants in 74 cities nationwide, 2013–2017 (unit: %)

	SO_2	NO_2	PM_{10}	$PM_{2.5}$	O_3	CO
2013	86.5	39.2	14.9	4.1	77.0	85.1
2014	89.2	48.6	21.6	12.2	67.6	95.9
2015	95.9	51.4	28.4	16.2	62.2	94.6
2016	98.7	54.1	37.9	18.9	62.2	95.9
2017	100.0	52.7	43.2	25.7	35.1	100.0

Source Bulletin on the State of China's Environment, 2013–2016; Bulletin on the State of China's Ecological Environment, 2017

By 2017, all monitored cities had achieved full compliance in SO_2 and CO concentrations. Unfortunately, the percentage of O_3 monitoring results in the 74 cities in China that met the standards has not increased over the past few years, and even showed an unusually large drop in 2017.

Given that $PM_{2.5}$ is the focus of air pollution prevention and alleviation in the new era, we now have more data about the changes in annual average PM2.5 concentrations monitored in key cities and regions across China from 2013 to 2017 (see Fig. 1.3).

As shown in Fig. 1.3, the annual average concentrations of $PM_{2.5}$ in major cities and key regions across the country have declined at different rates since 2013. The results show that:

- The annual average concentration of $PM_{2.5}$ in 74 cities nationwide decreased from 72 $\mu g/m^3$ in 2013 to 47 $\mu g/m^3$ in 2017.
- Among the key regions, the change in the annual average concentration of $PM_{2.5}$ in the Beijing-Tianjin-Hebei region was the largest, decreasing from 106 $\mu g/m^3$ initially to 64 $\mu g/m^3$ over the four years.

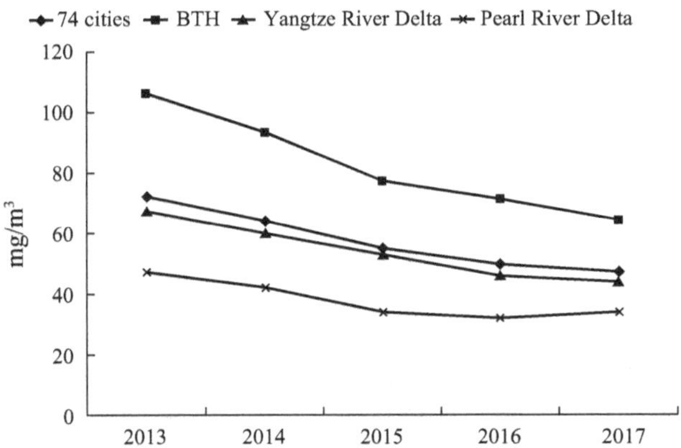

Fig. 1.3 Changes in annual average concentrations of $PM_{2.5}$ in key cities and key regions of China, 2013–2017 (*Source* Bulletin on the State of China's Environment, 2013–2016; Bulletin on the State of China's Ecological Environment, 2017)

- The Yangtze River Delta (YRD) region decreased from 67 μg/m^3 to 44 μg/m^3 and the Pearl River Delta region (PRD) decreased from 47 μg/m^3 to 34 μg/m^3.

Although the annual average concentration of $PM_{2.5}$ in the PRD is the only one that meets the national air quality standard (less than or equal to 35 μg/m3), on the whole, the above results show that $PM_{2.5}$ management has begun to bear fruit.

The effective reduction of air pollutants is directly reflected in improvements in air quality. According to the "Ambient Air Quality Index (AQI) Technical Provisions (for Trial Implementation)", China currently utilizes the ambient air quality index (AQI) to evaluate air quality, corresponding to the following values and descriptions:

0–50:	Excellent
51–100:	Good
101–150:	Mildly polluted
151–200:	Moderately polluted
201–300:	Heavily polluted
300+:	Extremely polluted

We can see the changes in the percentage of days with good or excellent quality in key cities and regions year-over-year since 2013 (see Fig. 1.4).

As shown from Fig. 1.4, the percentage of good days in key cities and regions in China has been increasing in recent years. The results of monitoring data show that from 2013 to 2017, the percentage of good days in the 74 cities increased from 60.5% to 72.7%. Among the key regions, the percentage of good days in the Beijing-Tianjin-Hebei region increased by nearly 20% over the five years (from 37.5% to 56.0%), and the AQI of the Yangtze River Delta and the Pearl River Delta regions also improved by about 10%.

The improvement in air quality is also directly reflected in the reduction in the number of heavily polluted days. To this end, we also examined the year-over-year changes in the percentage of heavily polluted days each year in key cities and regions from 2013 to 2017 (see Fig. 1.5).

As shown in Fig. 1.5, the percentage of heavily polluted days in key cities and regions in China has declined in recent years. The results of the

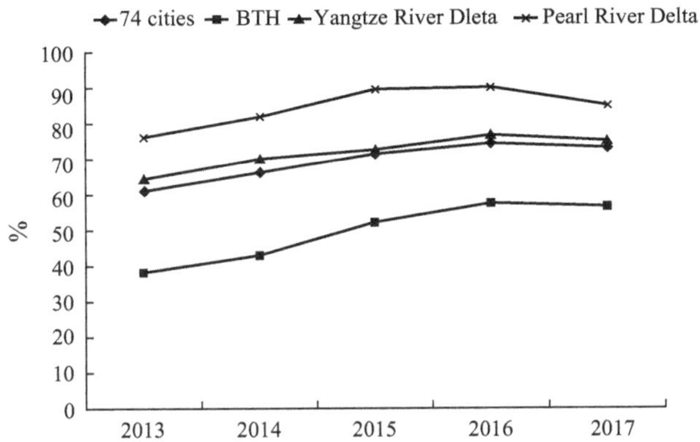

Fig. 1.4 Changes in the proportion of good days in key cities and key regions nationwide, 2013–2017 (*Source* Bulletin on the State of China's Environment, 2013–2016; Bulletin on the State of China's Ecological Environment, 2017)

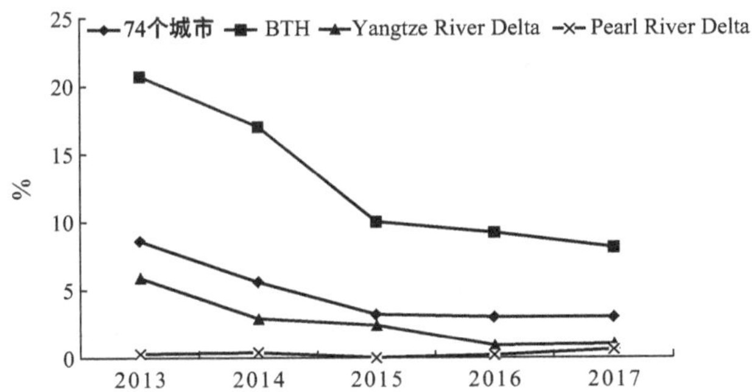

Fig. 1.5 Changes in the percentage of heavily polluted days in key cities and key regions nationwide, 2013–2017 (*Source* Bulletin on the State of China's Environment, 2013–2016; Bulletin on the State of China's Ecological Environment, 2017)

monitoring data from the 74 cities in China show that the percentage of heavily polluted days decreased from 8.6% in 2013 to 3.0% in 2017. In specific key regions, the percentage of heavily polluted days in the Beijing-Tianjin-Hebei region decreased by 12.6% over five years (from 20.7% to 8.1%), and the Yangtze River Delta region experienced a decrease from

5.9% to 1%. However, the percentage of heavily polluted days in the Pearl River Delta region has remained at an ultra-low level, below 0.6%.

In summary, from 2013 to 2017, China's key cities and regions effectively alleviated major air pollutants, with the percentage of good days increasing year-over-year and the percentage of heavily polluted days decreasing. This indicates that China's urban air quality has shown significant improvement in recent years. This improvement is largely due to the Chinese government's iron-fisted pollution management strategy and extraordinary air pollution management actions. However, urban air pollution in China remains serious. According to the 2018 *China Ecological Environment Situation Bulletin*, in 2018, only 121 of the country's 338 cities at or above the prefecture level had met ambient air quality standards. Although there has been significant improvement since 2017, 64.2% of the cities still fell short of the standards. Moreover, only 56.8% and 43.8% of the cities met the standards for PM_{10} and PM 2.5, respectively. The percentage of O_3 concentration days exceeding the standard have also increased compared to 2017. In addition, currently China's emissions of SO_2, nitrogen oxides, smoke (dust), and other air pollutants still rank among the world's worst, far beyond the acceptable capacity of the atmospheric environment. To achieve acceptable air quality standards, emissions still need to be reduced by at least 50% (Department of Atmospheric Environment, Ministry of Ecology and Environment 2018). This reminds us that air pollution management is a cause that is difficult to accomplish in a single attempt, and it is still necessary to continue to implement air pollution prevention and alleviation actions, and to prepare for a long-term war.

CHAPTER 2

Water Pollution and Its Governance in Urban Areas

Shi Chaoyi

Water is an indispensable resource all living organisms need to survive in the natural world. Although it is an essential element of the ecological environment, its scarcity and ecological significance have not received sufficient attention in recent years. Beginning with the Reform and Opening-up, with China's rapid industrialization and urbanization, secondary and tertiary industries were concentrated in highly populated city centers and their surroundings. Large amounts of untreated industrial sewage and household sewage were directly discharged into the local bodies of water, contaminating these bodies. By the late 1990s, this situation was becoming increasingly urgent. In the twenty-first century, Chinese people's environmental awareness has begun to gradually improve (Yan et al. 2010; Hong 2014) and the government has tightened the management of water pollution and the water environment. This has produced some results, but sewage discharge is still increasing

C. Shi (✉)
Department of Public Administration, East China University of Science and Technology, Shanghai, China
e-mail: shichaoyi@ecust.edu.cn

D. Hong and Y. Fan (eds.), *Toward a Green Society*,
https://doi.org/10.1007/978-981-96-5111-5_2

year-over-year. Coupled with decades of accumulated pollution, the situation has become extremely serious. Beginning with the 18th National Congress of the Communist Party of China (CPC), China has incorporated the construction of ecological civilization into the "Five-Sphere Integrated Plan" overall layout of the socialist cause with Chinese characteristics. Additionally, the 19th CPC National Congress proposed the goal of "Accelerating the Reform of the Ecological Civilization System and Building a Beautiful China". In this context, urban water pollution has been significantly curbed in recent years, but the situation is still grim. This chapter analyzes the development of urban water pollution, and its treatment.

2.1 Urban Water Pollution

China suffers from serious water shortages. Although China's total amount of water resources is the world's sixth largest, China's population is massive, and per capita water resources are small, less than 1/3 of the world's per capita average. For example, 2017 was an abundant year for water, yet water resources were only 2,069 m^3 per capita. In a dry year, there are even less water resources, with only 1,730 m^3 per capita in 2011 (see Table 2.1). As such, urban water shortages are particularly widespread. Around two-thirds of China's 600 municipal cities suffer water shortages. Furthermore, at least 110 cities experience serious water shortages. In Beijing, before the opening of the South-to-North Water Diversion Project, water resources were only about 150 m^3 per capita in years of water shortages, far below the internationally recognized warning level of 1,000 m^3 per capita.

At the same time, water pollution is also a cause for concern, and shortages of quality water have exacerbated China's water shortage. The shortage of water resources and the deterioration of the water environment have become bottlenecks for the sustainable development of the urban economy and society in most parts of China, and the deterioration of the water environment has only been curbed and improved in recent years. The following analysis and evaluations are based on statistical data published by the National Bureau of Statistics of China, the *Water Resources Bulletin* published by the Ministry of Water Resources, the *Environmental Quality Bulletin* published by the Ministry of Ecology and Environment, and the *Basin Water Resources Bulletin* published by the water conservancy committees of each river basin.

Table 2.1 Total water resources and per capita water resources in China, 2010–2018

	2010	*2011*	*2012*	*2013*	*2014*	*2015*	*2016*	*2017*	*2018*
Total water resources (trillion m^3)	3.09	2.32	2.95	2.79	2.73	2.79	3.25	2.88	2.79
Water resources per capita (m^3)	2,310	1,730	2,186	2,054	1,993	2,034	2,348	2,069	2,004

Note The total amount of water resources is based on data published on the official website of the National Bureau of Statistics of the People's Republic of China, and the per capita amount of water resources is calculated based on China's total population in that year

2.1.1 Massive Sewage Discharges, and the Proliferation of Domestic Sewage

Industrial and domestic wastewater discharges are the main sources of urban water pollution. This is why the *National Environmental Statistics Bulletin*, which is published annually by the Ministry of Environmental Protection of China, only included industrial wastewater and urban domestic wastewater before 2011. According to the bulletin data, the total amount of wastewater discharged in China has grown over the long term, from 42.84 billion tons in 2001 to 73.53 billion tons in 2015 (see Fig. 2.1). According to the National Bureau of Statistics' official website, China's total wastewater discharges began trending downward in 2016, with 71.1 billion tons in that year, and dropped further to 69.97 billion tons in 2017.

It is generally perceived that industrial pollution is the main cause of water pollution. However, the total amount of sewage discharged since the mid-1990s in China's cities and towns has exceeded the total amount of industrial wastewater. In the twenty-first century, this trend has been more pronounced. The total amount of industrial wastewater has decreased each year since 2007, from 24.6 billion tons to 19.95 billion tons in 2015. Moreover, the total amount of urban domestic sewage discharge has ballooned, from 23.23 billion tons in 2002 to 53.52 billion tons in 2015. The total amount of Chemical Oxygen Demand (COD) and ammonia nitrogen discharged from domestic sewage is also significantly higher than that from industrial sewage, and the total amount of ammonia nitrogen discharged from domestic sewage is three times higher

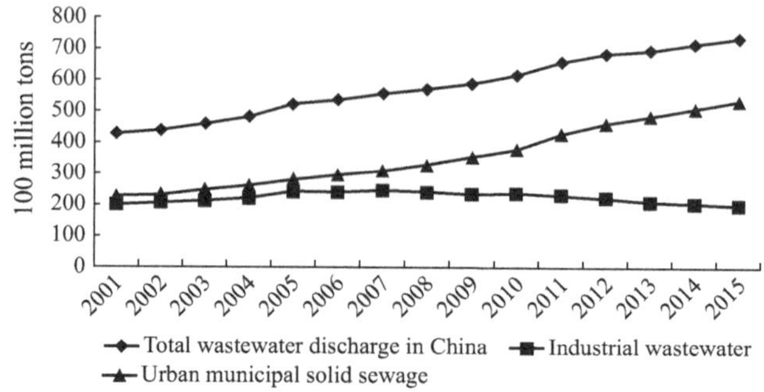

Fig. 2.1 Changes in urban wastewater discharge in China since 2001 (*Source* National Bulletin of Environmental Statistics, 2001–2015)

than that from industrial sewage. From a purely quantitative perspective, domestic sewage discharge has become China's largest source of water pollution. Of course, the toxicity and harmfulness of industrial sewage is still the main cause of environmental and ecological damage, and its treatment is more difficult.

2.1.2 *The Positive Correlation Between Sewage Discharge and the Economic Scale of Each Province*

In 2016, the seven Chinese provinces with the highest wastewater emissions were Guangdong, Jiangsu, Shandong, Zhejiang, Henan, Sichuan, and Hunan, in that order. The total wastewater discharge from these seven provinces amounted to 35.47 billion tons, accounting for 45.9% of the country's total wastewater discharge. In 2016, Guangdong, Jiangsu, and Shandong also ranked first, second, and third respectively in regional GDP, making them the three most economically developed provinces in China. Examining the 31 provinces, autonomous regions, and municipalities in China which are recorded in the statistics, the total sewage discharge and regional GDP rankings are roughly the same (see Fig. 2.2). Thus, it can be seen at this stage that the economic development of most provinces, autonomous regions, and municipalities in China was still highly dependent on resources and the environment, and the tension between economic development and environmental protection was still great.

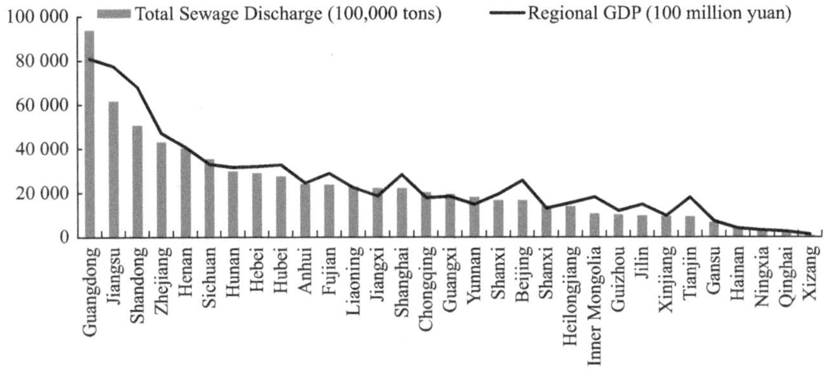

Fig. 2.2 Total sewage discharge vs. regional GDP in 31 provinces, regions, and municipalities in China, 2016 (*Source* Data from the Data Center on the official website of the National Statistical Office)

2.1.3 Water Quality in River Basins Has Improved, and Industrial Sewage Still Accounts for the Largest Proportion

The banks of major rivers and the surrounding areas of lakes are often the best places to promote industrialization and urbanization, due to their rich water resources. Important cities around the world are connected to important rivers, lakes, and reservoirs. In cities with weak pollution management capacity, rivers and lakes often become the most common places to discharge industrial and domestic sewage. Since the beginning of the twenty-first century, the words used to describe the water quality of China's rivers and lakes in the government's statistical bulletins have often included "seriously polluted", "moderately polluted", and "lakes with eutrophication (excess fertilizer runoff, mostly nitrogen and phosphorus) problems". This began to improve slightly in 2011, with the overall pollution of China's rivers improving to "mildly polluted" and the easing of the eutrophication of important lakes. However, the overall situation remains serious. Since the Third Plenary Session of the 18th Central Committee of the Communist Party of China (CPC), China has escalated its efforts in river basin management, and the overall water quality in river basins has gradually improved. To reflect the changes in river basin quality in recent years, the following section compares the water quality of China's seven major river systems between 2011 and 2017.[1]

2.1.3.1 The Yellow River Basin

The Yellow River is the mother river of China and the birthplace of Chinese civilization. However, since the middle of the Tang Dynasty, and especially since the Ming Dynasty, the Yellow River Basin's importance has been gradually declining. In the modern era, the Yellow River Basin has become a relatively underdeveloped region of China, yet there are still many cities (and much industry) along its banks, such as Lanzhou, Yinchuan, Hohhot, Zhengzhou, and Jinan. Most of the Yellow River Basin lies in a dry climate area, with an average annual precipitation of less than 500 mm; hence there is a shortage of water. With continuous industrialization and urbanization since the 1990s, water pollution in the Yellow River Basin is becoming increasingly serious. The water quality is categorized as moderately polluted, with about one-third of the evaluated river sections testing as worse-than Class V water, and more than 50% of the evaluated river sections testing Class IV or worse. The total annual wastewater discharged into the river has exceeded 4 billion tons. It was not until 2011 that there was a slight improvement in the Yellow River's water quality. For the first time in 10 years, less than 30% of the evaluated river length was labeled Class V. Of the 19,734.2 kilometers of river in the basin evaluated, 49.8% was labeled Class III or above, 21.1% as Class IV~V, and 29% labeled as poor, or Class V. In 2012, water quality continued to improve. Along the 20,545.3- km river length, Class IV to Class V water quality accounted for 17.1% of the total evaluated river length, and water quality worse-than Class V accounted for 27.4%. For the first time in ten years, less than 50% of the river was rated as Class IV or worse. Since then, the Yellow River's water quality has continued to improve. In 2017, of its 22,891.9 km, 69.9% had water quality rated at Class III or above; Class IV and Class V water was measured at 11% and 19.1%, respectively, a decline of 6.1% and 8.3% over the previous five years.

Most of the sewage discharged into the Yellow River is industrial sewage, followed by urban sewage and tertiary sewage. In 2012, Yellow River Basin wastewater discharge amounted to 4.474 billion tons, of

[1] The statistical data for the Songhua River and Liaohe River Basin are released together. Therefore, in this chapter they are referred to as the Songliao River Basin.

which urban sewage accounted for 27.7% of the total. Residential sewage (secondary wastewater discharge) accounted for 62.6%, and tertiary wastewater discharge accounted for 9.7%. In 2017, the Yellow River Basin wastewater discharge still amounted to 4.494 billion tons, of which industrial sewage, was still the main source of pollution, accounting for 50.3% of the total wastewater discharged. Urban residential wastewater discharge increased to 38.4%, while the increase in tertiary industry wastewater discharge was less (11.3%).[2]

2.1.3.2 The Yangtze River Basin

The Yangtze River is China's longest river. The Yangtze River Basin is in the subtropical warm and humid climate zone and the ecological environment is relatively good, compared to other regions of China. The Yangtze River Basin's water quality has been classified as mildly polluted. According to water quality statistics collected along the entire length of the river, in 2011, 29.7% of the river length was classified as Class III or worse (IV, V, and worse-than V accounted for 11.8%, 5.4%, and 12.5%, respectively); 70.3% of the of the river length was classified as Class III water quality. Furthermore, the total amount of sewage discharged into the Yangtze River Basin was massive. In 2011, it amounted to 34.21 billion tons,[3] over seven times that of the Yellow River Basin. Of that amount, industrial sewage accounted for the most—22.73 billion tons, or 66.4% of the total discharge. Domestic sewage was 7.88 billion tons, and the tertiary industry and the construction industry discharged another 3.60 billion tons, accounting for 33.6% of the total discharge. By 2017, Class IV, V, and worse-than Class V water quality was down to 16.1%, and Class III quality water accounted for 83.9% of the length of the river. But the total amount of sewage discharge remained high at 35.23 billion tons.[4] Industrial sewage discharge still accounted for the largest percentage of the total, amounting to 18.43 billion tons, or 52.3% of the total emissions. Domestic sewage increased to 10.13 billion tons, plus 6.67 billion tons discharged by the tertiary industry and construction industry, accounting for 47.7% of the total emissions.

[2] See the *Yellow River Water Resources Bulletin* for FY2011, FY2012, and FY2017.

[3] This data also excludes direct cooling water from thermal power plants and pit drainage, as well as Tibetan wastewater discharges.

[4] This data also excludes direct cooling water from thermal power plants and pit drainage, as well as Tibetan wastewater discharges.

The geographical distribution of the water pollution in the Yangtze River Basin is concentrated in the middle and lower reaches of the river. This is where cities are densely populated and economically developed, and where China's most important economic zones and largest urban clusters are concentrated, including the Yangtze River Delta cities led by Shanghai, and the urban belt of the middle reaches of the Yangtze River, led by the cities of Wuhan, Changsha, and Nanchang. The sewage discharge from the Yangtze River basin is concentrated in the Taihu Lake system and the Dongting Lake system, and the sewage discharge in these two tributaries has been reported to account for 81.1% of the entire basin's sewage discharge.[5]

2.1.3.3 *The Haihe River Basin*

The Haihe River is an important river in China. The Haihe River Basin covers the capital city of Beijing and the northern economic center of Tianjin. As such, the quality of its water resources and water environment is particularly important. However, the Haihe River Basin is located in the temperate zone in a semi-humid and semi-arid climate zone, and natural precipitation is low, little more than 500 mm per annum. Combined with the nearby dense population centers, industrial pollution is a serious issue in this region. After numerous treatments, the situation has improved, but the pollution remains serious. In 2011, 36.2% of the Haihe River Basin water was Class III or better. Class IV~V water accounted for 12.8%, and worse-than Class V water accounted for 51.0%. In 2012, the sections of the Haihe River Basin with water quality Class III or better accounted for 34.6% of the total evaluated river length, Class IV~V water accounted for 19.3%, and worse-than Class V water accounted for 46.1%. Worse-than Class V water had decreased slightly since 2011, but the situation had not changed significantly. By 2017, after years of continuous efforts, the relevant data showed that the situation was finally improving, and the section of the Haihe River Basin that had Class III or better water quality had increased to 39.3% of the total river length; Class IV~V water increased to 21.5%, while worse-than Class V water decreased to 39.2%.

In 2012, 5.363 billion tons of wastewater was discharged into the Haihe River Basin. Of that amount, wastewater discharged from industry and construction accounted 2.546 billion tons (47.5%). The amount

[5] According to the 2011 and 2017 *Water Resources Bulletin of the Yangtze River Basin and Southwest Rivers.*

of wastewater discharged from urban residents was 1.563 billion tons (29.1%), and the amount discharged from the tertiary industry was 1.254 billion tons (23.4%). Industrial wastewater is the main source of water pollution in the Haihe River Basin. Along with the escalating sewage discharge from urban residents and tertiary industry, the total amount of wastewater discharge in the Haihe River Basin is on the rise. In 2017, of the 5.985 billion tons of wastewater discharged, the amount of wastewater discharged by industry and construction dropped to 2.407 billion tons, accounting for 40.2%, while the amount discharged by urban residents increased to 2.87 billion tons, accounting for 48%. The amount discharged by the tertiary industry increased to 708 million tons, accounting for 59.8% of the total wastewater discharged.[6]

2.1.3.4 The Pearl River Basin

The Pearl River is located in Southern China, located in the tropical and subtropical monsoon climate zone, with a humid climate and annual precipitation of 1,000 to 2,000 millimeters. Some areas even reach 3,000 millimeters. Its length is second only to the Yangtze River, and as such, the water supply is abundant. The Pearl River Delta is the largest economic zone in Southern China, with its largest urban clusters. Its economy is dominated by exports. Since the Reform and Opening-up, with its rapid industrialization and urbanization, water pollution in the Pearl River Basin has become increasingly serious. However, since the river has a large volume of water, the pollution is less apparent. In 2011, the Ministry of Water Resources, Pearl River Water Resources Commission issued the "Pearl River Water Resources Bulletin" (the Pearl River includes the Pearl River Basin, the Han River Basin, the coastal rivers of Guangdong and Guangxi, and the rivers of Hainan Province). According to that 2011 report, along the total length of the Pearl River, 73.6% of the water was Class I~III. Class IV~V water accounted for 17.2%, and worse-than Class V accounted for 9.1%. Of 18.81 billion tons of wastewater discharged, the Pearl River Basin accounted for 14.65 billion tons, of which 12.53 billion tons of wastewater discharge was from Guangdong province. In the economically developed Pearl River Delta region, wastewater discharge accounted for 36% of the total amount in the actual Pearl River. Most of the wastewater discharge in the Pearl River

[6] According to the *Hai River Basin Water Resources Bulletin* for 2011, 2012, and 2017.

Delta comes from the secondary industry (industry and construction), amounting to 11.38 billion tons, accounting for more than 60.5% of the total wastewater discharge. By 2016, the Pearl River Basin's water quality had improved. Along the length of the major rivers in the Pearl River Basin, water quality of Class III or better increased to 87.9%, and the total amount of wastewater discharge declined to 17.42 billion tons. The main source of wastewater discharge was still the secondary industry (industry and construction), accounting for 50.2% of total wastewater discharge.[7]

2.1.3.5 *The Songliao Basin*

The Songliao Basin refers to the Songhua River, the Liao River, the rivers along the Yellow River and Bohai Sea, and the rivers along China's international borders in the Northeast. The administrative boundaries include the three provinces of Heilongjiang, Jilin, and Liaoning, and the eastern part of the Inner Mongolia Autonomous Region, the four leagues (cities),[8] and the city of Chengde in Hebei Province (Songliao area). Since the Ministry of Water Resources unified the Songhua River with the Liao River to create the Songliao Water Conservancy Commission, statistical bulletins are published together.

The Songliao basin is located in Northeastern China in the temperate continental monsoon climate zone, with annual precipitation between 350 and 1,000 mm. It is an old industrial base in Northeastern China, but also one of the earliest developments of China's urbanization and industrialization of the region. Water pollution in this region is also serious, particularly in the Liaohe area. The 2011 and 2012 bulletin data showed that water quality in both the Songhua River and the Liaohe River have declined. The percentage of water quality rated Class III or better has declined, and worse-than Class V water in the Liaohe River area has increased (see Table 2.2). By 2016, the water quality in the Songliao Basin had improved. An evaluation of the water quality along 22,087.7 km of river length showed that Class III water or better had increased to 64.1%, Class IV~V water had decreased to 25.3%, and worse-than Class V water had decreased to 10.6%.[9]

[7] According to the 2011 and 2016 *Pearl River Patch Water Resources Bulletin.*

[8] The four leagues (cities) in eastern Inner Mongolia Autonomous Region refer to Hulunbeier City, Xing'an League, Tongliao City, and Chifeng City, which are called the East Four leagues.

[9] According to the *Songliao Basin Water Resources Bulletin* for 2011, 2012, and 2017.

Table 2.2 Water quality in the Songliao Basin

	Year	*Evaluation of river length (km)*	*Class III or better (%)*	*Class IV~V (%)*	*Worse-than Class V (%)*
Songhua River Basin	2011	10,945.7	62.2	21.4	16.4
	2012	11,015.5	58.1	29.4	12.5
Liaohe Basin	2011	3,831.6	35.8	33.0	31.2
	2012	4,336.1	32.8	33.0	34.2

Source: *Songliao Basin Water Resources Bulletin*, 2011 and 2012

2.1.3.6 *The Huaihe River Basin*

The Huaihe River Basin is located in China's north–south climate transition zone. With annual precipitation of 600~1,400 mm, it is also a relatively water-scarce area. The Huaihe River area, which includes the Huaihe River Basin and the coastal rivers of the Shandong Peninsula, is a typical area in China in which the influence of industrialization and water pollution is serious. In 2011, along the 24,569 km of river length, only 38.0% was Class III or better; Class IV~V accounted for 37.6%; worse-than Class V water accounted for 24.4%. In the same evaluation, of the 22,085 km Huaihe River Basin, 38.5% was Class III or better, 38.6% was Class IV~V, and 22.9% was worse-than Class V. Along the 2,484 kilometers of the Shandong Peninsula, 34% was Class III or better, 28.7% was Class IV~V, and worse-than Class V water accounted for 37.3%. In 2011, the total amount of industrial wastewater (excluding direct flow cooling water and mine drainage from thermal power plants) and urban residents' domestic sewage in the Huaihe River was 9.098 billion tons, of which the annual discharge of waste water in the Huaihe River Basin was 7.630 billion tons and that of the Shandong Peninsula was 1.468 billion tons. Looking at the total amount of sewage discharged into the Huaihe River from each province, Henan Province discharged 2,855 million tons, Jiangsu Province discharged 2,146 million tons, Anhui Province discharged 1,835 million tons, Shandong Province discharged 784 million tons, and Hubei Province discharged 100 million tons, with the largest amounts being from Henan, Jiangsu, and Anhui Provinces.

By 2017, the Huaihe River's water quality had improved significantly. Along the 24,080 km length of the river, Class III or better water had increased to 55.2%. Class IV~V water had decreased to 33% and worse-than Class V water had decreased significantly, to 11.8%. Along the 20,874 km length of the Huaihe River Basin, Class III water or better had increased to 56.4%, Class IV~V water had decreased to 33.5% and worse-than Class V water had decreased to 10.1%. Along the 3,206 km of rivers in the Shandong Peninsula, Class III water or better had increased to 47%, Class IV~V water had decreased to 30.4%, and worse-than Class V water had declined to 22.6%.[10]

2.1.4 China's Overall Water Quality Has Improved Slightly, But the Situation Remains Grim

Before 2013, the *Bulletin on China's Environmental Situation* issued by the Ministry of Environmental Protection (MEP) usually gave a general description of water pollution in China. Based on data from the bulletins of previous years, the water quality of China's seven major water systems showed a marked improvement in 2009. Years of moderate pollution had reversed to light pollution, and the overall surface water quality had changed from years of serious or heavier pollution to light pollution in 2011.

The eutrophication of lakes and reservoirs has also improved. China's lakes have long had eutrophication issues, but by 2011, lake water quality as a whole had improved significantly, with the percentage of worse-than Class V water decreasing from 38.5% in 2010 to 7.7%. Taihu Lake also showed an impressive turnaround: after years of worse-than Class V water, it was now in Class IV (see Table 2.3). However, since the number of state-managed lakes increased to 62 in 2012, there has been polarization in the bulletin data, and the proportion of lakes superior to Class III and worse-than Class V has increased significantly. Combined with the overall water quality of rivers and lakes in China in recent years, water pollution management fluctuated, but showed no overarching trend (see Table 2.4). On the one hand, this shows that China has made obvious progress in the field of water pollution management over the past few years. On the other hand, it shows that the alleviation of water pollution in China is a battle and a long-lasting war. For example, the treatment

[10] According to the *Huaihe River Basin Water Resources Bulletin* for 2011 and 2017.

of Dianchi Lake has resulted in historic achievements, transforming long-standing heavy pollution into moderate eutrophication in 2016, and the water quality improved to lightly polluted in 2017.

Drinking water quality in China's cities has also improved. In 2008, China launched a survey of the basic environmental conditions of drinking water sources in cities and towns where county-level governments are located. The purpose of this survey was to annually assess the compliance of the water quality of the main centralized drinking water sources for the country's 113 cities that are key to environmental protection. The cities participating in the assessment are the 113 Key Cities for Environmental Protection first specified in the National Environmental Protection 11th Five-Year Plan announced by the State Council at the end of 2007. These include the four municipalities directly under the central government,

Table 2.3 Changes in the water quality of state-managed lakes, 2006–2013

Year	*Number of lakes under state management*	*Class III and Better (%)*	*Class IV~V (%)*	*Worse-than Class V (%)*	*Taihu Lake*	*Chaohu (Prefecture-level city in Anhui)*	*Dianchi Lake in Yunnan*
2006	27	29.0%	23.0%	48.0%	Worse-than Class V	Class V	Worse-than Class V
2007	28	28.5%	32.2%	39.3%	Worse-than Class V	Class V	Worse-than Class V
2008	28	21.4%	39.3%	39.3%	Worse-than Class V	Class V	Worse-than Class V
2009	26	23.1%	42.3%	34.6%	Worse-than Class V	Class V	Worse-than Class V
2010	26	23.0%	38.5%	38.5%	Worse-than Class V	Class V	Worse-than Class V
2011	26	42.3%	50.0%	7.7%	Class IV	Class V	Worse-than Class V
2012	62	61.3%	27.45	11.3%	Lightly Polluted	Lightly Polluted	Highly Polluted
2013	62	60.7%	27.8%	11.5%	Lightly Polluted	Lightly Polluted	Highly Polluted

Source: *Bulletin on the State of the Environment in China*, 2006–2013

Table 2.4 The overall water quality of rivers and lakes in China, 2014–2018

Year	*Cross-sectional water quality for the seven state-managed major river basins (%)*			*Water quality of state-managed lakes nationwide (%)*					
	Class III or better	*Class IV~V*	*Worse-than class V*	*Class I*	*Class II*	*Class III*	*Class IV*	*Class V*	*Worse-than Class V*
2014	71.2	19.8	9.0	11.3	17.7	32.3	24.2	6.4	8.1
2015	72.1	19.0	8.9	8.1	21.0	40.3	16.1	6.4	8.1
2016	71.2	19.7	9.1	7.1	25.0	33.9	20.5	5.4	8.0
2017	71.8	19.8	8.4	5.4	24.1	33.0	19.6	7.1	10.7
2018	74.3	18.9	6.9	6.3	30.6	29.7	17.1	8.1	8.1

Source: Bulletin on the State of China's Environment, 2014–2016; *Bulletin on the State of China's Ecological Environment*, 2017–2018

27 provincial capitals, five cities with separate programs, and 77 other cities. In 2009, the 113 Key Cities for Environmental Protection were the first to have the water quality of their main centralized drinking water sources meet the standard. In 2009, the water quality compliance rate of the 113 Key Cities for Environmental Protection for centralized drinking water sources was only 73%. The compliance rate increased year-over-year from 76.5% in 2010 to 90.6% in 2011, and to 97.3% in 2013. However, measurements taken since 2015 show that the water quality compliance rate has declined. In 2016, the compliance rate for 897 monitoring cross sections (points) in 338 cities was 90.4%. In 2017 the compliance rate for 898 monitoring cross sections (points) in 338 cities was 90.5%. This improved compliance rate points to the fact that China's water environment quality monitoring requirements have greatly improved since 2014, and the requirements for environmental data have become more stringent. On the other hand, it also shows that China's water environment conditions are still grim, and with fluctuating data, the pressure for sustained improvement remains immense.

2.2 Urban Sewage Treatment Capacity and Problems

Since the 1980s, water pollution in China has become increasingly serious and more pronounced, peaking in the mid- to late 1990s. However, the problem of urban sewage treatment has not received enough attention. The construction of urban sewage treatment facilities has been slow, and the capacity to treat urban sewage has been low for a long time. With the rapid annual growth of sewage discharge, the low sewage treatment capacity will inevitably lead to a spike in water pollution, aggravating China's water environment problems. It was not until the 2010s that there was significant improvement in China's urban sewage treatment plants and sewage treatment capacity, and the trend of deteriorating environmental water quality was initially reversed in 2011. Since the Third Plenary Session of the 18th Central Committee of the CPC Central Committee, China has increased its urban wastewater treatment efforts, and urban wastewater treatment facilities have continually improved with upgrades in treatment capacity.[11] China's urban wastewater treatment capacity and its associated problems are mainly reflected by the following factors.

2.2.1 Urban Sewage Treatment Has Long Been Neglected, and the Sewage Treatment Rate Is Low

In the 1990s, China entered a period of rapid industrialization and urbanization, yet urban wastewater treatment long remained neglected. It was only in 1991 that China began to compile statistics on wastewater treatment rates, and at that time, the treatment rate was only 14.86%. Previously, most of the sewage produced by urban life and production had been directly discharged with no treatment. Although China's sewage treatment efforts have increased since, in 2006 the sewage treatment rate was still only 55.67%. In China's county-level municipalities, sewage treatment is even more neglected, with a sewage treatment rate of only 7.55% in 2000.

[11] The data in this subsection is compiled from the Ministry of Housing and Construction's *Urban and Rural Statistical Yearbook* and the *Bulletin of China's Urban Drainage and Sewage Disposal Situation* (2006–2010).

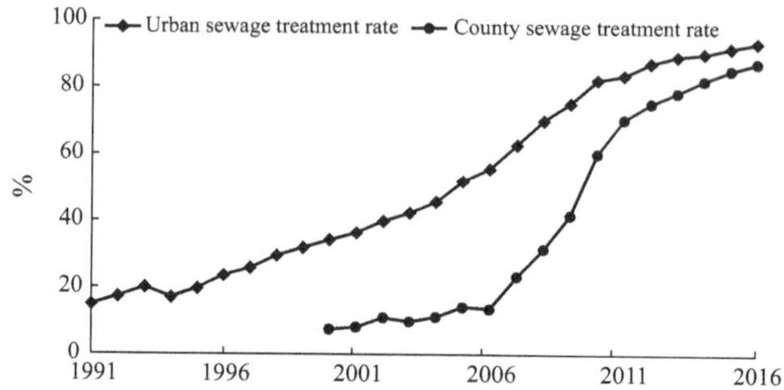

Fig. 2.3 Changes in sewage treatment rates, 1991–2016

It was not until after 2006 that there was rapid improvement in urban wastewater treatment, and by 2016 the wastewater treatment rate of China's municipal cities had reached 93.44%. The wastewater treatment rate at the county level had also dramatically increased, from 13.6% to 87.38% (see Fig. 2.3).

2.2.2 *Chronic and Serious Shortages of Urban Sewage Treatment Facilities and Sewage Discharge Facilities*

One reason for the low urban sewage treatment rate has been the shortage of sewage treatment facilities in China. In 1991, there were only 87 sewage treatment plants throughout China, with a sewage treatment capacity of only 3.17 million cubic meters per day. In 2000, there were only 54 sewage treatment plants at the county level, with a sewage treatment capacity of only 550,000 m^3/day.

Since 2006, China has increased its investment and construction of urban sewage treatment plants, and its urban sewage treatment plants grew in number from 815 to 2,039 in 2016. Meanwhile, the number of sewage treatment plants at the county level grew from 204 to its peak of 1,599 in 2015 (see Fig. 2.4). Cities' and counties' daily sewage treatment capacities have also increased, from 63.66 million m^3/day and 4.96 million m^3/day to 149.1 million m^3/day and 30.36 million m^3/day, respectively.

At the same time, construction of China's pipeline drainage network has been unable to keep up with demand. In 1991, China's urban pipeline

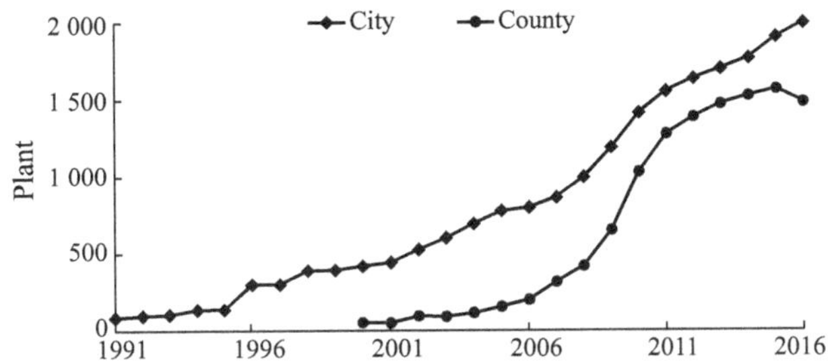

Fig. 2.4 Wastewater treatment plant construction, 1991–2016

drainage network measured only 61,601 km. Coupled with poor maintenance, the clogging of aging pipes, torrential downpours in the summers, and frequent floods of cities not only exacerbated China's water pollution problems, but also triggered several tragic disasters. A heavy rainstorm in Beijing on July 21, 2012, affected more than 1.6 million people, resulted in at least 79 deaths, and causing direct economic losses exceeding 11.6 billion yuan.

2.2.3 *The Underutilization of Sewage Treatment Facilities*

China's water pollution conditions are grim. Not only is there a severe shortage of sewage treatment facilities in cities and towns, but the operations of sewage treatment facilities in many Chinese cities is unsatisfactory. For example, in 2007 the national sewage treatment plant operating load rate was only 70.9% on average. By 2010, even after years of improvement, the load rate was still only 79.1% (see Fig. 2.5). The load rate for county-level sewage treatment plants is particularly low, and some sewage treatment plants are practically useless.

The distribution of urban sewage treatment plants' load rates in the 31 provinces, autonomous regions, and municipalities in China in 2010 reveals that some regions' sewage treatment plant load rates were below 60%. The operating load rates of sewage treatment plants in Shanghai, Beijing, Shandong, Yunnan, Guangdong, Chongqing, Henan, Zhejiang, and Liaoning were slightly higher, above 80%, and exceeded 90% only in Shanghai (see Fig. 2.6).

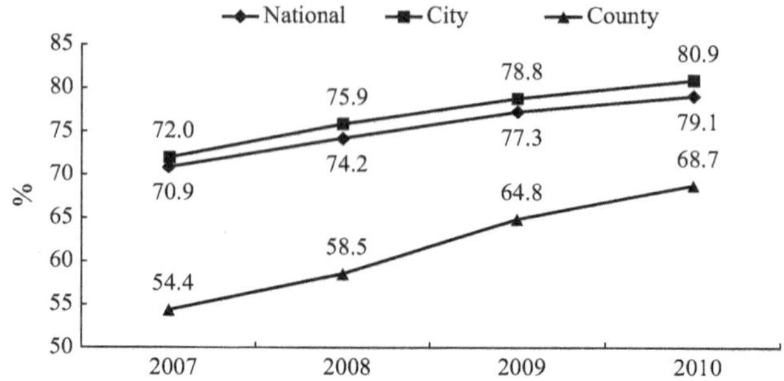

Fig. 2.5 National wastewater treatment plant operating load rates, 2007–2010

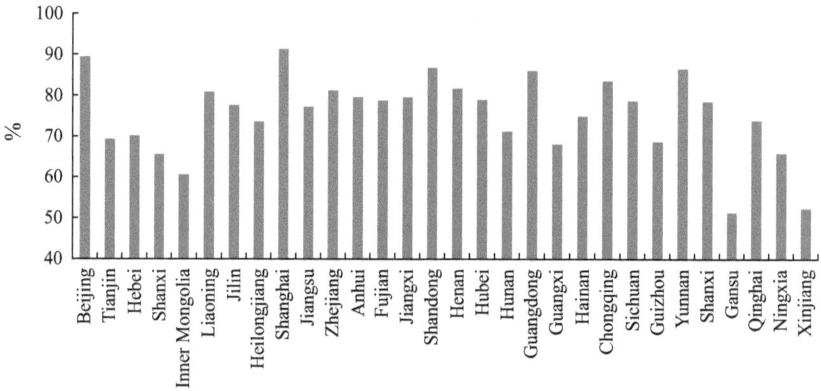

Fig. 2.6 Operating load rates of urban wastewater treatment facilities in 30 provinces, regions, and municipalities, 2010 (*Note* Data for the Tibet Autonomous Region are missing. *Source*: *Bulletin on the Status of Urban Drainage and Sewage Treatment in China*, 2006–2010)

2.2.4 A Single Mode of Sewage Treatment, Dominated by Centralized Treatment

There are two main methods of sewage treatment: centralized and decentralized. Centralized sewage treatment systems typically include urban sewage pipeline networks and sewage treatment plants which occupy large land areas. They are common especially in older cities, where demolition and relocation are difficult and land costs are high. Moreover, under normal circumstances, there is sewage leakage in the centralized sewage treatment system during transportation through the pipeline network, and the general leakage amount can be 10%~20% of the total water volume. Not only will this introduce pollution into the environment, but it is also detrimental to water pollution treatment. Decentralized sewage treatment systems generally only include the cost of sewage treatment devices, sludge collection, transportation, and treatment system costs. They cover a small area, eliminating the need to construct a drainage pipeline network, and therefore infrastructure and operational investment is lower. Moreover, decentralized treatment reduces the multiple transportation links for sewage and treated water resources over the pipeline network system. This prevents sewage leakage caused by long-distance transportation.

Sewage treatment in China is primarily through centralized treatment, and decentralized sewage treatment has received insufficient attention; most cities use only the single centralized sewage treatment method. For example, in 2010 the average urban sewage treatment rate in China was 79.28%, of which 72.15% was by centralized treatment. The sewage treatment rate in counties and towns was 50.69%, of which 45.49% was by centralized treatment.[12] In addition, China's long-term centralized sewage treatment level is low, and much source point pollution cannot be effectively disposed by ignoring decentralized sewage treatment. This affects China's sewage treatment level.

In recent years, China's sewage treatment rate has improved greatly and the centralized sewage treatment rate has continued to increase. Some individual cities such as Liaoyang, Panjin, and Tieling in Liaoning Province, and Liaocheng in Shandong Province have achieved 100% centralized sewage treatment rates. However, as of 2017 there remained some cities with centralized sewage treatment rates below 70%.

[12] According to the 2006–2010 *Communiqué on Urban Drainage and Sewage Treatment in China*.

2.3 The Original Characteristics and Dilemmas of Urban Water Pollution Control

Urbanization and industrialization are the main causes of water pollution in Chinese cities. Along with the proliferation of urbanization and industrialization, China's urban economy and society have developed rapidly, and China's GDP has grown to be ranked second in the world, contributing more than 30% to the world's economic growth, thanks mainly to cities and industries. However, for a long time, under the mechanism of fiscal decentralization and performance-based evaluation based on economic growth, many city governments adopted the practice of relaxing environmental supervision and lowering environmental standards to attract capital and production facilities. In this way, they could facilitate extensive development of their local economies. This has led to local ecological damage, environmental degradation, and increasingly, widespread water pollution. Since the Third Plenary Session of the 18th Central Committee of the CPC Central Committee, China has accelerated its institutional construction of ecological civilization. It has taken multiple measures to ensure legal protection against water pollution, regulate systems and mechanisms, and reform administrative departments. In the process, urban water pollution management has reached unprecedented heights, and institutional changes are on the rise. The following is an analysis of the characteristics of, and the problems with, the institutional mechanism of urban water pollution alleviation prior to the Third Plenary Session of the 18th Central Committee of the Communist Party of China.

2.3.1 A Dual Management System with Administrative Regions as the Mainstay

The history of environmental water management systems for China's river basins can be roughly divided into three stages. The first stage, from 1949 to 1984, was the initial stage of China's water pollution prevention and management work. Special water pollution prevention and alleviation legislation was created from scratch, and seven major river basin management agencies were established. Because China's industrial production was outmoded at that time, the total amount of pollutant discharge did not exceed the self-healing capacity of the water environment. Therefore, there was little degradation in the water environment. Thus, there was no conflict between water pollution and water environmental protection during this time.

The second phase, from 1984 to 2002, was the integrated management phase of water resource conservation in water basins. During the 1980s, with the rapid development of China's economy and urbanization, large amounts of pollutants were discharged into rivers and lakes, rapidly degrading the water environment and water ecology. In 1984, China issued the *Law of the People's Republic of China on the Prevention and Control of Water Pollution* which became the earliest separate law on pollution management in China. It formally established a management system for China's water pollution prevention and alleviation supervision, that is, the management system of sub-regions and sub-sectors. Since then, various laws and regulations on water resources and water environment management have been issued one after another. In 1988, the *Water Law of the People's Republic of China* was enacted. It became the foundational law for water management in China. In 1996, the Law of the PRC on the Prevention and Control of Water Pollution was amended, and the legal regulations on water management in China were gradually tightened. However, in terms of a management system, all of them required the implementation of sub-regional and sub-sectoral management systems. Although river basin management agencies had long been established in the seven major river basins, these management agencies are in fact agencies of the Ministry of Water Resources, and are public institutions with no law enforcement powers. As a result, their water basin management powers are limited.

The third phase covers the period from 2002 to this writing. Article 12 of *the Water Law of the PRC,* revised in 2002, stipulates that "the State shall implement a management system combining basin management and administrative area management of water resources". However, the dual leadership system for water resource protection in China's river basins exists in name only. This is reflected in the weak water pollution management and supervision at the river basin level, and the implementation of general administrative regional management (Zhong and Liu 2008).

However, water resources and water environments are different from fixed resources such as forests and grasslands; they are fluid and systematic. Since water resources and water environments are subject to a dual management system based on administrative regional management, a river basin's management capability is lower than that of provincial administrative regions in terms of power level and organizational level. Moreover, they have weak overall planning and coordination supervision capabilities. They also lack the statutory authority for water pollution prevention and alleviation, resulting in the integrity and systems of rivers or lakes being artificially divided according to administrative divisions. This affects the integrity and the systematization of water environment governance.

2.3.2 A "Multi-Regulator" with Numerous Management Rules and Regulations and a System with Divided Functions

Prior to 2014, there were numerous laws and regulations related to the management of water resources and water environments in China. Although *the Water Law of the PRC* and *the Law of the PRC on the Prevention and Control of Water Pollution* were the two most important laws, numerous others laws were in effect. These included *the Law of the PRC on the Protection of the Environment*, *the Law of the PRC on Flood Control*, *the Law of the PRC on Soil and Water Conservation*, *the Regulations of the PRC on the Management of Rivers*, and *the Regulations of the PRC on the Administration of Waterways*. In addition, dozens of rules and regulations were issued by various State Council ministries and commissions on water management, as were rules and regulations issued by local governments to support the management of water resources and the water environment. Although there were many relevant laws and regulations, they were unambiguous regarding the boundaries and scope of their specific management and protection. This resulted in the issues of undefined positions and overstepping in water management.

In terms of administrative management, local governments at all levels were vertically responsible for environmental quality management, and horizontally responsible for implementing the system of unified management of environmental protection departments and the division of labor and management of relevant departments. Therefore, many departments have been involved in water environment management in China. The administrative management of water pollution prevention and alleviation provides an exemplary case. China stipulates that the environmental protection departments of the people's governments at all levels are the entities that exercise unified supervision over the prevention and alleviation of water pollution. Along the same lines, the transportation departments and navigation departments at all levels are the entities that supervise pollution from ships. Municipal management departments and water source protection institutions in important river basins shall, in combination with their respective duties, cooperate with environmental protection departments to supervise the prevention and alleviation of water pollution. However, under the pursuit of GDP growth, environmental protection departments are often weaker than economic departments, so objectively they play little role in unified supervision.

In addition, China stipulates that the prevention and alleviation of water pollution be planned in a unified manner according to the river basin or region, and once a water pollution management plan is approved, it becomes the basis for water pollution prevention and alleviation. In actuality, many additional departments are either directly or indirectly involved in areas such as construction, land and resources, transportation, agriculture, forestry, health, science and technology, development and reform and finance. Although the division of labor in many departments is different, there are many overlapping powers. Without unified standards for policy implementation, it is difficult to achieve unified planning and coordination in management (He 1999). For example, the water conservancy department and the environmental protection department are the most important institutions for the management and protection of water resources and the water environment. There are many contact points between the two departments, but in actual operation, the water conservancy department is only responsible for the water itself, and not the shorelines. Conversely, the environmental protection department is only responsible for the shorelines, not the water itself. Such divisions have resulted in redundant work and the inability to enforce many powers and responsibilities. For example, in the same bulletin on China's water environment quality, the data between the Ministry of Water Resources and the Ministry of Environmental Protection do not match, because they are separate entities. Both reports are issued by the government, so it is difficult for the general public to understand the discrepancies in the data, and it also causes unnecessary waste of human, material, and financial resources.

2.3.3 Inadequate Supervision Under the Leadership of Administrative Management

Water environment management in China is implemented by the local government-led administrative management. Coupled with the insufficient use of market mechanisms, social supervision has yet to be effectively utilized, such that effective supervision of water pollution is still not in place.

From an administrative management perspective, although there are environmental protection departments specializing in environmental protection, China's local environmental protection departments still implement a dual leadership system led by local governments. The local environmental protection departments are dependent on the local government for financing and personnel. Under China's long-standing GDP-led government performance-based ideology, it is difficult for environmental protection authorities to supervise the management of governments at the same level. Therefore, it is difficult for local environmental protection departments at all levels in the river basin to effectively supervise environmental protection in the region.

From a market mechanisms perspective, the efficiency of water resource use could be improved through various economic levers such as taxes, fees, subsidies, and credits, and water pollution could be curbed through flexible water pollution compensation systems. However, for a long time, the Chinese government had both management and operational functions, and had the dual role of player and referee in water environment management. Many major polluters are themselves also major contributors to public economies and to local government tax revenue, making it difficult to implement water environment supervision and management. Some local governments even give prior warning to enterprises when higher-level departments are audited or inspected, becoming accomplices of environmental pollution.

At the same time, there is a serious lack of supervision in Chinese society, and the State has only given the public limited rights of supervision at the legal level, such as the right to report and the right to sue. Although the system of public hearings has been strengthened in recent years, this has often been a mere formality, making it difficult for public supervision to be effective.

2.3.4 *Urban Water Pollution Problems, and Their Governance Under the Perspective of Local Sociology*

At the Second China Environmental Sociology Symposium hosted by several organizations including Hohai University in April 2009, Hong Dayong gave a speech entitled "Sociological Analysis of Water Pollution in China". In the speech, Hong proposed that the problem of water pollution can be analyzed from the perspectives of functionalism, social conflict theory, and social construction theory.

Chen Ajiang (2000, 2007, 2008) argues that water pollution is fundamentally not a scientific and technological problem, but an economic and social one. His analysis of the causes of the deterioration of the water environment in the Taihu Lake basin and water pollution in the Dongcun case can be analyzed by applying a functionalist dimension. He has argued that the main reason for the water environmental problems caused by industrialization and urbanization has been the distortion of people's values. Therefore, the environmental problems are the natural results of certain social processes, and the study of the environment needs to be broadened to explore the organization of people's social lives. Social systems, on the other hand, evolve through continuous adaptation to the environment, and when environmental conditions continue to deteriorate, they adjust to respond constructively to environmental threats, such that changing the values of members of society is important for promoting environmental protection.

The social conflict theory of urban water pollution, on the other hand, argues that due to power disparities in society, elites control the economy, the law, and environmental orientation, such that environmental problems arise in favor of the elite's interests. Environmental problems are inevitable, and elites in pursuit of their own interests, either directly or indirectly, exacerbate the environmental problems, but are rarely penalized by society. Thus, they will continue depleting resources and risk creating environmental problems. Therefore, the key to solving environmental problems is to promote social equity. When analyzing the causes of urban water pollution, Jiang Ying found that enterprises are an important source of pollution. Due to the government's local protectionism, local interests, and other reasons, there will be many management vacuums in government protection of the urban water environment. Social groups struggle to influence urban water environmental protection due to environmental awareness, organizational levels and are typically too weak to act. Therefore, Jiang Ying (2007) noted that only through organizational innovation and the optimization of social structure to promote public participation can we further promote environmental protection. Similarly, Xu Genhong (2017) also observed a dominant social practice in the industrial water pollution field where actual practiced norms do not comply with formal rules. The result of this social fact is that there are logical outcomes in the industrial water pollution field when the formal rules are overridden by local policies; the local government is held hostage by the polluting enterprises, by violations which occur from behind the scenes to the front lines, and from endogenous violations to exogenous violations. The social reasons for deciding these logical outcomes are the evaluation mechanism under the imbalance of the institutional structure, the supervision mechanism under the imbalance of the power structure, and the limited drive to internalize the rules. Therefore, the governance mechanism of industrial water pollution includes three primary components: main structural optimization, rule culture reproduction, and effective social supervision.

Social construction theory posits that the problem of urban water pollution is an understanding of the relationship between human society and the natural environment. This is a cultural phenomenon. This cultural phenomenon emerges through the cognition and negotiation of different groups in society. People with different cultural and social backgrounds have different perceptions on the environment. Thus, environmental degradation is a symbol for different groups to express their own opinions, and the identification of a particular environmental situation as an environmental problem is the temporary result of the competition of opinions between different groups. This is the result of the use of a range of tools and methods of interaction, and it involves the exercise of power. Therefore, rather than focusing on what is currently wrong with the environment, it is important to analyze who is highlighting environmental problems, and to deconstruct them. Thus, the key to solving a given environmental problem is to use scientific knowledge, mass media, organizational tools and public action to construct the problem, and interject it into the decision-making agenda, and eventually into policy practice.

2.4 Recent Changes and Prospects for Urban Water Pollution Management

In November 2012, the 18th National Congress of the CPC proposed a grand blueprint of promoting "ecological civilization" and "building a beautiful China". Since the Third Plenary Session of the 18th CPC Central Committee, the construction of China's ecological civilization has moved to the fast track, and an era of unprecedented opportunity in the treatment of urban water pollution has begun. The report of the 19th CPC Central Committee National Congress in October 2017 states "adhering to the harmonious coexistence of man and nature" as the basic strategy for adhering to and developing socialism with Chinese characteristics in the new era, and proposes the goal of "accelerating the reform of the ecological civilization system and building a beautiful China". Specific requirements have been proposed for solving prominent environmental problems, increasing the protection of ecosystems, and reforming the ecological environment supervision system. In order to solve acute environmental problems, proposals were offered such as tightening pollution discharge standards, increasing polluters' accountability, improving environmental protection credit evaluation, mandatory information disclosure, and severe punishments. In addition, there were proposals to build an environmental governance system led by the government, with enterprises as the main body, and social organizations and the public participating together. Thus, urban water pollution management has entered a new era.

2.4.1 China's Water Pollution Prevention and Alleviation System Is Becoming Increasingly Comprehensive

Recent years have seen rapid advancements in China's system of water resource protection and water environment prevention and alleviation. In 2014, the strictest environmental protection law in China's history was implemented. The Ministry of Environmental Protection also issued supporting regulations such as daily fines, seizure and detention, the restriction and suspension of production, administrative detention, environmental information disclosure for enterprises and institutions, and the investigation and management of environmental emergencies. In 2015, the State Council issued the *Action Plan for the Prevention and Control of Water Pollution*, formulated and implemented a target responsibility letter, and delegated the tasks to the provinces (including autonomous regions and municipalities) based on 1,940 assessment sections. At the same time, the national and key regional water pollution prevention and alleviation coordination mechanism was established, and provinces (autonomous regions and municipalities) were required to prepare specific work programs for water pollution prevention and alleviation. In 2016, the Ministry of Water Resources issued the *Layout Plan for Water Intake, Sewage Discharge, and Emergency Water Sources Along the Yangtze River Economic Belt* and compiled the *Ecological Environmental Protection Plan for the Yangtze River Economic Belt*. This was a major step forward in exploring the prevention and alleviation of water pollution in the river basin. In 2017, the Ministry of Environmental Protection issued the *Measures for the Administration of Sewage Discharge* Permits (for Trial Implementation) and the *Classified Management List of Sewage Discharge Permits for Fixed Pollution Sources* (2017 Edition). This intensive introduction of various systems has provided an institutional guarantee for water pollution mitigation.

2.4.2 Water Pollution Enforcement and Administrative Control Mechanisms

Another major step in the management of water pollution has been the unprecedented strengthening of environmental law enforcement and administrative supervision. In 2014, with the enactment of the new Environmental Protection Law, environmental pollution was strictly enforced in order to correct the long-standing inertia of local governments sacrificing the environment for economic development. In 2014 alone, environmental protection departments across the country reported at least 2,180 cases of suspected environmental violations to police, twice as many as in the past 10 years combined. By 2016, the number of cases of routine penalties, sealing and seizure, production restriction and suspension, transfer to administrative detention, and transfer of suspected environmental pollution crimes nationwide had increased to 22,730. Since the General Office of the State Council issued the *Notice on Strengthening Environmental Supervision and Law Enforcement* in 2014, the Ministry of Environmental Protection has conducted extensive comprehensive environmental inspections and interviews of the main responsible persons in city governments, with increasing intensity every year. In 2014, 25 cities conducted comprehensive environmental inspections, and 6 city governments were interviewed. In 2017, environmental protection inspections were fully implemented, and 30 persons in power in cities (counties, districts), departments, and units were interviewed.

2.4.3 Urban Water Pollution Management Capacity Is Improving, Along with the Management System

With the rapid advancement of the legal system for water pollution and the reform of the administrative management system and its mechanisms, and with the guarantee of political attention and financial investment, China's facilities for water pollution prevention and alleviation have improved dramatically, and this has been bolstered by improvements in technology. By 2017, 93% of China's provincial-level and above industrial clusters had built centralized sewage treatment facilities, the sewage treatment capacity of industrial distribution areas had experienced great improvement, and black and odorous bodies of water in the built-up areas of 36 key cities had been mostly eradicated. At the same time, the government-led, enterprise-oriented, social organizations, and public participation in the water environment management system also took shape. Additionally, in 2017 the administration promoted the "Environmental Protection Manager" launched by the Ministry of Environmental Protection—a big step in the direction of environmental governance for social and professional management services. It also provided new ideas for enterprises to curb pollution. Social forces involved in environmental governance have also been improved. The new environmental protection law stipulates that as long as environmental protection social organizations are registered with the civil affairs department of the People's Government at the city level or above, they can conduct environmental protection activities that have harmed social public interests in the past or have the potential to harm social public interests. Those engaging in ecological damage are now subject to lawsuits.

2.4.4 *Reform of the Water Pollution Administrative Management System and Mechanism*

In response to the long-standing overlapping management in China's water environment governance administrative system, at the end of 2016, the General Office of the CPC Central Committee and the General Office of the State Council jointly launched the *Opinions on Comprehensively Implementing the River Supervision System*. By the end of June 2018, the river supervision system was established across the country. At the same time, various regions also followed the river supervision system and launched a lake supervision system, further expanding the scope of water environment supervision. The river supervision system is a collaborative basin governance system led by Party and government leaders. It is a water environment governance system created based on the shortcomings of the bureaucratic environmental management system, and has experienced significant problem-solving issues (Shi 2018). Therefore, in the short term, China's water pollution management has indeed improved. However, the river supervision system is hierarchical and based on authority. Therefore, it will inevitably face the challenges of "capability dilemma, organizational logic dilemma and responsibility dilemma" (Ren 2015). To this end, in order to increase environmental protection efforts, China has proposed environmental supervision by river basin, and piloted vertical management reforms for environmental protection agencies. At the same time, an environmental protection inspection office has been established, and six regional inspection centers have been transformed from public institutions into administrative agencies, and renamed inspection bureaus. This improved the administrative capacity of environmental inspections. At the same time, the national surface water monitoring section authority was centralized, separating the collection from the measurement process, and the monitoring data was interconnected and shared nationwide to improve the data's objectivity and authenticity. This led to thorough investigations of human interference in environmental monitoring activities, and severe penalties when applicable.

In 2018, the reform of the State Council's large-scale ministerial system led to further adjustments in the administrative groups related to water resources and water environment governance. The responsibilities of the Ministry of Water Resources for the preparation of water function zoning, the management of sewage outlet settings, and the protection of river basin water environments were merged with the responsibilities of the Ministry of Ecology and Environment. Additionally, the responsibilities of the Ministry of Water were merged with those of the Ministry of Natural Resources for the management of water resources investigation and confirmation of rights. As of this writing, the restructuring of institutions throughout the country remained ongoing.

Overall, since the construction of ecological civilization was included in China's "Five-Sphere Integrated Plan" goal of socialist construction with Chinese characteristics, China's urban water pollution management has achieved unprecedented results. The results have included the improvement of water pollution prevention and alleviation systems, the implementation and adherence to water pollution law enforcement and administrative mechanisms, the continuous improvement of industrial sewage and urban domestic sewage treatment facilities and technologies, and the continuous advancement of the water environment governance system led by the government. In this process, enterprises have acted as the main body, with social organizations and the public participating as well. With the ongoing changes in the administrative management system of water pollution, such as the "River and Lake Supervision System" and the "Large Department System", urban water pollution management will enter a new era of governance. However, questions remain over how to refine and implement various laws and regulations, how to coordinate economic development and water environmental protection, how to achieve cross-regional governance of water resources and the water environment, and how to sustain the enthusiasm and cooperation of local governments under vertical supervision. For example, what is the short-term effect of water pollution mitigation, and how can the long-term ecological effect and awareness of water environmental protection among the populace be ensured? Additionally, how can we further encourage behaviors which reflect the spirit of environmental protectionism? These questions underscore the fact that urban water environmental protection and water pollution management in China still have a long way to go.

CHAPTER 3

Municipal Solid Waste and Its Governance in Urban Areas

Gong Wenjuan and Zhao Zhao

This chapter analyzes the practice of municipal solid waste management. The production of municipal solid waste affects everyone, and its disposal is also one of the signs of the progress of social civilization. Since the turn of the twenty-first century, China's annual output of municipal solid waste has exceeded 100 million tons. This has steadily increased, and the "garbage siege" is grim. From a national perspective, whether it is the amount of waste removal, the number of waste disposal facilities, the availability of funds for treatment, or the rate of ineffective treatment, there is a disparity in progress between regions. In addition, the landfilling, incineration, and composting processes generate foul smelling gases which contain nitrogen and sulfur compounds and toxic substances such as dioxins. Groundwater and soil are also being polluted by leaching. These processes pose varying degrees of environmental and health risks to

W. Gong (✉) · Z. Zhao
Department of Sociology, Xiamen University, Xiamen, China
e-mail: gongwenjuan@xmu.edu.cn

Z. Zhao
e-mail: z2020029@sdaeu.edu.cn

D. Hong and Y. Fan (eds.), *Toward a Green Society*,
https://doi.org/10.1007/978-981-96-5111-5_3

the surrounding residential communities. As people become more aware of the environment and their health, environmental risks may transform into social risks, thus increasing the costs of urban management. In order to optimize the management of municipal solid waste, over the past decade or so, governments at all levels in China have been emphasizing the removal and disposal of solid waste, and waste management policies have improved due to a series of changes.

3.1 Municipal Solid Waste Treatment

3.1.1 The Sources and Characteristics of Municipal Solid Waste

Municipal solid waste refers to solid waste generated over the course of daily life in a city, or in activities providing services for daily life in a city, as well as solid waste that is regarded as municipal solid waste under the provisions of laws and administrative regulations.[1] This definition reveals that the scope of municipal waste is wide, covering waste from many sources, such as daily life, commercial activities, and public institutions in many facets of people's lives and work. According to the Classification and Evaluation Standard of Municipal Solid Waste issued by the Ministry of Housing and Urban–Rural Development in 2004, most of China's municipal solid waste can be divided into one of six categories: recyclables, bulk waste, compostable waste, combustible waste, hazardous waste, and other waste. Based on the different sources of waste, the Ministry of Housing and Urban–Rural Development divides municipal solid waste into residential waste, cleaning waste, gardening waste, waste from commercial service outlets, waste from commercial offices, waste from medical and healthcare institutions, waste from transportation and logistics stations, waste from construction sites, waste from industrial enterprises, and other types of waste.

With the rapid development of China's economy and the improvement in people's material standards of living, China's municipal solid waste presents the following characteristics.

[1] For details, see the *Technical Policy on the Treatment of Municipal Solid Waste and Prevention and Treatment of Pollution* (Urban Construction [2000] No. 120) from the Ministry of Housing and Urban–Rural Development, Ministry of Ecology and Environment, and Ministry of Science and Technology of the People's Republic of China.

Firstly, the total output of waste in China is immense. In recent years, the cumulative amount of annual municipal solid waste has reached seven billion tons, covering an area over 800,000 acres, with an average annual growth rate of 4.8% in recent years. At least 600 cities, (not counting counties) or two-thirds of China's large and medium-sized cities, are dealing with the garbage siege, and one-quarter of cities no longer have a suitable place to pile up waste (Yi 2013).

Secondly, Municipal solid waste has exhibited rapid growth. According to data released in *China Statistical Yearbook* 2001–2019, in 2001, China's municipal solid waste removal amounted to 135 million tons. In 2018, this amount grew to 228 million tons, an increase of 93 million tons in 17 years, with an average annual growth rate of 3.14%.

Thirdly, municipal solid waste is complex, varied, and in constant flux, complicating its management. Due to improvements in standards of living, lifestyles, and changing consumption patterns, waste composition is becoming an increasingly complex problem. Thus, municipal solid waste is no longer limited to food waste, paper, plastic, metal, and other conventional components; it now includes a large amount of waste that takes a long to decompose and which contains harmful components. At the same time, China's waste treatment technology is limited. In addition, Chinese people's dining customs result in a high proportion of organic waste, such as kitchen waste, and the high water content of the waste makes it difficult to sort, transport, and treat at the end of the process.

Fourthly, the no-sorting recycling and treatment methods waste useful resources in municipal solid waste, and cause serious environmental pollution. China uses four billion plastic fast food boxes, 500–700 million instant noodle bowls and billions of disposable chopsticks every year. Recycling 1,500 tons of wastepaper could prevent cutting down the trees used to produce 1,200 tons of paper. One ton of aluminum cans can be melted to refine one ton of good aluminum blocks, thus preventing the mining of 20 tons of aluminum ore. Kitchen waste includes food wastes such as leftovers, bones, roots, leaves, and peels. Through on-site composting by biotechnology, about 0.3 tons of organic fertilizer can be produced per ton of kitchen waste (Zhang 2011). However, inefficient waste sorting and recycling in China have not only failed to make good use of this misplaced wealth, but have also caused great harm to the environment. For example, waste batteries, waste plastics, and other special wastes that contain harmful chemical components and are difficult to decompose pollute the soil and endanger human health if they are discarded indiscriminately.

3.1.2 Municipal Solid Waste Removal

In the twenty-first century, the amount of municipal solid waste removed in China has been over 100 million tons annually, and it keeps rising. In 2005, China's municipal solid waste removal amount was 155.768 million tons, and in 2018 it reached 228.018 million tons, an increase of 46.38% compared with 2005. As shown in Fig. 3.1, the volume of municipal solid waste transportation has been growing since experiencing small fluctuations from 2005 to 2010, and in 2016, the volume of municipal solid waste transportation exceeded 20 million tons.

For this chapter, the 31 provinces, autonomous regions, and municipalities in China are divided into three regions according to the level of regional economic development and geographic location: the East, Central, and West (excluding Hong Kong, Macao, and Taiwan), and municipal solid waste removal in each region is statistically analyzed. The Eastern Region includes Liaoning, Beijing, Tianjin, Hebei, Shandong, Shanghai, Suzhou, Zhejiang, Fujian, Guangdong, and Hainan.

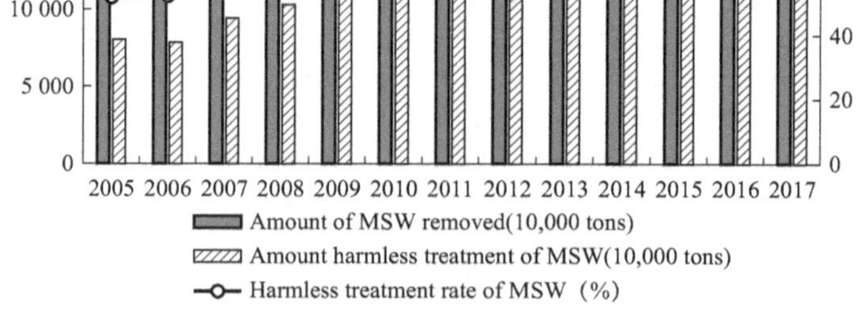

Fig. 3.1 Municipal solid waste treatment in China from 2005 to 2017 (*Source: China Statistical Yearbook* 2006–2018)

The Central Region includes Heilongjiang, Jilin, Shanxi, Inner Mongolia, Henan, Jiangxi, Hunan, Anhui, and Hubei. The Western Region includes Guangxi, Yunnan, Guizhou, Sichuan, Chongqing, Shaanxi, Xinjiang, Gansu, Qinghai, Tibet, and Ningxia. As shown in Fig. 3.2, from 2005 to 2017, the amount of municipal solid waste transportation in China trended upward gradually, but there are stark differences between the regions. The share of municipal solid waste transportation in the Eastern, Central, and Western regions was basically consistent with the three regions' levels of economic development, with the highest level in the Eastern Region, the second highest in the Central Region, and the lowest in the Western Region. The volume of waste removal in the Eastern Region accounted for more than 50% of the national waste removal volume, and in 2008 it exceeded 80 million tons. Unlike the upward trend in the volume of waste removal in the Eastern and Western Regions, the volume of waste removal in the Central Region has declined slightly.

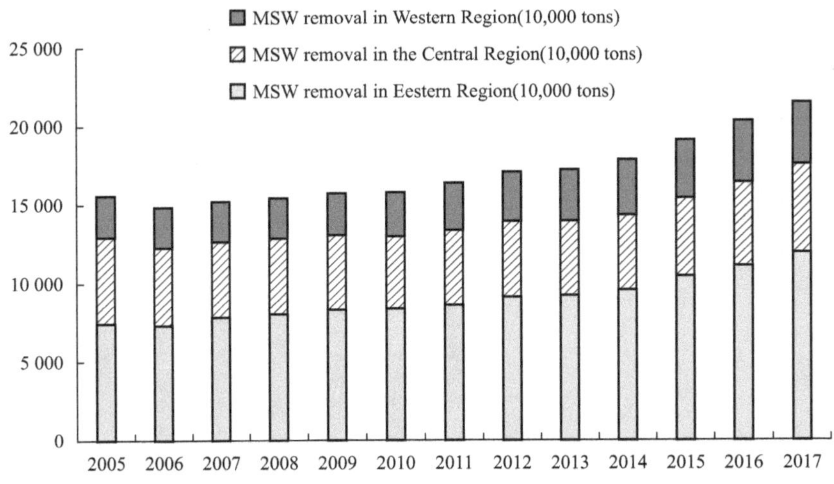

Fig. 3.2 Calendar year municipal solid waste removal in China's East, Midwest, and West Regions, 2005–2017 (*Source*: *China Statistical Yearbook* 2006–2018)

3.1.3 *The Harmless Disposal of Municipal Solid Waste*

3.1.3.1 Disposal Facilities

In recent years, China has been increasing its investment in environmental pollution management. Investment in urban environmental infrastructure construction is one of the three major components of environmental pollution management, accounting for over 50% of its annual expenditure. This grew from 146.69 billion yuan in 2005 to 608.57 billion yuan in 2017, with an average annual growth rate of 11.57%. Investment in urban sanitation also rose from 16.48 billion yuan in 2005 to 62.3 billion yuan in 2017, with an average annual growth rate of 10.77%. Compared with the 608.57 billion yuan invested in urban environmental infrastructure, the investment in amenities and sanitation seems insignificant. Figures released by the Ministry of Ecology and Environment show that from 2005 to 2017, China's annual investment in amenities and sanitation accounted for only about 10% of its investment in the construction of urban environmental infrastructure, compared with only 7.8% in 2012 (see Fig. 3.3).

The 2018 *China Environmental Statistical Yearbook* released by the Ministry of Ecology and Environment showed that as of 2017, a total of 2,209 urban sewage treatment plants had been surveyed and counted

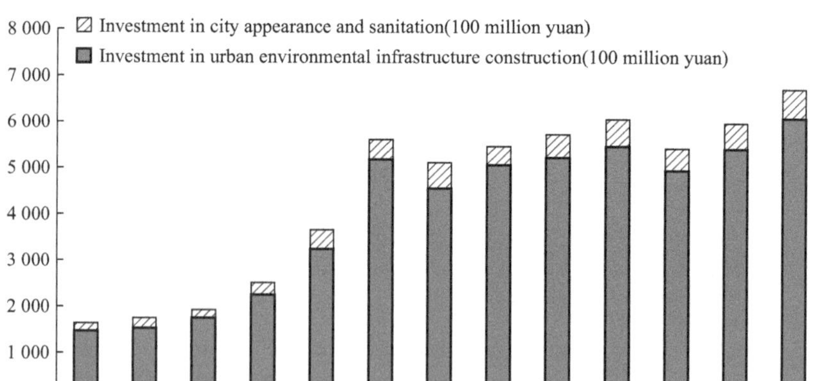

Fig. 3.3 National investment in urban environmental infrastructure construction and investment in amenities and sanitation, 2005–2017 (*Source*: *China Environmental Statistical Yearbook* 2018)

nationwide. This was an increase of 170 over the previous year, with treatment capacity of 157 million tons per day and a total of 45,289 million tons of sewage treated for the year. There were 1,013 safe waste treatment plants throughout China, with an annual volume of 210 million tons of sanitary treatment of municipal solid waste, including 654 sanitary landfill safe waste treatment plants with an average daily safe waste treatment volume of 360,500 tons. There were also 286 incineration safe waste treatment plants with an average daily safe waste treatment volume of 298,100 tons, and 73 other safe waste treatment plants with an average daily sanitary treatment volume of 21,300 tons.

As shown in Table 3.1, there are clear regional differences in the number of both sewage treatment plants and municipal safe solid waste treatment plants, decreasing from the East to the West. As of 2017, there were 661 cities in China, and 1,013 safe waste treatment plants. Theoretically, this represented an average of more than one plant per city, but careful examination of the 2018 *China Environmental Statistical Yearbook* revealed that there was uneven distribution of the municipal safe solid waste treatments plants. Some economically developed regions and provinces have as many as 80 waste treatment plants, while in Western provinces such as Qinghai and Tibet, waste treatment plants number only in the single digits. Prior to 2016, Tibet did not even have a single waste treatment plant.

3.1.3.2 Disposal Volume

The municipal solid waste treatment rate rose rapidly in 2007 after a period of fluctuation from 2000 to 2006, and the municipal solid waste treatment rate in China reached 99% in 2018. This was 36.97 percentage points higher than it was in 2007. The "The 13th Five Year Environmental Protection Plan" issued by the State Council in 2016 proposed that during the "13th Five-Year Plan" period, the municipal solid waste treatment rate nationwide would reach 95%. By the end of 2016, the actual municipal solid waste treatment rate in China was 96.6% (see Fig. 3.4), reaching the target ahead of schedule.

After 2006, the sanitary treatment rate in the Eastern, Central, and Western regions grew rapidly. From 2005 to 2017, the Eastern region maintained a high sanitary treatment rate which continued to rise steadily on this basis. The sanitary treatment rate in the Central and Western regions was not proportional to the two regions' economic development, and the sanitary treatment rate in the Western region was higher than

Table 3.1 China's municipal solid waste treatment plants in the eastern, central, and western regions, 2017

	Eastern region	*Western regions*	*Central region*	*National total*
Sewage treatment plants (buildings)	1,187	558	464	2,209
Sewage treatment rate (%)	92.55	93.24	89.94	91.91
Sanitary treatment plants for municipal solid waste	481	287	245	1,013
Sanitary landfill sanitary treatment plants (fields)	250	215	189	654
Incineration sanitary treatment plants (fields)	181	60	45	286
Other sanitary treatment plants (fields)	50	12	11	73

Source: *China Environmental Statistical Yearbook* 2018, *China Statistical Yearbook* 2018

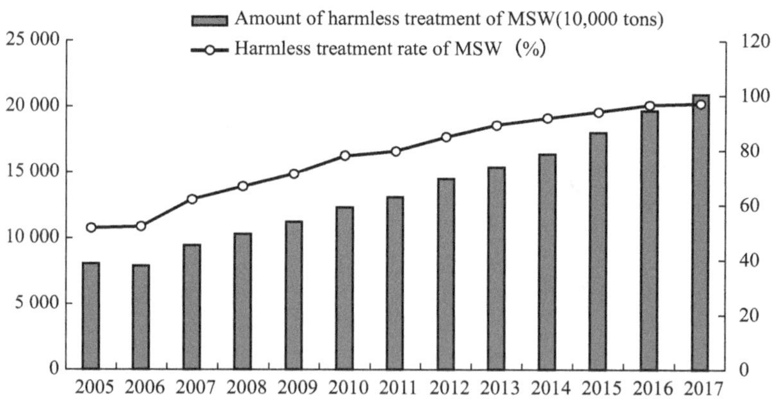

Fig. 3.4 Volume and rate of harmless treatment of municipal solid waste nationwide, 2005–2017 (*Source*: *China Statistical Yearbook*, 2006–2018)

that in the Central region. Moreover, the sanitary treatment rate in the Western region was higher than the national rate (66.80%) for the first time. It exceeded 70% in 2009 and reached 80.24% in 2010, with an average growth rate of 7.38% over the two years.

From 2005 to 2017, unlike the trend of continuous increase in the sanitary treatment rates of municipal solid waste in the Eastern and Western regions, the Central region showed a meandering trend. The sanitary treatment rate trended downward from 2005 to 2006, dropping from 39.55% in 2005 to 34.36% in 2006. The rate bottomed out in 2006 and then rose again, reaching 70.44% in 2011. By 2017, the municipal solid waste sanitary treatment rates in the Eastern, Central, and Western regions had each exceeded 97%.

3.1.4 *The Main Modes of Waste Disposal and Change*

As of this writing, China's municipal solid waste disposal is dominated by landfilling, incineration, and composting. The *National Environmental Statistics Bulletin* (2015) shows that at the end of 2015 there were 2,315 municipal solid waste treatment plants in China, treating a total of 248 million tons of municipal solid waste throughout the year, of which a total of 178 million tons was disposed by landfill, four million tons by composting, and an additional 66 million tons by incineration.

Landfilling is currently the most important waste disposal method in China. It can be divided into two major types: simple landfilling and sanitary landfilling. Simple landfilling, whether in the choice of landfill sites or in the construction of landfill facilities, lacks systematic, standardized scientific design. It also lacks strict seepage protection, resulting in serious groundwater pollution. During heavy rainfall, garbage at the surface can flow into lakes and rivers, damaging surface water supplies. Various kinds of waste simply pile up without any treatment, which can breed bacteria and produce toxic gases.

Sanitary landfilling is a safer method of waste disposal. It utilizes the methods of an impermeable bottom layer, layered landfills, and a top layer of soil covering after compaction. In this way, the garbage is isolated from the environmental ecosystem to the greatest extent possible, thus achieving the goal of safe disposal (Wen 1996). Although this method offers advantages over the simple landfilling method, its shortcomings are also obvious, such as the difficulty of selecting a site for a landfill at a time when suitable land is becoming scarce, and the inability to quickly dissipate waste. Both simple landfills and sanitary landfills consume large areas of land, and their use exerts considerable pressure on large cities where land resources are already scarce. At the same time, although sanitary landfills are systematically protected against infiltration, there is still the risk of the contamination of groundwater sources by seepage.

Composting is a treatment method primarily used for organic waste. Organic waste is mixed with soil and other materials, and under high temperatures and humid conditions, microorganisms are used to decompose it into organic fertilizer. Organic waste such as food waste, fallen leaves, and branches can be composted. However, this method is time-consuming and can damage the surrounding environment.

Incineration is the process of burning waste and using the heat generated to produce electricity and usable heat. This method is effective in waste minimization and resource utilization, but it is also prone to the production of toxic substances such as dioxins during the waste incineration process.

As of this writing, sanitary landfills remain the primary sanitary treatment method for municipal solid waste in China, and the majority of its safe waste is processed through sanitary landfills every year. From 2005 to 2018, the number of incineration plants in China has increased exponentially, from 67 in 2005 to 331 in 2018. In that same period, the incineration of municipal solid waste increased from 7.91 million tons to 101.849 million tons.

The percentage of incinerated waste in the total amount of safe waste is increasing year-over-year. The "13th Five Year Environmental Protection Plan" states that "by 2020, the waste incineration treatment rate will reach 40%". As of this writing, urban land is scarce and incineration has become the preferred method of safe waste disposal in more and more cities, especially big cities. However, the use of composting has declined, and in 2011 the State stopped sorting composting plants and treatment volume separately, and now classifies them both as other harmless treatment measures. In 2018, there were 97 composting and other sanitary treatment plants across the country. In 2005, 3.454 million tons of compost were treated, accounting for 4.32% of the total amount of safe waste that year. By 2018, the amount of composting and other safe waste treated totaled 6.744 million tons, which accounted for only 2.99% of the total amount of sanitary treatment in that year (see Table 3.2).

Table 3.2 Municipal solid waste sanitary treatment plants in China from 2005 to 2018

Year	*Number of sanitary treatment plants*			*Sanitary treatment amount (ten thousand tons/year)*		
	Sanitary landfill	*Incineration*	*Compost/ other*	*Sanitary landfill*	*Incineration*	*Compost/ other*
2005	356	67	46	6,857.1	791.0	345.4
2006	324	69	20	6,408.2	1,137.6	288.2
2007	366	66	17	7,632.7	1,435.1	250.0
2008	407	74	14	8,484.0	1,569.7	174.0
2009	447	93	16	8,898.6	2,022.0	178.8
2010	498	104	11	9,598.3	2,316.7	180.3
2011	547	109	21	10,063.7	2,599.3	426.6
2012	540	138	23	10,512.5	3,584.1	393.0
2013	580	166	19	10,492.7	4,633.7	267.6
2014	604	188	26	10,744.3	5,329.9	319.6
2015	640	220	30	11,483.1	6,175.5	354.4
2016	657	249	34	11,866.4	7,378.4	428.9
2017	654	286	73	12,037.6	8,463.3	533.2
2018	663	331	97	11,706.0	10,184.9	674.4

Note In 2011, compost was changed to "other" in the statistical indicators of harmless treatment plants and treatment capacity
Source: *China Statistical Yearbook* 2006–2019

3.1.5 *Regional Differences in Waste Disposal Patterns*

Based on the geographic location of each province, we further subdivided the 31 provinces and municipalities into seven regions (excluding Hong Kong, Macao, and Taiwan): Northeast China (HL, JL, and LN), Northern China (BJ, TJ, HE, SX, and NM), Eastern China (SD, SH, JS, ZJ, FJ, JX, and AH), Southern China (GD, GX, and HI), Central China (HA, HN, and HB), Northwestern China (SN, GS, QH, NX, and XJ), and Southwestern China (CQ, SC, YN, GZ, and XZ). The similarities and differences in waste treatment patterns among the seven regions were compared in detail using data and graphs. Table 3.3 shows that the three regions with the safest waste treatment plants in China were Eastern China, Northern China, and Southern China. Outside of Eastern China, sanitary landfills were still the main way to dispose of waste safely.

From 2005 to 2018, the number of safe sanitary landfill plants across China grew slowly, and even decreased in some regions. The number of

Table 3.3 Distribution of safe waste treatment plants in China in 2018

	Sanitary landfills (plants)	*Incinerators (plants)*	*Other*	*Total*
Northeastern China	82	15	6	103
Northern China	100	31	14	145
Eastern China	133	161	46	340
Central China	79	50	10	139
Northwestern China	98	24	9	131
Southwestern China	86	7	6	99
Northeastern China	85	43	6	134
National total	663	331	97	1,091

Source: *China Statistical Yearbook* 2019

sanitary landfill plants in Eastern China decreased from 209 in 2003 to 133 in 2018.[2] Although sanitary landfills offer the advantages of high treatment capacity and low investment, they occupy large parcels of land, and finding open space to dispose of waste is a difficult task for large cities already short on land (e.g., Shanghai in Eastern China, Beijing, and Tianjin in Northern China).

From 2005 to 2018, safe waste incineration proliferated across the country, but also showed uneven development between regions, with the Eastern Region growing faster than the Western region, and faster growth in the economically developed regions than in the underdeveloped regions. Eastern China was the fastest growing region, with the region's incineration plants increasing from 25 in 2005 to 161 in 2018, while the Northwestern region went from one incineration plant in 2005 to no waste incineration plants in 2011, and then to seven in 2018.[3] Waste incineration can expedite waste reduction and treatment, and alleviate urban land shortages, but constructing waste incineration plants also entails large capital investment and advanced technology, and also poses high risk.

Unlike sanitary landfills and waste incineration, the use of safe composting to dispose of municipal solid waste decreased in most regions of China from 2005 to 2018. By 2010, the three regions with the sharpest reductions were Eastern China, Central China, and Southwestern China.

[2] See *China Statistical Yearbook* 2006–2019.

[3] See *China Statistical Yearbook* 2006–2019.

Of the seven regions mentioned earlier, only Northern China and Northwestern China have increased the number of composting plants, and the increases are in the single digits, far less than the growth in the number of sanitary landfill plants in the two regions over the five-year period.[4]

3.1.6 Summary

Since the beginning of the twenty-first century, China has gradually shifted its attention to the disposal of municipal solid waste and related issues. It has also issued a series of policy documents requiring all regions of the country to strengthen municipal solid waste treatment with the slogan "Reduce, Recycle, Sanitize". As such, China's municipal solid waste removal and sanitary treatment volume has grown rapidly. By 2018 China's municipal solid waste sanitary treatment rate had reached 99%, but this does not mean that the waste problem has been solved. China now faces six major problems: huge stock, lack of treatment facilities, slow construction, low investment, difficulty eradicating secondary pollution, lack of public awareness, and deficiencies in the regulatory system.

Faced with the problems of a large population base and large amounts of garbage, under the current technical conditions, it would be possible to reduce the output of urban domestic waste by formulating effective comprehensive waste management regulatory systems and policies, and by promoting national participation.

3.2 Municipal Solid Waste Treatment Policy

As of this writing, China's municipal solid waste treatment policy system is based on the Constitution of the People's Republic of China and the Environmental Protection Law of the People's Republic of China as the basic law, as well as the Law on Prevention and Control of Environmental Pollution by Solid Waste in the People's Republic of China and the Regulations on the Administration of Urban Appearance and Environmental Sanitation. Policies and regulations such as the National Plan for the Construction of Harmless Treatment Facilities for Municipal Solid Waste, the Measures for the Administration of Municipal Solid Waste,

[4] See *China Statistical Yearbook* 2006–2019.

and the Technical Policy for the Treatment and Pollution Prevention of Municipal Solid Waste are also pertinent.

3.2.1 *Waste Management Policies, Regulations, and Changes*

3.2.1.1 *Constitution*

The Constitution of the People's Republic of China is the basic law of China. It provides the fundamental basis for the formulation of other environmental protection laws, regulations, and policies. Article 9 of *the Constitution of the People's Republic of China stipulates*, "natural resources such as mineral deposits, streams, forests, mountains, grasslands, wastelands and mudflats belong to the State, i.e., are owned by the entire population...The State guarantees the rational use of natural resources and the protection of precious animals and plants. Any organization or individual is prohibited from appropriating or destroying natural resources by any means whatsoever". This defines environmental protection as a basic state policy and sets the tone for environmental protection work throughout the country. Article 26, which states, "the State shall protect and improve the living and ecological environments, and prevent pollution and other public hazards", provides a further constitutional basis for waste management in special areas.

3.2.1.2 *Legislation*

Based on the Constitution, *the Environmental Law of the People's Republic of China* (for Trial Implementation) was introduced in 1979 in order to protect and improve living and ecological environments, prevent and alleviate pollution and other public hazards, safeguard human health, and promote the development of socialist modernization. The Act provides guiding principles for environmental protection in China in the areas of environmental regulation, prevention, and the management of environmental pollution and other public hazards. It also provides principles for legal responsibility, including the principles of coordinated development of economic construction and environmental protection, prevention as the mainstay, and integration of prevention and alleviation, the "polluter pays" principle, the government's responsibility for the quality of the environment, and reliance on the masses to protect the environment. Environmental impact assessment of construction projects was first established as a legal system in *the Environmental Law of the People's*

Republic of China (for Trial Implementation). Ten years after the introduction of the Trial Law, t*he Environmental Law of the People's Republic of China* was revised and implemented in 1989.[5] This law clarified and strengthened the monitoring responsibilities and powers of the relevant government departments and refined the relevant legal responsibilities of the central government, local governments at all levels, and enterprises. In 2014, the newly revised Environmental Protection Law explicitly included multiple environmental stakeholders in the environmental protection and management team, stating "citizens, legal persons and other organizations shall enjoy the right to obtain environmental information and to participate in and supervise environmental protection in accordance with the law" and "citizens shall abide by environmental protection laws and regulations, cooperate in the implementation of environmental protection measures, separate municipal solid waste in accordance with the regulations, and reduce the damage to the environment in their daily lives". It also increased the penalties for environmental damage incurred by governments, enterprises, and individuals. Citizens were required to abide by environmental protection laws and regulations, cooperate in the implementation of environmental protection measures, separate household waste in accordance with regulations, and reduce the damage caused to the environment in their daily lives. Additionally, it increased the penalties for environmental damage by governments, enterprises, and individuals.

The Law of the People's Republic of China on Environmental Impact Assessment,[6] which was discussed and adopted by the Standing

[5] The first version of the Environmental Law of the People's Republic of China was adopted by the Standing Committee of the Seventh National People's Congress at its Eleventh meeting on December 26, 1989, and promulgated by Decree No. 22 of the President of the People's Republic of China, to be implemented as of the date of its promulgation. The second version was amended and adopted at the eighth meeting of the Standing Committee of the Twelfth National People's Congress on April 24, 2014, and promulgated by Decree No. 9 of the second edition, which was revised and adopted at the Eighth Meeting of the Standing Committee of the Twelfth National People's Congress on April 24, 2014, and promulgated by Decree No. 9 of the President of the People's Republic of China. It came into force on January 1, 2015.

[6] First amended in accordance with the Decision on Amending the Energy Conservation Law of the People's Republic of China and Six Other Laws of the People's Republic of China of the Twenty-first Session of the Standing Committee of the Twelfth National People's Congress of July 2, 2016; and amended in accordance with the Decision on Amending the Labor Law of the People's Republic of China and Seven Other Laws of the People's Republic of China of December 29, 2018 of the Seventh Session of

Committee of the Ninth National People's Congress in 2002, is complementary to the Environmental Protection Law. The legislative purpose of the Law of the People's Republic of China on Environmental Impact Assessment is to prevent adverse effects on the environment resulting from the implementation of planning and construction projects. The law contains clear provisions on the concepts, principles, scope, procedures and legal responsibilities of environmental impact assessment, and explicitly includes public participation in environmental impact assessment in its statutes, such as Article 5 of Chapter I, which stipulates: "China encourages the participation of relevant organizations, experts and members of the public in the assessment of environmental impact in an appropriate manner". Article 11 of Chapter II stipulates: "for plans that may cause adverse environmental impacts and directly involve the public's environmental rights and interests, the planning authorities should hold demonstrations, hearings, or take other forms to solicit opinions from relevant units, experts and the public on the draft environmental impact report before the draft plan is submitted for approval". This clarified the public's role in environmental management matters, providing a legal basis for public participation in waste management, including the planning and siting of waste treatment projects.

The Law of the People's Republic of China on Prevention and Control of Environmental Pollution by Solid Waste, issued and amended by the Standing Committee of the National People's Congress, is a special law on municipal solid waste treatment. The Law covers the regulation of solid waste pollution prevention and alleviation, the prevention and alleviation of solid waste pollution, the prevention and alleviation of hazardous waste pollution, and legal liability. Article 3 of the Law states, "the State shall prevent and control the pollution of the environment by solid waste, implement the principles of reducing the amount and hazardousness of solid waste, making full and rational use of solid waste and disposing of solid waste in a harmless manner, and promote cleaner production and the development of a circular economy". In fact, this defines the basic principles for the management of municipal solid waste, i.e., reduction, recycling, and harmlessness. The revised Law on the Prevention and Control of Environmental Pollution by Solid Waste has several highlights. Firstly, the polluter-responsible system is codified in the form of a law,

the Standing Committee of the Thirteenth National People's Congress of December 29, 2018, Second Amendment.

and Article 5 of the Law stipulates, "the State implements the polluter-responsible principle according to the law for the prevention and control of environmental pollution by solid waste", clarifying for the first time the polluter's responsibility. Secondly, the burden of proof was changed from that of environmental victims to that of "whoever pollutes, whoever proves", i.e., the reversal of the burden of proof in compensation for pollution damage, with the burden of proof being borne by the victim in respect of exemptions provided in the law. This provides legal safeguards for protecting the lawful environmental rights and interests of disadvantaged groups. Thirdly, it forbade the shuttering or dismantling of municipal solid waste disposal facilities and places without authorization. It required that any substances recovered from municipal solid waste be used in accordance with the purposes and standards stipulated by the state, providing a legal basis for the rational disposal and management of municipal solid waste. Fourthly, in order to reduce the amount of solid waste generated and the associated hazards, the Act establishes the extended producer responsibility system, i.e., the producer not only has to assume responsibility for environmental pollution in the production process, but also has to assume responsibility for the recycling or disposal of end-of-life products or used packages. This addresses the problem of environmental pollution brought about by the disjunction between the responsibility for production, consumption, and waste disposal.

3.2.1.3 Administrative Regulations and Decrees

In 1986, the State Council approved the *Report on the Handling of Municipal Solid Waste to Improve Environmental Hygiene* by the Ministry of Housing and Urban–Rural Development, Ministry of Ecology and Environment, and other departments. With this approval, the State formally began municipal solid waste management. In 1992, the State Council promulgated *the Regulations on the Administration of City Appearance and Environmental Sanitation*, which was revised twice, in 2011 and 2017. Article 28 of the Regulations stipulates, "the administrative department of urban sanitation of the urban people's government shall supervise and manage the collection, transportation and disposal of municipal solid waste...Municipal solid waste shall be gradually collected, transported and disposed of in a classified manner". Article 30 states, "encouragement and support are given to the relevant departments to organize the movement of clean vegetables into the city and the recycling of waste materials, so as to reduce municipal solid waste". It also stipulates, "warnings and fines shall be imposed" on those who do not follow the regulations on the removal and disposal of waste. This provides the norms of implementation for the management of municipal solid waste. In addition, it mentions, "environmental sanitation management should be gradually socialized. Cities with the necessary conditions can set up environmental sanitation service companies. Where professional environmental sanitation units are commissioned to clean, collect, transport and dispose of waste, they shall pay a service fee". This introduced market forces into the municipal waste management system.

In 1992, the State Council approved the *Notice on Opinions on Solving the Problem of Municipal Solid Waste in China*, which was jointly formulated by the Ministry of Housing and Urban–Rural Development, the State Environmental Protection Administration, and other departments, laying the groundwork for China's professional management of municipal solid waste. The *Notice* denotes the severity of the pollution problem caused by municipal solid waste, and analyzes the reasons for it, including insufficient funds for waste disposal, the lack of a policy encouraging recycling and comprehensive utilization of waste, outdated waste disposal technology and equipment, and the poor treatment of professional staff. In response to these problems, countermeasures have been proposed to strengthen the management of the municipal solid waste disposal industry, to implement comprehensive utilization of municipal solid waste recycling, increase the recycling rate, and collect funds for the construction of harmless municipal solid waste disposal facilities through multiple channels.

In 1993, the Ministry of Housing and Urban–Rural Development issued the *Measures for the Management of Municipal Solid Waste*. A new version was issued in 2007 and amended in 2015. The measures state, "the management of municipal solid waste shall be based on the principles of minimization, resource utilization and harmlessness, and on the principle that whoever produces it shall be responsible for it in accordance with the law".

There are several major improvements in the amended measure. Firstly, it clarifies the parties responsible for the management of municipal solid waste and their rights and obligations. It not only stipulates the responsibility of sanitation business enterprises, but also stipulates the supervision and management responsibilities of environmental sanitation departments. Secondly, it emphasizes the requirements for garbage sorting and offers detailed regulations on the behavior of both work units and individuals in discarding garbage. Thirdly, it strengthens the regulations on the preparation of municipal solid waste management plans and the construction of waste collection and disposal facilities. Fourthly, the provisions on municipal solid waste disposal fees emphasize the necessity of paying municipal waste disposal fees. This is the first time that China has clarified domestic waste generators' obligation to pay garbage disposal fees in the form of administrative regulations, and established corresponding legal penalties. Fifthly, it establishes a franchise system in the field of waste treatment, and stipulates the market access conditions, licensing procedures, and responsibilities of enterprises engaged in urban domestic waste business activities. Market forces were introduced into the field of public utilities, alleviating the shortage of capital investment in the waste disposal industry and easing the pressure on the government's finances. However, the entry qualifications and obligations and responsibilities of the operating enterprises are strictly regulated, so as to ensure that the development of the waste disposal industry is standardized and conducted under the auspices of the law.

In 2000, the Ministry of Housing and Urban–Rural Development issued the *Notice on the Announcement of Pilot Cities for the Classified Collection of Municipal Solid Waste*. This identified Beijing, Shanghai, Guangzhou, Shenzhen, Hangzhou, Nanjing, Xiamen, and Guilin as pilot cities for the sorted collection of municipal solid waste, and clarified the objectives of the pilot work for the sorted collection of municipal solid waste for the year 2000. It was announced at a symposium on the sorted collection during the pilot work, and also proposed the formulation of methodology and standards for the sorted collection of waste and the indicators for the statistical evaluation of waste collection. Moreover, it called for a combination of the sorted collection of waste with the recycling of resources, and appealed to the State to perfect the relevant laws and regulations as soon as possible.

In 2006, the Ministry of Housing and Urban–Rural Development issued the Notice on the Issuance of China's Urban and Rural Environmental Sanitation System Construction. It specifies "the establishment of a sound environmental sanitation system and a standardized governmental supervisory mechanism, and the improvement of the charging system for the disposal of municipal solid waste", and "the improvement of waste disposal facilities" as the objectives of the construction of the urban and rural environmental sanitation system. It also establishes "adhering to the integration of waste management and pollution prevention into the circular economy track, vigorously promoting waste reduction, resource utilization and harmlessness, actively carrying out waste sorting, collection and treatment, expanding the regeneration and utilization of resources and energy, and treating waste at the end of the process as a whole process of remediation at the source" as a basic principle for the construction of urban and rural environmental sanitation systems. At the same time, it emphasizes the importance of "public participation" in the cause of waste management, and proposes the construction of four major systems—the governmental administrative system of environmental sanitation supervision, the market operation system of environmental sanitation management, the social participation system of environmental sanitation management, and the emergency response system of environmental sanitation emergencies.

In April 2011, the State Council approved and forwarded the *Notice on Opinions on Further Strengthening the Disposal of Municipal Solid Waste* proposed by the Ministry of Housing and Urban–Rural Development and the Ministry of Ecology and Environment. The *Notice* establishes basic principles for the management and treatment of municipal solid waste, including the mobilization of all people and scientific guidance; comprehensive utilization; integrated planning and rational layout; government leadership and social participation. The notice also elaborates upon strategies to improve the capacity and level of municipal solid waste treatment in terms of waste treatment planning and guidance, collection and transportation networks, technology selection, supervision and management, evaluation systems, policy support, the division of labor among departments, publicity, and education.

In February 2016, the Central Committee of the Communist Party of China and the State Council issued *Several Opinions on Further Strengthening the Management of Urban Planning, Construction and Management*, which emphasized the establishment of a coordination mechanism among the government, communities, enterprises and residents, and the promotion of waste reduction, resourcefulness and harmlessness through sorting, and collecting, and comprehensive recycling.

In March 2017, the Notice on the Implementation Plan of the Municipal Solid Waste Classification System proposed the basic establishment of laws, regulations and standard systems related to waste sorting by the end of 2020. It also proposed building a replicable and popularized model for the sorting of municipal solid waste, and that the recycling rate of municipal solid waste in the cities where there is mandatory sorting of municipal solid waste exceed 35%. Additionally, some regions were required to implement mandatory sorting of municipal solid waste, guide residents to sort municipal solid waste, strengthen the construction of support systems for the sorting of municipal solid waste, and improve organizational leadership and job security.

From 2018 to 2019, the Ministry of Education, Ministry of Ecology and Environment, Ministry of Housing and Urban–Rural Development, the State Council, and other departments issued a series of administrative laws and regulations. These included the Interim Measures for Examining the Work of Classifying Municipal Solid Waste, the Notice on the Issuance of a Pilot Work Program for the Construction of a Waste-Free City, and the Notice on the Comprehensive Launch of Work on the Classification of Municipal Solid Waste in Prefectural-level and Above Cities Across the Nation, and a series of administrative laws and regulations. This jumpstarted a national campaign to categorize waste. The Ministry of Housing and Urban–Rural Development and nine other departments issued the *Notice on the Comprehensive Launch of Work on the Classification of Municipal Solid Waste in Prefectural-level and Above Cities Across the Nation*. This requires that by the end of 2019, cities at all levels will have prepared and completed an implementation plan for the sorting of municipal solid waste, and defined the standards for the sorting of municipal solid waste, as well as the objectives and tasks, key projects, supporting policies and specific measures to promote the categorization of municipal solid waste. By 2020, 46 key cities will have established domestic waste sorting and treatment systems. As such, the subjects in recent administrative regulations and responsibilities are clearer, and the goals are more accurate.

3.2.1.4 Industry/Technical Standards

Since the beginning of the twenty-first century, China has further categorized and clarified technical industry standards on the management of municipal solid waste, ensuring that the implementation of waste treatment and pollution prevention and alleviation is well documented. In 2000, the Ministry of Housing and Urban–Rural Development along with several other departments issued the *Technical Policy for Municipal Solid Waste Treatment and Pollution Prevention*. This emphasized the principles of waste minimization and resource utilization and safety. It also embodied the determination to transform end-of-pipe treatment into source control, excessive packaging at the source to the development of comprehensive utilization technology, to sorted compression-type collection and transportation, and ultimately to landfill, incineration, and composting treatment. At the same time, the technical details of waste treatment were stipulated, such as the calorific value of waste incineration and the residence time of flue gas in the after-combustion chamber.

In 2004, the Ministry of Housing and Urban–Rural Development issued *Municipal Domestic Waste Classification and Evaluation Standards*, which focuses on the principles of the sorted collection and resource utilization of municipal solid waste. It also establishes detailed provisions on waste sorting categories, requirements, operations, and evaluation indicators, providing specific and operational indicators for waste sorting work.

In 2010, the Ministry of Housing and Urban–Rural Development, the National Development and Reform Commission, and the Ministry of Ecology and Environment jointly issued the *Technical Guidelines for Domestic Waste Disposal*, stating the aim of "protecting public environmental sanitation and human health". On the basis of the *Technical Policy on the Treatment of Municipal Solid Waste and Prevention and Treatment of Pollution*, specific requirements were proposed for the feasibility of sanitary landfills, incineration, composting and other waste treatment technologies, as well as for the construction of municipal solid waste treatment facilities. Detailed provisions were also provided on the controversial mode of waste incineration, including the applicability of incineration technology, requirements for the construction of waste incineration plants, and the supervision of their operation. Compared with the *Technical Policy on the Treatment of Municipal Solid Waste and Prevention and Treatment of Pollution*, the *Technical Guidelines for the Treatment of Municipal Solid Waste* place more emphasis on pollution management during waste disposal. For example, there are more specific provisions on the mitigation measures for dioxins generated by the municipal solid waste incineration process.

In addition to the principal provisions of the *Technical Policy on the Treatment of Municipal Solid Waste and Prevention* and the *Technical Guidelines for the Treatment of Municipal Solid Waste*, the State has also issued the following series of mitigation standards for different waste disposal modes.

- Technical Standards for Sanitary Landfilling of Municipal Solid Waste
- Construction Standards for Municipal Solid Waste Landfill Disposal Project Standards for Municipal Solid Waste Landfill Pollution Control
- Standards for Municipal Solid Waste Incineration Pollution Control
- Specifications for Municipal Solid Waste Incinerators and Waste Heat Boilers
- Municipal Solid Waste Incineration and Treatment Project Technical Specifications
- Municipal Solid Waste Incineration Air Pollutant Emissions Standards

These documents clarify the sorting and stipulate the selection of treatment modes, equipment construction, technological control, and emissions standards for municipal solid waste disposal.

3.2.1.5 Program Outline

In November 2007, the State Council issued the Notice on the Eleventh Five-Year Plan for National Environmental Protection. It proposed a plan for the construction of facilities for the environmentally sound disposal of municipal solid waste. It also added an increase of capacity of 240,000 tons of environmentally sound municipal solid waste per day, and a rate of environmentally sound treatment of municipal solid waste of no less than 60%. Additionally, it promoted the sorting of waste and strengthened the environmental supervision of waste disposal facilities. Moreover, it proposed improving environmental economic policy, and levying comprehensive municipal solid waste disposal fees.

In the same year, the National Development and Reform Commission, the Ministry of Construction, and the State Environmental Protection Administration jointly issued the *11th Five-Year Plan for the Construction of Harmless Treatment Facilities for Municipal Domestic Waste in China*, which set specific goals. By the end of the 11th Five-Year Plan, the national goal for the sanitary treatment of domestic waste was a rate of 60%. The rate for domestic waste in cities was 70%, and in counties it was 30%. It also set a target of the establishment or improvement of domestic waste collection and transportation systems in at least 90% of counties across the country.

On April 19, 2012, the General Office of the State Council issued the "12th Five-Year Plan for the National Municipal Solid Waste Sanitary Treatment Facilities Construction Plan". This plan clarified the goals, main tasks and safeguarding measures for the construction of national urban domestic waste harmless treatment facilities during the 12th Five-Year Plan period. The objectives of the plan were as follows: by 2015, municipalities directly under the central government, provincial capitals, and municipalities with separate plans will all realize the sanitary treatment of municipal solid waste, and the municipal solid waste treatment rate in cities will exceed 90%. By 2015, pilot projects for the comprehensive promotion of the sorting of municipal solid waste will be implemented, and multiple demonstration cities for the sorting of municipal solid waste will be built in each province (autonomous region and municipality). Compared with the "11th Five-Year Plan", the "12th Five-Year Plan" has the following highlights: Firstly, it proposes "government-led, social participation" to interject social capital into domestic waste treatment. It also encourages the public to participate in waste sorting, planning waste reduction from the source. Secondly, it proposes comprehensive promotion of pilot municipal solid waste sorting. Thirdly, for the first time, it proposes improving the collection and transportation system and improving the management of garbage stock. Fourthly, it proposes increasing capital investment and budgets for garbage disposal. Fifthly, instead of setting targets for safe waste disposal by region, detailed targets are set for each province, autonomous region and municipality.

On December 31, 2016, the National Development and Reform Commission and the Ministry of Housing and Urban–Rural Development jointly issued the "13th Five-Year Plan for the National Municipal Solid Waste Harmless Treatment Facilities Construction Plan". It proposed the following goals by the end of 2020:

- A sanitary treatment rate of 100% for municipal solid waste in major cities
- A sanitary treatment rate of 95% municipal solid waste in municipal cities
- A municipal solid waste treatment rate in the built up area of counties (*xiancheng*) of at least 80%
- A sanitary treatment rate of municipal solid waste in townships (*zhen*) of at least 70%

- Cities with separate plans and provincial capitals (built-up areas) will realize zero landfills for primary waste.
- Townships will realize full coverage of harmless treatment capacity for municipal solid waste.
- A minimum recycling rate of 35% for municipal solid waste

Compared with the "Twelfth Five-Year Plan for the National Municipal Solid Waste Harmless Treatment Facilities Construction Plan", the plan proposes strengthening the innovation leadership, promoting the new mode of "Internet + Resource Recycling", strengthening the construction and cultivation of professional and technical talent and management talent, developing vocational education and pre-employment and on-the-job vocational training, and improving employees' personal and vocational skills.

3.2.1.6 Local Legislation

In accordance with national laws and regulations on municipal solid waste management, local regulations have been issued to suit unique local situations.

For example, in 1995, the Nanjing Municipal Government issued *Interim Regulations on the Management of Municipal Domestic Waste Bags in Nanjing*, which stipulated detailed rules for the collection, transportation, and penalties for municipal solid waste disposal. In 2013, the Nanjing Municipal Government officially passed and implemented the *Nanjing Domestic Waste Classification Management Measures*. In 1999, Beijing promulgated the *Implementation Measures for the Collection of Municipal Solid Waste Disposal Fees in Beijing* (for trial implementation) to levy municipal solid waste disposal fees. Since then, domestic garbage disposal fees have been levied across the country. In 2012, Beijing promulgated the *Beijing Municipal Domestic Waste Management Regulations*, which defined comprehensive standards for the sorting of domestic waste. In December 2004, the Xiamen Municipal Government issued the *Measures for the Management of Municipal Domestic Waste in Xiamen*. In 2017, the Sixth meeting of the Standing Committee of the 15th Xiamen Municipal People's Congress passed the *Xiamen Special Economic Zone Domestic Waste Classification Management Measures* to clarify detailed rules for the sorting of municipal domestic waste. In 2011, Guangzhou issued the *Interim Regulations on the Classification and Management of Municipal Domestic Waste in Guangzhou*. On December 27, 2017, the

Regulations on the Classification and Management of Domestic Waste in Guangzhou was adopted at the 11th meeting of the Standing Committee of the 15th Guangzhou Municipal People's Congress. In 2014, the Shanghai Municipal Government promulgated and implemented the *Measures for Promoting the Classification and Reduction of Domestic Waste in Shanghai*. In March 2018, Shanghai issued the *Implementation Plan on Establishing and Improving the Whole Process Classification of Domestic Waste in the City*. On January 31, 2019, the Second Session of the 15th Shanghai Municipal People's Congress voted to pass the *Shanghai Municipal Domestic Waste Management Regulations*, which was officially implemented on July 1. To standardize the sorting and delivery behavior of domestic waste generators, the Shanghai Community Waste Classification and Reduction Project formulated the *Shanghai Municipal Domestic Waste Classification and Delivery Guidelines* in accordance with the requirements of the *Shanghai Municipal Domestic Waste Management Regulations*. Shanghai's detailed garbage sorting rules and strict implementation and supervision sparked a wave of heated discussion and learning across the country. Other pilot cities for waste sorting have also implemented relevant measures.

Although there are differences in how municipal solid waste is managed around the world, the purpose in all of them is to guide the participation of multiple social forces in the management of municipal solid waste sorting. This is done through means such as market regulation, rewards, and penalties, with the aim of reducing resource utilization and promoting safety in municipal solid waste.

3.2.2 Changes in Policies and Regulations and Existing Problems

Examining the history of policy documents on municipal solid waste management in China since the founding of the People's Republic of China, the following can be observed: First, before the 1970s, municipal solid waste management was not emphasized, but beginning in the 1990s, the issue gradually gained attention, and beginning in the mid-to-late 1990s, it was attracting mounting attention as a social issue. Second, among the policies and regulations on municipal solid waste management issued over the years, 62 (38.75%) were related to waste sorting, 52 of which were issued in the twenty-first century, and the idea of end-treatment has gradually changed to source classification management. Third, the number of industry technical standards guiding the precise management of waste has increased rapidly since the twenty-first century, and operationalization and precise management is becoming one of the goals of waste management.

China's municipal solid waste management policies have changed as follows. First, the idea of waste management has changed from "end treatment" to "comprehensive management". Whereas earlier regulations emphasized solutions to the problems of waste disposal, waste elimination, and sanitary treatment, in the twenty-first century, new regulations have been implemented to establish a comprehensive system of waste elimination at the source, recycling and sanitary treatment at the end (i.e., the creation of a closed cycle of waste minimization), resourcing and safety. This reflects the concept of a circular economy.

Second, there has been a change in the waste management participants. Recent legislation has given greater prominence to the involvement of multiple environmental stakeholders in waste management enterprises, rather than the government being overburdened with the task of the end-treatment of waste. In terms of source, regulations require producers (e.g., restrictions on packaging under the Law of the People's Republic of China on Prevention and Control of Environmental Pollution by Solid Waste and the Technical Policy on the Treatment of Municipal Solid Waste and Prevention and Treatment of Pollution) and consumers (e.g., restrictions on the use of plastic bags under the *Notice on Restrictions on the Production, Sale and Use of Plastic Shopping Bags* from the General Office of the State Council) to minimize waste production. In terms of sorting and recycling, the regulations require consumers (both work units and individuals) to collect and sort their waste, and impose fees for municipal solid waste disposal (e.g., the Measures for the Management of Municipal Solid Waste). This requires environmental protection units and waste handlers to sort and treat waste during the processes of waste collection, transfer and disposal. In terms of terminal treatment, the regulations establish a franchising system to introduce market forces into the field of public utilities. At the same time, the regulations stipulate the market access conditions, licensing procedures, and responsibilities of enterprises engaging in municipal solid waste business activities (e.g., the Measures for the Management of Municipal Solid Waste). These are intended to introduce social forces into the management of public affairs, and to encourage the participation of multiple environmental stakeholders, especially the general public, in the management and ecological protection of municipal solid wastes.

Third, the means of waste management have changed. Recent policies have emphasized the introduction of market principles and forces into waste management and environmental protection. For example, the *Notice on Implementing a Charging System for Municipal Domestic Waste Disposal to Promote the Industrialization of Waste Disposal* implements a charging system for municipal solid waste disposal, and calls for the establishment of reasonable charging standards. The decision of the Third Plenary Session of the 18th Central Committee stipulates: "Adhere to the principles of paying for the use of resources and whoever pollutes the environment or destroys the ecology pays, and gradually extend the resource tax to the occupancy of all kinds of natural ecological space" and "develop the environmental protection market, implement the trading system for energy saving, carbon emission rights, sewage rights and water rights, establish a market-oriented mechanism to attract social capital to invest in ecological environmental protection, and implement third-party treatment of environmental pollution". This means introducing market mechanisms and market forces into the public sphere of environmental protection.

Fourth, waste management has been gradually institutionalized. Prior to the twenty-first century, China had less specific legislation and policy regulations on waste management, and most were merely guiding opinions (For example, the 1986 *Report on the Handling of Municipal Solid Waste to Improve Environmental Hygiene*, and from 1992, *Several Opinions on Solving the Problem of Municipal Solid Waste in China*). Since the turn of the millennium, the government has frequently issued administrative laws and regulations on waste reduction, resource utilization, and sanitary treatment, such as the *Technical Policy on the Treatment of Municipal Solid Waste* and *Prevention and Treatment of Pollution and the Measures for the Management of Municipal Solid Waste*. To implement waste reduction, resource utilization, and safety into practice, a series of operable industrial and technical standards, such as the Classification and Evaluation Standard of Municipal Solid Waste and the Technical Guidelines for the Treatment of Municipal Solid Waste, and a long-term plan for the future development of municipal solid waste management, have also been formulated. In addition, a series of operational industrial and technical standards, such as the Classification of Municipal Solid Waste and its Evaluation Standards, have been issued to implement waste minimization, resource utilization, and harmlessness. In terms of penalties, the rules are becoming stricter and the penalties are increasing in severity.

These laws and regulations have provided a legal framework for waste management and made it possible to follow rules and regulations and to comply with the law. The Third Plenary Session of the 18th Central Committee proposed the implementation of the most stringent system of source protection—compensation for damages and accountability. These initiatives reveal the state's determination in recent years to systematically protect the environment.

Fifth, waste management is becoming more technical, professional, and industrialized. The Environmental Law of the People's Republic of China, revised in 2014, calls for "relevant departments of the State Council and local people's governments at all levels to take measures to promote the production and use of clean energy". It also requires that enterprises prioritize the use of clean energy, adopt processes and equipment with high resource utilization rates and minimal pollutant emissions, and utilize comprehensive technology for waste and harmless treatment of pollutants. This stipulates new requirements for the technologization of the environmental protection field. The *Notice on the Implementation of a Charging System for Municipal Solid Waste Disposal and the Promotion of the Industrialization of Waste Disposal* states: "Reform the system of waste disposal and implement entrepreneurial management", and "Introduce a competitive mechanism to select qualified enterprises to undertake municipal solid waste disposal through public bidding". This has prompted the gradual transition of waste disposal toward a path of specialization and industrialization. The Third Plenary Session of the 18th Central Committee of the Communist Party of China (CPC) also noted "develop the environmental protection market...Establish a market-oriented mechanism to attract social capital to invest in ecological environmental protection and implement the third-party treatment of environmental pollution".

Generally speaking, China's laws and policies on municipal solid waste management are gradually improving. However, problems still remain, and these should not be overlooked.

Firstly, some of the current laws and regulations on waste management are principled and general, but lack detailed provisions on a specific operational basis. Moreover, the relevant provisions are formalistic and difficult to implement. For example, the "Cleaner Production Promotion Law of the People's Republic of China" requires resource-based treatment of waste, but it does not stipulate what "resource-based" is, nor how to manage it, rendering this regulation ineffective in actual operations.

Secondly, there is a lack of economic and cultural policies supporting waste management policies. Environmental management policy (including garbage disposal policy), as a subsystem of social policy, should synergize with other subsystems such as economic policy and cultural policy. If, in order to deal with the problem of garbage disposal, only the improvement and innovation of a certain system is emphasized, this will only treat the symptoms, not the root cause of the problem. Looking at the policies related to garbage disposal, there are currently no systematic supporting economic policies. In terms of cultural policies, there is no systematic system for promoting the development of relevant science and technology, the integration of industry, academia, and research, and mechanisms for informing the public.

Thirdly, there is no system for public participation in waste management. Although the State has gradually emphasized public participation in waste management, there are currently no coherent regulations that provide detailed regulations on the ways and regulatory powers for the general public to participate in it. Correspondingly, there are no requirements for the public's responsibilities or obligations in waste management.

3.3 Reflecting on Municipal Solid Waste Management

China's municipal solid waste management policy is constantly improving, but there is still a long way to go before a complete system of policies and regulations is in place. Promoting China's urban domestic waste management in the direction of recycling and reducing waste at its source, recycling resources, and safe end-treatment requires mobilizing the entire country and the collective efforts of all stakeholders.

The government needs to consolidate its efforts to promote the construction and improvement of the waste management system. First, a multi-level and multi-stage waste management regulatory system should be established to systematically protect municipal solid waste management. China's municipal solid waste management laws and regulations are not sound, and some important systems that should be connected with each other are either missing or imperfect, such as the industrialized system of municipal waste management, the waste management charging system, the resource recycling system, and public participation in the waste management system. Second, the connection between laws and regulations and policies needs improvement. Some overlapping and contradictory laws and regulations should be systematically investigated and corrected to account for regional differences. Additionally, some reasons need the initial establishment of local waste management laws and regulations. Third, the operability of relevant regulations should be clarified. Some of the existing regulations on waste management are too vague and difficult to operate, and their enforcement standards and penalties should be clarified. Fourth, it is important to clarify which administrative authorities are responsible for each type of duty. This will not only prevent the occurrence of "swarming when it is advantageous and shirking responsibilities when it is not advantageous", but will also prevent the emergence of "multiple administrations and chaotic management". Fifth, improvement is needed in supporting economic and cultural policies to create a favorable market environment, and social and cultural environment, for waste management. This can be accomplished by increasing capital investment, rationalizing the allocation of resources, and the continuing improvement of the hardware and software facilities for waste management. This should be done while introducing social capital into the management of public utilities and consolidating and protecting them with a clear system. Sixth, improvement is needed in the information disclosure system to allow the public access to authoritative data on urban domestic waste management released by the government through formal channels. This can encourage the public to participate in urban domestic waste management, open channels for the public to participate in public affairs management, and regulate the public through their participation in legally sanctioned behavior. As the main environmental stakeholder in the urban waste management system, the government must not only work hard in system construction and personnel arrangements, but also shoulder the responsibility of creating a positive cultural atmosphere. In this way, it can cultivate citizenship, encouraging the public to participate in the governance of public affairs, and the completion of social tasks, resulting in the integration of cultural cultivation and institutional management.

If the decision-making structure and policy arrangements of the national political system can ensure fairness and justice in environmental decision-making, including waste management, then as an interest representation system, the government can integrate the public's organized interests into the national decision-making structure. This would be an ideal state. In fact, this problem is prevalent in environmental governance around the world, that is, governments collude with the interests of industrial capitalism, blocking the public's ability to participate in decision-making. When a state forges an alliance with private enterprises and important decisions are made by large trade union organizations behind closed doors to circumvent the normal democratic process, so-called cooperative political arrangements emerge. Therefore, this method of decision-making is also called the "political shutdown approach", and these political arrangements rarely benefit the general public (Hong and Gong 2008). Urban domestic waste management is a public matter, and the public should be able to listen to the opinions of various stakeholders, so that the public can understand, share, and bear the benefits and costs of public decision-making. Unfortunately, as of this writing, the public in China lacks formal participation channels and authoritative ways to obtain information on urban waste management matters (Gong 2016). People perceive risks, but lack channels for expression, and ultimately this affects their risk response behavior (Slovic 1993), potentially leading to risk amplification (J. K. Caspersen and R. E. Caspersen 2010). Therefore, we call for the gradual improvement of the public participation system, the standardization of public participation in public affairs, and the standardization of loose public participation.

As the most direct and major environmental stakeholder in waste management, the public's increased awareness of waste management, and their participation and support of government policies, are the keys to waste reduction, resource utilization, and harmlessness. As consumers, the public generates garbage in their daily lives and work. As participants in garbage management, they have the responsibility and obligation to sort and recycle garbage, and as a largest group of environmental stakeholders, their sorting and recycling behaviors contribute the most to garbage reduction, and have the most direct and obvious effect. The public participates in urban domestic waste management in both the private and the public sector. Work in the private sector includes paying attention to relevant information, improving personal environmental awareness, changing consumption habits and lifestyles that may be damaging to the environment, and gradually developing behavioral habits such as waste sorting and green consumption. Work in the public sector includes proactively obtaining waste management information, providing advice and suggestions on the formulation (or revision) of waste management systems and policies, breaking away from "NIMBYism", and building solid, interactive relationships with government departments. Public participation in the management of public affairs can prevent the abuse of public power, ensure the realization of citizens' rights, and make public policies more scientific and democratic, thereby improving their legitimacy (Yu 2006).

In the twenty-first century, technology has been the magic bullet for countries around the world in addressing the problem of waste disposal. The use of technology and the specialization of waste disposal is a trend in this industry. The improvement of waste treatment technology and strict technical standards are important guarantees for the reduction and neutralization of waste. Due to the trend of industrialization in waste disposal, private capital and enterprise behaviors are pouring into this public service field. This represents a comprehensive embodiment of marketization, socialization, and legalization, and also the interplay between the government, NGOs, and enterprises. Therefore, the qualification of enterprises' access, operations standards, and evaluation of the quality of treatment should be implemented with stricter standards. Additionally, enterprises should improve their technological standards and management norms.

Experts, media, and non-profit organizations are important stakeholders in the integrated waste management chain, representing the intersection of science/technology, public opinion, and public goods in waste management. The results of scientific research should be applied and continually improved. The specialization and technologization of waste treatment require technical and expert support, and combining industry, academia, and research is an important way to optimize waste management. Thus, the government should support and increase investment in scientific research, and encourage research and development in environmental protection science and technology related to waste treatment and social impact assessment research. It should also mobilize the energy of universities and scientific research institutes to fund environmental protection scientific research and social assessment research on the risks of waste treatment, and strengthen environmental protection scientific research and social assessment research.

The media can also guide the whole society to participate in waste management by publishing public opinions. The most important part of this is correcting public opinion when there is misinformation. Moreover, the media should be mobilized to promote and popularize an understanding of waste treatment to the public. In the greater system of society, the media plays an important role as the "social device" that conveys information and communicates with the world. Because of its powerful ability to communicate through time and space, it creates the effect of the "separation of time and space", so that even if people are not present at the scene of a situation, they can still be aware of it and form their own opinions through the media's broadcasts. Since the media is the main provider of information to society, its choices and presentation (especially intensive and centralized broadcasting) can influence people's prioritization of issues, and this has a direct effect on the process and speed of how issues are constructed. Due to the critical nature of the media, its reports exert public pressure on the governmental decision-making system to accept the aspirations and demands of the public, transforming the public agenda into the governmental agenda. In turn, this leads to the institutionalization of a given problem and the possibility of a solution. Since the turn of the millennium, China's media has been characterized by diversification and expansion of scale. This has provided new ways for social information to be disseminated for individuals to communicate and give feedback.

Furthermore, non-profit organizations, as providers of public goods, should play the role of communicating between the government, the public, and other stakeholders, and become intermediaries and bridges between the government and the public. They should encourage private environmental organizations to organize and mobilize the public to participate in waste separation and recycling. Starting waste disposal from the source is fundamental. We should mobilize civil environmental organizations to publicize and educate the public to raise awareness of the significance of waste sorting and recycling and environmental protection for their own lives, to expand the social base of concern for waste disposal, and to urge the government to prioritize the environment in the political agenda.

In 2019, Shanghai launched the first initiative on the management of municipal solid waste sorting. In Shanghai, the sorting of waste is no longer a slogan, but a practice. Shanghai's foray into waste sorting management offers the following experiences which are worth learning from. First, what municipal solid waste can be sorted and recycled must be clarified to facilitate any kind of public undertaking, and at the same time, the collection facilities for the sorting of municipal solid waste must be standardized to integrate with the sorting of public waste. Scheduled and regular waste collection is an effective way to promote waste sorting at the initial stage. Second, a system for the full sorting of waste has been established. Instead of the previous all-in-one treatment of municipal solid waste, mandatory sorting has been implemented in all facets of waste disposal, collection, transportation, and end-treatment. Third, the government has promoted the participation of all people and has strengthened social co-governance in public affairs. The public is now mobilized to participate throughout the entire process of waste sorting and supervision. This includes, for example, volunteer teams composed of party members, building leaders, and others who to take turns on duty, guiding residents to sort materials. Fourth, there is policy support and legislative guarantee. Shanghai has established a comprehensive supervision mechanism that combines the soft and the hard, that is, guidance and restraint. Fifth, there is lasting and comprehensive awareness and education. As such, the concept of household waste sorting has penetrated into the public consciousness, and the cultural environment is crucial.

Municipal solid waste governance is a massive, long-term public undertaking. It requires the mobilization and participation of all stakeholders, the establishment of a three-dimensional and multi-level regulatory system, and the construction of a healthy social culture. Only in this way can the best possible cycle of waste management be achieved.

CHAPTER 4

Non-Point Source Pollution (NSP) and Its Governance in Rural Areas

Ma Guodong

With the rapid growth of China's economy, environmental problems in China's rural areas are intensifying, against the backdrop of growing population and urbanization. Thus, more and more scholars are researching rural environmental problems and exploring their root causes, as well as countermeasures and mechanisms for solving them (Hong 2000a; Jiang and Jiang 2007; Geng 2012). Rural environmental problems are often closely linked to "non-point source (run-off) pollution (NSP)". Along with the proliferation of modern agriculture, chemical fertilizers, pesticides, and plastic film mulch have become widely used in production practices in the agricultural industry, as well as by individual farmers. Although the use of these products has led to increased agricultural yields, and can be credited with stimulating some of the rapid agricultural development,[1] the extent of the pollution and damage caused by their use

[1] This so-called development is more likely to represent the increase in economic returns following the expansion of agriculture.

G. Ma (✉)
School of Humanities and Management, Ningxia Medical University, Yinchuan, China

D. Hong and Y. Fan (eds.), *Toward a Green Society*,
https://doi.org/10.1007/978-981-96-5111-5_4

has been unexpected. They cause widespread contamination of bodies of water (rivers, lakes, bays, reservoirs, etc.) by large quantities of pollutants entering the water through the process of runoff and seepage from unspecified areas under the influence of precipitation and the draining effect of surface runoff.[2] Unlike point source pollution, such as industrial wastewater pollution and urban sewage pollution, NSP usually does not have a fixed point of discharge, so it is generally difficult to determine the source of the pollution and its geographic boundaries. In fact, in addition to chemical fertilizers and pesticides, the inappropriate discharge of organic and inorganic substances such as livestock and poultry manure and domestic garbage in rural areas is an important factor contributing to NSP. This makes prevention and alleviation of NSP challenging. In addition to the fact that NSP has entered the environmental protection agenda at a relatively late stage, many prevention and mitigation measures still remain at the engineering level. This means that in order to alleviate the problem of NSP in China, it is necessary to start from a holistic and multidisciplinary point of view, to explore in development of NSP in the countryside, and to understand the characteristics of its development.

Based on a detailed discussion of the current status, trends and characteristics of rural NSP in China, this chapter explains the driving mechanism behind the development of NSP, explaining that NSP is the result of the combined action of a variety of mechanisms. The chapter also discusses the enhancement of NSP management from the perspectives of technological treatment, institutional response, and social governance.

4.1 Current Status, Trends, and Characteristics of Rural NSP

Environmental problems in rural areas are intensifying and recent developments are not encouraging. The *Bulletin of the First National Pollution Census* shows that major pollutants such as chemical oxygen demand (COD), total nitrogen (TN), and total phosphorus (TP) emitted from agricultural sources have accounted for 44%, 57%, and 67% of the total national emissions, respectively.[3] In terms of COD emissions from

[2] The concept of non-point source pollution has been generally agreed upon; despite several minor disagreements over details, it has essentially the same meaning.

[3] Three departments jointly issued the *First National Pollution Census Bulletin* (2010-02-10) [2019-07-22]. http://www.gov.cn/jrzg/2010-02/10/content-1532174.htm.

Table 4.1 National discharge of chemical oxygen demand (COD) in wastewater, 2011–2015

Year	*Total emissions (tons)*	*Emissions from agricultural sources (tons)*	*Percentage of emissions from agricultural sources among total emissions (%)*
2011	2,499.9	1,186.1	47.4%
2012	2,423.7	1,153.8	47.6%
2013	2,352.7	1,125.8	47.9%
2014	2,294.6	1,102.4	48.0%
2015	2,223.5	1,068.6	48.1%

Source: *National Bulletin of Environmental Statistics*, 2011–2015

wastewater alone, Table 4.1 shows that from 2011 to 2015, China's total COD emissions, as well as COD emissions from agricultural sources, have both declined. However, the proportion of emissions from agricultural sources among total emissions has increased (from 47.4% to 48.1%). Thus, NSP's contribution to COD emissions, and to the deterioration of the rural environment, cannot be underestimated.

4.1.1 The Current Status of NSP

4.1.1.1 1The Manifestations of NPS

The manifestations of agricultural NSP are manifold, but can be summarized in three main ways.

The first is the fertilizer and pesticide pollution mentioned earlier. Out of self-interest, farmers ignore scientific suggestions for ingredients, and use pesticides and fertilizers inappropriately and in excessive dosages, especially by spraying excessive amounts of insecticides on crops. This causes serious contamination and harm to soil and bodies of water.

The second is pollution from livestock and poultry manure. Livestock farming has an important role in rural economic development, yet farming produces numerous inevitable environmental byproducts. For livestock and poultry, manure is produced while farming. If farmers do not render it harmless (treat is safely) but instead discharge it into ditches, it will pollute surrounding bodies of water, causing unrecoverable damage to the environment. It can also cause negative health effects on the surrounding population. However, China's safe treatment of livestock and poultry manure is still in its initial stages, and has not developed enough to constitute a large-scale, scientific, and rigorous treatment model.

The third is pollution from rural solid waste. This includes domestic waste from rural residents and solid waste pollution from farming, such as the hazards of plastic film mulch. Many farmers lack an appropriate understanding of environmental protection, and do not realize that if they do not dispose of the used plastic film mulch correctly but simply discard it, it will damage the rural ecological environment. In reality, we regularly see unrecycled plastic film mulch scattered throughout fields, and wind-blown mobile garbage, all of which will cause environmental pollution. To address this form of pollution, a new state-controlled monitoring network of more than 300 pilot sites for localized monitoring of residual plastic film pollution on agricultural land was established in 2012.[4] It should be noted that although the framework for a monitoring system with national coverage has been established, it is still in its primary iteration, and the tasks ahead remain daunting.

4.1.1.2 The Characteristics of NSP

NSP has the following characteristics. First, there are various sources of pollution, such as livestock and poultry and the manure they produce, sewage sludge, and chemical fertilizers. The organic and inorganic chemical oxygen demand (COD), total nitrogen (TN), and total phosphorus (TP) produced by these sources are capable of causing serious environmental strain. Second, pollution is dispersed and there are no precise sources, so it is difficult to determine where and to what extent the pollution is occurring. Third, NSP is difficult to monitor because it is decentralized and random. In recent years, China has undertaken many efforts in the field of NSP monitoring. In 2012, there were more than 160 state-controlled agricultural NSP monitoring points monitoring more than 1,200 plots.[5] By 2013, there were 270 state-controlled monitoring points for NSP from farmland.[6] However, the size of the monitoring sites is limited in absolute terms, and sustained energy efficiency is imperative.

[4] See *Bulletin on the State of the Environment in China*, 2012.

[5] See *Bulletin on the State of the Environment in China*, 2012.

[6] See *Bulletin on the State of the Environment in China*, 2013.

4.1.1.3 The Hazards of NSP

The hazards of NSP are far-reaching. First and foremost are the health hazards. NSP, such as fertilizer and pesticide residues, enter and accumulate in bodies of water and enter the human body through drinking water and agricultural byproducts, thus endangering human health. In addition, the direct entry of livestock and poultry manure into bodies of water may lead to the propagation of a large number of pathogenic microorganisms, which may induce lesions after entering the human body. Secondly, there are environmental hazards. NSP entering a body of water will cause "eutrophication", resulting in the death of a large number of aquatic organisms and disrupting the natural environment. Thirdly, there are economic hazards. NSP leads to the following problems:

- Higher drinking water costs
- Lower crop yields
- Lower quality of agricultural products
- Lower returns for farmers
- Higher capital investment costs for preventing erosion on farmland
- Higher costs of maintaining human and animal health
- Depreciation of natural assets due to the presence of NSP

Finally, NSP is a social hazard. It may lead to the emergence of various conflicts, such as the discharge of domestic sewage, which leads to tension between neighbors; the excessive use of chemical fertilizers and pesticides by farmers, which causes water pollution and losses to the interests of aqua culturists, thus triggering conflicts between farmers and aqua culturists; and the damage to environmental rights and interests that occurs in different regions and watersheds due to NSP, which also leads to conflicts.

4.1.2 NSP Development Trends

In China, NSP has undergone a long-term process. This process is intertwined with agriculture. Especially with modern agriculture's increasing dependence on chemical fertilizers and pesticides, the issue of NSP has escalated to a new level. In 2010, the *Bulletin on the State of the Environment in China* clarified that the NSP crisis in agriculture was bleak. The *National Environmental Statistics Bulletin*, which has been published since 2011, has begun to calculate and analyze emissions from chemical oxygen demand (COD) and ammonia nitrogen (AN) from agricultural sources, and their share in total emissions. This has indicated the seriousness of environmental pollution in rural China. In the future, trends in the development of rural NSP are likely to focus on the following areas.

First, it is unlikely that the NSP problem will be solved in the short term, and sustained investment in environmental protection will be needed. In the past, agricultural production was geared toward the pursuit of yields and profits, with little attention to the negative effects of the excessive use of chemical fertilizers and pesticides on soil and bodies of water. Thus, farmers have become overly reliant on these chemicals without anticipating the real consequences of the environmental damage they cause. The NSP problem will be difficult to solve in the short term due to the passing of time and its inertia effect, coupled with the lack of effective policy measures and technological means to deal with it. Therefore, sustained investment in environmental protection is needed to respond to NSP. State-controlled monitoring points for agricultural NSP have been established throughout China, and a number of demonstration zones for the prevention and alleviation of agricultural NSP have been established in the watersheds of Taihu Lake, Dianchi Lake, and Chaohu Lake, as well as in the Three Gorges Reservoir area. Yet, these investments still fall short, and a wider network of management and monitoring networks will be needed in order to build a broad and powerful platform for solving rural environmental problems in the future.

Second, the possibility of continued NSP deterioration persists, and the risk of the eutrophication of bodies of water will not recede. As people's living standards improve, the general public's demand for meat, eggs, fruit, and vegetables will increase. This means that production in industries such as planting and animal breeding must be intensified. However, since these industries have not been fully optimized, polluting behaviors and phenomena are inevitable. If the farming industry greatly expands the planting area and increases the use of chemical fertilizers and pesticides, the concentrations of nitrogen, phosphorus, and other elements in the soil will continue to increase, and the threat of the eutrophication of bodies of water will continue to escalate. Thus, it is conceivable that the negative effects of NSP will continue in the future.

Finally, alleviating the NSP problem will depend on increased scientific and environmental awareness among farmers, as well as effective management of both government and society. However, it will take time to stimulate farmers' participation in improving the environment, and to optimize the government's role in environmental protection. Improving farmers' environmental awareness and their understanding of environmental protection cannot be achieved overnight. This means that the government, the citizenry, and society as a whole should work together to deepen their understanding of NSP. At the same time, the government should strengthen its own functions in environmental protection management, environmental construction, and environmental protection publicity, so as to continually pursue and ensure the achievement of environmental protection and ecological restoration.

4.2 The Causes of Rural NSP

What is the cause of NSP in rural areas? Why is NSP on the rise? Why is NSP so difficult to treat? The answers to these questions are of practical significance and have a direct bearing on the path forward in solving rural environmental problems and the effectiveness of national environmental governance. Therefore, several explanatory models of the dynamic mechanisms have been proposed and explored, and which are conducive to an in-depth understanding of the causes of NSP.

4.2.1 Dualistic Social Structure and NSP

NSP, as a prominent representative of rural environmental problems, is a product of specific social structures and social processes.[7] Therefore, discussion of the causes of NSP and the intensification of the resulting pollution should be focused to an inquiry into the relevant social structure and social processes. Only in this way will the deeper structural dynamics of society be understood. In their article "Reproduction of Dualistic Social Structures: A Sociological Analysis of Rural Nonpoint Source Pollution in China" Hong Dayong and Ma Fangxin (2004) noted that China's specific dualistic social structure is the underlying cause of the growing problem of rural NSP. In this view, it is China's disparate dual urban–rural structure that exacerbates today's NSP problem.

According to Hong Dayong, this can be explained in at least five ways. First, the long-standing division between urban and rural areas slowed

[7] Scholars represented by Hong Dayong (2000b, 2001) generally believe that environmental problems are essentially social problems, which are products of social structures and social processes.

the process of urbanization in China, with many people being stranded in the countryside. This has exacerbated the tension between the population and resources. Second, the gap between urban and rural areas continues to widen in the dual urban–rural structure, with the rural population living in poverty and facing immense pressure to survive and improve their livelihoods. Thus, these individuals are typically unwilling to show much concern for pollution. Third, the economic structure of the countryside is too homogenous, with most people earning their living from agriculture as their main industry. Labor-intensive, small-scale agricultural production increases the difficulty of managing NSP. Fourth, as a result of the dualistic social structure, rural elites have been trying to migrate to the cities, resulting in those who remain in the countryside for employment being less qualified, less equipped to learn about the environment, and less aware of environmental protection. Fifth, environmental protection in rural areas has long been neglected, and environmental protection policies, environmental protection organizations, environmental protection personnel, and environmental protection infrastructure have been under-resourced (Hong and Ma, 2004). Increased NSP in rural areas is the result of the dual urban–rural structure.

This analysis is profound. Firstly, it provides a comprehensive and informative picture of the ways and processes through which social structures induce and exacerbate NSP. NSP is not merely a biological, physical, and chemical change process, but also as a social process. Secondly, this kind of explanation accounts for the complexity of social factors, as well as demographic factors, resource factors, industrial factors, and institutional factors that have all been included in the field of thought as explanatory elements. Finally, this explanatory model illustrates the problems associated with NSP in China and its causes. However, there are certain shortcomings. For example, it fails to reveal the interrelationship between NSP and social development from the micro level or from the perspective of needs, and fails to identify the incentives for NSP production in the path of the material cycle and energy flow.

4.2.2 *Metabolic Rift and Non-Point Source Pollution*

Metabolism is a concept from biology which refers to the process of continuous material renewal and energy exchange between the organic components of living organisms through the synthesis and degradation of chemical substances. In the middle of the nineteenth century, Karl Marx applied this concept to the field of social sciences to reveal the material-metabolic relations between human beings and nature, the processes of commodity circulation and capital accumulation in capitalism, the natural and social mechanisms by which ecological and environmental crises are created, and the possibilities of capitalism's progress toward ecological crisis (Marx and Engels, 1972). Later, Clark and Foster (2010) systematically elaborated on Marx with their theory of metabolic rift based on in-depth study of ecological Marxism. They argued that capitalism was the root cause of metabolic rift. In the pursuit of surplus value and capital accumulation, an almost predatory mode of production is used, leading to a disconnection between natural metabolism (the circulation of matter and energy flows within natural systems) and social metabolism (the circulation of matter and energy flows that exist between human beings and natural systems). The result is "metabolic rift".

According to the explanation of the theory of metabolic rift, the generation and development of NSP in China's rural areas is due to the existence of metabolic rift. NSP is caused by the disruption of material exchanges within the natural systems of the countryside due to modern factors, and at the same time, the disruption of regular material exchanges between farmers and the natural systems and the inability to circulate energy. For example, the emergence and use of chemical fertilizers, a modern product that enhances land fertility and increases crop yields, has rendered traditional materials such as farmyard manure and pond sludge useless. Meanwhile, waste materials such as used agricultural plastic film mulch cannot be eliminated by the cyclic metabolism of the agricultural system, and will even harm the rural ecological environment if mis-handled. Thus, the originally balanced network of material exchange and energy flow is disrupted.

This theory is still of theoretical and practical significance to the current NSP dilemma. The theory of metabolic rift provides a theoretical option for solving the current ecological predicament, that is, how to repair and reshape the normal natural and social metabolism of the ecosystem in due time, to resolve the contradiction between human beings and nature. Moreover, although the critique of metabolic rift is directed at capitalism and its mode of production, it still facilitates reflection on existing development paths and models so that new and better metabolically characterized development mechanisms can be created. Finally, natural and social metabolism require people to re-examine the relationship between human beings and human beings, and between human beings and nature, and to search for the factors that cause breaks in the metabolic chain from a more relational perspective. In this way, it can help restore balance in the ecosystem.

4.2.3 Demand and Environmental Pressure

Behavioral science generally supports the idea that human behavior is caused by certain motives, and motivation comes from individuals' own needs. People set specific behavioral goals to satisfy these needs. When a need is satisfied, another new need will arise, which will trigger a new behavioral goal. This creates a cycle of human behavior. In addition to the universal economic needs, there are many other needs. According to Maslow, human beings have a complex set of needs with a hierarchical distribution of levels including physiological needs, security needs, social needs, respect needs, and self-actualization needs. Alderfer proposed the ERG theory based on Maslow's needs theory, suggesting that human beings have three major needs: survival, interrelationship, and growth. In Alderfer's view, the existence of needs exerts a driving effect on behavior. The effect of this behavior on the environment may be either positive or negative. If it is negative, it will cause different levels of stress on the environment. In rural areas, since farmers generally have the need for survival and development (growth), they will set production and life goals based on these needs that will yield profits, and consciously or unconsciously take the action of discharging toxic and hazardous substances into the surrounding soil and bodies of water. This results in the accumulation of toxic and hazardous substances in the environment beyond its self-purifying capacity, thus causing and contributing to the emergence and development of NSP. For example, in order to satisfy the basic needs of production and life, and to obtain a certain economic income (or to satisfy a higher level of needs and earn a greater economic income), farmers will purchase and use chemical fertilizers and pesticides to boost the productivity of agricultural products. However, when fertilizers are applied inappropriately, the elements contained in excess pesticides and fertilizers enter the soil and bodies of water and become saturated, which may induce NSP.

It would be reasonable to explain the occurrence and development of NSP indirectly from the perspective of demand. From the viewpoint of demand theory, the process of satisfying demand is also the process of implementing environmental behavior. NSP is a negative result of inappropriate behavior undertaken to satisfy individual needs. Therefore, in order to eliminate the possibility of NSP, it is necessary to re-examine the different levels of farmers' needs, and help them set reasonable behavioral goals. However, this explanation has several limitations. For example, it over-emphasizes the individual psychological dimension of the developmental explanation of NSP, but neglects the influence of macro-social structural elements on environmental behavior and its behavioral consequences.

4.2.4 *Cultural, Institutional, and Technological Progress and NSP*

Although there is still a lack of significant research on the relationship between culture and NSP, the role of culture in environmental change is hard to deny. Ma (1993) noted that in order to conduct in-depth research on the environment, it is necessary to comprehend the relationship between cultural traditions and the environment in a timely manner. Looking at nomadic herders, mountain people, and farmers, he reveals the role of the environmental knowledge of different cultural groups in environmental management. Later, Chen (2000, 2007) used a case study approach to provide a sociological explanation for water pollution, suggesting that the loss of traditional ethical norms in a community and the erosion of inhabitants' traditional values are drivers of water pollution. Studies such as these show the importance of cultural factors in environmental change. In rural areas, there have been dramatic changes in traditional ways of production and lifestyles. As such, the way water and soil are used, as well as methods of planting and rearing, have changed. If there are no reformed values to guide them, the further proliferation of NSP will be inevitable.

Government-led environmental protection and environmental governance systems, as well as the formulation and implementation of environmental policies, are also factors influencing environmental change in rural areas. Wang (1999) has argued that it is precisely because of the characteristics of the household responsibility system, which is characterized by small-scale farming, that there are deficiencies in alleviating externalities' effects on the ecological environment. This is coupled with the lack of a relevant system to support it, which led to the deterioration of the natural environment in the 1980s. This suggests that institutional deficiencies are an important cause of environmental degradation. In fact, in addition to the imperfections of institutional policies, various other problems have also hindered sound environmental protection and practices. These have included differences in perceptions of policies and the environment, complementarity and tension between formal and informal norms, specification, tension, and coordination in policy implementation, and the feedback and monitoring of information (Lin Mei, 2003).

Technology is a double-edged sword, and its development has the potential to bring about both progress in modernization and deterioration of the environment. It can be said that the pollution of the atmosphere, the depletion of resources, and the destruction of the ecosystem are all intertwined with the development of technology. The development and application of unsuitable technologies can cause varying degrees of environmental damage. NSP is a prominent manifestation of this. For example, the popularization of plastic film technology has led farmers to use large quantities of plastic film mulch in the agricultural production process, and the discarded plastic film mulch, without proper treatment, can cause interference or even damage to the farmland environment. In this sense, technology is also an important factor in NSP.

4.3 Rural NSP Management Policies and Challenges

4.3.1 *The Meaning and Impact of NSP Management Policies*

The consequences of the development of rural NSP are becoming increasingly obvious, and this has seriously affected both the environment and the economies of China, and in particular its rural areas. In the face of this situation, rural NSP mitigation has become a necessity for social development. Not only does this require society to improve its understanding of the causes, characteristics, and hazards of NSP, but it also has prompted the government to introduce a series of policies and regulations to establish the necessary institutional conditions for effective NSP mitigation. Promoting NSP management policy is not an expedient measure, but the inevitable result of adapting to the long-term development of society. Some of the previous designs and arrangements have lost their effectiveness in the current state of affairs, and they are no longer suitable for guiding and regulating the environmental behavior of the actors in rural life and agricultural production activities, based on the concept of ecological balance. Especially when the agricultural industrial structure is in the phase of optimization and adjustment, the original pollution prevention and management system may be unable to play an efficient role in regulating behavior. Therefore, new management policies are necessary for promoting more effective prevention, mitigation, and management of NSP.

Existing policies on NSP management have several limitations. Firstly, the laws and regulations relating to NSP management are not sound enough to facilitate coordinated and mutually supportive synergy. This means that it is impossible to offer effective and holistic responses to the pollution problem. In the implementation process, the existing policy norms have not been strongly enforced due to the special characteristics of agricultural production and the inherent hidden, decentralized, random, and unmonitored nature of NSP. Thus, it is necessary to further strengthen and improve the NSP management system and to improve the efficiency of policy implementation. Secondly, in agricultural life and production, the guiding and mandatory technical norms and standards that should be in place have yet to be adequately formulated and optimized. This is inconsistent with the requirements of rural NSP management. Thirdly, policies such as promoting the use of chemical fertilizers still reflect the market-oriented development orientation driven by economic interests, with a clear utilitarian tendency. Fourthly, the existing policies for alleviating NSP overlook the participation and needs of farmers. In this way, they provide little benefit to farmers, but rather infringe on their interests (Hong and Ma, 2004). Specifically, some short-term external input projects which lack sustainable operations have limited effects on the alleviation of NSP. Fifthly, NSP management policy has failed to encourage the resource utilization of agricultural waste, which has weakened the effectiveness of NSP management. These constraints have limited the improvement to the rural environment.

In fact, the formulation of NSP management policies should not only consider the special needs of agricultural development, but also farmers' interests. At the same time, they should also promote the maintenance of the rural ecological environment to the greatest extent possible. Sensible institutional arrangements can exert positive effects on NSP management. Firstly, it can help to manage and reduce the number of decentralized agricultural activities, rationally optimize the scale of resource development, promote the scientific management of land and water, and strengthen sewage monitoring and rural environmental supervision.[8] Secondly, it can more effectively manage the decentralized discharge of farmers' domestic sewage, improve the centralized treatment rate of domestic waste, and help build the environmentally sound infrastructure that farmers need. Thirdly, it helps farmers to gradually acquire new living habits that are in harmony with the environment, and to increase their awareness of environmental protection.

4.3.2 Problems in Rural NSP Management

The main problems in managing NSP in rural areas are as follows.

Firstly, the policy and regulatory system for NSP alleviation is inadequate. As mentioned above, the existing NSP management system lacks an effective response to intensifying rural environmental problems, and it overlooks farmers' interests, instead tending toward utilitarianism. This is coupled with the lack of systematism.

Secondly, investment in NSP management has been insufficient. Environmental protection in China has long been implemented under the policy that the polluter is responsible for its clean-up. However, the sources of NSP tend to be widespread and difficult to identify. In these cases, the government needs to invest in prevention and mitigation measures. However, the solution is not so simple. The state's financial investment in environmental protection is still concentrated in urban areas and industry. In contrast, although the government's investment in rural environmental protection has increased in recent years, it remains insufficient.[9]

Thirdly, basic technology is weak. China has long lacked basic NSP monitoring capabilities, and the initial creation of the national NSP monitoring network took place in only in 2013. This was a significant milestone, with 270 formalized state-managed monitoring points

[8] In December 2012, the Ministry of Environmental Protection of the People's Republic of China *issued Guidance on the National Ecological and Rural Environment Inspectorate*, which clarified the significance of rural environment inspection. The implementation of this policy has created conditions for further solutions to non-point source pollution in rural areas.

[9] The *Bulletin on the State of the Environment in China* in 2015 and 2016 revealed that the central government invested 6 billion yuan as special funds for rural environmental protection in 2015 and 2016 respectively to support rural environmental governance.

for farmland NSP.[10] Despite this, there still remains a problem in the inability to collect a sufficient amount of basic data that would be useful for resolving NSP. This makes it difficult to introduce effective technical standards and measures for prevention and mitigation. In terms of technology alone, many NSP management technologies have yet to be developed, while point source pollution management technologies have been primitively utilized, and the actual effects that prevention and mitigation technologies can produce remain unclear.

Fourth, the awareness of NSP prevention and mitigation is weak. As the main unit of agricultural production and life, farmers should undertake the responsibility of environmental protection and environmental management. However, currently most farmers' awareness of environmental protection is low, as is their understanding of NSP and its hazards. Thus, people tend to focus on the massive economic benefits and value that agricultural production can produce, but ignore the negative environmental consequences of production.

4.4 The Advancement and Improvement of Rural NSP Management

In December 2018, China's Central Agricultural Office, the Ministry of Agriculture and Rural Affairs, and 18 other departments jointly issued the Rural Human Settlement Environment Remediation and Village Cleaning Action Program. This proposed a plan to begin cleaning up rural organic garbage, village ponds and ditches, livestock and poultry breeding manure and sewage, and other agricultural production waste, and changing the bad habits affecting the rural human settlement environment. The aim was to intensify the clean-up of the rural human settlement environment. This program has important guiding significance for solving rural environmental problems and rural modernization. To improve rural NSP management, it is necessary to consider the technical treatment model, the system response model and the social governance model.

[10] See the *Bulletin on the State of the Environment in China*, 2013.

4.4.1 *The Technical Treatment Model for NSP*

The resolution of NSP first depends on the application of scientific and technological means. Although there is the risk of the abuse of technology, this does not alter the fact that technology can be a developmental tool that can be applied over time. In other words, the proper application of the appropriate technologies can have a positive effect on NSP mitigation. However, the reality is that there remains much room for progress in technological development, such as in the weak foundation of preventative technology, the dated point-to-area treatment technology, monitoring technology, and technical standards.

Therefore, to prevent and alleviate NSP, it is necessary to establish a complete system of technological development, and to consolidate the basis for technological research, development, and application. In daily farm life and production, we advocate the comprehensive use of technology to develop and implement the following:

- Clean and environmentally friendly biogas
- A moratorium on plow planting
- Edible fungus cultivation
- Soil testing and formula fertilization
- Clean breeding
- Safe treatment of domestic waste

The implementation of all of these interventions will comprehensively reduce the probability of rural NSP. In addition, it must be emphasized that the prevention and mitigation of NSP must simultaneously focus on two technological development paths. The first is the preventive monitoring technology path, that is, the government needs to do the following:

- Increase capital investment in preventive technology
- Implement preventive monitoring standards
- Enhance the application of preventive monitoring technology
- Improve detection and early warning capacity

The second is the technical path of end-treatment, that is, after the occurrence of NSP, effective technical responses can be implemented, and physical, biological, and chemical tools can be applied rationally. At the same time, the transformation of technological achievements should be strengthened, and new environmental treatment and pollution treatment technologies should be applied to NSP prevention and alleviation to curb its effects. The synergistic development of the two paths is an important guarantee for alleviating rural environmental problems. It should be noted that the technology processing model is quite basic, and it likely needs institutional protection as well as societal involvement to reach its full capacity.

4.4.2 And Institutional Response Model for NSP Management

In the face of the current NSP crisis, breakthroughs are needed at the institutional level for effective prevention and alleviation. As mentioned above, system deficiencies and imperfections will likely intensify environmental pollution. This means that it is necessary to strengthen the awareness of institutional development, establish a set of practical institutional safeguards, and promote the institutional construction of NSP management. Ideas for accomplishing this can be expanded upon in three main ways.

First, it will be necessary to cultivate a cultural environment that strengthens the construction of an NSP management system. The cultural environment is a soft environment for system building. It not only provides reasonable value principles for system building, but also encourages farmers to gradually internalize the specific requirements of the NSP Management System, and helps farmers to form stable value judgments about the rural environment and the future sustainable development of the countryside. Therefore, to promote the construction of an NSP management system, it is necessary to cultivate a positive cultural environment. This requires publicizing the urgency of the NSP crisis by means of both raising public awareness and education, and improving societal awareness by means such as basic education, continuing education, and social education.

Second, a sound system of legal norms must be created in due course. Laws and regulations are not only important elements of institutional arrangements, but also effective means of promoting institutional construction. The establishment of a legal system can clarify the action power of policymakers and the obligations and responsibilities of NSP management work. Moreover, it can encourage governments at all levels to formulate, implement, and practice effective NSP management systems. In China, many laws, regulations, and policies have been introduced from the central to local governments to solve environmental problems. However, there remains a lack of specialized NSP laws and regulations. This also means that it is imperative to establish a safeguard mechanism to promote the construction of an NSP management system.

Finally, the leadership and supervision in charge of NSP prevention and alleviation must be strengthened to create a positive atmosphere for pollution management. In the process of promoting NSP management in rural areas, it is necessary to strengthen government leadership and supervision. The government is the leading force in the construction and implementation of the system. It provides mandatory means for the construction and implementation of the system, as well as the corresponding incentive structure to promote innovation and revision in NSP management systems. The role of leadership and supervision reflects the dominant character of the government, which is conducive to improving the NSP management system. Specifically, NSP management in rural areas is a long-term and complex systematic project which requires coordination and cooperation between different departments. Thus, it is necessary to strengthen leadership, and in doing so, combine the issue of NSP with agricultural optimization, farmers' happiness, and rural development. In this way, it can become an important item on the government agenda. At the same time, we need to integrate resources, strengthen comprehensive law enforcement, supervision and management, and guide farmers to follow a sustainable development path through various means such as the popularization of science education and raising awareness through the media.

4.4.3 A Social Governance Model for NSP Management

NSP management is a grand systematic project. It is difficult to alleviate pollution by means of technical responses and system improvement alone. Thus, over the long run, the macro model of social governance should be advocated.

First, the government, industry, and the public must reach a unified opinion and form a joint force on the issue of NSP management. With the development of the economy and society, the causes of environmental problems become increasingly complex. Especially for forms of pollution such as NSP, it is difficult to determine who the real polluters are, and who the preventors are. In a sense, all members of society are responsible for the occurrence and development of NSP. NSP is intertwined with rural areas, agriculture, and every farmer. Therefore, farmers should deepen their understanding of NSP and strive to restrict their own behavior in the process of farming and daily life. From the government's view, in addition to continuing to play a leading role, it should increase capital investment, and formulate preferential environmental protection policies on taxes and prices. Industry and the public must also become an important force in the governance structure. The full mobilization of their motivation is an important condition for the mitigation of rural environmental problems. Therefore, through guidance and advocacy, a three-in-one diversified investment mechanism consisting of government, enterprises and social organizations should be established.

Second, the social organizations' role needs to be regularly reaffirmed. As a social force, social organizations, especially rural civil environmental protection organizations, have crucial governance functions. They can not only boost farmers' awareness of NSP prevention and mitigation and related environmental protection through various environmental education activities, but also can assist government organizations in implementing environmental policies. At the same time, social organizations can supervise illegal acts involving the ecological environment, prompting both individuals and enterprises to internalize the concept of ecological environmental protection into their own codes of conduct, and isolate themselves from the production and lifestyle of NSP. Therefore, the cultivation of social organizations is of immense practical significance, and it is an important measure for optimizing rural environmental governance.

Finally, social governance should be oriented toward ecological economic development. It is indisputable that NSP is intertwined with agriculture, farmers, and the countryside, and agricultural production is a major source of NSP. To overcome the harm agricultural production causes to the environment, we should promote the following:

- Develop a circular agricultural economy
- Stress the concept of "reduce, reuse, recycle" in the agricultural production cycle
- Safely treat waste generated in the process of livestock and poultry breeding and planting

The government, enterprises, and social organizations should advocate and promote the development of organic agriculture through various channels and means, and ensure ecological benefits while improving agricultural economic benefits.

In summary, NSP is caused by the heavy use of pesticides, fertilizers, and herbicides, as well as the large-scale livestock and poultry breeding in rural areas. It not only causes the eutrophication of rivers and lakes, but also COD and heavy metal pollution, wreaking serious harm on rural areas.[11] This harm will persist in future social and economic development and modernization. To prevent the continuous escalation of NSP, it is necessary to recognize how NSP is produced and the dynamic mechanism underlying it. This chapter provides an analysis of it from the theoretical perspectives of social structure, metabolic rift, and demand. Although the government has made some effort to alleviate NSP, these efforts have been limited. In the process of prevention and mitigation, the problems of insufficient investment, inadequate policies and regulations, and weak basic technical work have yet to be solved, and thus, the future task of the prevention and alleviation of NSP in rural areas remains arduous. However, we believe that with the progress of technology and the rational use of technology, the improvement of the system and the strengthening of social governance, environmental governance in rural areas will produce more tangible results.

[11] According to data from the *Bulletin on the State of China's Ecological Environment* released by the Ministry of Ecology and Environment in 2018, among the 107 lakes (reservoirs) monitored for nutritional status in China, 25 were mildly eutrophic and 6 were moderately eutrophic. Among these, Taihu Lake, Chaohu Lake, and Dianchi Lake showed a mildly eutrophic state. As early as the beginning of the twenty-first century, the State Environmental Protection Administration (SEPA) disclosed the trend of eutrophication in Taihu Lake, Chaohu Lake and Dianchi Lake, but industrial pollution was not the main reason for this (the contribution of industrial wastewater to total nitrogen and phosphorus accounts for only 10–16%). Rather, NSP in rural areas is likely responsible for a large portion of the environmental deterioration in these bodies of water (Li et al. 2001).

CHAPTER 5

Water Pollution and Its Governance in Rural Areas

Tong Zhifeng

Water pollution is not only an important manifestation of urban environmental problems, but also an important component of rural environmental problems. This chapter discusses measures to optimize the management of water pollution, and proposes suggestions for improvement on the basis of an overview of the sources and hazards of rural water pollution in China and the evolution of water pollution management policy.

Throughout the process of China's rapid industrialization, water pollution, especially in rural areas, has been on the rise.[1] Hong (2013) has noted "China's environmental governance shows a relatively obvious tendency to emphasize urban areas over rural areas, and there is an increasing trend in the shift of pollution from urban to rural areas". On December 17, 2013, *Hangzhou Metropolis Express* reported a story that shocked the inhabitants of Zhejiang province. Two pesticide production giants, Jinfanda and Xin'an Chemical, had illegally dumped tens of

[1] "Half of China's urban underground water polluted." *China Daily*, 2012-05-28.

Z. Tong (✉)
Zhejiang University of Finance and Economics, Hangzhou, China

D. Hong and Y. Fan (eds.), *Toward a Green Society*,
https://doi.org/10.1007/978-981-96-5111-5_5

thousands of tons of waste liquid in Zhejiang, Shanxi, and Shandong provinces. The untreated waste liquid had caused widespread pollution to local farmland, streams, and rivers, with fish and shrimp dying out in some areas and contaminating tap water in Hangzhou with a foul smell. These two enterprises had each earned tens of millions of dollars in profits, but the economic losses caused by environmental pollution are conservatively estimated at over 300 million yuan.[2] According to the *Statistical Communique of National Environment*, there were 420 environmental emergencies in 2010, of which 135 involved water pollution. According to news from the Anhui Province Department of Ecology and Environment, in 2018, there were four environmental emergencies in Anhui Province, and each one was a water pollution incident.[3] This highlights the urgent need for rural water pollution alleviation measures.

5.1 Sources and Hazards due to Rural Water Pollution

5.1.1 The Sources of Rural Water Pollution

Water pollution in China began in the 1950s during the period of industrialization. It has intensified since the 1970s and is now one of China's preeminent environmental problems. Pollution in China doubled from the 1980s to the 1990s (Wang 1989). Rural water pollution is generally classified as either endogenous or exogenous pollution.

5.1.1.1 Endogenous Pollution in Rural Areas

Endogenous pollution includes pollution from agricultural production and rural domestic sewage. The former refers primarily to pollution caused by agricultural cultivation and livestock breeding. Excessive nitrogen content in surface and groundwater bodies caused by the overuse of fertilizers and pesticides in agricultural production is a major factor in the pollution of rural waters. Over the years, the use of chemical

[2] Two pesticide giants, Jinfanda and Xin'an Chemical, illegally dumped tens of thousands of tons of waste liquid. (2013-12-17)[2019-07-22]. http://zjnews.zjol.com.cn/system/2013/12/17/019762084.shtml.

[3] Anhui Provincial Department of Ecology and Environment. 2018 Provincial Information on Environmental Emergencies. (2019-01-08)[2019-07-22]. http://www.aepb.gov.cn/pages/ShowNews.aspx?NType=2&NewsID=162549.

fertilizer in China's agriculture has continued to rise. Hong et al. (2015) have noted "in terms of area sown per unit of crop, it has increased from 174.6 kg/hm^2 in 1990 to 351.45 kg/hm^2 in 2011, a 2.01-fold increase. Even after 2005, in the context of the country's increased support for soil testing and formulation technology and the alternative application of organic fertilizers, the growth rate of chemical fertilizer use has not significantly declined, but basically increased at about 1.5% per year". Fertilizer utilization is an important indicator of rural surface pollution. Generally speaking, a lower fertilizer utilization rate indicates a higher rate of fertilizer loss, which means that a large amount of fertilizer is lost with surface runoff, sediment, eluviation, etc. This in turn leads to serious surface pollution and damage to the watershed. Additionally, China's fertilizer utilization efficiency is still low. The study reported that the nitrogenous fertilizer use efficiency in China is only about 30%, and the utilization rate of phosphate fertilizer is 10–25% (Zhao et al. 2012). Moreover, the chemical fertilizer utilization rates for wheat, maize, and rice are 37%, 26%, and 37%, respectively (Li and Li 2011). This is much lower than the 60%~80% in developed countries around the world (Hong et al. 2015). The 2014 *Communique on China's Ecological and Environmental Situation* also reports: "currently, the seasonal utilization rate of chemical fertilizers nationwide is only about 33%, generally lower than the 50% level of developed countries. China is the world's largest country in terms of production and use of pesticides, but currently, the effective utilization rate is also only about 35%. The annual use of plastic film mulch is about 1.3 million tons, more than the entire total for all other countries. Thus, the "white revolution" and "white pollution" of the plastic film mulch industry coexist". Furthermore, the 2017 *Communique on China's Ecological and Environment Situation* states, "The utilization rate of chemical fertilizers for the three major grain crops—rice, corn and wheat—was 37.8%, while that of pesticides was 38.8%, and the comprehensive utilization rate of livestock and poultry wastewater reached 64%". Nitrogen fertilizers remaining in agricultural soils enter surface water and groundwater after water solubilization and irrigation, causing serious pollution to shallow groundwater in ponds, lakes, and rivers, and endangering drinking water sources.

According to the relevant data in Table 5.1, over the past decade or so, national ammonia nitrogen emissions (including only industrial ammonia nitrogen emissions and urban household ammonia nitrogen emissions) reached 1.498 million tons (as of 2005), and have decreased ever since.

However, in 2011, after adding the data on emissions from agricultural sources and concentrated emissions, ammonia nitrogen emissions reached 2.604 million tons, of which the emissions from agricultural sources was 827,000 tons, nearly three times the amount of industrial emissions. In 2015, ammonia nitrogen emissions from agricultural sources were 3.3 times higher than those from industry. This demonstrates the severity of the pollution of water bodies caused by rural farming production.

In addition, untreated manure from rural livestock farming can also pollute rural water. According to the Communique of the First National Census of Pollution Sources, chemical oxygen demand (COD) emissions from agricultural sources amounted to 13.2409 million tons in 2007, accounting for 47.6% of China's total COD emissions. Of that amount, livestock and poultry farming discharged 12.6826 million tons of COD,

Table 5.1 National ammonia and nitrogen emissions unit: 10,000 tons

	2002	*2005*	*2008*	*2009*	*2010*	*2011*	*2012*	*2013*	*2014*	*2015*
Total ammonia nitrogen emissions	128.8	149.8	127.0	122.6	120.3	260.4	253.6	245.7	238.5	229.9
Industrial ammonia nitrogen emissions	42.1	52.5	29.7	27.3	27.3	28.1	26.4	24.6	23.2	21.7
Ammonia nitrogen emissions from urban sources	86.7	97.3	97.3	95.3	93.0	147.7	144.6	141.4	138.1	134.1
Ammonia nitrogen emissions from agricultural sources						82.7	80.6	77.9	75.5	72.6
Centralized ammonia nitrogen emissions						2.0	1.9	1.8	1.7	1.5

Source Based on the ***National Communique of Environmental Statistics*** for the relevant years accounting for 96% of the total amount of COD discharged from agricultural sources. This means that COD discharged from livestock and poultry farming accounted for as much as 45% of the total amount of COD discharged throughout the country.[4] Zhang et al. (2010) pointed out that livestock and poultry manure pollution has increased due to the proliferation of large-scale farming:

> The annual production of livestock and poultry manure amounts to 2.7 billion tons, and the chemical oxygen demand content in the manure is nearly 80 million tons, which is about five times that of national industrial and domestic sewage discharges. When the Livestock Breeding Waste Emission Standards were officially implemented on January 1, 2003, about 90% of large-scale livestock and poultry farms failed to meet the emissions management standards, and a large amount of untreated manure and sewage was discharged directly into the water, resulting in serious environmental pollution.

As shown in Table 5.2, in 2011, COD emissions from agricultural sources amounted to 11.861 million tons, accounting for 47.4% of all COD emissions. In 2012 and 2015, the share of COD emissions from agricultural sources amounted to 47.6% and 48.1%, respectively. As for pollution from agricultural sources, livestock and poultry farming accounted for 96%, 38% and 56% of COD, total nitrogen, and total phosphorus, respectively. This reveals that livestock and poultry pollution have become a major source of pollution in rural areas.

Next, let us look at rural sewage pollution. The uncontrolled discharge of rural sewage has polluted the soil, surface water, and groundwater, and thus has become a significant source of pollution in the rural environment. This has led to the phenomenon of blackening and stench emanating from rural rivers, as well as the breeding of mosquitoes and flies. This in turn increases the spread of communicable diseases caused by germs and insects in sewage, thus posing a public health hazard. According to statistics from the 2010 *First National Pollution Source Census Communique*, China produces more than 9 billion tons of domestic sewage, more than 280 million tons of domestic garbage, and 260 million tons of human waste, the vast majority of which is dumped,

[4] From the *First National Pollution Source Census Bulletin* jointly issued by the Ministry of Environmental Protection and the National Bureau of Statistics and the Ministry of Agriculture. Proportion data is calculated based on the data in the communiqué.

Table 5.2 Chemical oxygen demand (COD) emissions unit: 10,000 tons

	2000	*2005*	*2008*	*2011*	*2012*	*2013*	*2014*	*2015*
COD total emissions	1,445.0	1,414.2	1,320.7	2,499.9	2,423.7	2,352.7	2,294.6	2,223.5
Industrial COD emissions	704.5	554.8	457.6	354.8	338.5	319.5	311.3	293.5
COD emissions from urban sources	740.5	859.4	863.1	938.8	912.8	889.8	864.4	846.9
COD emissions from agricultural sources				1,186.1	1,153.8	1,125.8	1,102.4	1,068.6
Centralized COD emissions				20.1	18.7	17.7	16.5	14.5

Source Based on the National Communique of Environment Statistics for the relevant years

discarded, or discharged without treatment. According to the National Bureau of Statistics, China's rural sewage discharge was 16.7 billion tons in 2013 and 20.2 billion tons in 2016, an increase of 21.0%. In 2011, only 6.7% of administrative villages in China even treated their domestic sewage, and even by 2016, that figure had only reached 20%. This indicates it will likely be quite some time before the problem of sewage pollution in rural areas subsides.

5.1.1.2 *Exogenous Pollution in Rural Areas*

Exogenous pollution refers to pollution transferred from outside the countryside, such as rural pollution caused by urban sewage and industrial emissions. First, let us examine pollution from industrial enterprises. Wang (1989) noted that 75% of China's sewage is industrial, and at that time, only 20% of the factories had sewage treatment facilities. According to the data in Table 5.3, the total volume of wastewater discharge has increased over the past decade or so, growing from 41.52 billion tons in 2000 to 73.53 billion tons in 2015. Of this, industrial wastewater discharge has remained fairly consistent, at around 20 billion tons, peaking at 24.31 billion tons in 2005, and declining only slightly ever since.

It should be noted that among the rural pollution caused by emissions from industrial enterprises, pollution from township and village enterprises is particularly damaging to the rural environment. The *National Survey Communique on Industrial Pollution in Township and Village Enterprises* published in 1997 shows that the proportion of pollution

Table 5.3 National total wastewater discharge table, unit: billions of tons

	2000	*2005*	*2008*	*2011*	*2012*	*2013*	*2014*	*2015*
Total wastewater discharge	415.2	524.5	571.7	659.2	684.8	695.4	716.2	735.3
Industrial wastewater discharge	194.2	243.1	241.7	230.9	221.6	209.8	205.3	199.5
Urban domestic sewage discharge	220.9	281.4	330.0	427.9	462.7	485.1	510.3	535.2
Centralized wastewater discharge				0.4	0.5	0.5	0.6	0.6

Source Based on the *National Communique of Environment Statistics* for the relevant years

from township and village enterprises in the overall industrial pollution increased from 11% in the 1980s to 45% in 1995. Moreover, the emissions of some major pollutants are close to, or have exceeded, 50% of the total pollutant emissions from industrial enterprises (Wang et al. 2012). In particular, pollution from rural waters near small paper mills has become one of the main culprits in the degradation of the rural environment.

Next, let us examine sewage sludge from urban life. In addition to industrial sludge, production and domestic sewage from the countryside itself, large amounts of pollutants from cities are discharged into rural areas in various ways. Table 5.3 shows that since 2000, urban domestic wastewater discharge has grown annually, increasing from 22.09 billion tons to 53.52 billion tons in 2015, a 140% increase. According to the National Urban Sewage Treatment and Recycling Facilities Construction Plan for the 12th Five Year Plan issued by the General Office of the State Council in 2012, the urban sewage treatment rate in 2010 was 77.5% for cities, 60.1% for counties, and less than 20% in towns, and the rate of safe disposal of sludge was less than 25% in 2010. According to the National Urban Sewage Treatment and Recycling Facilities Construction Plan for the 13th Five Year Plan published in December 2016, as of 2015, the national urban sewage treatment capacity had reached 217 million cubic meters per day, the urban sewage treatment rate had reached 92%, and the county sewage treatment rate had reached 85%. But at the same time, there were the following problems:

- There is still an uneven regional distribution in the construction of sewage treatment facilities.

- Support for the construction of pipeline networks is lagging.
- The facilities in townships (*zhen*) are insufficient.
- The old pipeline network has serious leakage issues.
- There is an urgent need for upgrading the facilities.
- Some sludge disposal creates secondary pollution hazards.
- Reclaimed water is under-utilized.
- There is a gap between the effectiveness of urban sewage treatment and people's expectations of an improved water environment.

In 2010, the safe disposal rate of sludge in cities, counties, and townships nationwide was less than 25%. In 2015, safe disposal rate of sludge in cities improved to 53%, compared with only 24.3% in counties. According to China Water Network's *China Sludge Treatment and Disposal Market Analysis Report* (2011 edition), "sewage treatment plants produce 5 to 10 tons of sludge for every 10,000 tons of sewage treated. China produces 0.175 million tons of wet sludge every day, and as of 2010, China's annual production of wet sludge reached 63.875 million tons" (Xie 2012). The sludge is not properly disposed of and 90% of the it flows out of the plant and is haphazardly disposed (Xie 2012). Most of that untreated sewage and sludge flows to rural areas, causing great harm to rural bodies of water. For example:

> At the end of 2011, a case of printing and dyeing sludge occurred in Dujiangzhai Village, Hecheng Street, Gaoming District, Foshan City, Guangdong Province. The five suspects hauled more than 60,000 tons of printing and dyeing sludge to the village for direct dumping. This also led to dangerously high levels of ammonia nitrogen content, total nitrogen, total phosphorus and other indicators for the sludge dump effluent and nearby surface water. Heavy metals such as lead, mercury, copper, nickel and zinc were also detected in samples of nearby water and sludge. (Lv 2012)

5.1.2 The Hazards of Rural Water Pollution

5.1.2.1 Water Pollution Jeopardizes Villagers' Health

Studies have shown a correlation between high rates of endemic cancers and organic water pollution (Lu et al. 2008). In the article "Nearly 100 Cancer Villages in Mainland China May Be Sacrificed" published by *Phoenix Weekly*, the author cited data from medical research to report that 80% of cancer cases are known to be related to the environment, and especially to chemicals in the environment, with water being a lethal cause (Deng 2009). In the same year, Sun Yuefei (2009) conducted a statistical survey of public reports by major media in recent years, noting that there were 247 cancer villages throughout China, covering 27 provinces, autonomous regions, and municipalities across the country. In January 2013, the Ministry of Environmental Protection issued "The 12th Five-Year Plan for the Prevention and Alleviation of Chemical Environmental Risks" which states:

> In recent years, a variety of chemical substances have been detected in some rivers, lakes, offshore waters, wildlife and human bodies in China, and the concentrations of persistent organic pollutants and endocrine disruptors in localized areas are higher than the international level, and toxic and hazardous chemicals have caused a number of acute water and airborne environmental emergencies, and drinking water crises have occurred in a number of places, and serious health and social problems have been observed in individual areas. The health and social problems have even emerged in some areas, such as 'cancer villages'.

Year-round haphazard sewage irrigation can cause serious organic, acid–base, and heavy metal contamination of agricultural land, reducing soil and crop productivity or quality. Contaminated soil, which in turn contaminates crops, enters the human body through the food chain and accumulates to produce a variety of chronic diseases, such as itai-itai disease, also known as cadmium poisoning disease. Sewage irrigation can also lead to groundwater or river water contamination, which, through the consumption of drinking water or aquatic products, can also lead to human diseases, such as Minamata disease in Japan.[5]

5.1.2.2 Water Pollution Harms Rural Ecology

Water pollution has led to significant damage to many river ecosystems in China. For example, studies have shown that the population of the Chinese river dolphin, a rare dolphin species that lives in the Yangtze River, has been declining since the 1950s, with an estimated population

[5] Heavy metal pollution of irrigated water is serious, and the use of sewage water for agricultural production is prohibited. (2013-02-05) [2019-07-22]. http://news.sina.com.cn/green/news/roll/2013-02-05/153726212047.shtml.

of 400 in the 1980s. It was estimated to be extinct in 2006 after an international team of scientists failed to find evidence of Chinese river dolphin activity during a two-month search. Water pollution has been cited as one of the main reasons why the Chinese river dolphin is endangered, and likely extinct.[6]

With the industrialization of rural areas, many rural villages have lost their beautiful scenery which was present in the early 1980s, and the ecological environment of rivers, ponds, and other water systems has been greatly damaged. There is no shortage of evidence of this in everyday life. For example, in a report in *Southern Weekly*, a deputy director of the Lanxi Environmental Protection Bureau who visited the Lan River in 1987 describes the changes in the Lan River: "previously, it was clear to the bottom...(but later)...first there was mud, then water plants, and finally the water plants could be taller than a person" (Lv 2014).

5.1.2.3 Water Pollution Leads to Massive Economic Losses

Scholars have estimated that the total economic losses caused by water pollution in 1998 amounted to 247.5 billion yuan, accounting for 3.1% of China's total annual GDP (Li et al. 2003). Zhang Zengjian (2005) estimated that the economic losses from water pollution in China in 2000 amounted to 232.307 billion yuan, accounting for 2.39% of national GDP. The *China Green National Accounting Research Report* 2004, jointly published by SEPA and the National Bureau of Statistics, is an authoritative government report. According to it, economic losses caused by environmental pollution nationwide amounted to 511.8 billion yuan in 2004, accounting for 3.05% of that year's GDP. Among them, the environmental cost of water pollution amounted to 286.28 billion yuan, accounting for 55.9% of the total cost (Bu 2006).

5.1.2.4 Water Pollution Indirectly Affects Social Stability

In 1993, there were roughly 8,700 mass protests in China, increasing to 87,000 in 2005 and more than 90,000 in 2006 (Jin and Zhao 2011). Among these mass protests, those protesting environmental issues accounted for about 20%. Statistics from the environmental protection department also show that environmental group events are growing at an

[6] US National Oceanographic and Atmospheric Administration: Chinese River Dolphin (2012-02-17) [2019-07-22]. http://www.nmfs.noaa.gov/pr/species/mammals/cetaceans/chineseriverdolphin.htm.

annual rate of 29% (Tong 2013). Water pollution is the main cause of rural environmental mass protests (Tong 2008).

5.2 The Evolution of Rural Water Pollution Management Policy

Analysis of the source of rural water pollution reveals that rural water pollution management is a comprehensive project involving both exogenous and endogenous pollution, both point and diffuse pollution. Because rural environmental pollution has long been under-emphasized, few policies or regulations have targeted rural pollution, and especially rural water pollution. Moreover, many of them are scattered in comprehensive environmental laws and regulations (refer to Table 5.4). Examining the introduction and revision of the Law of the People's Republic of China on the Prevention and Alleviation of Water Pollution, China's water environment policy can be roughly divided into the following stages.

5.2.1 Prior to the Mid-1990s, the Focus Was on Urban Water Pollution Management, While Rural Water Pollution and Its Prevention and Management Policies Were Neglected

In 1973, the Office of the State Council Leading Group for Environmental Protection was established. In the same year, the first national conference on environmental protection was held. During this period, the industrial water pollution crisis began to receive attention. It was also during this period that industrial wastewater pollution management intensified, while water pollution management was emphasized in the Bohai Sea, the Huanghai, and Baiyangdian. At the policy level, in 1979 a trial Implementation of Law of the People's Republic of China on Environmental Protection was implemented, with a special chapter on "Prevention and Alleviation of Pollution and Other Public Nuisances". This dealt primarily with the more serious pollution from industrial and mining enterprises and urban life at that time, without mentioning rural pollution.

In 1984, China issued and implemented the Law of the People's Republic of China on Prevention and Alleviation of Water Pollution. It made provisions on sewage irrigation and pesticide use. For example, Article 29 states, "Discharge of industrial wastewater and municipal

Table 5.4 China's (rural) water environment related laws and policies

	Title	*Implementation Dates*
Legislation	Law of the People's Republic of China on Environmental Protection	1989/2015
	Law of the People's Republic of China on the Prevention and Alleviation of Water Pollution	2008/2018
	Water Law of the People's Republic of China	1988/2002/2009/2016
	Law of the People's Republic of China on Environmental Impact Assessment	2003/2016/2018
	Law of the People's Republic of China on Promoting Clean Production	2003/2012
	Agricultural Law of the People's Republic of China	1993/2003/2013
	Law of the People's Republic of China on the Prevention and Alleviation of Environmental Pollution by Solid Wastes	1996/2016
	Law of the People's Republic of China on the Promotion of a Circular Economy	2009/2018
	Law of the People's Republic of China on Soil and Water Conservation	1991/2011
	Law of the People's Republic of China on the Prevention and Alleviation of Soil Pollution	2019
Administrative Regulations	Regulations on the Implementation of the Law of the People's Republic of China on Soil and Water Conservation	1993/2011
	Pesticide Regulation	1997/2001/2017
	National Contingency Plan for Environmental Emergencies	2014
	Plan Environmental Impact Assessment Ordinance	2009
	Water Pollution Management Action Plan	2015
Department Regulations	Regulations on the Management of Pollution Prevention and Alleviation in Protected Areas of Drinking Water Sources	1989/2010
	Measures for the Management of Livestock and Poultry Farming Pollution Prevention and Alleviation	2001
	Provisions on Procedures for Investigation and Handling of Pollution Incidents in Fishery Waters	1997
	Environmental Petition Scheme	2006

(continued)

Table 5.4 (continued)

	Title	*Implementation Dates*
	Interim Measures for the Management of Comprehensive Environmental Improvement Projects with Special Funds for Centralized Rural Environmental Protection	2009
	Measures for Managing the Work of the Environmental Reporting Hotline	2011
	Measures for Reporting Information on Environmental Emergencies	2011
	Measures for Public Participation in Environmental Protection	2015
	Interim Provisions on the Administration of Sewage Discharge Licenses	2016
	Measures for public participation in environmental impact assessment	2019

Source Organized by the author

wastewater into agricultural irrigation channels shall ensure that the quality of the water at the nearest downstream irrigation intake point is in accordance with the water quality standards for agricultural irrigation. The use of industrial wastewater and municipal wastewater for irrigation shall prevent the pollution of soil, groundwater and agricultural products". Article 30 states, "The use of pesticides shall be in accordance with national regulations and standards for the safe use of pesticides". The Environmental Protection Law of the People's Republic of China, which came into force in 1989, merely states in Article 20 "People's governments at all levels shall strengthen the protection of the agricultural environment...by the rational use of chemical fertilizers, pesticides and plant growth hormones". There is no mention of rural pollution in the text.

Generally speaking, before the mid-1990s, awareness of rural environmental protection in China was weak. Policies and regulations pertaining to rural environmental protection were scattered throughout comprehensive environmental laws and regulations. In this policy climate, rural environmental protection, including rural water environmental protection, had yet to be listed as a specialized topic, and the State's focus was still on industrial pollution prevention and urban pollution mitigation. It is also clear from the prohibitions in the legal provisions that the misuse of pesticides and fertilizers was more widespread at that time.

5.2.2 *Attention to Rural Environmental Management Since the Mid-1990s; Relevant Specialized Prevention and Alleviation Policies*

In 1995, the *China Environmental Situation Communique* for the first time singled out the environmental problems in rural areas, stating:

> With the rapid development of township industries, environmental pollution has shown a sharp trend of spreading from the cities to the countryside...Pollutant emissions from the township industries have shown a fast-growing trend, aggravating the damage to the ecological environment. The destruction of the ecological environment has been exacerbated.

During this period, there was greater progress than before in terms of policies for the protection of the rural water environment. First, terms such as "rural pollution" and "agricultural pollution sources" began to appear in relevant laws and regulations. Second, increasing attention began being paid to the pollution of rural production and living conditions. For example, China has introduced laws and regulations to regulate the abuse of pesticides and livestock and poultry farming, which were causing serious rural water pollution. In particular, the following progress was made in policy for protecting the rural water environment during this period.

5.2.2.1 *Regulating Public Participation*

In the amended Law of the People's Republic of China on the Prevention and Alleviation of Water Pollution of 1996, the following statement was added: "In the environmental impact report, there shall be comments from the work units and residents of the area where the construction project is located". This is further reinforced in the Law of the People's Republic of China on Environmental Impact Assessment, implemented in 2003, which states in Article 5, "The State encourages relevant units, experts and the public to participate in environmental impact assessment in an appropriate manner". Article 21 stipulates:

> Except in cases where confidentiality is required by State regulations, in the case of a construction project which may have a significant impact on the environment and for which an environmental impact report should be prepared, the construction unit shall, before submitting for approval an environmental impact report on the construction project, hold hearings or other forms of soliciting the views of the relevant units, experts and members of the public. The environmental impact report submitted for approval by the construction unit shall be accompanied by an explanation of the adoption or non-adoption of the opinions of the relevant units, experts and the public. The environmental impact report submitted for approval by the construction unit shall be accompanied by a statement on the adoption or non-adoption of the opinions of the relevant units, experts and the public.

The Interim Measures for Public Participation in Environmental Impact Assessment, implemented in 2006, contains detailed provisions on the general requirements and organizational forms of public participation. It is also the first interim approach to public participation at the ministerial level. The Interim Measures for Public Participation in Environmental Impact Assessment have also become a way for farmers to intervene in the face of pollution of the rural water environment, especially in the case of rural construction projects that may affect the rural environment. Additionally, public participation has a deterrent effect.

5.2.2.2 Raising the Threshold for Small Businesses Without Water Pollution Management Measures

Article 23 of the 1996 Law of the People's Republic of China on the Prevention and Alleviation of Water Pollution stipulates: "the State shall prohibit the construction of new small-scale chemical pulp, printing and dyeing, dyestuffs, tanneries, electroplating, oil refining, pesticides, and other enterprises that cause serious pollution of the water environment without water pollution prevention and alleviation measures". During the Ninth Five-Year Plan period (1996–2000), China outlawed and shuttered over 84,000 seriously polluting small enterprises. Many small coal mines, iron and steel mines, cement mines, glass mines, oil refineries, and thermal power plants that were technologically outdated, wasteful of resources, of low quality, polluting to the environment, or did not meet the conditions for safe production, were eliminated. In addition, high-sulfur coal production was restricted, effectively reducing total pollutant emissions.

5.2.2.3 *The Rational Application of Fertilizers and Pesticides*

Article 39 of the 1996 Law of the People's Republic of China on the Prevention and Alleviation of Water Pollution stipulates: "Agricultural administration departments of local people's governments at or above the county level and other relevant departments shall take measures to guide farmers to apply fertilizers and pesticides scientifically and reasonably, to curb the excessive use of fertilizers and pesticides, and to prevent water pollution". Article 58 of the Agricultural Law of the People's Republic of China which was implemented in 1993 and amended in 2002 contains a similar provision:

> Farmers and agricultural production and management organizations should maintain farmland, use chemical fertilizers, pesticides and agricultural films in a rational manner, increase the use of organic fertilizers, adopt advanced technologies, protect and improve the strength of the soil, and prevent the pollution, destruction and deterioration of the strength of the land used for agricultural purposes.

The Law of the People's Republic of China on Promoting Clean Production, implemented in 2003, similarly advocates that farmers:

> should scientifically use chemical fertilizers, pesticides, agricultural film mulch and feed additives, improve planting and breeding techniques, achieve high quality and safety of agricultural products and the resourcing of agricultural production wastes, and prevent the pollution of the agricultural environment.

The Pesticide Regulations, implemented in 2001, provide more detailed regulations on the registration, production, operation and use of pesticides.

5.2.2.4 *Regulating Livestock and Poultry Farming*

Livestock and poultry farming is a major source of environmental pollution in rural waters, and the Measures for the Management of Livestock and Poultry Farming Pollution Prevention and Alleviation, implemented in 2001, regulate this:

Article 65 of the Agricultural Law of the People's Republic of China states:

> straw and other residual materials after the harvesting of agricultural products shall be comprehensively utilized and properly disposed of, so as to prevent environmental pollution and ecological damage. Units and individuals engaged in the large-scale breeding of livestock and poultry and other animals shall carry out the safe treatment or disposal of manure, wastewater and other wastes, and units and individuals engaged in aquaculture shall reasonably bait, fertilize and use medicines, so as to prevent environmental pollution and ecological damage.

On the whole, since the mid-1990s, the State has gained a clearer understanding of the seriousness of the rural environmental problems, increasingly emphasized rural environmental protection (including water environmental protection), and introduced a series of laws and regulations in the light of realistic developments. The following two points are particularly worthy of attention. First, the environmental protection department has taken the lead in China in terms of policies and regulations on public participation. This has also created conditions which facilitate the protection of the rural water environment. Second, some specialized policies and regulations have begun to be introduced to address the realities of rural areas, such as the Pesticide Regulation and the Management of Livestock and Poultry Farming Pollution Prevention and Alleviation, which were implemented in 2001. These policies have had a significant positive impact on the rural water environment.

5.2.3 *Strengthening and Improving the Institutional Setup for Rural Water Environment Management Around 2011*

In 2008, the Law of the People's Republic of China on the Prevention and Alleviation of Water Pollution was amended to strengthen the responsibilities of local governments, enhance the protection of drinking water sources, and increase the penalties for environmental violations (including penalties for corporate executives).

The recently revised Law of the People's Republic of China on the Prevention and Alleviation of Water Pollution had added two important systems in the general provisions—an objective responsibility and assessment system and an ecological compensation mechanism for the water environment. Along with the emissions standards and the total amount management system, these constituted the three major systems in the general provisions. For example, with regard to the ecological compensation mechanism for the water environment, the law stipulates: "The State shall, by means of financial transfers and other means, establish and improve the ecological compensation mechanism for the water environment in areas located in drinking water source protection zones and the upstream areas of rivers, lakes and reservoirs".

In addition, some of the more important systems have been improved in the sub-provisions. First, the sewage charging system has been improved; the law before the amendment had established a "sewage charge for exceeding the standard", but the amendment has abolished this system and made the charging system more scientific. Second, the total management system was refined, marking a shift from total management over key bodies of water to the comprehensive implementation of total management. Third, the water pollution emergency response system has been strengthened in the revision. Fourth, the monitoring system has been improved, specifying, "The State shall establish a system for monitoring the quality of the water environment and the discharge of water pollutants". Also, a unified system for releasing information on the state of the water pollution environment was established. Fifth, the planning system has been improved, the procedures for the preparation and approval of water pollution prevention and alleviation plans have been refined, and it has been clarified that the prevention and mitigation of water pollution should be planned on a basin-by-basin or region-by-region basis. Sixth, the management system for drinking water source protection zones should be improved. These institutional settings are instructive for rural water environment protection. The specifics of the policy at this phase are discussed below.

5.2.3.1 Supporting the Comprehensive Utilization of Rural Crop Residues, Livestock, and Poultry Manure

The Law of the People's Republic of China on the Promotion of the Circular Economy, issued in 2008, stipulates:

> China encourages and supports agricultural producers and relevant enterprises to adopt advanced or applicable technologies, comprehensively utilize crop residues, livestock and poultry manure, byproducts of the agricultural product processing industry, waste agricultural film mulch, etc., and develop and utilize biomass energy sources such as biogas.

The 2017 *Report on the Work of the Government* proposed accelerating the straw comprehensive utilization rate such that it reaches 85% by 2020, an increase of nearly 5 percentage points from 2015. In December 2017, the General Office of the National Development and Reform Commission, the General Office of the Ministry of Agriculture, and the Comprehensive Department of the National Energy Administration jointly issued the Guiding Opinions on Carrying out Straw Gasification and Clean Energy Utilization Project Construction. This detailed the key tasks and safeguard measures for straw gasification and clean energy utilization.

5.2.3.2 Experimentation with Incentive-Based Environmental Policy Settings

With regard to the treatment of domestic waste in rural areas, the National Television and Telephone Conference on Rural Environmental Protection, convened by the State Council in 2008, proposed a "Reward-driven approach, where rewards replace subsidies". This would be a way to promote the comprehensive improvement of rural environments. The 2009 Implementation Program on a "Reward-and-Punishment Mechanism to Accelerate the Resolution of Outstanding Rural Environmental Problems" stipulates:

> Priority will be given to arranging funds for promoting comprehensive environmental improvement with incentives for those regions that have completed their treatment targets on time and have better assessment performance. Regions that fail to complete their governance objectives on time and have poor assessment performance will be notified and criticized, and will be disqualified from making declarations, stopping funding arrangements, or recovering funds that have already been disbursed.

Since the introduction of the "Encourage Sustainable Agricultural Practices by Offering Incentives" policy, much rural environmental infrastructure, such as sewage and garbage treatment facilities, has been built in various regions, and the rural environment has been improved. However, since the completion of some of the facilities, there have been problems such as unclear delegation of responsibility, lack of funds for operations and maintenance, insufficient management and care personnel, and unsound regulations. In order to ensure the long-term and stable operations of the facilities and to solve outstanding environmental problems in rural areas, the Ministry of Environmental Protection and the Ministry of Finance jointly issued the Opinions on Strengthening the Operation and Management of Rural Environmental Infrastructure under the Encourage Sustainable Agricultural Practices by Offering Incentives program in 2015.

5.2.3.3 *Specialized Financial Support for Rural Environmental Management*

For a long time, funding for environmental management has been skewed in favor of urban areas. Meanwhile, rural areas have suffered from financial constraints in the process of environmental management. In 2009, the Ministry of Environmental Protection and the Ministry of Finance issued the Interim Measures for the Management of Comprehensive Environmental Improvement Projects under the Central Special Funds for Rural Environmental Protection. This provides for the declaration and approval of projects, as well as their organization and implementation, assessment and acceptance, supervision and inspection. Specialized support from the central financial authorities has leveraged local financial support, which has helped to promote rural environmental management. In 2017–2018, the Ministry of Finance, in accordance with the *Notice of the Ministry of Housing and Urban–Rural Development and Other Departments on the Announcement of the List of Traditional Chinese Villages Included in the Scope of Central Financial Support in 2017 and Proposed to be Included in the Scope of Central Financial Support in 2018*, issued funds for improving rural environments (about 3 million yuan per village) to 1,044 villages to support the protection of traditional villages.

5.2.3.4 *Prohibiting the Use of Sewage Sludge in Agricultural Production*

On January 23, 2013, the General Office of the State Council issued the *Notice on the Arrangement for the Issuance of Recent Work on Soil Environmental Protection and Comprehensive Governance*. This directive called for a ban on the use of sewage and sludge in agricultural production. Article 28 of the Soil Pollution Prevention and Alleviation Law of the People's Republic of China, which went into effect on January 1, 2019, also stipulates, "it is prohibited to discharge into agricultural land sewage and sludge containing heavy metals or other toxic and hazardous substances in excess of the prescribed standards, as well as dredging sludge, tailings, and slag, etc., which may cause soil pollution".

5.2.3.5 *Regional Planning, Environmental Impact Assessment, and Public Participation*

In 2009, the Ministry of Environmental Protection issued the *Notice on Strengthening the Work of Plan Environmental Impact Assessment* which proposed to:

> Effectively strengthen the environmental impact assessment of regional, river basin and sea area planning, and take the integrity and long-term environmental impact of regional, river basin and sea ecosystems as the key point of evaluation. Taking fully into account the characteristics of planning and planning and environmental assessment, more attention should be paid to the professional opinions of the relevant departments and experts involved in planning that is more policy-oriented and macroscopic in nature. For development and construction plans with more specific content, attention should also be paid to the opinions of direct environmental stakeholders. An explanation of the adoption of public comments and the relevant reasons for them shall be an important part of the review opinions.

Regulations such as the *Measures for Public Participation in Environmental Protection*, which came into effect on September 1, 2015, and the *Measures for Public Participation in Environmental Impact Assessment*, which came into effect on January 1, 2019, encourage public participation to protect the public's right to know, participate, express and supervise environmental protection.

5.2.3.6 *Refinement of the Rural Water Environment Policy*

After the Third Plenary Session of the 18th Central Committee of the Communist Party of China, the Ministry of Environmental Protection issued the first four guiding documents. These included the *Guidelines for the Construction and Investment of Rural Domestic Sewage Treatment Projects*, the *Guidelines for the Construction and Investment of Rural Domestic Garbage Classification, Collection and Treatment Projects*, the *Guidelines for the Construction and Investment of Rural Drinking Water Sources Environmental Protection Projects* and the *Guidelines for the Construction and Investment of Rural Small-Scale Livestock and Poultry Breeding Pollution Prevention and Treatment Projects*. These documents covered important sources of pollution in the countryside such as rural sewage, domestic garbage, and small-sized livestock and poultry breeders. These policies are highly relevant and operational, and also serve to guide the development of the rural water market.

On the whole, in recent years, China has begun to explore more detailed and appropriate institutional settings, such as the ecological compensation system, and the policy design has been more detailed in terms of rural water environment management policies. At the same time, the management of rural water environments has received specific support from the central financial authorities. In addition, a number of institutional arrangements have been implemented to address emerging rural water pollution problems, such as sludge pollution.

5.3 Policy Optimization in Rural Water Pollution Management

After more than 40 years of development, the Chinese government has introduced a number of water pollution management policies and has made some achievements in rural water pollution management. Especially in recent years, the Chinese government has become increasingly concerned about rural environmental problems and has a clearer understanding of rural water pollution. For example, according to data published in the 2000 and 2012 Communiques on the State of the Environment in China, the number of construction projects for rural ecological protection increased from 158 in 2000 to 3,229 in 2012.

However, as some scholars have observed, "China's environmental policies are widely regarded as relatively successful in urban areas and relatively backward in rural pollution management" (Wang et al. 2008). So, what is the crux of China's rural water pollution prevention and alleviation? Moreover, how can China's governance policies be optimized?

5.3.1 Existing Problems in Rural Water Pollution Management

Rural water pollution is a comprehensive problem which is related to both exogenous industrial pollution management and endogenous agricultural and rural production and life. It is also related to the lack of existing rural environmental laws and regulations and the poor implementation of existing environmental laws and regulations. At the same time, weaknesses in rural environmental protection and the shortcomings of the environmental protection system will also affect rural water pollution management. The most immediate and urgent problems are related to the following factors.

5.3.1.1 *Industrial and Urban Pollution Are Shifting to Rural Areas*

The 2010 Communique on the State of the Environment in China noted: "industrial and mining pollution in rural areas has become prominent, the transfer of urban pollution to rural areas is accelerating". Additionally, the 2011 Communique on the State of the Environment in China states:

> With the continuous acceleration of agricultural industrialization and urban-rural integration, China's rural and agricultural pollutant emissions continue to increase, and the rural environmental situation is becoming increasingly severe. This is widely manifested by the intensification of pollution from rural life in some areas, the serious pollution of livestock and poultry breeding, and the transfer of industrial and urban pollution to the countryside.

Looking back at the 2006–2010 *Communique on the State of China Environmental Situation*, the shift of pollution from urban to rural areas has continued to be a major concern. Due to the seriousness of the problem of urban pollution transfer to rural areas, the first National Land Planning Outline (2016–2030) issued by the State Council in 2017 states, "Stricter environmental access for industrial projects is needed to prevent urban and industrial pollution from transferring to rural areas".

For example, in Guangdong Province, when the operating costs of enterprises in Guangzhou and Shenzhen were rising, some factories in the two cities relocated to neighboring areas. In recent years, the economically lagging eastern and western wings of Guangdong Province and the mountainous areas of northern Guangdong have continued to undertake polluting projects from the Pearl River Delta region, and the ecological deterioration in some areas has intensified. In Guangdong's large and medium-sized cities, 15 types of heavily polluting small enterprises that the state ordered to close have gradually disappeared, and many manufacturers have moved to remote mountainous areas (Li 2006). In another example, in August 2011, corrupt businessmen in Qujing City, Yunnan Province illegally dumped 5,222.38 tons of chrome slag deep in the local hills in order to cut transportation costs.[7] Such incidents are common, such as the Xin'anjiang phenol pollution incident in Hangzhou in 2011, cadmium pollution in Longjiang, Guangxi, and in Zhenjiang, Jiangsu in 2012, and phenol pollution of water sources.

5.3.1.2 *Long-Term Emphasis on Environmental Pollution Mitigation Investment in Cities, While Neglecting Rural Areas*

In recent years, China has invested heavily in pollution management. Although 2001is the lowest investment in recent years, it still accounted for 1.15% of GDP that year (110.66 billion yuan), while in 2010 it was 665.42 billion yuan, accounting for 1.67% of GDP. However, upon analysis of the data, it appears that these funds were used mainly for urban environmental protection. Since 2001, with the exception of 2007, investment in urban environmental infrastructure construction has accounted for over 50 percent of total investment in environmental pollution management, and in 2010 it was 422.42 billion yuan, or 63.5%. Beginning in 2008, the central financial administration began allocating special funds for rural environmental protection, and the following amounts were invested each year:

- 2008: 500 million yuan
- 2009: 1 billion yuan
- 2010: 2.5 billion yuan
- 2011: 4 billion yuan
- 2012: 5.5 billion yuan
- 2013: 6 billion yuan

Jin (2013) has commented, "this is a drop in the bucket for rural areas, which account for nearly 70% of the country's land area". In addition:

> The vast majority of counties (municipalities) have no investment in rural environmental protection. For example, only 6% of villages nationwide have funds for garbage removal. Compared with industrial enterprises, rural areas also receive very limited funds from financial sources for pollution

[7] Water contamination incidents across the region were frequent in 2019, and rural areas have become a regulatory gray area (2012-02-23) [2019-07-22]. http://news.xinhuanet.com/society/2012-02/23/c_122741395.htm.

management and environmental management capacity building, such as the difficulty of applying for sewage charges for specialized management. (Xi 2010)

5.3.1.3 Policy Gaps Remain in the Area of Rural Water Environment Management

In the prevention and alleviation of pollution from agricultural production, departmental rules and regulations have been introduced to prevent and alleviate pollution from livestock and poultry farming. However, there remains no system dedicated to the prevention and alleviation of pollutants such as chemical fertilizers, agricultural film mulch, and sludge. In 2009, the Ministry of Environmental Protection and the Ministry of Finance jointly issued the Provisional Method for the Management of Central Rural Environmental Protection Special Fund Environmental Comprehensive Treatment Projects. This document stipulated regulations on project application and approval, organization and implementation, evaluation and acceptance, and supervision and inspection. Another example is in the recycling of pesticide packaging waste. In January 2013, the General Office of the State Council issued the "recent work arrangements for soil environmental protection and comprehensive management". It proposed "establishing a pesticide packaging containers and other waste recycling system". However, there has been a lack of a series of complementary systems, as well as the corresponding financial incentives and support. Thus, this system is virtually null and void.

With regard to the excessive use of chemical fertilizers and pesticides, the 1996 Law of the People's Republic of China on the Prevention and Alleviation of Water Pollution states that the excessive use of chemical fertilizers and pesticides should be curbed. This is reiterated in the Law of the People's Republic of China on the Prevention and Alleviation of Water Pollution, which was revised in 2008 and amended in 2017. However, as of this writing, the problem of excessive use of chemical fertilizers and pesticides remains serious. In other words, many institutional settings or environmental laws and regulations lack specific implementation measures and promotion methods. This detracts from the laws and regulations' effectiveness.

5.3.2 *The Optimization of Rural Water Pollution Policy*

The first national pollution source census conducted by the Ministry of Environmental Protection in 2010 showed that major pollutants from agricultural sources such as chemical oxygen demand, total nitrogen, and total phosphorus, accounted for 43%, 57%, and 67% of total emissions, respectively. The census also showed that rural areas have become the areas hardest-hit by water pollution in China.

The media and the public are perceiving the environmental problems as increasingly serious. This has been due to the complex effects of China's environmental problems, the imbalance between urban and rural regional development, and environmental degradation approaching the limit of environmental capacity, and the relative failure of the system and institutions of environmental governance, as well as other compounding problems occurring simultaneously (Hong 2013). Thus, China's rural environmental problems, especially the water environment, will likely remain serious in the future.

Since the 18th CPC National Congress, the Central Committee of the CPC has elevated ecological civilization construction to unprecedented heights. The State Council has tasked the Ministry of Environmental Protection to take the lead in formulating three pollution prevention and alleviation action plans, the Clean Water Action Plan and the Rural Ecological Environment Protection Action Plan, each involving water pollution management. Additionally, the central government has emphasized the rural water environment, but this has not been enough. As such, policies are still in need of further optimization.

5.3.2.1 *Increasing Investment in Rural Environmental Management and Strengthening Policy Support for the Rural Environment*

Compared with urban environmental governance, investment in environmental governance in rural areas has been inadequate. In 2011, the state announced a five-year, 380 billion yuan investment plan to improve urban wastewater treatment facilities and to build some 14,000 monitoring stations across China to monitor water quality. However, the central government has invested far less in rural water pollution management. To say that support is lacking would be an understatement. According to the Interim Measures for the Administration of the Central Special Funds for Rural Environmental Protection, implemented in 2009, the special funds focus on supporting the protection of drinking water sources in rural areas, the treatment of sewage and garbage in rural areas, the treatment of livestock and poultry breeding pollution, the treatment of industrial and mining pollution in rural areas left over from the past, the prevention and alleviation of agricultural surface pollution and soil pollution, as well as other comprehensive environmental remediation measures relevant to improving the environment in villages. From 2009 to 2013, the cumulative investment in the centralized rural environmental protection program was only 26 billion yuan.

5.3.2.2 *For Rural Water Environment Protection, It Is Necessary to Strengthen Incentive-Based Environmental Policies*

Command and management, economic incentive, and persuasion-encouragement are the three main instruments of environmental policy, with the degree of regulation decreasing by an order of magnitude (Song 2008: 29). Command-and-manage policy instruments are characterized by certainty and the requirement of clear management targets. This policy system has been exceptional and has played a large role in industrial pollution alleviation. However, the implementation costs are high, and the scope of application in the field of agricultural and rural environmental protection is limited, and these instruments are only applicable to issues that are of greater impact and in need of strict enforcement, for example, the prohibition of dangerous pesticides (Le et al. 2003).

Regarding the practical experience of developed countries:

> The management of agricultural surface pollution usually takes the form of economic incentives of the preventive type. For example, the Environmental Quality Incentives Program in the United States provides financial and technical support to producers to increase agricultural yields while at the same time contributing to improved environmental quality. Many countries in the European Union have adopted environmental taxes and fees to limit the amount of fertilizers and pesticides used by farmers and reduce the pollution of bodies of water by agricultural practices. (Han and Jin 2013)

In China, the command-and-manage type of environmental policy is still dominant, as evidenced by the few policies targeting rural water environments. Incentive-based environmental policies are still being explored and piloted, such as the Implementation Program on Promoting Comprehensive Environmental Improvement with Incentives to Accelerate the Resolution of Outstanding Rural Environmental Problems, introduced in 2009, which is a typical incentive-based environmental policy. Based on the characteristics of rural environmental pollution, in terms of institutional setting, the policy department should incentivize rural villagers and neighboring enterprises to participate in water environmental protection. For example, fertilizer bags and pesticide containers are often discarded at random, causing great harm to the rural water environment. Some garbage collection stations are reluctant to accept these highly toxic wastes, and consideration could be given to adopting a government-subsidized approach to garbage collection station funding. This would promote collection by farmers, recycling by garbage collection stations on their behalf, and fixed-point treatment by the State.

5.3.2.3 *Strengthening Policy Innovation and Implementation for Exogenous Rural Pollution*

Exogenous pollution of the rural water environment consists primarily of pollution from industrial enterprises and urban domestic sewage. The first step in combating this pollution is to enforce the relevant environmental laws and regulations that have been enacted. For a long time, the State has invested heavily in industrial pollution and urban sewage treatment, and there have been many policies to regulate them. However, industrial pollution and urban pollution persist. One of the reasons is that the enforcement of the laws and regulations is not strict enough. This not only undermines the laws and regulations, but also weakens rural water environment management. The second is to innovate current environmental governance systems and mechanisms. The Law of the People's Republic of China on the Prevention and Alleviation of Water Pollution, as amended in 2017, involves at least a dozen systems, such as the target responsibility and assessment and evaluation system, the system of ecological compensation for the water environment, the total volume management system, the standards system, the planning system, the EIA system, the sewage charging and licensing system, the protected area system, the deadline treatment system, the monitoring system, the inspection system, and the system for eliminating outdated processes and equipment. These systems still need to be improved in the course of concrete practice, so as to make them suitable for the development of local practices. For example, a comprehensive sewage licensing system should be implemented, drawing on the established sewage rights systems in other countries, to prohibit enterprises from discharging pollutants directly or indirectly into bodies of without a license, or in violation of their licenses on a national scale. Some of the environmental governance mechanisms also need to produce new ideas.

5.3.2.4 *With Regard to Endogenous Pollution in Rural Areas, Emphasis Should Be Placed on Building a Sense of Home and Improving Environmental Participation Mechanisms*

With regard to endogenous water pollution in rural areas, it is necessary to start from the examination of the cultural community, to stimulate the villagers' sense of home, and to protect villages on their own initiative. Environmental policy alone cannot solve the problem of stimulating the sense of home, but needs to be promoted along with community policy, for example, through the intervention of community work, the reconstruction of village rules and regulations, the promotion of community residents' self-identification and homeland identification, and the formation of proactive environmental protection consciousness. Secondly, the social participation mechanism needs improvement. Livestock and poultry farms scattered around villages are one source of rural water pollution. The government should be stricter in enforcing water environment standards, and rectify, or even ban, any enterprises that fail to meet the sewage standards. The government should also encourage villagers to participate in the supervision of enterprises around the village to create a system of checks and balances on polluting enterprises.

To conclude, the improvement of rural water pollution policy is an ongoing and comprehensive project. The effectiveness of rural water pollution management is intertwined with both water pollution management policy and the overall environmental management institutional mechanism. For example, in the area of environmental management, we cannot avoid the question of how to solve the problem of the weakness and federation of local environmental protection departments, and the problem of sacrificing environmental protection by local governments in order to maintain economic growth, especially from a policy perspective. Therefore, it is equally important to promote institutional reform of environmental management at the rural level. When the government, society, and the market can synergize in rural water pollution management, rural water environment management will achieve better results.

CHAPTER 6

Rural Ecological Destruction and Protection

Zhang Jinjun

Ecological destruction is a direct manifestation of rural environmental problems, and this chapter focuses on rural ecological destruction and ecological protection. According to the explanation in the *Dictionary of Environmental Protection*, ecological destruction refers to certain changes in the ecosystem due to natural or man-made factors which upset the original equilibrium state, thus creating destructive ecological fluctuation or a vicious cycle (Zhu 2009: 88). In this chapter, ecological destruction ecological destruction refers to the consequences caused by human factors. The so-called ecological destruction caused by anthropogenic factors refers to the ecological problems caused by the direct action of human activities on ecosystems, resulting in a significant reduction in ecosystems' production capacity and significant changes in their structure, such as soil erosion caused by destruction of the vegetation cover, degradation of grasslands caused by overgrazing, and the extinction of rare species caused by indiscriminate mining and fishing. (Zhu 2009: 88).

J. Zhang (✉)
Law School, Anhui Normal University, Wuhu, China

D. Hong and Y. Fan (eds.), *Toward a Green Society*,
https://doi.org/10.1007/978-981-96-5111-5_6

6.1 Characteristics and Trends of Rural Ecological Destruction

The terms "ecological destruction" and "environmental pollution" are often used interchangeably, yet there are important differences between them that require explanation. "Environmental pollution" refers to the ecological environmental problems caused by human beings discharging harmful substances or harmful factors into the ecological environment in the process of industrial and agricultural production and daily consumption, resulting in changes in the structure and function of the ecosystem. Examples of this would include air pollution, water and soil pollution, noise pollution, and solid waste pollution (Zhu 2009: 179). Environmental pollution and ecological destruction are both secondary environmental problems caused by human activities, but their causes are different. It is generally believed that environmental pollution is caused primarily by rapid urbanization and the proliferation of industry and agriculture, while ecological destruction is caused primarily by the irrational exploitation and utilization of natural resources by human beings (Hong 2002). Moreover, the extent of environmental pollution is less than that of ecological destruction. Generally speaking, environmental pollution within the absorption capacity of the ecological environment rarely results in ecological destruction, and only when the environmental pollution is serious enough to exceed the self-cleansing capacity of the ecological environment will it cause ecological fluctuation and ecological destruction.

Generally speaking, pollutants are concentrated in urban areas due to the high density of transportation, industrial activities, and human settlement. Ecological and environmental problems are mainly manifested as environmental pollution, such as air pollution, water pollution, and noise pollution. In rural areas, because people use natural resources in improper or excessive intensity, ecological and environmental problems are manifested primarily as ecological destruction, such as soil erosion, desertification, soil salinization, forest reduction and water resource reduction (Jia 2008: 11). Since the founding of the PRC, there have been three main types of ecological and environmental problems: soil erosion, land desertification, and freshwater ecological problems. Since the Reform and Opening-up, the scattered rural industrial enterprises, continuous urban pollution transfer, and large-scale use of chemical fertilizers and pesticides have rapidly polluted the rural ecological environment (Li et al. 2005: 5–6).

6.1.1 Ecological Destruction in Rural Areas Is Grim

Ecological destruction in rural China has a long history, with some local areas already experiencing significant effects in the traditional agricultural era. From 1949 to 1957, some industrial enterprises, especially thermal power plants, were planned and constructed along rivers. Yet these power plants had little technical capability to dispose of wastewater. Instead, they used rivers as sewers for waste discharge, damaging the rural ecological environment (Qu 1988). From 1958 to 1965, due to large-scale iron and steelmaking, mass movements, and the arbitrary deployment of small steel plants, smog was widespread. Sewage and sludge were ubiquitous, and indiscriminate exploitation of mineral resources led to extensive ecological destruction in rural areas (Zhou et al. 1996: 128). Between 1966 and 1976, the unbalanced emphasis on "prioritizing grain production" in agricultural practices resulted in the advancement of grain production at the expense of forestry, animal husbandry, and fisheries. This led to escalated deforestation, overgrazing, land reclamation from lakes, as well as the development of artificial cultivated land. Thus, the agricultural ecosystem has already been seriously damaged, leading to a vicious cycle in rural ecosystems and frequent pollution and disastrous incidents. (Zhou et al. 1996: 128). Since the Reform and Opening-up, China has experienced a period of accelerated social transformation, and this social transformation has highlighted and aggravated China's ecological and environmental problems (Hong 2001: 85), including ecological destruction in rural areas. Scholars have estimated the percentages of anthropogenic disturbances which have caused ecosystem degradation. Overexploitation (including direct damage and environmental pollution) accounts for 35%, and deforestation accounts for 30%. Agricultural activities account for 28%, while the overharvesting of fuelwood accounts for 6%, and bioindustry for 1% (Zhang 2009: 23).

On the question of the severity of rural ecological destruction, Zhu Guangyao, former deputy director of the State Environmental Protection Administration, contends that in the 10 years from 1996 to 2005, the Chinese government adopted a series of major ecological environmental protection measures while developing the economy. Overall, China's environmental pollution and ecological destruction have slowed.[1] Ecological destruction in rural areas has also shown signs of slowing, but remains serious. When Li Keqiang was vice premier of the state council, he mentioned in his speech at the National Teleconference on Rural Environmental Protection that China's rural ecological environment degradation was still severe. Soil erosion, land desertification, and ecological function degradation continue to degrade the environment. In some locales, even though indiscriminate mining, deforestation, and land reclamation have been repeatedly banned, damage to the ecological environment in rural areas continues.[2] The academic community generally recognizes that ecological destruction in China's vast rural areas is serious. Furthermore, the problem of rural ecological destruction is expanding from local areas to larger regions (Fu et al. 2000; Liang 2009); the most notable issues include water shortages, soil erosion, desertification and sandification, an increasing area of damaged land and unchecked growth (Cui 2007).

In the early 1950s, 2.8 million square kilometers of China's land was affected by soil erosion, accounting for 29.1% of its total land area.[3] According to the results of the Second National Remote Sensing Survey on Soil Erosion released by the Ministry of Water Resources in 2002, by 2000, China's soil erosion had increased to 3.56 million km^2, accounting for 37% of the country's land area. According to the survey, soil erosion in China was widespread, diverse, and intense, and there were various types and degrees of soil erosion in mountainous, hilly, and sandy areas, as well as in rural and urban areas.[4] By 2004, some 48.67 million hectares of agricultural land in China had been eroded, accounting for 38% of its

[1] Cheng Gang. The trend of intensifying environmental pollution and ecological destruction in China has slowed over the past decade. (2006-06-05) [2019-07-22]. http://www.china.com.cn/chinese/kuaixun/1230001.htm.

[2] Li Keqiang, Vice Premier of China, delivered a speech at a national television conference on rural environmental protection. (2008-07-24) [2019-07-22]. http://www.china.com.cn/tech/zhuanti/wyh/2008-08/13/content_16210275.htm.

[3] Overview of soil erosion in China (2005–07-19) [2019–07-22]. http://scitech.people.com.cn/GB/25509/50262/50980/3553777.html.

[4] The Ministry of Water Resources has announced the findings from the second nationwide remote sensing survey on soil and water erosion. (2002–04-03) [2019–07-22]. http://www.h2o-china.com/news/8637.html.

cultivated land.[5] According to the 2015 *China Desertification and Desertification Status Communiqué*, as of 2014, China had 2.61 million km^2 of desertified land area, and 1.72 million km^2 of sandy land, indicative of the extent of land desertification.

Desertification of China's land is a serious issue. From the third century B.C. to 1949, there were a total of 70 major sand and dust storms recorded in Northwestern China, with an average of one every 31 years. In the 50 years since the founding of the PRC, there have been 71 major sand and dust storms in the same region. Although there are significant differences in the measurement methods used in historical records and those from modern meteorological observations, there are clearly more dust storms now than there were in the past.[6] In terms of freshwater ecological problems, relevant information shows that 90% of the rivers flowing through cities in China have been seriously polluted, and at least 300 million farmers are unable to drink clean, safe water.[7] By the end of 2010, over 298 million people in rural China had unsafe drinking water.[8]

6.1.2 Rural Environmental Pollution Has Gradually Developed into Ecological Destruction

Since the twentieth century, humans have both intentionally and unintentionally introduced many pollutants into the ecological environment via industrial and agricultural production. This has changed the environmental factors of the ecosystem, and thus, has affected entire ecosystems. The resulting air, water, soil, and solid waste pollution are key causes of ecological destruction (Zhang 2009: 22). Since the initiation of the Reform and Opening-up, there has been a notable increase in the spread of environmental pollution in China; it has expanded from land to

[5] "The overall status of soil erosion in China." (2005–07-19) [2019–07-22]. http://scitech.people.com.cn/GB/25509/50262/50980/3553777.html.

[6] Ministry of Natural Resources. *Overview of land desertification in China* (2018–03-22) [2019–07-22]. http://zrzy.wuhai.gov.cn/zwgk/zzglrz/201811/t20181122_783431.html.

[7] Li He. "Strategic EIA: Solving environmental problems at the source". (2007–06-24) [2019–07-22]. http://www.h2o-china.com/news/59136.html.

[8] See National Development and Reform Commission, Ministry of Water Resources, Ministry of Health, Ministry of Environmental Protection, National Twelfth Five-Year Plan for Rural Drinking Water Safety Project.

offshore waters, from surface water to groundwater, and from general pollutants to toxic and harmful pollutants. Point source pollution and NSP have occurred simultaneously, and there has been overlap between domestic pollution and industrial emission pollution. Various new and old pollution and secondary pollution have also compounded, and air, water, and soil pollution have interacted with each other. The threat to the ecosystem is increasing, and the scope of ecological destruction is gradually expanding (He et al. 2010: 55).

Some scholars categorize rural environmental pollution into two types: exogenous pollution and endogenous pollution. The former mainly refers to any pollution generated by industries transferred from urban areas to rural areas and any pollution generated by rural industries, while the latter refers to pollution created by farmers themselves (Chen 2007). Most endogenous pollution is NSP. In recent years, more and more development zones, industrial parks, and especially chemical parks, have been established in rural areas. This has caused the transfer of urban industrial wastewater, domestic sewage, and garbage to rural areas, thus deteriorating the rural ecological environment (Wan 2007). In 1995, the discharge of industrial wastewater in townships and towns accounted for 21.0% of the national industrial wastewater discharged that year. Compared with the 1989 survey of township industrial pollution sources, the discharge of industrial wastewater had increased by 121%.[9] According to estimates from researchers' in the field of agricultural natural resources, the discharge of industrial wastewater, COD, dust and solid waste in townships and towns in China has accounted for over 30% of its total industrial pollutant emissions (Zhang and Liu 2011: 89). Under normal circumstances, small paper mills in townships discharge 3 times as many pollutants per ton of paper produced as large state-owned enterprises, 4 times as much the amount of organic pollutants and 14 times as much the amount of suspended solids. Therefore, it is common for a small paper mill in a township to pollute a river, a reservoir, a piece of farmland, or a tidal flat (Zhang and Liu 2011: 41). The results of a survey of 100 villages showed that there were 57 polluting enterprises in and around the villages surveyed. Surface water was polluted by waste water

[9] See the *Communiqué on the Investigation of Sources of Industrial Pollution in Townships and Towns* issued by the State Environmental Protection Administration, the Ministry of Agriculture, the Ministry of Finance and the National Bureau of Statistics on December 23, 1997.

from industrial enterprises in 45% of the villages, shallow groundwater was polluted by industrial wastewater and waste residue in 20% of the villages, air quality was affected by waste gas and dust from industrial enterprises in 39% of the villages, and soil was polluted by waste water residue in 13% of the villages (Liu et al. 2007). Urban pollution transfer damages the rural ecological environment, such that the ecological and environmental problems in rural areas have evolved from resource degradation to now include both resource degradation and environmental pollution (Li et al. 2005: 36–37).

NSP is a type of environmental pollution related to point source pollution. Excessive and irrational use of pesticides and fertilizers in rural areas of China, livestock and poultry manure from small-scale livestock and poultry farming, pollution from large-scale farming (Geng 2017), as well as untreated agricultural production wastes, rural household garbage and wastewater are all direct factors contributing to rural NSP. The characteristics of NSP include decentralization, concealment, randomness, and uncertainty of the discharge entity and region. Its causes are complex, the incubation period is long, and it is difficult to monitor. In the context of the dual social structure of urban and rural areas, NSP has remained on the rise (Hong and Ma 2004). Li Keqiang once noted that China's rural domestic pollution and NSP are still serious, with over 9 billion tons of domestic sewage produced annually in rural areas being discharged arbitrarily, and 280 million tons of domestic garbage being dumped arbitrarily.[10]

Continuous industrial pollution and NSP in rural China have resulted in ecological destruction to rural areas. Environmental pollution is gradually and systematically destabilizing and destroying China's countryside, both covertly and overtly, seriously damaging the ecological environment in some rural areas (Zhang and Gu 2003). The extensive pollution of rural farmland and water sources means that the foundation of farmers' livelihoods has been undermined, the very land they occupy has become uninhabitable, and villages are being deserted or even disappearing altogether (Jinhai 2008: 83).

[10] Speech by Vice Premier Li Keqiang at the National Television and Telephone Conference on Rural Environmental Protection. (2008-07-24) [2019-07-22]. http://www.china.com.cn/tech/zhuanti/wyh/2008-08/13/content_16210275.htm.

6.1.3 The Regional Characteristics of Rural Ecological Destruction

China's rural ecological destruction has clear regional characteristics. The trend of ecological destruction caused by irrational exploitation and utilization of natural resources in Western China is becoming ever clearer. Most areas with the greatest ecological pressure caused by rural ecological resource degradation are in the West. However, this phenomenon has expanded and spread to some Central and Eastern rural regions as well (Liang 2009). As such, ecological destruction caused by environmental pollution in rural areas in Eastern and Central China is intensifying.

China's river-based soil erosion is characterized by several features: First, most soil erosion occurs in the upper reaches of the Yangtze River in Yunnan, Guizhou, Sichuan, and Hubei provinces, and Chongqing Municipality. It also occurs in Shanxi, Shaanxi, and Gansu provinces, Inner Mongolia and Ningxia Hui Autonomous Regions, and other regions in the middle reaches of the Yellow River. Second, the occurrence of river-based soil erosion in China increases as one travels from east to west. In terms of affected area, river-based soil erosion in the Eastern Region encompasses 90,000 km^2, while the affected areas the Central Region comprise 490,000 km^2, and the affected areas in the Western Region total 1.07 million km^2. Third, the region of China most severely affected by wind erosion is the Northwest. Fourth, the areas of water and wind erosion overlap in the regions bordering the Great Wall and the agricultural-pastoral transition zones within Xinjiang Uygur Autonomous Region.[11]

Examining land desertification and sandification, deserts in China are concentrated in the West. An analysis of Landsat image data of the same area in 17 typical sandy areas in China at different times showed that the Maowusu Sandy Land in the border zone of Inner Mongolia Autonomous Region, Shaanxi Province, and Ningxia Hui Autonomous Region in the West covered an area of about 40,000 km^2. The same images showed that the area comprised of quicksand had increased by 47% in 40 years. Additionally, forest land area had decreased by 76.4% and the grassland area had decreased by 17%. A similar analysis was performed in the southern part of the Hunshan Dak Sandy Land, located at the

[11] Ministry of Water Resources announces the results of the second national soil erosion remote sensing survey. (2002-04-03) [2019-07-22]. http://www.h2o-china.com/news/8637.html.

southern end of the Xilin Gol Grassland in the central Inner Mongolia Autonomous Region. The images showed that overgrazing and firewood harvesting had increased the quicksand area by 98.3%, and the grassland area had decreased by 28.6% in just nine years. The shrinking of the Minqin Oasis in Gansu, the degradation of grasslands in Alxa, and the disappearance of the Suosu Forest as well as poplar and red willow forests in the lower reaches of the Tarim River in Xinjiang each indicate the severity of desertification in Western China.[12]

Examining freshwater ecological problems, 2010 survey data from the China Rural Issues Research Center's 100 Villages Ten-Year Observation project team at Central China Normal University showed that 19.3% of surveyed farmers had suffered varying degrees of water shortages. Among them, the percentage of water-deficient rural households in the Western region was 31.8%. The percentage of rural households lacking water in decentralized villages was 20.6%, while in villages in Central China it was 14.4%. The percentages of water-deficient farmers in plateau and mountainous villages were 36.5% and 29.9% respectively, much higher than those in other terrain areas, and the water scarcity problem in these two village types was widespread.[13] Through its research, the "100 Villages Ten-Year Observation" project team concluded that there were four major problems with China's rural residents' drinking water, one of which was that the Western Region was the hardest-hit area, with 19.031 million water-deficient rural households.[14]

Rural environmental pollution, as exemplified by rural industrial pollution, is concentrated in the economically advanced Eastern Region, in provinces such as Zhejiang, Jiangsu, Shandong, Guangdong, and Fujian, as well as in the Central Region in provinces such as Henan, Anhui, and Shanxi. The regional differences in rural industrial pollution are clear. Rural industrial pollution in the Eastern Region is worse than in the

[12] Ministry of Natural Resources. *Overview of Desertification in China*. (2018-03-22) [2019-07-22]. http://zrzy.wuhai.gov.cn/zwgk/zzglrz/201811/t20181122_783431.html.

[13] "A Comprehensive Approach to Solving the Drinking Water Problems of Rural Residents is Urgently Needed" Report. (2010-10-12) [2019-07-22]. http://theory.people.com.cn/GB/12933577.html.

[14] *Report on The Imperative of a Comprehensive and Integrated Solution to the Drinking Water Problems of Rural Residents*. (2010-10-12) [2019-07-22]. http://theory.people.com.cn/GB/12933577.html.

Central Region. The same pollution in the Central Region is worse than that in the Western Region, and the rural industrial pollution in both the Eastern and the Central regions is intensifying. Heavily polluting and moderately polluting industries in rural areas in the Western Region account for a small percentage of China's total pollution, and the visible effect on the ecological environment is unclear (Liang 2009). Meanwhile, environmental pollution in rural areas in the Eastern and Central regions visibly damages the ecological environment. However, there are various indications that environmental pollution in the Eastern Region has begun to shift to rural areas in the Central and Western regions.[15] Many media sources have even reported that the Western region has become the hardest-hit area for environmental pollution.[16]

6.2 Rural Ecological Protection Practices and Achievements

Between the founding of the PRC and the Reform and Opening-up, the Chinese government's rural ecological protection work was primarily manifested in rural water and soil conservation, agricultural resource protection, and forest and mineral resource protection. This reflected the Chinese government's initial concerns over rural ecological protection. The Common Program of the Chinese People's Political Consultative Conference (September 29, 1949) proposed the principles of building water conservancy, protecting forests, and developing forestry in a planned manner. In *Consultation for Opinions on Seventeen Articles on Agriculture* (December 21, 1955), Mao Zedong demanded that within 12 years, most wastelands and mountains be eliminated, trees planted according to specifications, and greening be implemented. In January 1956, the Central Committee of the Communist Party of China proposed

[15] "High-pollution projects are gradually relocating to the Midwest, resulting in an escalation of pollution in rural areas." (2011-08-17) [2019-07-22]. http://www.legaldaily.com.cn/index/content/2011-08/17/content_2871878.htm?node=20908Investigation: Environmental pollution in eastern China has been transferred to the central and western regions. (2008-07-28) [2019-07-22]. http://news.ifeng.com/c/7fYQJ1MPUwb.

[16] Western China's ecological environment is fragile, and this limits its development (2012-03-08) [2019-07-22]. http://finance.ifeng.com/roll/20120308/5717531.shtml.

the *National Agricultural Development Outline*, calling for the construction of hydraulic engineering, river management, and the implementation of water and soil conservation work over vast rural areas. In July 1957, the State Council issued the *Interim Outline of Water and Soil Conservation of the PRC* which stipulated the establishment of a national and a provincial water and soil conservation committee (limited to provinces with water and soil conservation projects). Additionally, it stipulated the implementation of new water and soil conservation projects, including the planned closure of mountains, forest and grass cultivation, and the prohibition of land reclamation, indiscriminate reclamation of logging, grazing, mountain burning, and mining. In May 1963 and December 1965, the State Council issued the *Forest Protection Regulations* and the *Provisional Regulations on the Protection of Mineral Resources*, respectively. These regulations stipulated that only selective logging, sanitary logging, and reforestation logging were permitted for greening tree forests, seed collecting forests, and sanctuaries. Deforestation for farming and indiscriminate digging and mining were prohibited, with an emphasis on protecting mineral resources and underground water resources. The state council also mandated the establishment of forest and mineral resource protection organizations at all levels of government, while integrating the efforts of government departments into grassroots organizations. In June 1972, a Chinese government delegation participated in the Human Environment Conference, the first United Nations global environmental summit, an important turning point in China's rural ecological protection work. In October 1974, the State Council Leading Group for Environmental Protection and its offices were established. After 1974, a considerable number of counties in China gradually established environmental protection bureaus, and townships and towns in some developed areas also established corresponding environmental protection agencies.

Since the Reform and Opening-up, under the influence and role of various economic and social factors, ecological pressure and destruction in China's rural areas have intensified. In response to this problem, the Chinese government issued a series of ecological protection policies, including the prevention and mitigation of land desertification and soil erosion, forest protection, and returning farmland to forest, the establishment of ecological reserves, the development of ecological agriculture and the establishment of ecological compensation mechanisms and systems. Since 1978, the Chinese government has launched a number of large-scale ecological restoration and protection projects. In 1978, with the approval of the State Council, the shelter forest project of the "Three Norths" (Northwest, Northeast and Northern China) was officially launched. Over the past 40 years, this project has achieved impressive results which have drawn worldwide attention. The 13 years (from 1998 to 2010) that the Natural Forest Protection Project was in effect saw massive improvement in the ecological environment of the upper reaches of the Yangtze River, the middle and upper reaches of the Yellow River, the Northeast region, the Inner Mongolia Autonomous Region, and other key state-owned forest zones. Since the Project of Returning Farmland to Forest was launched in 1999, the forest coverage of the project area has expanded, and the ecological environment has generally improved. According to the 2018 *Communiqué on the Status of China's Ecology and Environment*, by the end of 2017, a total of 2,750 nature ecological reserves of various types and levels had been established in China, and the number of national nature ecological reserves increased to 474 by 2018. The ecological protection boundaries of 15 provinces, autonomous regions, and municipalities, including Beijing Municipality, Tianjin Municipality, Hebei Province, and Ningxia Hui Autonomous Region, have been preliminarily defined. Additionally, 16 provinces, autonomous regions, and municipalities, including Shanxi Province, have outlined a delineation plan. In the more than 40 years since the Reform and Opening-up, a series of rural ecological protection policies, measures and actions undertaken by the Chinese government have not only slowed rural ecological destruction, but have also accelerated the construction process of land greening and expanded the international influence of China's ecological civilization construction.

6.2.1 Alleviating Rural Ecological Destruction

Environment, soil erosion area in China that year was 2.949 million km^2, accounting for 31.1% of the measured area. The area affected by water erosion comprised 1.293 million km^2, while the area affected by wind erosion comprised 1.656 million km^2. Compared to the 3.56 million km^2 of soil erosion area in 1999, China's soil erosion problem has improved, and rural areas are no exception.

Additionally, land desertification has also been mitigated. As mentioned above, according to the 2015 *Communiqué on the Status of Desertification and Sandification in China*, by 2014, China's desertification area had reached 2.6116 million km^2, while the sandy land area was 1.7212 million km^2. In comparison to 2009, there was a reduction of 12,120 km^2 in desertification over the past five years, equating to an annual decrease of 2,424 km^2 and a decrease of 9,902 km^2 in sandy land over the same period, with an annual decrease of 1,980 km^2. Compared with 2009, there has been improvement in terms of land desertification, with a positive trend of overall containment, continuous reduction, functional enhancement, and clear results.

Finally, examining freshwater ecological issues, the 2018 *Communiqué on the Status of China's Ecology and Environment* shows that in 2018, 1,935 surface water quality sections (points) were monitored nationwide and 71.0% were measured as Class I~III, an increase of 3.1% from 2017. The percentage of sections worse-than Class V was 6.7%, a decrease of 1.6% from 2017. By comparison, the 2008 *Communique on China's Environmental Status* showed that of the 409 water quality sections (points) measured, 55% were Class I~III. This indicates that the freshwater ecological problems in rural areas have also improved over time.

In addition, the construction of nature reserves of various types and levels and the establishment of ecological protection boundaries have played an important role in water and soil conservation, and in maintaining ecological balance. Since the early 1980s, large numbers of surplus laborers from China's rural areas have migrated to urban areas. This has caused a shortage of rural labor in the outflow areas, and a considerable amount of arable land has been abandoned. However, these abandoned arable lands have gradually evolved into forest land, which has had a positive effect on the rural ecological environment (Qin 2009).

6.2.2 The Acceleration of Land Greening

Since the Reform and Opening-up, the Chinese government has launched a number of large-scale ecological restoration and protection projects, especially key forestry ecological projects such as the Three North Shelter Forest Project, the Natural Forest Protection Project, and the Project of Returning Farmland to Forest. This has expanded China's forest coverage and accelerated the land greening process.

Since the initiation of the Three North Shelterbelt Forestry Project in 1978, a total of 30,143,000 hectares of forestland had been planted and preserved as of 2018. The forest coverage rate in the project area increased from 5.05% in 1979 to 13.57% in 2015, owing to the concerted efforts of the project. This initiative also established a green Great Wall for wind and sand resistance, while maintaining soil integrity. Thus, it has served as an exemplary model for China's ecological civilization construction and global ecological governance.[17] During the construction period from 1998 to 2010, the natural forest area increased by 1.89 million hectares.[18] Since the implementation of the two rounds of farmland reforestation in 1999, more than 500 million mu of farmland have been returned to forest and grassland nationwide, resulting in an increase of 502 million mu of forest land area, accounting for 42.5% of the 1.18 billion mu of planted forests. Additionally, the artificial grassland area increased by 5.0261 million mu, accounting for 2.2% of the 225 million mu of planted grassland in China. On average, the forest coverage in the project area has increased by more than 4 percentage points, making a significant contribution to the new greening of China and a greener earth.[19]

According to data from the National Forest Resources Inventory, China's forest coverage rate increased from 12.7% in 1976 (First National Inventory of Forest Resources, 1973–1976) to 16.55% in 1998 (Fifth National Inventory of Forest Resources, 1994–1998). By 2013, China's forest coverage rate had risen to 21.63% (Eighth National Inventory of Forest Resources, 2009–2013). As such, forest resources have continued to expand in area, and improve in both quality and efficiency. According to the 2017 *Communiqué on the Status of China's Ecology and Environment*, China's forest area and forest stock ranked 5th and 6th in the world, respectively, and its planted forest area ranked first in the world. According to the 2018 *Communiqué on the Status of China's Ecology and Environment*, by the end of 2018, the Chinese government had completed afforestation and greening of another 106 million mu in the

[17] The Three North Program has raised forest coverage by 8.5 percentage points in the 40 years leading up to this writing.

(2018-12-01) [2019-07-22]. http://politics.people.com.cn/n1/2018/1201/c1001-30435883.html.

[18] See The Eighth National Inventory of Forest Resources (2009–2013).

[19] Li Xuelian. "The State Forestry and Grassland Administration of China implemented a policy to convert over 500 million mu of farmland into forest and grassland, achieving remarkable results." (2019-07-09) [2019-07-22]. http://news.ifeng.com/c/7oAeTv73Iwq.

overall promotion of large-scale land greening actions. As the government's ecological protection policy continues to improve and the concept of green development continues to be practiced, China's forest coverage will continue to expand, and the process of land greening will accelerate.

6.3 Strategies and Challenges in Rural Ecological Conservation

As previously mentioned, ecological conservation efforts in rural China have been ongoing since the establishment of the PRC. In August 1973, the State Planning Commission held its first national environmental protection conference in Beijing. The meeting determined the 32-Character Policy for China's ecological environmental protection, that is, *Comprehensive Planning, Rational Layout, Comprehensive Utilization, Turning Harm into Profit, and Relying on the Masses* and *Taking Action by All, Protecting the Environment and Benefiting the People.* At the meeting, the *Several Provisions on the Protection and Improvement of the Environment* (Trial Implementation) was adopted, and the State Council Leading Group for Environmental Protection and its offices were established. However, because the chaos caused by the Cultural Revolution had yet to be rectified, the spirit and related regulations of the first national environmental protection conference were never fully implemented (Wen 2010: 5).

Article 11 of the Constitution of the PRC, adopted by the First Session of the Fifth National People's Congress in March 1978, stipulates, "The State protects the environment and natural resources and prevents pollution and other public hazards". In September 1979, *China issued the Environmental Protection Law of the PRC* (Trial Implementation) for the first time, which legally affirmed the "32-Character Policy" (Article 4). This provided clear provisions for land use, water protection, mineral development, forest harvesting, pasture protection, and wildlife protection. (Articles 10 to 15). It also required the establishment of ecological environmental protection institutions and the strengthening of ecological and environmental management (Articles 26–28). In addition, it provided clear incentives and penalties (Articles 31–32). In December 1983, the State Council convened the Second National Conference on Environmental Protection, which established ecological environmental protection as a basic national policy of China. In July 1985, the Ministry of Agriculture, Animal Husbandry and Fisheries Agricultural Environmental Monitoring Center issued the *Report on China's Agricultural Environmental Quality* (1983). This was China's first systematic study of the country's rural ecological environment problems.

Ecological and environmental policy includes pollution management policy and ecological protection policy. In addition to various formal ecological environment management systems, China's ecological and environmental policies also include phased ecological environmental protection measures and programs. In reviewing China's ecological and environmental policies since 1949, some scholars believe that the 1970s was the era of the initial construction of China's ecological and environmental policies, the 1980s was the era of the formation of the framework system, the 1990s was the era of the strategic transformation, and the twenty-first century was the era of comprehensive and integrated decision-making (Wen 2010: 4–19). Based on the five levels of China's rural ecological environment policy system, i.e., party policies, laws and regulations, standards and norms, planning and programs, and local policies, some scholars have divided China's rural ecological environment policy system into three stages—germination (1949–1977), construction (1978–1999), and initial formation (2000–present) (Zhang 2018).

As of this writing, China had formulated at least 10 ecological and environmental laws, including the Environmental Protection Law of the PRC, the Water Pollution Prevention and Control Law of the PRC, and the Air Pollution Prevention and Control Law of the PRC. It has also implemented over 20 ecological resource laws, including the Forest Law of the PRC, the Grassland Law of the PRC, the Land Management Law of the PRC, the Water Law of the PRC, the Soil and Water Conservation Law of the PRC, and the Mineral Resources Law of the PRC. In addition, it has issued more than 200 regulations and normative documents on ecological and environmental protection departments. However, this has not prevented the continued deterioration of rural ecological destruction. The current rural ecological protection policy itself, and its implementation, still face several problems.

6.3.1 The Policy System Is Not Yet Sound or Complete

Some scholars divide China's ecological and environmental policies into mandatory policies and compensatory policies, believing that although mandatory policies have the effect of enforcement at the legal level, there are problems such as slow reaction time with policy updates, arbitrary standard formulation, one sidedness, and limited coverage. Meanwhile, compensatory policies have problems such as low absolute compensation standards and one-size-fits-all approaches, limited coverage, single sources of funding, poor management, and insufficient incentives for stakeholders (Zhou et al. 2013). China's current ecological and environmental policies generally show characteristics such as direct government control (Xia 2000: 113–129) and crisis response (Xun and Bao 2007), balance between ecological environmental protection and economic development and equal emphasis on pollution prevention and ecological protection (Wen 2010: 24–27).

Since the Reform and Opening-up, governments at all levels in China have issued a number of policies and regulations for rural ecological protection. However, a considerable number of policies and regulations are geared around crisis response or ecological environmental protection and economic development balance, and there remains a clear gap compared with the actual needs of rural ecological environmental protection. There are many problems in rural ecological protection policies and regulations, such as fragmentation, lagging content, and insufficient strength. These include many legal gaps in natural resources and biodiversity conservation, as well as the lack of existing procedural laws. This is not conducive to ecological environment law enforcement as there are no specific legal norms, and legal responsibilities are unclear (Xu 2004). In the system of rural ecological environment management, it is essential for ecological environment management agencies to exercise unified and coordinated authority. The gradual improvement of the rural ecological environment monitoring system is imperative. Furthermore, there is a shortage of research and development efforts for environmentally friendly technologies suitable for rural areas within the rural ecological environment technology system (Li 2012: 126–127).

Moreover, compared with urban ecological environmental protection, the foundation of ecological protection in rural areas in China is weak. Under the background of the dual structure of urban and rural economy and society, there is a clear disparity between rural and urban areas, and there are clear differences in ecological and environmental policy design and policy support. Additionally, the rural ecological environmental protection policy and the urban ecological environmental protection policy generally present a dual ecological environment policy structure.

While the legislative system for urban ecological environmental protection is comprehensive, rural ecological environment legislation remains inadequate (Jinhai 2008: 84).

6.3.2 Overlaps and Contradictions Between Policies

China's current rural ecological environmental protection system not only suffers from imperfection and deficiencies in the system, but there are also major overlaps and conflicts between existing systems. One example is the convergence of the Water Law of the PRC and the Mineral Resources Law of the PRC.

Both laws stipulate that groundwater is within the scope of their definition. According to the Water Law of the PRC: "The water administrative department of the State Council is responsible for the unified management and supervision of water resources nationwide, including the management of surface water and groundwater resources" (Article 12). According to the Mineral Resources Law of the PRC, "The geological and mineral resources department of the State Council is responsible for the supervision and management of mineral resource exploration and mining nationwide" (Article 11). In this regard, the State Council's geology and mineral resources department is also the department in charge of supervising and managing groundwater resources. This inevitably causes management overlap. More importantly, according to the provisions of the Water Law of the PRC, the extraction of groundwater is subject to water resource fees (Article 48). Likewise, according to the Mineral Resources Law of the PRC, mineral resource compensation fees are also required for groundwater extraction (Article 5). This has led to the phenomenon of duplicate fees being charged by the two sectors. In reality, the two departments are at odds with each other regarding management, and the two departments compete with each other when charging fees. This leaves resource users even more confused and at a loss. In addition, the New Five-Point Systems implemented after 1989 (namely, the Responsibility System for Ecological Environmental Protection Goals, the Quantitative Assessment System for Comprehensive Improvement of the Urban Ecological Environment, the Pollution Discharge Permit System, the Centralized Pollution Control System, and the Time-Limited Treatment System) overlap and compete with the previously implemented "Three Old Systems" and still continue. There are also obvious overlaps and contradictions within the "Three Simultaneous" systems, the Pollution Discharge Fee System, and the Ecological Environmental Impact Assessment System. This leads to difficulties in relevant departments' implementation of policies. Therefore, the inconsistency of various ecological environmental protection systems themselves further limits their binding force on people's behavior (Hong 2001: 189–190).

The rural ecological environment system is organically inter-linked. If it is artificially divided into land, agriculture and animal husbandry, minerals, water conservancy and many other industrial departments and administrative divisions in the system design, then the primary function of these industrial and administrative departments would not be to protect ecological environmental resources. Rather, it would be to create economic benefits through the development and utilization of natural resources. This would inevitably lead to confusion in the management system, and weaken the executive power of ecological environmental protection administration (Xiao et al. 2010: 192). As a result, rural ecological destruction persists.

6.3.3 The Consequences of Ecological Destruction to "Local and Informal Policies"

The term "Local and informal environmental policies" encompasses not only official documents and regulations issued by local governments, but also the verbal commitments and instructions of local leaders, as well as unspoken practical rules among stakeholders (Geng and Chen 2013).

Many localities in China have varying degrees of local environmental protection policies. Leaders of some localities and departments such as Hunan Province, Fujian Province, and Liaoning Province emphasize economic development and despise ecological environmental protection, while other localities have formulated local policies that contradict laws and regulations on ecological environmental protection (Hao 2017). Preliminary statistical findings from 2007 in Guangdong Province reveal the presence of over 30 unofficial environmental policies, concentrated at both extremities of the Eastern and Western Regions, as well as in economically underdeveloped counties and cities in the northern mountainous areas of Guangdong.[20] Hubei Province had 79 environmental

[20] Environmentally detrimental "backyard policies" are being eliminated. (2007-09-27) [2019-07-22].

http://news.sina.com.cn/c/2007-09-27/052612642272s.shtml.

local policy documents before 2008.[21] In addition, Hebei, Shandong, Xinjiang, Inner Mongolia, Yunnan, Henan, Sichuan, Fujian, Jiangxi, Guangxi, Shaanxi, Shanxi, Jiangsu, and several other jurisdictions have enacted their own local environmental protection policies.

The implementation of local environmental protection policies in various parts of China has led to environmental protection departments' void of ecological and environmental law enforcement power (Geng and Chen 2013). Meanwhile, departmental protectionism and local protectionism have become significant obstacles to ecological and environmental law enforcement (Hong 2001: 189). Local governments' focus on economic benefits has led to serious local protectionism, and the rule of man has become more important than the rule of law. This has interfered with the law enforcement of ecological and environmental law enforcement departments, weakening environmental protection law enforcement (Jiao 2011). Local environmental protection policies often deviate from the set goals of the central rural ecological protection policies in the process of local implementation, causing serious environmental pollution and ecological destruction to rural areas. In a study of the policy practice of returning farmland to forest in a county in Southern Shaanxi, Ma Juan found that the central and local governments have different understandings of ecological protection and construction; the state wants ecological protection, while the local government wants development. In the process of policy implementation, the central government's ecological protection policies often deviate from the original goals (Ma 2012).

6.3.4 Low Public Participation in the Policy Implementation Process

From the government's perspective, the power of non-governmental environmental protection is mainly reflected on two levels: groups and the public. Non-governmental environmental protection power is primarily a force at the social level. Its foundation is public environmental awareness and environmental protection behavior. Its cohesion mechanism is non-governmental environmental protection organizations, communities, and mass media. Its role is to urge and assist the government in

[21] Hubei Province is phasing out and rescinding localized environmental protection policies to improve the regulatory framework for enforcing environmental protection. (2007-11-15) [2019-07-22]. http://www.124.gov.cn/2007-11/15/cms501126article.shtml.

promoting ecological environmental protection. In addition, enterprises, especially environmental protection enterprises, should also be regarded as an important part of the private sector's environmental protection force (Hong et al. 2007: 12–14). In the implementation process of China's rural ecological protection policies, the participation of private environmental protection forces is limited. In many localities, the public's basic right to know about environmental pollution and the right to claim infringement are ignored. There is also a lack of channels and processes to participate in and promote environmental protection, and therefore the public cannot effectively supervise it. As a result, the public wants to participate, but cannot.[22] Scholars have analyzed the following reasons why the Chinese public pays attention to, but does not participate in, the process of ecological and environmental protection: the existing institutional factors fail to motivate positive group behavior, and the herd mentality causes the public to just tag along. The participatory concept of environmental protection is only a recent phenomenon, and the public's understanding of environmental protection is lacking (Wang 2008: 115–119).

Surveys and studies have found that urban residents in China have significantly more environmental protection knowledge and awareness of ecological and environmental problems than do rural residents (China Environmental Protection Foundation 1998: 71–73). However, they are more concerned about the ecological and environmental protection of the urban areas around them. In terms of the awareness of ecological environmental problems, the respondents are mainly concerned about various ecological environmental problems close to them, such as the air, water, noise, industrial waste, domestic waste, food, and other forms of pollution. Meanwhile, between 20 and 30% of the respondents do not know about ecological environmental problems that are distant from their daily lives (Hong 2005). Under the dual social structure of urban and rural areas, the elites in the countryside do their best to migrate to the cities, resulting in lower quality of rural employees, weakening their understanding of the ecological environment. This results in poor ecological environmental protection awareness (Hong and Ma 2004). In the vast

[22] Breaking down environmental "local policies" requires upholding the people's right to a clean environment. (2007-01-15) [2019-07-22]. http://news.sohu.com/20070115/n247617039.shtml.

rural areas, farmers participate in and influence the ecological and environmental policy process primarily through reporting and complaints, petitions, villagers' meetings and villagers' forums (Tan 2012). However, due to farmers' insufficient understanding of ecological protection issues, weak laws, and regulations on rural ecological protection, and the lack of specific operational regulations for public participation, farmers struggle to participate in rural ecological protection (Tan 2012).

Moreover, in some rural areas of China, when economic interests conflict with ecological interests, farmers will first choose economic over ecological interests as long as the ecological interests cause no direct harm to local farmers (Jin 2008: 148). Behind ecological and environmental problems lies the difficult question of how to choose between environmental protection and livelihood, which is particularly widespread in underdeveloped rural areas in China (Li 2018). China's ecological protection policies are strict and specific. There is a lack of an intermediary mechanism between the government and herders, leading to challenges in translating straightforward and consistent ecological policies into practical measures that are suitable for specific local conditions. As a result, herders in the northern grasslands of Inner Mongolia frequently express dissatisfaction with impractical ecological protection policies. Under a uniform ecological protection policy, the interests of local herders are inadequately represented, leading them to resort to widespread violations as a means of opposing ecological protection measures (Wang 2009: 24). Based on the practical case of a national and universal policy of returning farmland to forest, research has shown that farmers' ecological wisdom and local knowledge based on their own survival logic helped a policy evolve step-by-step. The final result was that the policy had facilitated the unique process of "The policy of reforestation is still being implemented, despite ongoing agricultural activities". This shows that the relationship between the implementation of ecological environment policies and local daily production and life practices directly determines the effect of ecological protection policy implementation. Standardized knowledge must return to diversified local knowledge and be embedded in daily production and life practices in order to be truly recognized and implemented by implementers (Zhong 2014).

China's non-governmental environmental protection organizations are concentrated in Beijing, Shanghai, Tianjin, Hunan, Hubei, Sichuan, Chongqing, Yunnan, and Inner Mongolia. There are less in other regions, and even fewer still in the vast rural areas. Some rural areas have no non-governmental environmental protection organizations at all. As far as the role of non-governmental environmental protection organizations is concerned, China's current environmental protection organizations are still in their infancy in terms of number, organizational construction, and business development, and are far from fulfilling their responsibilities and obligations (Wang 2008: 166). Moreover, non-governmental environmental organizations operate in a way that maintains close relationships with formal state agencies, and few environmental NGOs target industrial pollution. Additionally, only a few NGOs are involved in direct action against corporate pollution or government negligence, or in helping the public undertake such actions (He et al. 2010: 231–232).

6.4 Future Prospects for Rural Ecological Conservation

In view of the grim reality of China's rural ecological destruction, problems remain in rural ecological protection policies themselves, as well as in the actual implementation process. Thus, many scholars and other people of insight have offered suggestions to explore methods of rural ecological protection in China. Thus, the following countermeasures and suggestions are crucial: regular monitoring and evaluation of rural ecological conditions, further improvement of the rural ecological protection policy system, promotion of regional management and inter-governmental cooperation in rural ecological protection, more participation from non-governmental environmental protection forces in rural ecological protection, and gradual integration of urban and rural ecological environmental protection.

6.4.1 Regular Monitoring and Assessment of Rural Ecological Conditions

Developed Western countries such as the United States and the Netherlands emphasize regular monitoring and evaluation of rural ecological conditions. This is one area in rural ecological protection in which they have been successful. The United States has been consistently monitoring and evaluating agricultural NSP since 1972, leading to the implementation of a series of effective control programs for managing rural ecological systems (Liang 2009). The Netherlands also emphasizes regular monitoring and assessment of the rural ecological environment, and has developed a system to measure inorganic material at the farm-level and a total balance method to estimate nitrate loss per farm per year. On this basis, it formulates corresponding ecological environment management policies (Liang 2009).

Regarding ecological destruction in China's rural areas, a considerable number of members of the public, including the vast number of farmers, and government departments at all levels are aware of the problem's seriousness. However, there has been a lack of complete information and monitoring data to gauge the problem's severity. A survey of rural environmental conditions in Wengyuan County, Shaoguan City, Guangdong Province, showed that local farmers had repeatedly asked the government for information and monitoring data on local environmental conditions. However, the town, county and municipal governments could not provide the exact information on the quality of the ecological environment that local farmers needed, as no institutions have comprehensive understandings of the rural ecological environment (Li et al. 2009: 5). Therefore, China should aggregate the actual data from rural areas and learn from the successful rural ecological protection experience of developed Western countries. Additionally, we should gradually increase the deployment of rural ecological environment monitoring networks, and regular monitoring and assessment of rural ecological conditions should be conducted at least every two years. This would provide a scientific decision-making basis for rural ecological protection legislation, ecological protection planning and ecological environmental governance.

First, China should monitor and evaluate agricultural NSP in key river basins at least every two years. China has 10 key river basins—the Songhua River, the Huaihe River, the Haihe River, the Liaohe River, the middle and upper reaches of the Yellow River, Taihu Lake, Chaohu Lake, Dianchi Lake, the Three Gorges Reservoir Area and its upper reaches, and the Danjiangkou Reservoir Area and its upper reaches. These involve a total of 23 provinces, autonomous regions, and municipalities directly under the Central Government.[23] In April 2012, the State Council approved the Plan for the Prevention and Control of Water Pollution in Key River Basins (2011–2015). It emphasized that the plan is an important basis for the prevention and alleviation of water pollution and

[23] See the Ministry of Environmental Protection, the National Development and Reform Commission, the Ministry of Finance, and the Ministry of Water Resources for the Prevention and Control of Water Pollution in Key River Basins (2011–2015).

the management of the ecological environment in key river basins. Taking this as an opportunity, China should implement regular monitoring and assessment of agricultural NSP in key river basins in a timely manner, and implement corresponding agricultural NSP alleviation plans on this basis.

Second, China should monitor and evaluate the pollution status of rural industries in key areas at least once every two years. China's key areas include Beijing, Tianjin, Hebei Province, the Yangtze River Delta, the Pearl River Delta, as well as central Liaoning Province, Shandong Province, Wuhan City and its surroundings, Changsha City, Zhuzhou City, Xiangtan City, Chongqing City, Chengdu City, Eastern Fujian, the north-central part of Shanxi Province, Guanzhong in Shaanxi Province, Gansu Province, Ningxia Hui Autonomous Region, and the Urumqi Urban Agglomeration in Xinjiang Uygur Autonomous Region. This would involve a total of 19 provinces, autonomous regions, and municipalities directly under the Central Government.[24] China should also implement regular monitoring and assessment of rural industrial pollution in key areas in a timely manner, as well as effective rural industrial pollution management plans on this basis.

Third, China should monitor and evaluate rural ecological destruction in the Western Region at least once every two years. China's Western Region includes 12 provinces, autonomous regions, and municipalities: Chongqing City, Sichuan Province, Guizhou Province, Yunnan Province, Guangxi Zhuang Autonomous Region, Shaanxi Province, Gansu Province, Qinghai Province, Ningxia Hui Autonomous Region, Tibet Autonomous Region, Xinjiang Uygur Autonomous Region, and Inner Mongolia Autonomous Region. As the ecological environment in the Western Region is fragile, it is all the more important for China to conduct regular monitoring and assessment of rural ecological destruction there, so as to provide a solid basis for decision-making on ecological environmental protection and governance in the western rural areas.

Finally, in the era of big data, China should establish a sharing platform for monitoring data for rural ecological environmental conditions, and provide sufficient information support on rural ecological environmental

[24] See the Ministry of Environmental Protection, the National Development and Reform Commission, and the Ministry of Finance for the Twelfth Five-Year Plan for the Prevention and Control of Air Pollution in Key Areas.

conditions for government departments at all levels, so as to facilitate more scientific and reasonable decision-making on rural ecological protection.

6.4.2 Further Improving the Policy System for Rural Ecological Protection

Some developed countries, such as the United States, Japan, and the Netherlands, have gradually improved the policy system for rural ecological protection. However, China's current rural ecological protection policy system is neither sound nor complete, and there are points of intersection and contradictions between rural ecological protection policies. Therefore, China needs to further improve its rural ecological protection policy system in light of the actual conditions in rural areas.

First, China should gradually improve the legal and regulatory system for rural ecological protection. Although China has formulated and implemented a number of laws and regulations on ecological environmental protection, many problems remain. These include difficulties in implementing laws and regulations, and the lack of positive interaction between development planning and law enforcement protection (Zhang 2019). Moreover, due to gaps in relevant legislation, rural soil pollution, intensive livestock and poultry breeding pollution, and laissez-faire use and management of chemical fertilizers, pesticides and agricultural films, considerable damage has been caused to China's rural ecological environment (Jinhai 2008: 84–85). Therefore, China should gradually improve its legal and regulatory system, including the entry threshold for the ecological environment, agricultural ecological compensation, agricultural clean production, livestock and poultry breeding pollution prevention and mitigation, rural NSP prevention and alleviation, and rural industrial pollution prevention and alleviation. It should also continue to supplement and revise according to changes in the rural economy, as well as changes to social and ecological conditions.

Second, China should gradually coordinate the exercise of the functions and powers of rural ecological protection management agencies. Exercising the functions and powers of rural ecological protection management institutions should solve the problem of "who will manage and how to manage rural ecological protection". At present, in addition to the Ministry of Ecology and Environment, the National Development and Reform Commission, the Ministry of Agriculture and Rural Affairs, the Forestry Bureau, the Ministry of Water Resources, the Ministry of Natural Resources, and the Ministry of Housing and Urban–Rural Development have also undertaken the functions of rural ecological protection and management. Therefore, China should gradually coordinate the exercise of the functions and powers of rural ecological protection management institutions to ensure the coordination, systematization, and sustainability of rural ecological protection work.

Third, China should gradually improve the rural environmental investment system. For a long time, rural areas have received scant funds for building capacity for pollution mitigation and ecological environment management from financial channels. Additionally, it has been difficult to apply for special treatment pollution discharge fees (Su 2006). Most of China's investment in pollution prevention and alleviation has been invested in industry and cities (Pan 2004). Therefore, China should gradually increase the percentage and intensity of government financial investment in rural ecological protection. At the same time, China should attract social funds to invest in rural ecological protection. It should also encourage organizations and individuals to research ways and methods of investing social funds in rural environmental protection, and gradually improve the investment input, benefit sharing, exit mechanism and supporting policies of social funds in rural environmental protection (Li 2012: 173–174).

Fourth, China should gradually improve its rural environmental technology system. Promoting rural ecological protection with scientific and technological innovation is also an important aspect of improving the rural ecological protection policy system. China should accelerate research and development of applicable technologies for rural environmental protection, and promote the demonstration and promotion of applicable technologies for rural environmental protection (Li 2012: 174–175). China should be cautiously optimistic, while promoting technological innovation and transformation, gradually improving the evaluation and management system for technology, and preventing the negative consequences of technology (Hong 2001: 177–178).

Fifth, China should also introduce a rural ecological protection policy evaluation model. In the process of implementing rural ecological protection policies, the effect of implementation is the core of rural ecological protection policies. Some scholars have noted that China's current environmental policy has not been formulated in a timely manner after tracking feedback to get accurate information on the effect of policy implementation. Thus, the government cannot adjust the ecological and environmental policy in a timely manner, and enterprises cannot adapt to the requirements of the ecological and environmental policy in a short period of time. If evaluation models are introduced, these problems can be solved (Zhou et al. 2013). Scholars have established a comprehensive evaluation model system for ecological and environmental policies, which provides an evaluation method for the comprehensive evaluation of various effects and interactions of ecological and environmental policies (Jiang 2006).

6.4.3 *Promoting Regional Management and Inter-Government Cooperation in Rural Ecological Protection*

Due to the severity and complexity of China's rural ecological destruction, and the characteristics of cross-regional and cross-river basins, the crisis has exceeded the control of individual local governments. This is exacerbated by the tendency toward fragmentation among local government ecological environment management departments and local governments in the management of river basins and regional ecological environments. Thus, regional management and inter-government cooperation on rural ecological protection in China are becoming increasingly important.

First, China should gradually establish regional ecological environment administrative institutions to unify ecological environment management rights. In other countries, there are two general types of cross-regional ecological environment management institutions: the first is regional ecological environment management institutions, represented by the United States and Canada; the second is river basin ecological environment management institutions, represented by New Zealand, France, and Canada (Xiao et al. 2010: 201). In fact, the reform of China's regional ecological and environmental administrative institutions has led to the enactment of several useful changes. At the national level, there is the river basin management model established by the Water Law of the PRC, and the legal status of seven river basin water administrative agencies, including the Yangtze River Water Conservancy Commission. These have been clarified since the passage of the new water law. The responsibilities of river basin management agencies have been clarified, and the status of water administrative law enforcement subjects has been strengthened. At the local level, Zhejiang Province and Jilin Province have both tried to divide inter-provincial ecological regions and establish ecological construction demonstration zones in accordance with the national *Measures for the Evaluation and Management of Ecological Function Reserves and Interim Regulations for Ecological Function Zones*. China can learn from these experiences when establishing regional ecological and environmental administrative institutions (Zhan and Zhao 2009). Some scholars have proposed a plan for establishing regional ecological and environmental administrative institutions, which includes 5 national bureaus (Bohai Bureau, Taihu Bureau, Pearl River Delta, Three Gorges Bureau, and Sanjiangyuan District) and 12 provincial-level sub-bureaus, (Changzhutan Branch, Zhongyuan Branch, Jianghan Branch, Harbin Branch, Liaoshen Bureau, Guanzhong Bureau, Dianchi Bureau, Beibuwan Branch, Guiyang Bureau, Baotou Bureau, Urumqi Bureau, Heihe Branch). The program not only considers the urgency of controlling environmental pollution and curbing ecological degradation in different regions, but also accounts for future development trends (Zhou Chenghu et al. 2008).

Second, China should promote the coordination and cooperation of local governments to protect the rural ecological environment. Local governments must work together to clean up and break down the local policies that hinder environmental protection. It is encouraging that the local governments have begun to seek cooperation in ecological environmental management. In November 2003, the Water Conservancy Departments of eight provinces and autonomous regions in the Haihe River Basin, including Tianjin, Beijing, Hebei, Shanxi, Shandong, Henan, Inner Mongolia, and Liaoning, signed the *Declaration on Water Collaboration in the Haihe River Basin*. In December 2003, four provinces and autonomous regions, Jilin, Liaoning, Heilongjiang, and Inner Mongolia joined forces to manage pollution in the Songhua-Liao River basin. Scholars have described the current mechanism of ecological and environmental cooperation and governance among local governments in China as such: first, much of consensus on local intergovernmental ecological and environmental cooperation is guaranteed by leaders' commitments, and lacks legal effectiveness and stability; second, the degree of institutionalization of cooperative action is low, basically staying at the level of various meetings, taking the form of collective consultation; third, due to the imbalance in the economic and social development of various participants, there are great differences in the goals of ecological environmental protection; fourth, the model of local intergovernmental relations that plays a substantial role in ecological environment governance, especially river basin governance, is mainly a vertical operation mechanism (Yang and Sun 2009). In view of the problems in the ecological environment cooperation mechanism of local governments, the following improvement measures could be taken: first, improve the legal system of local governments' ecological environment governance cooperation; second, establish cooperative administration and change the relationship mode between local governments; third, transform the functions of local governments and create appropriate conditions for cooperative administration (Yang and Sun 2009).

6.4.4 Promoting the Non-Governmental Environmental Protection Forces' Participation in Rural Ecological Protection

In the process of modernization, developed countries have also faced serious ecological and environmental problems. Their environmental practices teach us that we must mobilize the effective participation of the general public through organizational innovation. The lessons of the deterioration of the ecological environment in developing countries tell us that ecological environmental protection cannot rely solely on elites and experts, and it is crucial that ordinary people participate in it in an appropriate way (Hong 2001: 246–249). Therefore, there is an urgent need to increase the participation of civil environmental protection forces in rural ecological protection.

First, China should further improve the mechanism for public participation in rural ecological protection. The establishment and improvement of mechanisms for public participation in rural ecological protection means that the government should take appropriate measures to enable the public to understand the ecological conditions in rural areas, and to have the right and ability to participate in rural ecological protection work. One of the measures is to cultivate public awareness of the ecological environment. On the basis of further promoting economic development and improving people's standards of living, it is necessary to further strengthen ecological and environmental education, and to disseminate and popularize ecological and environmental information (Hong et al. 2007: 71). The second measure is to guarantee the public's right to know about ecological conditions in rural areas. The government should establish a comprehensive system to ensure public access to information on rural ecological conditions, and develop an effective monitoring mechanism for the agricultural sector through transparent disclosure of ecological data. The third measure is to improve the mechanism for expressing farmers' ecological and environmental appeals. At present, in the face of rural environmental pollution and ecological destruction, the expression mechanism of China's farmers' ecological and environmental demands has many faults. As such, it is necessary to establish a "local government-social organizations-media-farmers" linkage mechanism to meet and protect farmers' ecological and environmental demands and wishes. The fourth measure is that the government should specify the channels and procedures for public participation in rural ecological protection in the basic regulations on ecology and the environment.

Second, China should give full allowance to the role of rural environmental protection organizations. The development of rural environmental protection organizations in China plays a crucial role in promoting rural ecological protection. Regarding the healthy development of rural ecological protection in China, the government should increase financial support for non-governmental environmental protection forces, adjust and improve relevant laws and regulations, encourage and cultivate non-governmental environmental protection organizations, and open up new paths for the growth and expansion of non-governmental environmental protection forces. A broader institutional space would provide various convenient conditions for the public to participate in ecological and environmental protection (Hong et al. 2007: 25–27). In contemporary rural communities, where farmers are increasingly isolated, the lack of farmer-organization has become more conspicuous. Therefore, local governments should also have a long-term vision, and allow, encourage, and support the development of rural ecological protection self-organization, so as to strengthen the non-governmental environmental protection power of rural society. This can also cut costs for local governments in rural ecological environment management and governance. At the same time, rural environmental protection organizations should improve their promotion and education capabilities, social supervision capabilities, and policy advocacy capabilities to participate in rural ecological protection. In terms of promotion and education, China should utilize radio, film, television, books, newspapers and periodicals, slides, the Internet, and other media to publicize and popularize rural ecological and environmental protection information and raise farmers' awareness of ecological and environmental protection, the legal system and society. In terms of social supervision, rural ecological protection supervision can be implemented in various forms such as plan supervision, process supervision, behavior supervision, and end-of-line supervision. In terms of policy advocacy, it is possible to influence the government's rural ecological protection decision-making by becoming involved in major rural environmental pollution and ecological destruction incidents, implementing collective actions, and mobilizing the media.

Finally, China should give full allowance to communities' role in rural ecological protection. The community is an important mechanism and carrier for rallying civil environmental protection forces, and it has unique advantages in promoting ecological environmental protection and governance (Hong et al. 2007: 100). In the face of the destruction of ecological and environmental resources in communities and the decline of modern communities, there are several feasible options for community participation in ecological and environmental protection and governance. The first option is to retreat from a radical view of the community to a moderate view of the community, trusting in community members' ability to negotiate and cooperate, and to work together to create new systems to pursue their own interests. The second option is community building, which involves a whole process, from empowering community members to building community organizations, to building a community culture. The third option is to build alliances between the community and other governance subjects, including the border with the government and the integration of private property rights. The fourth option involves venturing into domains increasingly intertwined with environmental pollution, ecological degradation, and related issues. The fifth option is that the construction of the community ecological environment should shift the environmental protection function from the government department to the community itself (Hong et al. 2007: 130–146).

6.4.5 *Integrating Urban and Rural Ecological Environmental Protection*

The integration of urban and rural ecological environment protection refers to the gradual change in the urban-centered approach which has long persisted in China's ecological environment protection, in which equal attention is given to ecological environment protection in both urban and rural areas. The integration of urban and rural ecological environment protection is a prerequisite for adhering to Xi Jinping's

Thought of Socialism with Chinese Characteristics in the New Era, Implementing the Scientific Outlook on Development, Practicing the Concept of Green Development, Realizing Social Harmony Between Urban and Rural Areas, and Promoting the Construction of New Towns and Cities. There is also a practical need to manage the rural ecological environment and promote its protection. Thus, the integration of urban and rural ecological environment protection may be the ultimate means to rural ecological protection.

First, China should clarify the goal of integrating urban and rural ecological environmental protection. The direct goal of the overall planning or the integration of urban and rural ecological environmental protection is the coordinated development of economic, social and ecological environmental protection in urban and rural areas. Realizing the coordinated development of urban pollution management and rural ecological environmental protection is also crucial (Song and Jin 2007). The integration of urban and rural ecological environmental protection requires comprehensive consideration of urban and rural areas, urban residents and rural residents, urban economic and social development, and rural economic and social development. In doing so, urban and rural ecological environmental protection should be viewed holistically.

Second, China should rationally plan an implementation strategy for the integration of urban and rural ecological and environmental protection. Regarding rural ecological protection, there are five main points in the implementation strategy for the integration of urban and rural ecological protection. Point No. 1 is to implement an ecological environment management policy that favors, or even prioritizes, rural ecological environment protection. Point No. 2 is the establishment of a mechanism of compensation from the city to the countryside, from industry to agriculture, and from the economy to the ecological environment. Point No. 3 is to transplant successful urban ecological and environmental management systems to rural areas. Point No. 4 is to coordinate the layout of industrial development in urban and rural areas, raise the threshold of access to environmental protection in rural areas, and prohibit the transfer of urban industrial pollution to rural areas. Point No. 5 is to delimit and improve the red line of ecological protection and scientifically implement a system of main function zones for ecological protection (Zhu 2005).

Third, China should clarify the path to the integration of urban and rural ecological environmental protection. The first path is to ensure legislation, strengthen the legal construction of urban and rural ecological environmental protection, and gradually change the status quo of the ecological and environmental legal system. As of this writing, this system emphasizes cities over rural areas, and heavy industry over agriculture. The second path is to ensure awareness, and strengthen the overall publicity of (and education on) urban and rural ecological environmental protection. The third path is to guarantee policy, promoting the integration of urban and rural ecological environment policies and economic policies. The fourth path is to provide technical support for management, and establish a coordination mechanism and monitoring and early warning system for the urban and rural ecological environment. The fifth path is public protection, and improving the public participation system for the overall planning of urban and rural ecological environmental protection. The sixth path is the industrial guarantee, and the implementation of the circular economy development model based on the concept of eco-industry (Sun 2009).

Finally, we also need to clarify that if China wants to realize the integration of urban and rural ecological environmental protection, it must also realize urban and rural political, economic and social integration, and expand the freedoms of the vast agrarian population. Therefore, protecting the rural ecological environment should be a proposition which benefits farmers' own interests, so that farmers have the ability to take responsibility. Only in this way will there be a solid foundation and driving force for rural ecological environmental protection (Jinhai 2008: 160–167).

PART II

Environmental Concern and Behavioral Tendencies

This section includes analysis of the changes in public environmental concernsandbehavioral tendencies on the basis of China's environmental problems and economic and social development. We also discuss urban-rural and generational differences in public environmental concerns and behaviors, and analyze the impact of economic growth on public environmental concerns and behaviors. Additionally, we explore the correlation between air pollution and residents' intention to relocate in the form of special topic-based data from a city survey. The focus of this research is the greening of Chinese society in terms of individual public awareness and behavior.

CHAPTER 7

Urban–Rural Differences in Environmental Concern

Fan Yechao and Hong Dayong

The urban vs. rural contrast has long played an important role in sociological analyses and research on inequality. Existing studies have shown that there are significant differences between China's urban and rural residents in many social dimensions, including income, educational opportunities, social security, social relationship networks, and lifestyles (Cai and Yang 2003; Wu 2013; Fang 2007; Zhang and Ruan 1999; Zhang 2009). In recent years, more and more urban–rural comparative studies have begun to explore issues such as birth planning, trust in the government, happiness, class consciousness, and mental health (Feng and Zhang 2002; Gao and Zhai 2013; Zhang 2010; Xing 2006; Zhao 2008). Conclusions from these studies have consistently suggested that in the context of this dualistic social structure, difference in objective social attributes is a cause for

Y. Fan (✉)
Minzu University of China, Beijing, China
e-mail: fanyc@muc.edu.cn

D. Hong
Renmin University of China, Beijing, China
e-mail: hongdy@ruc.edu.cn

D. Hong and Y. Fan (eds.), *Toward a Green Society*,
https://doi.org/10.1007/978-981-96-5111-5_7

subjective attitude and conceptual differentiation between urban and rural residents.

The urban–rural divide caused by the differing structures is also reflected in environmental concerns. According to objective environmental monitoring data, both urban and rural areas in China face serious environmental problems. However, since the 1990s, urban areas have been prioritized in terms of development and modernization. In addition, the focus of environmental management and protection has long been tilted toward urban areas. Consequently, certain urban environmental issues have gradually ameliorated over time. In contrast, the environmental conditions in rural areas have deteriorated rapidly and spun out of control (Hong 2000; Wang 2010). In the context of rapid urbanization, the environmental risks faced by both urban and rural areas are still escalating, which has brought great challenges to environmental governance, while concurrently shaping urban and rural residents' views on and understanding of environmental issues. How do urban and rural residents view environmental issues? Are there significant differences in their levels of concern for the environment? What factors affect this? This chapter examines this issue using authoritative survey data.

7.1 Literature Review

7.1.1 *Scholarly Research on the Differences in Environmental Concern Between Urban and Rural Residents*

Environmental concern refers to the extent to which people are "aware of and supportive of, or willing to contribute to, the resolution of ecologically related problems" (Dunlap and Jones 2002: 485). Comparative urban–rural studies of environmental concerns first appeared in the United States in the 1960s, with an initial consensus emerging in the 1970s and 1980s. Tremblay and Dunlap (1978) reviewed 12 studies of environmental concern published between 1965 and 1972, nine of which showed that urban residents had higher levels of environmental concern. Later, Van Liere and Dunlap (1980) included urban and rural residence in the social base variables of environmental concern studies, and proposed the "residence hypothesis": urban residents are more concerned about the environment than rural residents. There are three theoretical explanations for this hypothesis, namely, differential-exposure theory, extractive-commodity theory and the theory of human-modified vs. natural environmental orientations.

According to the theory of differential-exposure, the degradation of objective environmental conditions drives public concern for the environment. Generally, urban areas face more environmental problems such as air, water, and noise pollution than rural areas. According to the theory of extractive-commodity, most occupations in rural areas (e.g., farming, forestry, mining, animal husbandry, fishing, and byproducts) are directly related to the exploitation and utilization of natural resources. Thus, rural residents engaged in the relevant occupations will acquire a utilitarian value system, i.e., viewing the natural environment as a commodity to be exploited instead of a resource to be protected. With this mindset, they will care less about environmental issues. In the context of a shared rural culture, such utilitarian values also spread to other villagers who are not engaged in natural resource utilization. In contrast, urban residents are more likely to be employed in manufacturing, services, and other fields that are not directly involved in the extraction and utilization of natural resources. Moreover, their use of the natural environment is mostly ornamental or leisure-based, so they are more likely to accept relevant environmental protection concepts (Tremblay and Dunlap 1978).

Using data from the U.S. General Social Survey (GSS) during 1973–1978, Lowe and Pinhey (1982) found that past residence is a better predictor of environmental concern than current residence, and proposed a third competing explanation for urban–rural differences in environmental concern: the theory of human-modified vs. natural environmental orientations. It holds that socialization experiences in the human-modified and natural environments lead to the difference in environmental protection attitudes between urban and rural residents. Urban residents who grew up in human-modified environments (e.g., shopping malls, asphalt highways, and theme parks) are more likely to feel that humans have an active role in the natural environment, and are more likely to accept that humans are responsible for environmental problems. In contrast, rural residents who grow up in the natural environment may believe that the environment is "God's or nature's work". Thus, they are more inclined to think that the solution to environmental problems is the evolution of the natural environmental system itself, rather than recognizing humans' role in environmental protection. This is reflected in their indifference to environmental problems.

All three theoretical explanations for the residence hypothesis are controversial (e.g., Rickson and Stabler 1985; Freudenburg 1991; Alm and Witt 1997). However, this does not affect the research conclusion that "urban residents are more concerned about the environment than rural residents" which has long been accepted by many scholars (Greenbaum 1995: 145–146). However, the emergence of several new developments in the international community since the 1990s has brought unprecedented challenges to the above theoretical explanations and the nearly mature residence hypothesis.

First, new characteristics of environmental problems have appeared, which not only increase the complexity of measuring environmental concern, but also challenge the explanatory power of differential-exposure theory. In the early 1990s, the management of traditional environmental pollution problems begun to produce some results, but at the same time, new environmental problems, such as climate change, the hole in the ozone layer, and the reduction of biodiversity began to enter the public's awareness as a result of scientific research. These problems quickly amassed widespread attention. Environmental problems took on new characteristics, such as being holistic, abstract, and global. As a direct consequence, measurement of environmental concerns has become more complex, and some simple measurement tools may no longer accurately capture the differences in attitudes between urban and rural residents toward new environmental issues such as climate change (Hong 2006). Further, direct observation and quantification of these new environmental risks is often difficult, and the differential-exposure theory's claim that "environmental quality is more often observed to be in decline" may be outdated.

Second, in some Western countries, such as the United States, the economic and social structure of rural areas has undergone immense change, and the physical boundaries between urban and rural areas are no longer clear. Moreover, the practical foundation of the earlier theories no longer apply. Industrial transformation has gradually reduced economic growth's dependence on natural resources, and new industries such as tourism have emerged in rural areas (Bennett and McBeth 1998; Jones et al. 2003). Meanwhile, along with the process of urbanization (especially reverse urbanization), the movement between urban and rural areas has accelerated, and the extension of urban amenities (e.g., highways and environmental protection facilities) has led to more and more human-modified landscapes in rural areas, such that the "environment" of the countryside is no longer a single element of the natural environment (Huddart-Kennedy et al. 2009). As a result, the premise of both extractive-commodity theory and the theory of human-modified vs. natural environmental orientations has been shaken.

Finally, differential-exposure theory, extractive-commodity theory, and the theory of human-modified vs. natural environmental orientations are each facing new challenges. At the same time, a large body of evidence suggests that differences in environmental concerns between urban and rural residents are gradually converging or dissipating. With the globalization of environmental research, the residence hypothesis has been tested and supported in a number of countries outside the United States (e.g., Berenguer et al. 2005; Huddart-Kennedy et al. 2009). However, analysis of recent cross-country survey data suggests that the hypothesis does not hold in most countries (Marquart-Pyatt 2008). In addition, since the late 1980s, in the United States, the birthplace of the residence hypothesis, scholars have noted that the impact of urban and rural residence on environmental concerns has been weakening. In addition, by the early 1990s, there was no significant difference between urban and rural areas (e.g., Mohai and Twight 1987; Xiao and Dunlap 2007). This suggests that the findings of more recent studies tend to reject the residence hypothesis. Thus, the environmental concerns of urban and rural residents may be converging on a global scale.

7.1.2 The Current Status of Chinese Scholars' Studies on the Differences in Environmental Concerns Between Urban and Rural Residents

The earliest documented surveys on environmental concerns in Mainland China can be traced back to the mid-to-late 1990s. Based on data from the National Environmental Awareness Survey (NEAAS), which was conducted in 1995 in seven cities and seven rural suburbs of China, and included 3,662 samples, Hong Dayong analyzed the characteristics of the Chinese public's concern for the environment in the early stages. Examining the responses using a percentage scale, urban residents were more concerned about the environment than were rural residents (China Environmental Protection Foundation 1998). Other analyses of the data show that rural residents were less aware of environmental issues and policies and regulations than urban residents, and only 58.2% of rural residents had even heard of environmental protection (compared to 89.0% of urban residents). Using data from a survey of 300 samples conducted in 1997, Ma and Guo (2000) compared the environmental concerns of urban and rural residents using multiple measurement indicators. They found that urban residents in general had stronger awareness of environmental protection, and were more supportive of environmental protection than their rural counterparts. Data from the 2003 China General Social Survey (CGSS), suggests that the differences in place of residence on environmental concern are even prevalent in urban areas across China. For example, residents from municipalities and provincial capitals have higher levels of environmental concern and participate in environmental protection more often than do residents of prefectural and county-level cities (Xiao et al. 2013). In addition, most results from small-scale surveys in recent years have indicated that urban residents in China are more environmentally conscious than rural residents (e.g., Gao and Meng 2011; Zhou and Zhu 2012; Yu 2014).

Although most of the data used in these studies could be considered inadequate, it can paint a rough picture that since the mid-1990s, urban residents in Mainland China have had a higher level of environmental concern than rural residents. In this regard, the residence hypothesis has been validated in Mainland China. However, scholars' comparisons of environmental concerns between urban and rural areas have been limited to descriptive analyses, and lack in-depth theoretical explanations. Considering the current differences between urban and rural areas in China, we can test several of the theoretical explanations proposed by international scholars: First, although both urban and rural areas in China face serious environmental problems, environmental problems were first concentrated in urban China, and only surfaced in rural areas later. In terms of the duration of exposure to environmental problems, it can be said that urban residents have been exposed to environmental problems longer than their rural counterparts, and the scope of environmental hazards may also be greater in urban areas. Second, as of this writing, China's farming, forestry, animal husbandry, and fisheries, and other occupations related to the exploitation of natural resources are concentrated in rural areas, and the primary sector of the working population still accounts for a large proportion of this. Third, some rural areas in Central and Western China have yet to be fully developed due to geographical constraints, and are still dominated by natural environmental elements. In addition, the strict *hukou* system has long restricted urban–rural population mobility, and the majority of Chinese residents live near where they were registered at birth and where they were socialized (Lu 2008). Therefore, the above-mentioned differential-exposure theory, extractive-commodity theory, and theory of human-modified vs. natural environmental orientations each have room to be tested in China.

7.1.3 Research on the Mechanism of Convergence of Environmental Concern Among Urban and Rural Residents

As mentioned earlier, recent studies have tended to dismiss the differences in environmental concerns between urban and rural areas. Assuming that the limitations of the measurement tools do not seriously interfere with the findings, why is there a convergence of environmental concerns between urban and rural residents? The previous analysis is suggestive of two insights. First, environmental problems have changed over time, and the objective environmental risks borne by urban and rural residents have tended to equalize. Meanwhile, how they experience and view environmental problems has become increasingly similar. Second, the social structure has leveled, and social attributes of urban and rural residents have begun to converge under the general pattern of urban–rural integration, and there has been a growing consensus on attitudes and concepts. All of the explanations above are at the macro-social level. Thus, they are abstract, and their operational value and policy significance are limited. As such, we need to explore whether there is a specific explanation mechanism. Judging by some of the existing literature (Tremblay and Dunlap 1978; Freudenburg 1991), education and mass media may be important factors underlying the convergence of the environmental concerns of urban and rural residents.

First, education (especially environmental education) can directly contribute to the expansion of public environmental knowledge. In turn, this affects environmental concern. *Agenda 21*, proposed at the 1992 Earth Summit, called for the inclusion of environmental education in the national education of all countries. The aim was to incorporate it into the general knowledge-base of the citizens of the world. Governments quickly responded to this agenda strategically and enacted relative policy. As of this writing, environmental education is a compulsory subject in education in all countries. Through standardized education, and especially environmental education, the level of public environmental awareness has generally improved. However, controversy remains over how environmental knowledge affects environmental concern. One view is that those with higher levels of environmental knowledge generally show more environmental concern (Hayes 2001). Another view is that the public cares about environmental issues because of *limited* knowledge or ignorance, and that people with more environmental knowledge are less concerned about environmental issues (Davidson and Freudenburg 1996). In any case, the significant effect of environmental knowledge on environmental concern is well-recognized in the academic community.

Second, mass media has had a significant influence on environmental concerns. This influence is reflected in the media's function as a "source of information". Through news reports, features, and other forms of presentation, the public is informed about environmental issues. Especially since the 1990s, new environmental issues such as climate change and the hole in the ozone layer have been hotspots of global media attention. Many members of the general public first became aware of these environmental terms through the media, and therefore began paying attention to these issues (Stamm et al. 2000; Hannigan 2009: 83–97). Studies have also shown that public use of the media increases environmental knowledge (Chan 1999). In this sense, although environmental issues are in constant flux, the mass media fills the public's cognitive "blind spots", thus indirectly influencing environmental concerns. The second way in which the mass media influence environmental concerns is by guiding the attitudes of the audience. However, the direction of this influence is uncertain. This is because environmental issues presented in the media come from a variety of sources, including scientists, governments, local organizations, environmental groups, and government officials. They are often presented to the public as a constructed rather than as objective facts. Therefore, individuals' attitudes are influenced by the media's divergent positions (Gooch 1996).

In China, the influence of education and mass media on public environmental concern is also noteworthy. The Chinese government responded quickly to *Agenda 21* in the early 1990s by promoting environmental education, which achieved many results and contributed to the dissemination of environmental knowledge among the Chinese public (Yan et al. 2010). A study based on CGSS2003 data found that environmental knowledge has had a significant effect on public environmental concern in urban China (Xiao et al. 2013). In addition, many scholars have noted that mass media has exerted a heavy influence on the current level of public environmental concern and participation in China. However, in terms of the direction and magnitude of the influence, the conclusions are as divergent as those of studies from other countries (Hong 2001: 148–155; Paek and Pan 2004; Gong W.J. 2013).

Based on analysis of the literature above, this chapter presents authoritative data from a national urban–rural social survey to conduct an in-depth comparative analysis of the environmental concerns of urban and rural residents in China. This is done to test the explanatory power of the relevant academic theories, and to analyze and discuss the social mechanisms behind the emergence of the differences in the environmental concerns of urban and rural residents, as well as the developmental trends behind these differences.

7.2 Research Design

7.2.1 Data Description and Analytical Strategies

The data used in this study come from the CGSS 2010 survey, which covered 31 provincial administrative units in China (excluding Hong Kong, Macao, and Taiwan). The respondents were residents aged 16 and above, and the questionnaire was completed by face-to-face interviews. The total valid CGSS2010 sample count was 11,785, and the response rate was 71.32%. The main measurement items focused on the questionnaire's environment module, which was an optional module in the CGSS2010 survey. Respondents had a 1/3 probability of correctly answering this module by random selection, and the module's valid sample count was 3,716. Although the design sample was reduced, the statistical results can also be extrapolated to the national level. Excluding the small number of missing samples, the final valid sample count for analysis was 3,679. Within the sample, 64.3% of the participants were urban and 35.7% were rural; 47.3% were male, and 52.7% were female. 8.7% were under the age of 25, 15.7% were between 25–34, 44.1% were between 35–54, and 31.5% were 55 or above. 34.1% had only a primary school education, 29.2% had attended junior high school, 20.1% had attended senior high school, and 16.6% had attended schooling above the senior high school level.

The main question in this chapter is: Are there differences between urban and rural residents' environmental concerns in contemporary

China? If so, is it true that urban residents are more concerned about the environment than rural residents? Although international comparative studies have shown that the differences in environmental concern between urban and rural residents may converge, we believe that the phenomenon described by the residence hypothesis, that is, "urban residents care more about the environment than rural residents", can still be observed in China. This is the general hypothesis of this study (Hypothesis 1). Based on the questionnaire design of the CGSS, we also operationalized the three theoretical explanations surrounding the residence hypothesis into specific hypotheses.

> Hypothesis 2: Urban dwellers who have experienced environmental hazards and have directly observed the hazards of environmental problems are likely to be more concerned about the environment than urban dwellers who have not experienced environmental hazards, and especially rural dwellers.
> Hypothesis 3: Rural residents who are currently engaged in farming are less concerned about the environment than those who are not engaged in farming, and also less concerned than urban residents.
> Hypothesis 4: Urban residents who had a non-agricultural *hukou* before the age of 16 are more likely to have lived in the city during the period of socialization than those who had an agricultural *hukou* before the age of 16 (who moved to the city after being socialized in the countryside); they are likely to be more concerned about the environment than rural dwellers.

In this study, we adopted a dual analysis strategy to test the above hypotheses. Through the ANOVA bivariate analysis strategy, we compared the clusters involved in the above hypotheses, and conducted a preliminary exploration of the relationship between the urban–rural divide and environmental concerns. Then, we compared the differences in environmental concerns among the seven urban–rural clusters involved in the four operational hypotheses to test whether the urban–rural differences they describe are significant. Next, we conducted structural equation modeling of environmental concern to observe the relationship between urban–rural and environmental concern, controlling for other socio-demographic variables and introducing environmental knowledge and media use as mediating variables.

7.2.2 Measurement of Variables

7.2.2.1 Dependent Variable

The dependent variable in this study is environmental concern. Due to the complexity of measuring environmental concern, the direction and magnitude of the differences in environmental concern that researchers had previously observed between urban and rural areas may also have been affected.[1] Currently, the most commonly used environmental concern measurement tool is the NEP scale and its revised version, proposed by Dunlap et al. (Dunlap and Van Liere 1978; Dunlap et al. 2000). In recent years, more Chinese scholars have begun to use the revised NEP scale to study the environmental concern of the Chinese public (Hong Dayong, and Xiao Chenyang 2007). To explicate the current differences in environmental concern between urban and rural residents in China, we introduced as many environmental concerns and measurement items as possible into the measurement model according to the design of the questionnaire. Using confirmatory factor analysis (CFA), we examined the reliability of the combination of measurement items under different measurement dimensions,[2] and ultimately identified five dimensions of environmental concern (Table 7.1):

1. New Ecological Paradigm (NEP) (8 items)
2. Environmental Concern Degree (3 items)
3. Environmental harm assessment (4 items)
4. Willingness-to-pay (3 items)
5. Environmental behavior (3 items)

After identifying the five dimensions of environmental concern, we developed a high-order CFA measurement model (see Fig. 7.1). This model is the measurement model in structural equation modeling. It is

[1] For example, Van Liere and Dunlap (1981) have compared urban–rural differences in environmental concern across five different measures, and found that both the level of significance and the size of the correlation coefficient are somewhat affected.

[2] Using the CFA test, we initially dropped several measures with low factor loads, including the seven negative statement items in the NEP scale. Only a portion of the data analysis results are presented, and interested readers are welcome to email the authors to view additional results. For model simplicity, no data estimates control for measurement error correlations.

Table 7.1 Environmental concern measurement items

Inclination	*Index*	*Project description*	*Measurement scale*
New Ecological Paradigm (NEP)	Item 1	The current population is approaching the limits of what the planet can sustain	1 = totally disagree ~ 5 = totally agree
	Item 2	Human destruction of nature often leads to catastrophic consequences	1 = totally disagree ~ 5 = totally agree
	Item 3	Humans are currently abusing and destroying the environment	1 = totally disagree ~ 5 = totally agree
	Item 4	Plants and animals have the same right to exist as humans	1 = totally disagree ~ 5 = totally agree
	Item 5	Human beings, despite their special abilities, are governed by the laws of nature	1 = totally disagree ~ 5 = totally agree
New Ecological Paradigm (NEP)	Item 6	The Earth is like a spaceship with very limited space and resources	1 = totally disagree ~ 5 = totally agree
	Item 7	The balance of nature is fragile and easily disturbed	1 = totally disagree ~ 5 = totally agree
	Item 8	If things continue as they are, we will soon have a serious environmental disaster	1 = totally disagree ~ 5 = totally agree
Environmental Concern Degree	Item 9	Overall concern about environmental issues	1 = not at all concerned ~ 5 = very concerned
	Item 10	Level of understanding of the causes of environmental problems	1 = not at all ~ 5 = very well
	Item 11	Level of knowledge of solutions to environmental problems	1 = not at all ~ 5 = very well

(continued)

Table 7.1 (continued)

Environmental harm assessment	Item 12	Environmental harm due to air pollution caused by vehicle emissions	1 = not harmful at all ~ 5 = extremely harmful
	Item 13	Environmental harm due to air pollution caused by industrial emissions	1 = not harmful at all ~ 5 = extremely harmful
	Item 14	Environmental harm due to pesticides and fertilizers used in agricultural production	1 = not harmful at all ~ 5 = extremely harmful
	Item 15	Environmental harm due to pollution of rivers, streams, and lakes	1 = not harmful at all ~ 5 = extremely harmful
Willingness-to-pay	Item 16	Paying higher prices for the environment	1 = not harmful at all ~ 5 = extremely harmful
	Item 17	Paying higher taxes for the environment	1 = very reluctant ~ 5 = very willing
	Item 18	Lowering standards of living for the sake of the environment	1 = very reluctant ~ 5 = very willing)
Environmental behavior	Item 19	Reducing the amount of energy or fuel consumed at home for the sake of the environment	1 = never ~ 4 = always
	Item 20	Saving or reusing water for the environment	1 = never ~ 4 = always
	Item 21	Not buying certain products in order to be environmentally friendly	1 = never ~ 4 = always

assumed that the five different dimensions are jointly loaded on a second-order factor, which is the environmental concern variable to be measured. In Fig. 7.1, the rectangles represent the 21 measurement items in the questionnaire (observable variables), which are loaded on five different dimensions of environmental concern (first-order latent variables). These are in turn loaded on the second-order latent variable of environmental concern that we intend to measure. At the same time, each observed variable has a corresponding measurement error, e1 to e21, and each first-order latent variable has a corresponding regression residual, z1 to z5.

Table 7.2 presents some of the results for estimating the model in Fig. 7.1 for urban–rural subgroups using the CGSS2010 data. According to the results of the model fitting indicators, even though the chi-square test was significant, all other fitting indicators met the acceptable criteria.[3] When we used 0.25 and 0.40 as the loading standard for the first-order and second-order factors, respectively (Raubenheimer 2004), we found that all factor loadings for each item were up to the standard. This indicates that each item has good measurement reliability. Therefore taken together, the five-dimension measurement model is supported by the data and can be used as a tool for the study of Chinese urban and rural residents' environmental concern. According to the theory of the environmental belief system, there is no significant difference between the urban and rural group comparisons in the five-dimension environmental concern measurement model. This also indicates that there is a relatively coherent and similar belief system in the way urban and rural residents view environmental issues in China.[4] This is an important premise for the urban–rural comparisons in this chapter. Imagine if urban and rural residents' perceptions of environmental issues were fragmented, or if there

[3] In the analysis of structural equation modeling, the chi-square test cannot be used as an absolute criterion for assessing the fit of the model because it is easily affected by the sample size. Some scholars believe that a baseline fit index (NFI), a comparative fit index (CFI) greater than 0.9, and a root mean square error of approximation (RMSEA) less than 0.05 are stronger evidence of a better model fit (Qiu and Lin 2008: 77–84).

[4] Belief system means "a set of views and attitudes that are mutually binding and organically related" (Converse 1964). Research on environmental concern suggests that members of the public from the same social background share a coherent environmental belief system and share many similarities in the way they understand and perceive environmental issues (Dunlap 2008; Xiao et al. 2013).

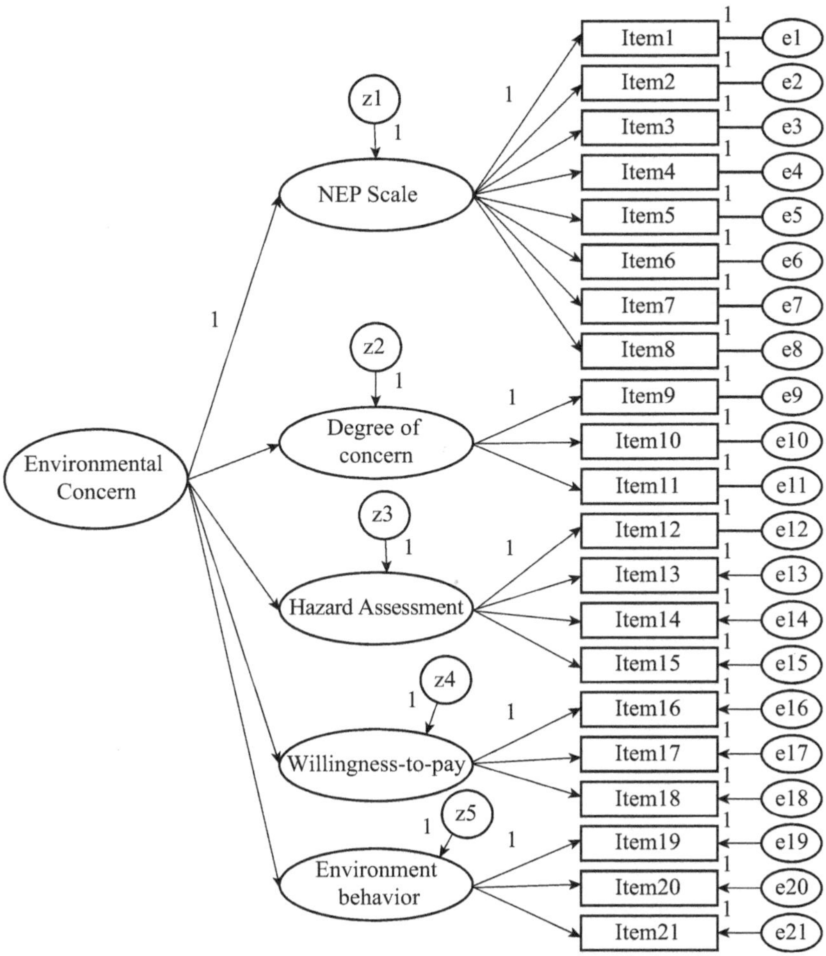

Fig. 7.1 A higher-order CFA measurement model of environmental concern

were significant differences in how they viewed environmental issues. This would limit comparisons on the same scale.

To facilitate the bivariate ANOVA analysis, five variables were obtained by adding up the scores of the items under each aspect of environmental concern, each of which is named by the aspect name. The higher the score

Table 7.2 Partial estimates of the high-level CFA measurement model of environmental concern

Variable		*NEP*		*Environmental concern degree*		*Environmental harm assessment*		*Willingness-to-pay*		*Environmental behavior*	
		Urban	*Rural*	*Urban*	*Rural*	*Urban*	*Rural*	*Urban*	*Rural*	*Urban*	*Rural*
Second load factor	EC	0.517	0.589	0.522	0.450	0.409	0.458	0.442	0.425	0.659	0.616
First order load factor	Item 1	0.361	0.351	–	–	–	–	–	–	–	–
	Item 2	0.572	0.583	–	–	–	–	–	–	–	–
	Item 3	0.546	0.476	–	–	–	–	–	–	–	–
	Item 4	0.564	0.500	–	–	–	–	–	–	–	–
	Item 5	0.578	0.454	–	–	–	–	–	–	–	–
	Item 6	0.579	0.460	–	–	–	–	–	–	–	–
	Item 7	0.585	0.562	–	–	–	–	–	–	–	–
	Item 8	0.610	0.568	–	–	–	–	–	–	–	–
	Item 9	–	–	0.389	0.316	–	–	–	–	–	–
Variable		*NEP*		*Environmental concern degree*		*Environmental harm assessment*		*WTP*		*Activism*	
		Urban	*Rural*	*Urban*	*Rural*	*Urban*	*Rural*	*Urban*	*Rural*	*Urban*	*Rural*
First order load factor	Item 10	–	–	0.827	0.695	–	–	–	–	–	–
	Item 11	–	–	0.749	0.882	–	–	–	–	–	–
	Item 12	–	–	–	–	0.712	0.740	–	–	–	–
	Item 13	–	–	–	–	0.723	0.668	–	–	–	–
	Item 14	–	–	–	–	0.600	0.498	–	–	–	–

Variable	*NEP*		*Environmental concern degree*		*Environmental harm assessment*		*WTP*		*Activism*	
	Urban	*Rural*	*Urban*	*Rural*	*Urban*	*Rural*	*Urban*	*Rural*	*Urban*	*Rural*
Item 15	–	–	–	–	0.544	0.490	–	–	–	–
Item 16	–	–	–	–	–	–	0.819	0.868	–	–
Item 17	–	–	–	–	–	–	0.853	0.918	–	–
Item 18	–	–	–	–	–	–	0.673	0.682	–	–
Item 19	–	–	–	–	–	–	–	–	0.771	0.757
Item 20	–	–	–	–	–	–	–	–	0.750	0.749
Item 21	–	–	–	–	–	–	–	–	0.710	0.671
Model Fit Indicators	χ^2/df		*p*-value		NFI		CFI		RMSEA	
	0.031		1632.527/368		0.000		0.920		0.937	

for a certain variable, the higher the level of environmental concern along the corresponding dimension (see Table 7.3).

7.2.2.2 Predictor and Control Variables

The predictor variable in this study is the type of urban–rural settlement, which is a categorical variable. In many studies conducted outside of China, urban and rural settlement types are distinguished by population. This is because the proportion of the rural population is miniscule in highly urbanized Western countries such as the United States. Obviously, this method of urban–rural delineation is not applicable to China, and therefore has rarely been used in studies conducted in China (Zhang Yulin 2013). The CGSS survey defines urban and rural residence according to the difference in whether the surveyed community is established as a neighborhood committee or a village committee. We follow this urban–rural delineation method in our study.[5] In order to clarify the relationship between urban and rural residence and environmental concerns, we introduce several control variables, including common socio-demographic variables such as gender, age, education, annual income, *hukou*, CCP affiliation, previous encounters with environmental hazards, whether or not individuals are currently working in agriculture, and *hukou* at the age of 16 (see Table 7.3 for a detailed description of the variables).

7.2.2.3 Mediating Variables

To explicate the relationship between urban–rural residential differences and environmental concerns, and especially to explore the social mechanism of urban–rural differences, we introduced two additional variables: environmental knowledge and media use.

[5] The reason for not using household registration type as a criterion for the division of urban and rural areas is based on two main considerations: first, there are many types of household registration in China as of this writing; in addition to the common non-agricultural household registration and agricultural household registration, there are also other types such as military, blue-stamp household registration, and "unregistered household". Second, and more importantly, there is a great deal of population mobility in Chinese society, and many people live away from where they are registered. Of course, in order to test the effect of household registration on environmental concerns, we also introduced this independent variable into the structural equation model, so that readers could compare the results with the type of residence according to the grassroots self-government organizations.

Table 7.3 Variables involved in the study

Variable	*Characteristic*	*Mean*			*Standard deviation*			*Clarification*
		Urban sample	*Rural sample*	*Combined*	*Urban sample*	*Rural sample*	*Combined*	
NEP	Progressive	31.15	28.70	30.27	4.590	4.376	4.664	Orientation of environmental concern I
Environmental Concern Degree	Progressive	9.13	8.06	8.75	2.281	2.312	2.348	Orientation of environmental concern II
Environmental harm assessment	Progressive	15.63	15.63	15.63	2.285	2.329	2.352	Orientation of environmental concern III
Willingness-to-pay	Progressive	9.05	8.63	8.90	2.758	2.874	2.807	Orientation of environmental concern IV
Environmental behavior	Progressive	7.15	5.70	8.75	2.292	2.164	2.348	Orientation of environmental concern V
Urban or Rural	Binary	–	–	0.64	–	–	0.479	0 = Rural, 1 = Urban
Gender	Binary	0.47	0.48	0.47	0.499	0.500	0.499	0 = Female, 1 = Male
Age	Progressive	46.54	48.74	47.33	16.038	15.055	15.728	Unit: years

(continued)

Table 7.3 (continued)

Variable	*Characteristic*	*Mean*			*Standard deviation*			*Clarification*
		Urban sample	*Rural sample*	*Combined*	*Urban sample*	*Rural sample*	*Combined*	
Education Level	Progressive	10.32	6.44	8.93	4.326	3.949	4.589	0 = no formal education; 6 = elementary school 9 = junior high school; 12 = high school (junior high school, vocational high school, technical school); 15 = vocational college; 16 = bachelor's degree; 19 = graduate school or above

Variable	*Characteristic*	*Mean*			*Standard Deviation*			*Scale*
		Urban Sample	*Rural Sample*	*Combined*	*Urban Sample*	*Rural Sample*	*Total Root*	
Annual income	Progressive	24.53	9.42	19.13	69.262	11.148	56.404	Unit: thousands of yuan
Hukou	Binary	0.77	0.06	0.51	0.424	0.243	0.500	0 = agricultural, 1 = non-agricultural
CCP Affiliation	Binary	0.17	0.07	0.13	0.374	0.251	0.339	0 = non-Party member, 1 = Party member
Encounter with environmental hazards	Binary	0.91	0.79	0.87	0.288	0.407	0.340	0 = Never encountered, 1 = encountered
Farming Status	Binary	0.05	0.56	0.23	0.214	0.497	0.422	0 = not farming, 1 = farming

(continued)

Table 7.3 (continued)

Variable	*Characteristic*	*Mean*			*Standard Deviation*			*Scale*
		Urban Sample	*Rural Sample*	*Combined*	*Urban Sample*	*Rural Sample*	*Total Root*	
Hukou at age 16	Binary	0.14	0.02	0.10	0.346	0.134	0.294	0 = agricultural, 1 = non-agricultural
Media usage	Progressive	15.37	11.08	13.84	2.652	2.538	4.546	High scores indicate frequent use of media
Environmental knowledge	Progressive	5.78	3.95	5.13	4.447	3.233	2.755	High scores indicate high levels of environmental knowledge

The 2010 CGSS survey followed the 10-item environmental knowledge scale from CGSS2003 (Hong and Xiao 2007), assigning a value of 1 to each item for correct actual awareness, and a value of 0 to each item for incorrect actual awareness or choosing "don't know". Since each item was a dichotomous variable, no validation factor analysis was conducted. However, the scale's alpha reliability coefficient was 0.805, indicating that its internal consistency was good. The continuous variable of environmental knowledge was obtained by totaling the scores of each item on the scale, with higher scores indicating higher levels of environmental knowledge (see Table 7.3).

The construct for the media use variable was based on the CGSS 2010 questionnaire which asked respondents about their use of different media over the past year, including newspapers, magazines, radio, television, the Internet (including cell phone Internet access), and customized messages on cell phones. The alpha reliability coefficient for all items on the scale was 0.668 with responses values of 1 = never, 2 = rarely, 3 = sometimes, 4 = often, and 5 = always. However, the results of the unidimensional CFA showed that the factor loading for TV use was lower when the latent media use variable was measured together with the other media use items. Further analysis reveals that the items for TV users have better discriminatory power, and the lower unidimensional factor loadings may be due to the fact that the public uses TV significantly more often than other media. Based on the face validity, we still regarded the scale items as a single-dimensional tool, and summed the scale items to obtain the media use variable. This variable is continuous, with higher scores indicating more frequent media use (see Table 7.3).

7.3 Data Analysis Results

7.3.1 Multi-faceted Comparison Environmental Concerns Between Urban and Rural Areas

Table 7.4 shows the results of bivariate ANOVA analysis on the differences between urban and rural areas and within urban and rural areas based on the CGSS2010 data. It respectively compares the scores of different urban and rural groups along five aspects of environmental concern.

As shown from the comparative results of Group 1, urban residents have higher scores than rural residents for the five environmental

Table 7.4 Multidimensional comparison of environmental concerns among urban and rural residents in different groups

Group sequence	*Comparison group*	*NEP*		*Degree of concern for environmental problems*		*Evaluation of environmental hazards*		*Willingness-to-pay*		*Environment behaviors*	
		Mean	F value	*Mean*	F value	*Mean*	F value	*Mean*	F value	*Mean*	F value
Group 1	Urban residents (n = 2,366)	31.15	249.07***	9.13	183.06***	15.63	211.60***	9.05	19.32***	7.15	351.75***
	rural residents (n = 1,313)	28.70		8.06		14.47		8.63		5.70	
Group 2	Urban residents who have experienced environmental hazards (n = 2,150)	31.30	275.99***	9.22	209.74***	15.68	223.83***	9.09	22.76***	7.18	359.63***
	Rural residents (n = 1,313)	28.70		8.06		14.47		8.63		5.70	
Group 3	Urban residents who have experienced environmental hazards (n = 2,150)	31.30	27.61***	9.22	37.07***	15.68	11.36**	9.09	6.04*	7.18	5.55*
	Urban residents who have not been exposed to environmental hazards (n = 216)	29.59		8.24		15.13		8.61		6.80	
Group 4	Rural residents who are currently engaged in agriculture (n = 736)	28.27	230.63***	7.91	163.61***	14.33	177.67***	8.60	15.23***	5.62	258.64***
	Urban residents (n = 2,366)	31.15		9.13		15.63		9.05		7.15	
Group 5	Rural residents who are currently engaged in agriculture (n = 736)	28.27	15.96***	7.91	7.65**	14.33	6.28*	8.60	0.20	5.62	2.27
	Rural residents who are not engaged in agriculture (n = 577)	29.24		8.26		14.66		8.67		5.80	
Group 6	Urban residents who had non-agricultural *hukou* before the age of 16 (n = 2,038)	31.07	222.27***	9.05	147.64***	15.62	197.71***	8.99	12.87***	7.12	317.15***
	Rural residents (n = 1,313)	28.70		8.06		14.47		8.63		5.70	
Group 7	Urban residents who had non-agricultural *hukou* before the age of 16 (n = 2,038)	31.07	4.36*	9.05	20.16***	15.62	0.01	8.99	8.23**	7.12	2.35
	Urban residents with agricultural *hukou* before the age of 16 (n = 328)	31.64		9.65		15.64		9.46		7.33	

* $p \le 0.05$, ** $p \le 0.01$, *** $p \le 0.001$

concerns: New Ecological Paradigm, degree of concern for environmental problems, evaluation of environmental hazards, willingness-to-pay, and environment behaviors, and each of these scores is statistically significant. This indicates that compared with rural residents, urban residents are more generally accepting of the pro-environmental concept embodied in the NEP, are more concerned about environmental problems, are more able to recognize the hazards of environmental problems, have stronger willingness-to-pay, and participate in more environmental protection in their daily lives. These results support Hypothesis 1 (the residence hypothesis). In short, in contemporary China, there is indeed a significant difference in the level of environmental concern between urban and rural residents, with urban residents showing more environmental concern than rural residents in many regards.

The comparison of Group 2 to Group 3 was to test Hypothesis 2. The results for Group 2 show that the level of environmental concern of urban residents who have encountered environmental hazards is significantly higher than that of rural residents. The results of Group 3 show that urban residents who have been exposed to environmental hazards are indeed more concerned about the environment than those who have not been exposed to environmental hazards. In other words, the differential-exposure theory is supported by the preliminary data.

The comparison of Group 4 to Group 5 was to test Hypothesis 3. The results for Group 4 show that rural residents who are currently engaged in agriculture have lower scores than urban residents on all five dimensions of environmental concern. The results for Group 5 show that rural residents who are currently engaged in farming have lower scores than those who are not engaged in farming along the three dimensions of NEP, degree of concern for environmental problems, and evaluation of environmental hazards. However, there is no significant difference between the two groups in terms of willingness-to-pay or environment behaviors. In other words, there is indeed a significant relationship between whether or not one works in agriculture and the level of environmental concern of urban and rural residents, but only in some aspects. Therefore, the extractive-commodity theory is partially supported at the initial stage.

The test of Hypothesis 4 can be seen in the comparative results for Groups 6 and 7. The results for Group 6 show that urban residents who had non-agricultural *hukou* before the age of 16 had significantly higher environmental concern scores than rural residents in different dimensions. However, the results for Group 7 show that the *hukou* type before the age of 16 is significantly associated only with the scores for NEP, the degree of concern for environmental problems, and the willingness-to-pay of urban residents. Meanwhile, the differences in the evaluation of environmental hazards and the daily environmental protection behaviors of urban residents are not reflected by the *hukou* type before the age of 16. Further, along the three dimensions where there are significant differences, urban residents with agricultural *hukou* before the age of 16 have significantly higher scores than those with non-agricultural *hukou* before the age of 16. This is in the opposite direction of what is described in Hypothesis 4. Therefore, it can be said that Hypothesis 4, and the theory of human-modified vs. natural environmental orientations on which it is based, are not supported by the data.

The results of the above analyses reveal that the residence hypothesis is still valid in contemporary Chinese society. Chinese urban residents' levels of environmental concern are significantly higher than those of rural residents. To further explore the causal relationship between urban–rural differences and environmental concern, we developed a structural equation model of environmental concern.

7.3.2 A Structural Equation Model of Environmental Concern

On the basis of the environmental concern measurement model (see Fig. 7.1), we used the second-order factor "environmental concern" as the dependent variable. Urban vs. rural, gender, age, education, personal annual income, *hukou* type, Party membership, past encounter with environmental hazards, current farming status, and *hukou* type at the age of 16 served as the independent variables, and environmental knowledge and media usage were the mediator variables, thus establishing a structural equation model (see Fig. 7.2). In the model, media usage has a direct effect on environmental concern and may also have an indirect effect on environmental concern through environmental knowledge. In addition, the model eliminated six pairs of correlations between independent variables that were not statistically significant.[6]

[6] The deleted relationships are urban and rural areas and gender, gender and household registration, gender and exposure to environmental hazards, gender and current farming, gender and household registration type at age 16, and age and household registration. The results of the multivariate collinearity test show that the variance inflation factor (VIF)

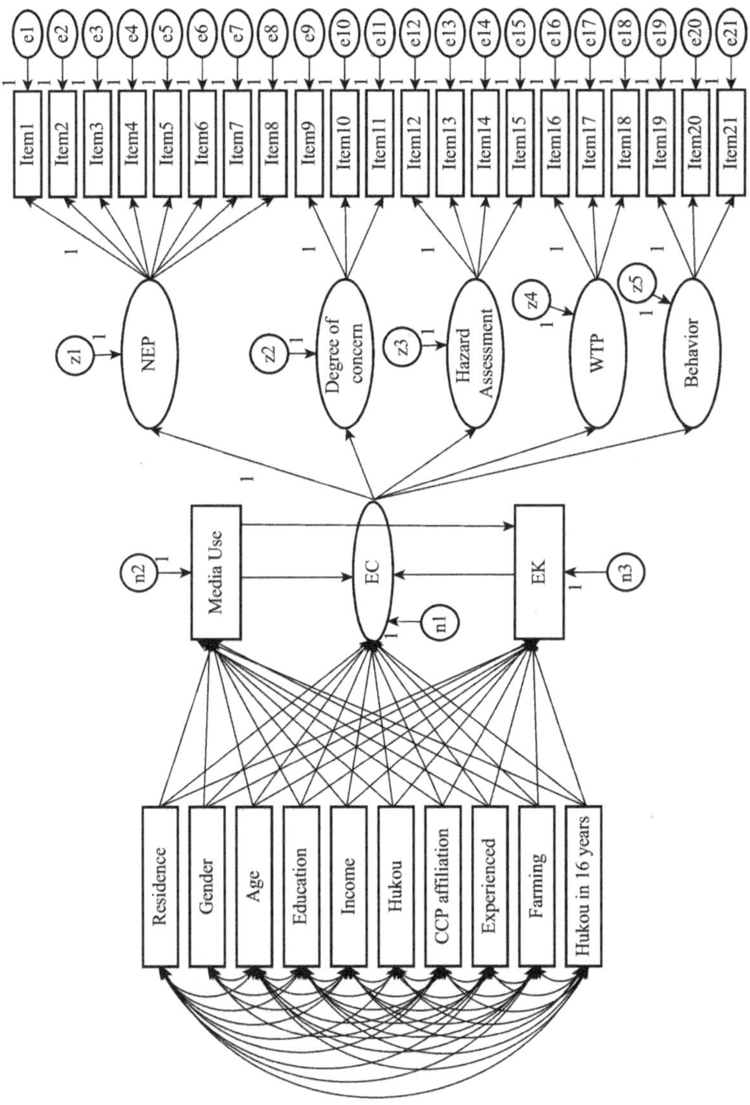

Fig. 7.2 Structural Equation Modeling of Environmental Concerns

Table 7.5 shows some of the estimated results of the model shown in Fig. 7.2. In addition to the chi-square test still being significant, all other model fitting indexes, including NFI, CFI, and RMSEA, reach acceptable standards. In summary, the model has a good fit.

First, each variable has a direct effect on environmental issues. As shown in Table 7.5, environmental concern is well explained (R^2

Table 7.5 Direct effects of variables on environmental concern, environmental knowledge, and media use and model fit

Variable	*Environmental concern*		*Environmental knowledge*		*Media use*	
	Standardized Regression Coefficient	*P-value*	*Standardized Regression Coefficient*	*P-value*	*Standardized Regression Coefficient*	*P-value*
Urban or rural	0.071	0.004	0.025	0.211	0.113	0.000
Gender	0.004	0.832	0.052	0.000	0.038	0.002
Age	0.064	0.002	−0.091	0.000	−0.091	0.000
Education	0.101	0.000	0.251	0.000	0.394	0.000
Annual income	0.013	0.452	0.012	0.378	0.027	0.027
Hukou	0.074	0.004	0.123	0.000	0.174	0.000
Party membership	0.028	0.117	0.042	0.004	0.084	0.000
Encounter with environmental hazards	0.112	0.000	0.136	0.000	0.022	0.068
Farming status	−0.021	0.307	−0.023	0.178	−0.071	0.000
Hukou at age 16	0.022	0.213	−0.062	0.000	−0.036	0.006
Media usage	0.251	0.000	0.160	0.000	–	–
Environmental knowledge	0.422	0.000	–	–	–	–
R^2	0.598		0.322		0.478	
Model Fit Indicators	χ^2/df	*P*-value	NFI	CFI	RMSEA	
	2 481.085/430	0.000	0.931	0.942	0.036	

of the respective variables ranged from 1.05 to 2.38, and the collinearity problem was not prominent.

measures 59.8%). Under the control of other variables, the following conclusions can be drawn:

1. Urban vs. rural background has a significant direct effect on environmental concern, and urban residents are more concerned about the environment than rural residents, which again verifies the hypothesis of residence.
2. Past encounters with environmental hazards have a significant direct effect on environmental concern, which supports the differential-exposure theory (Hypothesis 2).
3. Farming status and *hukou* at the age of 16 do not have a notable effect, indicating that these variables are not significant; Hypotheses 3 and 4 are rejected.
4. Media usage and environmental knowledge have significant effects on environmental concern, and they are the two variables with the greatest influence, judging from the absolute value of the regression coefficients.
5. Age, education, and *hukou* type also have significant effects on environmental concern, with older people, those with higher education levels, and those with non-agricultural *hukou* being more concerned about the environment.
6. Gender, annual income, and Party membership do not have a significant effect on environmental concern.

Secondly, Table 7.5 also shows that both environmental knowledge and media usage are also well explained by their respective variables ($R^2 =$ 32.2% and 47.8%, respectively). In the case of environmental knowledge, when controlling other independent variables, the variables that have a significant effect are gender, age, education, *hukou* type, Party membership, past encounter with environmental hazards, *hukou* type at the age of 16, and media usage; urban–rural difference, annual income, and current farming status have no significant effect. Judging from the absolute values of the standardized regression coefficients, the two independent variables that have the greatest effect on environmental knowledge are education and media usage, respectively. The higher the education level and the more use of media, the more environmental knowledge people have. These results suggest that environmental education and mass media contribute to the growth of environmental knowledge among the Chinese public. Moreover, in terms of media usage, all of the variables in the model, except for past encounter with environmental hazards, had a significant effect. While keeping other variables constant, urban residents have higher media usage than rural residents, as do males, young people, those with high education levels, those with higher annual incomes, those with urban *hukou*, Party members, those who are not currently farming, and those who had an agricultural *hukou* when they were 16 years old.

Finally, let us examine the relationship between the respective variables and environmental knowledge, media usage, and environmental concern. Since both environmental knowledge and media usage as mediating variables have significant effects on environmental concern, it can be assumed that a variable that has a significant effect on environmental knowledge or media usage would also have a significant indirect effect on environmental concern. Therefore, the indirect effect of each variable on environmental concern through environmental knowledge and media usage can be added to the direct effect to obtain the total effect of each variable on environmental concern (see Table 7.6).[7]

The mediating influence of environmental knowledge and media usage involves most of the independent variables in the model. Limited by space, we only examined the urban and rural variables. As shown in Table 7.6, there is a significant direct effect of urban vs. rural difference on environmental concern, with urban residents being more concerned about the environment than rural residents. This difference is amplified by the level of environmental knowledge and media usage, which shows that the total effect is greater than the direct effect. Therefore, environmental knowledge and media use are important mechanisms for the formation of differences in environmental concern between urban and rural residents. Urban residents have higher levels of environmental concern due to higher media usage. However, Table 7.6 also shows that although the direct effect of urban–rural difference on environmental knowledge is not significant, there is a strong indirect effect on environmental knowledge through media usage, which exacerbates the urban–rural difference in environmental concern.

[7] It should be noted that the total effect of any independent variable on environmental concern is significant if one of its direct or indirect effects on environmental concern is significant. In this regard, all independent variables in the model are significant in terms of their total effect on environmental concerns.

Table 7.6 Direct, indirect, and total effects of respective variables on environmental concerns

Variable	*Environmental knowledge*			*Environmental concern*		
	Direct effect	*Indirect effect*	*Total effect*	*Direct effect*	*Indirect effect*	*Total effect*
Urban or Rural	0.025	0.018	0.043*	0.071*	0.047	0.118*
Gender	0.052*	0.006	0.058*	0.004	0.034	0.038*
Age	−0.091*	−0.020	−0.111*	0.064*	−0.078	−0.014*
Education	0.251*	0.063	0.314*	0.101*	0.232	0.333*
Annual income	0.012	0.004	0.017	0.013	0.014	0.027*
Hukou	0.123*	0.028	0.151*	0.074*	0.107	0.182*
Party membership	0.042*	0.013	0.056*	0.028	0.045	0.073*
Farming status	−0.023	−0.011	−0.035	−0.021	−0.032	−0.054*
Hukou at age 16	−0.062*	−0.006	−0.068*	0.022	−0.038	−0.015*
Media Usage	0.160*	–	0.160*	0.251*	0.068	0.319*
Environmental knowledge	–	–	–	0.422*	–	0.422*

Note Direct effects are standardized regression coefficients; * $P \leq 0.05$; indirect effects were not tested for significance

7.4 Summary and Discussion

At this point, the following basic conclusions can be drawn. First, the data analysis based on CGSS2010 shows that urban and rural residents in China share a similar belief system in terms of how they view environmental issues. Second, there is indeed a significant difference between urban and rural residents in terms of their levels of environmental concern. Urban–rural differences have a significant effect on environmental concern. Urban residents show more environmental concern than rural residents in a number of aspects, which is consistent with the early foreign residence hypothesis. Third, differential-exposure theory can explain the differences in public environmental concern between urban and rural areas in China, while the other two theories cannot. Fourth, urban–rural differences in environmental concern are amplified by the mediating effects of environmental knowledge and media use.

As mentioned earlier, recent studies abroad have shown that at a global level, urban–rural differences in the public's environmental concerns have been converging. However, the findings in this chapter suggest that there are still significant differences in the level of environmental concern between urban and rural residents in China. From the point of view of the choice of research instruments, we have covered as many different dimensions of environmental concern as possible in the measurement of environmental concern, and the comparison of each dimension shows that urban residents' environmental concern is significantly higher than that of rural residents. Therefore, it is reasonable to rule out the possibility that the results may be different because of the different methods of measurement. From the viewpoint of the design of the research methodology, in the structural equation modeling, while controlling for the socio-demographic variables and other variables that have a significant effect on environmental concern, the urban vs. rural variable still shows a significant effect on environmental concern, and thus the possibility of a spurious correlation can be ruled out. Therefore, the residence hypothesis can be confirmed in China, and the finding that Chinese urban residents are more concerned about the environment than their rural counterparts is verified.

In this chapter, we systematically test three theoretical explanations for the residence hypothesis proposed by earlier studies conducted outside of China, but only the differential-exposure theory is supported by the data. In other words, in contemporary China, urban residents may indeed be more concerned about the environment than rural residents because of the higher levels of past encounters with environmental hazards. However, differential-exposure theory can only explain part of the urban–rural differences in environmental concern. The results of structural equation modeling show that while controlling the variable for encountering environmental hazards, urban–rural differences still have a significant effect on environmental concern. This at least suggests that differential-exposure is not the main reason for the urban–rural differences in environmental concern. One interesting finding is that people who have experienced environmental hazards also have increased environmental knowledge, which in turn has an indirect effect on environmental concern. Accordingly, the differential-exposure theory can be expanded: the fact that urban dwellers are more likely to have encountered environmental hazards than rural dwellers will cause them to be more concerned about the environment. The fact that urban dwellers may have more knowledge about the environment will also contribute to their concern for the environment.

In this study, we chose farming status as the measure of occupation, with natural resource extraction and *hukou* type at age 16 as the measure of residence during the socialization period. This enabled us to test the extra-commodity theory and the theory of human-modified vs. natural environmental orientations, respectively. The results show that rural residents who are currently engaged in farming do show less environmental concern in some of the orientations than do urban residents and rural residents who are not engaged in farming. However, urban residents who were not engaged in farming before the age of 16 do not show more environmental concern than those who were engaged in farming before the age of 16, and the latter scored even higher in some of the orientations. Further, controlling other variables, current farming status, and *hukou* type at the age of 16 have no significant effect on environmental concern.

Additionally, we found that although rural farmers have the lowest levels of environmental concern, this is likely because farmers have less environmental knowledge and less access to the media than other groups. Moreover, studies in China have shown that in the production and life of Chinese rural residents, there is a local endogenous knowledge system (local knowledge) about the environment. It is because of their high dependence on natural resources and their belief in "nature" that they show a tendency to follow nature. This objectively plays a role in protecting the environment and maintaining ecological balance (Ma 2001; Wang 2010; Zhong 2014). Although our study is insufficient to reject the extractive-commodity theory and the theory of human-modified vs. natural environmental orientations, we believe that these two theories rooted in Western societies might not be suitable for explaining the differences in environmental concerns between urban and rural residents in China.

This study also shows that media usage and environmental knowledge mediate the formation of urban–rural differences in environmental concern. It should be noted that mass media has become popular in rural areas of China in recent years, but rural residents still have less access to media than their urban counterparts.[8] Nowadays, with the popularity

[8] Cable television is one example. Statistics show that as of 2012, there were 84.32 million cable subscribers in China, but this only accounts for 33.5% of all households, while the number of broadcast television subscribers nationwide and their share of the total number of households was 215.09 million and 51.5%, respectively. In other words,

of new media (cell phones and the Internet), urban residents can obtain environmental information and knowledge through a variety of convenient media sources, which might not be possible in most Chinese rural areas as of this writing. Urban residents access media more frequently than rural residents, and it is precisely the different opportunities and variety of media that lead to the difference in the amount of environmental information available to urban and rural residents. The degree of acceptance of the clear "environmental stance" in current Chinese media reports will also be different. Regardless, even though there is no significant difference in the level of environmental knowledge between urban and rural residents when controlling other variables, urban residents with frequent media usage will learn more about environmental protection from the media than rural residents who use media less frequently. The result is that the urban–rural difference in environmental concern is magnified.

Taken together, there is reason to believe that the environmental concerns of urban and rural residents in China will continue to converge, and eventually become isomorphic. Studies have shown that the convergence of urban and rural residents' environmental concerns is a global phenomenon, and the results of surveys in some Western developed countries even show that there no longer are urban–rural differences. This shows that when a country's economic and social development reaches a certain stage, the convergence of urban and rural residents' environmental concerns may be inevitable. As of this writing, whether in terms of the level of economic development, urbanization level, or the ability to cope with environmental problems, there is still a gap between China and many Western countries, but the gap is shrinking. Furthermore, over the long run, the difference between urban and rural residents' concerns for the environment in China should dissipate, as findings for other countries have shown.

Additionally, according to recent studies, the gap between urban and rural residents' environmental concerns has begun to narrow. As mentioned earlier, the 1995 National Environmental Awareness Survey (NEAAS) showed that only 58.2% of rural residents had heard of environmental protection, while 90% of urban residents had heard of it (China Environmental Protection Foundation (CEPF) 1998). However,

although cable broadcasting and television is available in half of the country's households, nearly 70% of rural residents do not have direct access to it at home. See http://data.stats.gov.cn/workspace/index?m=hgnd.

the CGSS2010 results show that there is no significant difference between the knowledge levels of urban and rural residents regarding environmental protection when removing the influence of mass media and other factors. This shows that the gap between urban and rural residents' knowledge of environmental issues has narrowed over the past 15 years with the popularization of environmental education.

Moreover, in recent years, more and more environmental protests have been concentrated in China's rural areas and urban suburbs, and rural residents' protests of projects with environmental risks have gained attention. (Jing 2009; Li and Zhao 2012). This hints that the concept of environmental protection has become increasingly popular in rural China.

Our study also suggests that as urbanization advances, rural residents will become increasingly concerned about the environment. The popularity of mass media has long been an important sign of urbanization and modernization (Ingalls 1992: 321). When rural residents have more opportunities to learn about environmental protection through an increased variety of media, the result should be increased concern for the environment.

Finally, two major shortcomings of this study should be noted. First, although we have provided a systematic and comprehensive approach to measuring environmental concern, the complexity of environmental concern measurement suggests that there may be information omissions and methodological limitations. Environmental problems in rural areas are new social problems brought about by modernization and urbanization. Over thousands of years of agricultural society, rural residents have coexisted with the natural environment and developed lifestyles and customs with distinctive regional characteristics, including simplistic environmental concepts. How to recognize these local environmental protection concepts is beyond the capacity of quantitative research, but it can be an important topic for further qualitative research. Furthermore, due to the limitations of the questionnaire items, the indicators used in this study to test the Western-related theories were rather simplistic. We hope that in future studies, we will have the opportunity to re-test these theories with more comprehensive indicators, so as to deepen the theoretical explanations of the differences in environmental concern between China's urban and rural residents.

CHAPTER 8

Age Differences in Environmental Concerns

Hong Dayong, Fan Yechao, Deng Xiaqiu, and Qu Tianci

In the 1960s and 1970s, in Western countries such as the United States, the environmental movement was intertwined with the anti-war movement, the civil rights movement, and the feminist movement, all of which significantly impacted society. In the Western environmental movement, young people, particularly students, demonstrated high enthusiasm and were the primary participants (Buttel 1979). In recent years, the younger generation has been active in environmental mass demonstrations and often shapes their outcomes.

Currently, most domestic environmental protection organizations rely on the younger generation to spearhead environmental actions. This reliance is evident in the names of these organizations, such as the "China

D. Hong (✉) · X. Deng · T. Qu
Renmin University of China, Beijing, China
e-mail: hongdy@ruc.edu.cn

T. Qu
e-mail: qtc329@ruc.edu.cn

Y. Fan
Minzu University of China, Beijing, China
e-mail: fanyechao@ruc.edu.cn

D. Hong and Y. Fan (eds.), *Toward a Green Society*,
https://doi.org/10.1007/978-981-96-5111-5_8

Green Youth Environmental Protection Organization" (Green Youth) and the "China Youth Climate Action Network" (CYCAN).

Why do young people show a strong inclination toward environmental protection? Are young Chinese individuals more concerned about the environment than older generations? If so, how can we understand this phenomenon? Based on existing findings, this chapter uses national survey data to investigate the relationship between age and environmental concern, and proposes possible theoretical explanations.

8.1 Literature Review

8.1.1 Foreign Research and Theoretical Perspectives on Age and Environmental Concern

Environmental concern refers to an individual's awareness of environmental issues and support for environmental protection. In academic articles, exploring the social basis of environmental concern—comparing and explaining which groups of people care more about the environment—has been a common focus of researchers. Despite the increasing number of empirical studies, the social basis of environmental concern has not emerged as clearly as expected. Most socio-demographic variables, such as gender, ethnicity, and place of residence, have limited or uncertain influence on environmental concern. Only two variables, age and education, have shown a sustained and stable effect on environmental concern (Van Liere and Dunlap 1980; Jones and Dunlap 1992). Of these two variables, age is recognized as having the greatest impact on environmental concern. There is a significant negative correlation between age and environmental concern, with younger people being more environmentally concerned than older people (Greenbaum 1995: 125). How can we understand this "diminishing effect" of environmental concern across age distribution? Researchers tend to explain this from both life cycle and cohort perspectives.

The life cycle perspective suggests that as individuals age, their perceptions and attitudes change. Researchers have proposed various theories to explain why young people are more concerned about the environment. American environmental sociologist Buttel's (1979) analysis of social structure pointed out that, on one hand, because social institutions are not deeply embedded, young people are usually suppressed and lack power and resources. Therefore, they have a stronger desire to reform the social structure and reshape the social order. On the other hand, the environmental movement can be seen as a strategy for young people to improve their social status, and a higher level of environmental concern reflects their strong sense of resistance. Based on cultural construction analysis, Melucci (1985) argued that young people symbolize flexibility and variability in culture. The ecological movement can be regarded as a resistance to the domination of technological rationality in life. Its free and spontaneous social significance aligns well with the dominant "youth culture", thus garnering more support from young people. From a stakeholder analysis perspective, Murphy (1994) pointed out that young people are more likely to be victims of environmental damage in the long term, making them more attentive to environmental problems and more active in environmental protection than their parents and grandparents. Kanagy et al. (1994) argued that young people generally pay less tax due to their low income. Consequently, increasing government financial input to solve environmental problems does not impose a significant economic burden on them, making them more likely to form positive attitudes about environmental protection due to the low cost of participation.

The cohort perspective suggests that each generation grows up in a distinct social environment shaped by major historical events (e.g., social movements, economic crises, wars). This process of socialization results in differences in attitudes and values between age groups. When examining age differences in environmental concerns, researchers also consider intergenerational effects. For example, Inglehart's (1995) post-materialist theory proposes that the generation born after World War II grew up in an era of socioeconomic prosperity and stability. Consequently, their values have shifted from a focus on economic development, technological advancement, and material satisfaction to an emphasis on belonging, self-expression, and quality of life, which is reflected in a significant increase in public environmental concern. Bakvis and Nevitte (1992), based on data from a Canadian national survey, found that respondents born after 1964 exhibited greater concern for environmental protection compared to those born before 1964. Additionally, numerous surveys indicate that environmental concern peaked in North America and Australia among individuals born between 1942 and 1964 (Greenbaum 1995: 131). Therefore, the increase in environmental concern associated with the generational value shifts described by post-materialist theory is supported by empirical data.

The two perspectives of environmental concern about age differences reveal the biological and societal aspects of age variables. There are significant differences in the theoretical premises of these two perspectives. The life cycle perspective assumes that an individual's level of environmental concern fluctuates throughout different stages of life—showing more concern in youth and less in old age—reflecting a natural decline in concern for environmental issues. In contrast, the cohort perspective suggests that generations raised in similar social contexts share similar environmental values acquired during socialization, differentiating them markedly from other generations. Social changes have led to a new generation with heightened environmental concern, while intergenerational differences are evident in the lower levels of concern among older generations.

It is clear that the life cycle perspective offers a micro, individual-oriented explanation of age differences in environmental concern, while the cohort perspective provides a macro, social-oriented view.

8.1.2 The "Buttel Model" of Age and Environmental Concern Analysis

Are age differences in environmental concern attributable to life cycle changes or cohort effects? This question would be straightforward to answer with regular tracking survey data on environmental concerns. If such data reveal that the environmental concern of the same respondents diminishes gradually over time, it would indicate a significant life cycle effect. Conversely, if the data show that the environmental concern of respondents born within a specific age group remains consistently high or low, it would suggest that age differences within the same cohort are more explanatory. In this context, Honnold's (1984) research provides valuable insights. However, tracking survey data is often challenging to obtain, and early international environmental surveys typically offer only cross-sectional data at a single point in time. This raises the question of whether age differences in environmental concerns can be analyzed using cross-sectional data, and if so, how? To address this issue, the renowned American environmental sociologist Buttel (1979) synthesized the aforementioned perspectives and introduced a multi-path analysis model to examine age differences in environmental concern. This model, published in 1979, is now known as the "Buttel model" in subsequent research (see Fig. 8.1).

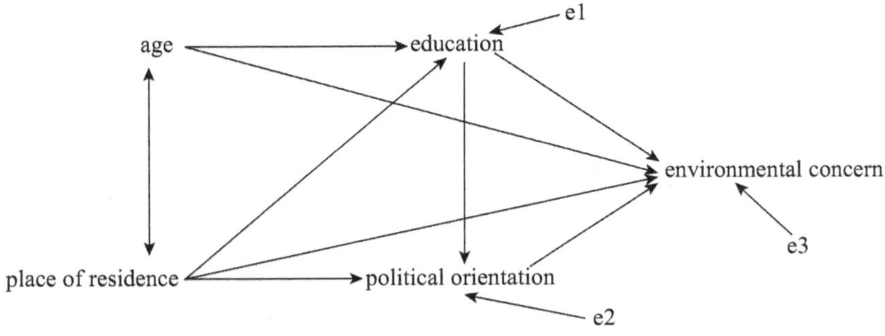

Fig. 8.1 Buttel's path analysis model to investigate age differences in environmental concern

A total of five variables are introduced into the model shown in Fig. 8.1, with *e*1 to *e*3 representing measurement errors. Among these, environmental concern is the dependent variable that requires explanation. The other four variables—age, place of residence, education, and political orientation—are assumed to influence environmental concern. The impact of the age variable on environmental concern is divided into indirect and direct effects. Buttel indicated that if age differences in environmental concern are primarily a cohort phenomenon, the age variable should significantly affect environmental concern through the intermediary variables of education and political orientation, with the indirect effect being greater than the direct effect. Conversely, if age differences are mainly a life cycle phenomenon, the age variable itself should have a significant direct effect on environmental concern, surpassing the indirect effect. Based on the results of a 1974 questionnaire conducted in Wisconsin, Buttel found that age had a significant direct effect on environmental concern, greater than the indirect effect through education and political orientation. Consequently, Buttel concluded that age differences in environmental concern are predominantly a life cycle phenomenon (Buttel 1979).

Despite some limitations, the Buttel model effectively addresses the challenge of examining age differences in environmental concern using cross-sectional data. Given the lack of cumulative tracking survey data on environmental concerns in Mainland China, the Buttel model remains a valuable tool for analyzing cross-sectional data to understand variations in environmental concern.

8.1.3 Existing Research and Shortcomings in China

Domestic empirical research on environmental concerns began in the 1990s. The results from the 1995 National Environmental Awareness Survey, which used a 100-point environmental concern scale, indicated that public environmental concern was generally low across all age groups. However, young people under the age of 29 exhibited higher environmental concern compared to other age groups (Hong 1998). Ren Liying (2002) found, based on the 1998 national public environmental awareness survey that public participation in environmental protection decreased with age. The first Chinese General Social Survey in 2003 revealed a significant negative correlation between the level of environmental concern in urban areas and age (Hong et al. 2012: 82–102). The 2007 national public environmental awareness survey also showed that young people had higher scores than the elderly in aspects such as environmental awareness, severity of environmental problems, and environmental behavior. Moreover, recent small-scale surveys have consistently shown that young people demonstrate higher levels of environmental concern compared to older individuals (e.g., Li 2011; Wu et al. 2012).

Based on the findings of domestic research mentioned above, two key conclusions can be drawn. First, the level of environmental concern among young people in China is generally higher than that of the elderly, a trend that is consistent with international survey results. Second, as surveys have been conducted over the years, age-related differences in environmental awareness have become increasingly evident. However, these studies have not provided in-depth theoretical explanations for the observed age differences in environmental concern, leaving the mechanisms underlying these differences undetermined. Additionally, there are notable shortcomings in the data sources and measurement tools used in these studies. Therefore, there is a need for further exploration and detailed analysis of age differences in public environmental concern across China. This chapter will utilize recent national survey data and the "Buttel model" to further investigate and analyze public environmental concern in China.

8.2 Data, Models, and Variables

8.2.1 *Data Description*

The data for this study comes from the environmental module of the 2010 China General Social Survey (CGSS2010). Conducted by the Department of Sociology at Renmin University of China in collaboration with other academic institutions, the survey employed a multi-level stratified probability sampling design and covered 31 provincial administrative units in China (excluding Hong Kong, Macao, and Taiwan). It was administered to residents aged 16 and above, with the questionnaires primarily completed through face-to-face interviews. In the CGSS2010 questionnaire, the environmental module was optional, and respondents had a one-third probability of being selected to complete this module through random sampling, ensuring its national representativeness. The final effective sample size for CGSS2010 was 11,785, with a response rate of 71.32%. Of these, 3,716 respondents completed the environmental module.

After excluding samples with significant deficiencies, the final number of samples included in this study was 3,510. Of these, 52.5% were women and 47.5% were men. Urban respondents comprised 65.6%, while rural respondents accounted for 34.4%. By age, 9.1% were under 25, 16.0% were between 25–34, 23.3% were between 35–44, 21.2% were between 45–54, and 30.4% were 55 years or older. By education, 32.2% had attained primary school or less, 29.7% had completed junior high school, 20.8% had finished senior high school, and 17.3% had a junior college or university degree.

8.2.2 *Model Setting*

This study employs the "Buttel model" (Buttel 1979) to investigate age differences in public environmental concern in China. However, as the "Buttel model" is primarily based on empirical findings and theoretical research from the United States in the 1970s, some adjustments are necessary for its application to the Chinese context. First, the "Buttel model" includes a political orientation variable to measure whether differences in political values between generations, due to cohort effects, impact environmental concern. Since this variable is seldom used in domestic studies, it will be excluded from the model. Second, while the "Buttel model" considers education an important aspect of the cohort effect, it does not specify which type of education affects environmental concern. Given that environmental education has been formally integrated into the Chinese education system since the 1970s, this factor is likely significant. Therefore, we introduce a new intermediary variable—environmental knowledge—between education and environmental concern. Third, the "Buttel model" uses the direct impact of age on environmental concern to test the life cycle effect, which may also be influenced by other mediating factors, such as perceived social status differences. Finally, the "Buttel model" is quite concise and only controls for the correlation between place of residence and age, neglecting other socio-demographic variables. Given the limited social research on public environmental concern in China, we believe that additional socio-demographic variables (such as gender and income) should be controlled to more clearly examine the relationship between age and environmental concern. The final analysis model established in this chapter is illustrated in Fig. 8.2.

The primary difference between the path analysis model and the Buttel model lies in the independent and mediating variables. First, in terms of independent variables, this study builds upon the "Buttel model" by incorporating additional variables: gender, current employment, annual income, marital status, and party membership, alongside age. We assume that gender directly affects all mediating and dependent variables, while

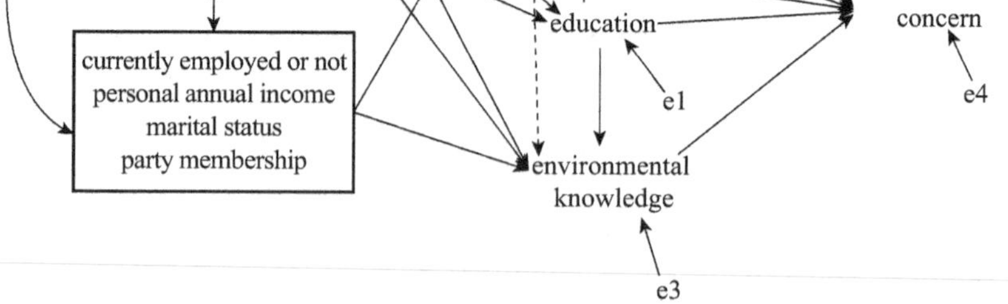

Fig. 8.2 Path analysis model of this study

other newly introduced independent variables directly affect the mediating and dependent variables, with the exception of the education variable. Second, regarding mediating variables, this study introduces two new variables: environmental knowledge and self-rated socioeconomic status. The self-rated socioeconomic status variable is a tentative decomposition of the life cycle effect from the original model. According to life cycle theories (Buttel 1979), age may indirectly influence environmental concern by affecting self-rated socioeconomic status. Existing research (Peng 2013) also suggests that self-rated socioeconomic status may impact environmental knowledge and concern, represented by a dotted path in the model. Additionally, e1 to e4 represent measurement errors for each mediating and dependent variable.

This study aims to explore the causes of age differences in environmental concern and test two theoretical explanations—life cycle and cohort effects—using the analytical model. Based on the theoretical background and the analytical model, we propose the following hypotheses: Hypothesis 1: If the life cycle effect is significant, age itself will have a direct effect on environmental concern or will have a significant mediating effect through self-rated socioeconomic status. Hypothesis 2: If the cohort effect is significant, age itself will have no independent effect on environmental concern but will have a significant mediating effect through education and environmental knowledge.

8.2.3 Operational Variables

According to the analytical model, the variables involved in this study are categorized into three groups: dependent variables, control variables, and mediating variables.

8.2.3.1 Dependent Variables

Environmental concern was measured using the "New Ecological Paradigm Scale" (NEP Scale) developed by Dunlap et al. (2000). The Chinese version of this scale, known as the Chinese New Ecological Paradigm Scale (CNEP Scale), has been locally modified and validated. It has been confirmed as a reliable and valid single-dimensional scale through tests conducted with CGSS survey data in 2003 and 2010 (Hong et al. 2014). Table 8.1 presents the data analysis results for the CNEP Scale.

Table 8.1 CGSS survey results of 2010 China environmental concern scale (*N* = 3510)

The CNEP project	*Completely disagree (%)*	*Somewhat disagree (%)*	*Neither agree or disagree (%)*	*Somewhat agree (%)*	*Completely agree (%)*	*CFA factor load*
1. The current population is approaching the limit that the earth can bear	2.5	10.0	31.7	40.9	15.0	0.38
2. Human destruction of nature often leads to catastrophic consequences	1.6	5.4	19.9	48.0	25.2	0.55
3. Humans are currently abusing and destroying the environment	2.9	7.9	18.2	47.6	23.5	0.46
4. Animals and plants have the same right to existence as human beings	1.4	4.6	17.2	43.3	33.5	0.52
5. The self-balancing capacity of nature is strong enough to cope with the shocks of modern industrial society	14.9	29.6	38.2	13.1	4.2	0.33
6. Humans, despite their special powers, is still subject to the laws of nature	1.5	4.2	25.3	42.4	26.6	0.49
7. It is an exaggeration to say that mankind is facing an "environmental crisis"	13.3	33.6	34.7	14.8	3.6	0.38

(continued)

Table 8.1 (continued)

The CNEP project	*Completely disagree (%)*	*Somewhat disagree (%)*	*Neither agree or disagree (%)*	*Somewhat agree (%)*	*Completely agree (%)*	*CFA factor load*
8. The Earth is like a spaceship, with only a limited amount of space and resources	2.2	7.5	31.1	36.3	22.9	0.53
9. The balance of nature is fragile and can be easily disturbed	2.0	6.8	29.6	40.2	21.5	0.56
10. If everything continues as it is at present, we will soon suffer a serious environmental disaster	2.5	9.1	31.6	33.5	23.4	0.61

Confirmatory factor analysis (CFA) results indicate that the CNEP scale used in this study meets the acceptable factor loading level (typically ≥ 0.3) for a single-dimension scale. Therefore, the scale scores can be directly summed to create a measure of environmental concern. For scoring, items 1, 2, 3, 4, 6, 8, 9, and 10 are positive statements. Responses are coded as 1 for "completely disagree", 2 for "somewhat disagree", 3 for "neither agree nor disagree", 4 for "somewhat agree", and 5 for "completely agree", in increasing order of agreement. Items 5 and 7 are reverse-coded, with scores assigned in decreasing order. By summing the scores from the 10 items, we obtain an environmental concern variable ranging from 10 to 50, representing a continuous variable.

8.2.3.2 Mediating Variables

To examine the impact of life cycle and cohort effects on age differences in environmental concern, this study introduces three mediating variables: self-rated socioeconomic status, education, and environmental knowledge. Self-rated socioeconomic status is assessed by asking respondents to rate their current status on a scale from 1 to 10, with higher scores indicating higher perceived socioeconomic status. Education is measured by the number of years of schooling completed, ranging from 0 to 19 years.

The environmental knowledge variable is based on a scale with 10 measurement items developed by Hong Dayong for the CGSS survey in 2003 (Hong and Xiao 2007). Each item is scored as 1 for agreement with the statement and 0 for disagreement or "don't know". Although confirmatory factor analysis was not performed due to the dichotomous nature of the items, the scale's alpha reliability coefficient is 0.805, demonstrating good internal consistency. The environmental knowledge variable is calculated by summing the scores across the 10 items, with higher scores indicating greater environmental knowledge (see Table 8.2).

8.2.3.3 *Control Variables*

To clearly illustrate the relationship between age and environmental concern, this study controls for several variables in the path model, including gender, urban or rural residence, current employment, personal annual income, marital status, and party membership (see Table 8.2 for detailed descriptions).

8.3 Research Findings

8.3.1 *Comparison of Environmental Concern Scores Across Different Age Groups*

Correlation analysis of age and environmental concern reveals a Pearson product-moment correlation coefficient of −0.117 ($p = 0.000$). This indicates a negative correlation between age and environmental concern in China, consistent with the findings of Dunlap et al. (2000) from the early 1990s in the United States. Additionally, respondents were categorized into seven distinct age groups based on their ages at the time of the survey. Variance analysis was performed on the environmental concern scores across these age groups (see Table 8.3).

The ANOVA F-test results in Table 8.3 indicate significant differences in environmental concern levels among different age groups. Overall, younger age groups exhibit higher environmental concern scores compared to older groups. Specifically, respondents under 20 years old have the highest environmental concern scores, while those aged 70 and above have the lowest. Scheffe's multiple comparison results reveal no

Table 8.2 Describes the main variables involved in the study

Variable name	*Characteristic*	*Mean*	*Standard deviation*	*Description*
Environmental concern	Continuous	36.61	4.679	Higher score correlates to a higher level of environmental concern
Environmental knowledge	Continuous	5.32	2.652	Higher score, correlates to a higher level of environmental knowledge
Education Level	Continuous	9.08	4.550	0 = No formal education, 6 = Primary school 9 = Middle school,12 = High school,15 = some college, 16 = Bachelor,19 = Graduate or above
Self-rated socioeconomic status	Continuous	4.07	1.766	Higher score correlates to higher self-rated socioeconomic status
Gender differences	Norminal	0.48	0.499	0 = Female,1 = Male
Rural vs Urban	Norminal	0.66	0.475	0 = Rural,1 = Urban
Current employment status	Norminal	0.63	0.483	0 = Not-employed,1 = Employed
Personal annual income	Continuous	19.58	57.543	Unit: Thousand yuan
Marital status	Norminal	0.90	0.303	0 = Unmarried,1 = Married (including widowed and divorced)
Party membership	Norminal	0.14	0.342	0 = Non-party member,1 = Party member

Table 8.3 Comparison of scores of public environmental concern in different age groups ($F = 12.17$, $p = 0.000$)

Age	*Mean*	*Std deviation*	*Sample size*	*Scheffe multiple comparisons*[1]
(A) Under 20 years	37.67	4.563	105	A ~ F > G
(B) 20 to 29 years	37.20	4.777	508	C > D
(C) 30 to 39 years	37.34	4.863	699	C > E
(D) 40 to 49 years	36.36	4.472	799	
(E) 50 to 59 years	36.31	4.566	666	
(F) 60 to 69 years	36.49	4.746	452	
(G) 70 and older	34.93	4.240	281	

significant differences in environmental concern scores among the three age groups under 40, nor between the two age groups between 40 and 59. The primary distinction lies between those younger than 40 and those older than 40, with the former displaying higher environmental concern. If these findings are applied to specific historical periods, it can be concluded that the level of environmental concern among Chinese individuals born after the 1970s is significantly higher than that of those born before the 1970s.

8.3.2 *Path Analysis of Age Differences in Environmental Concern*

If the life cycle were the primary cause of age differences in environmental concern, we would expect a gradual decline in concern levels with increasing age, even if the effect is not substantial. However, statistical results reveal that significant age differences in environmental concern are primarily observed between generations born around the 1970s. This result suggests that the age differences in environmental concern are more likely due to intergenerational differences arising from cohort effects. To further investigate this, we applied a multi-path analysis using the modified "Buttel model" to re-estimate the data. The results are presented in Tables 8.4 and 8.5.

[1] Only comparison results with statistical significance (p-value less than 0.05) are reported here.

Table 8.4 Direct effects of the respective variables on environmental concern, environmental knowledge, self-rated socioeconomic status, and education

Independent variable	*Environmental concern*		*Environmental knowledge*		*Self-rated Socioeconomic Status*		*Education*	
	Beta	p-*value*	*Beta*	p-*value*	*Beta*	p-*value*	*Beta*	p-*value*
Age	−0.014	0.473	−0.060	0.002	0.080	0.000	−0.389	0.000
Gender	0.025	0.126	0.052	0.001	−0.060	0.000	0.175	0.000
Rural vs Urban	0.089	0.000	0.140	0.000	0.009	0.644	0.384	0.000
Current employment status	−0.003	0.857	−0.018	0.287	0.056	0.003	–	–
Personal annual income	0.019	0.216	0.010	0.511	0.082	0.000	–	–
Marital status	0.020	0.239	−0.039	0.018	0.009	0.639	–	–
Party membership	0.019	0.240	0.059	0.000	0.031	0.069	–	–
Education	0.113	0.000	0.364	0.000	0.201	0.000	–	–
Self-rated socioeconomic status	0.004	0.776	0.053	0.000	–	–	–	–
Environmental knowledge	0.309	0.000	–	–	–	–	–	–
R^2	0.183		0.252		0.046		0.334	

Table 8.4 presents the direct effects of the respective variables in the analysis model on the dependent and mediating variables. It shows that environmental concern, environmental knowledge, and education are well explained by their respective variables, while the independent variables have low explanatory power concerning self-rated socioeconomic status. Due to space constraints, we focus on the direct effects of age and the three mediating variables on environmental concern. Notably, age does not have a significant direct impact on environmental concern when other independent variables are controlled. This suggests that the effect of age on environmental concern is mediated through other variables.

The question arises whether age influences environmental concern through self-rated socioeconomic status (indicating a life cycle effect) or

Table 8.5 Direct, Indirect, and Total impact of the respective variables on environmental concern (standardized regression coefficient)

	Direct impact	*Indirect impact*	*Total impact*
Age	−0.014	−0.106	−0.120*
Gender	0.025	0.055	0.080*
Rural vs. Urban	0.089*	0.132	0.221*
Current employment status	−0.003	−0.004	−0.007*
Personal annual income	0.019	0.005	0.024*
Marital status	0.020	−0.012	0.008*
Party membership	0.019	0.019	0.038*
Education	0.113*	0.117	0.230*
Self-rated socioeconomic status	0.004	0.016	0.021*
Environmental knowledge	0.309*	0.000	0.309*

* $p \leq 0.05$

through education and environmental knowledge (indicating a cohort effect). Statistical test results show that age has a significant positive direct impact on self-rated socioeconomic status, meaning that older individuals tend to rate their socioeconomic status higher. Conversely, age has a significant negative direct impact on both education and environmental knowledge, indicating that older individuals generally have fewer years of education and lower levels of environmental knowledge. These findings align with the expectations of both life cycle and cohort effects. However, environmental knowledge and education have a significant direct impact on environmental concern, while self-rated socioeconomic status does not independently affect environmental concern. The Beta coefficients indicate that the direct impact of education and environmental knowledge on environmental concern is greater than that of self-rated socioeconomic status. Thus, age does not independently influence environmental concern and does not indirectly affect it through self-rated socioeconomic status. Consequently, Hypothesis 1, which is based on the life cycle effect, is not supported by the data.

Further analysis of the indirect and direct impacts of each variable on environmental concern through the three mediating variables provides the total impact of each independent variable on environmental concern (see Table 8.5).

Furthermore, we focus solely on the relationship between age, the three mediating variables, and environmental concern. As shown in

Table 8.5, although age does not have a significant direct impact on environmental concern, education and environmental knowledge, which significantly influence environmental concern, are themselves significantly affected by age. Consequently, the total impact of age on environmental concern shows a significant negative correlation. Thus, Hypothesis 2, based on the Cohort Effect, is effectively supported by the data. According to these statistical results, Fig. 8.3 illustrates the relationships among the four variables: age, education, environmental knowledge, and environmental concern.

From Fig. 8.3, we can see that age significantly affects environmental concern through three main pathways: (1) Age → Education → Environmental Concern; (2) Age → Environmental Knowledge → Environmental Concern; and (3) Age → Education → Environmental Knowledge → Environmental Concern. Examining the path coefficients, it is evident that the first two pathways likely represent the primary mechanisms through which the cohort effect influences age differences in environmental concern. These pathways suggest that differences in environmental concern across age groups are primarily due to variations in years of education. The third pathway indicates that the effect of age on environmental concern through education is significantly mediated by environmental knowledge. This means that the impact of education on environmental concern is partly channeled through its effect on environmental knowledge.

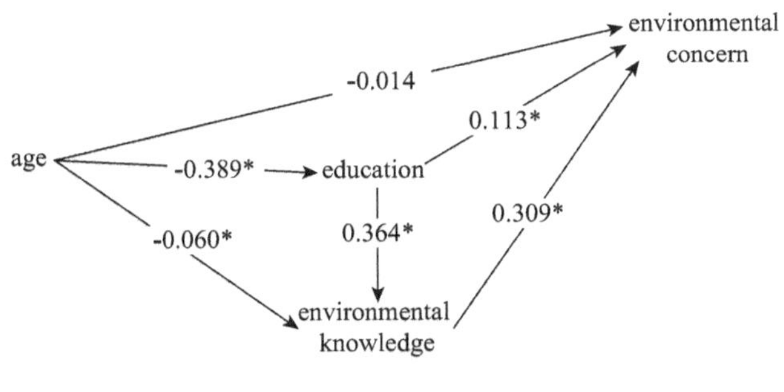

Fig. 8.3 Relationship among age, education, environmental knowledge, and environmental concern

8.4 Conclusions and Discussion

This chapter analyzes age differences in environmental concern among the Chinese public using data from the CGSS2010. The statistical analysis reveals significant variations in environmental concern levels across different age groups, with a notable difference between those born before and after the 1970s. The younger generation demonstrates higher environmental concern compared to the older generation. This finding indicates that the hypothesis based on the life cycle effect is not supported by the data. Instead, the results suggest that age differences in environmental concern are primarily influenced by the cohort effect, a phenomenon of intergenerational isolation.

What factors contribute to the higher environmental concern among China's younger generation? One key factor is access to environmental education. The data analysis shows that while age itself does not independently affect environmental concern, education plays a significant role. As illustrated in Fig. 8.3, education not only directly impacts environmental concern but also indirectly influences it through environmental knowledge. The main reason for the age differences in environmental concern among the Chinese public appears to be the disparity in educational opportunities that foster environmental knowledge.

The Chinese government's involvement in the United Nations Conference on the Human Environment in 1972 marked the beginning of modern environmental protection efforts in China. Since then, environmental protection and education have significantly developed. Before the 1970s, environmental protection in China was nascent and had limited impact. However, post-1970s, with the growing recognition of environmental protection's importance, environmental education gained momentum and was incorporated into formal education by the early 1990s (Qu 2013). Following the first National Conference on Environmental Protection in 1973, many universities introduced environmental protection programs. The Environmental Protection Law of the People's Republic of China (Trial Implementation), adopted in 1979, emphasized environmental education. The Environmental Education Development Plan (Draft) of 1980 was included in the national education plan. By 1990, the National Education Commission mandated environmental education in elective courses and extracurricular activities for high school students. In 1993, environmental education was integrated into compulsory education curricula, becoming a permanent subject in basic education (Hong et al. 2012: 87–88).

The research findings underscore the profound social impact of environmental protection over the past 40 years, evidenced by the higher environmental concern levels among those born after the 1970s. The exposure to formal environmental education appears to be a crucial factor in this generational difference: those born before the 1970s generally lacked formal environmental education and thus have lower environmental knowledge and concern. Conversely, the new generation, who benefited from formal environmental education, exhibit higher levels of environmental knowledge and concern. It is anticipated that, as generations evolve and environmental education becomes more widespread, the age differences in environmental concern will gradually diminish.

It is important to note that the reliance on cross-sectional data limits this study, as long-term tracking data are difficult to obtain. The cohort effect tends to assume that a generation's environmental concern level remains stable, without accounting for the overall growth of societal environmental concern. Additionally, the study found that age has a significant direct impact on environmental knowledge, beyond its influence through education. This direct impact may be attributable to informal environmental education methods, such as media reports and social publicity, which could have policy and operational significance for understanding age differences in environmental concern. Although this aspect is not explored in detail in this chapter, it presents a valuable direction for future research.

CHAPTER 9

Economic Growth and Environmental Concern

Xiao Chenyang and Fan Yechao

Economic growth generally leads to an increase in standards of living, which will lead to an increase in people's demand for quality of life. This includes an increase in demand for better environmental quality. In other words, there should be some degree of positive correlation between economic growth and public environmental concerns. However, existing studies show that the relationship between the two is complex and sometimes nonexistent. Whether China's rapid economic growth has simultaneously stimulated increased public environmental concern is the subject of this chapter.

C. Xiao (✉)
American University, Washington, DC, USA
e-mail: xiao@american.edu

Y. Fan
Minzu University of China, Beijing, China
e-mail: fanyechao@ruc.edu.cn

D. Hong and Y. Fan (eds.), *Toward a Green Society*,
https://doi.org/10.1007/978-981-96-5111-5_9

9.1 China's Economic Growth and Environmental Protection

Rapid economic growth is one of the most impressive achievements of China's Reform and Opening-up. From 1978 to 2018, China's gross domestic product (GDP) has grown at an average annual rate of 9.4%, from 367.9 billion yuan to 90,030.9 billion yuan. In 2010, it surpassed Japan to become the world's second-largest economy. During that same period, China's per capita gross national income (GNI) also increased from $200 to $9,732, exceeding the average for middle-income countries. In the context of the era of economic prosperity, the living standards of the Chinese people have also improved considerably. For example, since the 1980s, the proportion of poor people in China has been decreasing at a rapid clip, with 740 million rural people lifted out of poverty by the end of 2017. This brought the incidence of rural poverty down to 3.1% (Office of Household Surveys, National Bureau of Statistics 2018). Moreover, data released by the National Bureau of Statistics indicates that from 2013 to 2018, Chinese residents' per capita disposable income increased from 18,311 yuan to 28,228 yuan, a 50% increase in just six years.

While China has made remarkable achievements in economic development, the ecological and environmental conditions it faces are not optimistic. This manifests first and foremost in the urgent problem of water pollution. According to data released by the Ministry of Ecology and Environment in 2018, only 41 of the 111 important lakes and reservoirs monitored nationwide had achieved Class II water quality (Class I being the best), 25.8% of the rivers had water quality lower than Class III, and the water quality of the northern basins such as the Yellow River, Songhua River, Huai River, Haihe River, and Liao River were each suffering from some degree of pollution.[1] Second, frequent outbreaks of smog in major cities such as Beijing and Shanghai in recent years also illustrate the severity of air pollution in China's cities. Environmental monitoring data show that in 2018, 64.2% of the 338 cities at the prefecture level and above monitored in accordance with the new national air quality standards fell short of the standards. In addition, China overtook the United States as the world's largest emitter of carbon dioxide

[1] Ministry of Ecology and Environment, 2018 *Communiqué on the State of China's Ecology and Environment* (2019-05-22) [2019-07-22]. http://www.mee.gov.cn/hjzl/zghjzkgb/lnzghjzkgb/201905/P020190619587632630618.pdf.

in 2006 (Rosenthal 2008). These unprecedented environmental challenges, which can be seen as the cost of China's rapid economic growth over the past few decades, pose a direct challenge to the sustainability of China's economic growth. According to some estimates, in 2004, China's economic losses caused by environmental pollution were about 511.8 billion yuan, accounting for 3.05% of the country's GDP that year.[2] According to a research institute's 2005 environmental sustainability index of 145 major countries and regions around the world, China ranked 133rd, near the bottom (Esty et al. 2005: 47–46). Therefore, China will face the dilemma of choosing between economic growth and environmental protection for a long time to come, and environmental governance will be crucial to maintaining the sustainable growth of its economy.

Whether it is environmental governance or the practice of environmental policy, success depends on the public's attention to environmental issues and support for environmental protection, that is, environmental care. Previous studies have shown that public environmental concern is not only constrained by individual characteristics such as gender, age, place of residence, political party tendency, and socioeconomic status at the micro level, but is also the result of the co-construction of a specific level of economic development and the objective environment at the macro level of a society (Hong and Lu 2011; Brechin 1999; Xiao and McCright 2007). As some studies have noted, rapid economic growth and rapid environmental change are important dimensions for understanding the Chinese experience when economic development levels are low and environmental problems have not been fully exposed. In this regard, the weak environmental concerns revealed by surveys of the Chinese public at and before the beginning of the twenty-first century seem understandable (Bao and Chen 2011). This begs the question: since the beginning of the twenty-first century, against the backdrop of rapid economic growth and a sharp decline in the objective environment, how has the Chinese public's environmental concern changed?

[2] State Environmental Protection Administration, *National Bureau of Statistics China Green National Accounts Research Report* 2004 (2006–09–07) [2019–07–22]. http://www.gov.cn/gzdt/2006-09/07/content_381190.htm.

9.2 Review of Research on Economic Growth, Environmental

9.2.1 Degradation and Environmental Concern

9.2.1.1 Theoretical Controversy

In a developing country like China, where economic growth is strong and the environment is in decline, how do public environmental concerns evolve? A common assumption is that in a developing country, the public may be more concerned about economic issues than environmental ones. A related notion is that public environmental concern is more likely to occur in wealthy countries with developed economies. According to this assumption, economic growth will not only reduce the tension between the economy and the environment, but will also leave more space to environmental protection in the public agenda, thereby promoting the growth of public environmental concern.

Indeed, in the view of some proponents of ecological modernization theory and environmental Kuznets curve theory, a certain level of economic growth is indispensable to the success of environmental reforms and governance, even though some risks of accelerated environmental degradation can be expected in the process (e.g., Cohen 1997; Dinda 2004). Scholars who hold this view believe that economic growth provides the necessary financial support for the development and promotion of more environmentally friendly products and technologies. Furthermore, as environmental reforms deepen, it can be expected that political and cultural changes will follow: the public will become more and more environmentally concerned, which in turn will drive the ecological transformation of society (Givens and Jorgensen 2011). Regarding the question of how economic development can contribute to the growth of public environmental concerns, post-materialist value theory and the affluence hypothesis propose two different explanations.

The post-materialist value theory, proposed by Inglehart (1977, 1990, 1997), has been widely used to explain the rise of public environmental concern. According to the theory, the basic material needs of the new generation who grew up in the affluent environment created by affluent industrial societies after World War II were largely met, and the socialization process they underwent led to a greater focus on post-materialistic needs in their values, such as freedom of expression, quality of life, and environmental quality. This shift in values is considered to be the main driver of many new social movements in the West, including the environmental movement in the 1960s and '70s. As a result, China's economic growth is likely to lead to a similar shift in values among the Chinese public, especially in more developed urban areas, which in turn will lead to public concern for environmental issues.

Compared with the post-materialist theory of value, the affluence hypothesis is equally concerned with the promoting effect of economic growth on environmental concerns, but it offers a different explanation of the former's argument about the relationship between the two. According to the affluence hypothesis, the post-materialistic values are not mediated, but instead there is a direct link between environmental concerns and economic prosperity (Franzen and Meyer 2009). A high-quality environment is seen as an "amenity good" that is needed by both the rich and the poor, and thus it becomes a commodity that can be economically calculated and purchased. The increase in affluence increases the chances that members of the public will purchase a high-quality environment, and as a result, more interest and concern is generated around it.

In contrast to these two arguments is the global environmentalism thesis, according to which, a high level of concern for the environment can also occur in economically underdeveloped countries. Evidence cited has included the enthusiastic participation of many less developed countries in the United Nations Conference on Environment and Development in Rio de Janeiro in 1992, and the findings of many multinational surveys, such as the 1992 Gallup Planetary Health Survey (e.g., Dunlap and York 2008). According to the theory of global environmentalism, the rise of environmentalism is global and not limited to economically wealthy individuals or countries. Thus, rather than a one-sided emphasis on affluence or economic development, a more appropriate approach would be to assume that environmental concerns have multiple sources.

Proponents of post-materialist value theories have also noted the surge of environmentalism in less developed regions, and have revised their theories as a result (e.g., Inglehart 1995). In essence, they have acknowledged that environmental concerns have multiple sources, such as the transition to post-materialistic values in developed regions and the deteriorating environmental conditions in less developed regions. Kidd and Lee (1997: 6) further argue that both objective issues and subjective values can promote pro-environmental perceptions. Even in countries with less developed economies but more serious objective problems, all else being equal, individuals with post-materialist values should theoretically care more about the environment than those who hold materialistic values.

This theoretical revision ignited controversy at the end of the twentieth century, and in 1997, a special issue of *Social Science Quarterly* sparked heated debate in which scholars confronted each other on a variety of issues about the relationship between different variables. The debate first focused on whether it would be appropriate to examine the post-materialistic value transition at the individual level, or whether it is only applicable to state-level analysis. Additionally, would it be appropriate to use measures of affluence and economic development (e.g., GDP) as a proximity or direct measure of post-materialistic values? Furthermore, some scholars have argued that in the study of post-materialist value theory, the indicators used to measure environmental concern are usually related to economic payments, and may be affected by the bias of ability to pay. Additionally, the level of concern is not measured (e.g., Brechin and Kempton 1997). In addition, the relative magnitude of the effect of affluent/economic development or post-materialistic values on environmental concerns is also an important point of contention. While significant statistical results often appear in the analysis, some scholars have noted that the effects have been weak, and have questioned whether these statistically significant results were of any practical significance (White and Hunter 2009; Kvaløy et al. 2012).

In recent years, Papel et al. have noted the change in the scale of socioeconomic status (SES) factors. On this basis, the relationship between environmental concern and socioeconomic status has been re-theorized. In one study, by drawing inspiration from the diffusion of innovation theory, Papel and Hunter (2012) suggest that environmentalism may initially arise among people of higher socioeconomic status and then gradually spread to people of lower socioeconomic status. Accordingly, they argue that post-materialistic theories of value and affluence hypotheses can explain the embrace of environmentalism by those of higher socioeconomic status in the early days. Moreover, as the theory of global environmentalism argues, the spread of environmentalism and the objective problem of environmental degradation will attract even more environmental concern from the general public. In short, socioeconomic status may have a very strong initial effect, but this effect will diminish over time. Pampel and Hunter (2012) used 26 U.S. General Social Surveys (GSS) to analyze changes by cohort and revealed that education (a measure of socioeconomic status) did show a narrowing positive effect over the years. Interestingly, although they found that cohort changes in household income showed the same pattern as the effect of education, it was a persistent negative effect.

Overall, there has been no consensus on whether economic growth and affluence promote public environmental concern. However, most theoretical perspectives suggest that public environmental concerns intensify as exposure to a deteriorating environment increases, regardless of socioeconomic status.

9.2.2 *Empirical Findings in the Literature*

The literature on environmental concerns has been abundant to date, and most studies have included some measure of socioeconomic status, both for reasons of focus and control variables. This chapter focuses only on several recent studies (mainly since 1999) that have detailed the effects of socioeconomic status and/or post-materialistic values. Many studies have focused their analysis at the individual level (e.g., Hunter et al. 2010; Marquart-Pyatt 2007, 2008; Best and Mayerl 2013). Some studies entailed analysis at the national level (e.g., Knight and Messer 2012; Sandvik 2008; Duroy 2008). There are also studies that integrate the two levels, either in a separate form (e.g., Ahern 2012) or in the form of a complex multi-level design (e.g., Haller and Hadler 2008; Freymeyer and Johnson 2010; Givens and Jorgenson 2011). Some studies have directly measured post-materialistic values (e.g., Mohai et al. 2010; Nawrotzki 2012; Zhao 2012), while others have not (e.g., Brechin 1999; Sandvik 2008; Meyer and Liebe 2010). As is generally found in the literature, these studies have taken different approaches to measuring many aspects of environmental concern. Many studies (mainly those with multi-level designs or international comparison) have also made measurements of objective environmental conditions, such as CO2 emissions data (e.g., Kvaløy et al. 2012; Marquart-Pyatt 2012), and population density (Duroy 2008).

Research findings in this area are largely mixed and inconclusive. At the individual level, the effects of education have been consistent across all studies, with higher levels of education often associated with higher levels of environmental care. The effect of household income on environmental concern under various measures is generally consistent with the findings of studies prior to 1999 (e.g., Van Liere and Dunlap 1980). Greenbaum 1995). In some studies that include direct measurements of post-materialistic values (e.g., Ahern 2012; Franzen and Meyer 2009; Nawrotzki 2012), there have been reports of positive correlations, but the scale of the effect is generally weak. In addition, two studies involving China also reported that they did not find a significant effect of post-materialistic values on environmental concerns (Mohai et al. 2010; Zhao 2012).

In studies at the national level or at multiple levels, the effect of GDP, which is often used to measure economic development, on environmental concerns under different measures, has shown inconsistent results. Similar results have been observed in relation to the effect of environmental conditions (most commonly CO_2 emissions). This is indeed somewhat surprising when one considers that all theoretical perspectives predict that environmental degradation will stimulate public environmental concern. In most of those studies that reported significant results, there was a gap between environmental conditions and awareness of environmental issues, rather than willingness-to-pay or environmental donations (e.g., Duroy 2008; Marquart-Pyatt 2012).

In summary, although there are still disagreements, there is some evidence that post-materialistic values are positively correlated with environmental concern under different measurements. Nonetheless, since household income and GDP mostly have only a weak or insignificant effect on environmental concerns, the previously hypothetical post-materialistic value as an intermediary between economic development and environmental concern is uncertain. Moreover, empirical research appears to be consistent with the global environmentalist doctrine that environmental concerns come from diverse sources, and that economic affluence is unlikely to constitute a necessary condition for environmental concerns.

9.3 Research Design

9.3.1 Data Basis

This chapter examines how economic development and the rise in individual affluence affect Chinese citizens' level of environmental concern. We used data from the China Comprehensive Social Survey (CGSS) environmental module from 2003 and 2010. The 2003 CGSS survey, although confined to urban areas, was representative of the sample at the national level. The CGSS data for 2010 consisted of two separate samples from urban and rural areas. The 2003 and 2010 CGSS surveys used random sampling and were collected through face-to-face interviews, with response rates of 77% and 71%, respectively. CGSS 2010 included two samples, urban and rural, but only 1/3 of the total samples were surveyed by random selection in the environment module. After eliminating some responses due to insufficient data on key survey items, the urban and rural sample sizes for CGSS 2003 were 5,073 and 3,409, respectively. The urban and rural sample sizes for CGSS 2010 were 2,262 and 1,147, respectively. Using three different sample datasets at two time points, we can design a study at the individual level that includes cross-sectional and longitudinal analysis. Unfortunately, since it is not panel data in the true sense of the word, the vertical analysis in this chapter will be limited to a simple trend analysis.

From 2003 to 2010 (the two points in the study), China's economic growth grew by leaps and bounds, and achieved great success. During this period, China's gross domestic product (GDP) nearly tripled, from 13,582.28 billion yuan to 40,151.28 billion yuan. In just eight years, the per capita disposable income of urban and rural residents also increased from 8,472.2 yuan and 2,622.2 yuan to 19,109.4 yuan and 5,919.0 yuan, respectively (National Bureau of Statistics of the People's Republic of China 2011). During that same period, the vast majority of the Chinese population also effectively shared in the benefits of the country's economic prosperity. Medical insurance coverage offers an illustrative example. Between 2003 and 2010, the number of employees covered by medical insurance in urban areas increased from 79.749 million to 177.912 million. In 2003, a new type of rural cooperative medical insurance was also popularized in rural areas, and by 2010, the participation rate had reached 96%, covering 836 million people (National Bureau of Statistics of the People's Republic of China 2011).

From the perspective of environmental change, 2003 to 2010 was also an important period of intensification for China's environmental problems. Since the beginning of the twenty-first century, the Chinese government has increased its investment in environmental governance, and several environmental problems have begun to abate. As such, the environmental quality has improved in many locales. However, many of the environmental threats facing China have yet to be eliminated. On the contrary, the compounding effect of environmental problems caused by rapid economic development has intensified (Hong 2013). According to the *National Environmental Statistical Bulletin*, in just the eight years from 2003 to 2010, there were 7,306 environmental emergencies (environmental pollution and damage accidents) nationwide (an average of 913 incidents a year) resulting in direct economic losses (excluding the loss of the Songhua River pollution accident in 2005). This amounted to 1,305.396 million yuan.[3] At the same time, more and more Chinese people were beginning to realize, or had personally encountered, the dangers of many environmental problems, and environmental protests and environmental rights protection incidents have emerged one after another across the country (Zhang 2010; Lu and Qi 2019). Overall, the Chinese public's experience with environmental issues deepened during this period.

9.3.2 *Research Hypotheses*

In the cross-sectional study section, we will focus on the effects of socioeconomic status factors and post-materialistic values on environmental concerns under different measurements. According to the affluence hypothesis, there is a direct relationship between socioeconomic status factors and environmental concerns, while the post-materialist value theory offers a mediating effect model: socioeconomic status is the independent variable, environmental concern under different measures is the dependent variable, and post-materialistic values act as the mediating variable. As of this writing, with the exception of a handful of studies (e.g., Kemmelmeier et al. 2002; Gelissen 2007), few empirical studies have tested such a mediation model in practice. To align with the post-materialist theory of values, in this chapter we construct and test this mediation model. We will first test the following hypotheses (the specifics of the measurement are discussed below):

Hypothesis 1: There is a positive correlation between socioeconomic status and environmental concerns.

Hypothesis 2: There is a positive correlation between post-materialistic values and environmental concerns.

Hypothesis 3: When post-materialistic values are mediated in the model, socioeconomic status's effect on environmental concerns

[3] See *National Environmental Statistical Bulletin*, 2003–2010.

declines, at least in terms of the scale of the impact, or disappears altogether.

Given that all theoretical perspectives predict that deteriorating environmental conditions will increase environmental concerns, our analysis also includes a strategy for accounting for the experience of environmental problems, and we test the following hypothesis:

> Hypothesis 4: There is a significant positive correlation between environmental problem experience and environmental concern.

Since environmental conditions theoretically are often viewed as a source of environmental concern, and are a source of environmental concern beyond the scope of post-materialistic values, and since the latter often acts as an intermediary factor in the model, we also set the experience of environmental problems as a mediating variable in the model. However, the mediating effect of environmental experience is not the focus of our research.

In the longitudinal research part, we intend to test the following hypotheses based on the results of theoretical predictions:

> Hypothesis 5: From 2003 to 2010, there was a correspondingly significant increase in public environmental concern in China in the context of rapid economic growth.

In addition to the above correlations, as previously stated, a study by Papel and Hunter (2012) directs this chapter's attention to changes in the effects of socioeconomic status. They found that the effect of education (rather than income) in the United States diminished over time, and that this may have been the result of the spread of environmentalism. In light of this, we propose the following hypothesis:

> Hypothesis 6: The effect of socioeconomic status on environmental concerns was weaker in 2010 than in 2003.

To test the mediation model, we primarily used analyses that were shown to be particularly effective in analyzing mediation effects (e.g., Dietz et al.), as well as structural equation modeling (SEM), 2007. SEM

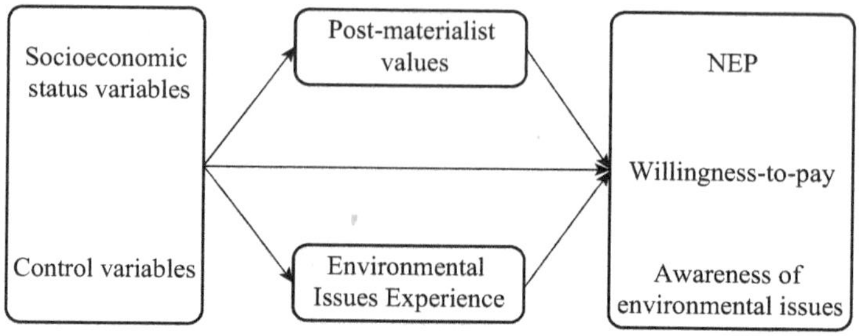

Fig. 9.1 Conceptual roadmap of the structural equation model in this study

also provides the ability to simultaneously analyze the differences in the comparison of urban and rural sample groups for a better fit, as well as to compare the differences in the latent mean and regression coefficients of a model from year to year (e.g., Bollen 1989). Figure 9.1 depicts the conceptual roadmap we used to perform the SEM analysis. In this diagram, each arrow represents a direct impact path.

9.3.3 Variable Measurement

An important dependent variable in this study is environmental concern, which we will measure along the multifaceted construct defined by Dunlap and Jones (2002). Environmental concern is defined as how much an individual cares about environmental issues and their willingness to support environmental protection. Given that some measures may bias the results of the analyses that have been discussed in the literature review, this chapter focuses on measuring three dimensions of environmental concern: the New Ecological Paradigm (NEP), the Willingness to Pay for Environmental Protection (WTP), and Awareness of Environmental Problems (AEP). These three dimensions were also chosen based on data availability and the consistency of survey items across years.

Both the 2003 and 2010 CGSS surveys included the 15-item 2000 version of the NEP scale (Dunlap et al. 2000). The application of the NEP scale in China shows that 10 of the 15 items on the scale can form a new scale with better measurement quality (Hong 2006; Hong et al. 2014). Therefore, we used these 10 items to measure acceptance of NEP by the Chinese public (NEP 1 ~ 10). These NEP items are 1, 3, 5, 7, 8,

9, 10, 11, 13, and 15 from the original scale (Dunlap et al. 2000: 433), scored as:

1 = Strongly agree
2 = Somewhat agree
3 = Unsure
4 = Somewhat disagree
5 = Strongly disagree

Prior to the analysis, we also inversely assigned two items with negative assignment.

As part of the 2010 International Integrated Social Survey (ISSP 2010), CGSS 2010's environmental module includes three items to measure the public's WTP: higher prices for environmental protection, higher taxes and willingness to reduce one's own standard of living (WTP1 ~ 3); the variable values are scored as:

1 = Very willing
2 = Somewhat willing
3 = Unsure
4 = Somewhat unwilling
5 = Very unwilling

CGSS 2003 also contains three similar survey items: willingness-to-pay higher prices, taxes, and donating for environmental protection, with the variable values scored as 1 = agree, 2 = unsure, and 3 = disagree. We use these programs to measure the public's WTP.

Finally, both surveys were designed to ask respondents to assess the severity or hazards of various environmental problems. There are 12 projects in the CGSS 2003, each dealing with environmental problems in residential communities, including air pollution, destruction of the forest cover, water pollution, degradation of cultivated land, noise pollution, freshwater scarcity, industrial waste pollution, food pollution, household waste pollution, desertification, lack of green space and wildlife extinction. These are scored as:

1 = Very severe
2 = Somewhat severe

3 = Fair
4 = Not severe
5 = Not Severe at all/not an issue

CGSS 2010 included seven projects with perceived environmental hazards, but there was no specific geographic level. Further examination revealed that two items in the CGSS 2010 (genetically modified food and nuclear power plant) had a large number of missing values (more than 40%). Therefore, these two projects had to be abandoned. The remaining five items were vehicle emissions, industrial air pollution, pesticides and fertilizers, water pollution, and global warming. The responses were given the following scores:

1 = Extremely harmful
2 = Very harmful
3 = Probably harmful
4 = Somewhat harmful
5 = Completely harmless

Together, these items measure the AEP. We used confirmatory factor analysis (CFA) to test the results of these measurements of environmental concern, and found that the reliability was generally good (see Table 9.1).

Regarding post-materialist values, eight measurement items were designed for CGSS 2003:

1. Maintaining social order and safety
2. In major decision making, the government should listen more to the opinions of the people.
3. Control unemployment and ensure sustained economic growth.
4. Guarantee the freedom of speech.
5. Ensure that future generations have access to a good environment and adequate resources.
6. Intensive development in science and technology
7. Improve the present generation's standards of living.
8. Reflect on the negative effects of modern science and technology.

Of the items above, the odd numbers are materialistic values, and the remaining four items are post-materialistic values. Respondents were

Table 9.1 CFA test results for environmental concern measurement items

Project	*2003*	*2010*	
	(n = *5,073)*	*Urban* (n = *2,262)*	*Rural* (n = *1,147)*
NEP 1	0.42	0.45	0.43
NEP 2	0.65	0.67	0.63
NEP 3	0.65	0.66	0.54
NEP 4	0.58	0.65	0.59
NEP 5	0.24	0.38	0.18
NEP 6	0.56	0.63	0.49
NEP 7	0.34	0.41	0.28
NEP 8	0.61	0.66	0.55
NEP 9	0.65	0.64	0.63
NEP 10	0.72	0.70	0.64
WTP 1	0.49	0.85	0.90
WTP 2	0.71	0.90	0.95
WTP 3	0.68	0.74	0.74
Local issue 1	0.59	–	–
Local issue 2	0.64	–	–
Local issue 3	0.58	–	–
Local issue 4	0.74	–	–
Local issue 5	0.68	–	–
Local issue 6	0.61	–	–
Local issue 7	0.64	–	–
Local issue 8	0.59	–	–
Local issue 9	0.61	–	–
Local issue 10	0.69	–	–
Local issue 11	0.65	–	–
Local issue 12	0.52	–	–
General issue 1	–	0.66	0.67
General issue 2	–	0.69	0.65
General issue 3	–	0.69	0.60
General issue 4	–	0.69	0.66
General issue 5	–	0.66	0.65

Note All factor loads were statistically significant ($p < 0.05$)

asked to select four of the eight items that were most important to them, and each respondent was assigned a score of 0 ~ 4 according to the number of post-materialistic value items chosen. In CGSS 2010, four items from the criteria designed for the ISSP survey are used to measure post-materialistic values. Respondents are asked to select the two projects to which China should give highest priority from the four items below:

1. Maintain domestic order.
2. Give the people more say in government decision-making.
3. Curb price increases.
4. Protect freedom of expression.

Similarly, odd-numbered terms are materialistic values, and even-numbered terms are post-materialistic values. We have a post-materialistic value item as the most important priority assignment (2), a post-materialistic value as a second priority (1), and a materialistic option (0). The sum of the scores of the two items can measure post-materialistic values, and the variable value range is 0 ~ 3.

Ideally, we would use actual monitoring data to measure environmental condition variables, such as physical readings of air pollution, at each of the sites visited. Unfortunately, there is no design for the CGSS survey. As a less than perfect alternative, we found that in both surveys, a question had been designed to ask respondents whether they and their families had experienced some environmental problems that required responses, and the responses were scored as 1 for "yes", or 0 for "no" to construct the respondents' "experienced environmental problems" variable.

Socioeconomic status factors pertained primarily to education and household income. In terms of educational variables, both surveys asked respondents about the highest educational degree they had earned, with options ranging from "no formal education" all the way up to "graduate degree". We assigned the answers to the standard number of years required for each qualification. The household income variable is measured using annual household income. To correct for any positive skewness common in income measurements, the model uses the logarithm of annual household income. In addition, this study also includes measures of respondents' CCP membership, which we believe also reflect respondents' socioeconomic status to a degree. Finally, full-time employment (defined as working at least 40 hours per week) served as a control variable in this study, with other control variables including gender (1 = female, 0 = male) and age (actual age at the time of interview). The independent variables and control variables involved in this study are detailed in Table 9.2.

Table 9.2 Basic descriptions of the independent variables and control variables

Variable	*2003*	*2010*	
	(n = 5,073)	*Towns (n = 2,262)*	*Rural (n = 1,147)*
Age (mean and standard deviation)	43.51 (13.18)	46.11 (15.94)	47.67 (14.85)
Percentage of women	51.84%	52.92%	50.57%
Education (mean years and standard deviation)	10.44 (3.70)	10.61 (4.28)	6.70 (4.00)
Annual household income (RMB, average and standard deviation)	24,390 (41,983)	54,349 (123,545)	23,816 (38,318)
Full-time employment	46.07%	43.24%	46.29%
Member of the Chinese Communist Party	18.57%	25.71%	9.50%
Post-materialist value index (mean score and standard deviation)	1.32 (0.80) (max = 4, min = 0)	0.67 (0.83) (max = 3, min = 0)	0.61 (0.82) (max = 3, min = 0)
Experienced environmental problems	76.62%	92.08%	83.63%

We use Mplus 7.11 for confirmatory factor analysis and structural equation model estimation, and the software uses the robustly weighted least squares technique (WLSMV), which is more suitable for cases with many categorical variables (Brown 2006). In order to deal with any missing values, we used a multi-imputation method to generate five imputed datasets for analysis, and the weighted average of the analysis results of these five datasets served as the final result (see Rubin 1987). To test the indirect effects' statistical significance, we used a bootstrap design (performed 1,000 times) to generate bias-corrected standard errors (see Hayes 2009).

9.4 Findings

Data analysis yielded a large number of results. To test the assumptions of the cross-section study section, we will first present the results of the structural equation model, with the results of the analysis of the three samples reported in Tables 9.3 and 9.4. Figure 9.1 shows the direct effect, i.e., the regression coefficient when the other indicators are controlled, with a straight one-way arrow. Indirect effects are the magnitude of the effects that are indirectly generated through mediating variables (post-materialistic values and experiences of environmental problems). The total effect is the sum of the direct and indirect effects (see Hayes 2009). For testing most of the hypotheses, only the total effect needed to be examined. However, when testing Hypothesis 3, the indirect effects needed to be explored as well.

Hypothesis 1 posits a positive correlation between socioeconomic status and environmental concerns. We have inconsistent findings about this. As explained in the literature review section, across all samples at both points in time, education has shown a sustained positive effect on both NEP and AEP; individuals with higher education levels tend to care more about the environment. Further, education is usually one of the most influential variables. Education also had the strongest effect on people's WTP, but only in 2003. More recently, in 2010, education does not seem to increase WTP.

Annual household income has a continuous positive effect on NEP; the wealthy are more receptive to it. In addition, in the 2003 and 2010 rural samples, we observed a weak but statistically significant effect of annual household income on WTP. This indicated that the wealthier urban dwellers in 2003 and the rural dwellers in 2010 had been more likely to make economic sacrifices. But this was not the case among the rural sample in 2010. It was only in the 2010 urban sample that we were able to observe a positive effect of annual household income on environmental awareness. This suggested that in urban areas in 2010, people with higher annual household incomes were more likely to perceive general environmental problems as more serious. However, this was not the case in rural areas. In addition, it is important to note that the effect of annual household income is small among all the variables. This indicates that annual household income is not an important determinant of environmental concerns.

Table 9.3 Predictions from three structural equation models of environmental concern: standardized direct, indirect, and total effects (CGSS 2003)

	New ecological paradigm			*WTP*			*Awareness of environmental problems*		
	Direct effect	*Indirect effect*	*Total effect*	*Direct effect*	*Indirect effect*	*Total effect*	*Direct effect*	*Indirect effect*	*Total effect*
Independent variable									
Gender (female = 1)	−0.09*	−0.01*	−0.10*	0.01	0.00	0.01	−0.07*	0.02*	−0.09*
Age	0.03	0.00	0.03	0.01	0.00	0.01	0.02	0.01	0.04
Education level	0.28*	0.02*	0.30*	0.19*	−0.01	0.18*	0.17*	0.06*	0.23*
Full-time employment	−0.02	−0.01	−0.03	0.03	0.00	0.04	0.01	−0.02	−0.01
Membership in the Chinese Communist Party	0.02	0.00	0.02	0.08*	0.00	0.08*	0.02	0.00	0.02
Logarithm of annual household income	0.07*	0.00	0.07*	0.09*	0.00	0.09*	0.02	−0.01	0.01
Post-materialism	0.05*	–	0.05*	−0.01	–	−0.01	0.08*	–	0.08*
Experienced environmental problems	0.12*	–	0.12*	−0.05	–	−0.05	0.40*	–	0.40*
R^2	0.14			0.08			0.23		
Model Fitting									
Chi-square	3 633.13								
Degree of Freedom	437.00								
RMSEA	0.04								
CFI	0.95								
TLI	0.94								

As mentioned earlier, CCP membership can also be used as an indicator of socioeconomic status. In the urban samples from both years, Party membership had a small positive effect on WTP. As a result, among urban dwellers, Party members were slightly more willing to pay for environmental protection than non-Party members. In rural areas in 2010, Party members were slightly more receptive to NEP than non-Party members.

Table 9.4 Environmental concerns predicting results from three structural equation models: standardized direct, indirect, and total effects (CGSS 2010)

	New ecological paradigm			*WTP*			*Awareness of environmental problems*		
	Direct effect	*Indirect effect*	*Total effect*	*Direct effect*	*Indirect effect*	*Total effect*	*Direct effect*	*Indirect effect*	*Total effect*
Independent variable (urban area)									
Gender (Female = 1)	−0.01	−0.01	−0.02	−0.01	0.00	−0.02	0.06*	0.00	0.07*
Age	0.00	−0.02	−0.02	0.03	−0.02	0.01	0.03	−0.01	0.03
Education level	0.17*	0.01	0.18*	0.04	0.01	0.05	0.19*	0.01	0.20*
Full-time employment	−0.04	−0.01	−0.04	−0.03	−0.01	−0.03	−0.05	0.00	−0.05
Membership in the Chinese Communist Party	0.04	0.00	0.03	0.08	0.00	0.07*	0.03	0.00	0.03
Logarithm of annual household income	0.08*	0.01	0.09*	0.04	0.01	0.05	0.13*	0.00	0.13*
Post-materialism	0.09*	–	0.09*	0.07*	–	0.07*	0.02	–	0.02
Experienced environmental problems	0.07	–	0.07	0.07	–	0.07	0.06	–	0.06
R^2	0.07			0.03			0.09		
Independent variable (rural area)									
Gender (female = 1)	−0.09*	0.01	−0.09*	−0.01	0.00	−0.01	−0.03	0.01	−0.02
Age	−0.01	−0.03	−0.03	−0.01	−0.03	−0.03	−0.03	−0.03*	−0.06*
Education	0.13*	0.02	0.14*	0.05	0.01	0.06	0.18*	0.02	0.20*
Full-time employment	0.03	0.00	0.02	0.01	0.00	0.01	−0.02	0.00	−0.02
Membership in the Chinese Communist Party	0.09*	0.01	0.10*	0.05	0.01	0.06	0.03	0.01	0.04

(continued)

Table 9.4 (continued)

	New ecological paradigm			*WTP*			*Awareness of environmental problems*		
	Direct effect	*Indirect effect*	*Total effect*	*Direct effect*	*Indirect effect*	*Total effect*	*Direct effect*	*Indirect effect*	*Total effect*
Logarithm of annual household income	0.09*	0.03	0.11*	0.06	0.02	0.08*	0.02	0.03*	0.05
Post-materialism	0.09*	–	0.09*	0.10*	–	0.10*	0.10*		0.10*
Experienced environmental problems	0.20*	–	0.20*	0.13*	–	0.13*	0.23*	–	0.23*
R^2	0.13			0.05			0.13		
Model fitting									
Chi-square	1 332.50								
Degrees of freedom	551.00								
RMSEA	0.03								
CFI	0.98								
TLI	0.98								
Independent variable (urban area)									
Gender (female = 1)	−0.01	−0.01	−0.02	−0.01	0.00	−0.02	0.06*	0.00	0.07*
Age	0.00	−0.02	−0.02	0.03	−0.02	0.01	0.03	−0.01	0.03
Education level	0.17*	0.01	0.18*	0.04	0.01	0.05	0.19*	0.01	0.20*
Full-time employment	−0.04	−0.01	−0.04	−0.03	−0.01	−0.03	−0.05	0.00	−0.05
Member of the Chinese Communist Party	0.04	0.00	0.03	0.08	0.00	0.07*	0.03	0.00	0.03
Logarithm of annual household income	0.08*	0.01	0.09*	0.04	0.01	0.05	0.13*	0.00	0.13*
Post-materialism	0.09*	–	0.09*	0.07*	–	0.07*	0.02	–	0.02

(continued)

Table 9.4 (continued)

	New ecological paradigm			*WTP*			*Awareness of environmental problems*		
	Direct effect	*Indirect effect*	*Total effect*	*Direct effect*	*Indirect effect*	*Total effect*	*Direct effect*	*Indirect effect*	*Total effect*
Experienced environmental problems	0.07	–	0.07	0.07	–	0.07	0.06	–	0.06
R^2	0.07			0.03			0.09		
Independent variable (rural area)									
Gender (female = 1)	−0.09*	0.01	−0.09*	−0.01	0.00	−0.01	−0.03	0.01	−0.02
Age	−0.01	−0.03	−0.03	−0.01	−0.03	−0.03	−0.03	−0.03*	−0.06*
Education	0.13*	0.02	0.14*	0.05	0.01	0.06	0.18*	0.02	0.20*
Full-time employment	0.03	0.00	0.02	0.01	0.00	0.01	−0.02	0.00	−0.02
Membership in the Chinese Communist Party	0.09*	0.01	0.10*	0.05	0.01	0.06	0.03	0.01	0.04
Logarithm of annual household income	0.09*	0.03	0.11*	0.06	0.02	0.08*	0.02	0.03*	0.05
Post-materialism	0.09*	–	0.09*	0.10*	–	0.10*	0.10*	–	0.10*
Experienced environmental problems	0.20*	–	0.20*	0.13*	–	0.13*	0.23*	–	0.23*
R^2	0.13			0.05			0.13		
Model fitting									
Chi-square	1 332.50								
Degree of freedom	551.00								
RMSEA	0.03								
CFI	0.98								
TLI	0.98								

Note * $p < 0.05$; The statistical significance test of the indirect effect is based on the standard error after bias correction produced by the boot method design

Overall, the data results partially support Hypothesis 1, but there were significant differences due to the following reasons: (1) specific socioeconomic status factors, (2) specific environmental concerns measure, (3) and different survey years. Therefore, it would be misleading to summarize these findings in general terms of socioeconomic status.

Hypothesis 2 posits that those who hold stronger post-materialistic values have higher levels of environmental concern. The results of the data partially support this hypothesis, but the evidence is inconsistent. In all years and in all samples, post-materialistic values do increase public acceptance of NEP. Moreover, in the 2010 urban and rural sample, those with stronger post-materialistic values were more willing to pay for environmental protection, but the results of the 2003 sample were different. In addition, those with stronger post-materialistic values in the 2003 and 2010 rural samples had higher overall AEP levels, but this was not found in the 2010 urban sample. Among all the variable relationships, the scale of the effect of post-materialistic values was small, indicating that the role of post-materialist values in environmental concern is limited.

To test Hypothesis 3 (that post-materialistic values mediate the effect of socioeconomic status on environmental concerns), we looked at the indirect effects of socioeconomic status (including education, annual household income, and CCP membership). In all samples for all years, with the exception of the 2003 education variable, there was no evidence of significant indirect effects for these three variables. Further analysis revealed that the indirect effects of the educational variables in 2003 were largely realized through the experience of environmental problems, rather than through post-materialistic values. This clarifies that Hypothesis 3 is not supported, and therefore post-materialistic values are not a mediating variable.

Hypothesis 4 suggests that there is a positive correlation between experiencing environmental problems and environmental concern, which is supported by the data analysis results as a whole. In the 2003 sample, those who had experienced serious environmental problems were more receptive to NEP, and were more likely to believe that local environmental problems were more serious, than those who had not. In fact, experiencing environmental problems has a stronger effect on environmental awareness than any other independent variable, even more so than education. However, it is interesting to note that an individual's experience of environmental problems does not increase their WTP. Analysis of sample data from 2010 showed that there were significant differences between urban and rural areas. In rural areas, people who have experienced environmental problems have higher environmental concerns under all measurements, and have the strongest effect in all areas. In the urban sample, we unexpectedly found that the experience of environmental problems had no significant effect on any aspects of environmental concern.

Finally, we examined two control variables. The first was the gender variable. The results of the data analysis showed that in 2003, women were less receptive to NEP than men, and were more inclined to believe that local environmental problems were less serious. There were no significant gender differences in WTP. The 2010 results showed that women's acceptance of NEP has remained low in rural areas. However, in urban areas, women were slightly more aware of general environmental issues than men, while gender differences regarding the other two environmental concerns were absent. These results suggest that over time, the level of environmental concern for Chinese women, especially in urban areas, has equaled that of Chinese men. It has even surpassed the latter in terms of awareness of environmental issues. Second, the full-time employment variable had no significant effect on any measures of environmental concern across the entire sample for all years.

Next, we turn to a vertical comparison, focusing on the analysis of the two urban samples, from 2003 and 2010. Hypothesis 5 predicts that we will observe higher levels of environmental concern among the Chinese public in 2010 than in 2003. Because of the differences in the measurement indicators used, it would not have been appropriate to directly compare the perception of environmental problems between the two points in time. Similarly, we cannot compare WTP. However, both surveys contained the same NEP scale items. As shown in Table 9.2, the two rural samples had consistent factor loads across the 10 NEP items, establishing the required measurement stability for cross-sample comparisons. We combined the two datasets and compared the latent mean using multiple sets of CFAs in Mplus. In 2010, when the potential mean of NEP was set to zero (0) as a reference point in the 2003 data, the estimated potential mean of NEP in the 2010 urban sample was – 0.027 ($p < 0.05$). The results showed that public acceptance of NEP in the urban sample in 2010 was on average lower than that in the urban sample in 2003. Because the latent mean is calculated synchronously with a single NEP item (1 ~ 5 points), the difference of 0.027 points was of little practical significance. Nonetheless, we found no evidence to support Hypothesis 5. In fact, from 2003 to 2010, acceptance of NEP in China's urban areas declined slightly. It is important to emphasize that the Chinese public was not less receptive to NEP. The results of the 2003 survey showed that on average 68% of respondents agreed or strongly agreed with the statements of the 10 NEP measurement items. By 2010, that same survey showed agreement by 70% of urban and 55% of rural respondents.

Finally, we examine Hypothesis 6, which states that socioeconomic status had a weaker effect on environmental concerns in 2010 than in 2003. Regarding this hypothesis, we focus only on the effects of socioeconomic status, i.e., the effects of education, annual household income, and CCP membership. We measured acceptance of NEP in the two urban samples, which is the only one with the same environmental concerns in the two samples. The results shown in Table 9.4 show that CCP membership has no statistically significant effect in either sample. Thus, it would be meaningless to draw further comparisons. At the same time, education and annual household income had a statistically significant effect on NEP in both samples. Therefore, we tested for statistically significant differences in both socioeconomic status variables. In the case of education, the standardized effect on NEP was 0.30 in 2003 and 0.18 in 2010, and the decrease of 0.12 was statistically significant ($p < 0.05$). The logarithm of the normalized effect of annual household income was 0.07 and 0.09 in 2003 and 2010, respectively, but the increase of 0.02 from 2003 to 2010 was not statistically significant. Taken together, Hypothesis 6 is supported by some data analysis results for socioeconomic status (mainly education) from 2003 to 2010. Thus, the effect on NEP has indeed declined.

Due to differences in operationalization, we could not perform statistical significance tests for post-materialistic values, WTP, or perceptions of environmental problems for the two years. For this purpose, we present the results of descriptive analysis. In the 2003 survey, there were five ordinal categories of indicators of post-materialist values, and their distribution was as follows: 13% = 0, 49% = 1, 32% = 2, 4% = 3, 1% = 4. In the 2010 survey, the distribution was as follows: 53% = 0, 29% = 1, 15% = 2, 3% = 3. In both indices, a high score represents stronger acceptance of post-materialistic values. The distribution in 2003 was clearly positively skewed, with a concentration between 1 and 2 (mean = 1.32, median = 1). In 2010, the distribution of the urban sample was more extreme, with a concentrated trend between 0 and 1 (mean 0.67, median and mean 0). The rural sample in 2010 showed a similar distribution: 58% = 0, 25%

= 1, 15% = 2, and 2% = 3. Taken together, we believe that the Chinese public was highly materialistic in both 2003 and 2010, which is similar to the findings of Kvaløy et al. (2012) based on data from the 2005–2009 World Values Survey.

Both surveys included a nearly identical item on paying higher taxes for the environment, but offered different options. In the 2003 survey, there were three options—agree, neutral, and disagree—with responses of 68% = agree, 14% = neutral, and 17% = disagree. The 2010 survey had five categories, from 1 = very willing to 5 = very unwilling. For the 2010 survey, we combined the two positive and two negative choices, thus simplifying the responses to the three categories with the following results: 39% = willing, 22% = neutral, and 39% = unwilling. The test results show that compared with the percentage of who "agrees" and "disagrees" in the 2003 urban sample, the percentage who responded "willing" in the urban sample in 2010 had decreased, while the percentage responding "unwilling" had increased (The p-value for both tests was less than 0.05). When asked whether they were willing to pay a higher price for environmental protection, CGSS 2003 data analysis showed that 51% = agreed, 18% = neutral, and 31% = disagreed. According to the CGSS 2010 survey, 50% = willing, 21% = neutral and 29% = unwilling; the results of the neither analyses were statistically significant. As a result, there is no evidence to support an increase in the Chinese public's WTP from 2003 to 2010.

Finally, the approximate results of the descriptive statistics of the measured items, such as the severity or hazard of the perceived environmental problem, were reported. In 2003, an average of 33% of urban respondents reported "severe" or "very serious" environmental problems (out of a total of 12 local environmental problems listed), from a lowest of 13% (desertification) to the highest of 47% (air pollution). In the 2010 urban sample, an average of 69% of respondents reported that environmental problems (five general environmental issues were listed) were harmful or very harmful, from a low of 60% (global warming) to a high of 86% (industrial air pollution). The responses in the rural sample averaged 54%, with a low of 37% (pesticide pollution) and a high of 78% (industrial air pollution).

9.5 Summary and Discussion

9.5.1 *Discussion of the Data Analysis Results*

The question this chapter addresses is how the Chinese public's concern for the environment might change during a period of rapid economic growth and rapid environmental degradation. While there are various debates in the social sciences about whether economic growth and individual affluence can increase public environmental concerns, there is near consensus that a sharp increase in public environmental concerns will be associated with rapid deterioration of environmental conditions. However, our research found no evidence of a significant increase in public environmental concern from 2003 to 2010, at least not in urban areas.

From 2003 to 2010, the majority of respondents reported experiencing environmental problems (77% in 2003 and 92% in 2010). Why, then, did their acceptance of the pro-environmental worldview and their WTP not change overall? The results of Tables 9.3 and 9.4 provide some clues regarding NEP. First, Tables 9.3 and 9.4 show that experiencing environmental problems had a significant effect on NEP in 2003, but this was absent in the 2010 urban sample. As a result, as the proportion of people experiencing environmental problems increases, its contribution to NEP dissipates.

Second, education seems to have the strongest positive effect on NEP. In most cases, there is also a positive effect on annual household income, but the impact is smaller. Table 9.2 shows that from 2003 to 2010, rural residents' average annual household incomes doubled, but their average number of years of schooling remained unchanged. We also examine the differences between the three samples in terms of NEP. Table 9.2 shows that the average number of years of schooling in the rural sample in 2010 was much lower than that of the other two urban samples. Similarly, the annual household income of the 2010 rural sample was much lower than that of the 2010 urban sample, but almost the same as that of the 2003 sample. The results of multiple groups of CFAs showed that the acceptance of NEP in the rural samples in 2010 was much lower than that in the urban samples in 2003 and 2010 (the differences in latent mean values were 0.256 and 0.230, respectively, and the p-values of the two tests were less than 0.05). Thus, we see a parallel congruence between differences in environmental concerns and differences in education, but we see no coherence between the former and the difference in annual household income. We believe that the overall educational access of urban residents in China changed little between 2003 and 2010, which may explain why their acceptance of NEP has also changed little.

It is not understood why there is no change in WTP. In 2003, the three socioeconomic status indicators—education, annual household income, and CPC membership—each had a significant positive effect on WTP. But by 2010, only the urban sample with CCP membership had a significant impact. These results show that the dependence on WTP due to socioeconomic status factors has declined in recent years. Therefore, a logical inference is that economic growth from 2003 to 2010 failed to boost WTP.

Then there is the influence of post-materialistic values. As predicted by post-materialist value theory, we find that post-materialist values have a persistent positive effect on environmental care under different measurements. Nonetheless, other findings underscore the validity of post-materialistic values. First, the scale of the effect of post-materialistic values has been smaller, which is consistent with the findings of previous empirical studies (e.g., Zhao 2012; Best and Mayerl 2013). Second, there is no evidence to support post-materialistic values as mediators between affluence and environmental concerns. Thus, while post-materialistic values and personal affluence do have some facilitating effects on the public's environmental concerns, they are not key predictors. In fact, the finding that strong materialistic values and environmental concerns can coexist among China's urban dwellers perhaps reflects the fact that economic growth and environmental quality are what the public wants.

Some of the findings in this chapter support the global environmentalist theory. First, the analysis results for all of the samples revealed that the public has a fairly high level of environmental concern, and this concern is not limited to those with higher socioeconomic status. This is because socioeconomic status factors only explain 10% ~ 15% of the variation in environmental concern under different measurements. Second, our results show that the variability in the interpretation of environmental concerns under different measurements was lower in 2010 than in 2003, even when accounting for the results in rural areas. In addition, education had less of an effect on NEP and WTP in 2010 than in 2003. These results not only support the global environmentalist theory, but also support Pampel and Hunter's (2012) argument that "there is a diffusion process of environmental concern across socioeconomic status". The arguments are consistent. Our measurements of public environmental concern in China are more accurate than the single measurement item used by Papel, taking into account the differences between China and the United States, this is an important finding.

9.5.2 Conclusions and Implications

From 2003 to 2010, despite China's rapid economic growth and environmental degradation, and contrary to all theoretical predictions, the pro-environmental worldview and WTP among China's urban dwellers remained largely unchanged. Although people with higher annual household incomes and greater post-materialistic values tended to have slightly higher levels of environmental concern, the idea that affluent or post-materialistic values are a key driver of environmentalism is not supported by the study. Instead, we found that in contemporary China, there is evidence that environmental concerns may have spread from the highly educated population to the rest of society. This is consistent with the global environmentalist view as a whole.

Our findings have some theoretical and practical implications. First, as many studies have found in other countries (Dunlap and York 2008; Hunter et al. 2010), affluence does not seem to be a prerequisite for the Chinese public's environmental concerns. Thus, the causal chain from economic development to increased affluence to rising levels of environmental concern is not empirically supported. Second, there is a lack of consistent support for the hypothesis that China's deteriorating environmental conditions will lead to greater environmental concerns. Our research shows that when looking longitudinally, there are different trends in different aspects of China's environmental concerns. Although an increasing number of people are reporting experiencing environmental problems, the pro-environmental worldview measured by NEP and the willingness of individuals to contribute to environmental protection showed no signs of increasing during our study period. Therefore, we need more elaborate conceptualization and measurement schemes when theorizing and examining sources of environmental concern. Third, education has a persistent and strong effect on various aspects of environmental concern, but not on annual household income. Accordingly, we argue that it would be more appropriate to separate socioeconomic status factors into different independent variables than to put them into a single latent construct when examining the effect of socioeconomic status factors on environmental concerns. This means that different levels of environmental concern might not be a reflection of overall socioeconomic status differences.

A practical takeaway from this chapter for environmental policymaking is that it would be unrealistic to expect that economic growth will increase affluence and naturally increase public environmental concern. Environmental activists are also steadfast that environmental degradation will increase environmental concern. Because the pro-environmental worldview (NEP) has not been strengthened, the current environmental activism of the Chinese public is more reactive than proactive, and thus, it is susceptible to the "issue-attention cycle" (Dunlap 1991). The findings of some environmental protests appear to be a commentary on this pattern. For example, in the case of the Xiamen PX case, Xiamen residents' attention to the environment was limited to their own community or region, and when the PX project was relocated to a neighboring city, the response was muted (Zhou 2011). In order to obtain sustained and long-term environmental policy support from the public, policymakers and environmental activists need to work to strengthen the public's pro-environmental worldview, which in turn promotes the adjustment of individual environmental behavior norms and actual behaviors (Stern et al. 1999).

Finally, it should be noted that the research reported in this chapter does have several limitations. First, the longitudinal comparison in this study is limited because we only have two years of survey data, and CGSS 2003 data only cover China's urban areas, which weakens our confidence in some of our more interesting findings (e.g., the diminishing effect of education). In future research, we suggest collecting multiple data points and using more rigorous panel design data. Second, inconsistencies in measurement design between the two CGSS surveys were a frequent challenge in this study. This will make direct comparisons and statistical significance tests difficult, or even impossible, in future surveys. In particular, it would be more effective to design more standard measurements for longitudinal trend studies. Third, we regret that we were unable to produce actual measurements of environmental degradation. To better test hypotheses related to the state of the environment, future studies should be use actual environmental status measurement like Mohai and other scholars (Mohai et al. 2010). Fourth, although we looked at three aspects of environmental concern, there remain several important elements that are not included in the analysis, the most prominent being environmental activism and environmental behavior. This is due both to data availability and to the limited size of a single study. Thus, future research should further expand upon this, and include additional measurements of environmental concern.

CHAPTER 10

Urban–Rural Differences in Environmental Behaviors

Peng Yuanchun

As in the study of environmental concern, the study of environmental behavior is also a core issue and mainstream topic of environmental sociology (Dunlap 2002). This chapter focuses on the analysis of urban and rural differences in public environmental behaviors in China. Generally speaking, high-quality academic research on environmental behavior in Chinese academic circles has been lacking. It was not until 2000 that public environmental awareness and environmental behavior became the focus of research (Peng 2011). Moreover, most research has been limited to exploring the environmental behavior of urban residents or rural residents and its influencing factors. Meanwhile, comparative studies on the environmental behavior of urban and rural residents nationwide have been rare. Therefore, this chapter uses authoritative data to systematically analyze urban and rural residents' environmental behaviors, whether there are differences between them, and what factors influence them.

Y. Peng (✉)
Renmin University of China, Beijing, China

D. Hong and Y. Fan (eds.), *Toward a Green Society*,
https://doi.org/10.1007/978-981-96-5111-5_10

Five basic assumptions in terms of socio-demographic characteristics are the most representative results of understanding and explaining environmental concern and environmental behavior at the individual level: the age hypothesis, the gender hypothesis, the social class hypothesis, the residence hypothesis, and the political hypothesis (Van Liere and Dunlap 1980). Of these, the residence hypothesis refers mainly to the fact that urban residents are more concerned about the environment, and implement more environmental behaviors than their rural counterparts, due to their higher education levels and incomes, and are more locally affected by pollution. Earlier studies supported this hypothesis (Tremblay and Dunlap 1978; Arcury and Christianson 1990; Fransson and Gärling 1999). Other studies found that with the gradual change in rural economic development patterns, increases in environmental protection facilities, and the improvement of environmental services, the urban–rural differences in environmental concern and environmental behavior are gradually narrowing and are no longer significant. Even after controlling for demographic variables (Tarrant and Cordell 1997; Jones et al. 2003), rural residents engage in more recycling and environmental management behaviors than their urban counterparts (Kennedy et al. 2009).

The relevant research on environmental behavior in China has shown that urban and rural residents have significant differences in environmental knowledge, awareness of environmental problems, environmental concern and environmental attitude (Hong 1997; Ma and Guo 2000). Additionally, urban–rural differences have an effect on environmental protection behavior (State Environmental Protection Administration, Ministry of Education 1999). Urban residents generally have environmental awareness, but their environmental behavior is lacking, while for rural residents, both environmental awareness and behavior are lacking (China Environmental Culture Promotion Association 2006). Urban residents' awareness of the concept of ecological civilization is much higher than that of farmers.[1] Other studies have explored the environmental behaviors of urban and rural residents, and found that big city residents are more concerned about the environment, and implement environmental behaviors more than do residents of small and medium-sized cities (Gong 2008; Peng 2013). Farmers also lack environmental knowledge

[1] China's first "national ecological civilization consciousness survey research report released." (2014–02–20) [2019–07–22]. http://www.gov.cn/jrzg/2014-02/20/content_2616364.htm.

and environmental awareness, and their environmental protection skills are in need of improvement (Zhu 2000). This is the basis for the analysis in this chapter.

10.1 Urban and Rural Residents' Environmental Behaviors

In the 2010 China General Social Survey, a multi-level stratified probability sampling design was adopted, and the survey covered 31 provincial administrative units in China (excluding Hong Kong, Macao and Taiwan). In the end, about 12,000 individuals in 100 counties (districts), 480 resident (village) committees and 12,000 families were surveyed, and 11,785 valid samples were obtained. In addition, the environmental module survey continued for respondents born in February, September, November, and December. The final effective sample size of the environmental module was 3,716, of which 2,392 urban residents and 1,324 rural residents were comprised, accounting for 64.4% and 35.6% of the environmental module samples, respectively.

10.1.1 Descriptive Analysis of the Environmental Behaviors of Urban and Rural Residents

According to the division of the private and the public spheres, we divided environmental behavior into two categories: private environmental behavior and public environmental behavior.

Private environmental behavior was measured by six activities:

- Sorting and recycling
- Buying fruits and vegetables grown without the use of chemical fertilizers or pesticides (hereafter referred to as organic)
- Reducing driving
- Reducing energy or fuel consumption
- Conserving or reusing water
- Avoiding consumption of certain non-environmentally friendly products

Public environmental behavior was measured by four activities:

- Participation in environmental groups
- Signing environmental petitions
- Donating money to environmental groups
- Participation in environmental protests or demonstrations

We analyzed the overall characteristics of a single type of environmental behavior and whether there was a difference between urban and rural residents, and the results are shown in Tables 10.1 and 10.2.

Overall, the proportion of urban and rural residents who engage in private environmental behavior is low. For example, due to limitations of the living environment, more than 40% of the respondents never separated garbage or waste products to facilitate recycling, and nearly half of them never bought organic fruits or vegetables. Also, only 3.5% of respondents reported significantly reducing their driving to protect the environment. In addition to the nearly 80% of the respondents who did not own a car or could not drive, the percentage of people who reduced their driving was even lower, only 2%. Nearly 30% of respondents reported never reducing their home energy or fuel consumption. 16.9% of the respondents never conserved or reused water, and only about half of the respondents often or always practiced this behavior. Slightly more than 30% of the respondents said they avoided purchasing certain products for the sake of environmental protection. Finally, the percentage of respondents who occasionally performed a certain behavior was higher than those who often or always performed the same behavior. It should be noted that the unfavorable built-in conditions such as insufficient basic environmental protection facilities and a lack of environmental protection services limit or hinder the implementation of environmental behavior. Thus, further improving environmental protection facilities and improving environmental protection services would be conducive to the cultivation and stimulation of positive environmental behavior.

As shown in Table 10.1, there are significant differences between urban and rural areas for each specific private environmental behavior, with urban residents implementing more private environmental behaviors than rural residents. Urban residents are also more likely than rural residents to always or often recycle, buy organic fruits and vegetables, reduce driving, reduce energy or fuel consumption, conserve or reuse water, and avoid consuming certain non-environmentally friendly products. They are also less likely than rural residents to ignore these behaviors. For example, 19.6% of urban residents reported never reducing their consumption of

Table 10.1 Private environment behavioral differences between urban and rural residents in a single domain

Activity	*Sample type*	*Response (%)*					*Chi-square test of urban–rural difference*
		Always	*Often*	*Sometimes*	*Never*	*Built-in limitation*	
E1. Sort glass, aluminum cans, plastic or newspaper for easy recycling	Total sample	11.9	19.7	23.9	17.3	27.1	$\chi^2 = 202.46$, *df* = 4, $p = 0.000$
	Urban	14.8	22.5	25.9	16.4	20.3	
	Rural	6.6	14.6	20.2	19.1	39.4	
E2. Buy fruits and vegetables that have not been treated with fertilizers or pesticides (organic)	Total sample	6.7	16.2	28.4	23.9	24.8	χ^2=178.21, *df* = 4, $p = 0.000$
	Urban	7.9	19.3	32.0	21.0	19.7	
	Rural	4.5	10.5	21.7	29.3	33.9	
E3. Reduce driving for the sake of the environment	Total sample	2.0	3.5	9.0	5.8	79.7	$\chi^2 = 87.503$, *df* = 4, $p = 0.000$
	Urban	2.6	4.4	11.5	5.2	76.4	
	Rural	0.8	1.8	4.7	7.0	85.8	
E4. Reduce the consumption of forms of energy or fuel such as gasoline, natural gas or electricity at home	Total sample	10.0	22.9	40.2	26.9	–	$\chi^2 = 210.08$, *df* = 3, $p = 0.000$
	Urban	12.2	26.6	41.6	19.6	–	
	Rural	5.8	16.2	37.8	40.2	–	

(continued)

Table 10.1 (continued)

Activity	*Sample type*	*Response (%)*					*Chi-square test of urban–rural difference*
		Always	*Often*	*Sometimes*	*Never*	*Built-in limitation*	
E5. Conserve or reuse water for environmental protection	Total sample	17.2	31.9	34.0	16.9	–	χ^2=252.12, df = 3, p = 0.000
	Urban	21.2	35.3	33.1	10.4	–	
	Rural	10.0	25.8	35.6	28.6	–	
E6. Avoid buying certain products for the sake of environmental protection	Total sample	7.4	16.9	41.7	34.0	–	χ^2=324.210, df = 3 p = 0.000
	Urban	9.7	21.0	45.4	24.0	–	
	Rural	3.2	9.6	35.2	52.0	–	

Note The constraints resulting from objective conditions

Table 10.2 Environmental behavior for a single public domain and its difference between urban and rural areas

Activity	*Sample type*	*Response (%)*		*Chi-square test of urban–rural difference*
		Yes	*No*	
E7. Joined any association for the purpose of environmental protection	Total sample	1.9	98.1	$\chi^2 = 6.707$, $df = 1$, $p = 0.010$
	Urban	2.4	97.6	
	Rural	1.1	98.9	
E8. Signed a petition on an environmental issue over the last 5 years	Total sample	1.3	98.7	$\chi^2 = 1.128$, $df = 1$, $p = 0.288$
	Urban	1.5	98.5	
	Rural	1.1	98.9	
E9. Donated money to an environmental group over the past 5 years	Total sample	5.3	94.7	$\chi^2 = 33.707$, $df = 1$, $p = 0.000$
	Urban	6.9	93.1	
	Rural	2.4	97.6	
E10. Participated in a protest or demonstration on an environmental issue over the past 5 years	Total sample	0.4	99.6	$\chi^2 = 0.040$, $df = 1$, $p = 0.842$
	Urban	0.4	99.6	
	Rural	0.4	99.6	

gasoline, natural gas, electricity, or other forms of energy or fuel at home to protect the environment, compared to 40.2% of rural residents; 52.0%

of rural residents never bought certain products for environmental protection, 28 percentage points higher than the corresponding percentage of urban residents.

The objective limitations of E1, E2, and E3 are that there is no recycling system in the respondents' place of residence, there are no organic fruits and vegetables available for purchase in the respondents' place of residence, or the respondents do not have a car or cannot drive.

As shown from Table 10.2, the percentage of urban and rural residents implementing environmental behaviors in the public domain is low, showing a lower participation level than that of private environmental behaviors. For example, only 1.9% of respondents had ever joined environmental protection associations. Over the past five years, 98.7% of the respondents had not signed a petition, 94.7% had not donated money to an environmental group, and 99.6% had not participated in a protest or demonstration on an environmental issue. Additionally, there was a difference between urban and rural areas in joining and donating money to environmental protection organizations. Also, the proportion of urban residents joining and donating money to environmental protection organizations was higher than that of rural residents. For example, 2.4% of urban residents had joined environmental protection organizations, compared to only 1.1% of rural residents. Furthermore, 6.9% of urban residents surveyed had donated money to environmental groups over the past five years, 4.5 percentage points higher than the corresponding proportion of rural residents. In addition, there was no significant difference between urban and rural residents in terms of whether they had signed environmental petitions or participated in environmental protests or demonstrations, and the participation level was low.

10.1.2 Comprehensive Comparative Analysis of Urban and Rural Residents' Environmental Behaviors

We have analyzed individual private environmental behaviors and public environmental behaviors and their differences between urban and rural areas. Next, we will analyze urban and rural residents' private and public environmental behaviors and whether there is a significant difference between them.

First, we assigned the following scores according to the frequency of implementation of private environmental behaviors: 0 = never; 1 = sometimes; 2 = often; 3 = always. In addition, due to the built-in limitations "there is no local recycling system in place" and "organic fruits and vegetables are not available locally", some residents are limited from implementing said recycling or corresponding purchase behaviors, which results in a score of "0". The behavior of protecting the environment is implemented by default due to "cannot drive or no car", which is scored as "3". The reliability analysis for the private environmental behavior scale is conducted with these adjustments. The reliability analysis results showed that after the third activity ("reducing driving for environmental protection") was excluded, the intrinsic consistency of the scale was higher, the alpha coefficient had increased from 0.694 to 0.776, and the correlation coefficients (Ri-t value) between E1, E2, E4, E5, and E6 activities and the total score for the scale respectively were 0.500, 0.397, 0.627, and 0. In addition, after deleting the corresponding activities, the alpha coefficient generally decreased or changed slightly, such that the internal consistency of the modified scale after the deletion of the third activity was high, and the scale reliability was acceptable. Next, we used exploratory factor analysis to study the validity of the revised private sphere environmental behavior scale, and found that all activities clustered on one factor. Therefore, we directly added the remaining five activities to generate private environmental behavior variables, with values ranging from 0 to 15 points, with a mean score of 5.44 and a standard deviation of 3.49. The higher the score, the higher the level of implementation of private environmental behavior. In addition, we assigned the values of "yes" and "no" to certain public environmental behaviors as "1" and "0" respectively. Since the corresponding activities are only divided into two values and have a concentrated negative bias toward one pole, they are directly added to generate a public environmental behavior variable with scores ranging from 0 to 4, with a mean score of 0.09 and a standard deviation of 0.35.

Then, in order to visually demonstrate the implementation of urban and rural residents' environmental behaviors, we measured private environmental behavior variables and public environmental behavior variables by percentage, as shown in Table 10.3. About 80% of the respondents scored below 60 points in their private environmental behavior, among which 8.3% never practiced any private environmental behavior, and only about 20% scored higher than 60 points; 99.7% of the respondents scored less than 60 points on public environmental behavior, and 92.8% of the respondents never engaged in any public environmental behavior. There was a significant difference between urban and rural areas in the scores for private and public environmental behavior: urban residents implemented more environmental behavior than rural residents. For example, 24.7% of urban respondents scored above 60 points for their private environmental behavior, compared to only 9.0% of rural respondents. Of the rural respondents, 16.5% never engaged in any private environmental behavior, 12.7 percentage points more than the urban respondents. 96.0% of the rural respondents never engaged in any public environmental behavior, 5.1 percentage points more than the urban respondents.

Finally, we tested the mean value of private and public environmental behaviors and found that there were significant differences between urban and rural residents in both private and public environmental behaviors (see Table 10.4). Specifically, urban residents engage in more private and public environmental behaviors than rural residents. It should be noted that this conclusion is based on the preliminary results of the correlation analysis, and the influence of other factors was not excluded. Whether this is valid needs to be further determined by statistical methods such as multiple linear regression.

Table 10.3 Frequency of environmental behavior variable scores (%)

	Private environment behavior			*Public environmental behavior*		
	Total sample	*Urban sample*	*Rural sample*	*Total sample*	*Urban sample*	*Rural sample*
0 points	8.3	3.8	16.5	92.8	90.9	96.0
1 ~ 19 points	13.2	10.0	19.0	–	–	–
20 ~ 39 points	33.1	31.0	36.9	6.0	7.6	3.0
40 ~ 59 points	26.3	30.6	18.6	1.0	1.1	0.8
60 ~ 79 points	13.2	16.6	7.0	0.2	0.3	0.2
80 points and above	5.9	8.1	2.0	0.1	0.1	–
Total	100.0	100.0	100.0	100.0	100.0	100.0
	$\chi^2 = 370.742$, $df = 5$, $p = 0.000$			$\chi^2 = 34.461$, $df = 4$, $p = 0.000$		

Table 10.4 Comparison of urban and rural residents' mean environmental behaviors

		Mean value	*Standard deviation*	*Test value*
Private environmental behavior	Urban	6.26	3.42	$F = 407.783$ $p = 0.000$
	Rural	3.93	3.08	
Public environmental behavior	Urban	0.11	0.38	$F = 24.820$ $p = 0.000$
	Rural	0.05	0.27	

10.2 Comparing the Influencing Factors of Urban and Rural Residents' Environmental Behaviors

10.2.1 Research Design

The dual structure of urban and rural areas has persisted for a long time in China, resulting in a wide gap between urban and rural areas in terms of environmental conditions, economic development, social differentiation, resource distribution, infrastructure construction, information dissemination, level of consciousness, and action ability. Based on this understanding and the academic research on environmental behavior, the basic hypothesis of this study is: There are significant differences in environmental behavior between urban and rural residents in China, with urban residents implementing more environmental behaviors than rural residents.

There are two major types of factors that influence environmental behavior: external constraints and internal constraints. External constraints mainly refer to the corresponding objective basis of environmental behavior. The more representative explanations are provided by pollution-driven theory and structural constraint theory. Pollution-driven theory focuses on the impact of objective environmental conditions on individual environmental behaviors. Urban residents are more likely than rural residents to suffer from pollution and other types of environmental deterioration, and thus they engage in more environmental behaviors. Therefore, we propose the pollution-driven hypothesis: Residents with more serious environmental problems in their residential areas will implement more environmental behaviors.

Structural restriction theory holds that individuals are often embedded in social structures, examples of which would be social status, social roles, social groups, social systems, and other patterns, which have corresponding influences and restrictions on individual social life and social behavior. Stratum structure is the core of social structure, and it is usually embodied as a social stratification system in modern society. Societal members with higher social status tend to have higher education levels and higher incomes, and thus their basic needs can be satisfied. As such, they pay more attention to the satisfaction of higher-level needs such as a comfortable living environment and high environmental quality, and are particularly sensitive to the decline and deterioration of the environment. Thus, they implement more environmental behaviors (Peng 2013). Therefore, we propose the class status hypothesis: The higher the residents' class status, the more environmental behaviors they implement.

In the specific prevention and control of environmental pollution and ecological damage, there are immense differences between urban and rural areas. These can be summarized as the duality of control system, which is an important reason for the disparity in urban and rural environmental problems. This has an even greater effect on the implementation of urban and rural residents' environmental behavior. For example, in terms of environmental protection, there is a tendency to focus on urban areas while overlooking rural areas. Urban environmental protection systems and environmental policies are relatively strong, and mass media plays a major role in overseeing urban public opinion on environmental protection and environmental governance. In contrast, rural environmental policies and regulations are relatively weak, and the media plays a minor role in overseeing rural public opinion. In addition, environmental protection agencies and environmental non-governmental organizations are more concentrated in cities (Hong 2001). Therefore, we propose the dual systems urban and rural environmental protection hypothesis: The greater the efforts of local environmental protection, the more the residents implement environmental behaviors.

With the proliferation of information technology, mass media such as TV, mobile phones, and the internet are increasingly embedded in people's daily lives. As such, they have a profound effect on individuals' social cognition and behavior. For example, the more ways there are to access environmental information, the more abundant the information about environmental issues and specific environmental behaviors is, and the more likely one is to implement environmental behaviors (Gamba and Oskamp 1994; Fransson and Gärling 1999; Peng 2013). However, the information gap between urban and rural areas is formidable. Mass media has a higher penetration rate in cities, while many rural residents have built-in limitations in obtaining information. However, due to the differences in work and lifestyles, urban residents have more exposure and greater appetites for media consumption than rural residents. In fact, mass media have different effects on urban and rural residents' environmental behavior. Therefore, we propose the information segmentation hypothesis: Residents with more exposure to mass media will engage in more environmental behaviors.

Psychologically orientated research has long occupied a dominant position in the field of environmental behavior research, which focuses on revealing the "black box" of implementing environmental behavior, that is, the complex internal process and psychological mechanism. Therefore, the internal constraints of environmental behavior mainly refer to the corresponding subjective motivation for generating environmental behavior. Only after a certain understanding of the relevant behavioral problems can conscious promotion of behavior be generated, and consciousness is the necessary prerequisite for the generation of behavior. Based on this, we propose the environmental awareness hypothesis: The higher residents' environmental awareness, the more environmental behaviors they will implement.

Social constructivism, on the other hand, holds that environmental problems are constructed, not only with their objective aspects but with their subjective aspects (Hong 2001). It is through the social construction process of international attention, promotion of governments at all levels, mass media focus, advocacy and the appeal of experts and scholars, and the intervention of environmental protection organizations that specific environmental conditions are recognized as problems. This awakens and stimulates environmental awareness and environmental behavior. Of course, if the members of a society encounter specific events such as pollution infringing on their daily lives, the role of constructing and stimulating environmental awareness and environmental behavior intensifies. For example, a study found that more than 50% of its respondents said that they would care about the environment only when they felt harmed by pollution (Ma and Guo 2000). As such, rural residents suffering from severe pollution were more aware of the environment (Hu 2007). Based on this, we propose the Event Construction hypothesis:

Residents who encounter environmental pollution events will implement more environmental behaviors.

10.2.2 Measurement of Variables

The dependent variables in this study are private environmental behavior and public environmental behavior. The independent variables include urban vs. rural residential setting, external constraints, and internal constraints. The external constraints include local environmental status, class status, local environmental protection efforts, and the degree of exposure to mass media, while the internal constraints include environmental awareness, and event construction.

Local environmental conditions: In this study, we measure local environmental status through environmental problems accurately perceived by the public. The questionnaire asks the respondents which problem has the greatest effect on them and their families. Selecting one of the nine types of environmental problems, such as air pollution or chemical fertilizer and pesticide pollution, indicates that the respondents are aware of the local existence of environmental pollution and other problems, and they are assigned a value of 1. A response of "no", "no choice", or "don't know" indicates that the respondents are not aware of the environmental problems that affect them locally, and these are assigned a value of 0.

Socioeconomic class status: Based on the relevant research results from both China and other countries, we measure individuals' objective class status by three indicators—income level, education level, and occupation; their self-rated socioeconomic status is measured by the social class to which the respondents belong. As for the measurement of specific variables, in terms of income level, we used annual personal income, that is, the respondents' total income during the past year. Education level was determined by the years of education, and respondents' education levels were assigned the following values:

0 = no education
6 = elementary school
9 = middle school
12 = high school/vocational high school/technical school
15 = junior college
16 = bachelor's degree
19 = graduate degree and above

Based on information about working conditions in the survey data, occupation was divided into three categories: 0 = unemployed, 2 = farming, and 3 = non-agricultural work. Individuals' self-rated socioeconomic status is scored by respondents' rating of their socioeconomic status at the time of the survey, with 10 points representing the top and 1 point representing the bottom.

Local environmental protection efforts: Due to the limited data, we could not obtain data on local environmental protection efforts such as the number of environmental protection agencies, the number of environmental non-governmental organizations, the amount of environmental protection investment, the number of environmental protection employees, or the objective environmental governance effectiveness at the respondents' local residences. Therefore, we only used the respondents' judgment of local governments' effectiveness in solving regional environmental problems over the past five years to measure local environmental protection efforts. The answers "one-sided attention to economic development, ignoring environmental protection work", "insufficient attention, insufficient investment in environmental protection", "Although efforts have been made, the effect has not been good" reflect weak local environmental protection efforts, and are assigned a score of "1". Responses such as "cannot choose" and "do not know" indicate that the respondents found it difficult to judge the local environmental protection efforts, and were assigned a score of "2". Responses such as "great efforts, there are certainly results" and "achieved great success" reflect that the local environmental protection efforts are reasonable, and were assigned a score of "3".

Mass media exposure: The survey asked respondents about their use of newspapers, magazines, radio, television, the internet, and mobile text messages during the past year, and assigned the following scores: 1 = never, 2 = rarely, 3 = sometimes, 4 = often, and 5 = always. Statistical analysis revealed that the alpha value of the 6 mass media access methods was 0.702, and after removing the corresponding items, the alpha coefficient generally decreased, that is, it had good reliability and internal consistency, and could be regarded as a single-dimension scale. Therefore, the above six items were directly added to generate the mass media exposure variable, whose scores ranged from 6 to 30, with a mean score of 13.78 and a standard deviation of 4.53.

Environmental awareness: This refers to the extent to which people are aware of and support the solutions to ecological and environmental problems, and individuals' willingness to contribute to the solution of such problems (Hong 2006). We measured environmental protection knowledge, environmental concern, and environmental behavior efforts from three perspectives. As for environmental protection knowledge, respondents were asked to judge whether the following 10 statements were true, false, or ambiguous, as shown in Table 10.5. Based on current knowledge, we know that 1, 3, 5, 7, 9 can be considered false statements, and 2, 4, 6, 8, 10 can be considered true statements. A score of "1" was given to each correct response and "0" to each incorrect response; "can't choose" and "don't know" were noted as errors. Table 10.5 shows that urban and rural residents' accuracy of environmental protection knowledge is low on the whole, with significant differences between urban and rural residents for each statement on environmental protection knowledge, that is, urban residents have higher levels of environmental protection knowledge than rural residents. The mean scores and standard deviations for environmental protection knowledge level were 5.15 and 2.76, respectively.

In the next study, we used the NEP scale revised by Dunlap et al. (2000) to measure environmental concern, as shown in Table 10.6; we also assigned scores to the revised NEP scale. Since statements 1, 3, 5, 7, 9, 11, 13, and 15 are considered true, the more in agreement their responses were, the higher their concern for the environment. Therefore, the following scores were assigned:

1 = totally disagree
2 = somewhat disagree
3 = neither agree nor disagree
4 = somewhat agree
5 = totally agree

Items 2, 4, 6, 8, 10, 12, and 14 were considered false statements. The more in agreement their responses were, the lower their environmental concern. Therefore, the following scores were assigned:

5=totally disagree
4=somewhat disagree

Table 10.5 Frequency and comparison of urban and rural residents' environmental protection knowledge

Item	*Sample type*	*Correct*	*Incorrect*	*Cannot choose*	*Test value*
(1) Vehicle exhaust does not pose a threat to human health	Total sample	12.4	81.2	6.4	
	Urban	9.9	86.5	3.6	$\chi^2 = 134.288$, $df = 2$,
	Rural	17.0	71.7	11.3	$p = 0.000$, $df = 2$, $p = 0.000$
(2) Excessive use of chemical fertilizers and pesticides can lead to environmental damage	Total sample	83.8	9.5	6.7	
	Urban	87.7	7.8	4.4	$\chi^2 = 82.498$, $df = 2$,
	Rural	76.8	12.4	10.8	$p = 0.000$
(3) The use of phosphorus-containing laundry detergent will not cause water pollution	Total sample	13.1	62.0	24.9	
	Urban	11.4	69.4	19.3	$\chi^2 = 157.736$, $df = 2$,
	Rural	16.1	48.7	35.2	$p = 0.000$
(4) Fluorine emissions from fluorine refrigerators will become a factor in destroying the atmospheric ozone layer	Total sample	51.7	9.7	38.6	
	Urban	62.0	9.1	30.0	$\chi^2 = 295.262$, $df = 2$,
	Rural	33.3	10.8	55.9	$p = 0.000$
(5) The production of acid rain has nothing to do with coal burning	Total sample	10.8	44.1	45.0	
	Urban	10.8	50.9	38.4	$\chi^2 = 131.519$, $df = 2$,
	Rural	11.0	32.1	57.0	$p = 0.000$

Item	*Sample type*	*Correct*	*Incorrect*	*Cannot choose*	*Test value*
(6) Species are interdependent, and the disappearance of one species will have a ripple effect	Total sample	52.3	5.8	41.9	
	Urban	61.7	5.1	33.3	$\chi^2 = 232.711$, $df = 2$, $p = 0.000$
	Rural	35.5	7.2	57.4	
(7) In the air quality report, Level 3 air quality means better than Level 1 air quality	Total sample	11.0	26.2	62.8	
	Urban	10.8	32.6	56.6	$\chi^2 = 142.915$, $df = 2$, $p = 0.000$
	Rural	11.4	14.7	73.9	
(8) A single forest with only a single species is more likely to cause pests and disease	Total sample	44.3	9.3	46.4	
	Urban	48.6	8.6	42.7	$\chi^2 = 49.883$, $df = 2$, $p = 0.000$
	Rural	36.6	10.4	53.0	
(9) In the water pollution report, Class V water quality means that it is better than Class I water quality	Total sample	7.9	16.4	75.7	
	Urban	7.6	19.3	73.1	$\chi^2 = 38.928$, $df = 2$, $p = 0.000$
	Rural	8.4	11.2	80.3	
(10) An increase in carbon dioxide in the atmosphere would be a warming factor	Total sample	53.2	5.0	41.8	
	Urban	63.4	4.7	32.0	$\chi^2 = 284.712$, $df = 2$, $p = 0.000$
	Rural	34.9	5.5	59.6	

Note Items 1, 3, 5, 7, 9 are false statements, and the others are true statements. Each correct response is assigned a score of 1, and each incorrect response is assigned a score of 0

Table 10.6 Comparison of item frequency and factor load for the NEP Revised Scale for urban and rural residents

Statement	*Sample type*	*1 = totally disagree; 2 = somewhat disagree; 3 = neither agree nor disagree; 4 = somewhat agree; 5 = totally agree*					*Factor load and test value*
		1	*2*	*3*	*4*	*5*	
(1) The current population is approaching the limit of what the earth can bear	Total sample	2.5	10.0	31.6	40.9	15.0	0.37
	Urban	2.1	10.3	26.2	44.3	17.1	$\chi^2 = 101.468$
	Rural	3.1	9.5	41.3	34.8	11.4	$df = 4$, $p = 0.000$
(2) Man is the most important and can change the natural environment to meet his own needs	Total sample	12.8	31.0	23.9	24.5	7.9	–
	Urban	15.4	34.0	19.9	23.3	7.4	$\chi^2 = 102.599$
	Rural	8.1	25.7	31.0	26.5	8.7	$df = 4$, $p = 0.000$
(3) Man's destruction of nature often leads to disastrous catastrophic consequences	Total sample	1.6	5.4	19.9	48.1	25.1	0.56
	Urban	1.4	4.5	15.2	49.3	29.6	$\chi^2 = 139.506$
	Rural	1.8	6.9	28.4	45.8	17.0	$df = 4$, $p = 0.000$
(4) Thanks to human wisdom, it is entirely possible to improve the earth's environmental conditions	Total sample	2.2	11.4	28.3	40.9	17.3	–
	Urban	2.3	13.5	24.1	42.6	17.7	$\chi^2 = 71.766$
	Rural	2.0	7.7	35.9	37.9	16.5	$df = 4$, $p = 0.000$
(5) At present, man is abusing and destroying the environment	Total sample	2.8	7.9	18.1	47.7	23.5	0.55
	Urban	2.1	6.4	14.0	51.4	26.1	$\chi^2 = 129.018$
	Rural	4.1	10.5	25.5	41.0	18.9	$df = 4$, $p = 0.000$
(6) The earth's natural resources are abundant as long as we know how to exploit them	Total sample	8.4	26.0	26.6	27.8	11.2	–
	Urban	10.1	30.2	21.6	27.4	10.7	$\chi^2 = 127.694$
	Rural	5.4	18.5	35.5	28.5	12.1	$df = 4$, $p = 0.000$
(7) Animals and plants have the same right to existence as humans	Total sample	1.4	4.6	17.2	43.3	33.4	0.49
	Urban	1.3	4.2	11.9	46.6	36.0	$\chi^2 = 143.721$
	Rural	1.7	5.3	26.9	37.3	28.7	$df = 4$, $p = 0.000$

Statement	*Sample type*	*1 = totally disagree; 2 = somewhat disagree; 3 = neither agree nor disagree; 4 = somewhat agree; 5 = totally agree*					*Factor load and test value*
		1	*2*	*3*	*4*	*5*	
(8) The balancing capacity of nature is strong enough to cope with the shocks of modern industrial society	Total sample	15.0	29.5	38.2	13.1	4.1	0.38
	Urban	18.6	34.2	30.8	12.9	3.6	$\chi^2 = 204.723$
	Rural	8.6	21.2	51.6	13.6	5.1	$df = 4, p = 0.000$
(9) Man, despite his special powers, is still subject to the laws of nature	Total sample	1.5	4.2	25.2	42.4	26.6	0.53
	Urban	1.6	4.1	18.2	46.1	29.9	$\chi^2 = 177.351$
	Rural	1.4	4.5	37.8	35.7	20.6	$df = 4, p = 0.000$
(10) The claim that mankind is facing an “environmental crisis” is an exaggeration	Total sample	13.3	33.6	34.7	14.8	3.6	0.42
	Urban	16.2	38.6	28.4	13.7	3.2	$\chi^2 = 172.855$
	Rural	8.2	24.7	46.0	16.8	4.3	$df = 4, p = 0.000$
(11) The Earth is like a spaceship, with only a very limited amount of space and resources	Total sample	2.2	7.5	31.1	36.2	22.9	0.63
	Urban	1.8	6.8	24.9	39.4	27.1	$\chi^2 = 158.208$
	Rural	2.8	8.8	42.3	30.6	15.5	$df = 4, p = 0.000$
(12) Man was born to be master, to rule over the rest of nature	Total sample	15.6	30.7	30.0	16.5	7.1	–
	Urban	18.7	34.9	24.2	15.4	6.8	$\chi^2 = 155.644$
	Rural	10.2	23.2	40.5	18.5	7.5	$df = 4, p = 0.000$
(13) The balance of nature is fragile and can easily be disturbed	Total sample	2.0	6.8	29.5	40.3	21.5	0.59
	Urban	1.8	6.3	23.2	43.3	25.3	$\chi^2 = 149.221$
	Rural	2.4	7.6	40.6	34.9	14.6	$df = 4, p = 0.000$
(14) Man will eventually know more about the laws of nature, and thus be able to control nature	Total sample	6.9	17.8	35.7	28.0	11.6	–
	Urban	7.9	20.9	29.8	29.2	12.2	$\chi^2 = 111.512$
	Rural	5.0	12.4	46.1	25.9	10.5	$df = 4, p = 0.000$
(15) If everything continues as it is at present, we will soon suffer a serious environmental disaster	Total sample	2.5	9.1	31.7	33.6	23.2	0.65
	Urban	1.8	9.4	24.6	36.7	27.5	$\chi^2 = 192.769$
	Rural	3.7	8.4	44.6	28.1	15.3	$df = 4, p = 0.000$

3=neither agree nor disagree
2=somewhat agree
1=totally agree

In addition, the answers "can't choose" and "don't know" in each item indicate that the response is ambiguous, which is close to "I don't care to agree or disagree", so it is assigned an intermediate score of "3". Table 10.6 shows that the overall level of environmental concern for urban and rural residents is low, and each item on the NEP revised scale has a significant difference between urban and rural residents, that is, urban residents have a higher level of environmental concern than rural residents. Reliability tests showed that the alpha value of the scale was 0.753, which indicated high reliability. Except for Statements 4 and 14 (whose Ri-t values were 0.022 and 0.197 respectively), the correlation coefficient between other statements and the total score for the scale was between 0.285 and 0.482, and after excluding Statements 4 and 14, the scale's alpha value increased slightly. Therefore, it was necessary to further investigate the scale's dimensions.

However, Hong (2006) used CGSS 2003 data to evaluate the application effect of the NEP revised scale in China, and argued that it could be a tool to measure public environmental concern in China, after proper modification. Then, through the application of confirmatory factor analysis, it was found that the factor load of the five false statements (2, 4, 6, 12, and 14) was too low. Therefore, they were eliminated and the remaining ten statements were constructed into a scale of environmental concern with high reliability and a single dimension suitable for the Chinese public (Xiao and Hong 2007). Based on the understanding above, the default value was re-encoded to the intermediate score 3 according to the common practice in the academic community, and the factor load obtained by the verification factor analysis[2] of the above ten-item scale (see Table 10.6) was weighted and aggregated to construct the environmental concern score variable; the higher the score, the stronger the environmental concern, with a mean score of 19.18 and a standard deviation of 2.92.

Environmental behavior efforts refer to the tendency to implement a specific environmental behavior as much as possible, which is measured by the respondents' answers to the questions of "the degree to which they are willing to pay higher prices, pay higher taxes, and lower living standards in order to protect the environment". In the analysis, we assigned the following scores:

5 = very willing
4 = somewhat willing
3 = neither willing nor unwilling
2 = somewhat reluctant
1 = very reluctant

The environmental behavior efforts variable was obtained by directly adding the scores of the above three items, and the total score ranged from 3 to 15. The higher the score, the more willingness to implement environmental behavior; the mean score was 8.91, and the standard deviation was 2.81.

Event construction: The social construction factor in this study is based on whether the respondents and their families have encountered environmental problems. The score for not having encountered environmental problems is 0, and the score assigned for having encountered environmental problems is 1, regardless of whether they have taken action.

[2] According to the modification suggestions for the model, the correlation between error variables was controlled, and the final chi-square value for the model was = 298.066, df = 27, p = 0.000, GFI = 0.98, NFI = 0.96, IFI = 0.96, CFI = 0.96, RMSEA = 0.052. Because the chi-square value is easily affected by the size of the sample, when the number of samples is large, the chi-square value will be large, the p-value will be smaller, and it is easy to reject the corresponding model. Therefore, multiple indicators should be adopted to measure the model's degree of fit. In this study, the chi-square test led us to reject the model, but the other indicators were good. Therefore, we considered the model to have good fit and accepted it.

In order to better explicate the urban–rural differences in environmental behavior, we introduced gender, age, and marital status as control variables. The various variables used in this study are described in Table 10.7.

10.2.3 Data Analysis

The variables for urban vs. rural residence, external constraints, and internal constraints were gradually incorporated into the model. Gender, age, and marital status served as control variables, and private environmental behavior served as a dependent variable for multiple linear regression analysis. The corresponding results are shown in Table 10.8.

As shown from Table 10.8, all models passed the F-test and were statistically significant and acceptable. Urban vs. rural residence passed the significance test for all models, indicating that there were significant differences between urban and rural residents in terms of private environmental behaviors, with urban residents exhibiting more private environmental behaviors than rural residents. In addition, with the gradual inclusion of external and internal constraints, the interpretation of the model increased from the initial 10.2% to 21.7% and 25.3%, and the urban vs. rural residence, external constraints, and internal constraints could ultimately explain 29.5% of the variation in private environmental behavior. This indicated that in addition to urban vs. rural residence, external constraints and internal constraints were also related to private environmental behavior.

After controlling for other variables, the awareness of local environmental conditions and mass media usage had significant positive effects on private environmental behavior; urban and rural residents who accurately perceived the local existence of environmental pollution and other problems, and urban and rural residents who had high mass media usage, implemented more private environmental behavior. Personal annual income had no significant effect on private environmental behavior, and neither education level nor self-rated economic status had any significant effect on private environmental behavior after the introduction of environmental awareness and social construction variables. This means that education level and self-rated economic status had no direct effect on the implementation of private environmental behavior, and may be influenced by intermediary variables such as environmental protection knowledge and environmental concern.

Table 10.7 List of study variables

Variable	*Characteristic*	*Explanation*
Private environment behavior	Progressive	Minimum score = 0, maximum score = 15, mean = 5.44, standard deviation = 3.49
Public environmental behavior	Progressive	Minimum sore = 0, maximum score = 4, mean = 0.09, standard deviation = 0.35
Local environmental conditions	Binary	1 = Accurately perceived local environmental problems, 0 = Did not accurately perceived environmental problems
Personal annual income	Progressive	Mean = 19,169.80 yuan, standard deviation = 60,770.698
Education level	Progressive	0 = No education, 6 = primary school, 9 = junior high school, 12 = high school/vocational high school/technical school, 15 = junior college, 15 = bachelor's degree, 19 = graduate degree and above, mean = 8.94, standard deviation = 4.60
Occupational type	Categorical	3 = Non-farm work, 2 = farming, 1 = unemployed
Self-rated socioeconomic status	Progressive	The higher the value, the higher the social class; mean = 4.05, standard deviation = 1.77
Local environmental protection intensity	Categorical	1 = Weak, 2 = difficult to judge, 3 = fair
Mass media usage	Progressive	The higher the score, the higher the media usage; mean = 13.78 standard deviation = 4.53
Environmental protection knowledge	Progressive	Minimum score = 0, maximum score = 10; mean = 5.15, standard deviation = 2.76
Environmental concern	Continuous variable	Minimum score = 7.68, maximum score = 25.85; mean = 19.18, standard deviation = 2.92
Environmental behavior efforts	Progressive	Minimum score = 3, maximum score = 15; mean = 8.91, standard deviation = 2.81
Encounter environmental problems	Binary	1 = Encounter, 0 = no encounter
Gender	Binary	0 = Male, 1 = female
Age	Progressive	Mean = 47.3, standard deviation = 15.73
Marital status	Progressive	0 = unmarried; 1 = married

Table 10.8 Standard regression coefficients of multiple linear regression (OLS) of private environmental behavior

	Model 1	*Model 2*	*Model 3*	*Model 4*
Urban vs. rural residence	0.320***	0.147***	0.193***	0.120***
	(0.149)	(0.116)	(0.155)	(0.114)
Local environmental conditions		0.090***		0.032#
		(0.161)		(0.179)
Personal annual income		−0.006		−0.009
		(0.000)		(0.000)
Education level		0.099***		0.029
		(0.018)		(0.018)
Farming status		−0.006		−0.010
		(0.186)		(0.177)
Current employment status		0.059**		0.049*
		(0.182)		(0.174)
Self-rated socioeconomic status		0.048**		0.024
		(0.033)		(0.032)
Local environmental protection at the place of residence is satisfactory		0.065*** (0.132)		0.063*** (0.126)
It is difficult to judge the intensity of local environmental protection at the place of residence		−0.112*** (0.181)		−0.048** (0.180)
Media usage		0.226***		0.176***
		(0.018)		(0.017)
Environmental protection knowledge			0.187***	0.126***
			(0.023)	(0.025)
Environmental concern			0.173***	0.152***
			(0.020)	(0.022)
Environmental behavior efforts			0.214***	0.191***
			(0.018)	(0.019)
Encounter environmental problems			0.053**	0.032#
			(0.158)	(0.195)
Control variable				
Gender	0.016	−0.026	−0.032*	−0.046**
	(0.112)	(0.119)	(0.104)	(0.114)
Age	−0.035*	0.048*	0.038*	0.048*
	(0.004)	(0.005)	(0.004)	(0.005)

(continued)

Table 10.8 (continued)

	Model 1	*Model 2*	*Model 3*	*Model 4*
Marital status	0.026	0.057***	0.039*	0.062***
	(0.207)	(0.225)	(0.190)	(0.215)
adjusted R^2	0.102	0.217	0.253	0.295
F	102.879	65.399	150.292	74.688
p	0.000	0.000	0.000	0.000

Note Agriculture served as the reference group for occupation type, and the environmental protection strength of residence was the weak reference group. The numbers in brackets are standard errors; #$p < 0.1$; *$p < 0.05$; **$p < 0.01$; ***$p < 0.001$

The effect of occupation type and local environmental protection efforts on private environmental behavior are more complex. There is no significant difference in the implementation of private environmental behavior between non-agricultural workers and farmers, but the non-workers implement more private environmental behavior than the farmers. The residents who think that the local environmental protection efforts are strong will implement more private environmental behaviors than the residents who think local environmental protection efforts are weak, while the residents who think that local environmental protection efforts are difficult to judge will implement less private environmental behaviors. Therefore, for private environmental behavior, the pollution-driven hypothesis and information segmentation hypotheses are confirmed, but the hierarchical status hypothesis is not supported, and the dual system hypothesis is only partially verified.

After controlling for other variables, environmental protection knowledge, environmental concern, environmental behavior efforts, and encountering environmental problems all have significant positive effects on private environmental behavior; the higher the environmental protection knowledge, the higher the environmental concern level, the stronger the environmental behavior efforts, and the more urban and rural residents who have personally (and as a family) encountered environmental problems, the more private environmental behavior they implement. Therefore, for private environmental behavior, both the environmental awareness hypothesis and the event construction hypothesis are confirmed. In addition, male, older, and married urban and rural residents engage in more private environmental behaviors. Relatively speaking, environmental behavior efforts, environmental concern, environmental protection knowledge, and urban and rural types have a greater effect on private environmental behavior.

In view of the fact that public environmental behavior is biased toward one end without implementation and does not meet the preconditions of multiple linear regression such as the normal distribution of residuals and the homogeneity of the variance of residuals, the value of the behavior of the public domain environment "1 ~ 4" is scored as "1", and "0" is still "0" for re-assignment. Then, the variables for urban and rural types, external constraints and internal constraints were incorporated into the model. Next, gender, age and marital status were taken as control variables, and the public domain environmental behavior was taken as the dependent variable for binary logistic regression analysis. The results are shown in Table 10.9.

As can be seen from Table 10.9, after controlling other variables, the difference between urban and rural environmental behaviors in the public domain is no longer significant, that is, there is no significant difference between urban residents and rural residents in the implementation of public environmental behaviors. Moreover, the environmental status of place of residence, personal annual income, education level, and employment status had no significant effect on the implementation of public environmental behavior; only the self-rated socioeconomic status had a significant positive effect on the implementation of public environmental behavior. Local environmental protection efforts had a significant effect on the implementation of public environmental behavior. Specifically, compared with urban and rural residents who think that local environmental protection efforts are difficult to judge, urban and rural residents who think that local environmental protection efforts are weak or fair were more likely to implement public environmental behavior, that is urban and rural residents who had a clear understanding and judgment of local environmental protection efforts were more likely to implement public environmental behavior. Additionally, the degree of exposure to mass media had a significant positive effect on the implementation of public environmental behavior, that is, the more urban and rural residents are exposed to mass media, the more likely they are to implement public environmental behavior. Therefore, for public environmental behavior, neither the pollution-driven hypothesis nor the hierarchical status hypothesis are supported, the dual system hypothesis is partially confirmed, and the information segmentation hypothesis is confirmed.

Table 10.9 Binary logistic regression analysis results for public domain environmental behavior

	Partial regression coefficient B	*Standard error S.E*	*Wald value*	*Degree of freedom*	*Significant level*	*Occurrence ratio Exp (B)*
Constant	−4.623	0.756	37.362	1	0.000	0.010
Urban vs. rural residence	0.420	0.232	3.297	1	0.069	1.523
Local environmental conditions	0.068	0.302	0.051	1	0.821	1.071
Annual income	0.000	0.000	0.718	1	0.397	1.000
Education level	−0.016	0.027	0.345	1	0.557	0.984
Employment status			1.312	2	0.519	
Farming status	0.311	0.283	1.207	1	0.272	1.365
Unemployed	0.133	0.198	0.449	1	0.503	1.142
Self-ranked socioeconomic status	0.119	0.046	6.553	1	0.010	1.126
Local environmental protection efforts			7.378	2	0.025	
Fairly effective	−0.046	0.171	0.071	1	0.789	0.955
Hard to judge	−1.293	0.476	7.366	1	0.007	0.274
Mass media exposure	0.101	0.022	22.079	1	0.000	1.107
Environmental protection knowledge	0.050	0.037	1.865	1	0.172	1.051
Environmental concern	−0.051	0.028	3.370	1	0.066	0.950
Environmental behavior efforts	0.175	0.030	34.774	1	0.000	1.191
Encounter environmental problems	0.095	0.338	0.080	1	0.778	1.100
Gender	0.230	0.159	2.083	1	0.149	1.258
Age	−0.028	0.007	16.748	1	0.000	0.973
Marital status	−0.196	0.243	0.650	1	0.420	0.822
Hosmer–Lemeshow test p-value = 0.800						

Note Non-agricultural occupation is the reference group for occupation type, and the environmental protection intensity in area of residence is the reference group

After controlling other variables, environmental protection knowledge, environmental concern, and environmental problems had no significant effect on the implementation of public environmental behavior. Meanwhile, environmental behavior efforts had a significant positive effect on the implementation of public environmental behavior. Therefore, for public environmental behavior, the environmental awareness hypothesis is only partially supported, while the event construction hypothesis is not supported. In addition, the younger the urban and rural residents, the more likely they are to engage in public environmental behavior. Gender and marital status had no significant effect on the engagement in public environmental behavior.

10.3 Summary and Discussion

China's urban and rural residents have generally low levels of environmental behavior. Both urban and rural residents engage in more private environmental behavior than public environmental behavior, and some residents are non-participants in environmental behavior, never engaging in any type of environmental behavior. Additionally, there is a significant difference between urban and rural private environmental behaviors, that is, urban residents engage in more private environmental behaviors than rural residents, and each specific private environmental behavior has significant differences between urban and rural residents. Additionally, urban residents engage in more specific private environmental behaviors than rural residents, such as sorting garbage and recycling, purchasing organic fruits and vegetables, reducing driving, reducing energy or fuel consumption, saving or reusing water, and avoiding the consumption of certain non-environmentally friendly products. There is no significant difference between urban and rural residents in terms of public environmental behavior, and the percentage of urban and rural residents who join environmental groups, donate money to environmental groups, sign environmental petitions, and participate in environmental protests or demonstrations is low.

The mechanism of environmental behavior varies from type to type, that is, different environmental behavior types have different influencing factors. For private environmental behavior, the pollution-driven hypothesis, information segmentation hypothesis, environmental awareness hypothesis and event construction hypothesis were all supported, but the class status hypothesis was not, and the dual system hypothesis of environmental protection was only partially supported. For public environmental behavior, the information segmentation hypothesis is confirmed, the pollution-driven hypothesis, the class status hypothesis and the event construction hypothesis are not supported, and the dual system hypothesis of environmental protection and the environmental awareness hypothesis are only partially confirmed.

10.3.1 Factors Influencing Private Environmental Behavior

10.3.1.1 Pollution-Driven and Private Environmental Behavior

Pollution-driven theory focuses on objective environmental problems' impact on environmental concern and environmental behavior implementation. Due to the limits of the data, this study only confirmed that urban and rural residents who believed that there were local environmental problems engaged in more private environmental behaviors. This shows that the public's direct perception in and experience with environmental problems has contributed to the implementation of private environmental behaviors. In follow-up research, based on the differences between urban and rural environmental problems, corresponding environmental status indicators from individual communities or villages, counties, provinces, and regions should be included. Additionally, multi-layer model analysis should be implemented in combination with the environmental status and problems that urban and rural residents actually feel and experience, so as to explicate the internal mechanism of the pollution-driven implementation of environmental behaviors.

10.3.1.2 Class Status and Private Environment Behavior

Contrary to the findings of Van Liere and Dunlap et al. (1980), class status has no significant effect on environmental behavior. This is consistent with our research results on urban residents' environmental behavior (Peng 2013). China's fragmented class status makes it difficult to tie to income, education level, and occupational status, and it is impossible to determine individuals' class status based on a single or comprehensive index. It is also difficult to use class status to guide individual social attitudes and behavioral orientations, due to varying interests and individualized social attitudes. In addition, the government-dominated environmental governance model has not been effectively combined with the change of class structure and the expansion of the middle class. This has resulted in a lack of class foundation in environmental behavior and environmental governance. Therefore, while focusing on expanding the middle class and promoting a middle-class-dominated society, we should also cultivate class consciousness and the ability to act together.

10.3.1.3 *The Urban–Rural Dual System of Environmental Protection and Private Environmental Behavior*

This study's findings reveal that urban and rural residents who had clear judgment about the efforts of local environmental protection implemented more environmental behaviors than those who did not. Compared with those who think it is difficult to judge local environmental protection efforts, those who think local environmental protection efforts are weak or fair may have a better understanding of the reasoning behind local environmental protection policies, the number of environmental protection institutions and organizations, the amount of environmental protection inputs, and the effectiveness of environmental protection. They may also have better awareness and understanding of the roles of (and interrelationships between) different actors such as the government, enterprises, and the general public. This may motivate them to implement more environmental behaviors. It should be noted that the data in this study only involve subjective aspects of environmental protection intensity, which may have affected the study's results. Therefore, subsequent research should include objective indicators such as the number of local environmental protection agencies and organizations, investment in environmental protection, the number of environmental protection employees, and the number of mass media reports on local environmental issues in the analysis.

10.3.1.4 *Information Segmentation and Private Environment Behavior*

With the advent of the information society, mass media is playing an increasingly important role in information dissemination, knowledge transfer, and topic focus. It can be argued that the more exposure urban and rural residents have to the mass media, the more likely they are to acquire more environmental knowledge and information, and the more likely they are to improve their environmental awareness and environmental concern level, thus prompting residents to implement more environmental behaviors. As shown in Table 10.8, after the inclusion of environmental awareness variables such as environmental protection knowledge, environmental concern, and environmental behavior efforts, mass media's effect on environmental behavior is weakened. This reflects that exposure level to mass media has a direct effect on environmental behavior, and also an indirect effect on environmental behavior through environmental awareness.

10.3.1.5 Environmental Awareness and Private Environmental Behavior

This study reveals that improving environmental awareness has a significant positive effect on the implementation of private environmental behavior. This is related to Chinese culture which emphasizes knowledge to guide daily life practice, and advocates the combination of knowledge and action, that is, before implementing a certain behavior, it is necessary to have a comprehensive understanding of the relevant knowledge. At the same time, the knowledge measured in this study is related to specific environmental problems such as air pollution and water pollution, which are less abstract and closely related to daily life. Furthermore, it would be of great significance to implement various forms of environmental education and elevate the public's understanding of the environment to promote their concern for the environment and the implementation of environmental behavior.

Similar to many studies that have found low correlations between environmental concern and environmental behavior (Dunlap and Van Liere 1978; Hines et al. 1987; Axelrod and Lehman 1993; Dunlap et al. 2000), environmental concern's effect on private environmental behavior was not as strong as expected in our study. This was because environmental concern is a complex system of attitudes, which not only covers the new environmental paradigm (NEP), but also includes many other attitudes such as natural utilitarianism, economic growth, and technological progress. These are inherently intertwined and implicitly contradictory. Even proponents of the NEP do not fully comprehend the balance of nature, the limits of growth, ecological crises, and anthropocentrism. Thus, they do not necessarily implement behaviors that are conducive to improving environmental conditions (Dunlap and Van Liere 1978). In addition, environmental concern's effect on private environmental behavior may also be mediated or hindered by other factors (Gardner and Stern 1996; Blake 1999; Dunlap et al. 2000).

Environmental behavioral efforts have a significant positive effect on both private and public environmental behavior. The reason is that behavioral efforts serve as statements that connect the subject of the participant with the future behavior, that is, the tendency to try to implement a certain behavior. Therefore, many studies have indicated that there is a strong correlation between behavioral efforts and actual behavior, and if the behavioral efforts can be correctly measured, most resulting behaviors can be predicted more accurately (Fishbein and Ajzen 1975; Taylor and Todd 1995). Of course, environmental behavior effort is only one of the factors that influence environmental behavior. In fact, the implementation of environmental behavior often needs to overcome certain obstacles or bear the corresponding costs. Thus, whether the conditions of behavior are available, whether the public opinion supports it, whether any important others expect it, and whether the money and time costs are appropriate, may regulate or otherwise affect the relationship between the efforts of environmental behavior and actual environmental behavior.

10.3.1.6 Event Construction and Private Environment Behavior

This study's findings show that urban and rural residents who have encountered personal and family environmental problems are more likely to engage in private environmental behaviors. One possible reason for this is that environmental problems have the appearance of objective facts and subjective constructions. Therefore, regardless of whether members of society (especially victims of environmental problems) realize the social causes of environmental problems, their impact on themselves and society, and the action strategies to prevent and resolve them, they need to go through the construction process from problem facts to subjective identification. This often requires the involvement, interaction, and co-construction of different social entities such as government departments, mass media, experts and scholars, and environmental protection organizations. However, if residents encounter specific events such as pollution infringement in daily life, these specific events are more likely to bring them stronger negative experiences. This can prompt them to consciously pay attention to relevant environmental information, and motivate them to take responsibility for environmental protection, and implement it into their daily lives. In this way, they can implement more private environmental behaviors such as sorting recyclable materials, garbage reduction, and green consumption.

10.3.2 Factors Influencing Public Environmental Behavior

This study has revealed that the percentage of urban and rural residents who implemented environmental behaviors is low. However, exposure to mass media, local environmental protection efforts, and environmental behavior efforts did have an effect on public environmental behavior. Neither local environmental status, social status, knowledge of environmental protection, environmental concern, nor encounters with environmental problems had any significant effect on public environmental behavior. The long-term government-led social management model has promoted the embedding of government in all aspects of social life, forming a pattern of "big government, small society". Moreover, society has been underdeveloped, resulting in limited opportunities and channels for public participation in public affairs, and a lack of awareness and ability to participate in them. This has affected the implementation of public environmental behaviors.

Another aspect may be the dominant model of environmental protection. In Western society, the public sphere is relatively developed, and multiple entities such as governments, enterprises, organizations, and the public consciously participate in environmental protection. Therefore, the public has more perception and experience with environmental conditions and environmental issues. This can stimulate the participation consciousness of corresponding subjects, such that they are more concerned about the environment and participate in more environmental protection activities. However historically, China's environmental protection work has been characterized by government domination, with the government being both the initiator and the main promoter of environmental protection, as well as the main coordinator and arbitrator of environmental protection. This has resulted in the failure to create a social atmosphere for public participation in environmental protection or to build diversified channels for public participation in environmental protection. This has led to a lack of awareness and public action to participate in environmental protection activities. Perhaps it can be understood that the implementation of public environmental behaviors in China is less out of concern for the environment and improvement of the environment, and more out of a response to the government's call and compliance with government guidelines.

CHAPTER 11

Residents' Smog-Related Out-Migration Intention (SOI) in Urban Areas

Hong Dayong, Fan Yechao, and Li Peifan

Research on behavioral choices in specific situations is more fruitful than general research on environmental concern and environmental behavior. Based on survey data from Beijing residents, this chapter explores the manifestation of people's intent to relocate and the factors which affect it within the context of smog-based air pollution. In addition to the constraints imposed by ecological conditions on human beings, which can be observed along various dimensions such as productivity, lifestyle, health conditions and cognitive experiences, it may also change the distribution

D. Hong (✉)
Renmin University of China, Beijing, China
e-mail: hongdy@ruc.edu.cn

Y. Fan
Minzu University of China, Beijing, China
e-mail: fanyechao@ruc.edu.cn

P. Li
China Energy Investment Corporation, Beijing, China

D. Hong and Y. Fan (eds.), *Toward a Green Society*,
https://doi.org/10.1007/978-981-96-5111-5_11

of population over a certain period of time and area, resulting in "environmental migration"; that is to say, "the migration activities that occur because of ecological degradation or in order to improve and protect the ecological environment, and the migratory population resulting from such activities" (Bao 2006). From a sociological perspective, for individuals who choose to relocate, this usually means not only a change in the living environment, but also a change in productivity and lifestyle, as well as social adaptation and any other problems pertaining to relocation and resettlement. And at the macro level, large-scale relocations of populations are bound to have a significant effect on the demographic, economic, social and ecological aspects of both sending and receiving regions.

For some time now, China's urban areas have been facing serious smog-based air pollution problems. Government monitoring data shows that in 2018, only 121 of the country's 338 cities at the prefecture level and above met ambient air quality standards, and although there has been significant improvement since 2017, 64.2% of cities still failed to meet air quality standards.[1] Since smog is largely the result of human activities, cities with high population concentrations like Beijing, Shanghai, and Guangzhou have become the "hardest-hit areas" affected by smog. Driven by the smog problem, "fleeing Beijing, Shanghai and Guangzhou" has become a hot social topics in recent years, and environmental migration intents and behaviors have received widespread attention.[2] According to media reports, in contemporary China, there is indeed a small number of elites who have moved away from first-tier cities to relocate to the countryside or abroad. In addition to the aversion to modern "urban diseases" such as traffic congestion and high costs of living, the fear and disappointment regarding environmental pollution of the metropolitan areas also spark the intent of these people to "leave one's native place, especially against one's will". Thus, the core research questions of this chapter are as follows: To what extent does smog-based air pollution influence residents' intent to relocate out of the city? What are the factors

[1] Ministry of Ecology and Environment. 2018 *Bulletin of China's Ecological and Environmental Conditions*. (2019–05–29) [2019–07–22]. http://www.mee.gov.cn/hjzl/zghjzkgb/lnzghjzkgb/201905/P020190619587632630618.pdf.

[2] *New York Times*: "Smog creates new 'environmental migrants' in China." (2013–11–25) [2019–07–22]. http://china.cankaoxiaoxi.com/2013/1125/306938.shtml.

"Smog contributes to 'environmental migration'". *Shenzhen Special Administrative Region Newspaper*, 2014–10-29(C6).

influencing the divergence in residents' propensity to relocate? What are the theoretical and policy implications of this?

11.1 Literature Review

11.1.1 Environmental Factors' Impact on Migration Decisions

In studies of population migration, ecological factors, as well as economic, political, and social factors, are important contextual variables of interest.[3] The sociologist William Petersen (1958) classified migration into four types: (1) migration triggered by ecological factors; (2) migration triggered by migration policies; (3) migration triggered by personal ambition; and (4) migration triggered by social momentum. Of these four types, ecologically triggered migration is the most basic type, in response to the relationship between human beings and nature. Its manifestations can be divided into wandering, ranging, and flight from the land. Those who relocate because of environmental factors are referred to as "environmental migrants", "environmental refugees" and individuals who go "back to the wilderness" (Hunter 1998; Myers 2005).

According to the push–pull theory in traditional migration studies, there is a gap between sending and receiving societies in terms of socioeconomic conditions and the stability of the political and social environment. Corresponding push and pull forces emerge, and migration occurs under the combined action of these two forces (Lee 1966; Portes and Böröcz 1989; Li 2003). In applying the push–pull theory to environmental migration, researchers have argued that environmental degradation and the deterioration of ecosystem services at the origin create an environmental push, while superior environmental quality and harmonious ecosystems at the destination create an environmental pull. The result is spontaneous environmental migration (Bogardi and Renaud 2006). The modified push–pull theory explanation of environmental migration has also been supported by several empirical studies. Analysis of multinational data by Reuveny and Moore (2009) has shown that environmental degradation, as measured by cultivated land degeneration, population growth and natural disasters, has a significant effect in models explaining migration, and is an important push factor in the

[3] Ecological factors include both primary ecological changes (e.g., natural disasters) and secondary environmental problems caused by human activities.

decisions of residents of different countries to relocate and emigrate to other countries. Using data from Nepal, Massey et al. (2010) also found that indicators of environmental degradation—e.g., land degradation, increased access to fuelwood and materials, increased population density and reduced agricultural productivity—are indeed strongly correlated with local people's decisions to relocate short distances.

The push–pull theory only considers the objective differences in socioeconomic characteristics between the places of origin and destination, but ignores individuals' subjective initiative and the intermediate factors that influence migrants' decisions. For example, in some cases of environmental migration, migrants move from large cities with a high level of socioeconomic development to small towns with good environmental quality but an underdeveloped economy. This is contrary to the direction of migration predicted by the classical push–pull theory. The reversal of this direction warrants a more reasonable explanation. More importantly, even if the push–pull theory could explain why people relocate, it does not answer why some people choose not to relocate in the same spatial and temporal context and in the face of the same environmental crisis (Richmond 1993). In other words, why do environmental forces have different effects on the relocation decisions of people in the same society? Thus, there are obvious theoretical shortcomings in using push–pull theory to explain spontaneous environmental relocation.

In response to the problems above, the stress-threshold theory proposed by Wolpert (1966) and Speare (1974) provides an explanation. The core idea of this theory is that the decision to relocate is a knee-jerk response to "stress". There is a threshold to the level of stress experienced by an individual in the sending region, and migration is likely when the stress experienced exceeds this threshold. Of these stressors, environmental stress (such as traffic congestion, air pollution, water pollution and noise pollution) is one of the most salient residential stressors individuals experience, and is an important reference standard for relocation decisions. When faced with an environmental risk, individuals will create simplified models of reality based on their own perceptions of risk. If the perceived environmental risk is within the threshold, they will remain where they are. On the contrary, if environmental pressure exceeds the limit of their ability to withstand it, environmental relocation will transpire. Using questionnaire survey data from a sample of 1,450 people in Los Angeles, CA (USA), Kiecolt and Nigg (1982) found that residents' assessment of the danger of environmental problems in their neighborhood and their perceived level of environmental risk were positively related to their desire to move. In a more recent study, Zhan et al. (2014) analyzed the relationship between Beijing residents' satisfaction with their residential environment and their intent to relocate, and found that the natural environment quality of a residential environment promoted residents' overall satisfaction with their residential environment, and then suppressed their intent to relocate. This provides additional empirical support for the pressure threshold theory.

In contrast to the push–pull theory, the stress-threshold theory distinguishes between migrants and non-migrants, and provides a better answer to the question of why some people might consider relocating by treating the intent to move as a knee-jerk response to a perceived level of environmental hazard that exceeds the limits of their tolerance. However, this theory does not adequately explain the phenomenon of "non-migration" (Fuguitt and Zuiches 1975). There are at least three problems with the stress-threshold theory. First, it fails to account for the effect of relocation costs on individual relocation decisions. Second, it narrows the types of behavioral choices individuals make in the face of environmental risks. Third, it ignores the dynamic evolution of environmental conditions. These problems not only illustrate the social complexity of relocation decisions, but also suggest that we should pay attention to the differentiation of residents' environmental relocation intents. The so-called differentiation of environmental relocation intent can be reflected not only in whether one considers relocation, but also in the type of relocation. For example, it has been found that while regions with more severe environmental hazards appear to be less attractive to newcomers than other regions, relocation is not as pronounced (Hunter 1998). Indeed, the divergence in residents' environmental relocation intents cannot be fully explained by environmental factors, and a better understanding of the reasons for this divergence requires exploring other factors influencing environmental migration intent.

11.1.2 Factors Influencing the Divergence in Environmental Migration Intent

Individuals' socioeconomic status affects their environmental relocation intent. Environmental justice theory suggests that differences in socioeconomic status result in corresponding differences in groups' coping capacities in the face of environmental risks. Sociologist Ulrich Beck

(2004: 38) said, "poverty is hierarchical and smog pollution is democratic". However, people with higher socioeconomic status can choose to relocate from their current residence to a higher-quality environment due to their stronger risk avoidance ability. When it comes to avoiding the risks to themselves and their families from problems such as smog pollution, people with higher socioeconomic status tend to have more ability and opportunities. Thus, they are more likely to choose to move to a new place of residence or to take better care of themselves (Brulle and Pellow 2006; Hong D. and Gong 2008). This is because relocation or protection itself entails economic and social costs (e.g., the costs of housing and social adjustment after relocation), and the socioeconomic status of an individual or family determines the likelihood that he or she will be able to bear such costs (Ritchey 1976; Fakiolas 1999). For example, analyzing data published by the United States Census Bureau on "seasoning migration of the elderly", Hogan (1987) found that favorable climatic conditions in the Sunbelt region were generally attractive to older Americans who chose to relocate, but that their ultimate ability to relocate to the Sunbelt region for the winter was largely determined by their economic status, i.e., "migrants tend to have higher incomes or be more affluent than non-migrants". In another example, in Bangladesh, Gray and Mueller (2012) found that despite the harsh environment created by floods, poverty factors limited local residents' relocation intent and actual relocation behavior. Thus, socioeconomic status remains an important variable to control when analyzing environmental relocation intent.

Environmental relocation intent is also influenced by individual behavioral adaptations: relocation is an individual choice for coping with environmental risks when they arise, but it is not the only choice. In fact, in addition to "fleeing", "hold-outs" can also adapt their behavior to prevent and mitigate the effects of environmental risks and achieve self-help (Wohlwill 1974; Vaughan 1993; Collins 2013). Evans et al.'s (Evans and Jacobs 1981; Evans et al. 1982) study of residents of Los Angeles who also faced issues with smog in the twentieth century showed that older residents were more likely to believe that smog had little effect on their health, because they had adjusted their daily activities at the right time to achieve "habituation" or "desensitization" to smog, despite perceiving the same smog severity level as new residents. Studies have also shown that the process of defining whether a location is habitable or not depends not only on the perception of environmental stress or risk, but also on the behavioral adaptability of the individual. Taking action to control risk can reduce the psychological stress caused by environmental factors and facilitate judgment of the livability of a place (Russell and Lanius 1984; Rishi and Khuntia 2012). Yin Lun (2011) found that when the negative effects of climate change detracted from the traditional livelihoods of Tibetans in Yunnan Province, they were able to mitigate these negative effects by adjusting their own behavior to cope with the environmental changes, and even seized the opportunities presented by climate change to achieve the transformation and sustainability of their livelihoods. The implication is that if individuals can adapt their behavior to counteract the effect of risks on themselves, or take action to mitigate them, they are unlikely to consider environmental relocation.

In addition, public confidence in (or expectations of) government efforts to protect the environment is also an important factor influencing relocation intent. We believe that environmental problems (or perceived environmental problems) evolve dynamically over time, with the potential to deteriorate, as described by pressure threshold theory. There is also a gradual transformation toward improvement through positive human intervention. Thus, even if residents perceive serious environmental risks, their confidence in environmental management technologies may lead them to positive expectations about the future environmental status of their neighborhoods, and thus be an important reason for them to remain in that neighborhood (Mileti 1980; Hunter 2005). Research has shown that in the contemporary global context, the public tends to assign primary responsibility for environmental management to the government, as in China (Dunlap 2002; Konisky 2011; Hong 2014). The manageability of environmental problems and the public's dependency on the government's assumption of responsibility for environmental protection give us reason to believe that the public's divergent expectations of the government's environmental governance will also affect environmental relocation intent.

As of this writing, urban smog issues have yet to be alleviated and have drawn attention from all walks of life in China. It has been suggested that in the long run, the smog problem may backfire on the urban residents and lead to a new wave of urban relocation (Tong and Wang 2014). Based on data from random telephone interviews in Beijing, we examine residents' intent to move out of the city due to smog-based air pollution, and analyze the differences in residents' intent to relocate from the city based on the relevant theoretical perspectives. Our hope is to provide insight for policy.

11.2 Research Design

11.2.1 Data Presentation

The data used in this study are from a questionnaire survey entitled "Beijing Residents' Perception of Smog and Behavioral Responses". It was conducted by the Institute of Environmental Sociology at Renmin University of China in Beijing toward the end of March 2014. The survey was conducted by telephone, using the national mobile phone number database provided by the Ministry of Industry and Information Technology (MIIT) as a sampling frame. This database includes all mobile phones whose owners were registered in Beijing. Using PPS, we extracted numbers based on their first three digits. Of the 600 valid numbers sampled, 308 valid responses were obtained, for a response rate of 51.33%.[4]

Of the valid responses, 60.7% were male and 39.3% were female; 5.2% of the respondents were aged 20 and under, 39.3% were 21 to 30, 29.9% were 31 to 40, 16.2% were 41 to 50, and 9.4% were over 50. In terms of education level, 5.6% had only primary school education or less, 10.7% had junior high school, 18.5% had high school/vocational high school/technical school/technical secondary school, 17.5% had junior college, 35.4% had bachelor's degrees, and 14.3% had master's degrees or above. In terms of local hukou, 46.4% of the respondents had a Beijing hukou, while 53.6% had a non-Beijing hukou.

11.2.2 Variable Measurement

11.2.2.1 Smog-Related Migration Intent

As it is difficult to obtain objective data on environmental relocation, this study focuses on the *intent* to relocate. Thus, we examined residents' tendency to move out of the country induced by the environmental conditions of the place of residence, and we focused on the factors

[4] We would like to thank Dr. Weidong Wang and the China Survey and Data Centre (NSRC) at Renmin University of China for their assistance with this survey. Due to the high refusal rate inherent in telephone surveys, data collected in this way are likely to be subject to sample bias. It is generally accepted that the current standard for an acceptable response rate for telephone interviews is 50% (Chambliss and Schutt 2013: 139). Therefore, the sample obtained in this study is representative enough to draw general inferences.

explaining the divergence in relocation intent. We hypothesized that environmental pollution influences the intent to relocate. In the telephone interview surveys, we asked respondents the following two questions, in order: (1) Do you intend to move out of Beijing because of air pollution? (2) Are you considering moving your children out of Beijing because of air pollution? The set of responses and the original responses for the entire sample are shown in Fig. 11.1.

As this survey design suggests, environmental factors' influence on the intent to relocate is no longer the focus of this study. Rather, the dependent variable in this study is the intent to move out assuming environmental impacts, i.e., "the intent to move induced by air pollution" (hereinafter referred to as "smog-related out-migration intention" (SOI). In order to describe this variable more precisely, we categorized the intent to relocate (see Table 11.1). We first divided the intent to

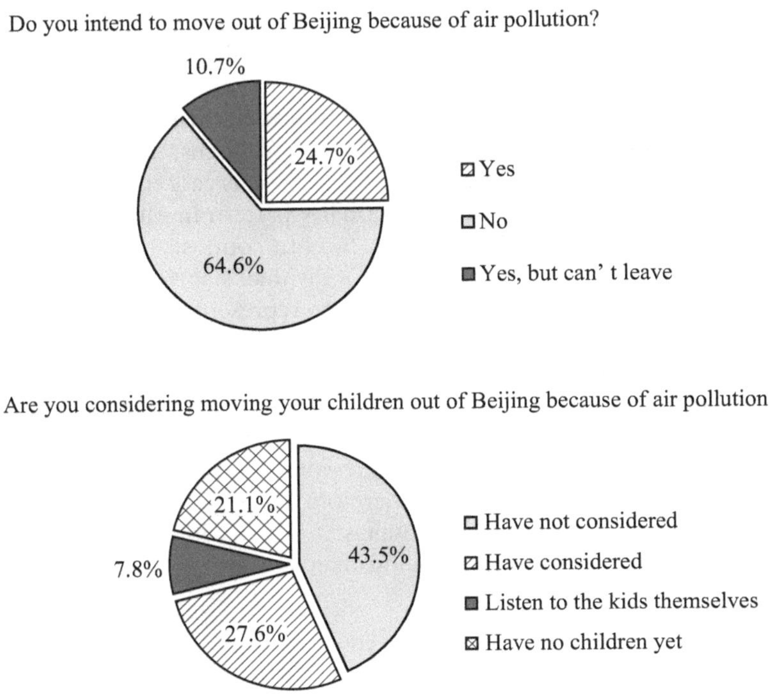

Fig. 11.1 Beijing residents' intent to relocate prompted by air pollution

Table 11.1 Classification of SOI

		Have considered relocating for their children	
		No	Yes
Have considered relocating for themselves	No	Staying put	Individual relocation
	Yes	Individual relocation	Family relocation

relocate into two broad categories: remaining put (have not considered relocating themselves or their children), and relocation (have considered relocating either themselves or their children or both). Within the relocation group there were two sub-categories: individual relocation (considering relocating only for either themselves or one of their children) and family relocation (considering relocating for both themselves and their children).[5]

The classification of SOI also considers the fact that existing studies have indicated that there are three levels of immigration behavior: individual, family, and community, and that the magnitude of its social effect is also progressive. Relocation at the community level generally occurs in the context of mandatory relocation, and is outside the scope of this study. Among the spontaneous relocators on which we focus, individual relocation is relatively flexible and temporary because it is easy to achieve due to its lower costs, and it is a common mobility pattern in modern big cities like Beijing where the population is in flux. In contrast, relocation at the family level is more dependent on the individual's socioeconomic status due to its higher costs, and is more likely to represent a permanent intent to move (Sandefur and Scott 1981). We believe that, in terms of Beijing residents' SOI, individual relocation is probably just a "stalling tactic" which residents have no choice but to employ (e.g., temporarily going to work outside of the city or sending their children to study abroad), while family relocation is a more realistic representation of the residents' intent to permanently "escape" the city. Therefore, the effects of the aforementioned variables, such as socioeconomic status, behavioral adaptability and confidence in the government's smog management, on the SOI can be

[5] Due to the limitations of the questionnaire, we are limited in our measurement of families moving out and have not included adult children's migration type with their parents. In other words, only cases where parents move out with their minor children are included.

reflected not only in terms of generating relocation intent, but also in terms of mediating residents' choices in family relocation.

11.2.2.2 Other Variables

Perceived Smog Hazard We introduced this variable to test the general hypothesis that environmental factors affect perceived relocation intent. We measured individual citizens' perceived smog hazard through the following questions. (1) How much do you think smog has negatively affected your daily work and life? (2) How much do you think smog has negatively affected your physical health? (3) How much do you think smog has affected your mental health? The response choices to these three questions were "no effect", "little effect", "unclear", "significant effect", and "great effect", with a range of values from 0 ~ 4 and an alpha coefficient of 0.788. The scores for the responses to these three questions were tabulated to obtain the perceived smog hazard variable; the higher the score, the higher the smog hazard level that residents felt. If the assumption that environmental factors affect the intent to relocate is true, then theoretically, there should be a high correlation between the perceived smog hazard and the intent to relocate.

Individual Socioeconomic Status In this study, the socioeconomic status variable consists of two factors: literacy and income. Literacy is a binary value corresponding to "no tertiary education" (assigned a value of 0) or "tertiary education" (assigned a value of 1). Income is based on the respondent's income the previous month. The higher the education level and monthly income, the higher the corresponding socioeconomic status of the population. We introduce this variable to explore the influence of a dependent variable.

Daily Behavioral Adaptation to Smog This variable was also designed to explore the influencing factors of a dependent variable. Based on existing studies, we divided residents' behavioral adaptations to smog into two categories: protective behavior (against smog) and mitigating behavior (against smog), and designed questions to measure the behaviors in telephone interviews, asking respondents whether they had adopted the listed behaviors to cope with air pollution, and assigning a value of 1 for "yes" and 0 for "no". To ensure the internal consistency of the measurement items, the corresponding measurement items were determined based on the change in the corresponding alpha coefficients after the removal of each item. The measurement of protective behaviors included four responses: "giving up outdoor activities", "going out as little as possible", "wearing a mask when going out", and "reducing window ventilation", with an alpha coefficient of 0.625. The measurement of mitigating behaviors included nine items: "not burning garbage in open air", "not having open barbecues", "not setting off fireworks in urban areas", "not over-decorating the house", "reducing the consumption of gas, natural gas, electricity and fuel at home", "choosing public transport (metro, buses) or bicycles when travelling", "not buying cars with high emissions", "buying high quality fuel for one's own car as much as possible", and "voluntarily choosing to live a simple green life", with an alpha coefficient of 0.721. We totaled the scores of the above items to obtain the "smog protection behavior" and "smog mitigation behavior" variables, with higher scores indicating more adaptation behaviors.

Confidence in the Government's Efforts to Mange Smog The introduction of this variable is not only a further empirical test of the findings of related studies, but also an attempt to enrich and expand new perspectives of environmental migration research. Confidence in the government's smog management was measured by asking the following three questions:

1. How do you think the Beijing Municipal Government is doing in terms of information disclosure in smog monitoring and forecasting and prevention? The response choices and values were:

   1 = very bad
   2 = not so good
   3 = hard to say
   4 = relatively good.
   5 = very good.

2. Do you believe the Beijing Municipal Government is really making great efforts to solve the smog problem? The response choices and values were:

   1 = no.
   2 = not really.
   3 = hard to say.
   4 = somewhat.
   5 = definitely.

3. Do you have confidence in the effectiveness of the Beijing Municipal Government's smog mitigation policies? The response choices and values were:

1 = no confidence.
2 = not much confidence.
3 = hard to say.
4 = some confidence.
5 = high confidence.

The alpha coefficient was 0.617. The scores for the responses to these three questions were tabulated to construct a new variable: confidence in the government's management of smog, with higher scores indicating greater confidence.

In addition, to better explore the relationship between the predictor variables and the dependent variable, we also introduced three control variables—gender, age, and local hukou—into the model analysis (see Table 11.2).

11.2.3 Analytical Framework and Research Hypotheses

This study can be divided into two parts: descriptive analysis and explanatory analysis. The descriptive part tests the stress-threshold theory in general and examines residents' perception of air pollution hazards and the related divergence of SOI; the explanatory part examines the influencing mechanism of the divergence of SOI, including the analysis of the influence of three groups of predictor variables—socioeconomic status, behavior adaptation to smog, and confidence in the government's smog management efforts—on the residents' consideration of whether or not to environmentally relocate, and what type of relocation to choose. Migration behavior is not included in this study.

The explanatory part is the focus of this study. Based on the analytical pathways and the description of the relationship between the three sets of predictor variables and environmental relocation intent based on the findings of the established studies, we identified the following research hypotheses for further testing.

> Hypothesis 1: Highly educated residents are more likely to have SOI and are more likely to consider family relocation than those without higher education.
>
> Hypothesis 2: The higher their monthly income level, the more likely residents are to have SOI, and the more likely they are to consider family relocation.

Table 11.2 Statistical description of study variables

Variable Name	*Type*	*Sample size*	*Average value*	*Standard deviation*	*Clarification*
Individual relocation due to smog	Categorical variable	308	0.25	0.432	0 = No, 1 = Yes
Family relocation due to smog	Categorical variable	243	0.35	0.478	For respondents with children only: 0 = No, 1 = Yes
SOI (Smog-related out-migration Intention)	Categorical variable	243	0.59	0.795	For respondents with children only 0 = Staying put, 1 = Individual relocation, 2 = Family relocation
Perceived smog hazard	Continuous variable	308	7.86	3.193	Cumulative score: 0 ~ 12 points
Protective behavior	Continuous variable	308	2.50	1.327	Cumulative score: 0 ~ 4 points
Mitigating behavior	Continuous variable	308	6.68	2.038	Cumulative score: 0 ~ 9 points
Educational attainment	Categorical variable	308	0.67	0.470	0 = No higher education, 1 = Higher education
Monthly income	Continuous variable	308	8.86	16.798	Unit: Thousands of yuan
Confidence in the government's smog management efforts	Continuous variable	308	9.06	2.872	Cumulative score: 3 ~ 15 points
Gender	Categorical variable	308	0.61	0.489	0 = Female, 1 = Male
Age	Continuous variable	308	35.47	12.019	Unit: years
Local hukou	Categorical variable	308	0.46	0.500	0 = non-local hukou, 1 = Beijing local hukou

Hypothesis 3: Residents with more smog protection behaviors are less likely to have SOI and are less likely to consider family relocation.
Hypothesis 4: The more smog mitigation behaviors the residents adopt, the less likely they are to have SOI, and the less likely they are to consider family relocation.
Hypothesis 5: The more confidence residents have in the government's smog management efforts, the less likely they are to have SOI, and the less likely they will be to consider family relocation.

11.3 Divergence in Residents' SOI

In the stress-threshold theory, the emergence of environmental migration intent requires two necessary conditions: deterioration of the objective environmental conditions, and members of society generally perceiving environmental risk (or "pressure") that exceeds one's own ability to bear. Therefore, before analyzing the divergence in Beijing residents' SOI, we examine the correlation between their perceived smog hazard and their intent to relocate, which is also a general test of the questionnaire design based on existing studies. Table 11.3 presents the self-reported negative effects of smog on daily working life, physical health, and mental health.

As indicated by the results in Table 11.3, the hazards of smog on various outcomes are generally felt by most residents, and are strong. The percentages of respondents who believe that smog has a "high impact" or a "very high impact" on their daily work life, physical health, or mental health were 68.2%, 70.8%, and 60.4%, respectively. This reflects the concern most residents have about the harmful effects of smog. Beijing residents feel the negative effects of smog on their physical health

Table 11.3 Hazards of smog perceived by Beijing residents

	Daily work life	*Physical health*	*Mental health*
No impact	5.2%	6.5%	13.3%
Little impact	17.9%	13.6%	17.5%
Hard to say	8.8%	9.1%	8.8%
High impact	39.3%	37.0%	37.0%
Very high impact	28.9%	33.8%	23.4%
Total	100.0% (308)	100.0% (308)	100.0% (308)

and daily work life stronger than on their mental health. At the same time, for their daily work life, physical health, and mental health, 23.1%, 20.1%, and 30.8%, respectively, of people still think that there is "no impact" or "little impact". This indicates that there are still some differences in the perception of the hazards of smog among Beijing residents, and that some still feel that the "environmental pressure" is insignificant. We also used bivariate ANOVA analyses to compare the differences in perceived smog hazard scores between residents of different genders, ages, hukou, education, and income (results are shown in Table 11.4).

The results in Table 11.4 demonstrate that there is no significant difference in the perceived smog hazard scores between male and female Beijing residents and hukou types. However, there are significant differences in the perceived smog hazard scores between residents of different ages, education levels and incomes. Residents aged over 50 years, the highest income quintile, and those with higher education have the highest

Table 11.4 Perceived smog hazards of Beijing residents with various socio-demographic characteristics

		Sample size	*Avg. value*	*Std. dev*	F/df
Gender	Male	187	7.82	3.269	0.07/1
	Female	121	7.93	3.085	
Age	20 years old and below	16	4.88	3.775	5.18/4***
	21 ~ 30 years old	121	7.74	3.121	
	31 ~ 40 years old	92	8.26	2.832	
	41 ~ 50 years old	50	7.70	3.536	
	Over 50 years old	29	9.03	2.706	
Local hukou	Beijing hukou	143	8.04	3.092	0.83/1
	Outside hukou	165	7.71	3.280	
Education	Higher education	207	8.33	2.881	14.25/1***
	No higher education	101	6.90	3.579	
Income	Lowest quintile	61	7.39	3.451	3.69/4**
	Second lowest quintile	38	6.34	3.961	
	Middle quintile	71	8.15	2.926	
	Next highest quintile	52	8.06	2.933	
	Highest quintile	86	8.51	2.768	

* $p \le 0.05$; ** $p \le 0.01$; *** $p \le 0.001$

perceived smog hazard, while those aged 20 years and younger, the second lowest income quintile, and those without higher education have the lowest perceived smog hazard. However, with the exception of the group aged 20 and younger, whose score is obviously low, the perceived smog hazard scores of the other groups are generally within the range of 6–9 (out of 12). This is on the high side overall, suggesting that the smog hazard is indeed generally perceived by members of different social backgrounds.

According to the role of environmental factors in population relocation and the stress-threshold theory mentioned above, the varying levels of "environmental pressure" members of society feel will lead to differences in whether they consider relocating, as well as the intensity of their intent. In terms of percentages, the majority of Beijing residents are still concerned about the smog hazard, even though the level of perceived smog hazard varies. Therefore, in theory, a high proportion of people should have relocation intentions. However, the survey shows that if asked whether they would move from Beijing because of air pollution, out of the 308 valid samples, only 114 residents (37.0%) explicitly expressed their intent to relocate (considered relocating themselves or their children), while 194 residents (63.0%) did not explicitly consider relocating. Though the questionnaire highlights the problem of pollution, and even though most people feel the harmful effects of pollution, the majority of Beijing residents still reported no relocation intention. This is inconsistent with the hypotheses that air pollution or perceived air pollution hazards cannot explain all of the differences in Beijing residents' intent to relocate due to smog, and that other social factors influencing residents' intent to relocate in this context warrant further exploration.

In fact, among Beijing residents who explicitly stated that they had considered relocation, there was also a wide divergence in the type of move, with a higher proportion of individual relocation than family relocation. The results of the survey show that of the 114 residents who had explicitly considered relocation, 67 (58.8%) were classified as individual relocation (either by themselves, or by one of their children relocating), while 47 (41.2%) were classified as family relocation (either by themselves, or by one of their children relocating). It is also clear that based on a simple binomial distribution of migration, the stress-threshold theory does not provide a convincing explanation.

In conclusion, based on the above preliminary analyses, we believe that based on objective pollution conditions and subjective pollution perceptions, there are still other factors underlying the divergence in Beijing residents' SOI. To this end, we propose developing a multiple regression model to explore further theoretical explanations.

11.4 Factors Influencing the Divergence in Residents' SOI

11.4.1 Factors Influencing Whether or Not to Relocate

Based on the analytical path, we first developed a binomial logistic regression model as follows:

$$In\left(\frac{P}{1-P}\right) = \beta_0 + \beta_1 X_1 + \ldots + \beta_k X_k, k = 1, 2, \ldots, j \quad (11.1)$$

This model (A) was developed to investigate the factors that influence whether residents develop SOI (having considered relocating themselves, or having their children relocate). Where P denotes the probability that residents have considered relocating or having their children relocate, $X1 \sim Xk$ denote k independent variables, βk denotes the regression coefficient of each independent variable at the time of a given outmigration intent, and $\beta 0$ is the intercept. To facilitate the interpretation of the model, we transformed the regression coefficients to odds ratios. The data estimation results for the model are presented in Table 11.5.

Table 11.5 shows the binomial logistic models based on the independent variables of whether respondents had considered relocating themselves, and whether they had considered relocating their children. Based on the respective goodness-of-fit indices from Models A1 and A2, both models have some explanatory power for the dependent variables (8.6% and 12.9% of the variance is explained by the pseudo coefficient of determination, respectively). Moreover, the variables in the models have significant effects, and as such, we judged both models to be valid. The effects of each variable are analyzed in detail below.

11.4.1.1 Gender, Age, Hukou, and Relocation Due to Smog

Controlling other independent variables, male respondents were 38.9% and 6.2% more likely than women to consider relocation themselves or their children, respectively. Additionally, age has a positive effect on intent

Table 11.5 Influences on Beijing residents' SOI: binomial logistic regression

	Model A1		*Model A2*	
	Have you considered relocating yourself?		*Have you considered relocating your children?*	
	Odds ratio	*Standard error*	*Odds ratio*	*Standard error*
Independent variable				
Male (reference = female)	1.389	0.409	1.062	0.329
Age	1.007	0.014	1.026	0.015
Beijing hukou (reference group = non-local hukou)	0.470*	0.147	0.553	0.184
Higher education (reference group = no higher education)	2.422**	0.850	1.862	0.654
Monthly income (thousands of yuan)	0.997	0.008	1.015	0.011
Behavioral adaptation to smog				
Protective behavior	1.492***	0.179	1.374*	0.172
Mitigating behavior	1.003	0.071	1.036	0.084
Confidence in the government's efforts to mitigate smog	0.906*	0.046	0.785***	0.046
Constant term	0.130*	0.116	0.435	0.420
Sample size	308		243	
Pseudo R^2	0.086		0.129	
χ^2/df	29.42/8***		40.45/8***	
Log likelihood	−157.382		−137.075	

* $p \leq 0.05$; ** $p \leq 0.01$; *** $p \leq 0.001$

to move, with the probability of relocating themselves or their children increasing 0.7% and 2.6%, respectively, for each year of increasing age. And finally, hukou has an inhibiting effect on relocation intent, with those holding Beijing hukou 53.0% and 44.7%, respectively, less likely to relocate themselves or their children than those holding non-local hukou. However, only the effect of Beijing hukou on whether respondents consider relocation is statistically significant in the above results. Therefore, the other conclusions above cannot be extrapolated to the overall picture. In other words, whether Beijing residents consider relocating is nearly independent of gender and age, and Beijing hukou constrains residents' intent to relocate, but does not determine whether they consider relocating their children.[6]

11.4.1.2 Educational Level, Monthly Income, and Smog-Related Relocation

Controlling other independent variables, compared with respondents without higher education, respondents with higher education were 142.2% and 86.2% more likely to relocate themselves or their children, respectively. The effect of monthly income on respondents' intent to relocate is inconsistent. For every 1,000 yuan increase in monthly income, the probability of relocating themselves decreased 0.3%, and the probability of relocating their children increased 1.5%. However, the test results indicate that only the relationship between education level and whether respondents have considered relocating is significant, while the other results cannot be extrapolated to the overall picture. In other words, income level has no significant effect on whether Beijing residents have considered relocation, and those with higher education are more likely to have considered relocating themselves, but whether they have considered letting their children relocate is hardly affected by education level.

11.4.1.3 Behavioral Adaptation to Smog and Smog-Related Out-Migration Intention

The survey results indicate that smog protection behavior has a significant positive effect on residents' SOI, while the effect of smog mitigation behavior is not significant. That is to say, the more smog protection behaviors residents adopt, the more likely they are to develop SOI; whether residents develop SOI has nothing to do with the corresponding mitigation behaviors they adopt. Controlling for the other independent variables, for every one percentage increase in SOI, the probability

[6] For the sake of brevity, we do not discuss the relationship between local hukou and outmigration intent in the final section of this chapter. We believe that the inhibitory effect of Beijing hukou on residents' outmigration intent can be understood from two perspectives: first, Beijing hukou can be seen as an indicator of higher socioeconomic status, which further challenges environmental justice theory; and second, whether or not one has a local hukou (to an extent) represents the length of time spent in the city, and residents who have lived in the city for a long time may develop a stronger community identity, which may also weaken their outmigration intent.

that the respondents themselves or their children have considered relocating is 49.2% and 37.4% higher, respectively. Compared to those who never adopted any of the listed smog protection behaviors, residents who adopted all of the protection behaviors were almost five times ($1.492^{(4-0)} \approx 4.955$) and four times ($1.374^{(4-0)} \approx 3.564$) more likely to have considered relocating themselves or their children out of the city, respectively.

11.4.1.4 Confidence in the Government's Efforts to Mitigate Smog and Smog-Related Relocation Intent

Controlling for other independent variables, respondents' confidence in the government's efforts to mitigate smog has a dampening effect on their likelihood of considering relocating. For every one percent increase in their confidence in the government's efforts to mitigate smog, the likelihood of respondents' intent to relocate themselves, or having their children relocate, decreases by 9.4% and 21.5% respectively. Therefore, respondents with the highest levels of confidence in the government's efforts to mitigate smog are 69.4% ($1-0.906^{(15-3)} \approx 0.694$) and 94.5% ($1-0.785^{(15-3)} \approx 0.945$) less likely, respectively, to consider relocating themselves or their children than those with the lowest levels of confidence. Again, both results are statistically significant. Therefore, it can be inferred that Beijing residents' confidence in the government's smog mitigation efforts inhibits their intent to relocate from the city, and the higher the confidence in government smog mitigation, the less likely people are to consider relocating.

11.4.2 Factors Influencing Different Types of Relocation Intent

Above, we discussed the factors that influence whether Beijing residents consider smog-based relocation. Now, among those who *are* considering smog-based relocation, what factors determine whether they choose individual relocation or family relocation? To address this question, we constructed an m logit regression model with the SOI type as the dependent variable, based on the SOI classification mentioned above.

$$P_{ij} = \frac{e^{\Sigma_1^n \beta_{nk} X_{ni}}}{\Sigma_{k=1}^{j} e^{\Sigma_1^n \beta_{nk} X_{ni}}}, i = 1, 2, \ldots, n;\ k = 1, 2, \ldots, j \qquad (11.2)$$

Model B was developed to explore the reasons why residents had different SOI types. We further differentiated residents with clear relocation intent into individual relocation and family relocation, resulting in a total of three different relocation intent types (including clearly staying put). In the model, i denotes each individual, k denotes the outmigration intent type, and X_{ni} denotes the respective variable. We adopted a latent variable model and used the m logit model for regression (with no relocation intent as the reference category). The model's sample estimation results are presented in Table 11.6. Again, the odds ratio results are presented to facilitate the model's interpretation. The model fit indicators indicate that the model is basically valid and has some explanatory power for the dependent variable. Each variable's effect on the dependent variable is analyzed below.

11.4.2.1 Gender, Age, Local Registration, and SOI Type

Controlling for the other independent variables, compared with women, men were 21.7% less likely to have considered relocating individually (as opposed to staying put), and 39.2% more likely to have considered relocating with their families (as opposed to staying put). For each one-year increase in age, the percentage of respondents considering individual relocation and family relocation increased by 1.5% and 2.7%, respectively. Compared with respondents with non-local hukou, those with Beijing hukou were 52.4% and 54.1% less likely to have considered individual relocation and family relocation, respectively. However, the above results do not pass the test of statistical significance, which means that Beijing residents' relocation intent type is not related to factors such as gender, age, and local hukou.

11.4.2.2 Education, Income, and SOI Type

Controlling for the other independent variables, individuals with higher education are 126.1% and 81.2% more likely to have considered individual relocation and family relocation, respectively, compared with those without higher education. For every 1,000 yuan increase in monthly income, the probability of considering individual relocation and family relocation increases by 1.3% and 1.0%, respectively. However, of all the relationships, only education's effect on individual relocation is significant. Thus, education level has an important influence on Beijing residents' consideration of individual relocation, and the more educated people are, the more likely they are to choose individual relocation, but

Table 11.6 Factors influencing Beijing residents' SJOI type: m logit regression

Independent variable	*Individual relocation/stay put*		*Family relocation/stay put*	
	Odds ratio	*Standard error*	*Odds ratio*	*Standard error*
Male (reference = female)	0.783	0.282	1.392	0.543
Age	1.015	0.018	1.027	0.018
Beijing hukou (reference group = non-local hukou)	0.476	0.185	0.459	0.190
Higher education (reference group = no higher education)	2.261*	0.952	1.812	0.792
Monthly income (thousands of yuan)	1.013	0.011	1.010	0.012
Behavioral adaptation to smog				
Protective behavior	1.149	0.163	1.772***	0.309
Mitigating behavior	0.972	0.091	1.020	0.104
Confidence in the government's efforts to mitigate smog	0.836**	0.058	0.786***	0.055
Constant term	0.707	0.789	0.125	0.157
Sample size	243			
Pseudo R^2	0.103			
χ^2/df	47.08/16***			
Log likelihood	−206.022			

*$p \le 0.05$; **$p \le 0.01$; ***$p \le 0.001$

education has no influence on whether they consider family relocation. There is also no relationship between the type of smog relocation intent that Beijing residents tend to have and their income level.

11.4.2.3 Behavioral Adaptation to Smog and SOI Type

The results of the significance test show that smog adaptation behavior has no significant effect on the respondents' consideration of individual relocation. Additionally, smog mitigation behavior has no significant effect on the consideration of family relocation, but smog protection behavior has a positive and significant effect on the respondents' consideration of family relocation. Controlling for the other independent variables, each point increase in smog protection behavior increases the probability of a family considering moving out by 77.2%, and the probability of considering family relocation is almost 10 times higher for those who have taken all protective measures than for those who have never taken any protective measures ($1.772^{(4-0)} \approx 9$ 0.859).

11.4.2.4 Confidence in the Government's Efforts to Manage Smog and SOI Types

Controlling for other independent variables, confidence in the government's efforts to alleviate smog has a significant negative effect on respondents' consideration of both individual and family relocation. For every one-point increase in confidence in the government's ability to combat smog, the probability of respondents' consideration of individual relocation and family relocation decreases by 16.4% and 21.4%, respectively. Compared with those with the least confidence in the government's efforts to alleviate smog, those with the highest confidence are 88.3% ($1-0.836^{(15-3)} \approx 0.883$) and 94.4% ($1-0.786^{(15-3)} \approx 0.944$) less likely to consider relocation individually and with their families, respectively. In other words, Beijing residents' confidence in the government's efforts to alleviate smog has a significant inhibiting effect on their consideration of individual relocation and family relocation due to smog.

11.5 Summary and Discussion

Based on the analysis of the survey data, we can draw the following four basic conclusions: First, the problem of smog-based air pollution has indeed aroused the general concern of Beijing residents, and some have even developed relocation intent. However, the divergence in the residents' SOI shows that the environmental factors' explanatory power is limited. Second, residents' SOI is less influenced by socioeconomic status factors. Third, residents' protective behavior against smog will generate SOI and will encourage them to consider family relocation. Fourth, residents' confidence in government smog management has a significant inhibiting effect on SOI. Specific discussions follow.

The results of the descriptive analyses in the previous section show that Beijing residents generally feel the seriousness of the smog hazard, but the corresponding SOI is not pronounced, and the divergence in the residents' SOI cannot be fully explained by the theory of environmental factors and the stress-threshold theory. There are indeed some residents who are affected by the smog problem and develop SOI, but those who insist on non-migration account for the majority. Yet even if they have considered relocation because of the smog, those who plan to relocate with their whole family are still in the minority, and a considerable portion of the residents are more inclined to choose the "stalling tactics" of moving themselves or their children. This is closer to the "wandering" than the "flight from the land" in the previous type of migration. Previous studies have also shown that large-scale, overall spontaneous "environmental migration" is rare, with more people choosing to "stay put" rather than to "flee" (e.g., Irwin et al. 2004; Hunter et al. 2015). As can be seen, there is a clear "under-motivation" problem regarding environmentally induced outmigration intent.[7] The apparent empirical shortcomings of environmental determinism led us to consider the social complexity of migration decisions. Individuals may be initially motivated to move by a single economic, political, social, or environmental factor, but the final decision to relocate is often influenced by a combination of factors (Goldhaber et al. 1983). Therefore, when studying a population's environmental relocation intent, it is important to resist the simplistic thinking of considering only environmental factors, and instead to examine them in the context of a dynamic process in which multiple factors, such as economic, political, social, and environmental factors, interact.

Another important finding of this study is that the influence of socioeconomic status on Beijing residents' SOI is limited. According to environmental justice theory, socioeconomic status has an important effect on SOI, and people with lower socioeconomic status are likely to abandon relocating or choose lower-cost relocation (e.g., individual relocation as opposed to family relocation) because they cannot afford the cost of relocation. This is the basis of our Hypotheses 1 and 2. However, the results show that the education variable has a significant effect only on the consideration of individual relocation and only at the individual level, but not on the consideration of having children relocate or on family relocation; the income factor has no significant effect in any of the models of the intent to move. Thus, Hypothesis 1 was only partially supported by

[7] Another item designed for the telephone survey confirmed this findings' reliability. When respondents were asked whether they had taken any action to reduce risks associated with smog, only 52 out of 308 (16.9%) of the valid responses explicitly stated that they had "gone out of town to avoid the smog", and 83.1% explicitly stated that they had never done so.

the data, and Hypothesis 2 was negated. Taken together, Beijing residents' SOI are less affected by individual socioeconomic status. If we consider environmental migration as an option for individuals to avoid environmental risks, the limited predictive power of socioeconomic status suggests that the effect of environmental risk cuts across social classes, and that different classes share the same concerns about risk. Their risk avoidance choices are also convergent; even if they have the ability to relocate or can afford the cost of relocation, residents still tend not to consider environmental relocation. The choice of risk avoidance is also convergent; even if they can afford to relocate, or can afford the costs of relocating, residents still tend not to consider environmental relocation.

The study also found that Beijing residents' different behavioral adaptations to smog had different effects on their intent to relocate from the smog. Inspired by existing studies, we proposed Hypotheses 3 and 4: if individuals can adjust their behavior to counteract the impact of the risk on themselves, or take actions to mitigate the risk, they are unlikely to consider environmental relocation. However, our results did not support these two hypotheses, and the self-help behaviors of residents facing the smog did not inhibit their relocation intent. Our findings revealed that smog mitigation behaviors showed no significant effects in any of the models. Instead of suppressing the SOI as expected, the residents' smog mitigation behaviors increased their intent to relocate individually and to consider relocating out of the city with their families. We believe that this result, which was contrary to our theoretical expectations, reflects Beijing residents' helplessness and anxiety in facing smog issues. Although residents have not given up on self-help in the face of the smog problem, their perceived environmental risks have yet to be effectively channeled. Overall, residents' behavioral adaptation to the smog is negative and expedient, and is close to failing in suppressing the intent to relocate.

In addition, this study found that positive expectations of environmental governance inhibit the intent of environmental relocation. Environmental relocation intent depends not only on sensitivity and adaptability to current environmental risks, but is also influenced by people's expectations of future environmental risks. The data suggest that confidence in the government's ability to alleviate smog has a dampening effect on Beijing residents' smog-based relocation intent to move out of the city, and also determines that they will not consider relocating individually or with their families. Thus, Hypothesis 5 is supported by the data. The more confidence Beijing residents have in the government's efforts to mitigate smog, the more likely they are to choose to "stay put". This suggests that we cannot simply assume that environmental conditions are constant when examining residents' intent to relocate out of Beijing. In fact, social problems such as environmental degradation will provoke social reactions and lead to dynamic changes over time, and residents' future expectations of these dynamic changes will also influence their current relocation decisions. Therefore, when studying environmental migration, special attention should be paid to the subjectivity and dynamism of people and the dynamics of environmental risks over time.

To further explore other theoretical explanations for environmental migration, we propose a new research perspective—the Expectation for Government Performance approach. It is based on both existing research and the empirical findings of this study. This approach refers to a form of confidence and future expectations held by the people who will make the decision to relocate about the social governance performance at the receiving location. If residents decide to relocate mainly in response to a particular social problem, then assuming that the problem has already been noticed by the government before it deteriorates further and that the government is making institutional arrangements to promote a solution, people will tend to believe that the problem is being addressed. They may even have confidence that the problem can be solved in the future. This will inhibit their intent to relocate. Specifically for environmental migration, the higher people's evaluation of the government's performance in environmental governance, the more likely they are to believe that the environmental problem is being solved, or will be solved in the future. This is likely to contribute to channeling the so-called "environmental pressure" in the stress-threshold theory, and thus, inhibit the intent to relocate due to the environment. While previous studies have suggested the theoretical impact of policy interventions on relocation intent (Mileti 1980; Hunter 2005), there has been little empirical support of this assertion. The results of this study suggest that positive expectations of government environmental policy performance do indeed dampen relocation intent. We argue that the Expectation for Government Performance approach is more dynamic than traditional environmental migration studies, and migration studies in general. This is because the Expectation for Government Performance approach considers the effects of the interaction between people and situational factors (environmental, economic, political, cultural, etc.) on the decision to relocate. Therefore, it is closer to empirical reality and more scientific in its explication of relocation intent in the context of the interaction between people and situations.

Given that relocation is costly and detrimental to social stability and urban image building, future institutional arrangements should pay sufficient attention to the issue of environmental relocation. The policy implications of this study can be summarized in three points: First, most residents have already felt the serious environmental risks, suggesting that the government needs more policy interventions to guide residents to cope with the risks. Second, few residents have the intention of spontaneous escape and self-help in the face of environmental risks. Rather, they hold on in the expectation of change, highlighting the necessity and urgency of policy interventions to improve the quality of the environment; the alternative is the stimulation of more social problems. Third, residents' confidence and expectations of policy intervention affect their relocation intent: the more confident, the more inclined they are to choose to stay and look forward to changes. Overall, those who choose to stay are in the majority. Therefore, it can be said that residents still have confidence in government and policy, which can be channeled to become an important supporting force for environmental improvement.

Finally, this study's limitations in terms of data and measurement leave us with several shortcomings and a lack of sufficient confidence in drawing conclusions. However, as an exploratory study, the findings of this study are of great value in revealing the complex relationship between pollution and residents' relocation intent, and especially the Expectation for Government Performance perspective. This can serve as a direction for us to examine and improve in future endeavors. In addition, because the scope of the study is limited to Beijing, it examines only one aspect of environmental migration—outmigration intent. Future studies could also explore environmental factors' influence on in-migration intent.

CHAPTER 12

Perceptions of Climate Change and Behavioral Tendencies

Hong Dayong and Fan Yechao

In the 1970s, more and more scientists started examining the trend of global warming and its human-induced factors. The declaration issued in 1979 at the First World Climate Conference, attended mainly by scientists, stated that if carbon dioxide levels in the atmosphere continued to increase, temperatures would rise to a measurable degree by the end of the twentieth century. Significant warming would then occur by the middle of the twenty-first century. In November 1988, the World Meteorological Organization (WMO) and the United Nations Environment Programme (UNEP) jointly established the Intergovernmental Panel on Climate Change (IPCC), whose mandate is to assess the current state of scientific knowledge on climate and climate change, analyze the potential

D. Hong (✉)
Renmin University of China, Beijing, China
e-mail: hongdy@ruc.edu.cn

Y. Fan
Minzu University of China, Beijing, China
e-mail: fanyechao@ruc.edu.cn

D. Hong and Y. Fan (eds.), *Toward a Green Society*,
https://doi.org/10.1007/978-981-96-5111-5_12

effects of climate change on society and the economy, and propose potential countermeasures for mitigation and adaptation to climate change. Since its establishment, the IPCC has organized thousands of experts worldwide to complete five assessment reports on climate change, of which the fifth assessment report has been completed in 2014. The report concluded that the warming trend of the global climate system is beyond doubt, which can be seen from the observed data on the increase of global mean temperature and sea temperature, the widespread melting of snow and ice, and the rise of global mean sea level. The primary cause of this warming trend is the massive emission of carbon dioxide and other greenhouse gases due to the burning of fossil fuels since the advent of industrialization.[1]

Judging from a large number of media reports and research works, climate change has become a major issue throughout the world. Thus, it has become an important global environmental issue, and an essential background that China must face in promoting ecological modernization and implementing ecological civilization. The United Nations initiated and formulated the *United Nations Framework Convention on Climate Change* in 1992, followed by the *Kyoto Protocol (1997), the Bali Action Plan (2007),* and other important documents. More than 190 countries and regions have ratified the United Nations Framework Convention on Climate Change, and 156 countries and regions have ratified the Kyoto Protocol. In addition to ratifying these two important documents, the Chinese government also established the National Leading Group on Climate Change and Energy Reduction in 2007 which formulated the China National Program on Climate Change. Since 2008, the Chinese government has successively issued national reports on *China's Policies and Actions in Response to Climate Change.*

In addition to the role of the government and enterprises in addressing climate change, documents from the UN and the Chinese government emphasize public awareness and participation in climate change. For example, Article 4, Paragraph 1 (i), of the United Nations Framework Convention on Climate Change requires all parties to "promote and cooperate in education, training and public awareness-raising related to climate change and encourage the widest possible participation in the

[1] IPCC Fifth Global Climate Assessment Report (1992–05-09) [2019–07-22] http://unfccc.int/resource/docs/convkp/convchin.pdf.

process, including the participation of various non-governmental organizations". Article 6 also stipulates that all parties should take steps at the national and international levels to implement six areas of education and training related to public climate change awareness.[2] China's National Plan to Address Climate Change also includes raising public awareness and the management as one of the four sub-goals:

> Through the use of modern information and communication technologies, strengthen climate change publicity, education, and training, encourage public participation, and other measures. By 2010, efforts will be made to popularize the knowledge of climate change, raise the awareness of the whole society, and create a good social atmosphere for effectively responding to climate change.[3]

The 2018 *Annual Report on China's Policies and Actions to Address Climate Change* clarifies that it is an important part of the government's work to "give play to the media's communication role, raise public awareness (of climate change), encourage enterprises and citizens to take active actions, and form a green and low-carbon development pattern with multi-participation".[4]

Public awareness and participation in the issue of climate change are significant in at least the following three aspects: First, climate change is ultimately directly related to everyone's interests, and the public has the right to more adequate and accurate information. Second, the public's perception and evaluation of climate change reflects the objectivity of climate change from another level, that is, the extent to which it is a social fact and an urgent social problem. Third, the public's necessary awareness and active response to climate change not only contribute directly to the solution to the problem, but also provide a social foundation for the implementation of various systems and policies for solving it.

Given this, based on authoritative multinational survey data, this chapter offers an international comparison of public perceptions and

[2] United Nations Framework Convention on Climate Change (1992–05–09) [2019–07–22] http://unfccc.int/resource/docs/convkp/convchin.pdf.

[3] China's National Plan on Climate Change (1992–05-09) [2019–07-22] http://www.china.com.cn/policy/txt/2007-06/04/content_8340931.htm.

[4] *China's Policies and Actions on Climate Change* 2018 Annual Report 2018–11-26) [2019–07-22] http://www.huanjing100.com/p-4774.html.

behavioral tendencies toward climate change in certain countries. To provide readers with a more comprehensive understanding and perspective on climate change issues, it reveals the basic attributes of climate change as a social fact from a level other than technology.

12.1 Research Questions and Data Sources

In the 1990s, national surveys in certain countries (such as Gallup polls in the United States and the 1993 American General Social Survey) and large-scale multinational surveys (such as the Planetary Health Survey and the 1993 and 2000 International Social Survey) began to address the issue of climate change. Some projects specifically ask respondents to rate the importance of climate change and their understanding of it. Based on these survey data, scholars have conducted preliminary studies on public awareness and actions on climate change. These have included an international comparison of public awareness of climate change and willingness to respond to climate change, climate change information dissemination, and claims of climate change denial and the reasoning behind them. Studies have also shown that there are regional and national differences in public awareness and willingness to act on climate change, however national education and economic development levels cannot fully explain these differences (Dunlap 1998; Bord et al. 1998; Brechin 2003, 2010). Public perception of climate change depends on information disseminated by the media (Boykoff and Boykoff 2004; Boykoff 2007; Boykoff and Roberts 2007). With the development of climate science and geopolitics, the authenticity, human causes, and severity of climate change are increasingly being questioned, and right-leaning think tanks, scientists, politicians, and media around the world constitute the primary entities denying climate change (McCright and Dunlap 2000, 2010, 2011). These studies and findings contribute to a deeper understanding of climate change and serve as a basis for this study. However, the researchers behind these studies did not have the opportunity to take advantage of the latest data, especially data from China. Thus, there is room for expansion in analyzing the theoretical implications of the data and findings. In addition, although a few studies have been conducted in China (Brechin 2010), there remain major deficiencies in the data in terms of survey scope, sample size, and scientific sampling.

In contrast, Chinese scholars began researching public cognition and climate change behavior relatively late, due to the lack of large-scale scientific social survey data. The few research results that have been produced are primarily based on small-scale survey research (Lv and Chen 2010; Tan 2011; Yin 2011; Zhou, Feng 2011). The most extensive survey available was completed by Horizon Research Consulting Group in August–September 2009. For the survey, seven big cities, seven small towns, and their surrounding rural areas were selected for a questionnaire survey, and the preliminary analysis results have been released (He 2010). Strictly speaking, this survey was not a nationwide scientific random sampling, and no international comparisons were made.

This study is primarily a descriptive study. The questions on which we focus are: What are the general characteristics of public perceptions and behavioral tendencies toward climate change in countries around the world? How do they differ from country to country, and what are the potential reasons for this? What are the theoretical and policy implications of the findings?

This study is based on two recent authoritative social surveys: the 2010 International Social Survey (ISSP 2010) and the 2010 China General Social Survey (CGSS 2010). The International Social Survey Program, which has cooperative survey agencies in 48 countries and regions worldwide, has conducted three surveys on the theme of the environment around the world since 1993. The 2010 survey expanded the number of countries surveyed and the number of items on climate change awareness based on the 1993 and 2000 surveys, and the survey data for some countries have been published on the ISSP website since 2012.[5] The China General Social Survey, launched in 2003, is the first nationwide, comprehensive, and continuous large-scale social survey project in China. Its purpose is to summarize the long-term trends of social change, explore social issues that are of theoretical and practical significance, and promote the openness and development of Chinese social science research by collecting multifaceted data on the Chinese people and Chinese society. Sharing provides data for government policy formulation and international comparative research.

CGSS Phase II (2010–2019) uses a multi-order stratified probability sampling design, and its survey covers 31 provincial-level administrative divisions in China (excluding Hong Kong, Macao, and Taiwan). The survey was conducted among residents aged 16 and above, and the sample

[5] Data for Australia, Hungary, China, and other countries and regions have yet to be released.

was randomly collected in both urban and rural areas. CGSS 2010 is an integral part of ISSP 2010 in the sense that CGSS 2010 incorporates all of ISSP 2010's environmental projects and was implemented concurrently with ISSP. For the environment module in the CGSS 2010 questionnaire and the three modules in parallel with the environment module, the investigator decided whether to include the environment module randomly. The final valid sample size for CGSS 2010 was 11,785, with a response rate of 71.32%, of which 3,716 were environment modules.

The authors of this study applied for the ISSP 2010 data released on August 28, 2012, which covered 30 countries: Argentina, Austria, Bulgaria, Canada, Chile, Croatia, Czech Republic, Denmark, Finland, France, Germany, the UK, Israel, Japan, Korea, Latvia, Lithuania, Mexico, New Zealand, Norway, Philippines, Russia, Slovakia, Slovenia, South Africa, Spain, Sweden, Switzerland, Turkey, and the United States.[6] The survey was conducted among the general public over the age of 16, and data was randomly collected in both rural and urban areas (mainly using multi-stratum probability sampling). Sample sizes for each country ranged from 1,000 to 3,000, and there was a total sample of 41,848 from 30 countries. According to the World Bank's 2010 income classification of countries based on per capita GNI, the 30 countries in the ISSP 2010 data are divided into two categories: mid-income countries and high-income countries. There are 10 countries in the mid-income group and 20 countries in the high-income group.[7] In order to draw a more intuitive international comparison, we analyze China as a separate country category.

12.2 Public Perception of the Importance of Climate Change

Climate change is different from environmental problems in the traditional sense, especially in terms of the depth and breadth of its potential impact and the complexity of dealing with it. However, to the extent

[6] In this study, the data from Flanders (Belgium) and Taiwan were excluded from the analysis.

[7] The 10 countries are Argentina, Bulgaria, Chile, Latvia, Mexico, the Philippines, Russia, South Africa, Turkey, and Lithuania. The World Bank's classification of countries' income levels can be found at http:data.worldbank.org/country.

climate change is limited. Among the nine choices offered by ISSP 2010 and CGSS 2010, healthcare was the most popular (23.7%), followed by the economy (23.3%) and education (17.1%). The environment ranked sixth (5.2%). As shown in Table 12.2, there are some differences between mid-income countries and high-income countries. Healthcare (21.8%), poverty (19.2%), and education (18.5%) were the most important issues in mid-income countries, with the environment (2.5%) in seventh place. High-income countries ranked the economy (29.7%), healthcare (23.9%), and education (15.4%) as the most important issues in their countries, with the environment ranking sixth (6.6%). China has the characteristics of a mid-income country, but at the same time, it is closer to high-income countries in terms of emphasizing environmental issues. The three most important issues in China according to the responses to the survey were healthcare (30.7%), education (23.5%), and poverty (16.3%), with the environment ranking sixth (5.5%).

Among all 31 countries, including China, the three countries with the highest percentage of the public responding that the environment was currently the most important issue in their country were Norway (15.6%), Switzerland (13.5%), and Canada (13.4%). However, even in these countries, the environment was not the most important issue; the

Table 12.2 Public perception of the importance of environmental issues (percentage + number of respondents)

Item	*Mid-income countries*	*High-income countries*	*China*	*Total*
Healthcare	21.8% (3,196)	23.9% (6,247)	30.7% (1 064)	23.7% (10,507)
Education	18.5% (2,715)	15.4% (4,038)	23.5% (814)	17.1% (7,567)
Crime	16.1% (2,362)	8.5% (2 225)	6.1% (210)	10.8% (4,797)
The environment	2.5% (360)	6.6% (1,736)	5.5% (190)	5.2% (2 286)
Immigration	2.4% (355)	4.8% (1,251)	0.3% (11)	3.7% (1,617)
Economy	13.8% (2,029)	29.7% (7,770)	15.0% (520)	23.3% (10 319)
Terrorism	5.3% (777)	2.0% (526)	1.1% (38)	3.0% (1 341)
Poverty	19.2% (2 820)	8.1% (2,130)	16.3% (565)	12.5% (5,515)
None of the above	0.4% (56)	0.9% (240)	1.4% (50)	0.8% (346)
Total	100.0% (14,670)	100.% (26,163)	100.0% (3,462)	100.0%(44,295)

Note There were a total of 45,564 responses; some responses were removed due to missing values

biggest concern was healthcare. The three countries choosing healthcare as the most important issue were Canada (42.9%), Norway (40.6%), and Switzerland (19.0%).

12.3 Public Perception of the Causes and Consequences of Climate Change

Further analysis of the public's understanding of the causes and consequences of climate change will help us to better judge the actual level of public awareness of climate change.

12.3.1 Public Understanding of the Causes of Climate Change

The ISSP 2010 and CGSS 2010 designed two statements related to the causes of climate change for respondents to assess as true or false:

1. Climate change is caused by a hole in the Earth's atmosphere.
2. Humans contribute to climate change every time we use coal, gasoline, or natural gas.

Respondents were given the option to select "completely true", "probably true", "probably false", "completely false", or "unable to choose". The first statement is a false statement, with the responses "probably false" and "totally false" deemed correct, and the responses "totally true" and "probably true" deemed incorrect. The second statement is a true statement, thus the responses "completely true" and "probably true" are correct and the responses "probably false" and "completely false" are incorrect. Due to differences in the implementation of national surveys, the above two statements on the causes of climate change were only asked in the following 18 countries: Austria, Czech Republic, Denmark, Finland, Germany, South Korea, Latvia, Lithuania, Mexico, New Zealand, Philippines, Russia, Slovakia, Spain, Switzerland, Turkey, United Kingdom, and China. As such, this data is limited to these countries.

As shown in Table 12.3, the public's understanding of the causes of climate change is limited. Among the responses, 23.0% of the public responded that the first statement was true, while 57.9% correctly identified it as being false. For the second statement, 74.5% of the public agreed with the statement, while 14.0% disagreed with it. The results of the Chinese public's responses were not satisfactory, with 38.4% and 22.3% of the public unable to respond correctly to Statements (1) and (2), respectively. The percentages of correct responses to Statements (1) and (2) were 16.3% and 65.4%, respectively, lower than the average of the surveyed countries.

A comparative analysis showed that the percentage of the public in high-income countries who incorrectly agreed with the false first statement (28.1%) was significantly higher than that in middle-income countries (16.8%), but the percentage who agreed correctly to the true second statement was nearly the same. The countries with the highest percentage of people responding to both statements correctly were Finland (31.3%), Denmark (26.9%), Switzerland (23.7%), and the United Kingdom (23.7%).

Table 12.3 Perceptions of the causes of climate change (percentage + number of responses)

	False	*True*	*Unable to choose*	*Total*
Statement 1) Climate change is caused by a hole in the Earth's atmosphere				
Mid-income countries	66.1% (5,369)	16.8% (1,368)	17.0% (1,382)	100.0% (8,119)
High-income countries	56.5% (8,344)	28.1% (4,151)	15.4% (2 270)	100.0% (14,765)
China	45.3% (1,659)	16.3% (595)	38.4% (1,405)	100.0% (3,659)
Total	57.9% (15,372)	23.0% (6,114)	19.1% (5,057)	100.0% (26,543)
Statement 2) Humans contribute to climate change every time we use coal, gasoline, or natural gas				
	False	True	Unable to choose	Total
Mid-income countries	13.2% (1,075)	76.5% (6,208)	10.3% (834).	100.0% (8,117)
High-income countries	14.8% (2,191)	75.7% (11,223)	9.5% (1,409)	100.0% (14,823)
China	12.3% (451)	65.4% (2,398)	22.3% (816)	100.0% (3,665)
Total	14.0% (3,717)	74.5% (19,829)	11.5% (3,059)	100.0% (26,605)

Note There were 45,564 total responses; some responses were removed because of missing values

12.3.2 Public Understanding of the Consequences of Climate Change

The ISSP 2010 and CGSS 2010 studies each asked a question regarding climate change's impact on the public and their families, and how the public understands the danger of global temperature elevation caused by climate change. Respondents were asked: "Which environmental issue do you think has the greatest impact on you and your family?" Respondents could choose from one of the nine environmental issue options listed, or "none of the above".

As shown in Table 12.4, the environmental issues that the public chose as having the greatest impact on individuals and families were air pollution (19.2%), household waste disposal (12.5%), and water pollution (12.2%), respectively. Climate change ranked fourth (11.2%). In mid-income countries, the responses were air pollution (18.6%), water pollution (15.6%), and water scarcity (12.6%). Climate change ranked fifth (10.0%). In high-income countries, the responses were air pollution (18.7%), climate change (12.9%), fertilizer and pesticide pollution (12.3%), a significant difference. In contrast, the Chinese people were more pessimistic about the impact of climate change on themselves and their families, choosing air pollution (25.6%), household waste disposal (20.9%), and water pollution (18.6%) in order, with climate change ranking only seventh (3.8%).

Among the 31 countries, including China, the countries with the highest percentage of the public who believe that climate change has the greatest impact on the public and individuals were, in order: Japan (28.0%), Austria (20.7%), Germany (20.3%), and the Philippines (20.2%). At the same time, climate change was also considered the environmental issue with the greatest impact on individuals and families. The countries with the smallest percentage listing climate change as having the greatest impact on their personal and family lives were the United States (6.9%), Latvia (6.6%), Israel (5.5%), and China (3.8%), with the United States (24.5%), Israel (24.9%), and China (25.6%) each being more concerned about the impact of air pollution. In Latvia (22.4%), genetically modified foods (GM) were the most important environmental issue. Combined with the previous analysis of the most important environmental issues in each country, we can see that some countries consider climate change to be their most important environmental issue. However, regarding the impact of climate change at the individual and household levels, the

Table 12.4 Environmental issues with the greatest impact on individuals and families (percentage + number of responses)

Items	*Mid-income countries*	*High-income countries*	*China*	*Total*
Air pollution	18.6% (2,621)	18.7% (4,607)	25.6% (852)	19.2% (8,080)
Fertilizer and pesticide pollution	7.6% (1,077)	12.3% (3,025)	15.4% (513)	11.0% (4,615)
Water shortages	12.4% (1,753)	5.3% (1,296)	5.3% (176)	7.7% (3,225)
Water pollution	15.6% (2,196)	9.5% (2,339)	18.6% (617)	12.2% (5,152)
Nuclear waste	4.0% (569)	3.5% (855)	0.1% (3)	3.4% (1,427)
Household waste disposal	11.4% (1,600)	12.1% (2,983)	20.9% (696)	12.5% (5,279)
Climate change	10.0% (1,408)	12.9% (3,176)	3.8% (126)	11.2% (4,710)
Genetically modified food	9.6% (1,358)	9.0% (2,221)	1.8% (59)	8.6% (3,638)
Depletion of natural resources	5.6% (783)	8.0% (1,974)	0.9% (29)	6.6% (2,786)
None of the above	5.1% (717)	8.9% (2,207)	7.6% (252)	7.5% (3,176)
Total	100.0% (14,082)	100.0% (24,683)	100.0% (3,323)	100.0% (42,088)

Note There were 45,564 total responses, and some responses were removed due to missing values

public's assessment decreased in most countries. For example, it decreased from 51.7% to 28.0% in Japan and from 5.7% to 3.8% in China.

According to analysis by natural scientists, one of the most direct and important signs and consequences of climate change is the rise in global temperatures, which leads to a series of harmful consequences such as the melting of ice sheets, rising sea levels, high-temperature droughts and a reduction in biodiversity (Sun 2006). ISSP 2010 and CGSS 2010 asked the public in various countries: "In general, to what extent do you think the global warming caused by climate change will be harmful to the environment?" The response choices were "extremely harmful to the environment" "very harmful," "somewhat harmful," "not very harmful," "not at all harmful" and "unable to choose." As shown from Table 12.5, across all responses, 85.0% of the public thought that global warming global warming was harmful, and 25.3% of the public thought that it was extremely harmful, to the environment. This indicated that all countries had a clear understanding of the danger of global warming global warming.

Note the variation between countries by income level. The perception of harm was much stronger in mid-income countries, where 33.7% of the public said climate change was "extremely harmful to the environment", compared with 22.4% in high-income countries. If the responses "extremely harmful to the environment", "very harmful", and "somewhat harmful" are combined, the percentage of people in middle-income countries who think that global warming is harmful is 87.8%. In comparison, the corresponding proportion of people in high-income countries is 84.7%. It is worth noting that in China, although 76.6% of the public think global warming is harmful, nearly one in five (19.0%) of the public say they "cannot choose" whether global warming is harmful or beneficial.

Table 12.5 Awareness of the danger of global temperature rise caused by climate change (percentage + number of responses)

- *In general, to what extent do you think the global warming caused by climate change will be harmful to the environment?*

	Mid-income countries	*High-income countries*	*China*	*Total*
Extremely harmful	33.7% (4,981)	22.4% (5,973)	13.2% (484)	25.3% (11,438)
Very harmful	34.4% (5,075)	34.2% (9,128)	36.0% (1,321)	34.4% (15,524)
Somewhat harmful	19.7% (2,904)	28.1% (7,508)	27.4% (1,004)	25.3% (11,416)
Not very harmful	6.1% (901)	9.0% (2,412)	3.9% (142)	7.7% (3,455)
Not harmful at all	1.6% (230)	1.7% (466)	0.5% (20)	1.6% (716)
Unable to choose	4.6% (677)	4.6% (1,236)	19.0% (699)	5.8% (2,612)
Total	100.0% (14,768)	100.0% (26,723)	100.0% (3,670)	100.0% (45,161)

Note There were 45,564 responses in total; some responses were removed due to missing values

A country-by-country analysis shows that more than 90% of the public in 11 countries view the rise in global temperatures caused by climate change as harmful: Argentina (95.4%), Chile (95.3%), Japan (93.4%), South Korea (93.3%), the Philippines (92.9%), Croatia (92.7%), Switzerland (92.3%), Israel (91.1%), Spain (90.7%), Mexico (90.5%), and Turkey (90.4%). The countries with the highest percentage of the public saying global warming is "extremely harmful to the environment" are Chile (45.5%), Turkey (43.8%), Mexico (42.7%), Japan (38.3%), and the Philippines (38.1%), and this may be related to these countries' geographic endowments.

12.4 Public Behaviors in Response to Climate Change

In addition to the manufacturing sector, public behavior in daily life is also closely related to climate change, especially energy consumption related to transportation and household life. ISSP 2010 and CGSS 2010 contain three survey questions on garbage classification, automobile consumption, and household consumption.

As shown in Table 12.6, in terms of sorting and recycling daily household garbage, 39.6% of the total sample said that they "always" sort and recycle. However, there are immense differences among people in countries with different income levels. The percentage of people in high-income countries who said they "always" separate and recycle their daily household waste was 58.3%, much higher than the 12.6% of people in middle-income countries. It was only 11.9% in China. Of course, recycling facilities are more widespread in high-income countries than in mid-income countries, with 17.8% of the public reporting that they lack such facilities locally, compared with 27.1% in China. However, excluding the absence of garbage collection facilities, even 35.6% of the public in middle-income countries said that they "never" separate their daily household waste, compared with 4.9% in high-income countries and 23.8% in China. Meanwhile in high-income countries, garbage sorting and recycling have been institutionalized and popularized.

In terms of automobile use, when respondents were asked, "How often do you deliberately reduce your driving for the sake of environmental protection?" only 16.3% reported "always" or "often", and the public in both middle-income and high-income countries reported similar results. Additionally, in high-income countries, cars are more common.

Table 12.6 Adjustment in public behavior due to climate change (percentage + number of responses)

	Always	*Often*	*Sometimes*	*Never*	*Not applicable*	*Total*
How often do you make a point of sorting glass bottles, aluminum cans, plastic or newspapers, etc., for easy recycling?						
Mid-income countries	12.6% (1,863)	14.9% (2,196)	25.4% (3,742)	29.3% (4,314)	17.8% (2,630)	100.0% (14,745)
High-income countries	58.3% (15,640)	22.9% (6,156)	12.1% (3,238)	4.8% (1,295)	1.9% (511)	100.0% (26,840)
China	11.9% (441)	19.7% (725)	23.9% (880)	17.3% (638)	27.1% (998)	100.0% (3,682)
Total	39.6% (17,944)	20.1% (9,077)	17.4% (7,860)	13.8% (6,247)	9.1% (4,139)	100.0% (45,267)
How often do you deliberately reduce your driving for the sake of environmental protection?						
	Always	Often	Sometimes	Never	Not Applicable	Total
Mid-income countries	3.3% (481)	7.9% (1,157)	17.6% (2,577)	25.4% (3,713)	45.8% (6,699)	100.0% (14,627)
High-income countries	4.6% (1,234)	16.0% (4 263)	31.9% (8,517)	32.4% (8,651)	15.0% (3,997)	100.0% (26,662)
China	2.0% (72)	3.5% (127)	9.0% (330)	5.8% (212)	79.7% (2,913)	100.0% (3,654)
Total	4.0% (1,787)	12.3% (5,547)	25.4% (11,424)	28.0% (12,576)	30.3% (13,609)	100.0% (44,943)
How often do you deliberately reduce your consumption of gasoline, natural gas, electricity, and other energy or fuels in your home to protect the environment?						
	Always	Often	Sometimes	Never	Not Applicable	Total
Mid-income countries	13.4% (1,940)	20.0% (2,891)	31.8% (4,597)	34.8% (5,039)	-	100.0% (14,467)
High-income countries	13.5% (3,582)	33.1% (8,788)	34.2% (9,095)	19.2% (5,105)	-	100.0% (26,570)
China	10.0% (363)	22.9% (836)	40.2% (1,467)	26.9% (981)	-	100.0% (3,647)
Total	13.2% (5,885)	28.0% (12,515)	33.9% (15,159)	24.9% (11,125)	-	100.0% (44,684)

Note Daily household waste sorting and recycling was not applicable to the responses "there is no garbage sorting and recycling facility in the place where you live". Reducing car travel did not apply to responses of "no car" or "cannot drive". The total sample size was 45,564, with some samples deleted because of missing values

In high-income countries, the percentage of the public who said they would "always" drive less for environmental protection was only 4.6%, and the percentage who would "often" drive less was 16.0%. Car access is low in middle-income countries and China, where 79.7% of people report "not owning a car" or "not being able to drive". However, among respondents who had access to a car, 46.8% in middle-income countries and 28.6% in China also reported "never" reducing their driving for environmental protection, compared with 38.2% in high-income countries.

In terms of energy consumption at home, the data analysis showed that 41.2% of the total respondents reported "always" or "often" reducing their consumption of energy or fuels, such as gasoline, natural gas, and electricity, to protect the environment. In comparison, 24.9% reported "never" reducing their consumption. There were also significant differences between different types of countries. More than 80% of the public in high-income countries have deliberately reduced their consumption of gasoline, natural gas, electricity, and other energy or fuels at home to protect the environment, while 65.2% of the public in middle-income countries and 73.1% in China report doing so.

Country-by-country analysis showed that among the 31 countries, including China, the 18 countries where the public reported the highest rate of separation and recycling of daily household waste were high-income countries, with a participation rate exceeding 84.7%. Russia had the lowest rate of public waste sorting and recycling, at 26.5%. As for reducing car travel for environmental reasons, the countries with the highest percentage of people reporting doing so were all high-income countries, except for Mexico, with China having the lowest percentage (14.5%). As for reducing energy or fuel use at home to protect the environment, the 11 countries with the highest participation levels were also high-income countries, with Mexico in 12th place (83.2%) and Israel being the lowest (39.3%).

12.5 Summary and Discussion

This study provides fresh and authoritative data to explicate public awareness and behavior in light of climate change in different countries, from a comparative perspective. Based on the above analysis and previous research, we can generally summarize the following conclusions.

First, climate change is indeed an important issue in today's world, but it is far from being the most important issue. The publicity and coverage of various media have an effect, but the extent of the effect is limited. 21.8% of respondents believed that air pollution was the most important issue, while 13.8% considered climate change the most important. This ranked climate change a distant second, trailed by water pollution at 13.0%. Among the various social issues surveyed, only a small percentage of the public in both high-income and mid-income countries rated the environment as the most important issue in their country, ranking it only sixth in terms of public concern, after healthcare, the economy, and education.

Second, although the public's understanding of the causes of climate change remains limited, a majority of the public believes that global warming caused by climate change is harmful to the environment. The above analysis shows that even in high-income countries, only 28.1% of respondents correctly identified the statement that climate change is caused by holes in the Earth's atmosphere as false.[8] At the same time, 85.0% of respondents in the countries surveyed believe climate change is harmful. Moreover, the public perception of harm is stronger in middle-income countries, where the proportion of people who think that climate change is "extremely harmful to the environment" is 33.7%, significantly higher than in high-income countries (22.4%). This is likely linked to the mass media's highlighting of global warming and its dangers.

Third, while climate change is rated by the public in each country surveyed as the second most important environmental issue in their own country, it is not the one that affects their individuals and families the most. Regarding effects at the individual and household level, the public's assessment of the importance of climate change has declined in almost every country. For example, in Japan, 51.7% of people believe that climate change is the country's most important environmental issue. However, only 28.0% believe it has the greatest effect on individuals and families. Of the total sample, 19.2% of the public chose air pollution, 12.5% chose household waste disposal, and 12.2% chose water pollution as the environmental issues with the greatest effect on individuals and families. Climate change ranked fourth at 11.2%. This reveals that issues that can be directly felt in daily life tend to be assessed as having a greater effect.

[8] Previous findings (Dunlap 1998; Berchin 2003) have shown that it is gradually increasing, indicating some increase in public knowledge of climate change.

Fourth, in terms of the public's coping behavior, although the public has the necessary information, the implementations of the behavior are inconsistent. Of the total sample, nearly six in ten (59.7%) respondents said they "always" or "often" engage in recycling. This indicated that recycling is highly institutionalized, especially in high-income countries. However, only 16.3% said they would "always" or "often" reduce their driving, and only 41.2% said they would reduce energy consumption at home in order to protect the environment. In high-income countries in particular, their willingness to drive less was disproportionate to their concern about climate change, with 32.4% saying they never reduce their driving for environmental reasons. This shows how difficult it is to change core behaviors in our lifestyles, even when we consider it important to address environmental issues such as climate change.

Fifth, comparative analysis shows that public awareness and behavioral adjustments to climate change vary across countries. Generally speaking, people in high-income countries are more concerned about climate change, and are more likely to consider it their country's most important environmental issue. For example, 51.7% of respondents in Japan, 26.9% in Norway, and 26.6% in Germany shared this view (see Fig. 12.1). At the same time, the general public in high-income countries are also more informed about climate change and adjust their behavior more. These data support the post-materialistic hypothesis.[9]

However, further analysis shows that, as the previous studies have indicated, national economic development levels cannot fully explain the differences in public perception and behavior adjustment to climate change (Dunlap 1998; Bord et al. 1998; Berchin 2003, 2010). In this study, only a small percentage of the public in developed countries such as the United States identified climate change as the environmental issue with the most impact on their families and individually. Meanwhile, countries like Chile, Mexico, and the Philippines had high percentages of respondents who viewed global warming as extremely harmful to the environment. There was little difference between high-income and middle-income countries in recognizing that people are contributing to

[9] According to Inglehart's (1990: 66) theory of post-materialism, since the 1960s, there has been a cultural shift in public values in developed countries: "from prioritizing physiological and safety needs to a greater emphasis on belonging, self-expression and quality of life". This is most prominently manifested in the growing public concern for the environment.

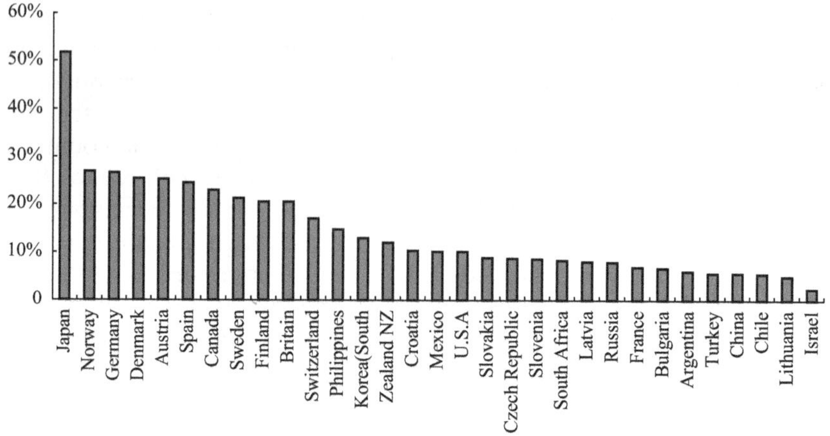

Fig. 12.1 Which issue do you think is the most important environmental issue in your country right now (% who selected "climate change")?

climate change every time they use coal, gasoline, or natural gas, and high-income countries showed no particularly positive behavior in terms of reducing driving for the sake of the environment.

Research has also shown that domestic opinion has an important influence on a given public. For example, in the United States public concern over global warming caused by climate change peaked in the late 1980s and early 1990s, accompanied by overwhelming media coverage (McCright and Dunlap 2000). However, in recent years, the level of public concern over climate change in the United States has stagnated, or even declined, as media have reported on discrepancies in the way climate change is reported and the effects of financial crises. (Boykoff and Boykoff 2004; Scruggs and Benegal 2012). Therefore, it should be said that the reasons for the differences in public awareness and the subsequent behavioral adjustment to climate change in different countries are complex. This is true not only in terms of the effects of the level and stage of economic development, but also in terms of the influence of each country's own resource and environmental endowment and the guidance of the mass media. Environmental protection policies and facility levels, public values, and lifestyles are interrelated, and this warrants further in-depth study.

Sixth, the data show that the Chinese public's awareness and behavior adjustment to climate change has been limited, and generally on par with the public in mid-income countries, and in some respects even lower. According to the Chinese public, the most important environmental problems are air pollution, water pollution, and household waste disposal, with climate change ranking fifth (5.7%), slightly higher than middle-income countries, but significantly lower than high-income countries. In contrast, the Chinese public is more pessimistic about climate change's effect on themselves and their families. They chose air pollution, household waste disposal, and water pollution in that order, with climate change ranking only seventh. On both knowledge measurements of the causes of climate change, the Chinese public gave poor responses, with 38.4% and 22.3% unable to even respond to Statements 1 and 2, respectively. This was below the average among the countries surveyed. Meanwhile, while 76.6% of the Chinese public believe global warming is harmful, nearly one-fifth of the public said they could not choose whether global warming is harmful or beneficial. The Chinese public performed slightly better than middle-income countries but worse than high-income countries in deliberately reducing their consumption of gasoline, natural gas, electricity, and other energy or fuels at home in order to protect the environment. Overall, the goal: "by 2010, strive to popularize the relevant knowledge of climate change and raise the awareness of the whole society" proposed in China's National Plan on Climate Change mentioned above was only partly achieved. On the other hand, the 2012 *Annual Report on China's Policies and Actions to Address Climate Change* emphasizes "promoting the publicity and popularization of scientific knowledge to address climate change and guiding the people to participate extensively in action to address climate change", which is reasonable; the task ahead remains arduous.

Theoretically, this study also underscores that climate change research and related policy actions must be based on climate change as a social fact. It also demonstrates the differences in social responses to climate change and the complexity of actions to address it.

Climate change should be understood as having both natural and social dimensions. However in practice, it is often framed as a fact measured by the research of natural scientists, and its seriousness is taken for granted, despite evidence that scientists have not reached a consensus. From a sociological perspective, even if scientists were to consistently and accurately measure climate change, it would only reveal a surface-level understanding. To promote social action against climate change, we must focus on the social context of climate change, the general state of awareness and its definition by members of society. People take action depending on their definition of the goals, means, and circumstances of a given action. By studying public awareness of climate change, we reveal the extent to which climate change is accepted by the public as an "objective" fact that influences people's actions. Only by holistically studying the social context of climate change can we derive a more comprehensive understanding of the phenomenon, and fairly judge the social actions and social changes that climate change may cause. The results of this study show that the social context of climate change is emerging, but its universality and constraints remain limited. To an extent, public perception of climate change may be related to the social construction of the media, and the empirical correlation with its daily life experience is weak. Thus, its direct and sustained binding force on behavior is limited.

Furthermore, climate change research should explore the diversity of social responses to climate change, and provide a comprehensive understanding of the public's various perceptions of climate change. Some overly technologically oriented studies have assumed that the public will respond to climate change coherently, and even enact arbitrary policy choices. Countries and regions differ in their geographical environments and resource endowments, in their stages of socioeconomic development, and in their consequent capacity to adapt to and mitigate climate change. They also differ in the methods, content, and goals of disseminating climate change information, and in their social structures and means of social organization. Differences in social values, attitudes, and lifestyles and types of social issues make it almost inevitable that the public will have varying perceptions and behavioral choices regarding climate change. Addressing and reconciling these differences, rather than ignoring or suppressing them, is an important prerequisite for avoiding simplistic policy actions and developing more effective policies. One goal of this study is to explicate the differences in public perceptions on climate change across countries.

Finally, given the limitations of climate change as a social phenomenon as revealed in this study, and the objective differences in public responses, we must not overlook the complexity of climate change action in the process of further research and policy action. Assuming that climate change is an undisputable fact of nature requires the mobilization of global action. However, to promote such action we cannot rely on simplistic coercion and threats, but instead need more extensive and effective information dissemination and communication and consultation. Moreover, we need to further construct the social reality of climate change by promoting collective awareness of it with more intensity and a broader scope. At the same time, to address climate change, we should implement the principle of "common but differentiated responsibilities" according to the actual conditions of different countries and regions, and formulate a more reasonable policy mix to unite the efforts of all countries around the world. In this regard, tackling climate change is bound to be a difficult and long-term process of action.

PART III

Governance Transformation and the Green Society

This section highlights climate change and air pollution management as examples, focusing on the analysis of the governance transformation trend reflected in the development of China's environmental policy, as well as the macro trends and challenges of China's social greening.

CHAPTER 13

China's Climate Change Practices

Hong Dayong

This focus of this chapter is the Chinese government's efforts to address climate change and the main challenges it faces. We then analyze the sociological significance of climate change practices, with a view to promoting more valuable research in the social sciences (particularly sociology), on climate change, and paying attention to new trends in social transformation in the context of climate change.

13.1 Unbalanced Climate Change Awareness

Within the scientific community, climate change is considered by many to be the greatest environmental risk facing human society since the Industrial Revolution. This risk is manifested in the increasing greenhouse gases in the atmosphere, and this basic consensus of the scientific community is increasingly recognized by heads of state around the world. Thus, many countries are promoting the global governance of climate change. In 1992, the United Nations Intergovernmental Negotiating Committee agreed on the United Nations Framework Convention on

D. Hong (✉)
Renmin University of China, Beijing, China
e-mail: hongdy@ruc.edu.cn

D. Hong and Y. Fan (eds.), *Toward a Green Society*,
https://doi.org/10.1007/978-981-96-5111-5_13

Climate Change (UNFCCC). This was a landmark event. On November 4, 2016, the Paris Agreement, which had been negotiated in a painstaking international manner, finally entered into force. The agreement has been formally ratified by 74 countries, which account for 58.82% of global greenhouse gas emissions. The agreement arranges for global action on climate change after 2020, and is another important milestone in the global governance of climate change.

However, within the scientific community, there has been far more discussion of climate change in the natural sciences than in the social sciences, with discussion of climate change in sociology being particularly limited. For example, in China's well-known full-text journal database, CNKI, a total of 11,626 articles can be found by searching for articles whose titles contain the term "climate change" (as of November 8, 2016). However, if natural science journals are excluded, that number drops to 1,844. In other words, only 15.9% of the literature on climate change has been published in humanities or social science journals. Among them, sociological literature on climate change is particularly scant. Of the 2,889 articles published in *Sociological Studies*, China's most elite sociology journal, only one contained the term "climate change" in the title (Zhang 2011). Thus, it can be argued that Chinese sociologists have paid little attention to the social causes and social impacts of, and the social responses to, climate change, with many Chinese people taking it for granted that climate change is a subject for natural scientists.

As far as the general public is concerned, if you interview a random person and ask him if he knows anything about climate change, chances are he has only heard about it, but knows little about it, or can only talk to you about "weather change". According to the 2010 China Comprehensive Social Survey (CGSS) conducted by the Chinese University of China, only 5.7% of respondents believe that the most important environmental issue in China is "climate change" (see Table 12.1). This was despite a recent study showing that about 63% of respondents have heard of "global climate change", another 23.6% said they had "never heard of it", and 13.4% said they "don't know". In their analysis, the researchers also noted that Chinese citizens' knowledge of global climate change is "shallow and inaccurate" (Huang et al. 2016).

In fact, like many countries around the world, the Chinese public is beset by a number of issues in the midst of social transformation, not just the environment. For example, according to 2010 China General Social Survey (CGSS) data, respondents ranked the social issues healthcare, education, crime, the environment, immigration, the economy, terrorism, and poverty in the following order of importance: health care (30.7%), education (23.5%), poverty (16.3%), the economy (15.0%), and crime (6.1%). The environment ranked sixth in importance at 5.5%. Even in developed countries, environmental issues are not at the forefront of the public mind.[1] If we look at environmental issues alone, Chinese respondents are more concerned about issues such as air pollution (34.7%), water pollution (20.0%), and domestic waste disposal (17.7%) that are closely related to their daily lives; climate change is relegated to the back burner. This is a clear difference from developed countries (see Table 12.1).

13.2 China's Efforts in Coping with Climate Change

Despite the above-mentioned imbalance in research and understanding regarding climate change, the Chinese government has long recognized the seriousness of global climate change, and has undertaken various measures in response. China has not only ratified a series of important documents to address climate change, such as the United Nations Framework Convention on Climate Change, the Kyoto Protocol, and the Paris Agreement, but has also taken various actions to mitigate and adapt to climate change on its own. Since the United Nations Conference on Environment and Development in 1992, the Chinese government has taken the lead in organizing the formulation of *China's Agenda 21—White Paper on China's Population, Environment and Development in the 21st Century*. Since then, a wide range of work has been undertaken in areas such as the formulation and coordination of policies on climate change. Since 2001, the National Coordinating Body for Climate Change Countermeasures has organized the preparation of the Initial National Communication on Climate Change of the People's Republic of China, which was formally submitted to The 10th Meeting of the Conference of the Parties to the United Nations Framework Convention on Climate Change at the end of 2004. In 2007, China established the

[1] According to the 2010 International Social Survey Program (ISSP 2010), the most important issues in high-income countries (by percentage of the public ranking each first in importance) are the economy (29.7%), healthcare (23.9%), education (15.4%), with the environment ranking sixth (6.6%).

National Leading Group for Climate Change, Energy Conservation, and Emission Reduction, and formulated and issued China's National Plan for Climate Change. Since 2008, the Chinese government has regularly released national reports on China's policies and actions to address climate change, disclosing China's progress on climate change, both at home and abroad.

In China, the National Congress of the Party has had a massive impact on the country's internal and foreign affairs. The report of the 17th National Congress of the Communist Party of China CPC in 2007 included the topic of climate change for the first time, stating that it is necessary to "strengthen capacity building to cope with climate change and make new contributions to the protection of the global climate". In 2012, the report of the 18th National Congress of the Communist Party of China further stated that China should "adhere to the principles of common but differentiated responsibilities, fairness, and respective capabilities, and work with the international community to actively respond to global climate change". This clarified China's path to addressing climate change. It should be emphasized that the Chinese government has recognized in practice that protecting the environment and responding to climate change need to be combined with better development and the promotion of comprehensive societal change. In 2003, China proposed the establishment of a scientific outlook on development. In 2007, the report of the 17th National Congress of the Communist Party of China proposed building an "ecological civilization"—that is, to create an industrial structure, growth model, and consumption pattern that conserves energy resources and protects the ecological environment. In 2012, in the report of the 18th National Congress of the Communist Party of China, it was further proposed to prioritize the construction of ecological civilization and integrate it throughout economic, political, cultural and social construction, strive to build a "Beautiful China", realize the sustainable development of the Chinese nation, and contribute to global ecological security. Following the Third Plenary Session of the 18th CPC Central Committee, the process of building China's ecological civilization system has continued to accelerate, and a systematic and complete ecological civilization system is taking shape. Since 2015, China has implemented a series of important policies, including a new environmental protection law, which has been described as the "strictest in history", and the *Overall Plan for the Reform of the Ecological Civilization System*. The Fifth Plenary Session of the 18th Central Committee of the Communist Party of China held at the end of 2015 proposed five major concepts to guide China's future development, which emphasized adherence to the concept of "green development": (1) adhere to the basic national policy of saving resources and protecting the environment; (2) firmly follow the development of production; (3) build an affluent life and ecology; (4) speed up the construction of a resource-saving and environment-friendly society; (5) forge a new pattern of harmonious development and modernization between man and nature.

As a national "five-year plan" to implement the spirit of the central government, the government plays a direct role in promoting green development and addressing climate change. The 11th Five-Year Plan (2006–2010) included environmental indicators such as energy consumption per unit of GDP, total emissions of major pollutants, and forest coverage as binding indicators.[2] Such indicators have been included in the 12th Five-Year Plan (2011–2015) and 13th Five-Year Plan (2016–2020). The scope of these plans is constantly expanding, the content is constantly being enriched, and the requirements are becoming more specific. Among the 25 main indicators in the 13th Five-Year Plan, 10 are resource and environmental indicators, and all are binding indicators, including a 15% reduction in energy consumption per unit of GDP compared with 2015, and a 3% increase in the proportion of non-fossil energy in primary energy consumption, and a 18% reduction in CO_2 emissions per unit of GDP. The plan also has a special chapter on "actively responding to global climate change". Judging from statistics, China's efforts to alleviate climate change have achieved some success. For example, since 2008, China's GDP has outpaced its total energy consumption. Moreover, since the Reform and Opening-up, China's energy consumption per 10,000 yuan of GDP has continued to decline, and by 2014 it had dropped to 0.7 tons of standard coal (see Fig. 13.1). Since the implementation of the

[2] The binding indicators are indicators that further clarify and strengthen the responsibilities of the government on the basis of expectations. They are the central government's work requirements for local governments and relevant departments of the central government in the areas of public services and public interests. The government ensures this through the rational allocation of public resources and the effective use of administrative power.

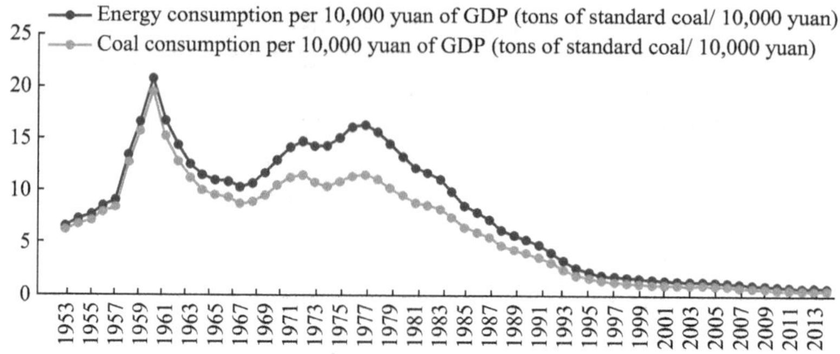

Fig. 13.1 Energy consumption per 10,000 yuan of GDP and coal consumption per 10,000 yuan of GDP in China, from 1952 to 2014 (*Source* China National Bureau of Statistics official website)

12th Five-Year Plan, carbon intensity has dropped by 20%, exceeding the 17% target set by the 12th Five-Year Plan.[3]

At the same time, China's energy mix continues to improve, with energy coming from the following sources in 2014 (See Fig. 13.2): coal (66.0%); oil (17.1%); natural gas (5.7%); and non-fossil energy (11.2%). In 2015, the proportion of non-fossil energy in energy consumption reached 12%, exceeding the target set in the 12th Five-Year Plan, and the proportion of non-fossil energy consumption continues to grow as of this writing.

The first *China's Policies and Actions to Address Climate Change* white paper released in 2008 noted:

> China will combine climate change with the implementation of sustainable development strategies, accelerate the construction of a resource-saving and environment-friendly society, and build an innovative country. With economic development as the core, energy conservation, optimization of energy structure, strengthening ecological protection and construction as the focus, and scientific and technological progress as the support, we will

[3] "The Information Office introduced the 2016 *Annual Report on China's Policies and Actions on Climate Change*" (2016–11–01) [2019–07–22]. http://www.gov.cn/xinwen/2016-11/01/content_5127079.htm.

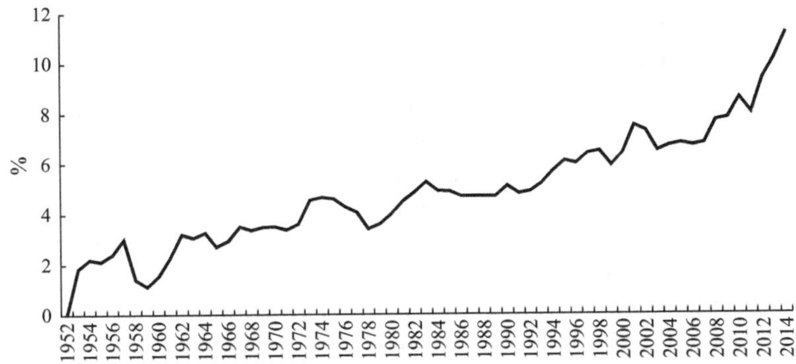

Fig. 13.2 Proportion of non-fossil energy consumption in China from 1952 to 2014 (*Source* official website of the National Bureau of Statistics)

> strive to control and mitigate greenhouse gas emissions and continuously improve the ability to adapt to climate change.[4]

This clarified China's basic roadmap for addressing climate change. Along this path, China is adjusting its economic structure, promoting technological progress, improving energy efficiency, developing low-carbon and renewable energy, and implementing afforestation to manage population growth. In addition, it is strengthening the formulation of laws, regulations, and policy measures, improving the construction of relevant systems and institutions, and improving the scientific research support capacity related to climate change. In the future, China will continue to implement climate change education and raise awareness. It should be said that China's path to climate change is in line with reality, on the right path, and fully considers promoting the coordinated linkage and coordinated transformation of the economy, politics, culture, society, and the environment. This demonstrates China's autonomy in addressing climate change.

[4] Information Office of the State Council of the People's Republic of China. "China's policies and actions on climate change" (2018–10–29) [2019–07–22]. http://www.gov.cn/zwgk/2008-10/29/content_1134378.htm.

13.3 Challenges Facing China in Coping with Climate Change

The main reason why China has been on the right path in tackling climate change and has achieved some success is that China's political system has a strong capacity to cope with crises and can "focus on big things". China's ruling party, the Communist Party of China, has a broad mass base, a sound organizational system, rich political experience, and strong social mobilization capacity. It is able to integrate climate change responses into an array social and economic work, seeking to unify environmental protection and economic development. In fact, the series of reforms that China is currently implementing, with the supply-side reform of the economy as the focus, and including the construction of values, also plays an important role in guiding the reasonable expectations of the public; it influences Chinese people to understand environmental protection's importance to building a better life. Of course, China's vast territory, massive population, complex climatic conditions, fragile ecological environment, and complex and volatile international environment still face formidable challenges in its response to climate change.

In terms of domestic challenges, the Chinese government first needs to disseminate its knowledge and recognition of climate change to a wide region, complex industries, and diverse populations. This will secure social support and cultivate the drive to address climate change from within society. As mentioned earlier, this is a challenge, and the Chinese public's awareness of climate change remains limited. In particular, there are stark development gaps between urban and rural areas, between regions, between industries, and between different groups of people, and the existence of such gaps affects the interests of all parties involved. For example, according to data released by the National Bureau of Statistics, in 2015, the Gini coefficient for China's household income was 0.462, even though it had gradually declined since 2008. However, it is still above the "warning line" and above the global average of 0.44. Based on the rural poverty alleviation standard of 2,300 yuan per capita per year, there were 70.17 million poor people living in rural areas in China in 2014. At the same time, nearly 20 million people in urban areas were eligible for subsistence allowances.

Second, China needs to strike a balance between tackling climate change and promoting economic development. China is still a developing country with a low level of economic development, and the contradiction between economic development, poverty eradication, and environmental protection remains prominent. Accounting for the per capita income and wide disparities in domestic development, as well as the gap between China and developed countries, it is in its overall and long-term interests to continue to promote national development.

Third, China needs to balance its ambitions to combat climate change with the resources it has available, especially technology. Mitigation and adaptation to climate change require a lot of resources, and especially advanced technologies. Although China emphasizes climate change research and capacity building, and continually improves its capacity to support climate change-related scientific research, the technical means that China has mastered are rudimentary. Thus, China still relies on developed countries for many technologies. At the same time, China also needs to raise a lot of money to combat climate change, another challenge.

Finally, China needs to balance the tension between its policy objectives and policy implementation systems to address climate change. A fragmented and multi-layered administrative system may seem comprehensive, but it also suffers from systemic inefficiencies. One of the key goals of China's ongoing political and administrative reform is to improve administrative efficiency. For example, China's ongoing reform of the vertical management system for monitoring, supervision, and enforcement of environmental protection agencies below the provincial level is an attempt to break down local protectionism and improve the quality and efficiency of environmental protection work. However, its effects still need more observation.

Regarding the challenges at the international level, first, the implementation of the principle of common but differentiated responsibilities needs improvement, and developed countries have yet to fulfill their responsibilities for their historical emissions. As of 2012, China's per capita emissions are still lower than those of the United States (see Fig. 13.3). At the same time, the trend of wealth polarization on a global scale has not eased. According to Credit Suisse's 2014 Global Wealth Report, global wealth is 20% higher than its peak before the 2008 financial crisis. In the report, wealth in North America increased the most, accounting for 34.7% of the world's wealth. Europe is in second place, accounting for 32.4% of global wealth. There were about 128,000 wealthy people with assets of at least $50 million worldwide, nearly half of whom were in the United States and nearly a quarter in Europe. Moreover, it is also unfair that developed countries have failed to fulfill their responsibilities, and China

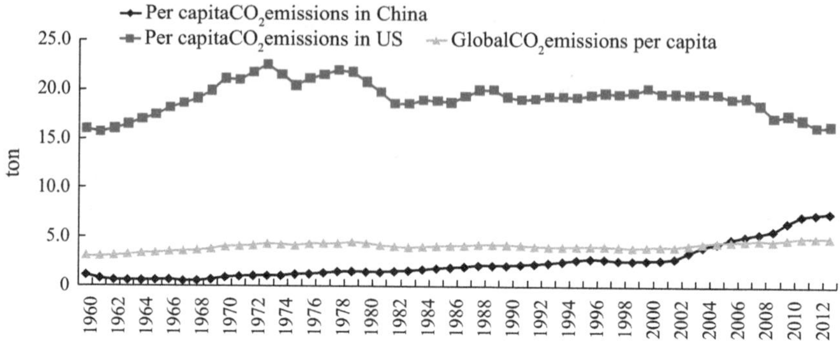

Fig. 13.3 Per capita CO_2 emissions in the agricultural and natural sectors of China, the United States, and globally, from 1960 to 2013 (*Source* World Bank Statistical Yearbook)

needs to work for a more equitable sharing of responsibilities, and resist an unequal world political and economic system.

Second, as China's economy continues to expand, its total greenhouse gas emissions continue to increase, accounting for an increasing share of the world's total emissions. As a result, China is not only being asked to incur more responsibilities by developed countries, but also by some developing countries and countries with greater vulnerability to climate change, thus bearing greater pressure to fulfill its responsibilities. The assumption of these responsibilities is intertwined with the relations between states. Therefore, China should consider making more commitments and contributions to the international community.

Finally, in accordance with the provisions of various international treaties, developed countries have pledged financial support to developing countries in the transfer of advanced technologies and to help them improve their ability to cope with climate change. However, these commitments are often paid in lip service and do not meet the needs of developing countries. Thus, China should implement more supervision and promotion in this regard, and at the same time work harder to promote independent innovation. Incidentally, as a developing country, China's experience in participating in global governance and responding to global crises is also expanding, and there is a process of continuous learning and creation.

In the face of complex domestic and international challenges, China's efforts to address climate change must be embedded in its own development process, and any effort that is divorced from China's development practice will likely not produce solid and sustainable results. While mitigating greenhouse gas emissions is important, and China has been working to do so, adaptation to climate change is equally important. Thus, China should continue strengthening its capacity to adapt to climate change through innovation and construction. China has its own position and process in reducing carbon emissions, and it is promoting independent emission reductions regardless of whether other countries have done so. Moreover, green development has been identified as a basic direction in the transformation of China's development strategy. China is striving to identify development opportunities in the process of responding to environmental crises, including climate change, creating new development paths and models, reshaping social life, and building new green social forms. Of course, we also want to mention that China increasingly hopes for closer and more effective international exchanges and cooperation, and increasingly hopes to leverage the strength of a community with a shared future for mankind to respond to global crises such as climate change.

13.4 The Sociological Significance of Practices to Address Climate Change

China's approach to climate change, which we have analyzed earlier, has in fact highlighted the social complexity of the climate change issue. The objective existence of the phenomenon of climate change and its potential real impact on human beings and the earth system is observable from the perspective of natural science, this is only one aspect of climate change. If we emphasize that climate change is caused by human causes, and that human society must take action to address climate change, then it is necessary to explore its social complexity. Thus, we must examine the complex social agents, social dynamics, and social processes that both cause, and are responses to, climate change. In this sense, climate change also has a social component, which is manifested as a social fact, and which requires in-depth research in social sciences (especially sociology). It should be said that there remains a significant lack of research on climate change in the social sciences, which hinders both understandings and responses to it.

As we mentioned above, climate change has rarely been studied in the Chinese sociological community, and there is a similar phenomenon in the international sociological community (Dunlap and Brulle 2015). In terms of the political innovation needed to combat climate change, as Anthony Giddens (2009) states, "we don't have the politics of climate change yet". In fact, we face not only a lack of political innovation, but also a lack of innovation in economic, social, and cultural systems. However, this innovation is currently transpiring in an uneven form in different countries and regions. To better tackle climate change, we need more in-depth and pragmatic social science research to discover real social system innovation, that is, innovation that transcends both the conservative and the radical.

Observing and analyzing social practices in response to climate change allows us to further examine the biophysical factors that influence the functioning of social systems, which have been known to have a wide-ranging impact, even before the dawn of modern sociology. It can be observed that under the influence of climate change, people's perceptions, attitudes, and behaviors are changing. Additionally, the types of social conflict and the level of social injustice are in flux, and the political and economic systems of societies are shifting along with emerging technological innovation and the institutional designs that drive them. Thus, it would be difficult to conclude that biophysical factors are unrelated to the functioning of modern society, and therefore there is no reason to ignore biophysical factors in the analysis of social operations.

China has taken the initiative to promote the overall reform of the social system, created a new form of social civilization through practical institutional construction, and has encountered some important challenges while making progress in some areas in response to the increasingly severe environmental crisis and climate change. In the future, we must focus on the continuation of life practice and explore a new path of civilization development. China's experience may tell us how the role of the state should be positioned in response to climate change. How is political consensus formed? How can climate change be integrated into economic development? How can we advocate and consolidate new social values? If China's practices continue to make significant progress, it will bring new hope to the future of our entire society.

Of course, the practice of coping with climate change has also brought new opportunities and created new space for many empirical studies in sociology. First, sociology can better describe the social face of climate change. Sociology can downplay the natural aspects of climate change, but the sociological approach can tell us who is speaking of "climate change" in our society. Sociology can intuitively reveal the imbalance in society's perception and actions on climate change, and can explicate the existence of this disequilibrium by borrowing various theories about power, familiar interests and values, as well as the methods of analyzing social structure, social processes, and social practices.

Second, sociology can be used to analyze "human beings" and the complex processes of human society in more detail, to more comprehensively reveal the complexity and diversity of the social, economic, political, and cultural effects of climate change, especially the differential distribution of these effects and the consequences of the social injustice and social conflicts they cause.

Third, due to the above two reasons, sociology can make a positive contribution to climate governance, provide better alternatives to climate governance, develop more detailed climate governance assessments, and promote climate governance systems. As such, it can promote the continued improvement of structures, policies, mechanisms, and practices.

Finally, the emergence of climate change and the complexity of coping with climate change once again remind sociologists that they must be reflective, critical, and constructive about their research objectives, and that of other sociologists. The development of modernity often brings unexpected consequences, and only by maintaining a sober reflective and critical lens can we regularly revise our understanding of the operation and development of society, uncover unexplained research and practical presuppositions, and improve the selectivity of social action.

CHAPTER 14

Changes in the Environmental Policymaking Process

Wu Liufen and Hong Dayong

Since the Reform and Opening-up, the development of the socialist market economy has changed the pattern in the relationship between the state and society in China. It has also changed the scope of citizens' rights of association, and the space for social organizations to participate in public affairs has been expanding. The interaction between various fields and the government has also undergone sharp and profound changes. In recent years, more and more members of the public and non-governmental environmental protection organizations have publicly appealed, complained, and protested to the government and relevant departments about urgent environmental problems and the environmental damage or hidden environmental risks in the existing policies, or those to be introduced by the government. In this way, they have

L. Wu (✉)
Guangxi University of Finance and Economics, Guangxi, China

D. Hong
Minzu University of China, Beijing, China
e-mail: hongdy@ruc.edu.cn

D. Hong and Y. Fan (eds.), *Toward a Green Society*,
https://doi.org/10.1007/978-981-96-5111-5_14

participated in the formulation and adjustment process of relevant environmental policies, thus reflecting an important trend in China's social green transformation. This chapter uses the formulation process for China's smog management policy as an example to explore the characteristics and effects of the interactive relationship between the public and the government.

14.1 The Smog Problem: One Air, Two Voices

There have been many large-scale smog incidents across China in recent years. According to the 2013 *China Climate Bulletin* issued by the China Meteorological Administration, the average number of smog days in Central and Eastern China in 2013 was 16 days, 8 days fewer than average, and the fewest since 1961. The average number of haze days was 36 days, 27 days more than historical average, and the highest since 1961.[1]

"Smog" is not a scientific concept. As of this writing, the Chinese scientific community uses the terms "haze" or "dust-haze" more often, with "smog" mainly referring to the general air turbidity phenomenon caused by fog and haze, which is collectively referred to as "hazy weather" by the public, and is one manifestation of serious air pollution. Therefore, smog management still falls under the scope of air pollution prevention and mitigation.

In 1973, the Chinese government enacted the "Trial Standards for the Discharge of Three Industrial Wastes" which tentatively set the emissions standards for 13 hazardous substances. This marked the first time that the prevention and alleviation of air pollution was put on the agenda of the Chinese government. For more than 40 years, the Chinese government has implemented air pollution prevention and alleviation mainly by strengthening the legal system and tackling key scientific and technological problems (Hao 2013). In terms of the legal system, in addition to the *Trial Standards for the Discharge of Three Industrial Wastes* (1973), the central government and environmental protection departments have enacted a series of policies and regulations, such as the *Environmental Air*

[1] The China Meteorological Administration issued the 2013 *China Climate Communique*. (2014–01–14) [2019–07–22]. http://www.cma.gov.cn/2011xwzx/2011xqxxw/2011xqxyw/201401/t20140114_236245.html.

Quality Standards (1982), *Provisions on Technical Policies for the Prevention and Control of Soot Pollution* (1984), *Law of the People's Republic of China on the Prevention and Control of Air Pollution* (2000), and the *Clean Production Promotion Law of the People's Republic of China* (2002), which have provided legal protection for China's air pollution prevention and alleviation. It has also created a legal system for coal-smoke air pollution management. At the same time, four environmental science research systems—the Chinese Academy of Sciences system, the institutions of higher learning system, the various departments of the State Council system, and the Environmental Protection Management system—have gradually taken shape (Editorial Board of 30 Years of Environmental Protection in China during Reform and Opening-up 2010). Several major topics in the prevention and alleviation of air pollution in environmental science research have been included in the "Seventh Five-Year Plan", "Eighth Five-Year Plan", "Ninth Five-Year Plan", and "Tenth Five-Year Plan" of national scientific development. The development of this environmental scientific research not only provides practical technical support for the prevention and alleviation of air pollution, but also promotes the corresponding policy formulation, the improvement of laws and regulations and the introduction of standards.

With institutional support and advancements in technology, China has made remarkable achievements in the prevention and alleviation of air pollution, especially in the past 10 years leading up to this writing. The national ambient air quality has improved significantly, and has remained stable overall. According to statistics from the *Bulletin of China's Environmental Situation* on the Ministry of Environmental Protection's website, from 2003 to 2012, in the annual monitoring of air quality levels in cities at the prefecture level and above, the percentage of air quality rated at Grade II (meeting the standard) or better increased from a low of 38.6% in 2004 to a high of 91.4% in 2012. The proportion of Grade III (exceeding the standard) air quality decreased from a peak of 41.2% (2004) to 7.1% (2012); the proportion of worse-than Grade III air quality dropped from a peak of 26.8% in 2003 to 1.2% in 2011. As shown in Fig. 14.1, China's air quality has been trending in a positive direction.

However, with the frequent occurrence of smoggy days, the public has questioned whether air pollution alleviation is in fact "gradually getting better". In November 2010, the U.S. Embassy in Beijing, using its Twitter account BeijingAir, posted an air quality index reading above 500 with the caption "Crazy bad". But because Twitter had few users in China

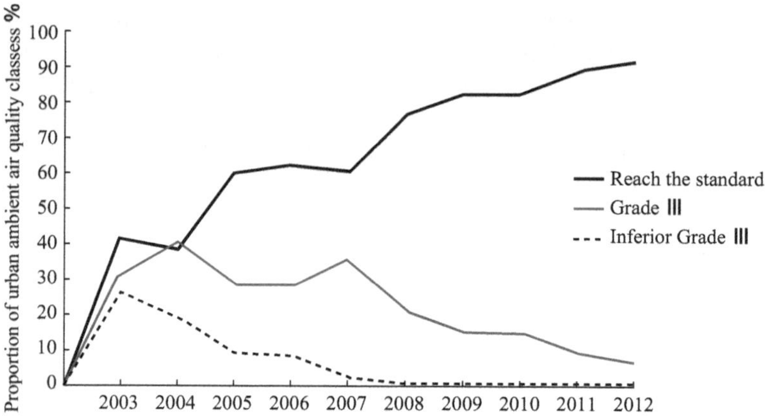

Fig. 14.1 Change in ambient air quality class in cities at the prefecture level and above, 2003–2012 (*Source* Compiled according to *China's Environmental Status Bulletin* issued by the State Environmental Protection Administration/ Ministry of Environmental Protection from 2003 to 2012)

at the time, its messages had limited impact. Later, with the popularization of modern media, $PM_{2.5}$ (particulate matter with a diameter of 2.5 micrometers or less) and smog became popular social issues discussed by the public through various media.

From the perspective of content analysis, there are five main categories of public concern: (1) "the Beijing air quality data gap controversy"; (2) reporting on smog; (3) reporting on the harm smog causes; (4) Government releases of information on smog management; (5) The popularization of information on smog protection. Among these, the "Beijing air quality data gap dispute" caused the most heated online discussion. In addition to the data released by the US embassy in Beijing showing Beijing air quality being "off the charts", most residents of China also feel that the air quality is very bad. However, the Beijing Municipal Environmental Protection Bureau released an air quality report showing that Beijing air is only slightly polluted. Thus, it can be said that government monitoring data contradicts the public's perception of air quality, raising questions about environmental protection departments' effectiveness in combating air pollution.

In summary, in the new stage of air pollution management in China, there has been a phenomenon of "one air, two voices". This phenomenon can be understood on two levels. Firstly, the difference between the US Embassy in China and the Beijing Environmental Protection Bureau in the monitoring of Beijing's air quality has triggered the interpretation of multiple parties throughout society, and constructed the smog problem. According to government monitoring data, Beijing's air quality has gradually improved in the decade leading up to this writing, and especially in 2011 and 2012. However, the smog problem "exploded" during these two years. In other words, smog was not considered a serious environmental problem until it began receiving public attention. With the online discussion, mass media reports and scientists' and government officials' "voice", as well as the introduction of relevant national policies, the smog problem became an urgent environmental problem. As an environmental issue, smog is a process, and a result of social consensus and co-construction. The second level is the inconsistency between objective monitoring and the subjective perception of air quality, which indicates tension between the government and the public in determining air quality. In addition to reflecting the evolution of how the government's monitoring indicators, monitoring methods, and governance priorities have lagged behind environmental issues, this also highlights the public's demand for an improved environment, along with improved standards of living. The awakening of public environmental awareness and the development of mass media have directly accelerated the process of the public expressing their will and participating in environmental governance.

14.2 Smog Management: A Combination of Push and Pull Factors

Regarding smog management, on the surface, public participation directly affects the formulation of smog alleviation policies. However, in-depth analysis shows that the formulation of smog alleviation policies is the result of the joint action of the dual forces of public participation and government leadership. This has the effect of slowing the combination of push and pull factors.

14.2.1 The Driving Force of Public Participation on the Evolution of Smog Issues

Firstly, public participation elevates the smog issue from strictly a scientific issue to a public issue. Like other environmental problems, smog has also undergone a social process of scientific research, public concern, and policy response. Smog entered the scientific community's field of view as an object of scientific research and an academic issue during the 1980s, when China had already pioneered research on atmospheric aerosols. From 2003 to 2007, the Chinese government designed and built a network of atmospheric composition observation stations for the Pearl River Delta cluster (PRD), the Beijing-Tianjin-Hebei cluster (BTH), the Yangtze River Delta cluster (YRD), and the central Liaoning City cluster (CL) (Wu 2012). However, smog as a scientific issue was rarely discussed by the public. After the controversy over $PM_{2.5}$ in 2011, the issue of smog transformed from a scientific issue into a public issue, creating public opinion pressure.

According to the weekly search frequency of the term "$PM_{2.5}$" provided by the Baidu search engine from January 1, 2011 to April 30, 2014 (see Fig. 14.2), prior to October 2011, the average weekly search frequency for $PM_{2.5}$ was miniscule (close to 0); However, after the "$PM_{2.5}$ storm" in October of the same year, related search counts ballooned, peaking in autumn 2013.

Secondly, the fact that smog became a public issue increased the public's awareness and understanding of haze. A telephone survey was conducted in Beijing in March 2013.[2] 76.6% of its participants responded

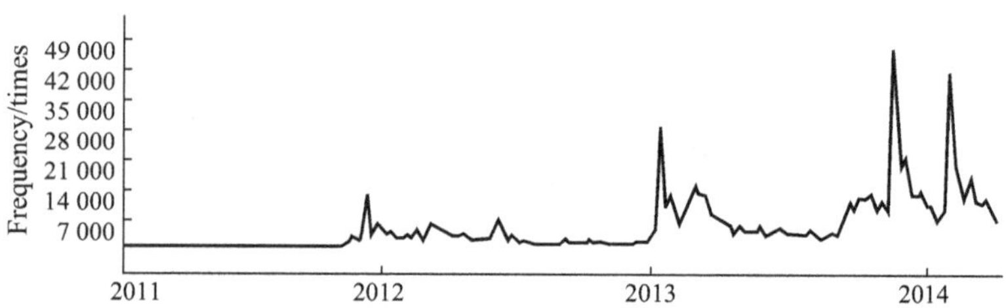

Fig. 14.2 Weekly Baidu search frequency for the term "$PM_{2.5}$", January 1, 2011–April 30, 2014

[2] This telephone survey was supported by the China Survey and Data Center at Renmin University of China and Dr. Wang Weidong. The sampling frame used in the survey was the national mobile phone number segment database provided by the Ministry of Industry and Information Technology. 600 valid numbers were randomly selected from all mobile phones registered in Beijing by prefix (the first three digits), and 308 of them were accessed (for a response rate of 51.3%). Due to the inherent high rejection rate

that the smog issue in Beijing was serious (54.6% rated it as very serious); only 10.4% responded with not serious or not very serious, and the remaining 13.0% responded that it was not serious; In terms of the public's behavioral tendency to deal with smog, 63.0% of the respondents agreed that the public should also take responsibility for smog management (27.6% of the respondents agreed), 23.7% disapproved, and the remaining 13.3% could not say whether they approved or disapproved. In terms of the public's expectations and support for the smog management policy, 29.9% of the respondents gave a positive evaluation of the government's information disclosure work in the monitoring, forecasting, and prevention of smog. However, only 4.6% of the respondents thought it was doing a good job; 35.1% thought it was doing a bad job or not a very good job, and the remaining 35.0% said it was not good. On the whole, the majority of the public have similar opinions on the severity of smog, and realize that they should bear relevant responsibilities, yet they are not satisfied with the government's policy response.

Third, the public's concern about the haze problem has gradually taken a clearer policy direction. This policy direction is manifested in two ways: one is to report it to the government and expect it to solve the problem. In the first half of 2014, cases involving air pollution accounted for 80.2% of the total number of cases accepted by the Ministry of Environmental Protection, a significant increase from 71.8% in the first half of 2013.[3] The second way is to employ various exploratory self-help measures to establish a model for public policy. For example, some ordinary citizens and enterprises voluntarily send masks to traffic police, cleaners, migrant workers, and other groups exposed to the smog; the Institute of Public and Environmental Affairs (IPE) released the *2012 Urban Air Quality Information Disclosure Index (AQTI) Evaluation Report* on the newly added $PM_{2.5}$ concentration index. Five environmental volunteer groups—Green Line Qilu, Tianjin Green Collar, Rock Energy and Environment Research Institute, China Air Watch Hebei Volunteer Group, and Beijing

of telephone interviews and the particularity of samples (for example, teenagers and the elderly may be less covered because they do not often use mobile phones), as well as the small sample size of the survey design, the representativeness of the data is limited, but it should have significant reference value for further in-depth research.

[3] "The environmental protection department hotline '12,369' environmental protection on June 1, 2014—the masses to report the case processing." (2014-07-22) [2019-07-22]. http://www.mee.gov.cn/gkml/sthjbgw/qt/201407/t20140722_280408.htm.

Water Resources Protection Foundation Nature University Foundation—have conducted research on coal management in 12 cities in Beijing, Tianjin, Shandong and Hebei since August 2013 by means of data analysis, field visits, and information disclosure applications. They also jointly launched the "Defender of Good Air" initiative, building a strong "public supervision" civil action network (Zhu 2014). In addition, Li Guixin, a resident of Shijiazhuang, sued the Shijiazhuang Environmental Protection Bureau on February 20, 2014, demanding compensation on the grounds that the annual average $PM_{2.5}$ in Shijiazhuang exceeded the standard limit by a factor of 3.4 and infringed on citizens' right to life and health. This incident prompted the first environmental lawsuit in China in which a citizen filed a compensation claim against a government department due to air pollution (Zhang 2014).

The pressure of public opinion and public participation has prompted the government to reflect on air quality monitoring indicators and monitoring methods, and it has begun to introduce more intensive smog management policies. From November 16 to December 5, 2011, the Ministry of Environmental Protection solicited public comments on the *Ambient Air Quality Standards* for the second time. In February 2012, the Ministry of Environmental Protection officially released the *Ambient Air Quality Standards* for new $PM_{2.5}$ air quality detection indicators, which were implemented in advance in key areas such as the Beijing-Tianjin-Hebei region, the Yangtze River Delta, and the Pearl River Delta. With this directive, many cities such as Beijing, Guangzhou, and Shanghai began to publicly release $PM_{2.5}$ monitoring data. On January 1, 2013, the China Environmental Monitoring Station's portal began to release real-time $PM_{2.5}$ monitoring data from 496 monitoring points in 74 cities.

14.2.2 The Government's Improvement of Environmental Governance is the Driving Force for the Introduction of Haze Management Policies

The prevention and mitigation of air pollution has long been a priority of the Chinese government's environmental protection work. The Chinese government enacted the *Law of the People's Republic of China on the Prevention and Control of Air Pollution* in 1987, amended it in 1995, and revised it again in 2000 to update its contents. The 2000 revised law reflects an increase from the original 41 articles in 1987 to 66 articles, including the general provisions, supervision and management of air pollution prevention and alleviation, the prevention and alleviation of air pollution from coal burning, the prevention and alleviation of pollution from vehicles and ships, the prevention and alleviation of waste gas, dust and odor pollution, and legal liabilities and supplementary provisions.

From the perspective of the enforcement effect of air pollution prevention and alleviation laws, although the overall industrial SO_2 emissions in China remain on the rise due to the sustained and rapid growth of energy consumption and economic agglomeration, large differences have begun to appear between regions, and the overall emissions intensity of industrial SO_2 continues to decrease (Li et al. 2010). At the same time, several studies have shown that from 2000 to 2007, the main pollutants in the atmospheric environment, SO_2, NO_2, and PM_{10}, showed a significant downward trend, of which SO_2 decreased the most. If the new monitoring indicators are not considered, Beijing air quality actually shows a significant trend of improvement (Han et al. 2009).

In terms of smog prevention and alleviation, megacities such as Beijing, Shanghai, and Guangzhou, driven by large-scale events, have also implemented monitoring and management of $PM_{2.5}$ earlier than planned. In 2007, Beijing cooperated with neighboring provinces, regions, and municipalities to jointly formulate the *Beijing Air Quality Assurance Measures for the 29th Olympic Games* to ensure good air quality during the Beijing Olympics. It was approved by the State Council in October of the same year. In fact, this is already a regional air pollution mitigation action. Since 2008, China's Ministry of Environmental Protection has built three atmospheric background stations, implemented the construction of a "Pilot Program for Monitoring Air Quality caused by Smog" in Guangdong and Jiangsu provinces and six major cities (Shanghai, Tianjin, Chongqing, Guangzhou, Shenzhen, and Nanjing), and built 16 haze monitoring stations (Wu 2012). In November 2010, the Ministry of Environmental Protection began soliciting opinions from society as a whole for the first time, on the newly revised *Ambient Air Quality Standards*. This was also the first time it had provided a reference limit for $PM_{2.5}$. In June 2011, the pilot monitoring work of the Urban Ambient Air Quality Assessment Method (trial) was quietly implemented in 26 cities across China, and pilot cities were required to monitor to the maximum extent of their capacity, including $PM_{2.5}$. In September of the same year, the Ministry of Environmental Protection issued the *Determination of Ambient Air PM_{10} and $PM_{2.5}$ Gravimetric Method*, which formally stipulated a measurement method for $PM_{2.5}$ in ambient air.

After the smog issue changed from a scientific issue to a public issue, the government responded quickly on the basis of the existing work, expediting the process of policy design, release, and implementation. For example, in May 2012, the Ministry of Environmental Protection issued the *Implementation Plan for the First Phase of Monitoring the New Air Quality Standards*. In September 2012, the State Council approved the *Emergency Plan for Prevention and Control of Air Pollution in Key Regions (for trial implementation)*. In September 2013, The State Council issued the *Action Plan for Air Pollution Prevention and Control (National Ten Measures)*. In October 2013, the Beijing Municipal Government issued the *Emergency Plan for Severe Air Pollution in Beijing (interim)*. As of January 7, 2014, the Ministry of Environmental Protection and 31 provinces (autonomous regions and municipalities) had signed the *Air Pollution Prevention and Control Target Responsibility Letter*. On January 22, 2014, the Beijing Municipal People's Congress also reviewed and passed the *Regulations on the Prevention and Control of Air Pollution in Beijing*, marking that there was a special local legal guarantee for smog management.

It could be said that the impetus for public participation had emerged and been manifested because of the Chinese government's improvement of environmental governance methods and encouragement of public participation. Since the beginning of the twenty-first century, there has been significant improvement in the Chinese government's institutional arrangements for public participation in environmental protection, and especially the mandatory provisions on environmental information disclosure. This has provided a legal basis for the public to obtain and disseminate environmental information, thus ensuring the proliferation of public issues. For example, *The Law of the People's Republic of China on Environmental Impact Assessment* came into effect on September 1, 2003, *The Interim Measures for Public Participation in Environmental Impact Assessment* came into effect on March 18, 2006 and *The Measures for Environmental Complaints and Visits* came into effect on July 1, 2006. *The Measures for the Disclosure of Environmental Information (trial implementation)* also came into effect on May 1, 2008. Moreover, the non-governmental organization Friends of Nature has applied to the Beijing Municipal Environmental Protection Bureau to disclose the causes of smog in Beijing and the proportion of pollution sources, and submitted a proposal to the Ministry of Environmental Protection through media platforms to alleviate smog (Wang 2012). It could be said that they all have benefitted from the existing institutional resources and social space.

In summary, the effective interaction between the government and the public has played a key role in the formation of China's smog management policies. The government has been promoting the improvement of environmental governance and exploring new environmental policies. At the same time, public participation has also promoted government decision-making, expediting the process of policy formulation, promulgation, and implementation.

14.3 Emergency Response and the Risk of Smog Management Policies

The above analysis shows that public participation plays an important and positive role in the formulation and implementation of smog alleviation policies. First, it changes the characteristics of the policy formulation process, transforming it from a relatively closed process within the government to a relatively open process of social participation. The second is to increase the subject of policymaking, so that policymaking develops from the interaction between experts and officials to the interaction between experts, officials, non-governmental organizations, and the public. Third, it accelerates the process of policy formulation and implementation, shortening the policy introduction cycle, and improving the efficiency of policy formulation. The government had planned to implement the new *Ambient Air Quality Standards* in 2016, and the apparent early implementation of the public opinion is a good example of this acceleration.

However, the smog management policies which have accelerated under the influence of public participation have the characteristics of emergency, and the professional and technical support of the policies is insufficient. Furthermore, some difficulties in the implementation of the policies may be render them insufficient to warrant consideration, or they may pose (potential or real) risks in the implementation process.

First, the current policies are insufficient to predict the long-term and arduous nature of smog management. Examining the experiences of other countries, smog management is a protracted process. When smog in Los Angeles gained public attention in 1943, the city's mayor promised comprehensive alleviation within four months (Jacobs and Kelly 2014), but in fact, it took decades for Los Angeles's air to improve substantially.

China's current policies are biased toward short-term and immediate results. Although it is possible to expedite the process of smog mitigation, and even achieve certain results in the short term, the long-term sustainability of this effect is questionable. After all, smog management is a complex systematic issue, involving many facets of social and economic development.

Second, there are practical difficulties in the implementation of regional prevention and management. In the Beijing-Tianjin-Hebei city cluster, the Yangtze River Delta city cluster, and the Pearl River Delta city cluster, external sources' contribution to the concentration of breathable particulate matter in some cities has varied from 16 to 26%.[4] Therefore, in order to improve smog management, the coordination of prevention and treatment among various regions is crucial. China's long-standing regional imbalances, which stimulate competitive economic growth and conflicts of interest, and which impede consensus and concerted action on environmental protection, have largely become endemic (Hong 2012).

Third, it is difficult to adjust and upgrade industrial structure during the process of transforming the concept of environmental protection. Without further optimization of the industrial structure, no matter how severe the pollution management measures are, they are unlikely to curb the increase in total pollution caused by economic expansion and mass consumption. In addition, China's urbanization process is still advancing rapidly. In 2013, 53.73% of China's population lived in urban areas. *The National New Urbanization Plan (2014–2020)* proposes that by 2020, China's urbanization rate should reach about 60%.[5] In the foreseeable future, the size of China's cities will continue to expand, and the urban population will continue to increase. The impact of rapid urbanization on resources and the environment is multifaceted (Hong 2014). For example, construction dust, the production of building materials, and urbanization consumption habits each mean that the task of energy conservation and emissions reduction is arduous. On this basis, smog management faces a formidable challenge.

Fourth, there is a long way to go in implementing extensive social mobilization. Alleviating smog is not only the responsibility of the

[4] Key areas "twelfth five-year" plan for the control of air pollution. (2012–12–05) [2019–07–22]. http://www.gov.cn/zwgk/2012-12/05/content_2283152.htm.

[5] National new urbanization planning (2014–2020). (2014–03–16) [2019–07–22]. http://www.gov.cn/xinwen/2014-03/16/content_2639841.htm.

government, but also of enterprises and citizens. Judging from the current conditions, the general public has many complaints about the smog problem, considerable criticism of the government's ineffective governance, and high expectations of smog alleviation. However, when smog alleviation involves the adjustment of individuals' own lifestyles and consumption concepts, the public resists. In our telephone interview survey of the Beijing public, only 12.0% of the respondents clearly understood the *Beijing Air Pollution Prevention and Control Regulations* (of which only 1.0% clearly understood them very well), while nearly 80% (77.0%) of the respondents said they were unaware of the new policy on smog prevention and alleviation, and 11.0% of the respondents could not say or did not understand. When asked whether they approved of the government raising taxes or consumer prices to solve the smog problem, only 20.5% of the respondents agreed (10.7% strongly agreed), while 60.7% of the respondents strongly disapproved or disapproved, and 18.8% of the respondents could not say whether they approved or disapproved. It can be seen that the public's understanding of government policies is not sufficient, and the willingness to promote smog management by increasing personal economic costs is also insufficient. Considering that China is still a developing country on the whole, the public's desire to continue to improve their standards of living is still urgent, and the psychological, intellectual, and material readiness to consciously assume the responsibility of environmental protection is insufficient. Thus, it is indeed difficult to mobilize the masses to participate.

14.4 Summary and Discussion

The above analysis reveals that in terms of the formulation and implementation of smog management policies, public participation has become an important force to promote China's environmental policy formulation. Moreover, the formulation model of China's environmental policy is changing, and becoming more open. In addressing environmental issues together, governments have become more responsive to public demands, and an effective interactive relationship between public participation and government decision-making is emerging.

However, in the interaction process between the public and the government at this stage, both sides still have certain limitations. The public's own professional knowledge of environmental problems is limited, and it is easy to overlook the environmental problems and the complex factors behind them. Thus, the public tends to be simplistic and emotional in solving environmental problems. They also lack rational thinking, and place too much blame and dependence on the government, and its willingness (or lack thereof) to act. Especially in the era of new media, the catharsis of public emotions has created powerful public opinion platforms and exerted immense pressure on the government. However, the government remains on a path dependent on the original decision-making mode and communication channels, and it is unable to cope with the new expansion of public participation. In particular, the government is not adept in the use of new methods and new skills in communicating with the public, often responding to the demands of the public in slow and improper ways, and without sufficient content. When public participation generates public opinion pressure, some officials are prone to rush policy responses or offer simplistic promises under the pressure of political correctness and stability maintenance. The limitations of the public and the government have both institutional and conceptual reasons which are closely related to specific stages of socioeconomic development and specific stages of environmental policy development. This is practically inevitable. Thus, it takes some practice and time to progress toward mature public-government interaction.

In practice, there remain limitations in the interaction between the government and the public, which increases the complexity of the environmental policymaking process, and can lead to environmental policies with incomplete design and risky implementation. As mentioned above, although the current smog mitigation policy has gradually systematized, the difficulty and long-term evaluation of smog management is underestimated, and in the implementation process, there remain risks such as effective social mobilization, the transformation of industrial structure, and the realization of regional joint prevention and alleviation. Therefore, in the future, we should emphasize the construction of more reasonable institutions and mechanisms, better integrate the strengths of the public and the government, and routinize, institutionalize, and rationalize the interaction between the public and the government. This can bring into full play the combined strengths of the public and the government in environmental protection in a more efficient way, to promote complex environmental policies with long-term effects embedded in all aspects and processes of society and the economy. In this way, we can facilitate better environmental governance and efforts to build a beautiful China.

CHAPTER 15

Toward Composite Environmental Governance

Hong Dayong

In recent years, under the backdrop of building an ecological civilization, China's environmental governance model has undergone a major transformation. This has laid the material, institutional, and value foundations for a green society. This chapter focuses on the connotations of environmental governance transformation.

In Party and government documents, "ecological civilization" was first proposed in the report to the 17th CPC National Congress. The 18th CPC National Congress proposed giving prominence to ecological civilization and integrating it into all aspects of the economy, politics, culture, and society in an effort to "build a beautiful China" and realize the sustainable development of the Chinese nation. At the Third Plenary Session of the 18th CPC Central Committee, several ways to accelerate the construction of an ecological civilization system and establish a systematic and complete ecological civilization system were proposed. In 2015, the construction of China's ecological civilization system entered

D. Hong (✉)
Renmin University of China, Beijing, China
e-mail: hongdy@ruc.edu.cn

D. Hong and Y. Fan (eds.), *Toward a Green Society*,
https://doi.org/10.1007/978-981-96-5111-5_15

a stage of rapid progress. The new environmental protection law (the strictest to date) was implemented on January 1. On April 25, the CPC Central Committee and The State Council officially issued the *Opinions on Accelerating the Construction of Ecological Civilization*. On July 13, the Ministry of Environmental Protection issued the *Measures for Public Participation in Environmental Protection*. On August 9, the General Office of the CPC Central Committee and the General Office of the State Council enacted the *Measures for Holding Party and Government Officials Accountable for Ecological and Environmental Damage* (trial). On September 11, the Political Bureau of the CPC Central Committee adopted the *Overall Plan for the Reform of the Ecological Civilization System*. The Fifth Plenary Session of the 18th CPC Central Committee held at year-end, reaffirmed its commitment to the concept of green development, incorporating the construction of ecological civilization into the 13th Five-Year Plan. It emphasized that improving environmental quality was the core, and proposed the implementation of a strict environmental protection system, and the goal of overall improvement of ecological and environmental quality by 2020.

The proposal and construction of ecological civilization directly addresses China's intensifying environmental crisis. It emphasizes green and sustainable development, and adherence to the basic state policy of conserving resources and protecting the environment. It also emphasizes adherence to the path of civilized development featuring increased production, prosperous living, and sound ecology, accelerating the building of a resource-saving and environment-friendly society, and producing a spatial pattern and industries that conserve resources and protect the environment. The structure, mode of production, and way of life will achieve a new pattern of modernization in harmonious development between man and nature. Historically, with the central government promoting the construction of ecological civilization, China's environmental governance has produced new trends and new characteristics. It has now entered a new stage of complex environmental governance. On the basis of a clear awareness of the environment and improved environmental policy design, environmental governance is increasingly showing Chinese characteristics.

15.1 Growing Environmental Awareness in China

Increasing environmental awareness is the premise of environmental governance. Environmental awareness can be defined by people's understanding and awareness of environmental conditions. However, environmental awareness is not limited to these two conditions; it includes at least five basic concepts. The first concept is awareness of the immediate environmental conditions, including what has happened to the environment, the environmental and social economic consequences, and the trend of environmental change. The second is attitudes toward changes in the environment, including whether the changes have serious consequences, whether the changes warrant attention, and how and when to deal with them. The third is the choice of environmental governance strategies, including the use of technology or the importance of institutional change, and whether to implement administrative regulation, market stimulus, or social supervision, or to rely on voluntary constraints. Fourth is the judgment on the socioeconomic effect of environmental governance, including whether to increase socioeconomic costs or promote socioeconomic transformation. The fifth is the overall attitude toward the relationship between human society and the natural environment, including whether to challenge nature, respect nature, conform to nature or protect nature.

It should be said that the process of China's expanding environmental awareness is in line with the development law of environmental awareness, as this awareness is affected by people's understanding of the following three laws. First is the operation law of the environmental system itself. This entails the absence or addition of elements in the environmental system, and will determine to what form, what degree, and the threshold at which the environmental system can withstand change. Furthermore, what are the limits and capabilities? The second is the law of interaction between the environmental system and the social system, including the environmental system's form, scope, and ability to support the social system, and the social system's form, scope, and degree to affect the environment, as well as the long-term trend of the interaction between the environment and society. The third is the law of social operation, including the composition of the social system, the correlation state, and the interaction relationship between each subsystem, and the correlation state and interaction relationship between various elements within each subsystem. People's understanding of these laws is a process of gradual deepening and continuous improvement.

Since China's delegation attended the first United Nations Conference on the Human Environment in 1972, China has experienced over 40 years of modern environmental governance. Looking back on this process, we can see that with the deepening of environmental scientific research and social and economic development, the CPC and the government's understanding and judgment of the environment have become increasingly clear and complete. This has resulted in the following six changes.

First, it has shifted from avoiding environmental problems to facing them head-on. In the initial stages of China's environmental governance, there was heated debate within the government over whether there even were environmental problems under socialist conditions. Even though environmental protection was identified as a basic national policy in 1983, it gained attention slowly. Since 1990, the State Environmental Protection Bureau has regularly released the *Bulletin of China's Environmental Status*, which has become an important window for understanding the changes in China's environmental status.

Second, China has moved from recognizing only local environmental threats to understanding the overall environmental threat. With an understanding of the trend of environmental change, we have expanded from an initial focus on industrial "waste gas, industrial wastewater and residue" to awareness of overall environmental risk, recognizing the severity of environmental pollution and ecological degradation, and realizing that strengthening environmental governance is a long-term plan related to the well-being of the people and the future of the nation.

Third is the movement from a "development first, then treatment" development strategy, to a shift to prioritizing environmental governance. Before the 1990s, although some environmental protection results had been achieved by strengthening environmental management, overall deterioration of environmental conditions continued. The theory of economic priority and economic determinism had actually restricted the process of environmental governance. Since the start of the twenty-first century, and specifically since the 18th National Congress of the CPC, the Party and the government have clarified the principle of prioritizing conservation, protection, and natural restoration, emphasizing that the trend of ecological and environmental deterioration should be addressed at the source.

The legislative purpose of the new Environmental Protection Law implemented at the beginning of 2015 has also been adjusted from the initial statement "to protect and improve the living and ecological environment, prevent pollution and other public hazards, safeguard human health, and promote the development of socialist modernization" to "to protect and improve the environment, prevent pollution and other public hazards, safeguard public health, promote ecological civilization construction, and promote sustainable economic and social development".[1]

Fourth is the shift from general environmental governance advocacy and planning to the construction of a practical, sustained, and specific system of environmental governance. In September 1979, the Environmental Protection Law of the People's Republic of China (for trial implementation) was issued. This market the first time that departments and governments at all levels had been legally required to consider environmental protection when formulating plans for national economic and social development. In the 1990s, because of the official formulation of the national annual work plan for environmental protection in 1992, the government officially incorporated the environmental protection plan into the overall plan for national economic and social development from the beginning of the Ninth Five-Year Plan. Since the turn of the millennium, attention has shifted toward institutional construction in environmental governance. In particular, the Third Plenary Session of the 18th CPC Central Committee systematically elaborated upon the goals of institutional construction, proposed the strictest source protection system, damage compensation system, and accountability system, improved the environmental governance and ecological restoration system, and used institutions to protect the ecological environment. The proposal of the CPC Central Committee on the 13th Five-Year Plan further included green development as an important dimension of and guideline for development, rather than just a specific content of development.

Fifth is a shift from treating environmental governance as a hindrance to economic development to using opportunities for environmental governance to promote economic transformation and upgrading. In the early days of environmental governance, lack of funding was a significant

[1] The Environmental Protection Law of the People's Republic of China came into effect on January 1, 2015. (2014–04–25) [2019–07–22]. http://www.gov.cn/xinwen/2014-04/25/content_2666328.htm.

impediment, and the investment of limited financial resources in environmental governance was believed to hinder economic development and increase financial costs. The state had no choice but to enhance environmental benefits by strengthening management links and improving enterprise management. With a growing understanding of the interaction between the environment and society, it has been recognized that environmental governance can foster new development opportunities and promote economic transformation and improvement.

Sixth, it is necessary to shift from extensive development that directly challenges the environment to reflective and inclusive development that adapts to environmental constraints. In the early stages of environmental governance, economic growth was in the extensive stage of extension and expansion, and simple environmental resource utilization was regarded as the only way to achieve modern economic growth; the resulting environmental pollution and destruction was regarded as the inevitable cost of economic development. Further acceleration of technological development and economic development will help alleviate environmental problems, and there should be no limit to economic growth. However, experience has shown that this perception is both inaccurate and dangerous. Since the mid-1990s, it has become apparent that a change in economic growth mode is needed. In the twenty-first century, especially since the 18th National Congress of the Communist Party of China, this understanding has solidified. A new consensus has emerged highlighting the need to adhere to the laws of nature, develop a circular economy, promote social change and green development, and promote development based on resources, the environment, and ecological protection.

According to the questionnaire survey data, there is a trend of an increasingly clear understanding of China's environment; environmental issues have become a major focus of both the public and the media. In 1995, Hong Dayong participated in the national environmental awareness survey, and the resulting data showed that 23.6% of the respondents said they were not knowledgeable of the concept of environmental protection. Of those responding, 16.5% thought their knowledge of environmental protection was "very low", 66.9% thought it was "low", 16.1% thought they had "some", and only 0.5% thought they had "a lot" of environmental protection knowledge. At the same time, most urban and rural residents lack understanding of policies and regulations related to environmental protection. Only 31.8% said they knew "a lot" or "some" about them, and just 0.5% responded that they knew "a lot" about them. Additionally, 42% said they had "only heard about it". Additionally, 26.2% said they had not heard anything about environmental policies or regulations. However, data from the 2010 China General Social Survey, which Hong helped design, showed that 70% of respondents recognized that China's environmental problems were "very serious" or "relatively serious". Moreover, 65.7% of the respondents said they were "very concerned" or "relatively concerned" about environmental problems, while only 3.1% said they were "not concerned at all" (Hong 2014).

15.2 Improvements in China's Environmental Policies

Environmental policy is an important tool for implementing environmental governance. It is usually formulated, promulgated, and implemented by a government through legal procedures, and reflects policymakers' understanding of the environment. With the gradual deepening of our understanding of the operation laws of the environmental system, the interaction law between the environmental system and the social system, and the laws of social operations, our understanding of the environment and its governance has solidified. China's environmental policy is also improving in the development and evolution to the present, and a more scientific and reasonable environmental policy system is emerging. China is moving toward a new era of integrated environmental governance, that is, it is oriented to the environment, relying on the environment, for the overall environmental comprehensive governance and social change era. This governance transition is roughly reflected in the following seven ways.

First, there is a more scientific understanding and definition of the objectives of environmental policy, from the management of a single environmental element and a single environmental function to the management of the overall environmental system and complex environmental functions. In addition, there is more emphasis on improving the environmental quality as the core of overall improvement to the quality of the ecological environment. For example, in the past, the main indicators for monitoring water pollution were chemical oxygen demand and total ammonia nitrogen emissions, while the indicators for monitoring air pollution included inhalable particulate matter (e.g., PM_{10}, $PM_{2.5}$), sulfur dioxide, and nitrogen oxides. For the prevention and alleviation of water pollution, the environmental protection department only supervises the operations of enterprise sewage treatment and urban sewage treatment plants, and is not involved in the management of the functions of any other body of water. The Third Plenary Session of the 18th CPC Central Committee and the Fifth Plenary Session of the CPC Central Committee and the Opinions on Accelerating the Construction of Ecological Civilization proposed utilizing China's entire territory and establishing a spatial planning system, delineating the control boundaries of production, developing living and ecological space, and using satellite remote sensing and other technological means for all-weather monitoring of natural resources and the ecological environment, and improving the coverage of all resources. The monitoring network system for source and environmental factors provides an overall monitoring and early warning for the environment's resource carrying capacity. Relevant documents stress that with human health at the core, environmental quality improvement as the goal, and environmental risk prevention as the baseline, we will strictly monitor the discharge of all pollutants, implement a total pollutant discharge control system for enterprises and public institutions, and implement ecological protection and restoration projects that account for mountains, rivers, forests, fields, and lakes.

The second way is to expand the constraints of environmental policies from targeting direct polluters to restricting all related subjects. For example, previous environmental policies have focused on direct polluters and saboteurs, emphasizing who pollutes, who pays, who develops, and who protects. These policies have indeed promoted environmental governance and will continue to be followed and improved in specific areas of environmental governance in the future. However, in the process of promoting ecological civilization, all social entities, including producers and consumers, saboteurs and beneficiaries, enterprises and institutions, the public and the government, have an array of environmental responsibilities, and all need to accept the constraints and regulations of environmental policies. The Third Plenary Session of the 18th CPC Central Committee highlighted the need to expedite the reform of the pricing of natural resources and their associated products to better reflect market supply and demand, resource scarcity, the costs of ecological and environmental damage, and the benefits of restoration. Also highlighted was the gradual extension of the resource tax to cover the use of natural and ecological space. Improving the ecological compensation mechanism for key ecological functional zones and promoting the establishment of a horizontal ecological compensation system among regions was also included. Also mentioned were ways to compile a balance sheet of natural resources, and audit leading officials for their natural resources assets when they leave office.

The third way is to gradually expand the environmental policy tools from relying primarily on administrative control to the comprehensive use of legal, economic, technical, social, administrative, and other means. The Sixth National Conference on Environmental Protection held in 2006 proposed "three changes"[2] in environmental protection work, one of which was to emphasize the combination of environmental policy tools. This has been regulated and emphasized in the new Environmental Protection Law implemented at the beginning of 2015. As mentioned in the *Opinions of the CPC Central Committee and The State Council on Accelerating the Construction of Ecological Civilization*, "improving the system of ecological civilization" includes improving the following: laws and regulations, the standards system, the property rights system, the usage control system for natural resource assets, the ecological environment supervision system and economic policies, while adhering to the red line of resources, the environment and ecology. This includes addressing and improving fiscal policies involving prices, taxes and financial and other policies to encourage and guide all types of subjects to participate in the construction of ecological civilization. Also included are the implementation of market-oriented mechanisms, improving the ecological protection compensation mechanism, improving the performance evaluation system, improving the accountability system and much other more comprehensive content.

The fourth way pertains to the focus of innovation in environmental policies. The focus has gradually shifted from relying mainly on the

[2] The first is to shift from emphasizing economic growth over environmental protection to paying them equal attention, and seeking development in protecting the environment; the second is to change from environmental protection lagging behind economic development temporally to contemporaneous environmental protection and economic development, thus alleviating the mentality of pollution first, then treatment, and an acceptance of destruction during treatment; third, it is necessary to change from a focus on administrative methods to protect the environment to comprehensively using legal, economic, technical, and necessary administrative methods to solve environmental problems, consciously following economic laws and natural laws, and improving environmental protection work.

government to collaborative innovation between the government, the market, and society. The Third Plenary Session of the 18th CPC Central Committee explicitly called for the development of an environmental protection market, the implementation of a trading system for energy conservation, carbon emission rights, pollutant discharge rights and water rights, the establishment of a market-based mechanism to attract private capital into ecological and environmental protection, and the implementation of third-party governance environmental pollution management. Article 6 of the new Environmental Protection Law, implemented in early 2015, stipulates "all units and individuals have the obligation to protect the environment". Local governments at all levels shall be responsible for the environmental quality in their respective administrative areas. Enterprises, public institutions, and other producers and business operators shall prevent or reduce environmental pollution and ecological damage, and bear responsibility for any damage caused in accordance with the law. Citizens shall increase their awareness of environmental protection, adopt a low-carbon and economical lifestyle, and conscientiously fulfill their environmental protection obligations. Article 9 further stipulates:

> People's governments at all levels shall strengthen publicity and popularize environmental protection, encourage the self-governance of grassroots mass organizations at a mass level, social organizations and environmental protection volunteers to carry out publicity of environmental protection laws and regulations and environmental protection knowledge, and create a good atmosphere for environmental protection. Administrative departments of education and schools should incorporate environmental protection knowledge into school education to cultivate students' awareness of environmental protection. The news media shall carry out publicity of environmental protection laws and regulations and environmental protection knowledge and supervise environmental violations by public opinion.[3]

There are also specific provisions on information disclosure and public participation.

[3] The Environmental Protection Law of the People's Republic of China came into effect on January 1, 2015. (2014–04–25) [2019–07–22]. http://www.gov.cn/xinwen/2014-04/25/content_2666328.htm.

Fifth, there is a shift in the basic orientation of environmental policy from expanding and improving supply to more stringent demand management. In environmental governance work in the past, it could be said that there have been some unscientific policy orientations. It was assumed that the supplies of environmental resources were unlimited, or at least that supplies could be continuously improved and expanded through technological progress and institutional construction. This policy orientation, while reducing the urgency of environmental risks, is in fact continuing to escalate the actual environmental risks. With deepening understanding of the laws of environmental governance, the new orientation of environmental policy emphasizes the concept of ecological civilization in terms of respecting nature, conforming to nature, and protecting nature, and emphasizes the scientific and rational management of human social needs. According to the report to the 18th National Congress of the CPC:

> In accordance with the principle of balancing population, resources and the environment and unifying economic, social and ecological benefits, we should control development intensity and adjust spatial structure, promote intensive and efficient production space, livable and moderate living space, and beautiful ecological space. This, so as to reallocate more land for natural restoration, designate additional arable areas for agricultural purposes, and establish sustainable habitats featuring clear skies, verdant landscapes, and unpolluted water sources for the benefit of future generations.[4]

The Opinions of the CPC Central Committee and The State Council on Accelerating the Construction of Ecological Civilization also emphasizes:

> establishing a bottom-line thinking, setting and strictly observing the upper limit of resource consumption, the bottom line of environmental quality and the red line of ecological protection, and limiting all kinds of development activities to the carrying capacity of resources and the environment." Set the "ceiling" of resource consumption reasonably, strengthen the control of strategic resources such as energy, water and land, strengthen

[4] *Unswervingly advancing along the path of socialism with Chinese characteristics and striving to build a moderately prosperous society in all respects: Hu Jintao's report at the 18th National Congress of the Communist Party of China* (full text) (2012–11–18) [2019–07–22]. http://politics.people.com.cn/n/2012/1118/c1001-19612670.html.

the control of energy consumption intensity, and do a good job in the management of total energy consumption.[5]

Sixth, in terms of policy relevance, there has been a trend from segmentation to high integration. In previous environmental governance, there was a tendency for separation between environmental policies and other social and economic policies. In this policy climate, environmental protection occasionally became talking point for environmental protection departments. Even specific pollution management often involved multiple administrative departments, and the policies of various departments lacked coordination and overall planning. This detracted from environmental governance's efficiency. For example, it would seem that the environmental protection department is the party responsible for water pollution management, but in fact, an array of government entities is involved. This includes the housing and construction commission, city management, agriculture, water conservancy, development and reform commissions, planning, land and resources, health, fisheries, water resources, protection agencies, and other public utilities. There are simply too many cooks in the kitchen. In order to promote the further correlation and integration of environmental policies, the 18th National Congress stated that ecological civilization construction should be placed in a prominent position and integrated into all aspects, and the entire process, of economic construction, political construction, cultural construction, and social construction. This had the effect of emphasizing that systematic, holistic, and coordinated social reform should be promoted to improve environmental governance. The Third Plenary Session of the 18th CPC Central Committee further clarified several directions for institutional development, such as improving the national natural resource asset management system. It also included improving the natural resources supervision system and exercising the responsibility for controlling the use of all national land space in a unified manner, establishing a regional linkage mechanism for ecosystem protection and restoration and pollution prevention on land and at sea. *The Opinions on Accelerating the Construction of Ecological Civilization* issued by the CPC Central Committee and The State Council emphasized "establishing

[5] *Opinions of the CPC Central Committee and the State Council on accelerating the construction of ecological civilization* (2015–04–25) [2019–07–22]. http://www.scio.gov.cn/xwfbh/xwbfbh/yg/2/Document/1436286/1436286.htm.

an environmental management system with human health as the core, environmental quality as the goal, and environmental risk prevention and control as the baseline, and improving the trans-regional coordination mechanism for pollution prevention and control".[6]

Seventh, in terms of the accountability for implementing environmental policy, there has been a trend from emphasizing the accountability of environmental protection departments to strengthening the overall accountability of party committees and governments. At the Third Plenary Session of the 18th CPC Central Committee, it was proposed that leading officials' natural resource assets be audited after they leave office and establishing a lifetime accountability system for ecological and environmental damage. The new Environmental Protection Law, which went into effect at the beginning of 2015, included detailed provisions on the accountability of local people's governments at all levels, environmental protection authorities of people's governments at or above the county level, and other departments responsible for environmental supervision and management. *The Measures for Holding Party and Government Leading Officials Accountable for Ecological and Environmental Damage* (trial implementation), implemented in August 2015, states that the regulations apply to leading members of local Party committees and governments at and above the county level and their relevant working departments, leading members of the relevant working departments of central and state organs and leading personnel of the relevant institutions of the above-mentioned working departments. The measures emphasize that local party committees and governments at all levels must bear the overall responsibility for protecting the ecological environment and resources in their own regions, and the main leading members of the party committees and governments bear the main responsibility; other relevant leading members bear their corresponding responsibilities within the scope of their duties.[7] Therefore, the accountability for environmental policy implementation has actually evolved into the accountability of the governance ability of the party committees and governments.

[6] *Opinions of the CPC Central Committee and the State Council on accelerating the construction of ecological civilization.* (2015–04-25) [2019–07-22]. http://www.scio.gov.cn/xwfbh/xwbfbh/yg/2/Document/1436286/1436286.htm.

[7] *Measures for Accountability of Party and Government Leading Officials for Ecological and Environmental Damage (Trial) was issued.* (2015–08–17) [2019–07–22]. http://news.xinhuanet.com/2015-08/17/c_1116282540.htm.

Furthermore, the modernization of the environmental governance system and governance capacity has been regarded as an important part of the modernization of the national governance system and governance capacity, which is related to the improvement and development of the socialist system with Chinese characteristics and the overall transformation of Chinese society toward green modernization.

15.3 Chinese Characteristics in Environmental Governance

Along with the increasing awareness of the environment and improving formulation and implementation of environmental policy, China has become more determined to adhere to green development and build an ecological civilization. In this context, the step-by-step progress of compound environmental governance is expected to improve China's environmental governance capacity, shorten the time span of environmental governance to overcome difficulties, and accelerate the process of improving environmental quality, so as to embark on the road of environmental governance with Chinese characteristics. The Chinese characteristics of the road of environmental governance are determined by China's environmental problems, basic national conditions, institutional basis, and international environment; it is a process of gradual practice and increasing manifestation.

First, China's road to environmental governance must address complex environmental challenges. At present, the compound effects of environmental problems caused by China's rapid development are intensifying, and environmental governance is becoming more difficult. Due to the latecomer advantage, those who are late to industrialize tend to accomplish it in a compressed timeframe. For example, it took 200 years for the United Kingdom and 135 years for the United States to complete their respective industrializations, while it only took 65 years for Japan and 33 years for South Korea (Hong 2013). China has maintained a high growth rate for a long time because of the positive impetus of a specific development model. In this context, complex environmental challenges are first manifested in their spatial universality. It can be said that from the sky to the earth, from the earth to the ground, from the land to the sea, from central cities to remote rural areas, we all face environmental challenges. In addition, compound environmental challenges are also manifested in the superposition of time. In the process of rapid and large-scale industrialization, environmental problems of various nature are concentrated and superimposed. In addition, complex environmental challenges are also manifested in the diversity of environmental demands, which are intensified by differences between regions, sectors, industries, and groups of people. Finally, compound environmental challenges are also manifested in the coexistence of domestic environmental and global environmental pressures, thereby reducing our time and space to address environmental issues. In order to address this unprecedented environmental challenge, what we can learn from the environmental governance model is extremely limited; our practice is a form of creation, and therefore must be tailored to China's unique circumstances.

Second, China's road to environmental governance is a pathbreaking example for major developing countries. Since the Reform and Opening-up, China has made remarkable achievements in economic development, especially in alleviating poverty and improving standards of living. By the end of 2014, China's GDP ranked second in the world. However, China's population is massive. China had a total population of 1,367.82 million at the end of 2014 (excluding Hong Kong, Macao, and Taiwan), and its per capita GDP was about 7,485 US dollars (about 46,531 yuan), still lagging behind many countries and only 13.7% of that of the United States. This figure was at least 50 years behind the United States, and ranked around 90th in the world. Therefore, China is still a developing country, and the contradiction between outdated productive forces and the growing material and cultural needs of the people remains a basic contradiction in Chinese society. Moreover, as a large developing country, China is also characterized by weak institutions, poor resources and environmental endowments, and unbalanced development. This further complicates environmental governance. For example, China's per capita cultivated land, fresh water, and forest account for only 32%, 27.4%, and 12.8% of the world average, respectively. China's per capita share of mineral resources is only half of the world average, and the per capita share of coal, oil, and natural gas is only 67%, 5.4% and 7.5%, of the world average, respectively. Additionally, the per unit output of energy resources is significantly higher than that of the world average. China's imports of oil, iron ore, and other imports, and foreign dependence have also been increasing, among which the foreign dependence on oil has risen from 32% in the early twenty-first century to 57% in 2012 (Hong 2013). Moreover, due to the complex operations of the environmental system, the long-term cumulative compound environmental damage has made the environmental damage in some areas difficult to repair in the short term, or even irreversible. Furthermore, the long-term unbalanced development between regions and between urban and rural areas has complicated environmental governance, created the possibility and opportunity for environmental pressure to transfer between regions, and regularly induced new problems. Therefore, China must promote compound environmental governance as it develops. This will be an unprecedented challenge. Therefore, there is no ready-made governance model from which China can learn. As such, China must forge its own path of environmental governance.

Third, China's road to environmental governance is the way forward based on socialist public ownership. The value orientation and institutional basis of socialism provide an intrinsic possibility for effective environmental governance. The essence of socialism is to liberate and develop the productive forces, eliminate exploitation, eliminate polarization, and ultimately achieve common prosperity. China adheres to the principle of "putting the people first", focuses on the overall and long-term interests of mankind, aims for the comprehensive and free development of all members of society, and pursues the harmony of all social relations. With its institutional structure based on public ownership of the means of production, it is designed to curb "production" and "development" for the sake of the selfish interests of capital groups. On the contrary, the value orientation and institutional arrangement of capitalism are root causes of the global ecological and environmental crisis, because its essence is the endless pursuit of the private interests of capital groups, focusing on the immediate interests of a few people and widening the gap between the rich and the poor. This inherently creates social segmentation, social tension and social conflicts, and thus cannot unite society and build consensus to promote environmental governance. Inevitably, capitalism will continue to aggravate the ecological and environmental crisis. For example, ecological colonialism is a new issue created in the process of globalization. At present, China is still in the primary stage of socialism. This stage not only provides an important institutional premise for improving environmental governance, but also faces great challenges. The road of environmental governance with Chinese characteristics is the road of continuous reform and development of the socialist system, maximizing the system's superiority, and continually improving the quality of the environment based on continual liberation and development of the productive forces. In this way, the evils of capitalism can be curbed and the threats and pressures of capitalism can be resisted on a global scale. Thus, the path of continuous environmental quality improvement is fundamentally different from the path of environmental governance under the conditions of Western capitalism.

Fourth, China's path to environmental governance is for the fundamental interests of the people, with a special emphasis on the role of the "critical minority". One strength of the Chinese socialist system lies in its capacity to mobilize resources to address large-scale projects. In undertaking major projects, the government's role in guiding, coordinating, organizing, and supervising is crucial and the leading officials of governments at all levels are particularly important. The direction is clear, the goals are set, and the key factor lies in the officials. In giving clear direction and setting the goal, the key factor is the officials. The opening ceremony of the seminar on the study and implementation of the spirit of the Fourth Plenary Session of the 18th Central Committee of the Communist Party of China for major leading officials at the provincial and ministerial levels to comprehensively promote the rule of law was held on February 2, 2015. At this ceremony, Xi Jinping stressed that leading officials at all levels must shoulder important responsibilities in promoting the rule of law. This will facilitate comprehensive governance of the country according to the law. Additionally, Xi said we must emphasize our focus on the "critical minority" of leading officials. This model also applies to promoting environmental governance in China. Vis-a-vis most Party members and the masses of people, leading officials are a minority. However, they are in key positions, key fields, and key links. Only when the leading officials are clear-headed, determined, qualified, and competent can China's environmental governance be effectively promoted. Perhaps based on this understanding, the central government formulated and issued the *Measures for Investigating the Responsibility of Party and Government Leading Officials for Ecological Environmental Damage* (Trial) to strengthen the responsibilities of Party and government leading officials for ecological environment and resource protection. Detailed provisions were outlined on the accountability of the main leading members of local party committees and governments, relevant leading members, and leading members of relevant government departments. It required the Party committees and their organizational departments to regard resource consumption, environmental protection, and ecological benefits as important content in their assessment and evaluations in appointing members of local party and government leadership groups. Officials who are responsible for causing serious damage to the ecological environment and resources must not be promoted, given responsibilities, or transferred to important posts. Such a top-down approach to environmental governance emphasizing leadership responsibilities does not exclude adhering to the principal position of the people, and arouses the enthusiasm, initiative, and creativity of the broad masses. However, it is more suitable to China's basic national conditions and has obvious differences from the environmental governance approach of Western countries.

Fifth, China's path of environmental governance is one of self-adjustment, self-processing, and self-innovation. In the context of strengthening environmental protection as the basic concept of global development and increasing pressure on environmental protection in the international context, China's environmental governance can no longer repeat the path of the West, and there is little or no opportunity to improve domestic environmental governance through the international transfer of environmental pollution and resource pressure. More importantly, China has endured pollution transfer and environmental squeeze from Western developed countries and has suffered immensely from it. "Do not do to others what you do not want to be done to yourself" is an old Chinese proverb. As a responsible major developing country, China can only rely on internal processing to promote environmental governance. China has independently adapted to, mastered, and guided the new normal of economic development. It has also proposed new ideas for innovative development, and focused on changing the driving force of economic growth, the economic development model, and the old development model. These are the concrete measures China has taken to follow the path of environmental governance with Chinese characteristics. In the process of promoting the construction of ecological civilization, China will promote technological innovation, organizational innovation, institutional innovation, and concept innovation in environmental protection. In this way, it will improve the resource and environmental benefits of economic development, and develop the environmental protection industry. China will also strengthen and improve demand management, form a spatial pattern, industrial structure, production mode, and way of life that conserves resource and protects the environment, so as to creatively embark on a new path of harmonious development between man and nature.

All in all, due to the constraints of various subjective and objective factors, the path of environmental governance that China is exploring and practicing must have Chinese characteristics. The Fifth Plenary Session of the 18th CPC Central Committee proposed the five development concepts of innovation, coordination, green development, openness and sharing, providing clearer and more specific theoretical guidance on the continued exploration of China's path to environmental governance. As long as social entities make concerted efforts and conscientiously follow the arrangements of the Central Committee, they will regard the realization, safeguarding, and development of the fundamental interests of the broadest masses of the people as the fundamental purpose of development, and the improvement of the people's well-being and the promotion of all-around human development as the fundamental starting point and goal of development. By accelerating the construction of ecological civilization, we can expect that the road of environmental governance with Chinese characteristics will expand and be followed. As such, it will offer important contributions to global environmental governance.

CHAPTER 16

The Factor Model of Public Evaluation of Government Environmental Protection

Lu Chuntian and Hong Dayong

As previously discussed, public participation in environmental protection is a crucial indicator of China's transition to a green society. This participation is manifested through various channels, one of which is the perception and assessment of the government's environmental protection efforts. China's rapid economic growth over the years has led to environmental problems that permeate all aspects of daily life and production. These issues not only cause economic losses, but also result in social conflicts and damage to public health. Faced with these daunting challenges, the Chinese government is increasingly shifting from a solely top-down administrative approach to a modern governance model that emphasizes environmental legislation, public engagement, and oversight. Public assessment of the government's environmental protection efforts

C. Lu (✉)
Department of Sociology, Xi'an Jiaotong University, Xi'an, China
e-mail: luchuntian@xjtu.edu.cn

D. Hong
Renmin University of China, Beijing, China
e-mail: hongdy@ruc.edu.cn

D. Hong and Y. Fan (eds.), *Toward a Green Society*,
https://doi.org/10.1007/978-981-96-5111-5_16

has become a significant component of government performance assessments, with the government and its constituent departments as the subjects of assessment and the public as the evaluators. Examining the extent of public participation in performance assessments, we can observe two main categories: (1) citizen groups or third-sector organizations that independently initiate and conduct assessments of government performance; (2) citizens who participate in performance assessment activities initiated and organized by government departments (Zhou 2008). In China today, both types of assessments are applied. For example, the Chinese General Social Survey (CGSS), organized by Renmin University of China, conducted surveys in 2003 and 2010 to assess public perceptions of the environmental protection efforts of both the central and local governments.

In this chapter, we investigate the factors that influence public perceptions of the central government's environmental protection efforts. In doing so, we provide an analytical framework for assessing the factors that influence environmental protection efforts at various levels of local government.

16.1 Factors Influencing the Assessment of Government Environmental Protection Efforts and Related Hypotheses

This chapter focuses on the factors affecting the public's subjective view of the government's environmental protection work, especially those influencing factors other than individual social characteristics. Media often emphasize the influence of individual socio-demographic and economic characteristics on assessment attitudes from the perspective of different disciplines. For example, economists are concerned about the impact of individual income, employment status, and the accumulation of family wealth on the perception of the work of the government (Kinder and Kiewiet 1979). Meanwhile, sociologists may be concerned about the impact of education level, social status, political orientation, and gender when evaluating government policy (Dietz et al. 2007). Social psychology examines the impact of public trust and risk perception on the assessment of the works of the government (Cin 2012). In this chapter, we utilize a multi-dimensional and comprehensive perspective to investigate the factors that affect the assessment of government environmental protection work.

The first level is the socioeconomic characteristic variables of individuals. Studies from both China and abroad have shown that individuals' social demographics and economic characteristics influence the government's public policy opinions, and the assessment of the government's environmental protection work is one form of the public assessment of government policy. The public holds a more positive view of the government when they perceive that the government can satisfy their needs for both public and private goods, while effectively managing economic, social, and political risks such as inflation, unemployment, and diplomatic crises. If the government is unable to meet their needs, then they will have a negative view of the government.

A series of both Chinese and overseas studies have shown that individuals' socioeconomic characteristics are related to their assessment of government environmental policies, but the proportion of the total variance that can be explained by socioeconomic characteristics is small. For example, some scholars have noted that age, gender, and political orientation have significant correlations with the government's attitude toward environmental policy (Konisky et al. 2008). Existing Chinese empirical studies have also shown that the public's assessment of the government's environmental protection work is intertwined with their own social attributes, but in the assessment of the central government and local government's environmental protection work, perceptions within the same social group can vary. For example, low-income groups may have a favorable view of the central government's environmental protection work, but an unfavorable view of the local government's environmental protection work (Lu et al. 2014). Although individuals' socio-economic characteristics influence the assessment of government environmental protection work, their social psychological variables have an even greater effect.

The second level of influence comes from the psychosocial variables of the public. First, we examine the effect on the level of trust in government. Trust is the foundation of good social order and is the simplification of a complex social system (Luhmann 2005: 10–11). Similarly, government trust is an interactive relationship between citizens and the government. It refers to the public's perception of the behavior of government authorities and organizations, and is based on whether the public's expectations are met (Mishler and Rose 1997). A high level of trust in the government indicates that the public's expectations of the government have been met. Conversely, a low level of trust indicates that the public is unsatisfied with, or does not recognize, the work of the government. Studies conducted outside of China have shown that the public's assessment of government performance or support for policies is related to their trust in the government (Chanley 2002; Chanley et al. 2000). Therefore, we propose Hypothesis 1: The higher the level of public trust in the central government, the higher the public's assessment of the central government's environmental protection work.

Second is the effect of the level of environmental concern. Although there remains some controvery about environmental concern measurement both in China and overseas (Dunlap and Jones 2002; Hong 2006; Lu and Hong 2011), there is a positive correlation between the level of environmental concern and environmentally friendly behavior. When the public's environmental concern level increases, not only are they more willing to engage in environmentally friendly behavior, but they will also have similarly higher expectations of the public. There is reason to believe that the public will request stricter environmental governance requirements as the main component of environmental supervision, management, and governance. Even if objectively the environment has not deteriorated, the public will still think that the government has not fulfilled its environmental protection responsibilities, because of their own increased level of environmental concern. Therefore, the perception of the government's environmental protection work will decline. Thus, we propose Hypothesis 2: the greater the public's environmental concern, the higher their expectations of the central government's environmental responsibility, and thus the lower their assessment of the central government's environmental protection work.

Finally, there is the effect of the public's perception of the seriousness of environmental problems. The judgment of environmental problems' severity depends largely on public awareness and perception. Some environmental problems exert a significant impact on human life and productivity, but if the public is unaware of these problems, they may ignore the risks they bring. On the contrary, if the public perceives the existence of environmental problems and hazards from different channels, they will think that the government should take measures to mitigate the harm caused by environmental risks to the public. Therefore, there is reason to think that when the public has a high perception of the severity of environmental problems, they may think that the government has failed to fulfill its responsibility of environmental protection, and therefore, the assessment of environmental protection by the government is low. Thus, we propose Hypothesis 3: the higher the public's perception of the severity of environmental problems, the lower their assessment of the central government's environmental protection work.

The third level of influence comes from macro-social background variables. There is a complex relationship between macro-economic growth and environmental pollution, with the most famous being the environmental Kuznets curve (EKC). This curve was first proposed by American scholars Grossman and Krueger (1991). They proposed that by analyzing data from 42 countries, the relationship between the emission of some environmental pollutants (soot, sulfur dioxide, etc.) and economic growth is similar to the Kuznets curve, reflecting income distribution and economic growth, and also presenting an inverted U-shaped curve. In other words, in the early stages of economic development, economic growth will aggravate environmental pollution, but once economic growth breaks through a turning point, continuous growth is conducive to the improvement of environmental quality. This hypothesis has received much scholarly attention since it was proposed, and many relevant empirical studies have been conducted, mainly testing whether the inverse U-shaped EKC relationship between various environmental pollutants and economic growth is consistent. Assuming this curve exists, where is the inflection point?

Empirical studies conducted by both Chinese and overseas scholars have examined the relationship between environmental pollution and economic growth from an economic perspective. They have found a variety of manifestations, including monotone decline and U-shaped, inverted U-shaped, N-shaped, and inverted N-shaped relationships. Which one appears is primarily dependent on the selection of regions and pollution indicators (Zhang et al. 2012). Regardless of the shape, the inflection points of whether the relationship is win–win or lose-lose depend on the scale effect, technical effect, and structural effect. From a win–win perspective between economic growth and environmental pollution, it can be inferred that as economic development increases income, environmental protection receives more attention, and more resources are invested. On the one hand, this objectively improves the quality of the environment. On the other hand, there is growing public demand for a healthy environment. When the public's demand for a healthy environment is matched to the public goods that the government can provide, the public will take a more optimistic view of the government's environmental protection work; When the public's demand for a healthy environment far exceeds the good products that the government can provide, the public's perception of the government's environmental work may be much lower than their perception of the government's economic work. From the lose-lose perspective, economic development will be accompanied by environmental destruction, and environmental destruction will make economic growth unsustainable. This will cause the public to more negatively perceive the government's work (including the economy and environmental protection). Since China's economy has risen from that of a low-income country to that of a middle-income country after more than 30 years of rapid development, the central government's requirements for environmental governance have remained far lower than the public's expectations for the environment. Thus, we propose Hypothesis 4 at the macro level: the richer the region, the lower the public's assessment of the central government's environmental protection work.

Individual attitudes emerge in a specific social background. Previous studies on personal attitudes have paid more attention to the influence of variables at the individual level, overlooking that the emergence of personal attitudes is inherently rooted in a specific social interaction context and cannot be separated from the influence of variables at the social macro level. Similarly, the assessment of the government's environmental protection work is not only related to the level of social and economic development in a given region, but also to the degree of pollution. Thinking further, it can be assumed that the level of pollution in the local area inevitably affects the public's support for environmental protection, and thus also affects the public's assessment of the central government's environmental protection work. This naturally leads to Hypothesis 5: The higher the pollution in an area, the lower the public's assessment of the central government's environmental protection work.

In sum, although the factors affecting the public's assessment of the government's environmental protection work are multi-layered and multi-dimensional, this chapter explores the impact of social psychology and objective social situation variables. Through the analysis of China's comprehensive social survey, we explore the factors that affect the public's subjective assessment of the central government's environmental protection work from multiple levels. Our focus is the effects of the public's psychosocial variables (the level of trust in the central government, the perception of environmental problems, and the level of environmental concern) and economic development and industrial pollution on the public's perception of the government's environmental protection work. In doing so, we explicate the changes in the public's subjective assessment of the central government's environmental protection work between 2003 and 2010.

16.2 Data and Methods

The data collected for this chapter combines data from both the individual and the provincial level. The data at the individual level consists mainly of the data from the China General Social Survey (CGSS2010), which adopts a multi-level stratified probability sampling design and covers 31 provincial administrative divisions in China (excluding Hong Kong, Macao, and Taiwan). Subsequently, CGSS2 003 data was added to the comparative analysis, and there were 5,073 valid samples in the environmental portion of the 2003 questionnaire.

In addition to the core modules, CGSS 2010 also contains the International Social Survey Cooperation (ISSP) environment module, the International Social Survey Cooperation (ISSP) religion module, and the East Asian Social Survey (EASS) health module. For these three modules, the surveyors decided which module the respondents would answer by random selection. In this way, the probability of respondents answering each module was equal, and the three sub-samples formed by these three modules also had equal national representation and equal sampling accuracy. There were 3,716 environment module samples. Missing values are treated in two ways. For the missing values of some important continuous variables with a large percentage, such as income, education, and environmental concern level, we used the mean value replacement method. For the categorical variables, missing values accounted for a small percentage of the sample, less than 1%, so the analysis was conducted directly after deleting these missing values, and the final sample size was 3,663.

Provincial-level data are from the 2010 China Urban Statistical Yearbook, including macro-economic development and environmental pollution indicators from 30 provincial-level administrative units (excluding Hong Kong, Macao, and Taiwan; Tibet had only 2 samples, and thus was also excluded). From the perspective of the CGSS sampling process, hierarchical cluster sampling has the potential to produce a cluster effect, which violates the assumption that all individuals are independent of each other in the ordinary least squares regression method. At the same time, considering the embedded data structure and the different levels of economic development and pollution emissions in China, we adopted a multi-level analysis model to test the effect of the individual-level and provincial-level variables on the subjective assessment of government environmental protection work.

16.2.1 *Individual-Level Variables*

The dependent variable was set in the form of the question: "How well do you think the central government has done in addressing China's domestic environmental problems in the past five years?" The response choices to this question were:

1) single minded emphasis on economic development, ignoring environmental protection
2) insufficient attention and environmental investment
3) effort made, but little achieved
4) great efforts and some results
5) great achievements
6) cannot choose
-1) refuse to answer
-2) don't know
-3) not applicable

Since the total percentage of responses to -1, -2, and -3 were less than 1.5, their responses were combined with "cannot choose" for ease of comparison. Those who responded 1, 2, 3, 4, and 5 were assigned values of 1, 2, 3, 4, and 5, respectively, with higher scores indicating higher assessment of the government. In order to include the "cannot choose" response in the analysis, we assumed it to be a neutral response and assigned it a value of 3. Note that the dependent variable is an ordered variable with 5 categories, which is defined as a continuous variable in the model for the convenience of interpretation.

The variables for individual socioeconomic characteristics include age, gender, education level, type of residence, income level, political status, and religious belief. Age is a continuous variable. The response value for gender is 1 for male and 0 for female. The following values are assigned for education level:

0) no education
6) elementary school
9) junior high school
12) high school and secondary school
14) junior college
16) bachelor's degree
19) graduate degree and above

Residence type is a binary variable with urban area = 1 and rural area = 0. Income level is an individual's total income the previous year, and is a continuous variable. Political status is a binary variable, with Party members = 1 and non-Party members = 0. Religious beliefs is also binary, with religious beliefs = 1 and no religious beliefs = 0.

The psychosocial variables at the individual level included: the level of trust in the central government, the level of environmental concern, and the perception of the severity of environmental problems. The responses to the question about the level of trust in the central government were:

1) no trust at all
2) little trust
3) between credible and untrustworthy
4) trustworthy or credible
5) highly trustworthy

The five responses above were given values of 1, 2, 3, 4, and 5, respectively. A higher score indicated a higher level of trust in the central government. Missing values accounted for 0.5% and 0.6% of the total sample, respectively, and were replaced with the mean.

Chinese scholars have discussed the application of this table in China, and have concluded that the Chinese version of the NEP scale (CNEP) includes 10 items that give a more accurate measurement; these are survey questions 1, 3, 5, 7, 8, 9, 10, 11, 13, and 15 (Xiao and Hong 2007), which we selected. Based on CGSS 2010 data, Hong et al. (2014) reanalyzed this scale and concluded that the Chinese version of the NEP scale was more suitable for China. Therefore, for this chapter, we used the Chinese version of the NEP scale (10 items in total) (Hong et al. 2014). The responses to each statement were:

1) completely disagree
2) somewhat disagree
3) neither agree nor disagree
4) somewhat agree
5) completely agree
8) cannot decide

Statements 1, 3, 5, 7, 9, 11, 13, and 15 are true statements; Statements 8 and 10 are false statements. The response "cannot choose" is grouped with "neither agree nor disagree". For true statements, the values assigned from "completely disagree" to "completely agree" are 1, 2, 3, 4, and 5, respectively. For false statements, the values assigned from "completely disagree" to "completely agree" are 5, 4, 3, 2, and 1, respectively. In order to simplify the analysis, the Kronbach coefficient for CNEP was determined to be 0.77 through reliability analysis, which can be considered a high reliability scale. The environmental concern level score is obtained by summing these 10 items, ranging from 10 to 50.

From the "stimulus–response" perspective of psychology, the "response" to the government's environmental protection work assessment and the public's perception of environmental protection are also related to the "stimulus" factor. In the CGSS 2010 questionnaire, respondents were asked about their overall judgment of the environment: "In your opinion, how serious are China's environmental problems?" There were six responses to this question:

1) very serious
2) relatively serious
3) cannot judge
4) not too serious
5) not serious at all
8) cannot choose

For consistency of analysis, "cannot choose" is grouped with Option 3. In the questionnaire, the 18 respondents who "refused to answer", "did not know", or selected "did not apply" were counted as missing values and were not included in the data analysis. In order to facilitate the study, the responses are reversely weighted, with the following scores assigned in the reverse weight: from 5 for "very serious" to 1 for "not serious at all".

16.2.2 Provincial-Level Variables

There were four variables at the provincial level; two indicators were used for economic development. The first was the per capita GDP for each province (in ten thousand yuan); the second was each province's GDP growth rate. Industrial pollution also included two indicators, the first was sulfur dioxide emissions, including industrial sulfur dioxide and domestic sulfur dioxide emissions; the second was soot emissions, including the total amount of industrial soot and domestic soot emissions. China's current energy structure relies mainly on coal and oil, which generate sulfur dioxide when burned, while soot is a particulate pollutant whose levels have a strong correlation with daily production and daily life. According to particle size, dust can be divided into falling dust and floating dust. Iron and steel, non-ferrous metal smelting, thermal power generation, cement and petrochemical production processes, vehicle and aircraft exhaust, as well as waste incineration, heating boilers, and household stoves' exhaust are the main sources of soot pollution. Among them, combustible fuel exhaust contributes the greatest amount. The variables are described in Table 16.1.

16.2.3 Model Setting

In order to verify the above hypothesis, we took the following analytical steps. The first was the zero model, also known as the one-way analysis of variance model, which has no explanatory variables at either the individual or the regional level. The model can be illustrated in the following Formula 16.1:

Level 1 Individual Level:

$$Y_{ij} = \beta_{0j} + r_{ij} \quad r_{ij} \sim (0, \sigma^2) \tag{16.1}$$

Level 2 Provincial Level:

$$\beta_{0j} = \gamma_{00} + u_{0j} \qquad u_{0j} \sim (0, \tau_{00}) \tag{16.2}$$

Table 16.1 Variable description

Variable name	*Mean value*	*Standard deviation*	*Number of samples*	*Variable description*
Assessment of the central government's environmental protection works	3.16	1.01	3,663	Continuous variable
Sociodemographic and economic characteristic variables				
Age	47.31	15.74	3,663	Continuous variable
Educational level	8.87	4.46	3,663	Continuous variable
Income (in ten thousand yuan)	1.91	5.65	3,663	Continuous variable
Gender	0.47	0.49	3,663	Male = 1, female = 0
Political status	0.13	0.34	3,663	Member of Communist Party of China = 1, other = 0
Religious beliefs	0.12	0.32	3,663	Religious = 1, non-religious = 0
Place of residence	0.64	0.48	3,663	City = 1, village = 0
Psychosocial variable				
Level of trust in the central government	4.37	0.79	3,663	Continuous variable
Environmental concern level	37.02	5.48	3,663	Continuous variable
Awareness of the severity of environmental problems	3.78	0.93	3,663	Continuous variable
Provincial-level variable				
GDP growth rate	13.47	1.82	30	Continuous variable
Per capita GDP (in ten thousand yuan)	3.35	1.81	30	Continuous variable
Sulfur dioxide emissions (in ten thousand tons)	73.79	42.06	30	Continuous variable
Soot emissions (in ten thousand tons)	28.25	17.67	30	Continuous variable

where Υ_{ij} is the score of member i's assessment of the central government's environmental protection work in Province j, β_{0j} is the average score of the government's assessment of environmental protection work in Province j, r_{ij} is the residual, following a normal distribution with mean 0 and variance σ^2, and σ^2 represents the degree of variation of environmental protection assessment in the same province. γ_{00} is the overall rating of the government's environmental efforts, u_{0j} follows a normal distribution with a mean of 0 and a variance of tau 00. τ_{00} represents the degree of variation in the government environmental assessment scores among different provinces. The purpose of this model is to decompose the total variance at both the individual and the regional level, and to calculate the intra-class correlation coefficient (ICC). ICC can be defined as $\tau_{00}/(\tau_{00+}\ \sigma^2)$, where a high coefficient indicates a large amount of inter-group variation and a high total variance, which can be explained by intra-group variation.

In the following model, variables related to the hypotheses are added to the model separately. In Model 2, socioeconomic characteristic variables are added, which tests the effect of socioeconomic characteristic variables on the assessment of government environmental protection work. In Model 3, social psychological variables are added, namely, the level of trust in the central government, the level of environmental concern, and the perception of the severity of environmental problems, to verify the first three hypotheses. In Model 4, provincial-level variables such as GDP per capita, GDP growth rate, sulfur dioxide emissions, and soot emissions are added to evaluate the effects of provincial-level variables on the assessment of the central government's environmental protection work, and to test the latter two hypotheses.

In this chapter, we use a random intercept model in which the intercept of the model is the average score of the provincial-level assessment of government environmental protection work. In the random intercept model, the difference between each group varies according to the mean of the dependent variable. The random intercept is the only group effect, and each regression coefficient at the individual level is fixed within these models. We used HLM software for the data analysis, and thus, the software presupposes the use of the full maximum likelihood method to estimate each parameter's value. For ease of comparison, we standardized all of the independent variables because they had different measurement levels. The final model results are shown in Table 16.2.

Individual-level model

$$Y_{ij} = \beta_{0j} + \beta_{1j}(X_1) + \beta_{2j}(X_2) + \beta_{3j}(X_3) + \beta_{4j}(X_4) + \beta_{5j}(X_5) + \beta_{6j}(X_6) + \beta_{7j}(X_7) + \beta_{8j}(X_8) + \beta_{9j}(X_9) + \beta_{10j}(X_{10}) + r_{ij} \quad (16.3)$$

Table 16.2 Multi-layer analysis of public assessment of the central government's environmental protection work

Model *Fixed effect*	*Model 1* *Coefficient (standard error)*	*Model 2* *Coefficient (standard error)*	*Model 3* *Coefficient (standard error)*	*Model 4* *Coefficient (standard error)*
Intercept	3.24*** (0.057)	3.24*** (0.057)	3.24*** (0.057)	3.24*** (0.057)
Individual-level variable				
Age		0.066*** (0.014)	0.031** (0.013)	0.031** (0.013)
Educational level		−0.116*** (0.022)	−0.066*** (0.021)	−0.066*** (0.021)
Income (ten thousand yuan)		−0.027 (0.019)	−0.022 (0.015)	−0.022 (0.015)
Gender (male = 1)		0.053*** (0.018)	0.05*** (0.018)	0.05*** (0.018)
Political status		0.031* (0.017)	0.034** (0.017)	0.034** (0.017)
Religious beliefs		−0.006 (0.014)	−0.001 (0.014)	−0.001 (0.014)
Place of residence		−0.038 (0.027)	−0.005 (0.026)	−0.005 (0.026)
Level of trust in the central government			0.164*** (0.018)	0.164*** (0.018)
Environmental concern level			−0.081*** (0.028)	−0.081*** (0.028)
Awareness of severity of environmental problems			−0.091*** (0.023)	−0.091*** (0.023)
Provincial-level variable				
GDP growth rate				−0.01 (0.059)
Per capita GDP (ten thousand yuan)				−0.133** (0.057)
Sulfur dioxide emissions (ten thousand tons)				0.077 (0.067)

(continued)

Table 16.2 (continued)

Model *Fixed effect*	*Model 1* *Coefficient (standard error)*	*Model 2* *Coefficient (standard error)*	*Model 3* *Coefficient (standard error)*	*Model 4* *Coefficient (standard error)*
Soot emissions (ten thousand tons)				−0.183*** (0.057)
Model *Random effect*	*Model 1* *Variance component* *(χ2)*	*Model 2* *Variance component* *(χ2)*	*Model 3* *Variance component* *(χ2)*	*Model 4* *Variance component* *(χ2)*
Average scores for environmental protection work assessment of provincial governments	0.089*** (252.79)	0.089*** (260.58)	0.081*** (272.73)	0.074*** (182.91)
Level 1 effect	0.98	0.954	0.913	0.914

*$p < 0.1$, **$p < 0.05$, ***$p < 0.01$

Provincial-level model

$$\beta_{0j} = \gamma_{00} + \gamma_{01}(W_1) + \gamma_{02}(W_2) + \gamma_{03}(W_3) + \gamma_{04}(W_4) + \mu_{0j} \tag{16.4}$$

$$\beta_{qj} = \gamma_{q0}, q = 1, 2, \ldots, 10 \tag{16.5}$$

In the model, the individual-level variables are X_1 (age), X_2 (education level), X_3 (income), X_4 (gender), X_5 (political status), X_6 (religious beliefs), X_7 (place of residence), X_8 (level of trust in the central government), and X_9 (environmental concern level), X_{10} (perception of the severity of environmental problems). Variables at the provincial level are W_1 (GDP growth rate), W_2 (GDP per capita), W_3 (sulfur dioxide emissions), and W_4 (soot emissions).

16.3 Model Results

Model 1 in Table 16.2 shows a two-tier completely unconditional model, from which we know how much of the total variance can be explained by the individual level and the regional level, respectively. The square handicap estimate for the Layer 1 effect is 0.98, much greater than the square handicap estimate for Layer 2 (0.089). The intra-group correlation coefficient (ICC) was calculated to be 0.08, which means that 8.6% of the variance per capita in the assessment of the central government's environmental work is attributable to the differences between provinces. Further analysis shows that the Tier 2 variance estimation is actually an analysis of the variance of the per capita subjective assessment score for each province. If the per capita subjective assessment score for each province is not significantly different, then the chi-square statistical test for Tier 2 variance should not be significant. However, the data results show that the test of Tier 2 variance is significant, and the chi-square value is 252.79, with 29 degrees of freedom. This also shows that the scores for different provinces in the assessment of the central government's environmental protection work can be explained from the individual-, regional economic-, and environmental-level characteristics.

In Model 2, analyzing all of the individual-level variables, we found that age, education level, gender, and political status had significant correlations with the assessment scores of the central government's environmental protection work. Within the results, the higher the age, the higher the assessment of the central government's environmental protection work. Men also scored higher on the government's environmental efforts than women. Additionally, political status has a significant effect on the assessment of the government's environmental protection work. Considering the difference in political loyalty between Party members and non-Party members, it is apparent that Party members have a higher positive assessment of the government's environmental protection work. In addition, the results of Model 2 show that per capita annual income, religious beliefs, and residence type have no significant effect on the assessment of government environmental protection work. The comparison of standardized regression coefficients at the individual level revealed that education level has the greatest effect on the government's environmental protection work, and the higher the education level, the lower the assessment.

In Model 3, social psychological variables were added: the level of trust in the central government: the level of environmental concern, and the perception of the severity of environmental problems. The variances at the individual level ranged from 0.98 to 0.953, while the variances at the provincial level changed little. This change suggests that psychosocial variables explain some of the variance at the individual level in the model. Additionally, there is a significant positive correlation between the level of trust in the central government and the subjective assessment score for the government's environmental protection work. This indicates that the higher the level of public trust in the government, the higher their assessment of the central government's environmental protection work. Thus, Hypothesis 1 is supported by the data. The standardized regression coefficients for the level of environmental concern and the perception of the severity of environmental problems are -0.081 and -0.091, respectively. This indicates that the higher the level of environmental concern, the higher the public's environmental protection requirements for the central government, and the lower the assessment of the central government's environmental protection work. Thus, Hypothesis 2 is supported. Similarly, the more serious the public's perception of environmental problems, the more dissatisfied they are with the government's environmental protection work, and the more likely they are to disapprove of the government's environmental protection work. Thus, Hypothesis 3 is also confirmed by the data. The standardized regression coefficients of the above three psychosocial variables reveal that the trust level in the central government has the greatest effect. From the perspective of the proportion of variance explained, when we add social psychological variables, the variance at the individual level declines from 0.089 to 0.081. This is equivalent to 9.0% of the individual-level variance being explained by social psychological variables.

In Model 4, two economic development indicators are added: GDP growth rate and per capita GDP (ten thousand yuan); and two regional industrial pollution indicators, sulfur dioxide emissions and soot emissions, are added. Table 16.2 shows that after controlling for variables at the individual level, the regions with higher per capita GDP have a significant negative correlation with the assessment of the central government's environmental protection work. This indicates that after the public meets certain material needs, they have more urgent requirements for a good environment. Therefore, it can be said that the wealthier a region, the more urgent its public demand for a good environment, and the more stringent its assessment of the government's environmental protection work. Thus, Hypothesis 4 is verified. However, it must be pointed out that there is no significant correlation between the GDP growth rate and the assessment of the central government's environmental protection work, and there is no significant correlation between the GDP growth rate and per capita GDP. This shows that the economic growth rate does not necessarily promote a higher assessment of the government's environmental protection work. At a time when the demand for a good environment exceeds material needs, the government's pursuit of GDP growth has led the public to believe that the government has neglected environmental protection.

Based on the industrial waste gas pollution index, we can conclude that the higher the soot emissions, the lower the opinion of the central government's environmental protection work, while sulfur dioxide emissions and the assessment of the central government's environmental protection work have no statistical correlation. A significant difference between soot and sulfur dioxide emissions is that soot emissions are easier for the public to observe, because the main components of soot are dust particles of fuel, unburned (black carbon) particles, and other particulate matter. Most of these particles can be seen by the naked eye, and in recent years, haze and fine particulate matter PM2.5 have rapidly entered the public eye, alerting the public of this link. This has brought environmental issues into the public spotlight. In contrast, sulfur dioxide is a colorless, pungent gas that can cause acid rain when it is discharged into the atmosphere in large quantities. Although it is also a great danger to public health, there is less public concern about it than the various particles that cause smog. It can be said that the more visible air pollution is to the public, the more the public feels that the government's environmental protection work is inadequate. Thus, Hypothesis 5 is partially confirmed. It could be argued that the more severe the air pollution easily observed by the public, the lower the public's assessment of the central government's environmental protection efforts. From the perspective of the proportion of variance explained, when we add the regional variable, the variance at the regional level declines from 0.081 to 0.074. This is equivalent to 8.6% of the variance being explained by the regional-level variable.

16.4 Summary and Discussion

It must be recognized that the CGSS2010 data only shows the public's subjective assessment of the central government's environmental protection work at this point. By looking back at the CGSS 2003 data, we can further understand the historical changes in the public's assessment of the central government's environmental protection work over the past eight years. Since the CGSS environmental data for 2003 only surveyed urban residents, it was also limited to cities in the historic comparative analysis (see Table 16.3).

The data from 2003 and 2010 indicate that the proportion of urban residents' negative and neutral assessments of the central government's environmental protection work (Items 1, 2, and 3) increased from 2003 to 2010, while the positive assessment (Items 4 and 5) showed a decreasing trend over the 8 years. Although there are different organizations or individuals which are held responsible for environmental problems, the public entrusts great hope in the government's environmental responsibility. According to CGSS 2010 data, 49% of respondents believe that the government should be held responsible for environmental degradation; In contrast, only 6.6% believe that individuals are responsible for the environment. It is important to recognize that the public's positive assessment of the central government's environmental work is on a downward trend, and the reasons for this are complex and multi-layered.

First, in terms of individual socioeconomic characteristics, the analysis shows that there is no significant correlation between public income

Table 16.3 Comparison of the assessment of the central government's environmental protection work at different time points (unit: %)

Assessment of the central government's environmental protection work *Response options*	*2003 年* *City (1)*	*2010 年* *City (2)*
1. One-sided emphasis on economic development and neglect of environmental protection work	3.55%	8.51%
2. Insufficient attention to and investment in environmental protection	11.89%	17.09%
3. Effort has been made, but the effect has not been good	29.37%	39.79%
4. We have made great efforts and achieved some results	40.76%	27.56%
5. We have made great achievements	10.33%	7.05%

levels and individuals' assessment of government environmental protection work. However, the younger generation tends to have a more negative view of the government's environmental protection work, and people with higher education are more cautious about the government's environmental protection work because of their access to a variety of sources of information. From a gender perspective, men hold the government's environmental protection work in higher regard than women. Whether this is because of their different socialization processes or other reasons remains to be further explored. Women are socialized to be more compassionate, which extends to a protective attitude toward nature, and thus they tend to evaluate the government's environmental protection efforts more conservatively. Meanwhile, men are socialized to be breadwinners, which makes them more concerned about economic growth and resource development. From the political perspective, party members' assessment of the government's environmental protection work is higher than that of non-Party members, which also reflects that political loyalty is an important factor not to be ignored in the government's various forms of performance assessment work.

Second, the social psychological variables in the regression analysis have a significant effect on the assessment of the government's environmental protection work. With improving public education levels and the popularization of mass media, the public's environmental concern level has also increased. This has intensified the public's demand for a clean and safe environment. It has also brought the government's environmental protection efforts under more scrutiny. In addition, whether the objective changes in the environment caused by economic development can be perceived by the public is also an important factor in determining the public's attitude. From an environmental constructivism perspective, the public perceives the seriousness of environmental problems through two channels, one is through mass media's reporting and dissemination of environmental issues, and the other is through the public's own experience. The perception of the severity of environmental problems that emerges through these two channels will inevitably affect public assessment of the government's environmental protection work.

The comparison of CGSS city data between 2003 and 2010 shows that there has been little change in urban residents' perceptions of the severity of environmental problems in terms of responses of "not at all serious", "not too serious", and "relatively serious". However the percentage of responses of "not sure" decreased from 24.74% in 2003 to 14.0% in

2010. Those responding "very serious" increased from 17.31% in 2003 to 24.38% in 2010. Additionally, more people perceived China's environmental problems as "very serious" in 2010 than in 2003. This also reflects the changes in the public's assessment of the government's environmental protection work. Alternatively, it may be that the objective environment is gradually improving, but public perception of the severity of environmental problems has not improved.

Another important factor is that perceptions of the government's environmental work are intertwined with the public's trust in the government. The higher the level of public trust in the government, the higher the assessment of the government's environmental protection work. Thus, the increasing proportion of the public's negative assessment of government environmental protection work may be related to declining trust in the government.

Finally, from the perspective of regional macro-economic indicators, there is a significant negative correlation between economic affluence and the public's assessment of the government's environmental protection work, while the GDP growth rate has no significant correlation with the public's assessment of the government's environmental protection work. This also implies that China's current developmental strategy should be adjusted, i.e., the primary goal should be the construction of ecological civilization, not merely GDP growth. It must be noted that although economic development has promoted regional affluence, it has also led the public to adopt a more stringent attitude toward assessing the government's environmental protection work. This is also reflected in that with improvements in living standards, the public has intensified its pursuit of a high-quality natural environment.

In the foreseeable future, with increasing public affluence, pressure on the government to protect the environment will intensify, mainly for two reasons. First, public concern for the environment will increase, offering more hope to the government's environmental regulatory role. The second is the increase in energy and resource consumption brought about by economic development. From the perspective of industrial pollution indicators, the more visible and intuitive industrial pollutants are discharged, the lower the public's assessment of the government's environmental protection work. On the contrary, some subtle industrial pollution, even if the total amount of emissions is acute, is not easily perceived by the public. A comparison between the two also shows that the public's assessment of the government's environmental protection work has not been comprehensive, but based more on their own perceptions and needs.

In summary, through the analysis of multi-layer factors that affect the public's assessment of the central government's environmental protection work, we can conclude that the public's assessment of the government's environmental protection work is not only based on their subjective feelings, but is also intertwined with the objective existence of regional affluence and environmental pollution. In terms of subjective feelings, this chapter examines the public's assessment of the government's environmental protection work from the level of public concern for the environment, the level of public perception of the seriousness of environmental problems, and the level of public trust in the central government. A comparative analysis shows that the public's perception of the severity of environmental problems has increased over the past eight years. Another factor not to be ignored is the level of public trust in the central government, which also shapes the public's assessment of the government's environmental protection work. What type of relationship there is between these three factors and whether there is a mediating effect of public trust level needs further research.

From the perspective of objective economic indicators, the GDP growth rate cannot enhance the public's sense of identity with the government's environmental protection work, and the development model centered on the GDP growth rate must be adjusted. Moreover, according to Maslow's hierarchy of needs theory, the wealth of the public will elevate the public's expectations for environmental protection, but the increase in per capita income also means that the government can secure more financial support for environmental governance. This study also shows that the environment's objective pollution level is related to the public's assessment of the government's environmental protection efforts. It must be noted that the public's assessment of the government's environmental protection work is based more on what they see and perceive to be environmental pollution.

Public assessment of government environmental protection work is the process of the interaction between the individual-level characteristics of social actors and the macro-social and economic background in which they are placed. This requires that the formulation of national environmental protection policies and their implementors should not only pay attention to the environmental protection needs and feelings of social individuals, but also focus on improving the social environment in which these needs and feelings are located. In this chapter, we construct a multi-level, subjective, and objective model to investigate the various factors affecting the public's assessment of the government's environmental protection work. We hope that the analysis results can provide some references for the government's environmental policy formulation and implementation.

CHAPTER 17

Modern Chinese Environmentalism

Hong Dayong and Fan Yechao

The formation of an ideology of environmental development is another important indicator of what is called "social greening", or green and sustainable development of society. In contemporary China, whether raised by the public or the government, concerns about and discussions of environmental issues are on the rise. And the importance of environmental protection has been deeply rooted in public consciousness. Reports on environmental issues and protection are frequently seen in domestic newspapers and on the internet, film, and television programs, suggesting the rise of modern environmentalism, which at the core, appeals to the public to protect the ecological and natural environment. The rise of modern environmentalism in Chinese society awakens more and more people to environmental issues and the negative impacts of human behavior on the environment. It has important bearing upon the current ecological practices and environmental governance in China.

D. Hong (✉)
Renmin University of China, Beijing, China
e-mail: hongdy@ruc.edu.cn

Y. Fan
Minzu University of China, Beijing, China
e-mail: fanyechao@ruc.edu.cn

D. Hong and Y. Fan (eds.), *Toward a Green Society*,
https://doi.org/10.1007/978-981-96-5111-5_17

Based on the theory of ideology in sociology, this chapter attempts to trace the development of modern environmentalism in the West and the corresponding development in China since the 1970s, and then identify the driving forces and the practical constraints of environmentalism in contemporary China.

17.1 Modern Environmentalism as an Ideology

Although environmentalism is a common term in current academic research, few researchers have seriously reflected on it. Therefore, it is difficult for us to find a clear academic definition. It is generally thought that environmentalism refers to an ideology, broad philosophy, and social movement which considers the concerns of environmental protection and environmental health improvement, particularly the measures which integrate the effect on animals, plants, humans and abiotic factors due to environmental changes. American ecologist F. J. Mazzotti (2001) defines environmentalism as "a way of thinking and a political practice movement based on the consensus that the natural environment should be protected"; environmental protection activities from the local level to the national and even the global level are the manifestation of various forms of environmentalism. Mazzotti also points out that the views of environmentalists can be divided into the three categories: health-related, that is, to prevent environmental pollution from poisoning the human body; economic-related, that is, to protect valuable natural resources for sustainable use; and lastly, aesthetic-related, that is, to seek a place that is more suitable for human life and living.

From the two aforementioned concepts of environmentalism, three characteristics of environmentalism can be summarized. First, environmentalism is oriented toward elements of the natural environment in the social system and points to specific ecological and environmental problems. Second, environmentalism has a clear value orientation, that is, human beings should protect ecological systems and the natural environment. Third, many ideas of environmentalism are fundamentally different, or even directly opposite, from other social trends of thought, such as anthropocentrism and materialism, which have long prevailed in Western society with "man conquers/dominates nature" at their core. For this study, environmentalism is defined as follows: environmentalism is a group of interrelated ideas and values that focus on the relationship between the environment and human society, and it clearly aims to protect the ecological and natural environment. Also, it is divided into traditional environmentalism and modern environmentalism.

From the perspective of historical origins, the concept of environmentalism can be traced back to the "Arcadianism" of the European and American social elites in the eighteenth century. And the resource conservationism of American society, which originated in the late nineteenth and early twentieth centuries is also regarded as the predecessor of environmentalism (Worster 1999). The former aims to pursue a way of life in harmony with nature, while the latter advocates the controlled exploitation and utilization of natural resources. It should be said that in traditional Chinese culture, there are also social ideas that are in line with the concept of environmentalism, such as "harmony between man and nature" and "respect nature and fear of the nature", all of which advocate conforming to the laws of nature and praising the harmonious and symbiotic relationship between man and nature. It should be mentioned that these early social ideas at home and abroad were confined to a small number of intellectuals and elites in history, and their influence on the general public was very limited, with little significant changes in social action. Nevertheless, these thoughts generally conform to our definition of environmentalism and can therefore be seen as traditional environmentalism.

In the 1950s and 1960s, with the rapid advancement of industrialization and urbanization, the concentrated outbreak of pollutions in Western countries became the direct cause of modern environmentalism. In 1962, American biologist Rachel Carson published her book *Silent Spring*, which expresses deep concern about environmental pollution and further ecosystem degradation caused by pesticides. In the book, Carson lashes out at the economic production sectors that were liable, causing strong repercussions not only in the United States but also across the global community (Carson 2014). Her book is recognized as the first work on environmental protection and the work that started modern environmental protection movements all over the world. Since then, the public began to pay attention to and seriously think about the relationship between environment and society. In the following decade, environmentalism developed vigorously and a succession of environmental protection movements took place in Europe and America. In 1970, the first "Earth Day" event was held in the United States. It was estimated that more than 20 million people across the United States had participated in demonstrations and speeches. This event is also considered by researchers to be a symbol of the widespread popularity of modern environmentalism (Dunlap and Mertig 1992).

The emergence and popularity of modern environmentalism is actually a revolution on the conceptual level and the belief system of society as a whole, and it is essentially a new ideology different from the traditional environmentalism and other ideologies in the past. Ideology refers to "a set of interrelated and relatively stable value beliefs" (Liu 2012), and it is the reference value standard for individuals to understand the objective world and reflect on themselves (Yu 2009). For one thing, as mentioned above, the ultimate value of modern environmentalism is the harmony between man and the natural environment, and it is a concept, and a way of thinking, that explicitly takes environmental protection as its value orientation. For another thing, modern environmentalism came into being in the context of continuous degradation of the ecological environment. In today's world, where environmental problems are still very severe, it has developed into a concept that is generally adhered to by governments and people in different countries around the world and has a solid social foundation. Accordingly, it can be argued that modern environmentalism essentially conforms to the characteristics that an ideology should have. It directly confronts ecological crises resulting from industrialization and urbanization in modern society and advocates collective and social actions for environmental protection to reshape the relationship between humans and the environment (Harper 2012). Modern environmentalism has surpassed traditional environmentalism in content and influence and has become a dominant new ideology.

Modern environmentalism has various manifestations. Ideology is not only embodied in the conceptualized and logicalized theoretical forms, but also exists in the visualized and symbolized perceptual forms (Liu 2015). As an ideology, modern environmentalism has both theoretical and perceptual forms. The theoretical form refers to systematic and theoretical ideas and views on environmental protection, which can be divided into two types. The first one is the theoretical understandings of the causes, influences, and solutions of environmental problems established by natural and social scientists through scientific research. For example, "ecological footprint theory" measures the environmental capacity of a country or region, and "ecological modernization theory" discusses future environmental governance trends. The second type is embodied in a systematic and institutionalized political ideological system aimed at environmental protection, such as the concept of "sustainable development" in the economic and social development strategies of most countries and regions and the program of "construction of ecological civilization" proposed by the Chinese government in recent years. In addition to its theoretical form, modern environmentalism often exists in perceptual forms, that is, the environmental belief systems formed by people in daily life practices. The perceptual form of modern environmentalism not only is reflected by the demands of environmental movements and the public's concern about and awareness of environmental problems but also includes simple "local knowledge" about environmental protection in some regions.

In terms of the believer, ideologies may be divided into three different levels: the global and/or the national, the communal, and the individual (Liu 2011). From this perspective, modern environmentalism can also be examined at the three levels. The first one is the global and/or national level. Second, the local and communal level, also known as the non-governmental environmentalism, is generally seen in social organizations, environmental movements, and public environmental concern with the aim of environmental protection. Third, the individual level can be understood as an individual's concern for the environment and tendencies to engage in activities promoting environmental protection. Modern environmentalism at the global or national level, often manifested in institutional programs, value system, or official ideology of environmental protection, is characterized by integrity, abstraction, and stability. In contrast, the local and individual levels are characterized by s locality, concreteness, and fluidity.

17.2 Modern Environmentalism in China

Modern environmentalism began in post-World War II American society, but it soon spread around the world. From the founding of the People's Republic of China in 1949 to the 1970s, due to successive foreign policies from "uniting with the Soviet Union against the United States" to "containing the Soviet Union against the United States", modern environmentalism as a Western social ideology did not spread in China. At that time, other ideologies dominated Chinese government plans and social thinking, characterized by the idea of "Conquering nature". Slogans such as "Man Will Conquer Nature", "Change Heaven and the Earth", "Fight with the Heaven and the Earth, and the Joy is Endless", and "Socialism has No Pollution" were widely circulated in Chinese society. In 1972, the first United Nations Conference on the Human Environment was held in Stockholm. More than 1,300 delegates from 133 countries and regions all over the world attended the conference. The government of China also sent a delegation and signed the conference documents, promising to cooperate with all parties to jointly solve environmental problems. If this event is taken as the beginning of China's modern environmental protection movement, the spread of modern environmentalism in China has gone through more than 40 years and may be divided into four stages.

17.2.1 Beginning (1972–1978)

In 1972, China sent a delegation to attend the United Nations Conference on the Human Environment, which was also the first large-scale international conference that China participated in after resuming its seat in the United Nations. In August of the following year, the Chinese government held the first national conference on environmental protection. More than 300 people, including heads of local administrative bodies, representatives from factories, and scientists and researchers attended the conference. For the first time, this meeting formally acknowledged that China's environmental problems were "occurring" and some were "rather severe", established a 32-character policy for China's environmental protection, and issued "Regulations on Protecting and Improving the Environment". Immediately after the meeting, the State Council set up a committee for environmental protection and initiated programs to monitor, evaluate, and provide key treatment for environmental pollution in some areas of China in the following years.

At the beginning of its introduction into China, modern environmentalism was received "courteously" by the Chinese government. However, the spread of environmentalism across the population did not take place at the same rate as in other countries. At this stage, under the influence of the policy of "class struggle as the guideline" and the ultra-left ideological trends in Chinese society, as well as the view held by many that environmental problems in the country were not yet serious, societal responses to modern environmentalism were inactive. Out of synch with the vigorous development of government programs, modern environmentalism was not accepted by the Chinese public, and it received a chilly reception from other competing ideologies. For example, on November

11th, 1978, the national newspaper *Guangming Daily* put forward the slogan "Let us Give Our Heartfelt Praise to the Tiger-Fighting Heroes in All Fields"; on the 19th of the same month, China National Radio broadcast three programs on how to catch giant pandas (Hong 2001). Nevertheless, despite public discourse that clashed with modern environmentalism, it was also during this period that environmental issues began to truly attract public attention, and importance of environmental protection began to establish itself in public consciousness.

17.2.2 Institutionalization (1979–1992)

The year 1979 was a landmark year in environmental protection. The "Law of Environmental Protection of the People's Republic of China (For Trial Implementation)" was promulgated for the first time, marking the beginning of China's environmental protection within the legal system. In 1982, the Chinese government established the Environmental Protection Bureau, which later developed into the Ministry of Ecology and Environment. In 1989, the revised "Law of Environmental Protection of the People's Republic of China" was approved by the National People's Congress and officially implemented. It was also during this period that the Chinese government successively announced the "Law of Marine Environmental Protection of the People's Republic of China"(1982), the "Law of Water Pollution Prevention and Control of the People's Republic of China"(1984), the "Law of the People's Republic of China on Forest"(1984), the "Law of the People's Republic of China on Grassland" (1985), the "Law of the People's Republic of China on the Prevention and Control of Atmospheric Pollution" (1987), the "Law of the People's Republic of China on Wild Animal Protection" (1988), the "Law of the People's Republic of China on Soil and Water Conservation" (1991), the "China's Ten Countermeasures for the Environment and Development" (1992) and a series of laws, policies, and regulations on the protection of the environment and ecological resources. Environmental protection was recognized as a basic national policy and a national strategy for sustainable development was established. In general, modern environmentalism at the national level grew and expanded rapidly during this period.

At the same time, non-governmental modern environmentalism, though not without problems, was developing. On May 15, 1990, the National Bureau of Environmental Protection used the "Investigation and Echo" program of the Central People's Broadcasting Station to ask national audiences for their opinions on environmental pollution and received responses from more than 1,600 listeners across the country. The results showed that, at that time, 99% of the audience were "serious" about environmental pollution and ecological damage in the country, and 94.8% of the listeners said they were "worried" about the harm of environmental pollution to their personal health (Xi and Xu 1998). These results showed that modern environmentalism had begun to be recognized by some discerning eyes across the country. However, the "Survey on Environmental Awareness of Chinese Urban Residents" carried out in cities across the country in the following year showed that the urban public at that time paid attention to the living environment but did not realize the close relationship between the ecological environment and individual acts, and respondents with lower education levels showed greater indifference to environmental problems than better educated respondents (Quality of Life Research Group 1991). In addition, while non-governmental environmental organizations came into existence in China in 1985, as of 1992, there were only two such organizations in China (Yang 2005). It is not difficult to see that the momentum to develop modern environmentalism in the Chinese population was not as strong as it was at the level of the national government. Although there were significant improvements and some notable achievements compared with the previous stage, progress was relatively slow.

17.2.3 Nationwide Action (1993–2002)

In 1993, the year when China clearly proposed a socialist market economic system China responded to the "21st Century Agenda" and established environmental education as a permanent subject and an important part of basic education. During this period, modern environmentalism at the national level was further steadily institutionalized, and the environmental protection system and environmental protection work plans established in the beginning stage began to be fully implemented. In 1993, the National People's Congress established the "Environment and Resources Committee", and the National Committee of the Chinese People's Political Consultative Conference also established the "Environment and Population Committee". Governments at all levels set up environmental protection departments in response to the increasingly severe damages to local ecological environment. During the "Ninth

Five-Year Plan" from 1996 to 2000, the Chinese government attached great importance to pollution control, concentrating on solving environmental problems that endangered people's health and lives, seriously affected the landscape, and hindered economic and social development. Among forms of ecological pollution, priority was given to water resource management, the control of major atmospheric pollutants, and controlling pollution in major cities, and the national government carried out the "33211" ecological environmental protection project in areas with prominent environmental problems.[1]

Particularly striking is the wide popularity of modern environmentalism among the general public during this period. First, with rapid economic growth, industrial pollution in urban areas became increasingly prominent and began to spread to rural areas, and people became increasingly aware of the harm of environmental problems. Second, some major environmental events aroused public attention to environmental issues, such as the severe pollution spill in the lower reaches of the Huaihe River in 1994 and the severe flood in the middle and lower reaches of the Yangtze River in 1998. The level of environmental awareness of the Chinese public continuously improved through these events. At the same time, the number of non-governmental environmental organizations in China also increased. As of 2002, there were 71 non-governmental organizations focusing on environmental protection in China (Yang 2005). In addition, according to the 2003 National Urban Environmental Awareness Survey (CGSS2003), although there were still obvious materialistic tendencies in public environmental awareness as a whole, the population were generally aware of the importance of the natural environment to human society, and a considerable proportion of respondents were actively protecting environmental in their daily lives (Hong 2005). These facts show that modern environmentalism at the non-government level in China made great progress during this period.

[1] The numbers in the 33211 "Ecological and Environmental Protection Project", respectively represent three rivers (Haihe, Huaihe, Liaohe), three lakes (Taihu, Dianchi, Chaohu), two control areas (sulfur oxide pollution and acid rain), one sea (Bohai Sea) and one city (Beijing).

17.2.4 Upgrading (2003–Present)

Since 2003, the development of modern environmentalism in China has entered a new stage at which it is integrated as an important part of China's mainstream ideology. In 2003, science-based developmental policies organized concepts around the objectives of "people-oriented", "comprehensive, coordinated, and sustainable" development and "promotion of the comprehensive development of economy, society and people"; these ideas were formally written into the party constitution at the 17th National Congress of the Communist Party of China. In 2005, the Chinese government proposed establishing a society that was environmentally friendly and resource-saving. In 2007, the report of the 17th National Congress of the Communist Party of China took "building an ecological civilization" as one of the new requirements for China to achieve the goal of all-round development of a well-off society and clearly stated that by 2020, the industrial structure, mode of economic growth and consumption should be oriented toward saving energy resources and protecting the ecological environment. The 18th National Congress of the Communist Party of China held in 2012 further proposed more conscious implementation of scientific development, giving priority to the construction of ecological civilization[2] by integrating it into all aspects of development and the whole process of economic, political, cultural, and social construction. The proposal and construction practices for ecological civilization were significantly explored by the Chinese government in the circumstance of increasingly shrinking natural resources. These policy movements indicated that the development of modern environmentalism entered a new stage with deeper implications.

At the same time, modern environmentalism at the non-government level has been flourishing, and the most prominent manifestation being a succession of environment-related protests across the country, including the 2003 "Yunnan Nujiang Dam Anti-Construction Movement", the 2007 "Xiamen Anti-PX Movement", the recent "Shifang Anti-Molybdenum and Copper Movement", the "Ningbo Anti-PX

[2] The 17th National Congress of the Communist Party of China proposed "Building an Ecological Civilization". Ecological civilization is a social form with the basic purpose of harmonious coexistence, all-round and sustained development between man and nature, man and man, and man and society.

Movement", and the "Panyu Anti-Waste Incineration Plant Construction". Although environmental protection is not the only reason behind these movements, they reflect to some extent the strong appeal of modern environmentalism. Meanwhile, modern environmentalism at the national level has begun to actively explore the mechanisms driving public participation in environmental programs, relax restrictions on the development of non-governmental environment-related organizations, and actively seek opportunities for dialogue with modern environmentalism as practiced in non-governmental settings. In 2003, the "Environmental Impact Assessment Law of the People's Republic of China" was officially implemented, encouraging relevant units, experts, and the public to participate in environmental impact assessment in an appropriate manner. With the announcements of the "Interim Measures for Public Participation in Environmental Impact Assessment" (2006), the "Measures for Disclosure of Environmental Information" (For Trial Implementation) (2007) and the revision of the new Environmental Protection Law (2014), there have been increasing institutional channels for the expression of environmentalism at the civic level.

Looking back at the development of modern environmentalism in China over the 40 years, one can easily find that there has been a process of ideological construction in which the state played a leading role. In other words, the development of modern environmentalism in China has been inseparable from the country's active acceptance, steady promotion, active practice, and continuous enrichment of this new ideology. In that process, modern environmentalism first gained considerable development at the national level and was finally integrated into the mainstream ideology of socialism with Chinese characteristics. In the new era, modern environmentalism at non-government level has continued to grow and will continue to lead and support China's social change and ecological environmental governance with as well as national policies.

17.3 Driving Factors of the Growth of Modern Environmentalism in China

The rise of modern environmentalism in contemporary China was not accidental. As the rise of a new social trend in thinking within a certain society often stems from the changes in its social system and the transformation of its social structures, so the development of modern environmentalism in China has also been socioeconomically driven.

17.3.1 The Conflict Between Environmental Deterioration and Economic and Social Development Is the Fundamental Reason Why Modern Environmentalism Can Be Accepted Within Government Ideology and Institutionalized

The reason why modern environmentalism was not introduced into China at its inception had to do not only with the foreign policy pursued by the mainstream socialist government toward European and American capitalist countries but also with the relative mildness of environmental problems. Since the initiation of Reform and Opening-up, China's economic and social growth has witnessed Great Leap Forward, and people's living standards have generally been greatly improved. However, with the continuous advancement of industrialization and urbanization, the pressure on the ecological environment is increasing (Qu 2013). Rural environmental conditions have also been deteriorating, characterized by non-point source pollution (Hong and Ma 2004; Zhang 2015).

It is apparently true that with the increased investment in environmental protection since the start of the twenty-first century, China's recent ecological and environmental crisis has been alleviated to a certain degree, yet the overall situation does not seem optimistic. In recent years, the large-scale outbreaks of smog across the country are a best example of the negative effect of rapid economic development. According to research estimates, the smog in January 2013 alone caused a minimum of 23 billion yuan in direct economic losses from national traffic and health problems (Mu and Zhang 2013). It can be seen that severe ecological and environmental problems have obviously compromised the country's sustainable socioeconomic development.

Even if the importance of modern environmentalism may not have been fully realized when it was introduced into China, the continuous deterioration of the ecological environment from the 1990s to the present has increasingly raised awareness of how pollution endangers economic and social development and people's health. The Chinese government's recognition of this new ideology is deepening, which provides an opportunity for the mainstreaming of modern environmentalism in the Chinese government's own ideology. In the context of the current rapid economic and social development, it can be safely assumed that the balance between ecological protection and economic development will depend on the combination of modern environmentalism and government ideology. A closer alignment of government and environmental goals will in turn give greater momentum to modern environmentalism.

17.3.2 *The Popularization of Environmental Education Has Enabled the Rapid Growth of Modern Environmentalism in China*

Admittedly, schools are an important space for individual socialization, and school education is one of the most important channels through which individuals learn specific social ideas and attitudes. School education plays a decisive role in the acquisition of mainstream ideology and the popularization of these ideas across society at large. The rapid growth of modern environmentalism in China has also been inseparable from the popularization of environmental education in China. After the First National Environmental Protection Conference in 1973, many colleges and universities established majors in environmental studies. The Environmental Protection Law of the People's Republic of China (Trial) passed in 1979 clearly stipulated environmental education. Enacted in 1980, and the "Environmental Education Development Plan (Draft)" was included in the national education plan. By 1990, the National Education Commission proposed that environmental education should be merged in elective courses and extracurricular activities for high school students. In 1993, environmental education was included in the teaching materials for compulsory education and became a permanent subject in elementary education (Hong et al. 2012). More than 40 years of environmental education have had far-reaching social influences, creating generations of citizens with increasing awareness of modern environmentalism.

In Table 17.1, the 2013 China General Social Survey data (CGSS2013) is used to compare the environmental concern, environmental knowledge, and environmental protection behaviors of respondents born in different generations. Notably, the younger generation is generally more concerned about environmental issues than the older generation, has a higher level of environmental knowledge, and is more active in environmental protection. Modern environmentalism is more popular among young people in China today. A recent study finds such intergenerational difference is typically seen between the generations born before and after the 1970s, and the introduction of environmental education in formal education can largely explain this difference (Hong 2015).

Table 17.1 Differences in Environmental concern, environmental knowledge, and environmental protection behaviors of the public for different generations (CGSS2013, *n* = 11 438)

	Focus on environmental problems (in %)	*Average score for environmental knowledge (out of 10)*	*Average score for environmental protection behavior (Out of 30)*
Born before 1950	10.1	3.48	14.40
Born in 1950s	13.4	4.11	14.87
Born in 1960s	15.0	4.45	15.02
Born in 1970s	17.9	5.27	15.52
Born in 1980s	17.8	5.82	15.91
Born in 1990s	21.8	6.64	16.04

Note (1) The variable "Proportion of Concerns about 'Environmental problems'" is constructed according to Question B10 in the CGSS2010 survey, and the statistics here represent the proportion of the public who listed environmental problems as one of the top three social issues; (2) Environmental Knowledge: The variable "average score" is constructed according to the cumulative sum of the item scores for the ten-item environmental knowledge scale in question B25 in the CGSS2010 survey. Each correct answer is scored as 1 point; otherwise, it is scored as 0 points. The ten-item environmental behavior scale assigns "never", "occasionally", and "often" a score of 1 point, 2 points, and 3 points, respectively, and the average is also constructed from the cumulative sums of respondents

All in all, the popularization of environmental education has had a far-reaching effect on the public, as can be seen from their greater concern about environmental issues and increasing enthusiasm in environment-related actions. Education is one of the motivating forces. with which modern environmentalism became popular in China.

17.3.3 *The Development of the Mass Media Has Brought Both Opportunities and Challenges to the Spread of Modern Environmentalism in China*

Another channel of the spread of modern environmentalism is the mass media. Remarking on the increasing infiltration of media in cultural life, especially visual media, British sociologist John Thompson says that the visualization or symbolization of cultural information as a result of the rapid development of media and network technology has not only changed the forms and ways that ideologies are disseminated but also triggered the profound transformation of contemporary social life

(Thompson 2012). The rapid development and wide application of modern media and tools of communication such as the internet, digital technology, film, and television have significantly sped up the spread of environmentalism in China and around the world.

Specifically, the mass media has been promoting the spread of modern environmentalism in China mainly in the following three ways. First, with vivid images, visual media awaken the public's aesthetic experience of the natural environment more easily and inspires the pursuit of the harmonious coexistence of man and nature. For example, since its launch in 1994, China Central Television (CCTV)'s "Man and Nature" series have been organized around "eulogizing life and paying attention to the environment", focusing on "introducing animals and plants and knowledge of nature, exploring the interaction between man and nature, and exploring effective methods for sustainable development of society, economy and ecology". This program has won a wide audience all over China. Second, environmental problems can be presented to the public in an immediately visible form, further enhancing public awareness of environment-related issues. The actual hazard of environmental problems, for example, were recorded in images, like "smog photography" by people from different parts of the country, and presented directly to people online. At the same time, satellite images of environmental problems such as the ozone holes and global climate changes that cannot be immediately seen with the naked eye, are circulated on the internet and accessible to general public. These programs allow the audience to grasp the reality and seriousness of abstract environmental problems and encourage them to consider their role in combating the problems. In 2014, photos of "skinny polar bears" published on the internet and in print media around the world caused public concern and discussions about its possible "killer"—namely global climate change—across China. Third, the mass media provide a platform on which environmentalists can publicize ideas about environmental protection and carry out dialogues with people having different notions. In the process, the influence of modern environmentalism has been further enhanced.

17.3.4 *The Awakening of Public Environmental Awareness Has Contributed to the Development of Modern Environmentalism in China*

As is visible in the results of national surveys at different points in time, the environmental awareness of the Chinese public has been growing steadily. A National Environmental Awareness Survey conducted in 1995 by the China Environmental Protection Foundation showed that the average environmental awareness score of the Chinese public at that time was only 44.13 points out of 100, with the lowest and highest scores were 2 points and 87 points respectively with a standard deviation of 12.86. As a whole, public environmental awareness was below the passing mark (60 points). When asked "Do you know what environmental protection is?" 23.6% of the participants answered "don't know"; responses of "a little" and "some" accounted for 66.9% and 16.1% respectively, and only 0.5% of the participants thought they had "a lot" of knowledge about environmental protection. In the CGSS2003 and CGSS2010 survey projects, the same internationally popular environmental awareness scale (the NEP scale proposed by Dunlap et al.) was used to measure the level of public environmental awareness. The data analysis shows that the level of public environmental awareness reflected in CGSS2010 was higher than that reflected in CGSS2003 with both overall measurements and urban residents only. CGSS2003 conducted a sampling survey with urban residents only, and the overall environmental awareness level of the participants was found to be above the passing mark, with an average score of 61.24 points out of 100. The lowest and highest scores were 13.33 points and 100 points respectively, with a standard deviation of 12.07. The level of environmental awareness among urban residents measured by CGSS2010 was 70.7 points (with a standard deviation of 9.7), which is more than 9 points higher than that in 2003. The total environmental awareness of both urban and rural residents measured by CGSS2010 was 68.7 points (with a standard deviation of 9.6), and the average score of rural residents was 65.3 points (with a standard deviation of 8.31), both of which are higher than that of urban residents measured in 2003 (Hong 2014). If we take into account the continuous increase in the number of public environmental complaints, protests, and the number of environmental protection organizations over the years, as well as public participation in various environmental protection policymaking processes and the substantial increase in the frequency of environment-related news reports, there are good reasons to believe that the level of environmental awareness of the Chinese public is rising.

The awakening of public awareness of the environment means that more and more people are concerned about environmental issues, which is itself a manifestation of the development of modern environmentalism. In addition, the increase in public attention to environmental issues has further promoted the development of modern environmentalism, which is an important factor driving integration with the political governance ideology of the Chinese government. Notably, the institutionalization of modern environmentalism is an indication of a positive response of the Chinese government to the growing demand of the public for increased environmental quality.

17.3.5 The Globalization of Environmentalism Created Part of the Conditions for the Development of Modern Environmentalism in China

Modern environmentalism is a global phenomenon. There are three main reasons for this. First, environmental problems are becoming increasingly global in nature. This is because the earth's environmental system is extremely complex, interrelated beyond national boundaries. Coupled with the increasing economic globalization, local environmental problems will eventually cause global impacts in one way or another. Global climate change, holes in the ozone layer, and other environmental issues are some best examples of the global nature of environmental problems. Second, international cooperation in the global environmental protection community has been highly frequent if not routine. Due to the global nature of environmental problems, their solutions naturally require close cooperation and joint efforts between various countries and regions. For that reason, a series of international environmental protection conferences (such as the Conference on Climate Change) have been jointly held by governments in recent years. The Chinese government attended various international conferences and responded actively to conference decisions since the First International Environmental Protection Conference. At the same time, environmental cooperation among countries at the non-governmental level has risen, as can be seen from the increased number of international organizations for environmental protection. Influential international organizations such as Greenpeace and the WWF have established offices or liaisons in China since the mid-1990s. Third, environmental concern has been shared worldwide. The results of a global survey show that since the 1990s, environmental concern is no longer peculiar to developed countries, and developing countries have shown similar levels of concern for environmental issues (Dunlap and Mertig 1997; Hong, Fan 2013).

The popularity of modern environmentalism around the world has not only created good external conditions for the development of modern environmentalism in China but also greatly promoted the dialogue of environmentalism between China and other countries in the world.

17.4 Trends and Constraints of Modern Environmentalism in China

As an ideology changes across different times and spaces due to changes in the underlying social context, its degree of influence will also change. In the United States, after more than half a century's development, modern environmentalism has gradually moderated. Generally speaking, modern environmentalism has not been particularly successful in many countries, including the United States. First, ecological and environmental issues have not been properly resolved, and second, their influence in the policy field remains very limited (Harper 2012). According to the American journalists Michael Shellenbergr and Ted Nordhaus in a 2004 conference article titled "The Death of Environmentalism", modern environmentalism had lost its vitality in modern society, which caused great repercussions in American society. In their eyes, despite decades of mobilization and substantial investments, environmentalist movements have not achieved much. In the United States, the environmentalist movements were represented only by special interest groups who speak in an elitist technocratic language. They failed to develop a public vision or strategy for reform, and more importantly, the movements seemed seriously incongruous with mainstream social values in the United States. While this view has itself been much criticized for being too harsh (Brulle and Jenkins 2006), a critique like this may reminds one to think again about the trends of development and degree of influence of modern environmentalism in China.

Since the 1970s, the development of China's modern environmental protection movement has made remarkable achievements. As has been indicated above, at the national level, China's environmental protection laws, policies, and regulations have been established and improved step-by-step. Environmental education has become an important part of national education at different stages, and environmental protection has been established as part of national policies. In the meantime, the disadvantages of the crude mode of economic growth characterized by high consumption of natural resources have become increasingly apparent, and ideas of green development such as sustainable development, scientific development, and low-carbon economy have become the consensus. Non-governmental environmental organizations are rapidly increasing in number. By the end of 2017, there were as many as 6000 registered ecological and environmental organizations and 501 private non-business bodies nationwide. At the same time, the results of national surveys in different years show that the level of environmental awareness and knowledge among the Chinese public has been growing steadily over the past few decades (Hong 2014). All this shows that modern environmentalism has become a rising social force in contemporary China. Compared with the social influence of modern environmentalism in other countries, the influence and momentum of environmental protection in contemporary China appears stronger, and it is leading to profound changes in China.

Although modern environmentalism has developed into an important part of the mainstream ideology in contemporary China, it has still to deal with the following constraints.

First, there is still tension or even opposition between China's modern environmentalism and other parts of the mainstream ideology and other ideologies. At present, China is still in the early stage of socialism, and the central task is still to liberate and develop productive forces to meet people's growing material and cultural needs. Generally, China is still in the middle stage of industrialization and urbanization, and the mode of development in government policy continues to emphasize high-speed, high-input production with inadequate consideration of environmental costs. This mode of production necessarily leads to the contradiction between economic and social development, and environmental protection will remain a difficult task for some time. The government is often faced with the predicament of balancing between them. Moreover, modern environmentalism is challenged by other ideologies. Some people describe environmentalism as an imperialist conspiracy that threatens the ideological security of contemporary China; others characterize environmentalism as a questionable trend of thought, arguing that the development of environmentalism will hinder China's social progress. Although the above anti-environmentalist views represent only nonmainstream—and often individual—voices, they prove a test of the capability of environmentalism as a mainstream ideology to accommodate and neutralize critiques.

Second, there are still some deficiencies in the institutionalization of China's modern environmentalism in practice. The first problem is the lax enforcement of environmental laws. As a result, environmentalism falls short in practice. The second is the lack of an effective channel for the public to participate in environment-related initiatives. Establishing an effective mechanism for public participation is extremely significant for promoting dialogues and the integration of environmentalism at the government and non-governmental levels. Since the start of the twenty-first century, environmental protests have occurred one after another across the country, which to a certain extent reflects the urgent desire of China's non-governmental environmental groups to express their demands through effective channels. Finally, it is imperative to establish a system for ecological compensation. Ecological compensation can make up for the long-existing structural absence in China's environment policies that focuses on the prevention and control of pollution. Ecological compensation directly accounts for the ecological and environmental damages in the country's important ecological functional areas, watersheds, and regions of mineral resource development. In addition, the goal of modern environmentalism is to encourage more people to join in environmental protection. Experience from other countries have shown that, as an incentive, the establishment and implementation of ecological compensation is highly significant for raising funds, improving public enthusiasm for environmental protection, and promoting social equity.

Third, modern environmentalist practices in China have been faced with high costs. The first economic costs. Although economic development and environmental protection are not necessarily opposing goals, adopting environment-friendly modes of development means changing the current extensive mode of economic growth, which will inevitably lead to economic slowdown and more expenditures on environmental protection in the short term. As far as the individuals are concerned, a green lifestyle will lead to increased costs of living. The second, the costs of time. Most environmental problems result from the long-term cumulative impact of human activities, and can rarely be solved overnight. Many will require joint efforts over decades or even generations. The third is social costs. The solution to environmental problems requires the transformation of the social system. In addition to the transformation of the economic growth mode, environmental solutions also include the strengthening of basic scientific research on environmental protection, the innovation of environmental protection systems, and the mobilization of society at large to engage in environmental protection. Therefore, it will also bring corresponding social costs.

CHAPTER 18

The Rise of the Green Society

Hong Dayong

The previous analysis shows that under the background of evolving environmental problems and the development of environmental governance, an important social trend in contemporary China is to move toward a green society. This chapter aims to analyze how social development in China since the beginning of Reform and Opening-up has incorporated environmental factors and gradually moved toward a green society. Green society here refers to a social process and state in which human beings, on the basis of understanding the interaction between society and environment, intentionally promote social changes to seek coordination between society and environment. This is an important aspect of contemporary social development in China and has the important connotations of dispersion and permeability.

In fact, since the beginning of humanity, the relationship between human beings and the environment has embraced both opposition and unity. On the one hand, obtaining resources from the environment is fundamental for human survival and development, and human production and living activities always have a certain environmental impact,

D. Hong (✉)
Renmin University of China, Beijing, China
e-mail: hongdy@ruc.edu.cn

D. Hong and Y. Fan (eds.), *Toward a Green Society*,
https://doi.org/10.1007/978-981-96-5111-5_18

including the consumption of resources, the decline and destruction of the environment. On the other hand, excessive resource exploitation and environmental destruction will eventually affect the survival and development of human beings. At different stages of productivity and under different social systems, human beings will incorporate specific environmental factors into various acts of social construction and strive to seek harmony between human society and the environment depending on the understanding of their relationship with the environment. In this sense, social construction has always had an environmental dimension, and the only difference is its historical stages. This phase-based difference is reflected in the recognition of environmental conditions and their impact on different stages of social development. It is also shown in the breadth, depth, and intensity of environmental factors incorporated into social construction.

18.1 Social Construction: From Developing the Environment to Protecting the Environment

Since ensuring and improving the people's livelihood has been the focus of social construction, the primary task at the beginning of the reform period was to eliminate poverty and improve the living standards. In 1978, China's per capita GDP was only 385 Yuan (RMB), ranking very low in the world. According to the current poverty standard, 97.5% of the rural population were living under the poverty line at that time, lacking food and clothing. Under such circumstances, it was imperative to transform the resources quickly and efficiently in the environment into goods and services on a large scale to eliminate poverty and generate wealth. Therefore, the development and utilization of the environment was a major focus of social action.

The Poverty of Abundance (Wang and Bai, 1986) was an influential book at that time. The book discusses the reasons why western China lagged its eastern counterparts and explores the routes out of poverty. Its core viewpoint lies in improving the quality of human resources, reforming social infrastructure, and adjusting how environmental resources can be used. The authors point out that despite the astonishingly rich resources in the west, "with which anything would seem achievable once attempted, people have generally failed wherever they attempted" (ibid.: 40). This happened because "the traditional socio-economic structure and people's inability of commodity production made it hard to effectively develop and utilize various resources to create more social wealth; at the same time, inefficient resource exploitation and a shortage of skilled labor have hindered the development of the social infrastructure, hence a vicious cycle of weak social system and poverty formed" (ibid.: 92). The authors believe that agriculture and animal husbandry are the sources of poverty and backwardness in the western region of China. As they state, "In terms of the relationship between human production and natural resources, the modern mode of production is manifested in multilevel three-dimensional development and multiple utilization of natural resources" (ibid.: 217–218). Therefore, it is necessary to change people's concept of development and create new modes of production and lifestyles, and develop environmental resources following the laws of the commodity economy to eliminate poverty. Although this book focuses on the western region, it is a valuable account of China's development broadly. Their views on the relationship between human beings and environmental resources represent the initial stages of the reform.

Indeed, marketization, industrialization, and urbanization have transformed social development and the utilization of resources, promoted economic growth, and improved living standards. Since the reform began, the achievements in anti-poverty and economic growth have benefited the entire nation and have attracted worldwide attention. However, we have also observed that in the progress of the reform period, the voices for protecting and improving the environment have become stronger than those for exploiting environmental resources. In 1983, environmental protection became a national policy in China, and later in 1995, it was adopted as a sustainable development strategy. Furthermore, at a symposium on population, resources, and the environment in March 2005, the Central Committee of the Communist Party of China (CPC) proposed to build an environment-friendly society. The Fifth Plenary Session of the 16th CPC Central Committee held in October of that year further clarified the goal of "Building a Resource-Saving and Environment-Friendly Society". In 2007, the 17th National Congress of the Communist Party of China proposed "Building an Ecological Civilization". Along the same lines, in 2012, the 18th National Congress of the Communist Party of China proposed that human and nature are a community of life, and humans must respect, conform to, and protect nature. Only by following the laws of nature can human being effectively prevent detours in the development and utilization of nature. The country must adhere to the policy of prioritizing conservation, protection, and natural restoration and form a spatial pattern of development, industrial structure, production mode, and lifestyle that conserve resources and protect the environment. The original tranquility, harmony, and beauty of nature should be restored. It is necessary to prioritize the construction of an ecological civilization and integrate it into the whole process of economic, political, cultural, and social development. The goal is to build a beautiful China that achieves sustainable development of the nation. In 2017 the 19th National Congress of the Communist Party of China further clearly defined pollution prevention and control as one of the three tough battles to fight during the period of building a well-off society in an all-round way.

Particularly, The General Secretary Xi Jinping gave a series of important lectures on environmental protection, and vividly and profoundly expound the connotations of environmental protection in social development. These ideas are reflected in some quotes from his lectures, including "there is no replacement for the ecological environment; if we do not value it when we use it, we will lose it and will not survive without it", "ecological prosperity leads to the prosperity of the civilization, while ecological destruction leads to the decline of the civilization", "we should protect the ecological environment as if it were eyes and cherish it as if it were our own life", "protecting the ecological environment means protecting productivity, and improving the ecological environment means developing productivity", and "lucid waters and lush mountains are invaluable assets".[1] Under the leadership of the Central Party Committee with Comrade Xi Jinping at its core, China has accelerated top-level designs for ecological civilization and the construction of institutional systems that focus on environmental protection following the 18th National Congress of the Communist Party of China. It also adopted the strictest systems under the rule of law, while accelerating innovation, strengthening implementation, and developing a series of fundamental, pioneering, and long-term work. Ecological environmental

[1] Xing Yuhao. The Prosperity of Ecology Leads to the Prosperity of Civilization: A Review of the Construction of Ecological Civilization Promoted by the Party Central Committee with Comrade Xi Jinping at the Core since the 18th National Congress. (2017-06-19) [2019-07-22]. http://www.qstheory.cn/zoology/2017-06/19/c_1121167567.htm.

governance has embarked on the fast track to treat both symptoms and root causes of environmental degradation, marking a historic and overall turning point. As a result, environmental factors are integrated into the process of social development in a new sense and promote a profound transformation of society itself.

18.2 Main Endogenous Drivers of Social Transformation

If the beginning of China's environmental protection practices was influenced, to a certain extent, by the wave of international environmental movements, then our current ongoing and in-depth promotion of environmental protection and the strengthening of an ecological civilization reflect more conscious efforts to respond to the needs of domestic development. In contrast to the regression of environmental protection in many developed countries and the resulting countermovement against global environmental protection, the greening of our society highlights its independence and autonomy from external trends and forces. In this case, what is the endogenous power that promotes the green transformation of our society? Some comprehensive, multi-level, and multitype forces are involved, and the following five are the most significant forces.

First, the conflict between economic development and the environment has become increasingly acute, and the quality of the environment has been facing serious threats. After decades of traditional high-speed growth at the cost of the ecological environment, the consumption of resources and the destruction of the environment in China have been very serious. In 2012, China produced 11.5% of the worlds' economic but consumed 21.3% of the world's energy, 45% of steel, 43% of copper, and 54% of cement, and the total amount of sulfur dioxide and nitrogen oxide discharged ranked first in the world (Dong et al., 2017). In 1985, China's wastewater discharge was only 34.1542 billion tons and it has been consistently rising ever since, reaching 71.10954 billion tons in 2016. Sulfur dioxide emission was 13.25 million tons in 1985 but climbed gradually and peaked at 25.888 million tons in 2006 and declined gradually to 11.028643 million tons in 2016 (see Fig. 18.1).

According to the China Ecological Environment Bulletin issued by the Ministry of Ecology and the Environment in 2017, among the 338 cities at the prefecture level and above, only 99 cities have reached the standards for ambient air quality, accounting for 29.3% of all cities. Two hundred

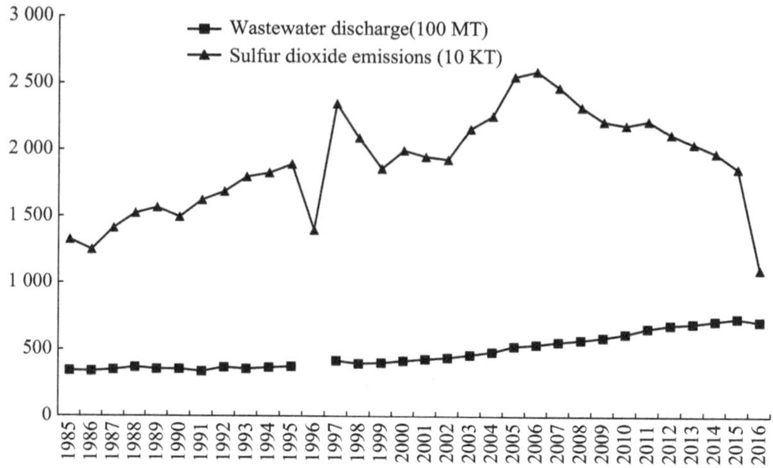

Fig. 18.1 National wastewater and sulfur dioxide emission trends from 1985 to 2016 (*Sources* Wastewater data were missing in 1996, and the data for other years came from the "China Statistical Yearbook" from 1985 to 1989, the "China Environmental Status Bulletin" from 1990 to 1994, the "National Environmental Statistical Bulletin" from 1995, and the "China Environmental Statistics Bulletin" from 1997 to 1998. The Environmental Status Bulletin from 1999 to 2015, the National Environmental Statistical Bulletin, and the 2016 data published on the website of the National Bureau of Statistics (http://data.stats.gov.cn/easyquery.htm?cn=C01) provide the remainder of the data, among which data from 1990 to 1995 do not include township industries. Sulfur dioxide data come from the "China Statistical Yearbook" from 1985 to 1989, the "China Environmental Status Bulletin" from 1990 to 1994, the "National Environmental Statistical Bulletin" from 1995 to 2015, and the 2016 data published on the website of the National Bureau of Statistics (). The data from 1990 to 1996 do not include township industries, and the data in 1996 are labeled "industrial sulfur dioxide emissions")

and thirty-nine cities did not meet the standards for ambient air quality, accounting for 70.7% of all cities. Among the 112 important lakes (reservoirs) in China, 6 of them have Grade I water quality, 5.4% of the total population; 27 (24.1%) have Grade II water quality; 37 (33.0%) have Grade III; 22 (19.6%) have Grade IV; 8 (7.1%) have Grade V; and 12 (10.7%) have poorer than class V. The monitoring of groundwater quality shows that he sites with excellent, good, better, poor, and extremely poor water quality accounted for 8.8%, 23.1%, 1.5%, 51.8%, and 14.8% of the total population, respectively. In addition to serious issues in air and water, there are other types of serious pollution, such as solid wastes and soil contamination, ecological damage is also a major concern. Among the 2,591 counties in China, only 42.0% of the country's land area can be classified as "excellent" and "good", 24.5% classified as "average", 33.5% classified as "below average" and "poor". The threat to food and drug safety, and health issues caused by declines in environmental quality is also becoming increasingly serious. These are the basic conditions and important driving forces for restructuring our society.

Second, People's needs have changed significantly. One of the most prominent achievements in social development since the reform period is the substantial improvement in the living standards of all people, meeting their basic needs and solving problems in food and clothing. Overall, the development has resulted in a well-off society. According to current rural poverty standards, the percentage of those in poverty in the rural population has dropped from 97.5% in 1978 to 3.1% in 2017. Moreover, a minimum living guarantee system has been established in both urban and rural areas throughout the country to meet the basic living needs of all people. In 2017, the disposable per capita income of all residents reached 25,974 Yuan (RMB). In 1978, the Engel coefficients of urban and rural residents were 57.5% and 67.7% respectively. However, in 2017, the overall average of the Engel coefficients of all residents dropped to 29.3%, meeting the United Nations' standard of affluence. More importantly, Chinese residents' assets have increased, and their ability to withstand risk has improved. For example, the total household deposits increased from 21.1 billion yuan in 1978 to 62.6 trillion Yuan in 2017. Consequently, people can pursue more extensive and diverse lives, and the level of needs is constantly improving, and they prioritize safety, comfort, and sustainability. Eating safe food, drinking clean water, breathing unpolluted air, enjoying a comfortable environment, and living a sustainable life have increasingly become basic needs. As a result, the public is more and more concerned about environmental quality, and environmental issues have become one of the most important and familiar issues to the general public and the media. In 1995, Dayong Hong organized a national environmental awareness survey. According to the survey, 23.6% of the respondents said that they were "not aware" of the concept of environmental protection. 16.5% of the people responded that their environmental protection knowledge was "very limited", 66.9% responded that they had "limited" awareness, 16.1% thought that they had "moderate" awareness, and only 0.5% of people responded that they had "a lot" of environmental protection knowledge. At the same time, most urban and rural residents lacked an understanding of the policies and regulations related to environmental protection. Only 31.8% of respondents thought they "know it well" or "know of", among which only 0.5% think they "know a lot"; 42% thought they "have only heard of it", and 26.2% had not heard of policies and regulations at all. However, according to the data from the 2010 China General Social Survey that Hong co-designed, 70% of respondents realized that China's environmental problems are "very serious" or "relatively serious", 65.7% of respondents said they were "very concerned" or "relatively concerned" about environmental issues, and only 3.1% said they were "not at all concerned" (Hong, 2014).

Third, social tensions and conflicts caused by environmental damage (risk) are becoming increasingly obvious. Easing social relations and resolving social conflicts is an important implication of social construction. During the social transformation period, labor disputes, land requisition and demolition, social security and so on were the main causes of social contradictions and conflicts. With the improvement of people's living standards and the awakening of awareness of environmental rights and interests, actual environmental damage and possible environmental risks have also become an important cause of aggravating social contradictions and conflicts, and promoting the green transformation of society has become an internal need to promote social harmony. From the data released by the state, over a period of time, the number of people and groups of petitioners due to environmental pollution have shown an upward trend. In 1987, 77,673 people filed petitions regarding environmental pollution. Iin 2000, the number reached 139,424. Statistics could not be found for 2001–2011, but there were still 104,323 petitioners in 2015 (see Fig. 18.2).

Since the start of twenty-first century, some major environmental mass incidents have involved tens of thousands of people, with wide-ranging impact and drawing widespread attention. Examples include the PX incident in Xiamen, Fujian Province in 2007, the cadmium pollution incident in Liuyang, Hunan Province in 2009, the "blood lead" incident in Fengxiang, Shaanxi Province, the Panyu waste incineration power plant construction incident in Guangdong Province, the PX incident in Dalian, Liaoning Province in 2011, the PC project incident in Tianjin in 2012, the Qidong Japanese Prince Paper Group incident in

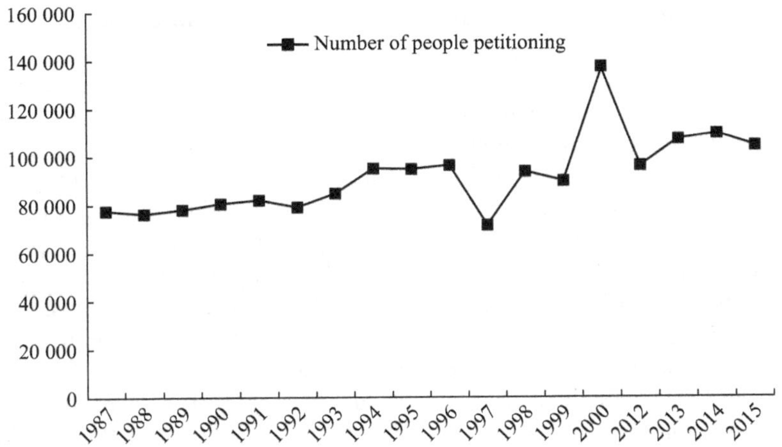

Fig. 18.2 Number of people petitioning for pollution in China (*Source* China Statistical Yearbook, 1987–1996. National Bulletin of Environmental Statistics, 1997–2000 and 2012–2015)

Jiangsu Province, and the Hongda Molybdenum Copper Co., LTD incident in Shifang, Sichuan. Some of these events triggered protests and conflicts during the Environmental Impact Assessment (EIA) phase of the project, such as the Qidong incident in Jiangsu Province, while others sparked clashes during the construction of the project, and others sparked clashes after the project was completed and operational, including the Dalian PX incident. Studies have shown that during the decade from 2003 to 2012, there were 230 large-scale environmental mass incidents disclosed by the media, which showed a significant increase year by year in number, reaching 58 in 2011 (Zhang Ping and Yang Zuchan, 2015). This situation is also confirmed by the statements of environmental protection department leaders and contrasts with the decline in other forms of conflict. Zhou Shengxian, former Minister of Environmental Protection, is reported to have pointed out that "while the overall number of mass incidents in China has decreased, the number of mass incidents caused by environmental problems has increased by more than 30 percent every year".[2]

Fourth, the focus of the Party and the government's work is adjusted, and the initiative has been taken. The system of socialism with Chinese characteristics is the fundamental system of our country. The most essential feature of socialism with Chinese characteristics is the leadership of the Communist Party of China. The Party adheres to the principal position of the people, practices the fundamental purpose of serving the people wholeheartedly, takes the people's aspiration for a better life as its goal, and constantly adjusts the direction and focus of its work considering changes in the principal contradictions facing society. At the beginning of the Reform and Opening-up period, faced with the low level of productivity and widespread poverty, it was an inevitable priority to accelerate the liberation and development of productivity, increasing the development and utilization of resources and the environment, and adhering to economic development as the goal. Even in this case, the Party and the government are still concerned about environmental protection, and while promoting economic development, they continue to strengthen the construction of environmental protection teams, institutions and systems, and enhance environmental protection forces (see Fig. 18.3).

Since the beginning of the twenty-first century, specifically since the 18th National Congress of the Communist Party, the Central Committee has made an in-depth analysis of the changing trend of the principal conflict in society, and clearly pointed out in the report of the 19th National Congress of the Party: "Socialism with Chinese characteristics has entered a new era, the principal conflict in Chinese society has been transformed into the conflict between unbalanced and inadequate development and the people's ever-growing needs for a better life. China has steadily solved the problem of food and clothing for more than a billion people, and overall achieved a moderately prosperous society, and will soon complete the building of a moderately prosperous society in all respects. The public's needs for a better life are increasingly extensive. They not only put forward higher requirements for material and cultural life, but also have growing demands for democracy, rule of law, fairness, justice, security and the environment. At the same time, the level of

[2] The rise of China needs to cross the "environmental protection door", and the incident of environmental protection groups is heavy. (2009-08-28) [2019-07-22]. http://news.sohu.com/20090828/n266295203.shtml.

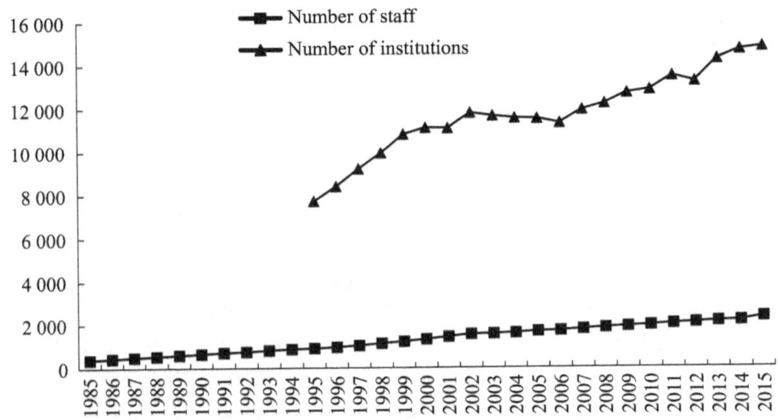

Fig. 18.3 The development trend of personnel and institutions in China's environmental protection system from 1985 to 2015 (*Source* China Statistical Yearbook, 1985–1996; National Environmental Statistical Bulletin, 1995–2015; National Statistical Yearbook of the Environment, 1996–2015)

productivity has improved significantly, and China's productive capacity has become one of the highest in the world in many aspects. A more prominent problem is unbalanced and inadequate development, which has become a major constraint on meeting the people's ever-growing needs for a better life".[3]

The Third Plenary Session of the 18th CPC Central Committee pointed out that it is necessary to establish a systematic and complete ecological civilization system, implement the strictest source protection system, damage compensation system, accountability system, improve the environmental governance and ecological restoration system, and use the system to protect the ecological environment. Since 2015, the construction of China's ecological civilization system has notably entered a rapid and substantial stage of advancement. Following the formal implementation of the new "strictest in history" environmental protection law

[3] Xi Jinping. Decisive Victory in Building a Moderately Prosperous Society in all Respects and Achieving the Great Victory of Socialism with Chinese Characteristics for a New Era: Report at the 19th National Congress of the Communist Party of China. (2017-10-27) [2019-07-22)]. http://www.xinhuanet.com/2017-10/27/c_1121867529.htm.

in January 2015, a series of important documents, such as the Opinions on Accelerating the Advancement of the Construction of Ecological Civilization, Measures for Public Participation in Environmental Protection, Environmental Protection Supervision Program (Trial), Measures for the Responsibility of Leading Cadres of Party and Government for Damages to the Ecology and Environment (Trial), the Overall Program for the Reform of Ecological Civilization Institution, Guidance on the Pilot Reform of the Vertical Management System for Monitoring, Supervision and Law Enforcement of Environmental Protection Institutions Below Provinces, Action Plan for the Prevention and Control of Air Pollution, Action Plan for the Prevention and Control of Water Pollution, Action Plan for the Prevention and Control of Soil Pollution, Reform Plan for the System of Reimbursement of Ecological Damage to the Environment and Opinions on the Delimitation of the Ecological Red Line and Strictly Observing were issued one after another. The construction of an ecological civilization has also been incorporated into the Thirteenth Five-Year Plan. In particular, the environmental protection inspection mechanism established based on the "Environmental Protection Inspection Program (Trial)" has achieved full coverage of the first round of central environmental protection inspectors. According to the data of the 2017 China Ecological Environment Status Bulletin released by the Ministry of Ecology and Environment, the inspectors held more than 18,000 party and government leaders accountable during the period of inspection, 135,000 environmental reports were received from the public, and more than 80,000 environmental problems from the public were directly promoted and solved. In 2017 alone, the environmental protection supervision work interviewed 30 cities (counties, districts), departments, and units, and the country implemented 233,000 cases of administrative penalties, with fines amounting to 11.58 billion Yuan, an increase of 265% over 2014 before the implementation of the new environmental protection law. In fact, the increasingly strict and detailed system design and implementation will transmit the pressure of environmental protection from the central government to local governments, from the government to enterprises, and from the state to individuals. The green movement initiated by the Party and the government to supervise enterprises and transmit pressure is opening up the path of composite environmental governance in China (Hong, 2016). For the Party and the government, which always take the people's interests as the center, this kind of active adjustment and action has an inherent inevitability.

Fifth, enterprises have found new profit opportunities in the environmental decline, changes in people's consumption preference and the government's regulation and governance investment, showing an increasingly obvious tendency to green behavior, and accelerating the development of new industries, new business forms, new models and new products, which not only meet the new needs of society but also promote social transformation. Since Reform and Opening-up, China's investment in environmental protection has gradually increased, accounting for more than 1% of GDP in 1999 for the first time and accounted for 3.5% during the "Twelfth Five-Year Plan" period, which directly promoted the rapid development of environmental protection industry. In 2000, the annual output value of the environmental protection industry reached 108 billion Yuan, and by 2010, it had reached 1.1 trillion Yuan.[4]

In addition to the environmental protection industry, in other types of enterprises, resource-based enterprises that mainly develop mineral resources and provide mineral products and primary products for the society have an important position, but at the same time, they also have serious environmental impacts in the production process. In 2013, the amount of industrial solid waste produced by resource-based enterprises, the total amount of industrial wastewater discharged, and the amount of industrial waste gas discharged accounted for 97.1%, 77.7%, and 92.4% of all industrial emissions, respectively. However, recent studies have shown that the green behavior of resource-based enterprises has become noticeable, although there are still some deficiencies. For example, 84.5% of the resource-based enterprises in the survey have incorporated environmental protection into their corporate target system, 80.4% pay attention to their corporate environmental image, 70.3% carry out regular training for their employees on environmental awareness and environmental management skills, 69.4% of their employees are able to actively participate in practical activities on corporate environmental management, 83.5% consider energy conservation and recycling when designing production, 77.6% give priority to renewable and easy-to-recycle materials when choosing production materials, 79.4% adopt environmentally friendly production processes, and 80.4% adopt material and waste recycling systems (Xie

[4] The annual growth rate of the environmental protection industry may exceed 20%, with a total investment of 17 trillion yuan. (2015-11-02) [2019-07].

et al., 2015). These signs indicate that the greening behavior of enterprises based on profit-seeking rationality may also become an endogenous driving force for social transformation.

18.3 Achievements and the Future of the Green Society

The effect of green society construction is multifaceted, and environmental impact is one of the main aspects. Based on the perspective of environmental protection, the head of the Ministry of Ecology and Environment used five "unprecedented" to describe the profound social changes aimed at improving environmental quality since the 18th National Congress of the Party: the depth of ideological understanding is unprecedented, the intensity of pollution control is unprecedented, the frequency of system introduction is unprecedented, the standard of supervision and law enforcement is unprecedented, and the speed of environmental quality improvement is unprecedented.[5]

Indeed, relevant data show that in the five years after the 18th National Congress of the Party, environmental protection and ecological civilization construction has indeed achieved outstanding phased results. For example, China's forest coverage continued to increase, from 21.38% in 2012 to 22.3% in 2016. The average concentration of inhalable particulate matter (PM10) in 338 cities at or above the prefecture level was 22.7% lower than in 2013. The average concentration of fine particulate matter (PM2.5) in the Beijing-Tianjin-Hebei region, the Yangtze River Delta, and the Pearl River Delta dropped by 39.6%, 34.3% and 27.7%, respectively from 2013. The percentage of surface water sections rated Class I to III increased from 6% to 67.8%, and the percentage Class V sections decreased from 9.7% to 8.6%.[6] The 2017 Bulletin on the State of China's Ecological Environment summed it up this way: "The quality of the country's air and water environment has been further improved, soil environmental risks have been contained, the overall pattern of the

[5] The central environmental protection inspectors are powerful: from 2016 to 2017, they completed the full coverage of provinces in the country. (2017-11-07) [2019-07-22]. http://www.xinhuanet.com/2017-11/07/c_1121916536.htm.

[6] The central environmental protection inspectors are powerful: from 2016 to 2017, they completed the full coverage of provinces in the country. (2017-11-07) [2019-07-22]. http://www.xinhuanet.com/2017-11/07/c_1121916536.htm.

ecosystem has been stable, nuclear and radiation safety has been effectively guaranteed, and the people actually feel the positive changes in the quality of the ecological environment".

In terms of energy conservation and emission reduction, China's GDP has grown significantly faster than its total energy consumption since 2008. Since Reform and Opening-up, China's energy consumption per 10,000 Yuan of GDP has continued to decline. According to the data released by the National Bureau of Statistics, it has fallen to 0.588 tons of standard coal in 2016. During the implementation of the "Twelfth Five-Year Plan", China's carbon intensity fell by a cumulative total of 20%, exceeding the target of 17% set in the 12th Five-Year Plan.[7] Figure 18.1 above also shows that in terms of sulfur dioxide emissions, there is a continuous and accelerating downward trend after reaching a peak in 2006.

If the construction of a green society has produced some remarkable environmental improvement effects, then we should have two basic attitudes. First, we should fully realize the correctness of the direction of green society construction, unswervingly promote the green transformation of society, continue to be committed to the realization of the harmonious coexistence of man and nature, and provide more high-quality ecological products to meet the people's growing needs for a beautiful ecological environment. The second is to maintain scientific calmness, have a spirit of continuous reflection, fully understand the sudden, phased, and partial nature of the current environmental improvement effect, and fully realize the locality, process, stage, and complexity of the construction of a green society. Without comprehensive, in-depth, and sustained construction of a green society, the current effect of environmental improvement is unsustainable, and the harmonious symbiosis between man and nature is difficult to achieve or effectively maintain.

Building a green society is undoubtedly a difficult and long-term process. We believe that there are at least several reasons for this. First, relative to the evolution of the environmental system itself, human intervention and influence are still limited. Some environmental problems are complex, with both mankind and natural causes, as well as human interaction with nature. For example, we have made great efforts to

[7] The Information Office introduces the 2016 Annual Report on China's Policies and Actions to address climate change. (2016-11-01) [2019-07-22]. http://www.gov.cn/xinwen/2016-11/01/content_5127079.htm.

control air pollution, but it is still difficult to profoundly affect climate change and the earth's environmental system over a long period of time, which are often important factors that aggravate air pollution or inhibit the effectiveness of air pollution control. It can be said that our current understanding of the earth and even the laws of the evolution of the cosmic system is still very limited, and we need to respect nature more consciously, protect nature, and follow the laws of nature. Second, compared with air pollution and water pollution, which are highly visible, fluid, and have clear causes of pollution, some pollution with low visibility, easy solidification, and complex causes are often easily ignored, due to its continuous accumulation, extreme complexity, and lagging social impact. This type of pollution is also more difficult to control, such as soil pollution, genetic pollution, biodiversity losses, etc. In fact, such pollution may continue to pose deeper and more comprehensive threats to human health and our current response to these aspects is weak. Third, in social transformation, the current focus is on strengthening environmental protection from the sphere of the State while readjusting the structure of the economy and industry. This is a very difficult task, especially since sustained transformation requires consideration of the objective challenges it faces. In contrast it is more difficult and difficult to achieve quick results by adjusting the way of life, guiding the public's behavior, and building the consensus of society as a whole. Our current efforts in this area are still insufficient, and effective measures are still very limited. Fourth, compared with constructing the system, the implementation of the system is more complex and difficult, specifically the internalization of the system into the conscious behavior and habits of social members is a long-term and complex process. Even so, there will be distortions, conflicts, and repetitions, which is what we need to pay special attention to, and it is also an important aspect that we fully discern the wisdom of sociology, psychology, and other social sciences. We need to pay more attention to the greening of the people's daily life practice, reconstruct the infrastructure in daily life more carefully, reconstruct the opportunities and spaces in daily life, and set up convenient and effective daily life guidance, to promote the construction of deep and essential green society. Otherwise, superficial changes in society will be delayed, malfunction and even subverted for deep reasons. Fifth, although the principal conflicts in our society have changed, the basic national condition that we are still in the primary stage of socialism and will remain so for a long time to come has not changed. Neither has China's international status as the world's largest developing country changed. Therefore, conflict between economic development and the environment is still long term, and we still need to balance economic development and environmental protection and achieve higher-quality economic development in promoting environmental protection. In particular, considering the imbalance of China's development, the development gap between urban and rural areas, between regions, and between groups is relatively large, and the social value is diversified, so the green society construction process will also face more prominent environmental equity problems. Facing up to and properly dealing with the issue of environmental equity will increase the endogenous impetus of the construction of a green society. Ignoring and failing to deal with this problem will undermine the green consensus and increase the internal resistance to the construction of a green society.

Therefore, the current construction of China's green society can only be said to be the beginning of the dawn, and the future has a long way to go. A truly green society requires not only the formation of a wide range of dominant green consensus, scientific, comprehensive, systematic, and detailed institutional arrangements, but also rigorous and effective routine system implementation practices. Also needed are the development of appropriate technical means and the dissemination of knowledge and information, a wide range of active green social organizations and green social activities, and the systematic restructuring and reconstruction of public daily life practices. In an era of globalization, the regional green society construction will also be affected by the external social environment, and it is necessary to carry out effective interaction and coordination with external society. Under the current development trend, the ultimate green society must be global, which requires profound and coordinated changes in the global society, and requires people all over the world to truly respect nature and cherish the community with a shared future for mankind in which we live.

References

Chapter 1

Dong Jie, Li Mengru, Sun Ruodan, et al. The implementation status of China's air quality standards and comparative study with foreign standards. Environment and Sustainable Development,2015(5):87–92.
Fan Yechao. Environmental mobility: an environmental sociology agenda in the age of globalization. Sociological Review,2018(1):56–68.
Gong Wenjuan. The construction mechanism of environmental problems: cognitive differences and competing claims. Journal of China University of Geosciences (Social Sciences Edition),2011(5):33–40.
Gu Shengzu, Zheng Chao, Fang Lang. Air pollution control under the conditions of rapid urbanization and industrialization. Journal of Theory,2014(6):42–45,127.
Hannigan. Environmental Sociology: 2nd Ed. Hong Dayong, et al. Trans. Beijing: China Renmin University Press,2009.
He Hong, Wang Xinming, Wang Yuesi, et al. Causes and control of atmospheric haze. Proceedings of Chinese Academy of Sciences,2013(3):344–352.
Hong Dayong. Economic growth, environmental protection and ecological modernization: from the perspective of environmental sociology. Chinese Social Sciences,2012(9):82–99,207.
Hong Dayong. The growth and limitation of public environmental awareness. Green Leaf,2014(4):4–14.
Hong Dayong. Environmental Sociology: Facts, theories and values. Ideological Front,2017(1):78–92.
Hong Dayong, Fan Yechao. In the face of haze: how to see, how to do. Chinese Journal of Science,2014–06–06(7).

D. Hong and Y. Fan (eds.), *Toward a Green Society*,
https://doi.org/10.1007/978-981-96-5111-5

Ji Bin, Chen Zhenhua. Acid rain pollution in our country. Environmental Protection,1982(12):24–27.

Jiang Baichen, Li Zhou. Study on environmental impact and countermeasures of rural industrialization. Management World,1994(5):192–197.

Xie Shuyan, Wang Ruibin, Zheng Haohao. Analysis of acid rain status in China from 2005 to 2011. Environmental Monitoring and Early Warning, 2012(5):33–37.

Li Aizhen, Sun Chengsan, Qi Shenghui. Introduction to atmospheric environmental impact assessment. Beijing: China Ocean Press,1997.

Li Jinju, Shen Yiqin. Comparison of ambient air quality standards in China and the United States. Environmental Monitoring Management and Technology,2003(6):24–26.

Li Xiaofei, Zhang Mingjun, Wang Shengjie, et al. Change characteristics and influencing factors of air pollution index in China. Environmental Science,2012(6):1936–1943.

Li Yizhong. Overview of Chinese industry. Beijing: China Machine Press,2009.

Li Zhou, Yin Xiaoqing, Bao Xiaobin. Township enterprises and environmental pollution. China Rural Observation,1999(3):3–12.

Liu Kefeng, Zhang Ying. Introduction to Environmental science. Beijing: China Forestry Publishing House,2012.

Lu Shuhua. Sociological research on urban ecological environment: Environmental pollution and residents' location distribution in Benxi City. Sociological Research,1994(6):22–40.

Qian Jinping. Introduction to Environmental Science. Beijing: China Environmental Science Press, 2011.

Qu Geping. Summary of the development of environmental protection in China. Trends in Environmental Science,1988(6):1–8,14.

Qu Geping. Review and Prospect of environmental protection in China. Journal of China Executive Academy of Environmental Management,1999(3):1–6.

Qu Geping, Peng Jinxin. Environmental Awakening: Human Environment Conference and China's first Environmental Protection Conference. Beijing: China Environmental Science Press,2010.

Department of Atmospheric Environment, Ministry of Ecology and Environment. Progress and suggestions on national air pollution prevention and control. Environmental Protection,2018(19):11–15.

Song Guojun. On Total emission Control and concentration control of pollutants in China. Environmental Protection,2000(6):11–13.

Wang Jinnan, Lei Yu, Ning Miao. The Chinese model for improving air quality: implementation and evaluation of the "Ten Atmospheric Principles". Environmental Protection,2018(2):7–11.

Wang Junxiu. Blue Book of Automobile Society: A report on the development of Automobile Society in China. Beijing: Social Sciences Academic Press,2011.

Wang Yuesi, Yao Li, Liu Zirui, et al. Air haze pollution and control strategies in Beijing-Tianjin-Hebei region. Proceedings of Chinese Academy of Sciences,2013(3):353–363.

Wang Yuesi, Zhang Junke, Wang Lili, et al. Research significance, present situation and prospect of air haze pollution in Beijing-Tianjin-Hebei region. Advances in Earth Science,2014(3):388–396.

Wu Dui, Wu Xiaojing, Li Fei, et al. Spatial and temporal variations of haze in mainland China from 1951 to 2005. Journal of Meteorology,2010(5):680–688.

Zhang Yongan, Wu Long. Characteristics and policy improvement direction of air pollution control in China from the perspective of policy combing. Environmental Protection,2010(5):48–50.

Chinese Academy of Engineering, Ministry of Environmental Protection. Research on China's environmental macro Strategy: Synthesis Report volume. Beijing: China Environmental Science Press,2011.

China Meteorological Administration. Specification for surface meteorological observation. Beijing: China Meteorological Press,2003.

Environmental health monitoring station, Chinese Academy of Medical Sciences. Global Environmental Monitoring System Air Pollution Monitoring Report of five cities in China (Discussion draft). Research Report,1983.

Bullinger M. Psychological Effects of Air Pollution on Healthy Residents:A Time-Series Approach. Journal of Environmental Psychology, 1989,9(2): 103–118.

Kelly F J, Fussell J C. Air Pollution and Public Health: Emerging Hazards and Improved Understanding of Risk. Environmental Geochemistry and Health, 2015,37(4): 631–649.

Pope III, Arden C, Burnett R T, et al. Lung Cancer, Cardiopulmonary Mortality, and Long-Term Exposure to Fine Particulate Air Pollution. JAMA, 2002,287(9): 1132–1141.

Shapiro J. Mao's War against Nature: Politics and the Environment in Revolutionary China. Cambridge: Cambridge University Press, 2001.

Chapter 2

Chen A Jiang. Sociological Explanation of water pollution: a case study of Dongcun. Journal of Nanjing Normal University (Social Science Edition),2000(10):62–69.

Chen A Jiang. From exogenous pollution to endogenous pollution: Social and cultural logic of water environment deterioration in Taihu Basin. Xuehai,2007(1):36–41.

Chen A Jiang. Separation of text norms and practice norms: An interpretative framework for industrial pollution in Taihu Basin. Xuehai,2008(4):52–59.

He Dawei. Water Environmental Management in our country: Problems and countermeasures. Science and Technology Review,1999(8):58–60.

Hong Dayong. The growth and limitation of public environmental awareness. Green Leaf,2014(4):5–14.

Jiang Ying. Interaction and integration: A sociological study on urban water pollution and treatment. Nanjing: Southeast University Press,2007.

Shi Yucheng. Normative Construction of "river chief system" model of watershed water environment governance: Based on dual perspectives of law and political system. Modern Law,2018(6):95–109.

Xu Genhong. Action logic, social causes and treatment mechanism of industrial water pollution. Journal of Hohai University (Philosophy and Social Sciences Edition),2017(4):59–64,91–92.

Yan Guodong, Kang Jiancheng, Xie Xiaojin, et al. The changing trend of public environmental awareness in China. China Population, Resources and Environment,2010(10):55–60.

Zhong Yuxiu, Liu Baoqin. Thoughts on the reform of watershed water environment management system. Water Resources Development Research,2008(7):10–14,31.

Chapter 3

Caspersen, J. K., Caspersen, R. E. Social Perspectives on Risk: Part I: Public, risk communication, and Social amplification of risk. Tong Yunzhi, trans. Beijing: China Labor and Social Security Press,2010.

Giddens. The Consequences of modernity. Tian He, trans. Nanjing: Yilin Publishing House,2000.

Cao Zuozhong, Gao Haicheng, Chen Junping, et al. Discussion on the development direction of domestic garbage disposal at present. Environmental Protection,2001(1):13–15,18.

Gong Wenjuan. Public participation and system trust in environmental risk communication. Sociological Research,2016(3):47–74,243.

Ministry of Construction. CJJ/T 102–2004 Classification and evaluation of municipal solid waste. Beijing: China Architecture and Construction Press,2004.

Hong Dayong, Gong Wenjuan. A review of the theories and methods of environmental justice research. Journal of Renmin University of China,2008(6):70–79.

Ministry of Construction, State Environmental Protection Administration, Ministry of Science and Technology. Municipal solid waste treatment and pollution control technology policy. Environmental Protection,2000(9):10–11.

Liu Ping, Tang Hongshou, Wang Rusong. Technical and economic analysis of incineration treatment of municipal refuse in China. China Population, Resources and Environment,2001(2):23–25.

Pan Yi. Garbage siege, city emergency: China's garbage disposal faces six major problems. China Environment News,2013–07–25(6).

Qu Zhiyun, Wang Jingmin, Liu Tao, et al. The choice of the treatment technology of municipal solid waste in China. Environmental Health Engineering,2006(3):58–60.

Wen Zhizhong. Discussion on the treatment and utilization of municipal garbage. China Population, Resources and Environment,1996(3):78–83.

Yu Keping. Some theoretical issues of citizen participation. Study Times,2006–12–19(5).

Zhang Chunyan. How to classify urban garbage. China Environment News,2011–08–23(8).

Arnstein S. R. A Ladder of Citizen Participation. Journal of the American Institute of Planners,1969,35(4):216–224.

Slovic P. Perceived Risk, Trust, and Democracy. Risk Analysis, 1993,13(6):675–682.

Chapter 4

Marx, Engels. The Complete Works of Marx and Engels: Volume 23. Beijing: People's Publishing House,1972.

Clark, Foster. Marxist ecology in the twenty-first century. Sun Yaoliang, compiler. Marxism and Reality (Bimonthly),2010(3):127–132.

Chen A Jiang. Sociological Explanation of water pollution: a case study of Dongcun. Journal of Nanjing Normal University (Social Science Edition),2000(1):62–69.

Chen A Jiang. From exogenous pollution to endogenous pollution: Social and cultural logic of water environment deterioration in Taihu Basin. Xuehai,2007(1):36–41.

Geng Yanhu. Three-dimensional "fracture": Sociological interpretation of environmental problems in suburban villages: a case study of Xiashi Village. Journal of China Agricultural University (Social Sciences Edition),2012(1):73–80.

Hong Dayong. China's urban-rural dual control system and environmental problems. Journal of Renmin University of China,2000a(1):62–66.

Hong Dayong. Social Transformation and Environmental Problems in contemporary China: A preliminary analysis framework. Southeast Academic,2000b(12):83–90.

Hong Dayong. Social Change and Environmental Problems: A Sociological Interpretation of environmental problems in contemporary China. Beijing: Capital Normal University Press,2001.

Hong Dayong, Ma Fangxin. Reproduction of dual social structures: a sociological analysis of non-point source pollution in rural China. Sociological Research,2004(4):1–7.

Jiang Liqiang, Jiang Lijuan. Farmer production practice and reproduction of rural environmental quality: A case study of Y village in Shandong Province. China Rural Observation,2007(5):65–72.

Li Guibao, Yin Qingming, Zhou Huaidong. Water environment problems and prevention and management of "three lakes" in China. Water Issues Forum,2001(3):36–39.

Lin Mei. Research on the implementation mechanism of environmental policy: an institutional analysis framework. Sociological Research,2003(1):102–110.

Ma Guoqing. Sociocultural view of environmental research. Sociological Research,1993(5):44–49.

Wang Yuesheng. Family responsibility system, peasant household behavior and environmental and ecological problems in agriculture. Journal of Peking University (Philosophy and Social Sciences Edition),1999(3):43–50.

Zhang Yulin. Serious integrated development mechanism and environmental conflict in rural China. Exploration and Controversy,2006(5):26–28.

Chapter 5

Bu Xuelin. Environmental Pollution Causes Annual Economic Losses of Over 500 Billion Yuan. China Environment News, 2006–09–08(1).

Deng Fei. Nearly 100 "cancer villages" in the mainland may be sacrificed. Phoenix Weekly, 2009(11):2–3.

Han Dongmei, Jin Shuqin. Analysis of China's agricultural and rural environmental protection policies. Review of Economic Research,2013(43):11–18.

Hong Chuanchun, Liu Moucheng, Li Wenhua. Evaluation of China's fertilizer input non-point source pollution control policy. Journal of Arid Land Resources and Environment,2015(4):1–6.

Hong Dayong. New thinking on China's environmental problems and the construction of ecological civilization. Exploration and Controversy,2013(10):4–10,2.

Jin Shuqin. Tracing, coping and suggestions of rural environmental pollution: a survey of rural water pollution in Hunan Province. Reference of Economic Research,2013(43):30–34.

Jin Taijun, Zhao Junfeng. Ecological analysis of the mechanism of mass incidents. Journal of Shandong University (Philosophy and Social Sciences Edition),2011(5):82–87.

Le Xiaofang, Luan Shengji, Wan Jinbo. On the innovation of China's rural environmental policy. China Environmental Management,2003(3):1–4.

Li Jinxiu, Liao Wengen, Chen Minjian, et al. Estimation of economic loss of water pollution in our country. China Water Resources,2003(21):63–66,5.

Li Jing, Li Jingyu. Study on fertilizer use efficiency and its determinants in grain production in China. Research of Agricultural Modernization,2011(5):565–568.

Li Yang. Pollution migration Routes in China. China News Weekly,2006(4):28–29.

Lv Minghe. "Poison mud" siege. Southern Weekend,2012–02–09(B11).

Lui Minghe. Unwelcome "positive" interviews with 15 Environmental Secretaries after swimming in the river. Southern Weekend,2014–01–09(green edition).

Song Guojun. Environmental policy analysis. Beijing: Chemical Industry Press,2008.

Sun Yuefei. Geographical distribution of cancer villages in China. Wuhan: Central China Normal University,2009.

Tong Zhifeng. Course and Characteristics: A study of environmental resistance in the social transition period. Gansu Journal of Theory,2008(6):85–90.

Tong Zhifeng. The State and farmers' environmental struggle: a preliminary analysis. Journal of Zhejiang Shuren University,2013(5):21–53.

Tong Zhifeng. Development and challenges of water pollution control policies in rural China. Journal of Nanjing University of Technology (Social Sciences Edition),2016(1):89–96.

Wang Qingxia, Gong Weiwei, Zhang Shanshan, et al. Current situation and cause analysis of rural environmental emergencies in China. Environmental Pollution and Control,2012(3):89–94.

Xi Beidou. Comprehensively Promoting Rural ecological Environment Construction: Technology and Countermeasures of urban and rural environmental protection in New rural construction. Environmental Protection,2010(19):11.

Xie Dan. Ten billion sludge business: half seawater, half flame. Southern Weekend,2012–02–09(B11).

Zhang Keqiang, Huang Zhiping, Wang Feng, et al. Rural surface pollution and its prevention and control measures. Agricultural Engineering Technology(New Energy Industry),2010(2):22–27.

Zhang Zengqiang. Research on economic loss of water pollution in China. Beijing: China Research Institute of Water Resources and Hydropower,2005.

Zhao Zhijian, Hu Xiaojuan, Peng Cuiting, et al. Analysis of the impact of fertilizer input and grain output changes on environmental costs in Hunan Province. Journal of Ecology and Environment,2012(12):2007–2012.

Lu W, Xie S, Zhou W, et al. Water Pollution and Health Impact in China: A Mini-Review. Open Environmental Sciences,2008,10(2): 1–5.

Wang J. Water Pollution and Water Shortage Problems in China. Journal of Applied Ecology, 1989,26(3): 851–857.

Wang M, Webber M, Finlayson B, et al. Rural Industries and Water Pollution in China. Journal of Environmental Management, 2008,86(4): 648–659.

Chapter 6

Chen A Jiang. From exogenous pollution to endogenous pollution: Social and cultural logic of water environment deterioration in Taihu Basin. Xuehai,2007,(1):36–41.

Cui Lianxiang. Study on the causes and countermeasures of rural ecological environment problems in China. Fuzhou: Fujian Normal University,2007.

Fu Bojie, Chen Liding, Yu Xiubo. The new characteristics of ecological environment in China and its countermeasures. Environmental Science,2000(5):104–106.

Geng Yanhu. Pollution of rural large-scale breeding industry and its control dilemma: Based on field investigation of pig breeding in Beizhen, Chaohu Basin. Journal of China University of Mining and Technology (Social Science Edition),2017(1):50–59.

Geng Yanhu. De-embedded development: An explanatory framework for rural environmental problems. Journal of Nanjing Agricultural University (Social Sciences Edition),2017(3):21–30,155–156.

Geng Yanhu, Chen Tao. Environmental protection "local policy": An explanation of the failure of environmental law. Journal of Hehai University (Philosophy and Social Sciences Edition),2013(1):34–38,90.

He Zhenyi, Wang Wuyi, Ye Jingzhong, et al. Environment and health: Interdisciplinary perspectives. Beijing: Social Sciences Academic Press,2010.

Hong Dayong. Social Change and Environmental Problems: A Sociological Interpretation of environmental problems in contemporary China. Beijing: Capital Normal University Press,2001.

Hong Dayong. On environmental problems and its sociological interpretation model. Journal of Renmin University of China,2002(5):58–62.

Hong Dayong. Environmental awareness of urban residents in China. Jiangsu Social Sciences,2005(1):127–132.

Hong Dayong, Ma Fangxin. Reproduction of dual social structures: a sociological analysis of non-point source pollution in rural China. Sociological Research,2004(4):1–7.

Hong Da Yong, et al. The growth of non-governmental environmental protection forces in China. Beijing: China Renmin University Press,2007.

Jia Zhenbang. Environment and Health. Beijing: Peking University Press, 2008.

Jiang Lin. Comprehensive Impact assessment model system and application of environmental policy. Environmental Science,2006(5):1035–1040.

Jiao Jie. Research on the legal system of new rural ecological environment protection. Taiyuan: Shanxi University of Finance and Economics,2011.

Jinhai. The pursuit and realization of urban environmental justice. Beijing: China Founder Publishing House,2008.

Li Bin. Research on rural environmental policy from the dual perspective of urban and rural areas. Beijing: China Environmental Science Press,2012.

Li Dechao. Breaking environmental protection policy. Reporter Observation,2007(16):10–17.

Li Xiaoyun, Zuo Ting, Jin Leshan, et al. Environment and poverty: Chinese practice and international experience. Beijing: Social Sciences Academic Press,2005.

Li Yaolei. The game between environmental protection and livelihood in rural ecological environment governance: A case study of A village in North China. Journal of Guangxi University for Nationalities (Philosophy and Social Sciences Edition),2018(6):37–43.

Li Zhiping, Chen Chunsheng, et al. Rural environmental control and protection of farmers' environmental rights. Beijing: Peking University Press,2009.

Liang Liutao. Study on temporal and spatial characteristics of rural ecological environment and its evolution law. Nanjing: Nanjing Agricultural University,2009.

Liu Hailin, Wang Zhiqin, et al. Rural environmental problems from 100 villages survey. Chinese Reform,2007(4):70–72.

Ma Juan. A sociological study on the practice of ecological policy in rural areas. Xi 'an: Northwest Agriculture and Forestry University, 2012.

Pan Yue. Environmental protection and social equity. Xinhua Monthly News,2004(12):69–73.

Qie Jianrong. Central environmental protection inspectors reveal local governments' fancy and chaotic behavior, and many governments have introduced "local policies" to protect illegal enterprises. Legal Daily, 2017–08–01(6).

Qu Geping. Summary of the development of environmental protection in China. Environment and Sustainable Development,1988(6):1–8,14.

Song Guojun, Jin Shuqin. On the Integration of Urban and Rural Environmental Protection. Environmental Protection, 2007(21):29–31.

Su Yang. Environmental pollution in the process of rural modernization. Journal of Macroeconomic Management,2006a(2):50–52.

Su Yang. Investigation of environmental pollution in rural China. Economic Information Daily,2006b–01–14(6).

Sun Jiaxiu. Research on the overall planning and coordinated development of urban and rural environmental protection under the background of dual structure. Chengdu: Southwest University of Finance and Economics,2009.

Tan Jiao. Public Participation in the policy process of rural ecological environment governance. Changsha: Hunan Normal University,2012.

Wan Bentai. The implementation of the "action Plan" to solve the rural 5 environmental problems. Environmental Protection,2007(1):15–17.

Wang Feng. Study on the mechanism of public participation in environmental protection. Beijing: China Environmental Science Press,2008.

Wang Xiaoyi. Grassland communities under environmental stress: A survey of six Gacha villages in Inner Mongolia. Beijing: Social Sciences Academic Press,2009.

Wen Zongguo. Environmental Policy in contemporary China: Formation, characteristics and trends. Beijing: China Environmental Science Press,2010.

Xi Xiaolin, Xu Qinghua. Survey of public environmental awareness in China. Beijing: China Environmental Science Press,1988.

Xia Guang. Environmental Policy Innovation: An Economic analysis of environmental policy. Beijing: China Environmental Science Press,2000.

Xiao Jianhua, Zhao Yunlin, Fu Xiaohua. Research on ecological and environmental governance towards multi-center cooperation. Changsha: Hunan People's Publishing House,2010.

Xu Xiaoyun. Research on existing problems and countermeasures of rural ecological environment protection in China. Changchun: Northeast Normal University,2004.

Xun Lili, Bao Zhiming. Government mobilization environmental policy and its local practice: a sociological analysis of eco-migration in S Banner, Inner Mongolia. Chinese Social Sciences,2007(5):114–128,207.

Yang Yan, Sun Tao. Research on cross-regional environmental governance and local government cooperation mechanism. Chinese Administration,2009(1):66–69.

Zhan Hongxu, Zhao Yixin. Study on setting up of regional environmental administration in China. Entrepreneur World · Next ten days,2009(5):3–5.

Zhang Guoqiang. Constructing legal barrier for rural ecological environment. People's Forum,2019(14):94–95.

Zhang Hongyan, Liu Pingyang. Research on incentive mechanism of rural environmental protection and development. Beijing: Economic Management Press,2011.

Zhang Jianqiang. Ecology and Environment. Beijing: Chemical Industry Press,2009.

Zhang Jinjun. Evolution and development trend of China's rural environmental policy system: Based on the perspective of modernization of rural environmental governance system. Henan Social Sciences,2018(6):97–101.

Zhang Xiaowen. On the construction of China's rural environmental information disclosure system. Agricultural Economics,2010(10):3–5.

Zhang Yulin, Gu Jintu. "Three rural issues" in the context of environmental pollution. Strategy and Management,2003(3):63–72.

China Environmental Protection Foundation. A preliminary study of Chinese public environmental awareness. Beijing: China Environmental Science Press,1998.
Zhou Chenghu, Liu Haijiang, Ouyang. Regional joint prevention of environmental pollution in China. Geoinformation Science,2008(4):431–437.
Zhou Xuezhi, Tang Wenkui, et al. Rural environmental protection in China. Beijing: China Environmental Science Press,1996.
Zhou Yingnan, Li Jie, Qu Yi. Research on the problems and countermeasures of China's existing ecological policies. China Population, Resources and Environment,2013(S1):95–98.
Zhu Deming. Environmental protection countermeasures for urban and rural integrated development. Reference of Economic Research,2005(71):35–36.
Zhu Hongfa. Dictionary of Environmental protection. Beijing: Golden Shield Publishing House,2009.
Qin H. The Impacts of Rural-Urban Labor Migration on the Rural Environment in Chongqing Municipality Southwest China:Mediating Roles of Rural Household Livelihoods and Community Development. PhD Thesis of University of Illinois at Urbana-Champaign, 2009.

Chapter 7

Cai Fang, Yang Tao. Urban-rural income gap and the critical point of institutional reform. Chinese Social Sciences,2003(5):16–25,205.
Fang Lijie. Research on Medical security for urban and rural poor in China. Population Journal,2007(2):48–53.
Feng Xiaotian, Zhang Qingsong. Study on the change of fertility intention of urban and rural residents in the past 20 years. Market and Demographic Analysis,2002(5):21–31.
Gao Caiyun, Meng Xiangyan. Empirical analysis of raising public environmental awareness. People's Forum,2011(11):156–157.
Gao Xuede, Zhai Xuewei. Government trust in urban and rural comparison. Sociological Research,2013(2):1–27.
Gong Wenjuan. Regulation and Construction: Presentation mechanism of environmental issues: Reflections on citizens' opposition to the construction of A waste incineration plant in A City. Society,2013(1):161–194.
Hannigan. Environmental Sociology: 2nd Ed. Hong Dayong, et al. Trans. Beijing: China Renmin University Press,2009.
Hong Dayong, Xiao Chenyang. Analysis of gender differences in environmental concern. Sociological Research,2007(2):1–27,242.
Hong Dayong. Measuring environmental concern: An application assessment of the NEP scale in China. Society,2006(5):71–92,207.

Hong Dayong. China's urban-rural dual control system and environmental problems. Journal of Renmin University of China,2000(1):62–66.

Hong Dayong. Social Change and Environmental Problems: A Sociological Interpretation of environmental problems in contemporary China. Beijing: Capital Normal University Press,2001.

Jing Jun. Cognition and Self-consciousness: Environmental Struggle in a Northwest village. Journal of China Agricultural University (Social Sciences Edition),2009(4):5–14.

Li Chenlu, Zhao Xudong. Primitive resistance in mass incidents: A case study of environmental protests in Donghai Village, Zhejiang Province. Society,2012(5):179–193.

Lu Chuntian, Hong Dayong. Constructing a measurement model of environmental concern: based on 2003 China General Social Survey data. Society,2011(1):35–52.

Lu, Yilong. Does registered permanent residence still work: household registration system and social stratification and mobility. Chinese Social Sciences, 2008(1):149–162, 207–208.

Ma Guoqing. Grassland ecology and Mongolian folk environmental knowledge. Inner Mongolia Social Sciences (Chinese version),2001(1):52–57.

Ma Rong, Guo Jianru. Urban and rural differences in environmental awareness and attitudes of Chinese residents. Social Science Front,2000(1):201–210.

Qiu Haozheng, Lin Bifang. Principle and application of structural equation model. Beijing: China Light Industry Press,2008.

Wang Xiaoyi. Vassal villages and environmental degradation. Xuehai,2010(2):60–62.

Wu Yuxiao. Educational Opportunity Inequality and its Evolution in Urban and rural China (1978–2008). Chinese Social Sciences,2013(3):4–21,203.

Xing Zhanjun. A comparative study on subjective quality of life of urban and rural residents. Society,2006(1):130–141,208–209.

Yan Guodong, Kang Jiancheng, Xie Xiaojin, et al. The changing trend of public environmental awareness in China. China Population, Resources and Environment,2010(10):55–60.

Ingalls. From Traditional Man to Modern Man: Personal Change in six developing countries. Gu Xin, trans. Beijing: China Renmin University Press,1992.

Zhang Junhua. A meta-analysis of the difference between urban and rural well-being. Society,2010(2):144–155.

Zhang Wenhong, Ruan Danqing. Social support network for urban and rural residents. Sociological Research,1999(3):14–19,22–26.

Zhang Yulin. Urban Belief and Rural Governance in China Today. Social Sciences,2013(10):71–75.

Zhang Yunwu. Interpersonal trust and social interaction of residents in different scale areas. Sociological Research,2009(4):112–132,244.

Zhao Yandong. Social network and physical and mental health of urban and rural residents. Society,2008(5):1–19,224.

China Environmental Protection Foundation. A preliminary study of Chinese public environmental awareness. Beijing: China Environmental Science Press,1998.

Zhong Xingju. Local practice of environmental concern: A case study of the policy of returning farmland to forest in Dongxi Village, Dabashan District. Journal of China University of Geosciences (Social Sciences Edition),2014(1):55–61.

Zhou Kui, Zhu Mingjiao. Analysis of the current situation and influencing factors of environmental awareness of urban and rural residents in China: survey data from Dujiangyan, Hefei, Ningbo, Huangshi and corresponding rural areas. China Population-Resources and Environment, 2012(Special Issue):262–266.

Alm L R, Witt S L. The Rural-Urban Linkage to Environmental Policy Making in the American West: A Focus on Idaho. The Social Science Journal, 1997, 34(3): 271–284.

Bennett K, McBeth M K. Contemporary Western Rural USA Economic Composition: Potential Implications for Environmental Policy and Research. Environmental Management,1998, 22(3): 371–381.

Berenguer J, Corraliza J A, Martín R. Rural-Urban Differences in Environmental Concern, Attitudes, and Actions. European Journal of Psychological Assessment, 2005, 21(2): 128–138.

Chan K. Market Segmentation of Green Consumers in Hong Kong. Journal of International Consumer Marketing, 1999, 12(2): 7–24.

Converse P E. The Nature of Belief System in Mass Public//Apter D E. Ideology and Discontent. New York: The Free Press of Glencoe, 1964:206–261.

Davidson D J, Freudenburg W R. Gender and Environmental Risk Concerns: A Review and Analysis of Available Research. Environment and Behavior, 1996, 28(3): 302–339.

Dunlap R E, Van Liere K D, Mertig A G, et al. Measuring Endorsement of the New Ecological Paradigm: A Revised NEP Scale. Journal of Social Issues, 2000, 56(3): 425–442.

Dunlap R E. The New Environmental Paradigm Scale: From Marginality to Worldwide Use. The Journal of Environmental Education, 2008, 40(1): 3–18.

Dunlap R E, Van Liere K D. A Proposed Measuring Instrument and Preliminary Results: The New Ecological Paradigm. Journal of Environmental Education, 1978, 9(1): 10–19.

Dunlap R E, Jones R E. Environmental Concern: Conceptual and Measurement Issues//Dunlap R E, Michelson W. Handbook of Environmental Sociology. Westport, CT: Greenwood Press, 2002:482–524.

Freudenburg W R. Rural-Urban Differences in Environmental Concern: A Closer Look. Sociological Inquiry, 1991,61(2): 167–198.

Gooch G D. Environmental Concern and the Swedish Press:A Case Study of the Effects of Newspaper Reporting, Personal Experience and Social Interaction on the Public's Perception of Environmental Risks. European Journal of Communication, 1996, 11(1): 107–127.

Greenbaum A. Taking Stock of Two Decades of Research on the Social Bases of Environmental Concern//Mehta M D, Ouellet E. Environmental Sociology: Theory and Practice. Ontario: Captus Press, 1995:125–152.

Hayes B C. Gender, Scientific Knowledge, and Attitudes toward the Environment: A Cross-National Analysis. Political Research Quarterly, 2001, 54(3): 657–671.

Huddart-Kennedy E, Beckley T M, McFarlane B L, et al. Rural-Urban Differences in Environmental Concern in Canada. Rural Sociology, 2009,74(3): 309–329.

Jones R E, Fly J M, Talley J, et al. Green Migration into Rural America: The New Frontier of Environmentalism? Society and Natural Resources, 2003, 16(3): 221–238.

Lowe G D, Pinhey T K. Rural-Urban Differences in Support for Environmental Protection. Rural Sociology, 1982,47(1): 114–128.

Marquart-Pyatt S T. Are There Similar Sources of Environmental Concern? Comparing Industrialized Countries. Social Science Quarterly, 2008, 89(5): 1312–1335.

Mohai P, Twight B W. Age and Environmentalism: An Elaboration of the Buttel Model Using National Survey Evidence. Social Science Quarterly, 1987, 68(4): 798–818.

Paek H, Pan Z. Spreading Global Consumerism: Effects of Mass Media and Advertising on Consumerist Values in China. Mass Communication and Society, 2004, 7(4): 491–515.

Raubenheimer J. An Item Selection Procedure to Maximize Scale Reliability and Validity. South African Journal of Industrial Psychology, 2004, 30(4): 59–64.

Rickson R E, Stabler P J. Community Responses to Non-Point Pollution from Agriculture. Journal of Environmental Management, 1985, 20(3): 281–293.

Stamm K R, Clark F, Eblacas P R. Mass Communication and Public Understanding of Environmental Problems: The Case of Global Warming. Public Understanding of Science, 2000, 9(3): 219–238.

Tremblay Jr K R, Dunlap R E. Rural-Urban Residence and Concern with Environmental Quality: A Replication and Extension. Rural Sociology, 1978,43(3): 474–591.

Van Liere K D, Dunlap R E. The Social Bases of Environmental Concern: A Review of Hypotheses, Explanations and Empirical Evidence. Public Opinion Quarterly, 1980(2):181–197.

Van Liere K D, Dunlap R E. Environmental Concern:Does It Make a Difference How It's Measured?. Environment and Behavior, 1981, 44(2): 181–197.

Xiao C, Dunlap R E. Validating a Comprehensive Model of Environmental Concern Cross-Nationally: A US-Canadian Comparison. Social Science Quarterly, 2007, 44(2): 181–197.

Xiao C, Dunlap R E, Hong D. The Nature and Bases of Environmental Concern among Chinese Citizens. Social Science Quarterly, 2013, 94(3): 672–690.

Yu X. Is Environment“A City Thing” in China? Rural-Urban Differences in Environmental Attitudes. Journal of Environmental Psychology, 2014, 38: 39–48.

Chapter 8

Hong Dayong. Comprehensive evaluation and sampling analysis of citizens' environmental awareness. Science and Technology Review,1998(9):13–16.

Hong Dayong, Fan Yechao, Xiao Chenyang. Testing the Chinese version of the Environmental Concern Scale (CNEP): a reanalysis of CGSS2010 data. Sociological Research,2014(4):49–72,243.

Hong Dayong, Xiao Chenyang. Analysis of gender differences in environmental concern. Sociological Research,2007(2):111–135,244.

Hong Dayong, Xiao Chenyang, et al. The Social basis of environmental friendliness: An empirical study of Chinese citizens' environmental concern and behavior. Beijing: China Renmin University Press,2012.

Li, Xiaohong. Socio-demographic characteristics and environmental concerns: data based on rural areas. China Population-Resources and Environment, 2011(12):121–128.

Peng Yuanchun. Structural constraints on urban residents' environmental behavior. Sociological Review,2013(4):29–41.

Qu Geping. Review and Reflection on China's environmental protection in the past 40 years: A review. Environmental Protection,2013(10):10–17.

Ren Liying. Public Participation in environmental protection // Yang Ming. Environmental problems and environmental awareness. Beijing: Huaxia Publishing House,2002:89–113.

Wu Jianping, Zi Fei, Liu Xianwei, et al. Measurement of new ecological paradigms: Revision and application of the NEP scale in China. Journal of Beijing Forestry University (Social Sciences Edition),2012(4):8–13.

Bakvis H, Nevitte N. The Greening of the Canadian Electorate: Environmentalism, Ideology and Partisanship//Boardman R. Canadian Environmental Policy. Toronto: Oxford University Press, 1992:144–163.

Buttel F. Age and Environmental Concern: A Multivariate Analysis. Youth & Society, 1979, 10(3): 237–256.

Dunlap R E, Van Liere K D, Merti A G, et al. New Trends in Measuring Environmental Attitudes: Measuring Endorsement of the New Ecological Paradigm: A Revised NEP Scale. Journal of Social Issues, 2000, 56(3): 425–442.

Greenbaum A. Taking Stock of Two Decades of Research on the Social Bases of Environmental Concern//Mehta M D, Ouellet E. Environmental Sociology: Theory and Practice. Ontario: Captus Press, 1995:125–152.

Honnold J A. Age and Environmental Concern: Some Specification of Effects. Journal of Environmental Education, 1984, 16(1): 4–9.

Inglehart R. Public Support for Environmental Protection: Objective Problems and Subjective Values in 43 Societies. Political Science & Politics, 1995, 28(1): 57–72.

Jones R E, Dunlap R. The Social Base of Environmental Concern: Have They Changed over Time? Rural Sociology, 1992, 57(1): 28–47.

Kanagy C L, Humphrey C R, Firebaugh G. Surging Environmentalism: Changing Public Opinion or Changing Publics? Social Science Quarterly, 1994, 75(4): 804–819.

Melucci A. The Symbolic Challenge of Contemporary Movements. Social Research, 1985, 52(4): 789–816.

Murphy R. Rationality and Nature: A Sociological Inquiry into a Changing Relationship. Boulder: Westview Press, 1994.

Van Liere K D, Dunlap R. The Social Base of Environmental Concern: A Review of Hypotheses, Explanations and Empirical Evidence. Public Opinion Quarterly, 1980, 44(2): 181–197.

Chapter 9

Bao Zhiming, Chen Zhanjiang. Environmental Dimensions of Chinese Experience: Dimensions and Limits: A review and reflection on Chinese environmental sociology. Sociological Research,2011(6):196–210,245.

Household Survey Office, National Bureau of Statistics. China Rural Poverty Monitoring Report 2018. Beijing: China Statistics Press,2018.

Hong Dayong. Measuring environmental concern: An application assessment of the NEP scale in China. Society,2006(5):71–92,207.

Hong Dayong. New thinking on China's environmental problems and the construction of ecological civilization. Exploration and Controversy,2013(10):4–10,2.

Hong Dayong, Fan Yechao, Xiao Chenyang. Testing the Chinese version of the Environmental Concern Scale (CNEP): a reanalysis of CGSS2010 data. Sociological Research,2014(4):49–72,243.

Hong Dayong, Lu Chuntian. Multi-level analysis of public environmental concerns. Sociological Research,2011(6):154–170,244–245.

Lu Chuntian, Qi Xiaoliang. Farmers' environmental struggle and government governance. Theoretical Investigation,2019(2):159–165.

Zhang Yulin. The Chinese experience of environmental struggle. Xuehai,2010(2):66–68.

National Bureau of Statistics of the People's Republic of China. China Statistical Yearbook:2011. Beijing: China Statistics Press,2011.

Zhou Zhijia. Environmental protection, group pressure, or interest spread: Motivation analysis of Xiamen residents' participation in PX environmental movement. Society,2011(1):1–34.

Ahern L. The Role of Media System Development in the Emergence of Postmaterialist Values and Environmental Concern: A Cross-National Analysis. Social Science Quarterly, 2012, 93(2): 538–557.

Best H, Mayerl J. Values, Beliefs, Attitudes: An Empirical Study on the Structure of Environmental Concern and Recycling Participation. Social Science Quarterly, 2013, 94(3): 691–714.

Bollen K A. Structural Equations with Latent Variables. New York: Wiley, 1989.

Brechin S R, Kempton W. Beyond Postmaterialist Values: National versus Individual Explanations of Global Environmentalism. Social Science Quarterly,1997, 78(1): 16–20.

Brechin S R. Objective Problems, Subjective Values, and Global Environmentalism: Evaluating the Postmaterialist Argument and Challenging a New Explanation. Social Science Quarterly, 1999, 80(4): 793–809.

Brown T A. Confirmatory Factor Analysis for Applied Research. New York: Guildford, 2006.

Cohen M J. Risk Society and Ecological Modernisation Alternative Visions for Post-Industrial Nations. Futures, 1997, 29(2): 105–119.

Dietz T, Dan A, Shwom R. Support for Climate Change Policy: Social Psychological and Social Structural Influences. Rural Sociology, 2007, 72(2): 185–214.

Dinda S. Environmental Kuznets Curve Hypothesis: A Survey. Ecological Economics, 2004, 49(4): 431–455.

Dunlap R E. Trends in Public Opinion toward Environmental Issues: 1965—1990. Society & Natural Resources, 1991, 4(3): 285–312.

Dunlap R E, York R. The Globalization of Environmental Concern and the Limits of the Postmaterialist Values Explanation: Evidence from Four Multinational Surveys. The Sociological Quarterly, 2008, 49(3): 529–563.

Dunlap R E, Jones R E. Environmental Concern: Conceptual and Measurement Issues//Dunlap R E, Michelson W. Handbook of Environmental Sociology. Westport, CT: Greenwood Press, 2002:482–524.

Dunlap R E, Van Liere K D, Mertig A, et al. Measuring Endorsement of the New Ecological Paradigm: A Revised NEP Scale. Journal of Social Issues, 2000, 56(3): 425–442.

Duroy Q M H. Testing the Affluence Hypothesis: A Cross-Cultural Analysis of the Determinants of Environmental Action. The Social Science Journal, 2008, 45(3): 419–439.

Esty D C, Levy M, Srebotnjak T, et al. Environmental Sustainability Index: Benchmarking National Environmental Stewardship. New Haven: Yale Center for Environmental Law & Policy, 2005.

Franzen A, Meyer R. Environmental Attitudes in Cross-National Perspective: A Multilevel Analysis of the ISSP 1993 and 2000. European Sociological Review,2009,26(2): 219–234.

Freymeyer R H, Johnson B E. A Cross-Cultural Investigation of Factors Influencing Environmental Actions. Sociological Spectrum, 2010, 30(2): 184–195.

Gelissen J. Explaining Popular Support for Environmental Protection:A Multi-level Analysis of 50 Nations. Environment and Behavior, 2007, 39(3): 392–415.

Givens J E, Jorgenson A K. The Effects of Affluence, Economic Development, and Environmental Degradation on Environmental Concern: A Multilevel Analysis. Organization & Environment, 2011, 24(1): 74–91.

Greenbaum A. Taking Stock of Two Decades of Research on the Social Bases of Environmental Concern//Mehta M D, Ouellet E. Environmental Sociology: Theory and Practice. Ontario: Captus Press, 1995:125–152.

Haller M, Hadler M. Dispositions to Act in Favor of the Environment: Fatalism and Readiness to Make Sacrifices in a Cross-National Perspective. Sociological Forum, 2008, 23(2): 281–311.

Hayes A F. Beyond Baron and Kenny: Statistical Mediation Analysis in the New Millennium. Communication Monographs, 2009, 76(4): 408–420.

Hunter L M, Strife S, Twine W. Environmental Perceptions of Rural South African Residents: The Complex Nature of Environmental Concern. Society & Natural Resources, 2010, 23(6): 525–541.

Inglehart R. The Silent Revolution: Changing Values and Political Styles among Western Publics. Princeton, NJ: Princeton University Press, 1977.

Inglehart R. Culture Shift in Advanced Industrial Society. Princeton, NJ: Princeton University Press, 1990.

Inglehart R. Public Support for Environmental Protection: Objective Problems and Subjective Values in 43 Societies. Political Science & Politics, 1995, 28(1): 57–72.

Inglehart R. Modernization and Postmodernization: Cultural, Economic, and Political Change in 43 Societies. Princeton, NJ: Princeton University Press, 1997.

Kemmelmeier M, Krol G, Kim Y H. Values, Economics, and Proenvironmental Attitudes in 22 Societies. Cross-Cultural Research, 2002, 36(3): 256–285.

Kidd Q, Lee A. Postmaterialist Values and the Environment: A Critique and Reappraisal. Social Science Quarterly, 1997, 78(1): 1–15.

Knight K W, Messer B L. Environmental Concern in Cross--National Perspective: The Effects of Affluence, Environmental Degradation, and World Society. Social Science Quarterly, 2012, 93(2): 521–537.

Kvaløy B, Finseraas H, Listhaug O. The Publics' Concern for Global Warming: A Cross-National Study of 47 Countries. Journal of Peace Research, 2012, 49(1): 11–22.

Marquart-Pyatt S T. Concern for the Environment among General Publics: A Cross-National Study. Society & Natural Resources, 2007, 20(10): 883–898.

Marquart-Pyatt S T. Are There Similar Sources of Environmental Concern? Comparing Industrialized Countries. Social Science Quarterly, 2008, 89(5): 1312–1335.

Marquart-Pyatt S T. Contextual Influences on Environmental Concerns Cross-Nationally: A Multilevel Investigation. Social Science Research, 2012, 41(5): 1085–1099.

Meyer R, Liebe U. Are the Affluent Prepared to Pay for the Planet? Explaining Willingness to Pay for Public and Quasi-Private Environmental Goods in Switzerland. Population and Environment, 2010, 32(1): 42–65.

Mohai P, Simões S, Brechin S R. Environmental Concerns, Values and Meanings in the Beijing and Detroit Metropolitan Areas. International Sociology, 2010, 25(6): 778–817.

Nawrotzki R J. The Politics of Environmental Concern: A Cross-National Analysis. Organization & Environment, 2012, 25(3): 286–307.

Pampel F C, Hunter L M. Cohort Change, Diffusion, and Support for Environmental Spending in the United States. American Journal of Sociology, 2012, 118(2): 420–448.

Rosenthal E. China Increases Lead as Biggest Carbon Dioxide Emitter. New York Times, 2008–06–14.

Rubin D B. Multiple Imputation for Nonresponse in Surveys. New York: Wiley, 1987.

Sandvik H. Public Concern over Global Warming Correlates Negatively with National Wealth. Climatic Change, 2008, 90(3): 333–341.

Stern P C, Dietz T, Abel T, et al. A Value-Belief-Norm Theory of Support for Social Movements: The Case of Environmentalism. Human Ecology Review, 1999, 6(2): 81–97.

White M J, Hunter L M. Public Perception of Environmental Issues in a Developing Setting: Environmental Concern in Coastal Ghana. Social Science Quarterly,2009,90(4):960–982.

Xiao C, McCright A M. Environmental Concern and Sociodemographic Variables: A Study of Statistical Models. The Journal of Environmental Education, 2007, 38(2): 3–14.

Zhao X. Personal Values and Environmental Concern in China and the US: The Mediating Role of Informational Media Use. Communication Monographs, 2012, 79(2): 137–159.

Chapter 10

Gong Wenjuan. Gender differences in environmental friendly behavior of urban residents in China. Journal of Women's Studies,2008(6):11–17.

Guo Qingguang. Communication Course. 2nd edition. Beijing: China Renmin University Press,2011.

State Environmental Protection Administration, Ministry of Education. National Public Environmental Awareness Survey report. Beijing: China Environmental Science Press,1999.

Hong Daiyu. Survey and Analysis of Public Awareness of Environmental Protection in China. China Population-Resources and Environment, 1997(2):27–31.

Hong Dayong. Social Change and Environmental Problems: A Sociological Interpretation of environmental problems in contemporary China. Beijing: Capital Normal University Press,2001.

Hong Dayong. Measuring environmental concern: An application assessment of the NEP scale in China. Society,2006(5):71–92,207.

Hong Dayong, Lu Chuntian. Multilayer analysis of public environmental concerns: data application based on China CGSS2003. Sociological Research,2011(6):154–170,244–245.

Hu Rong. Analysis of factors affecting urban residents' environmental awareness. Journal of Fujian Executive College of Economics and Management,2007(1):48–53,98.

Ma Rong, Guo Jianru. Urban and rural differences in environmental awareness and attitudes of Chinese residents. Social Science Front,2000(1):201–210.

Peng Yuanchun. Review of environmental behavior research in China. Social Science Research,2011(1):104–109.

Peng Yuanchun. Study on urban residents' environmental behavior. Beijing: Guangming Daily Press,2013.

Xiao Chenyang, Hong Dayong. A reanalysis of the Environmental Concern Scale (NEP) in China. Journal of Social Sciences,2007(1):55–63.

China Environmental Culture Promotion Association. China Public Environmental Protection and Livelihood Index Green Paper 2005. Green Leaf,2006(supplement).

Zhu Qizhen. Problems and countermeasures of farmers' environmental awareness. World Environment,2000(4):24–26.

Arcury T A, Christianson E H. Environmental Worldview in Response to Environmental Problems: Kentucky 1984 and 1988 Compared. Environment Behavior, 1990, 22(3): 387–407.

Axelrod L J, Lehman D R. Responding to Environmental Concern: What Factors Guide Individual Action? Journal of Environmental Psychology, 1993, 13(2): 149–159.

Blake J. Overcoming the"Value-Action Gap" in Environmental Policy: Tensions between National Policy and Local Experience. Local Environment, 1999, 4(3): 257–278.

Dunlap R E, Van Liere K D. The"New Environmental Paradigm": A Proposed Instrument and Preliminary Results. Journal of Environmental Education, 1978, 9(4): 10–19.

Dunlap R E, Van Liere K D, Merting A G, et al. Measuring Endorsement of the New Ecological Paradigm: A Revised NEP Scale. Journal of Social Issues, 2000, 56(3): 425–442.

Dunlap R E. Environmental Sociology: A Personal Perspective on Its First Quarter Century. Organization & Environment, 2002, 15(1): 10–29.

Fishbein M, Ajzen I. Belief, Attitude, Intention, and Behavior: An Introduction to Theory and Research. MA: Addison-Wesley, 1975.

Fransson N, Gärling T. Environmental Concern: Conceptual Definitions, Measurement Methods, and Research Findings. Journal of Environmental Psychology, 1999, 19(4): 369–382.

Gamba R J, Oskamp S. Factors Influencing Community Residents' Participation in Commingled Curbside Recycling Programs. Environment and Behavior, 1994, 26(5): 587–612.

Gardner G T, Stern P C. Environmental Problems and Human Behavior. Boston: Allyn and Bacon, 1996.

Hines J M, Hungerford H R, Tomera A N. Analysis and Synthesis of Research on Responsible Environmental Behavior: A Meta-Analysis. The Journal of Environmental Education, 1987, 18(2): 1–8.

Jones R E, Fly J M, Talley J, et al. Green Migration into Rural America: The New Frontier of Environmentalism? Society and Natural Resources, 2003, 16(3): 221–238.

Kennedy H E, Beckley T M, McFarlane B L, et al. Rural-Urban Differences in Environmental Concern in Canada. Rural Sociology, 2009, 74(3): 309–329.

Tarrant M A, Cordell H K. The Effect of Respondent Characteristics on General Environmental Attitude-Behavior Correspondence. Environment and Behavior, 1997, 29(5): 618–637.

Taylor S, Todd P. An Integrated Model of Waste Management Behavior: A Test of Household Recycling and Composting Intentions. Environment and Behavior, 1995, 27(5): 603–630.

Tremblay K R, Dunlap R E. Rural-Urban Residence and Concern with Environmental Quality: A Replication and Extension. Rural Sociology,1978, 43(3): 474–491.

Van Liere K D, Dunlap R E. The Social Bases of Environmental Concern: A Review of Hypotheses, Explanations and Empirical Evidence. Public Opinion Quarterly, 1980, 44(2): 181–197.

Chapter 11

Bao Zhiming. Definition, classification and some problems of ecological migration. Journal of Minzu University of China (Philosophy and Social Sciences Edition),2006(1):27–31.

Baker. Risk Society. He Bowen, trans. Nanjing: Yilin Publishing House,2004.

Hong Dayong, Gong Wenjuan. A review of the theories and methods of environmental justice research. Journal of Renmin University of China,2008(6):70–79.

Hong Dayong. The growth and limitation of public environmental awareness. Green Leaf,2014(4):5–14.

Li Qiang. Analysis of thrust and pull factors affecting China's urban and rural floating population. Chinese Social Sciences,2003(1):125–136,207.

Tong Yufen, Wang Yingying. Urban population and smog in China: an analysis of interaction mechanisms and pathways. Social Sciences in Beijing,2014(5):4–10.

Yin Lun. Tibetan cognition and response to climate change: An investigation of Guonian Administrative Village, Deqin County, Yunnan Province. Ideological Front,2011(4):24–28.

Zhan Dongsheng, Meng Bin, Zhang Wenzhong. A study on the perception of residence satisfaction and behavioral intention of Beijing residents. Geographical Research,2014(2):336–348.

Bogardi J J, Renaud F G. Migration Dynamics Generated by Environmental Problems. Paper for the 2nd International Symposium on Desertification and Migrations, Almería, 2006.

Brulle R J, Pellow D N. Environmental Justice: Human Health and Environmental Inequalities. Annual Review of Public Health, 2006, 27: 103–124.

Chambliss D F, Schutt R K. Making Sense of the Social World: Methods of Investigation. CA: Sage Publications, 2013.

Collins A E. Applications of the Disaster Risk Reduction Approach to Migration Influenced by Environmental Change. Environmental Science & Policy, 2013, 27(S1): 112–125.

Dunlap R E. An Enduring Concern. Public Perspective, 2002, 13(5): 10–14.

De Jong G F. Expectations, Gender, and Norms in Migration Decision-Making. Population Studies, 2000, 54(3): 307–319.

Evans G W, Jacobs S V. Air Pollution and Human Behavior. Journal of Social Issues, 1981, 37(1): 95–125.

Evans G W, Jacobs S V, Frager N B. Adaptation to Air Pollution. Journal of Environmental Psychology, 1982, 2(2): 99–108.

Fakiolas R. Socio-Economic Effects of Immigration in Greece. Journal of European Social Policy, 1999, 9(3): 211–229.

Fischer P A, Martin R, Straubhaar T. Should I Stay or Should I Go//Hammar T, Brochmann G, Tamas K, et al. International Migration, Immobility and Development. Berg: Oxford, 1997:49–90.

Fuguitt G V, Zuiches J J. Residential Preferences and Population Distribution. Demography, 1975, 12(3): 491–504.

Goldhaber M K, Houts P S, DiSabella R. Moving after the Crisis a Prospective Study of Three Mile Island Area Population Mobility. Environment and Behavior, 1983, 15(1): 93–120.

Gray C L, Mueller V. Natural Disasters and Population Mobility in Bangladesh. Proceedings of the National Academy of Sciences, 2012, 109(16): 6000–6005.

Hogan T D. Determinants of the Seasonal Migration of the Elderly to Sunbelt States. Research on Aging, 1987, 9(1): 115–133.

Hsieh C, Liu B. The Pursuance of Better Quality of Life: In the Long Run, Better Quality of Social Life Is the Most Important Factor in Migration. American Journal of Economics and Sociology, 1983, 42(4): 431–440.

Hunter L M. The Association between Environmental Risks and Internal Migration Flow. Population and Environment, 1998, 19(3): 247–277.

Hunter L M. Migration and Environmental Hazards. Population and Environment, 2005, 26(4): 273–302.

Hunter L M, Luna J K, Norton R M. Environmental Dimensions of Migration. Annual Review of Sociology, 2015, 41(1): 377–397.

Irwin M, Blanchard T, Tolbert C, et al. Why People Stay: The Impact of Community Context on Nonmigration in the USA. Population, 2004, 59(5): 567–592.

Kiecolt K J, Nigg J M. Mobility and Perceptions of a Hazardous Environment. Environment and Behavior, 1982, 14(2): 131–154.

Konisky D. Public Preferences for Environmental Policy Responsibility. The Journal of Federalism, 2011, 41(1): 76–100.

Lee E S. A Theory of Migration. Demography, 1966, 3(1): 47–57.

Massey D S, Axinn W G, Ghimire D J. Environmental Change and Out-Migration: Evidence from Nepal. Population and Environment, 2010, 32(2): 109–136.

Mileti D S. Human Adjustment to the Risk of Environmental Extremes. Sociology and Social Research, 1980, 64(3): 327–347.

Myers N. Environmental Refugees: An Emergent Security Issue. Paper for the 13th Economic Forum, Organisation for Security and Cooperation in Europe, Prague, 2005.

Petersen W. A General Typology of Migration. American Sociological Review, 1958, 23(3): 256–266.

Portes A, Böröcz J. Contemporary Immigration: Theoretical Perspectives on Its Determinants and Modes of Incorporation. International Migration Review, 1989, 23(3): 606–630.

Reuveny R, Moore W H. Does Environmental Degradation Influence Migration? Emigration to Developed Countries in the Late 1980s and 1990s. Social Science Quarterly, 2009, 90(3): 461–479.

Richmond A H. Reactive Migration: Sociological Perspectives on Refugee Movements. Journal of Refugee Studies, 1993, 6(1): 7–24.

Rishi P, Khuntia G. Urban Environmental Stress and Behavioral Adaptation in Bhopal City of India. Urban Studies Research, 2012, 2012: 1–9.

Ritchey P N. Explanations of Migration. Annual Review of Sociology, 1976, 2(1): 363–404.

Russell J A, Lanius U F. Adaptation Level and the Affective Appraisal of Environments. Journal of Environmental Psychology, 1984, 4(2): 119–135.

Sabates-Wheeler R, Taylor T, Natali C. Great Expectations and Reality Checks: The Role of Information in Mediating Migrants' Experience of Return. European Journal of Development Research, 2009, 21(5): 752–771.

Sandefur G D, Scott W J. A Dynamic Analysis of Migration: An Assessment of the Effects of Age, Family and Career Variables. Demography, 1981, 18(3):355.

Speare A. Residential Satisfaction as an Intervening Variable in Residential Mobility. Demography, 1974, 11(2): 173–188.

Vaughan E. Individual and Cultural Differences in Adaptation to Environmental Risks. American Psychologist, 1993, 48(6): 673–680.

Wolpert J. Migration as an Adjustment to Environmental Stress. Journal of Social Issues, 1966,22(4): 92–102.

Wohlwill J F.Human Adaptation to Levels of Environmental Stimulation. Human Ecology, 1974, 2(2): 127–147

Chapter 12

He Fan. Tackling climate Change: What does the Chinese public think? Chinese Statistics,2010(2):1–3.

Lv Yarong, Chen Shufen. Analysis of farmers' cognition and adaptive behavior to climate change. Chinese Rural Economy,2010(7):75–86.

Sun Jiaju. Global concern: Ecological environment and sustainable development. Nanchang: Jiangxi People's Publishing House,2006.

Tan Zhixin. Farmers' cognition and cognitive behavior of climate change: evidence from Shandong Province. Chongqing Social Sciences,2011(3):56–61.

Yin Lun. Tibetan cognition and response to climate change: An investigation of Guonan Administrative Village, Deqin County, Yunnian Province. Ideological Front,2011(4):24–28.

Zhou Jingbo, Feng Xiangzhao. Cognition and policy evaluation of climate change adaptation. China Population-Resources and Environment, 2011(7):57–61.

Bord R J, Fisher A, O'Connor R R. Public Perception of Global Warming: United States and International Perspectives. Climate Research, 1998, 11(1): 75–84.

Boykoff M T. Flogging a Dead Norm? Newspaper Coverage of Anthropogenic Climate Change in the United States and United Kingdom from 2003 to 2006. Area, 2007, 39(4): 470–481.

Boykoff M T, Boykoff J M. Balance as Bias: Global Warming and the US Prestige Press. Global Environmental Change, 2004, 14(2): 125–136.

Boykoff M T, Roberts J T. Media Coverage of Climate Change: Current Trends, Strengths, Weaknesses. Human Development Report 2007/2008. Human Development Report Office Occasional Paper, 2007.

Brechin S R. Comparative Public Opinion and Knowledge on Global Climatic Change and the Kyoto Protocol: The US versus the World. International Journal of Sociology and Social Policy, 2003, 23(10): 106–134.

Brechin S R. Public Opinion: A Cross-National View//Lever-Tracy C. Routledge Handbook of Climate Change. London: Routledge, 2010:209–239.

Dunlap R. Lay Perceptions of Global Risk: Public Views of Global Warming in Cross-National Context. International Sociology, 1998, 13(4): 473–498.

Inglehart R. Culture Shift in Advanced Industrial Society. New Jersey: Princeton University Press, 1990.

McCright A M, Dunlap R E. Challenge Global Warming as a Social Problem: An Analysis of the Conservative Movement's Counter-Claims. Social Problems, 2000, 47(4): 499–522.

McCright A M. Anti-Reflexivity: The American Conservative Movement's Success in Undermining Climate Science and Policy. Theory, Culture and Society, 2010, 27(2/3): 100–133.

McCright A M. The Politicization of Climate Change and Polarization in the American Public's Views of Global Warming (2001—2010). The Sociological Quarterly, 2011, 52(2): 155–194.

Scruggs L, Benegal S. Declining Public Concern about Climate Change: Can We Blame the Great Recession? Global Environment Change, 2012, 22(2): 505–515.

Chapter 13

Huang Lele, Ren Lei, He Wei. Perceptions and attitudes of Chinese citizens towards global climate change. Science Research,2016(3):45–52,118.

Zhang Qian. Herdsmen's social vulnerability to climate change: A case study of Gacha in desert steppe, Inner Mongolia. Sociological Research,2011(6):171–195,245.

Giddens A. The Politics of Climate Change. Cambridge: Polity Press Ltd., 2009.

Dunlap R E, Brulle R J. Climate Change and Society: Sociological Perspectives. New York: Oxford University Press, 2015.

Catton Jr W R, Dunlap R E. Environmental Sociology: A New Paradigm. American Sociologist, 1978, 13(1): 41–49.

Chapter 14

Years of Environmental Protection in China during Reform and Opening Up, Editorial Board. 30 years of environmental protection in China during reform and opening up. Beijing: China Environmental Science Press,2010.

Hao Jiming. A Long way to go through wind and rain: 40 years of air pollution control review and prospects. Environmental Protection,2013(14):28–31.

Han Yunfeng, Ma Mingtao, Song Lingyan. Analysis of the change trend of atmospheric environmental quality in Beijing in recent years. Environment and Sustainable Development,2009(6):4–7.

Hong Dayong. Economic growth, environmental protection and ecological modernization: from the perspective of environmental sociology. Chinese Social Sciences,2012(9):82–99,207.

Hong Dayong. Research on resource and environmental issues in the process of green urbanization. Environmental Protection,2014(7):19–23.

Jiao Yujie. "I measure the air for the Motherland": interview with Feng Yongfeng, the founder of Dar Q Nature Curiosity Society. World Environment,2012(1):28–29.

Li Mingsheng, Yu Yang, Li Mingxuan, et al. Analysis of dynamic change of industrial SO2 emissions in China. Journal of Ecology and Environment,2010(4):957–961.

Wu Dui. Review of research on haze weather in China in recent ten years. Journal of Environmental Sciences,2012(2):257–269.

Wang Tao. Seven proposals of the Southern Weekend cooperation with six ngos. Southern Weekend,2011-11-24(C14).

Wang Tao. The "big truth" about Beijing's air: A conversation with Du Shaozhong, former deputy director of the Beijing Environmental Protection Bureau. Southern Weekend,2012-07-19(C14).

Jacobs, Kelly. Los Angeles Smog apocalypse. Cao Junji, trans. Shanghai: Shanghai Science and Technology Press,2014.

Zhang Shuning. Sue the government because I have a kind wish. Beijing Times,2014–02–27(23).
Zhu Yan. Environmental groups jointly released the "First round of research report on coal problems in North China" to combat smog encountered "numbers game". Environment and Life,2014(7):105.

Chapter 15

Hong Dayong. New thinking on China's environmental problems and the construction of ecological civilization. Exploration and Controversy,2013(10):4–10,2.
Hong Dayong. The growth and limitation of public environmental awareness. Green Leaf,2014(4):4–14.
Xi Jinping. Ecological prosperity means civilization prosperity: Promoting ecological construction and building "green Zhejiang". Qiushi,2003(13):42–44.

Chapter 16

Hong Dayong. Measuring environmental concern: An application assessment of the NEP scale in China. Society,2006(5):71–92,207.
Hong Dayong. Economic growth, environmental protection and ecological modernization: from the perspective of environmental sociology. Chinese Social Sciences,2012(9):82–99,207.
Hong Dayong, Fan Yechao, Xiao Chenyang. Testing the Chinese version of the Environmental Concern Scale (CNEP): a reanalysis of CGSS2010 data. Sociological Research,2014(4):49–72,243.
Hobbs. Leviathan. Li Sifu, Li Tingbi, trans. Beijing: The Commercial Press, 1985.
Lu Chuntian, Hong Dayong. Constructing a measurement model of environmental concern: based on 2003 China General Social Survey data. Society,2011(1):35–52.
Lu Chuntian, Hong Dayong, Cheng Gong. Comprehensive analysis of urban residents' evaluation of government environmental protection: based on CGSS2003 and CGSS2010 data. Theoretical Exploration,2014(2):95–100.
Lu Man. Trust: a simplifying mechanism for social complexity. Qu Tiepeng, Li Qiang, Trans. Shanghai: Shanghai People's Publishing House,2005.
Xiao Chenyang, Hong Dayong. A reanalysis of the Environmental Concern Scale (NEP) in China. Journal of Social Sciences,2007(1):55–63.
Zhang Cheng, Zhu Qianlong, Yu Tongshen. The relationship between environmental pollution and economic growth. Statistical Research,2012(1):59–67.
Zhou Zhiren. Citizen Participation in Government Performance Evaluation: Practice and prospect in China. Chinese Administration,2008(1):111–118.

Chanley V A. Trust in Government in the Aftermath of 9/11: Determinants and Consequences. Political Psychology, 2002, 23(3): 469–483.

Chanley V A, Rudolph T J, Rahn W M. The Origins and Consequences of Public Trust in Government: A Time Series Analysis. The Public Opinion Quarterly, 2000, 64(3): 239–256.

Cin C K. Blaming the Government for Environmental Problems: A Multilevel and Cross-National Analysis of the Relationship between Trust in Government and Local and Global Environmental Concerns. Environment and Behavior, 2012, 45(8): 971–992.

Dietz T, Dan A, Shwom R. Support for Climate Change Policy: Social Psychological and Social Structural Influences. Rural Sociology, 2007, 72(2): 185–214.

Dunlap R E, Jones R E. Environmental Concern: Conceptual and Measurement Issues//Dunlap R E, Michelson W. Handbook of Environmental Sociology. Westport, CT: Greenwood Press, 2002:482–524.

Frank D J, Hironaka A, Schofer E. The Nation-State and the Natural Environment over the Twentieth Century. American Sociological Review, 2000, 65(1): 97–116.

Grossman G M, Krueger A B. Environmental Impacts of a North American Free Trade Agreement. NBER Working Paper No.3914, 1991.

Inglerhart R. Public Support for the Environmental Protection: Objective Problems and Subjective Values in 43 Societies. PS: Political Science & Politics, 1995, 28(1): 57–72.

Kinder D R, Kiewiet D R. Economic Discontent and Political Behavior: The Role of Personal Grievances and Collective Economic Judgments in Congressional Voting. American Journal of Political Science, 1979, 23(3): 495–527.

Konisky D M, Milyo J, Richardson L E. Environmental Policy Attitudes: Issues, Geographical Scale, and Political Trust. Social Science Quarterly, 2008, 89(5): 1066–1085.

Mishler W, Rose R. Trust, Distrust and Skepticism: Popular Evaluations of Civil and Political Institutions in Post-Communist Societies. The Journal of Politics, 1997, 59(2): 418–451.

Weber M. The Protestant Ethic and the Spirit of Capitalism. New York: Scribner's Son, 1958.

Chapter 17

Carson. Silent spring. Xu Liang, Trans. Beijing: Beijing Institute of Technology Press,2014.

Wurster. The Economic System of Nature: A History of ecological thought. Hou Wenhui. Trans. Beijing: The Commercial Press,1999.

Thompson. Ideology and Modern Culture. Gao Tian, et al. Trans. Nanjing: Yilin Publishing House,2012.

Hong Dayong. Social change and environmental problems. Beijing: Capital Normal University Press,2001.

Hong Dayong. Environmental awareness of urban residents in China. Jiangsu Social Sciences,2005(1):127–132.

Hong Dayong. The growth and limitation of public environmental awareness. Green Leaf,2014(4):4–14.

Hong Dayong, Fan Yechao, Deng Xiaqiu, et al. Analysis of age differences in public environmental concern in China. Youth Research,2015(1):1–10,94.

Hong Dayong, Fan Yechao. International comparison of public environmental risk perception and environmental protection tendency and its theoretical implications. Social Science Research,2013(6):85–93.

Hong Dayong, Ma Fangxin. Reproduction of dual social structures: a sociological analysis of non-point source pollution in rural China. Sociological Research,2004(4):1–7.

Hong Dayong, Xiao Chenyang, et al. The Social basis of environmental friendliness: An empirical study of Chinese citizens' environmental concern and behavior. Beijing: China Renmin University Press,2012.

Liu Shaojie. The formation and change of ideological hierarchy types. Academic Monthly,2011(2):5–12.

Liu Shaojie. Ideological Changes in Contemporary China. Beijing: Central Compilation Publishing House,2012.

Liu Shaojie. Theoretical form and perceptual form of ideology. Jiangsu Social Sciences,2015(5):14–20.

Mu Quan, Zhang Shiqiu. Assessment of direct social and economic losses caused by large-scale haze events in China in January 2013. China Environmental Science,2013(11):2087–2094.

Qu Geping. Review and Reflection on China's environmental protection in the past 40 years: A review. Environmental Protection,2013(10):10–17.

Quality of Life Research Group. Survey of urban residents' environmental awareness in China. Management World,1991(6):171–173.

Xi Xiaolin, Xu Qinghua. Survey of public environmental awareness in China. Beijing: China Environmental Science Press,1998.

Yu Wujin. Theory of Ideology. Revised edition. Beijing: People's Publishing House,2009.

Zhang Yulin. Rural areas have become the "pain in the pain" of pollution. Global Times,2015-02-06(15).

Brulle R J, Jenkins J C. Spinning Our Way to Sustainability? Organization & Environment, 2006,19(1): 82–87.

Dunlap R E, Mertig A G. American Environmentalism: The US Environmental Movement, 1970—1990. Abingdon: Taylor & Francis, 1992.

Dunlap R E, Mertig A G. Global Environmental Concern: An Anomaly for Postmaterialism. Social Science Quarterly, 1997, 78(1): 24–29.

Harper C L. Environmentalism: Ideology and Collective Action//Environment and Society: Human Perspectives on Environmental Issues.5ed. New York: Routledge, 2012:chap.8.

Mazzotti F J. Confusing Ecology and Environmentalism. University of Florida Cooperative Extension Service, Institute of Food and Agricultural Sciences, EDIS, 2001.

Yang G B. Environmental NGOs and Institutional Dynamics in China. The China Quarterly, 2005, 13(2): 113–130.

Chapter 18

Dong Jun, Wang Libin, Gao Jing, et al. Create a new situation of ecological civilization: The CPC Central Committee with Comrade Xi Jinping as the core has led the construction of ecological civilization since the 18th CPC National Congress. Economic Daily News,2017–08–03(6).

Hong Dayong. The growth and limitation of public environmental awareness. Green Leaf,2014(4):4–14.

Hong Dayong. China's approach to compound environmental governance. Journal of the Party School of the CPC Central Committee,2016(3):67–73.

Xie Xiongbiao, Wu Yue, Feng Zhonglei, et al. Research on green behavior of resource-based enterprises in China. China Population-Resources and Environment,2015(6):5–11.

Zhang Ping, Yang Zuchan. A Brief analysis on the characteristics of environmental group events in China in the past ten years. Journal of China University of Geosciences (Social Sciences Edition),2015(2):53–61.

Wang Xiaoqiang, Bai Nanfeng. Rich Poverty: An economic survey of China's backward regions. Chengdu: Sichuan People's Publishing House,1986.

Index

D. Hong and Y. Fan (eds.), *Toward a Green Society*,
https://doi.org/10.1007/978-981-96-5111-5